Lecture Notes in Computer Science 16291

The series Lecture Notes in Computer Science (LNCS), including its subseries Lecture Notes in Artificial Intelligence (LNAI) and Lecture Notes in Bioinformatics (LNBI), has established itself as a medium for the publication of new developments in computer science and information technology research, teaching, and education.

LNCS enjoys close cooperation with the computer science R & D community, the series counts many renowned academics among its volume editors and paper authors, and collaborates with prestigious societies. Its mission is to serve this international community by providing an invaluable service, mainly focused on the publication of conference and workshop proceedings and postproceedings. LNCS commenced publication in 1973.

Erik Bergström · Bernhard Hämmerli ·
Agnieszka Kitkowska · Joakim Kävrestad
Editors

Critical Information Infrastructures Security

20th International Conference, CRITIS 2025
Jönköping, Sweden, October 21–23, 2025
Revised Selected Papers

Springer

Editors
Erik Bergström
Jönköping School of Engineering
Jönköping, Sweden

Bernhard Hämmerli
Lucerne University of Applied Sciences
Luzern, Switzerland

Agnieszka Kitkowska
Jönköping School of Engineering
Jönköping, Sweden

Joakim Kävrestad
Jönköping School of Engineering
Jönköping, Sweden

ISSN 0302-9743 ISSN 1611-3349 (electronic)
Lecture Notes in Computer Science
ISBN 978-3-032-19539-5 ISBN 978-3-032-19540-1 (eBook)
https://doi.org/10.1007/978-3-032-19540-1

This Springer imprint is published by the registered company Springer Nature Switzerland AG
The registered company address is: Gewerbestrasse 11, 6330 Cham, Switzerland

Preface

The 20th International Conference on Critical Information Infrastructures Security (CRITIS 2025) was held on 21–23 October 2025 at the School of Engineering, Jönköping University, Sweden. The conference was hosted by the Cybersecurity and Privacy Research Group at the School of Engineering and organised by a local team consisting of Joakim Kävrestad, Erik Bergström, and Agnieszka Kitkowska.

Building on the long-standing CRITIS tradition, the 2025 edition provided an interdisciplinary forum for researchers, industry representatives, public-sector experts, and critical infrastructure practitioners, welcoming 38 participants. The conference addressed the increasing complexity of the threat landscape affecting critical infrastructures and emphasised the interplay between technological, organisational, and societal factors. This year's program particularly highlighted developments in cyber-physical systems security, resilience against hybrid threats, information sharing across sectors, and the human and strategic dimensions of critical infrastructure protection.

All submitted papers underwent a rigorous double-blind peer-review process, where 22 papers were ultimately accepted out of 38 submissions. Each paper was reviewed by three members of the program committee. Continuing a CRITIS initiative, the conference also hosted the Young CRITIS Award, highlighting the community's commitment to supporting emerging researchers in the field. This year, three promising scholars received a prize.

The conference combined academic and professional contributions with opportunities for networking and exchange. Participants were welcomed to Jönköping through a series of social activities, including a guided walking tour of the city, and a visit to the Husqvarna Museum.

The keynote program featured speakers who offered complementary perspectives on the challenges of securing critical infrastructures. Marco Nilsson, School of Education and Communication, Jönköping University, opened the event with reflections on societal resilience in the light of the last year's increasingly complex threat landscape. Annelie Mannerström, Chief Information Security Officer at Jönköping Energi, provided insights into how a medium-sized energy company manages an evolving and demanding threat environment. Katarina Boustedt, Research Project Manager at RISE and Cybercampus Sweden, concluded the keynote series with an examination of future directions for the governance of critical information infrastructures and national strategic initiatives in this area.

The editors warmly thank all CRITIS 2025 participants for their valuable contributions in an ever-changing technological and security landscape.

December 2025

Erik Bergström
Bernhard Hämmerli
Agnieszka Kitkowska
Joakim Kävrestad

Organization

General Chairs

Erik Bergström	Jönköping University, Sweden
Agnieszka Kitkowska	Jönköping University, Sweden
Joakim Kävrestad	Jönköping University, Sweden

Steering Committee

Bernhard M. Hämmerli	Lucerne University of Applied Sciences, Acris GmbH, Switzerland
Javier Lopez	University of Málaga, Spain
Stephen D. Wolthusen	Royal Holloway, University of London, UK and Norwegian University of Science and Technology, Norway

Program Committee

Steven Furnell	University of Nottingham, UK
Maria Riveiro	Jönköping University, Sweden
Jerome Landre	Jönköping University, Sweden
Bilal Naqvi	LUT University, Finland
Görkem Kilinç Soylu	Jönköping University, Sweden
Hazel Murray	Munster Technological University, Ireland
Magdalena Glas	University of Regensburg, Germany
Martin Lundgren	University of Skövde, Sweden
Florian Skopik	Austrian Institute of Technology, Austria
Gabriele Oliva	University Campus Bio-Medico of Rome, Italy
Linas Martišauskas	Lithuanian Energy Institute, Lithuania
Peter Popov	City St George's, University of London, UK
Vladimir Stankovic	City St George's,University of London, UK
Simon Tjoa	St. Pölten University of Applied Sciences, Austria
Vimala Nunavath	University of South-Eastern Norway, Norway
Jose Ferreira	University of South-Eastern Norway, Norway
Stephen Wolthusen	Norwegian University of Science and Technology, Norway

Eliana Stavrou	Open University of Cyprus, Cyprus
Magnus Almgren	Chalmers University of Technology, Sweden
Anne Remke	Westfälische Wilhelms-Universität Münster, Germany
Stefan Pickl	University of the Bundeswehr Munich, Germany
Peter Burgherr	Paul Scherrer Institut, Switzerland
Basel Katt	Norwegian University of Science and Technology, Norway
Sokratis Katsikas	Norwegian University of Science and Technology, Norway
Tom Chothia	University of Birmingham, UK
Rolf Blom	RISE, Sweden
Chris Hankin	Imperial College London, UK
Joe Gardiner	University of Bristol, UK
Mikel Iturbe	Mondragon University, Spain
Cristina Alcaraz	University of Málaga, Spain
Simin Nadjm-Tehrani	Linköping University, Sweden
Kurt Tutschku	Blekinge Institute of Technology, Sweden
Johanna Karvonen	Laurea University of Applied Sciences, Finland
Federica Pascucci	Roma Tre University, Italy
Stefano Panzieri	Roma Tre University, Italy
Panayiotis Kotzanikolaou	University of Piraeus, Greece
Karl Andersson	Luleå University of Technology, Sweden
Giuseppe Nebbione	Mälardalen University, Sweden
Graziana Cavone	Roma Tre University, Italy
Sebastian Obermeier	Lucerne University of Applied Sciences and Arts, Switzerland

Contents

Methods and Practice

What Makes Information Critical? Information Classification in Organizational Practice ... 3
Simon Andersson, Åsa Ericson, Johan Lugnet, and Christine Große

Reducing SOC Analysts Alert Fatigue via Real-Time CTI Correlation and Deduplication ... 20
Sotiris Koumourou, Adamantini Peratikou, Eliana Stavrou, Savvas Theodoulou, and Stavros Stavrou

Power Grids

Human and Organizational Factors in Smart Grid Cybersecurity: A Systematic Literature Review ... 39
Ronak Tejas Shah, Michel van Eeten, Wolter Pieters, and Simon Parkin

The Dark Side of Flexibility: How Aggregated Cyberattacks Threaten the Power Grid ... 58
Daniel Myrén, Zeeshan Afzal, and Mikael Asplund

Optimal Pathways in Hierarchical Smart Distribution Grid Models with Large Scale Adversarial Attacks and Dynamic Adversaries ... 82
Nataša Gajić and Stephen Dirk Bjørn Wolthusen

Security and Safety Large and Small

Risk Assessment of Wind Power Accidents: Safety and Health Impacts ... 105
Peter Burgherr and Adolfo Alejandro Uribe Poblete

Designing Cyber Security Communities of Support to Improve SME Cyber Hygiene and Resilience ... 123
Neeshe Khan, Ram Herkanaidu, Steven Furnell, Jason R. C. Nurse, Maria Bada, and Matthew Rand

Vehicles

Towards a Holistic and Multi-modal Vehicle Security Monitoring 143
Ali Recai Yekta, Dominik Spychalski, Cenk Yekta, Markus Heinrich, Christoph Krauß, and Stefan Katzenbeisser

A Systematic Literature Review on Cybersecurity in Autonomous Vehicles 163
Issa Morad, Yousef Yako, and Görkem Kılınç Soylu

Methods

A Workflow for Secure and Tamper Resistant Software Test Reporting 185
Jakob Rechberger and Steffen Heinzl

Breaking the Android Code: A Decade of Methods, Tools and Trends in Mobile Forensics 200
José María Gil-Delgado del Pozo, Lander Aguirregomezcorta Belinchon, and Görkem Kılınç Soylu

Operational Technology Network Anomaly Detection Using N-Grams 224
Jack Nunnelee, Alex Howe, and Mauricio Papa

Knowledge, Skills and Education

Blueprint for K-12 Cybersecurity Education: Integrating Cybersecurity Throughout All K-12 Subjects 245
Timothy Crisp and John Hale

Joining the Dots Between Cybersecurity Career Roles, Skills and Knowledge 265
Eliana Stavrou and Steven Furnell

Phase-Driven Transitions in Cyber-Physical Incident Command Systems: Communication Dynamics from Tabletop Exercises 284
Kenta Nakayama, Kenji Watanabe, and Ichiro Koshijima

AI and Critical Infrastructures

AI-Augmented Scenario Design: Experiences from a National Cybersecurity Exercise 305
Lenhard Reuter, Paul Smith, and Florian Skopik

Sow Smarter, Not Harder: Evaluating LLM-Generated Seeds for Fuzzing Critical Infrastructure 326
Jorge Barredo, Maialen Eceiza, Jose Luis Flores, and Mikel Iturbe

A Multi-dimensional Cyber Range-Powered Scoring Framework for Evaluating Cyber Resilience of Critical Infrastructures 347
Savvas Theodoulou, Eliana Stavrou, Adamantini Peratikou, and Stavros Stavrou

Security Frameworks

CY-TRUST: A Sectorial SOC Framework for Enhanced National and Cross-Border Cybersecurity Resilience 369
Adamantini Peratikou, Evagoras Charalambous, Eliana Stavrou, Panayiota Smyrli, George Hadjichristophi, and Stavros Stavrou

CPSTRIDE: A Threat Modeling Framework for Cyber-Physical Systems 384
Dallas Elleman and John Hale

Next-Generation Threat Risk Management by Integrating GenAI for Security Compliance and Controls 404
Šarūnas Grigaliūnas, Rasa Brūzgienė, Ilona Veitaitė, Renata Danielienė, Paulius Astromskis, Živilė Nemickienė, Dovilė Vengalienė, Rokas Stankūnas, Ieva Andrijauskaitė, and Ieva Šilingaitė

A Comparison of Security ICS Communication Protocols 424
Daniel Clark and Tom Chothia

Author Index 445

Methods & Practice

What Makes Information Critical? Information Classification in Organizational Practice

Simon Andersson(✉), Åsa Ericson, Johan Lugnet, and Christine Große

Luleå University of Technology, 97187 Luleå, Sweden
simon.andersson@ltu.se
http://www.springer.com/gp/computer-science/lncs

Abstract. This paper investigates how information classification is conducted in practice. Despite being a foundation of risk management work, information classification remains understudied from a practical perspective. This study uses semi-structured interviews and a small-scale experiment with professionals from a consultancy firm operating at a national level to explore how information assets are identified, valued and classified. The findings show that information classification is not a purely formalized process, but a collaborative and interpretative activity in which formal models are often adapted or bypassed in favor of context-specific reasoning. Key challenges in practice include inconsistent use of terminology, subjective judgments, and the limitations of classification schemes. The study highlights a need for a shared understanding and trust among participants, which were important factors for successful classification activities, especially in inter-organizational contexts. A three-step approach is thus proposed that emphasizes the value of information in organizational processes before assessing its protection needs. This new approach contributes to a more value-oriented understanding of assets instead of viewing them solely from the perspective of loss or damage. Future research could extend the findings presented.

Keywords: Information classification · Information security · Risk Management · Organizational practice

1 Introduction

The importance of information continues to grow and is often defined as one of, if not the most critical asset of value for an organization. According to [15], information assets are essential for business processes, interactions with stakeholders, all kinds of decisions and the strategic planning of an organization. Both the importance of information as an asset and the increasing number and severity of security breaches and cyber-attacks over the last decade emphasize the necessity of properly managing and protecting the information [14,49].

As a result, many organizations employ risk management methods to assess and reduce the associated risks [8,21]. Usually, the approaches start with an

E. Bergström et al. (Eds.): CRITIS 2025, LNCS 16291, pp. 3–19, 2026.
https://doi.org/10.1007/978-3-032-19540-1_1

identification of the assets that possess value for an organization and thus should be protected. The further steps of risk management include the assessment of threats, vulnerabilities, and consequences, including a representation of concepts like the frequencies of events and conditional probabilities for different consequences given the event, together with assessments of the severity of these consequences (e.g. [32]). In addition, the identification and selection of mitigation strategies, their implementation and monitoring, the external monitoring of emerging and developing threats and the learning from incidents are part of the risk management process [23]. In this paper, the focus is on the initial step, the identification and classification of the information within an organization that is worthy of protection. As previous literature has shown, identifying (information) assets that are of value for an organization is a difficult task, which among others also include capturing intellectual ones. Leming [33] thus stresses the problem that organizations seem to know more about computers and filing cabinets than the information they contain. Today, the same can be said about a greater variety of devices, databases, and cloud services. Therefore, research has regularly emphasized that information governance, including recognizing the value of information, should be a high-level corporate function to ensure maintenance and alignment with strategic development of the organization. Despite a great body of research considering risk assessment methods, there is still a lack of empirical studies investigating how information classification is done in practice and how the value of information is assessed prior to risk assessment and management.

This study aims to fill this gap and investigates information classification as it is done in practice to better understand the main considerations of the people responsible and the use of classification models in such efforts. For this purpose, several professionals tasked with risk management in their own and other organizations participated in this study. Based on interviews and a small-scale experiment, the results show that information classification is in practice a collaborative and interpretative process where formal models are often adapted or bypassed in favor of context-specific reasoning. Moreover, it has been demonstrated that the creation of a common understanding of the criticality of information in the organizational value creation processes and an appropriate level of trust between participants in classification workshops are crucial for the practical application of information classification. This is particularly important for consulting firms as they must confront particular challenges in information classification and risk management due to their vulnerable position as subcontractors [37].

The contribution of this study is twofold. First, it offers empirical evidence on how information is classified in practice, providing valuable insights into the key challenges and possible solutions in an organizational practice. This enables a better understanding of both the problem at hand and the need for further research. Second, it proposes a renewed perspective on information classification that focuses more on the value of information assets in the value chains of organizations before determining the need for protection in terms of specific attributes.

Following this introduction, the next section provides more details on the main concepts underpinning this study, and the method section describes the data collection and analysis. In the result section, findings from interviews and the classification experiment are presented, related to how professionals identify and assess information assets in practice, including approaches, challenges, criteria, and the role of trust. The discussion and conclusion sections complete the paper.

2 Information Classification

2.1 Key Concepts

A central feature of information is that it "represents some part of the world as being a certain way" [17]. In particular, information is an artifact that has semantic or representational content. Other research has recognized objects or documents that contain certain descriptions or summaries as such forms of representation [12]. However, further attributes are needed to distinguish between different levels of importance, that is, to classify the value of a piece of information for an organization. Information classification provides the base for subsequent risk assessments [7,16,47]. The first step is to identify the relevant information assets, describing which they are, how and where they are stored, who uses them, and for which tasks. In general, information is an essential prerequisite for business processes and strategic planning and decision making (see e.g. [15,24]). Information must therefore meet the specific criteria of an organization in terms of its quality and security, for which information classification lays ground. Information assets can be tangible, in the sense that they exist in a directly observable form on items such as paper or digital documents, and intangible, such as business strategies, employee knowledge, or the reputation of an organization. In addition, important information assets can be intellectual property, such assets are often formalized in (digital) documents and stored in hardware and software systems, such as servers, clouds, databases, and networks. Users can retrieve information from those systems to a variety of devices like laptops, tablets and mobile phones. Digital information can be in textual, audio and visual forms, including documents, videos, voice recordings, emails, web sites, text and multimedia messages.

It has been shown that identifying and classifying an organization's information assets are challenging, especially when they are abstract elements, for example, associated with the brand, reputation, and core know-how of an organization [3]. Likewise, digital information assets seem difficult to recognize. For example, a logistics company that fell victim for the NotPetya attack consequently realized that their transport management system was critical to their business [27]. Previously, the executives had seen the company's business as purely physical. From the loss of access to their information system they learned how much the company relies on the digital systems [27]. Hence, all information asset that can be associated with organizational value should be included in the classification process. Identifying and classifying information assets, their locations and interdependencies therefore necessitates a team of different professionals from the organization.

A deeper understanding of an organization, including its purpose and how value is created, is a precondition for information classification. In addition, established models can guide information classification, for example, ISO 27002 is a widely used and known standard [29]. Common information security qualities are confidentiality, integrity, and availability, which refer to the extent to which the information is protected from disclosure by unauthorized persons; is verifiable, well-documented, and free from unauthorized alteration; and is accessible for authorized persons at the right time, in the right place and with correct permission (see e.g. [24]).

Preferably, the classification is conducted by the mentioned team responsible, often in a workshop format [7]. Valuing information is difficult, and it is often considered one of the major problems within risk management [9,18]. The classification assesses the criticality of information to core business operations, for example, by investigating replacement costs and consequences associated with the loss, compromise or leakage of information [2]. Consequence categories can be used to emphasize different effects of misuse, disclosure, alteration or loss of information, such as financial, reputational or operational consequences [6]. However, the lens of compromise and loss may be insufficient to recognize the value of information, as it implies that value only arises in the presence of risk. Such a perspective runs the risk of overlooking the strategic and enabling role that information plays in everyday operations. Therefore, valuation should ideally be done upfront and based on how information supports business processes and creates value, not just how its absence might cause damage or loss.

2.2 Challenges with Information Classification

As mentioned, confidentiality, integrity, and availability are common qualities in information classification (see e.g., [24]), whereby assessing their importance intends to support representing the value of the information for an organization. Often, a classification scheme detailing a few levels of impact, which a compromise of these qualities could bring to the organization, is adapted to the organization of interest [10]. However, there is a scarcity of research considering how such classification scheme can be successfully used, apart from the finding that impact levels should have speaking names in the organizational context of application [7]. In addition, the number of such levels is commonly chosen by an organization itself; typically, it ranges between three and five [29,48]. The classification includes determining the importance of each factor in the context of the organization, while the highest classification of each aspect finally determines the classification for this information asset. In addition, there is a dilemma with the design of the schemes intended to support the information classification: they need to be detailed but also understandable for information owners and users [7,19]. Too complex schemes without sufficient instructions and assessment methods can instead lead to inconsistent valuation [19] whereas too simple schemes are associated with the "bias to the middle", that is, if unequal (e.g. three or five) alternatives are presented, users tend to choose the middle option, similar to the "center-stage effect", described in [41]. Additional issues that previous research has identified include weak, or a lack of, classification guidelines, insufficient inventories of assets, unclear ownership and incomplete classification processes [4,10,19,20,48].

Moreover, professionals entrusted with information classification and risk management in organizations need to legitimate their decisions and to appear confident and knowledgeable about the classifications made. That implies that trust in the role or person can play an important role in organizational information classification and risk management processes. Robinson [40] described trust as the attitude someone or a party adopts (trustor) towards somebody else or another party (trustee), such as a person, a role, an organization, a piece of information, a technical device or a system (e.g., [43]). According to [39], trust is a combination of five components: i) perceived competence, ii) objectivity, iii) fairness, iv) consistency, and v) faith (good will). In addition, it is emphasized that low performance on some attributes can be compensated by higher performance on others [39].

As indicated, information classification is associated with uncertainty in several ways. One concern is how to properly assess the criticality of information, another one is associated with the identification and assessment process within a particular context, and a third concern includes the professionals who act on behalf of an organization [23]. Furthermore, group settings may increase individually perceived uncertainty, including prevalent group values, the ambiguity of information that can emerge and the feeling of being forced into action [34]. Previous studies have shown that group decisions, whether collective or distributed, may tend to trust the opinions of experienced group members, meaning that not all alternatives are adequately considered [44]. In information classification practice, such behavior can lead to incomplete identification of information assets or over-valuing of assets that in turn imply inappropriate protection measures [4]. Consequently, this study involves a focus on trust, which also addresses the issue that trust is poorly understood from an organizational perspective [35].

3 Method

3.1 Data Collection

This study addresses the scarcity of empirical studies investigating how information classification is done in practice and how the value of information is assessed by the people responsible with the aid of classification models. For this purpose, four experienced professionals with different positions and backgrounds tasked with risk management on behalf of their organization, an information security consultancy firm, participated in this study. The consultancy firm operates at a national level and works extensively with public sector organizations, mainly in Sweden. It is of particular interest as consulting firms occupy a vulnerable position as subcontractors. As sub-contractors have access to multiple clients' data, they are at higher risk of being targeted by cyber-attacks [38], while at the same time needing to build and maintain a reputation as a trustworthy business partner. In addition, perspectives on information classification from a consultancy perspective were deemed interesting, as they assist others in the process, often users who are inexperienced. However, there is still a significant lack of research on specifically IT consulting firms [28]. The respondents in this study work in different locations and have different roles, but are all involved in information classification, allowing for a variety of valuable insights into the practice of information classification. Table 1 provides further details about the respondents.

Table 1. Respondents from an information security consultancy firm

Respondent	Length of interview	Experience in role
Business developer/project leader	60 min	> 20 years
Senior information security consultant	72 min	2 years
Senior consultant/IT-Archivist	28 min	> 20 years
IT-Archivist	40 min	1.5 years

Semi-structured interviews [1,30] with practitioners constitute the base for this study, which is a sufficient method for investigating the outlined topic in greater detail. Semi-structured interviews facilitate the collection of opinions, values and thoughts allowing for the enrichment of a study with extensive data [30]. Semi-structured interviews are generally described as conversations with a purpose; here, the focus was on in-depth dialogues exploring the experiences of the professionals with information classification in practice.

During the interviews, a set of open-ended questions were used to guide the dialogue. Examples of such questions were: *"Could you explain how you conduct information classification?"* and *"How do you use classification models in the classification work?"*. Follow-up questions were asked when answers needed further clarification. Upon consent of the respondents, the interviews were voice-recorded and transcribed verbatim. At the end of each interview, a small-scale experiment using two different classification schemes was conducted with the purpose of observing the process of information classification done by professionals. The respondents were asked to explain their reasoning while conducting the classification, and to "think aloud" to further explain the criteria they considered. In addition, notes were taken alongside the interviews and included in the analysis.

It should be noted that the empirical material consists of 4 interviews with professionals from a single consultancy firm. While this limits the breadth and generalizability of the findings, the respondents' extensive experience offers valuable insight into the practice of information classification.

3.2 Data Analysis

The analysis began while gathering the data, which is consistent with interviewing people [1]. For example, an interviewer seeks to identify hesitation or changes of wording while conducting interviews and follow-up questions. An initial analysis was done when listening to and transcribing the recorded interviews [13]. The in-depth analysis included further a thematic analysis of the transcripts by identifying, analyzing and interpreting patterns within the data [11]. The thematic analysis included the generation of initial codes, the organization of the material into themes, and the interpretation [11,42,46]. The interview guide provided the starting point for coding the material. The collected textual material was then arranged by identified relationships to form cohesive themes. The descriptions and examples provided during the interviews were interpreted using the introduced theoretical perspectives, namely the identification and classification of information assets, and challenges with the information classification process including a focus on trust [31]. The thematic analysis resulted in the following themes: (i) identification and classification of information assets, considering approaches, techniques and organizational prerequisites; ii) common criteria in practice, including reflections on what makes information critical; and iii) security communication and trust, involving contemplations on interpersonal and interorganizational challenges. The interpretations made were verified by returning to the interview recordings to confirm that they were grounded in the context of the investigated topic and mirrored the respondents' own words.

4 Results

4.1 Identification and Classification of Information Assets

There was consensus among the respondents about the importance of information classification for organizations regardless of their size. However, the perceptions varied in terms of how information should be identified and classified and what variables should guide the assessment. The classification scale was perceived as a dilemma by most respondents. According to the business developer, it is vital to identify the information asset, the owner or carrier of it and the classification of confidentiality, availability and integrity (CIA) demands:

"There are information objects and the scale of it, then there is the carrier of information, where does this information exist. This is often done within the borders of what we call information security... So, carrier of information, information object and a classification of the object... There are always variants of CIA but then you need a classification system that you agree with the customer about. Either high, medium, low or a scale of 1–5." - Business Developer

The Senior Information Security Consultant emphasized instead the understanding of the objectives for information classification in an organization and the completeness of the asset inventory

"First you are to value the information, but before it is important to create an inventory of it, it is far from always that has been done fully... You must understand what the purpose is, what is it that we want to

achieve? It is an asset inventory and [...] a valuation of this inventory that ends with [...] a valuation of our information."- Senior Information Security Consultant

In addition, the Senior Information Security Consultant highlighted issues with the naming of classification levels if they are not adapted to the needs of an organization.

"The worst scenario in a business with people is that someone dies. [And] we have handled information in a way that caused someone to lose their life. That's the worst case; another worst case is to go out of business. That is not severe, instead devastating would be better suited. If that happens it is over, goodnight!" - Senior Information Security Consultant

All respondents highlighted that providing guiding examples would be helpful for learning and understanding the information identification and classification task, especially when it comes to examining consequences of the loss of information qualities by unexperienced employees. Another issue brought up was the level of aggregation applicable during information identification. Not only was the type of information, such as financial data of a customer, perceived as too vague, but also the relationship to process flows and the relevance for the organization were considered difficult to assess without further insight into the key processes of a specific organization.

Although the respondents stated that the ordering of the classification scale would not matter, the small experiment at the end of the interviews revealed that all of them preferred to place the assets with the highest protection demands at the top of the list followed by the others in descending order.

The results of the interviews show that forming a heterogeneous team of various professions from an organization's different departments is a necessary precondition for performing information identification and classification. As different formal roles and responsibilities as well as individual experiences affect how the criticality of information is perceived, the classification work involves relational and knowledge complexity. This includes the representatives' differences in reasoning and comprehension of the organization's core values and the importance of information assets in organizational value generation along key processes. Information classification models are regularly used as communication tools facilitating negotiation and group decision-making.

4.2 Common Criteria in Practice

The respondents regularly helped other organizations, primarily in the public sector, with identifying and classifying information assets prior to risk analysis. Although quality criteria like confidentiality, integrity and availability are common in the information security field, all respondents explained that they often must rephrase them when talking with people in client organizations. The Business developer detailed it as follows:

"You must ask the right questions [...] if this is secret or sensitive information if it leaks? Yes, or no. Then you might have to value how sensitive it is. And if it is important that this information is always within reach and so on." - Business Developer

A few main reasons were regularly mentioned by the respondents, including the experience of experts involved in the classification of information, the vocabulary that is common in some professions and the terminology that is used in a specific organization. The Senior Consultant/IT Archivist exemplified the issues:

"If you are a system administrator and enter a classification workshop... This [the classification] is nothing that people I meet think about all the time. So, a lot of what I do also involves explaining why I do things and why I use the terms that I am using." - IT Archivist

The Business Developer explained the importance of establishing common ground to facilitate information identification and classification by the following example:

"When I arrive at a new customer and mention the term document it can mean a word-document for one person, a collection of 40 appendixes and one missive for another, and for a third person it could simply be a paper. It is very important that you agree on the meaning of certain terms." - Business developer

The Senior Information Security Consultant confirmed that the terms confidentiality, integrity and availability are less frequently employed as assumed and argued that they are not useful in the preparatory phase of risk analysis including information identification and classification in practice. He further declared:

"When I arrive at customers that use the terms a lot, I usually tell them that they are on the wrong track... I've done this for many years, and I know one thing. There is no point in classifying confidentiality [integrity and availability] 1 to 4, you will get a C2, I2 and A2, and what do you do with that?" - Senior Information Security Consultant

Instead of such superficial classification, where neither the term nor the numbers provide sufficient clarity on how to proceed, the assessment must therefore focus on the value of the information for the specific organization looking at the information in its context and how its value comes about. However, the study results reveal that discussing different scenarios is an approach to assessing consequences. The scenarios, naturally worst-case scenarios, are then compared with each other, which refers to risk analysis rather than to information classification as a precondition for the former.

4.3 Security Communication and Trust

The respondents reflected on the role of trust in their work with information classification in two ways, internally and externally. The internal perspective included trust within their organization among colleagues and the external perspective considered clients and customers of their consultancy services. Main prerequisites for trust that the respondents identified as one part's willingness to put faith in another individual, function or item, were the fulfilment of expectations regarding conducting tasks, adhering to agreements and behaving reliably. The business developer perceived that trust can be placed both on information and persons and explained it in the following way:

> *"When I help customers, trust is the connection to integrity [...], how much can I trust that this information that I take part in or receive is correct and not altered, and what believe do I put in it? And if we turn around and talk about colleagues then trust is [...] the ability to have faith in that the colleagues I have do what they are supposed to do and that they will do their work in the best possible way". - Business Developer*

Transparency and commitment to agreements were also considered important to create and enhance trust among business partners. All respondents expressed a clear distinction between trust in items, such as information, and people. Mainly, the interviewees discussed how one part's behavior affects the other part's trust in the former. When talking about trust in information, they rather reflected on one's belief in information qualities, such as accuracy, correctness and originality. The Senior Information Security Consultant emphasized the relation between information Security and trust:

> *"When connecting trust with Information Security, trust lies in the quality of the information. That it is correct, available and that there is some sort of quality-protection of confidentiality that often surrounds information or a task... within information security, it [trust] is what is important, it is the 'be-all end-all". - Senior Information Security Consultant*

The interviewees also provided the insight that trust is an important prerequisite in organizational and inter-organizational contexts to ease and streamline cooperations. The IT Archivist underlined the importance of a certain level of trust in such contexts:

> *"If you can trust each other, it makes transactions between people and things more effective. If you assume that you can't trust anything things will be far more cumbersome and complicated." - IT Archivist*

The results of the interviews emphasize that a common language and terminology regarding information classification and security requirements is considered a good start to build trust within the team and the organization. However, the extent to which trust in teamwork roles and responsibilities is expressed or taken for granted remains questionable.

5 Discussion

5.1 Implications for Information Identification and Classification

A few key issues can be discussed based on the analysis of the study's empirical evidence, including the complexity of the information classification task in an organizational context. To begin with, clarification of the general process steps appears necessary. Although defined as prerequisite for organizational risk analysis, the presented findings reveal that identification and classification of information tends to tamper into risk assessments, through the use of scenarios based on threats, vulnerabilities and consequence as well as probability estimations. As a consequence, the value of information in a specific organizational context, for example to enable and support core business processes and value realization is regularly overlooked. Moreover, the task remains unstructured and overly complex as all aspects of risk analysis are involved simultaneously. Therefore, a more structured approach is advisable. The upper row of activities in Fig. 1 illustrates a three-step process related to information classification, including the identification, valuation and classification of information, in an organizational context. The first step relates to an inventory of information assets, the second one intends to create an understanding of the value of the information to the organization and the third step results in determining the protection needs of the information assets.

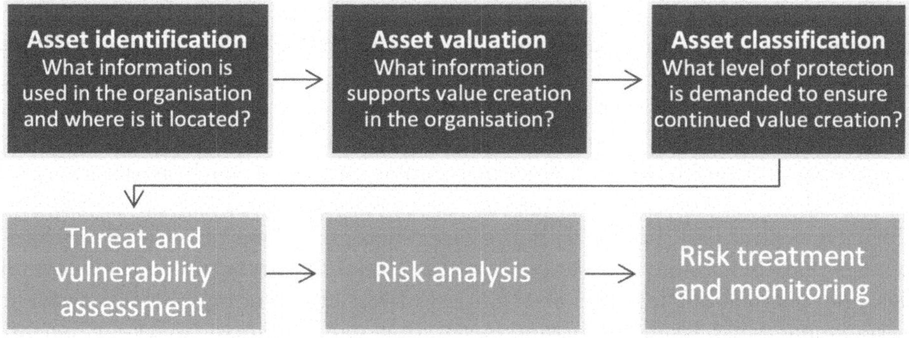

Fig. 1. A three-step process of asset identification and classification as input into risk analysis, (Newly originated by the authors).

This study has found that challenges appear in the identification step, for example, concerning the level of granularity that should be adopted, which also aligns with findings in previous research in different contexts (e.g., [4,25,26]). As emphasized by the empirical results, these steps preferably are conducted by a heterogenous team of various professions in a format that enables dialogue among participants and facilitates mutual understanding of the organizational values and security needs. In addition, the group also needs to discuss the level of detail and the terminology that is appropriate in the specific organization. Moreover, the employed tools and methodology require consideration. For example, the valuation of the identified assets could be based on a mapping of key processes prepared in advance following a structures quality management approach (cf. e.g., ISO 9001). An alignment of information security and quality management can help with both identifying information assets and processes that are critical to the organization and determining the value and protection needs of those information assets [22,24]. Process models and descriptions facilitate the identification of relevant information objects and their owners, carriers, and users, as well as interrelated systems and devices, as this study's results emphasize. Moreover, such alignment is likely to improve the various professions' understanding of the purpose of information classification in particular and the impact of information security work as a facilitator of business continuity in general.

As presented above, the classification of information, that is, the determination of the targeted level of protection, is accompanied by methodological issues. For example, the selection of the classification scheme or tool and the criteria for describing the level of protection required. The information qualities of confidentiality, integrity and availability are useful for describing the level of protection that is needed from the view of these three perspectives. However, the choice of one number or word that summarizes these three different dimensions regularly appeared as the key challenge, that also leads to an oversimplification and misalignment between information classification; threat, vulnerability and risk assessments; and mitigation strategies that facilitate organizational value creation by socio-technical processes. It would therefore be advisable to document the argumentation and considerations underpinning the group decision-making during the three-step process in a sufficient manner [5] to inform the following assessments, as depicted in the lower row in Fig. 1.

Moreover, the study's findings highlight trust as a means to cope with the uncertainty and ambiguity inherent in complex problems, such as determining the criticality of assets in societal contexts to prioritize resource allocation and security measures [25]. In the study presented here, trust was put on other professionals when their behavior was perceived reasonable in relation to their formal roles and responsibilities (see also [45]). Further, the findings also show that interpersonal trust is an important factor that can facilitate relational performance (e.g., [43]), especially in interorganizational collaboration by consultancy firms and in group settings.

5.2 Implications for Further Research

The findings of this study indicate several remaining issues that deserve further attention. First, organizational processes and contexts, as well as the information in use, are subject to regular and dynamic changes. Therefore, asset registries are incomplete and the determination of the value and protection needs of information assets changes over time. Further empirical research could examine how organizational procedures, and methodological approaches can be designed to better reflect the complex realities of public and private organizations. In addition, experiments on group settings and dialogue-based approaches could expand the findings presented in this study. In particular, the presented results emphasize a stronger focus on organizational value creation instead of premature risk analysis that arises when using consequence categories in information classification. Therefore, suggestions for further research include studies evaluating the applicability and usefulness of value assessments to determine the criticality of information. Inspiration can be found in the research area of critical infrastructure and vital societal function, in which infrastructure is considered critical if the survival, well-being and progress of society depend on its maintained functionality [25]. Similarly, information can be considered critical if the survival, well-being and progress of an organization (or society) depend on its maintained quality in terms of confidentiality, integrity and availability. Additional research could investigate the role of additional qualities that are gaining attention, such as privacy and truthfulness (see also [24]).

Moreover, the application of scales to describe and determine the protection needs of information assets regarding various information qualities is common but their meaningfulness has been questioned. In addition to terms that better describe the thresholds, the granularity of such scales can be subject to future research. The aggregation of the protection levels determined for each criterion into a value protection index that actually captures the significance of information under consideration remains a further area for research.

This study also reveals that providing examples was an important tool to convey the message to stakeholders involved in information classification. It could therefore be further explored whether the use of narrative or fiction-based methods of storytelling [36] can provide alternative approaches. In addition, the effects of such approaches on trust-building mechanisms among professionals may be of interest. Based on the empirical material presented, trust remains an important factor for group work and inter-organizational collaboration, especially with respect to security-related tasks conducted by consultants. Assessments include critical information, business secrets and dependencies on assets, knowledge and people. Hence, a certain level of interpersonal trust is also precondition for information classification, regardless of the involvement of internal or external professionals. Follow-up research could deepen the insights presented in this paper by analyzing how trust in partner organizations, individual professionals, information assets and different types of information systems affect the conduct of information classification and risk analysis in organizations. It could further investigate what secondary risks may arise from an inappropriate level of trust on both responsible people, implemented approaches and technical tools as well as their implications for supply chain security.

6 Conclusion

This paper investigated information classification as done in practice to better understand the main considerations of the people responsible, the use of classification models, and the interrelated challenges. To this end, several professionals who are regularly entrusted with such tasks in their own and other organizations, mainly in the public sector in Sweden, participated in this study.

The results highlight that a deeper understanding of an organization, including its purpose and how value is created, is necessary to perform meaningful information classification. For example, the type of information, such as financial data of a customer, and the relationship to core processes as well as the relevance for the organization were considered difficult to assess without further insight into a specific organization. In addition, the findings emphasize that a common language regarding information classification terms and security requirements helps to build trust within the team. However, the extent to which trust in teamwork roles and responsibilities is expressed or taken for granted remains a question for further investigation.

The classification of information includes determining the importance of different criteria in the context of the organization, while the highest classification of each usually determines the criticality of this information asset. However, the choice of one number or word that summarizes these different requirements regularly appeared as the key challenge, that also tended to lead to an oversimplification and misalignment between information classification; threat, vulnerability and risk assessments; and mitigation strategies. In particular, the presented study stresses a stronger focus on organizational value creation by socio-technical processes instead of premature risk analysis that arises when using consequence categories, which focus on compromise and loss, in information classification. Such a focus may overlook the strategic and enabling role that information plays in day-to-day business. Therefore, the findings underline that valuation should ideally be done upfront and based on how information supports business processes and creates value, not just how its absence might cause damage or loss.

The contribution of this study is thus twofold. First, it contributes empirical evidence on the classification of information that provides valuable insights into the key challenges and possible solutions in organizational practice. This enables a better understanding of both the problem at hand and the need for further research. Second, it offers a renewed three-step perspective on the classification of information that focuses more on the value of information assets in the value chains of organizations before determining the need for protection in terms of specific attributes.

Further research that seeks to advance the knowledge presented in this study could explore the development and evaluation of methods that better integrate value-based assessments into information classification processes. In addition, the impact of organizations' prerequisites, subcontractors in the supply chain and key narratives for problem recognition and trust building are further areas for future research. Further research could expand the study presented here with additional empirical material and take other contexts into account, such as the private sector or international organisations.

Disclosure of Interests. The authors have no competing interests to declare relevant to this article's content.

References

1. Adams, W.C.: Conducting semi-structured interviews. In: Handbook of Practical Program Evaluation, pp. 492–505 (2015)
2. Agrawal, V.: A framework for the information classification in ISO 27005 standard. In: 2017 IEEE 4th International Conference on Cyber Security and Cloud Computing (CSCloud), pp. 264–269. IEEE (2017)
3. Ahlin, K.: Measuring the immeasurable? The intangible benefits of digital information. In: Hawaii International Conference on System Sciences, pp. 6176–6185. Hawaii International Conference on System Sciences (2019)
4. Andersson, S.: Problems in information classification: insights from practice. Inf. Comput. Secur. **31**(4), 449–462 (2023)
5. Andersson, S., Bergström, E., Lundgren, M., Bernsmed, K., Bour, G.: Information security risk management tools in the air traffic management domain: what are practitioners' needs? Inf. Secur. J. A Global Perspect., 1–18 (2025)
6. Bergquist, J.H., Tinet, S., Gao, S.: An information classification model for public sector organizations in Sweden: a case study of a Swedish municipality. Inf. Comput. Secur. **30**(2), 153–172 (2021)
7. Bergström, E., Karlsson, F., Åhlfeldt, R.M.: Developing an information classification method. Inf. Comput. Secur. **29**(2), 209–239 (2021)
8. Bergström, E., Lundgren, M.: Stress amongst novice information security risk management practitioners. Intl. J. Cyber Situational Awareness **4**(1), 128–154 (2019). https://doi.org/10.22619/IJCSA.2019.100128, https://c-mric.com/100128
9. Bergström, E., Lundgren, M., Ericson, A.: Revisiting information security risk management challenges: a practice perspective. Inf. Comput. Secur. **27**(3), 358–372 (2019). https://doi.org/10.1108/ICS-09-2018-0106
10. Bergström, E., Åhlfeldt, R.-M.: Information classification issues. In: Bernsmed, K., Fischer-Hübner, S. (eds.) NordSec 2014. LNCS, vol. 8788, pp. 27–41. Springer, Cham (2014). https://doi.org/10.1007/978-3-319-11599-3_2
11. Braun, V., Clarke, V.: Using thematic analysis in psychology. Qual. Res. Psychol. **3**(2), 77–101 (2006)
12. Buckland, M.K.: Information as thing. J. Am. Soc. Inf. Sci. **42**(5), 351–360 (1991)
13. Denscombe, M.: EBOOK: The Good Research Guide: For Small-Scale Social Research Projects. McGraw-Hill Education (UK) (2017)
14. European Union Agency for Cybersecurity (ENISA): ENISA Threat Landscape 2024 (2024). https://doi.org/10.2824/0710888, https://www.enisa.europa.eu/sites/default/files/2024-11/ENISA%20Threat%20Landscape%202024_0.pdf
15. Evans, N., Price, J.: Development of a holistic model for the management of an enterprise's information assets. Int. J. Inf. Manage. **54**, 102193 (2020)
16. Everett, C.: Building solid foundations: the case for data classification. Comput. Fraud Secur. **2011**(6), 5–8 (2011). http://www.sciencedirect.com/science/article/pii/S1361372311700604
17. Fallis, D.: What is disinformation? Libr. Trends **63**(3), 401–426 (2015)

18. Fenz, S., Heurix, J., Neubauer, T., Pechstein, F.: Current challenges in information security risk management. Inf. Manage. Comput. Secur. **22**(5), 410–430 (2014), https://doi.org/10.1108/IMCS-07-2013-0053
19. Fibikova, L., Müller, R.: A Simplified Approach for Classifying Applications, pp. 39–49. Vieweg+Teubner, Wiesbaden (2011)
20. Ghernaouti-Helie, S., Simms, D., Tashi, I.: Protecting information in a connected world: a question of security and of confidence in security. In: 2011 14th International Conference on Network-Based Information Systems, pp. 208–212 (2011). https://doi.org/10.1109/NBiS.2011.38
21. Gritzalis, D., Iseppi, G., Mylonas, A., Stavrou, V.: Exiting the risk assessment maze: a meta-survey. ACM Comput. Surv. **51**(1), 1–30 (2018)
22. Große, C.: Towards an integrated framework for quality and information security management in small companies (2016)
23. Große, C.: Sources of uncertainty in Swedish emergency response planning. J. Risk Res. **22**(6), 758–772 (2019)
24. Große, C.: Enhanced information management in inter-organisational planning for critical infrastructure protection: case and framework. In: ICISSP, pp. 319–330 (2021)
25. Große, C., Larsson, A., Björkqvist, O.: Information-flawing filters in critical infrastructure protection: the deficient information basis in a Swedish approach. Int. J. Crit. Infrastruct. **19**(1), 40–57 (2023)
26. Große, C., Olausson, P.M., Wallman-Lundåsen, S.: Left in the dark: obstacles to studying and performing critical infrastructure protection. Electron. J. Bus. Res. Meth. **19**(2), 58–70 (2021)
27. Hepfer, M., Powell, T.C.: Make cybersecurity a strategic asset. MIT Sloan Manag. Rev. **62**(1), 40–45 (2020)
28. Hove, C., Tårnes, M., Line, M.B., Bernsmed, K.: Information security incident management: identified practice in large organizations. In: 2014 Eighth International Conference on IT Security Incident Management & IT Forensics, pp. 27–46. IEEE (2014)
29. ISO/IEC 27002: Information security, cybersecurity and privacy protection – information security controls. Standard ISO/IEC 27002:2022, International Organization for Standardization, Geneva, CH (2022). https://www.iso.org/standard/75652.html
30. Kallio, H., Pietilä, A.M., Johnson, M., Kangasniemi, M.: Systematic methodological review: developing a framework for a qualitative semi-structured interview guide. J. Adv. Nurs. **72**(12), 2954–2965 (2016)
31. Kvale, S.: The 1,000-page question. Q. Inq. **2**(3), 275–284 (1996)
32. Larsson, A., Große, C.: Data use and data needs in critical infrastructure risk analysis. J. Risk Res. **26**(5), 524–546 (2023)
33. Leming, R.: Why is information the elephant asset? An answer to this question and a strategy for information asset management. Bus. Inf. Rev. **32**(4), 212–219 (2015)
34. March, J.G.: Understanding how decisions happen in organizations. Organ. Decis. Making **10**(2), 9–32 (1997)
35. Marcial, D.E., Launer, M.A.: Towards the measurement of digital trust in the workplace: a proposed framework. Int. J. Sci. Eng. Sci. **3**(12), 1–7 (2019)
36. McBeth, M.K., Jones, M.D., Shanahan, E.A.: The narrative policy framework. Theor. Policy Process **3**, 225–266 (2014)
37. Nyman, M., Große, C.: Are you ready when it counts? It consulting firm's information security incident management. In: ICISSP, pp. 26–37 (2019)

38. General Data Protection Regulation: Regulation (EU) 2016/679 of the European Parliament and of the council. Regulation (EU) 679, 2016 (2016)
39. Renn, O., Levine, D.: Credibility and trust in risk communication. In: Kasperson, R.E., Stallen, P.J.M. (eds.) Communicating Risks to the Public. Technology, Risk, and Society, vol. 4. Springer, Dordrecht (1991). https://doi.org/10.1007/978-94-009-1952-5_10
40. Robinson, S.L.: Trust and breach of the psychological contract. Adm. Sci. Q., 574–599 (1996)
41. Rodway, P., Schepman, A., Lambert, J.: Preferring the one in the middle: further evidence for the centre-stage effect. Appl. Cogn. Psychol. **26**(2), 215–222 (2012)
42. Saldaña, J.: The Coding Manual for Qualitative Researchers, 4th edn. SAGE Publications Inc., Thousand Oaks, CA, USA (2021)
43. Söderström, E.: Trust types: an overview. Discourses Secur. Assur. Priv. **15**(16), 1–12 (2009)
44. Stasser, G., Kerr, N.L., Davis, J.H.: Influence processes and consensus models in decision-making groups. Psychol. Group Influence **2**, 279–326 (1989)
45. Svensson, Å., Lundberg, J., Forsell, C., Rönnberg, N.: Automation, teamwork, and the feared loss of safety: air traffic controllers' experiences and expectations on current and future atm systems. In: Proceedings of the 32nd European Conference on Cognitive Ergonomics, pp. 1–8 (2021)
46. Vaismoradi, M., Turunen, H., Bondas, T.: Content analysis and thematic analysis: implications for conducting a qualitative descriptive study. Nurs. Health Sci. **15**(3), 398–405 (2013)
47. Webb, J., Maynard, S., Ahmad, A., Shanks, G., et al.: Information security risk management: an intelligence-driven approach. Australas. J. Inf. Syst. **18**(3) (2014)
48. Whitman, M.E., Mattord, H.J.: Principles of Information Security, 7th edn. Cengage Learning (2022)
49. Yadav Ph D, S.B., Dong, T.: A comprehensive method to assess work system security risk. Commun. Assoc. Inf. Syst. **34**(1), 8 (2014)

Reducing SOC Analysts Alert Fatigue via Real-Time CTI Correlation and Deduplication

Sotiris Koumourou, Adamantini Peratikou(✉), Eliana Stavrou, Savvas Theodoulou, and Stavros Stavrou

Open University of Cyprus, Nicosia, Cyprus
Adamantini.peratikou@ouc.ac.cy

Abstract. Security Operations Centers (SOCs) grapple with analyst fatigue driven by over-whelming alert volumes and repetitive, low-value notifications. This work investigates whether verified Cyber Threat Intelligence (CTI) feeds can be leveraged, in real time, to suppress noise and surface genuine risk across a distributed Network Intrusion Detection System (NIDS) of Suricata sensors. We present a streaming methodology that (i) correlates each alert group with curated, verified CTI indicators (e.g., URL, Domains, IPv4, IPv6, SHA256, MD5 etc.) and (ii) deduplicates and groups recurrent, identical alerts across sensors within a configurable time window, to adjust triage priority. Suricata's native severities (1–3, with 3 being lowest) are treated as an initial signal that can be dynamically recalibrated by CTI context, campaign prevalence, indicator freshness, and observed recurrence across sites. Using this approach, we demonstrate that the total number of alerts presented to analysts can be reduced to a small fraction of the baseline over the same interval—without sacrificing coverage—by suppressing groups with negative or stale CTI evidence and by collapsing duplicates. Conversely, we show that alerts initially labeled with severity 3 can warrant promotion when corroborated by high-confidence CTI (e.g., active infrastructure, recent sightings, or linkage to ongoing campaigns), thereby preventing critical misses hidden among "low" severity events. The results suggest that real-time CTI correlation paired with alert grouping meaningfully lowers cognitive load, improves prioritization fidelity, and provides a principled path to balancing recall and workload in production SOCs.

Keywords: Security Operations Center · SOC · Alert fatigue. NIDS · Real-time correlation · Alert grouping · deduplication · Triage automation · False-positive suppression · Workload reduction · IOC

1 Introduction

Cybersecurity today is defined by a paradox: while organizations have access to increasingly advanced monitoring tools, defenders are often overwhelmed rather than empowered by the flood of information these tools generate. Security Operations Centers

E. Bergström et al. (Eds.): CRITIS 2025, LNCS 16291, pp. 20–35, 2026.
https://doi.org/10.1007/978-3-032-19540-1_2

(SOCs), which function as the central hubs of defense, must process very large volumes of alerts daily. Yet this constant stream of notifications often hinders rather than helps. Analysts face repetitive, low-value alerts that dilute attention, resulting in fatigue, slower response times, and a greater risk of overlooking genuine threats [1]. The challenge is compounded by the nature of modern adversaries. Advanced persistent threats are designed to evade traditional defenses, frequently bypassing signature-based mechanisms [2]. As a result, critical incidents can be buried among large volumes of benign or redundant alerts. Traditional SOC workflows, reliant on static rule sets and manual triage, struggle in this environment. Analysts are left with an unmanageable workload, where distinguishing between noise and actionable intelligence becomes increasingly difficult [3].

In response, research has explored ways to reduce alert fatigue, filter false positives, and improve triage accuracy. Proposed approaches include refining intrusion detection rules, adopting collaborative intelligence-sharing models, and structuring workflows to streamline alert handling [4–7]. Other work highlights the importance of systematically refining triage policies to reduce unnecessary escalations, emphasizing the need for continuous adaptation in SOC practices [8, 9]. Complementary research underscores the role of data-driven methods in enhancing consistency and efficiency across distributed SOC environments, where geographically dispersed sensors can amplify complexity [10, 11]. Despite these advances, most efforts focus on single aspects of the problem such as deduplication, enrichment, or workflow optimization without integrating them into a unified framework. This gap leaves SOCs without a principled approach to simultaneously suppress low-value alerts, highlight high confidence threats, and dynamically recalibrate priorities in line with the evolving threat landscape.

This work addresses that gap by introducing a novel methodology that leverages deduplication and real-time Cyber Threat Intelligence (CTI) to enhance the effectiveness of distributed Network Intrusion Detection Systems (NIDS). The proposed approach is twofold: (i) each alert group is correlated with verified CTI indicators such as URL, Domains, IPv4, IPv6, SHA256, MD5, TTPS, to recalibrate triage priorities [12, 13], and (ii) recurrent, identical alerts across sensors are aggregated within configurable time windows, reducing duplication. In this way, NIDS's baseline severity levels are transformed from static values into adaptive signals that account for CTI context, campaign prevalence, and indicator freshness. The outcome is a system that reduces the total number of alerts presented to analysts while ensuring that low-severity events linked to strong CTI evidence are not overlooked. For example, alerts initially tagged with severity 3 may warrant promotion if corroborated by intelligence tied to active campaigns. Conversely, duplicate or stale alerts can be suppressed, allowing analysts to direct their attention where it matters most. By lowering the manual burden of triage, SOC personnel can focus resources on proactive threat hunting and incident response [14].

This paper therefore presents a robust framework for real-time alert management that unifies CTI correlation, alert grouping, and dynamic severity recalibration into a single methodology. In doing so, it addresses the shortcomings of static rule-based approaches and fragmented solutions, offering a principled way to balance recall and workload in production SOCs. The overarching goal is to transform the reactive SOC model into a proactive, intelligence-driven operation, where genuine threats are surfaced with minimal delay and maximum accuracy.

2 Related Work

Numerous studies have highlighted the persistent challenges faced by Security Operations Centers (SOCs), particularly the overwhelming volume of alerts generated by intrusion detection systems and the resulting analyst fatigue [5]. This constant flood of notifications reduces analysts' ability to discern meaningful threats, increasing the risk of delayed responses or missed incidents. If one also considers extended threats [15] and the costly organizational and financial fallout of major data breaches [16], one can highlight how modern adversaries exploit all possible technical vulnerabilities in wired and wireless domains, and human shortcomings, emphasizing the need for SOC processes that leverage Cyber Threat Intelligence (CTI) to surface high-impact threats while reinforcing resilience through proactive defences and awareness training. The human dimension of cybersecurity is equally critical. Effective awareness and training require competencies tied to cyber threats and threat actors, noting the Cyber Incident Responder role from the ECSF as central for tailored programs [17]. In sector-specific contexts, [18] highlights the need to detect cyber threats in complex maritime environments, demonstrating how OT sensor data fusion can enhance situational awareness. Complementing this, [19] stresses that realistic cyber range scenarios, especially in critical infrastructures, allow trainees to build both technical and organizational skills. Integrating SOC practices into such exercises strengthens preparedness by simulating real-world detection and response workflows.

Building on this, researchers consistently stress the critical need for improved alert prioritization frameworks to combat the inefficiencies inherent in current SOC operations [8]. Traditional network intrusion detection systems, though effective in capturing signatures, often generate large volumes of low-fidelity alerts, which can consume analyst time without contributing to actual security improvements [3]. False positives represent a significant bottleneck, accounting for a large proportion of alerts that ultimately prove to be benign. Without intelligent filtering and contextual enrichment, analysts are forced to spend considerable time investigating irrelevant events, leading to fatigue, slower mean-time-to-detect, and heightened risk of overlooking genuine compromises.

Beyond these operational challenges, recent work has focused on the integration of CTI with varying types of intrusion detection systems to improve detection precision. Studies highlight that combining CTI with such systems allows external threat information such as Indicators of Compromise (IOCs) to enrich raw alerts, prioritize critical incidents, and suppress irrelevant notifications [20, 21]. By reducing noise and highlighting verified, high-confidence signals, IOC-driven CTI correlation enhances both the precision and recall of intrusion detection systems, thereby strengthening SOC resilience against evolving adversaries.

The literature therefore points to the importance of adaptive alert management systems that can dynamically prioritize threats based on context. Shah et al. [11] emphasize that such systems are particularly critical in distributed SOC environments, where alerts originate from geographically dispersed sensors and must be triaged consistently across sites. Adaptive systems that minimize non-analysed alerts at the end of each shift not only preserve operational continuity but also reduce analyst burnout, a persistent human-factor challenge in security operations.

Artificial intelligence (AI) and machine learning (ML) have also been explored as tools to streamline alert handling and reduce analyst burden. Recent work demonstrates their potential to automate aspects of false-positive detection and to assist in structuring workflows for handling large volumes of security data [6, 7]. These contributions highlight the value of data-driven methods for improving consistency and efficiency across complex SOC environments [10]. While promising, such approaches are often presented as standalone solutions and do not fully address the need for unified frameworks that integrate CTI correlation with alert grouping and prioritization.

Systematic reviews further underscore the evolution of CTI methodologies, techniques, and data handling strategies [22]. A central challenge remains the integration of heterogeneous CTI sources into a coherent operational picture, enabling timely transformation of raw intelligence into actionable signals. By reducing the time from intelligence ingestion to mitigation, SOCs can accelerate response while maintaining situational awareness [23]. Standardized CTI formats such as STIX 2.1 facilitate this process by enabling seamless exchange and integration across organizational and national SOCs [24], while collaborative real-time sharing practices bolster collective defence against transnational and highly coordinated adversaries [24]. Beyond data handling, researchers are increasingly exploring advanced analytical paradigms. Deep learning, generative AI, and other emerging approaches enable nuanced interpretations of CTI indicators, helping analysts differentiate between benign anomalies and genuinely malicious activity [25, 26]. These methods not only improve the fidelity of alerts but also address long-standing challenges such as class imbalance in threat datasets and the complexity of domain-specific signals. The application of such methods is not purely operational but also regulatory; effective CTI integration supports compliance with frameworks such as GDPR and NIS2 by improving incident detection and response capabilities [24].

Automated threat intelligence platforms represent another critical development, orchestrating the acquisition, processing, and dissemination of intelligence across diverse environments. Many of these platforms now dynamically recalibrate threat priorities, moving beyond static severity levels toward context-aware assessments that reflect ongoing campaigns, indicator freshness, and adversary tactics [27, 28]. By aligning detection systems more closely with the evolving threat landscape, these platforms play a key role in ensuring that SOC analysts can focus on high-value alerts while suppressing noise.

Collectively, the literature demonstrates that the challenges of alert fatigue, false positives, and distributed SOC management cannot be solved by technology alone. Hybrid approaches that integrate IOC scoring, standardized CTI formats, collaborative intelligence sharing, and sustained awareness training offer promising paths toward resilience. However, most existing efforts either focus narrowly on reducing false positives, improving analyst awareness, or standardizing CTI exchange. Few works operationalize real-time CTI correlation in conjunction with alert grouping, IOC scoring, and severity recalibration across distributed NIDS environments. Addressing this gap, the present study proposes a streaming methodology that directly integrates verified CTI feeds into the alert triage process, with the goal of lowering cognitive load while preserving detection coverage.

3 Proposed SOC Alert Reduction Model

This section details the architecture and operation of our real-time CTI-aware alert reduction pipeline for distributed NIDS (and complementary HIDS). The design goal is to (i) recalibrate NIDS's native severities using verified CTI indicators enriched with confidence and freshness and (ii) collapse duplicate alerts across sensors within an event time window. The approach operationalizes insights from the literature on SOC alert triage and CTI integration [2–4, 11–13, 20, 21, 27, 30, 31].

3.1 Proposed Model Architectural Overview

The proposed model integrates real-time CTI correlation, alert grouping, and dynamic severity recalibration into a unified streaming pipeline (Fig. 1). Incoming alerts from distributed NIDS sensors are not directly forwarded to analysts; instead, they are passed through a multi-stage reduction engine designed to suppress redundancy, enrich alerts with intelligence context, and surface only high-confidence signals.

The pipeline consists of the following main components:

CTI Ingestion and Caching. Verified CTI is periodically pulled from a CTI platform, a MISP instance, which is populated by external CTI feeds, filtered by taxonomy and source, and stored in a local low-latency cache to ensure correlation continuity even under transient connectivity loss. The CTI includes URLs, domains, IP addresses, SHA256 and MD5 hashes, together with metadata such as source reliability, sightings, TLP markings, and ATT&CK tags, in line with the CTI model and standards reviewed in [2, 23, 27, 31].

Real-Time CTI Correlation and Feature Extraction. Each alert group is key matched to CTI indicators by type, including IP addresses, domains and URLs at the effective top-level domain, and file hashes. From these groups, features are extracted such as the base severity from Suricata (ranging from one to three), the normalized confidence of the indicator based on reliability, sightings, and corroboration, the freshness of the indicator expressed as a decay with time since it was last seen or until its expiration, and the recurrence of the group in terms of size and spread across sites [20, 21, 29, 31].

Alert Normalization and Grouping. NIDS alerts from multiple distributed sensors are streamed over a Kafka cluster into a Logstash/OpenSearch cluster. Logstash normalizes key fields such as rule identifiers, source and destination tuples, and fully qualified domain names, then applies a session-based, windowed grouping procedure to collapse recurrent, identical alerts observed across sensors within a configurable event time window. Each resulting group retains its first and last seen timestamps, the total count of occurrences, and the number of sensors in which it appeared [4, 21].

Alert Prioritization. A prioritization algorithm is assumed to promote high-risk items (even when NIDS/Suricata severity = 3) and suppress low value/stale cases. To achieve this, the process combines CTI correlation, deduplication, the IOC severity prioritization

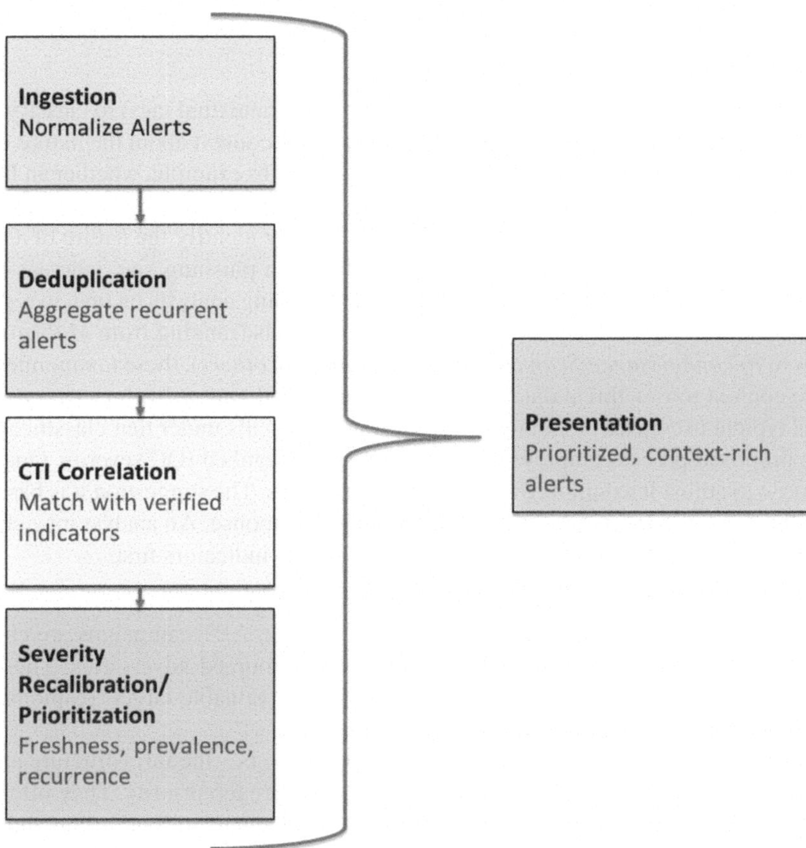

Fig. 1. Conceptual architecture of the proposed SOC alert reduction model

(Sect. 3.2), and the confidence levels provided by the IOC feed. A feedback loop could be used to update severity weights and thresholds periodically [3, 8, 9, 11, 13].

The design of the proposed architecture was informed directly by prior research on SOC alert triage, CTI enrichment, and distributed NIDS operation. The integration of real-time CTI correlation builds on insights from works demonstrating that IOC-driven enrichment significantly improves detection precision and contextual prioritisation [2, 20, 21]. The cross-sensor deduplication and grouping mechanism is motivated by studies on alert correlation within distributed SOCs, which stress the importance of collapsing redundant, multi-site events into unified incident representations [11, 21]. Finally, our IOC semantic taxonomy aligns with established CTI standards and data-exchange models, including MISP and STIX 2.1, [2, 23, 27] ensuring compatibility with widely adopted threat-intelligence practices. Together, these prior contributions shaped the unified streaming pipeline presented in this study.

3.2 IOC Threat Categories, Classification Taxonomy and IOC Severity Prioritization

CTI feeds use a set of predefined threat type categories (contextual tags) to classify indicators of compromise (IOCs). These threat types provide context about the nature of the malicious activity or intent associated with an indicator – for example, whether an IOC is related to malware, phishing, command-and-control (C2) infrastructure, reconnaissance scanning, etc. This classification helps analysts to quickly identify the nature of a given IOC. For example, a domain tagged as *Phish* indicates a phishing site, whereas an IP tagged *C2* suggests a command-and-control server – guiding analysts on how to respond to that indicator. By providing consistent threat type labels (ranging from *Malware* and *Exploits* to *Reconnaissance/Scan* and *Anonymization* and *others*), these taxonomies add valuable context to raw threat data, improving threat intelligence. Each category above includes typical use-cases or examples to illustrate what falls under that classification.

The proposed process employs the following typical ranked IOC severity. One may also choose to adjust it to suit its own threat type priorities. The suggestion it is based on relative threat severity, typical impact, and urgency of response. An analyst may choose to use this as a triage aid to focus on the most dangerous indicators first.

1. **Advanced Persistent Threat (APT):** This category denotes IOCs linked to known state-sponsored or highly sophisticated threat groups. APT campaigns are characterized by stealthy, long-term intrusions by well-resourced adversaries. These are considered critical because APT actors often pursue valuable targets (espionage or sabotage) and use advanced tactics.
2. **Command-and-Control (C2):** Indicators of C2 servers – the infrastructure attackers use to remotely control compromised systems – are top priority. They often signal an active breach, since adversaries rely on C2 channels to issue commands and extract data. Detecting C2 communication means an intrusion has likely occurred, making immediate containment essential.
3. **Data Exfiltration/Leakage:** Indicators that data is being stolen or leaked (such as exfiltration server IPs/domains or paste sites where stolen data is dumped) are extremely critical. A successful exfiltration can result in severe data loss, regulatory penalties, and extortion attempts, so these indicators demand an urgent response (identifying affected data, blocking channels, and eradicating the threat).
4. **Malware: Malware-related IOCs** (malicious file hashes, URLs, payload delivery domains, etc.) are a core threat and warrant high priority. Malware infections can lead to devastating outcomes like ransomware attacks or widespread compromise. Because malware often directly enables breaches and disruption, any active malware IOC typically requires immediate investigation, containment, and removal.
5. **Phishing:** Phishing-related indicators (phishing domains, fraudulent URLs, phishing email senders) rank very high, as phishing is one of the most prevalent entry vectors for attacks. Because phishing attempts can steal credentials or deliver malware, organizations respond rapidly to phishing IOCs – for example, by blocking or taking down malicious sites and alerting users – to prevent compromise before it occurs.
6. **Exploitation (Vulnerabilities):** Indicators of active exploitation – such as URLs or IPs hosting exploit kits, or signatures of known exploits – are high priority due to

their potential impact. An exploit IOC suggests attackers are attempting to leverage a software vulnerability to breach systems. These often require immediate action like patching the vulnerability or blocking the malicious host.

7. **Compromised Infrastructure/Accounts:** IOCs marked as 'compromised' indicate that a legitimate asset has been breached and co-opted by attackers. Such indicators are high priority because compromised third-party infrastructure can be used as trusted pivots to attack others. Must be treated as an active threat – block traffic and notify asset owners while investigating for broader compromise.
8. **Hacking Tools (Post-Exploitation Tools):** This category covers known attacker tools and dual-use utilities used during or after intrusions (e.g., credential dumpers, C2 frameworks, exploit tools). The presence of a hacking tool indicator is a strong sign of adversary activity in an environment and warrants rapid containment and hunting.
9. **Botnet Activity:** Indicators that an IP or domain is part of a botnet are a significant threat. Botnet controllers and nodes are used to conduct attacks like DDoS, spam campaigns, or further malware distribution. Botnet C2 servers are critical to block; individual bot IPs are generally medium priority but still worth filtering and monitoring.
10. **Distributed Denial-of-Service (DDoS):** IOCs related to DDoS attack infrastructure (e.g., IPs of known DDoS botnets or booter services) are important for preserving availability, though they generally rank below espionage or malware threats. Prioritize mitigation during active events and include known sources in pre-block lists.
11. **Peer-to-Peer (P2P) C2 Infrastructure:** Some advanced malware and botnets use P2P networks for command-and-control, making them more resilient. Indicators tied to P2P botnet nodes or malware using P2P are moderately high priority – block where possible and monitor for infection, recognizing the sophistication of such threats.
12. **Cryptocurrency Threats (Crypto):** This category includes indicators related to malicious or illicit cryptocurrency activity – illicit mining pools, wallets used by criminal operations, or crypto-related malware. Crypto-miner infections are typically medium priority (resource drain and security lapse), but crypto IOCs tied to major attacks should be handled as part of those higher-severity incidents.
13. **Fraud/Fraudulent Activity:** Fraud indicators encompass scam websites, fake e-commerce or banking sites, and fraudulent emails aimed at financial gain. Operationally important but often external to your network, these are typically medium priority: pursue takedowns, warn users, and block URLs after containing direct technical attacks.
14. **Scanning/Reconnaissance:** Indicators that an IP or host is performing network scans or reconnaissance are generally lower priority than indicators of an actual attack. Scanning is common background noise; handle via filtering and tuned detections while keeping focus on higher-severity threats.
15. **Brute-Force Attack Sources:** IOCs of systems engaged in brute-force password attacks (e.g., repeated SSH or RDP login attempts) are low-to-medium priority. They indicate malicious intent but are common and often opportunistic. Ensure rate limiting, MFA, and account lockouts; block chronic offenders as needed.

16. **Dynamic DNS (DynDNS) Usage:** Dynamic DNS services are frequently abused by attackers to evade blocking. On its own, a dynDNS IOC is a moderate-priority context indicator. Correlate with other signals (malware, C2) before acting; treat dynDNS-only indicators as suspicious but not definitive.
17. **Anomalous Activity:** The 'anomalous' category covers indicators that are unusual or deviate from normal patterns, yet not conclusively malicious. These warrant investigation but rank below confirmed malicious IOCs to prevent alert fatigue and focus on clear threats first.
18. **Anonymization Services (Non-Tor):** Indicators tied to VPNs, proxies, or anonymization services are often legitimate and thus primarily informational. Use as context (e.g., to flag riskier logins) but treat as lower priority unless corroborated by other malicious activity.
19. **Tor Network Traffic:** Tor is commonly used for anonymity by both legitimate users and threat actors. A Tor exit-node IOC is usually low priority on its own, serving as a signal for heightened monitoring rather than immediate blocking without additional malicious evidence.
20. **I2P Network Activity:** Like Tor, I2P provides anonymous communication and can be abused by adversaries. Treat I2P IOCs as low-to-medium priority context indicators unless combined with concrete malicious activity (e.g., malware callbacks).
21. **Suspicious (Uncategorized Suspicion):** Indicators that appear questionable but aren't confirmed malicious. Useful for watchlists and threat hunting; generally addressed after high-severity alerts to balance thoroughness with efficiency.
22. **Social Media Threats:** Covers malicious social media accounts, posts, or URLs used for phishing or abuse. Important for brand protection and user safety, but typically lower priority for SOC operations compared to direct technical threats.
23. **Adware:** Adware indicators are usually nuisance-level. Handle through routine endpoint hygiene and user education; they rarely require urgent incident response.
24. **Spam Infrastructure:** Spam-related IOCs (spamming IPs, spam domains) are generally low priority unless overlapping with phishing/malware. Address primarily via mail security controls and blocklists.
25. **VPS/Cloud Hosting:** Marks infrastructure from cloud/VPS providers. Widely used by both benign services and adversaries; treat as contextual and low priority unless coupled with malicious indicators.
26. **Informational Markers:** Not threats themselves but contextual artifacts (e.g., disposable email domains, public resolvers). Lowest priority; often excluded from alerting pipelines to reduce noise.
27. **Parked Domains/IPs:** Registered but inactive assets. Generally inert and very low priority unless they later activate with malicious content or resemble your brand (monitor for potential abuse).
28. **Sinkhole:** Infrastructure controlled by researchers/law enforcement to capture malicious traffic. Not an active threat. Traffic to sinkholes may indicate infection attempts, but the sinkhole IOC itself typically requires no blocking action.
29. **Suppress (False Positive Suppression):** Tag used to mark indicators that should be ignored due to being false positives or not relevant. Lowest priority; effectively removed from consideration except for periodic rule reviews.

Although the above typical taxonomy includes 29 IOC categories, not all appear in the evaluated dataset. Nevertheless, the ranking remains essential: it defines how correlated alerts are ultimately ordered and ensures that high-severity categories (e.g., APT, C2, Malware, Exploitation) are consistently surfaced ahead of low-impact categories such as Spam Infrastructure or general scanning.

4 Data Collection and Results Analysis

4.1 Data Collection Method

To evaluate the proposed SOC alert reduction model, we collected alerts from multiple distributed NIDS for a 24-hour period, resulting in 69,029,689 security events of security severity one, two, and three. Each alert record included fields such as source and destination IP, signature ID, and baseline severity. The alerts were then correlated against curated CTI feeds ingested from a MISP instance, fed by a commercial CTI feed, which included indicators of multiple types (IPv4, IPv6, domains, URLs, file hashes etc.) annotated with metadata for reliability, sightings, and freshness. A windowed grouping mechanism was also applied to collapse recurrent, identical alerts observed across sensors within the 24-hour interval. To ensure that the evaluation reflects realistic SOC conditions, all data was collected from a fully operational, production Security Operations Center (SOC). The monitored environment consists of 40 distributed NIDS sensors deployed across multiple network segments, including perimeter gateways, internal VLANs, and datacenter zones. These sensors inspect both internal east–west traffic and north–south traffic entering or leaving the organisation. The system therefore captures genuine user activity, external internet traffic, automated scanning, opportunistic attacks, and benign background noise typical of enterprise environments. Each sensor forwards alerts into a centralised streaming pipeline, maintaining consistent timestamping, rule metadata, and sensor ID. The alerts represent a true production traffic profile. During the 24-hour collection window, the system generated 69,029,689 raw NIDS events across severity levels 1–3, corresponding to unique Suricata signatures and diverse traffic patterns from normal business operations. The MISP-backed CTI platform provided verified indicators, updated multiple times per day from commercial and open-source feeds, and filtered through source-reliability and taxonomy criteria before ingestion.

We selected a 24-hour window to capture a complete daily operational cycle including peak working hours, automated nightly processes, and routine background scanning from the internet. This 24-hour period reflects a typical timeframe used by SOCs for daily handover and shift-based triage metrics. While the dataset cannot be made public due to operational sensitivity, we provide full characterization of its composition and collection methodology to support reproducibility of the evaluation approach.

Analysis was carried out in a sequential manner. First, the total number of alert events, and correlated events were analyzed to capture the scale of reduction achieved through correlation. Second, the aggregate impact of deduplication was quantified by comparing the correlated alert volume against the deduplicated volume across the specified 24-hour period. Finally, alerts were stratified by IOC severity to further prioritize the final bin of correlated alerts. This multi-layered analysis enabled us to assess both the efficiency of noise suppression and the fidelity of severity preservation.

4.2 Results and Discussion

The analysis of CTI alert reduction reveals significant benefits from the application of correlation, deduplication, and prioritization processes. As shown in Fig. 2, uncorrelated alerts were extremely high, especially at Severity Level 3, counting to 67,890,869 events. After correlation, the number of alerts dropped dramatically across all severity levels. The effect was particularly pronounced at Severity Level 1, where the initial 398,001 alerts were reduced to only 3, demonstrating the capability of correlation to suppress redundant or low-value signals. The reduction effectiveness is quantified in Table 1, which illustrates the percentage decrease in alerts. Both Severity Levels 1 and 3 exhibited 99.99% reduction, while Severity Level 2 achieved a reduction of approximately 99.78%. These results highlight the critical role of correlation in mitigating alert fatigue by filtering out events not flagged by CTI. Complementing correlation, deduplication provided further refinement. Figure 3 compares CTI correlated alerts, counting 1,584, where after deduplication the resulting alerts are down to 663, achieving a further 58.16% alert reduction. This underscores the value of normalization and aggregation steps in minimizing redundancy and ensuring that analysts focus on distinct incidents rather than duplicate events.

The final stage of the analysis stratifies correlated alerts by IOC severity according to the ranking defined in Sect. 3.2. Figure 4 has been updated to reflect this prioritization scheme rather than sorting categories by alert count. Accordingly, higher-severity categories such as Command-and-Control (3 alerts) and Malware (29 alerts) appear at the bottom of the vertical axis, followed by Exploitation (4 alerts), Botnet Activity (73 alerts), Scanning/Reconnaissance (438 alerts), Brute-Force Attack Sources (9 alerts), and Spam Infrastructure (107 alerts). Although the dataset is dominated numerically by low-severity categories (e.g., scanning and spam), this ordering ensures consistency with the methodological IOC hierarchy and surfaces the categories with the greatest operational relevance. Together, these findings demonstrate that a layered reduction approach combining correlation, deduplication, and prioritization substantially decreases alert volumes while preserving high-value indicators. This reduces analyst workload and enhances the efficiency of SOC operations by enabling focus on alerts most relevant to organizational risk.

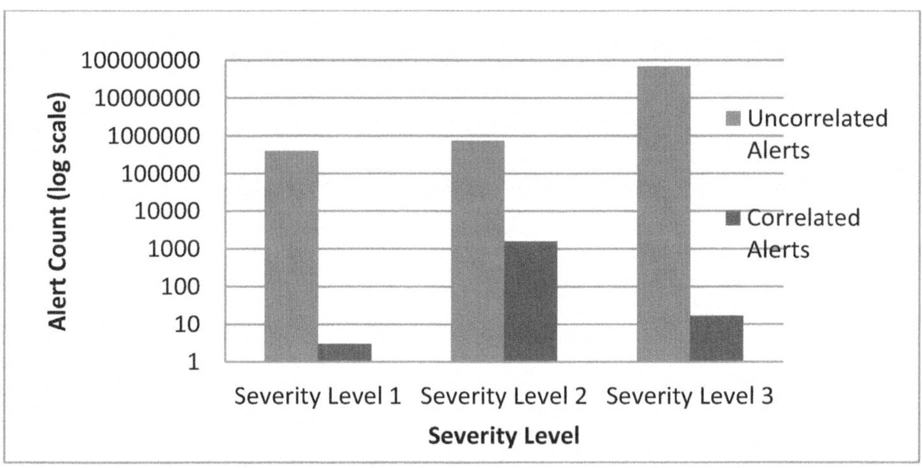

Fig. 2. Comparison of CTI Alerts (Uncorrelated vs. Correlated) across severity levels

Table 1. Reduction of CTI Alerts After Correlation (%) across severity levels

Alert Severity Level	CTI Uncorrelated	CTI Correlated	Alert Reduction (%)
Level 1	398001	3	99.999246
Level 2	740819	1564	99.788882
Level 3	67890869	17	99.999975

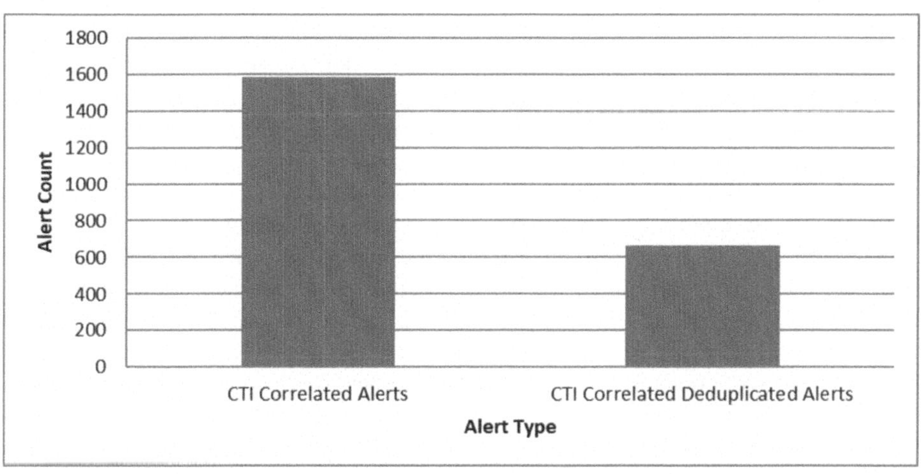

Fig. 3. Reducing CTI correlated Alerts through deduplication.

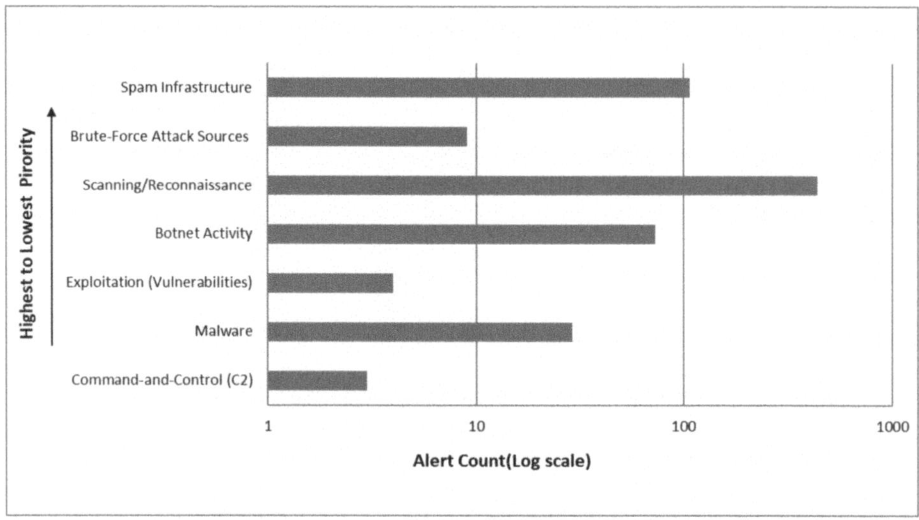

Fig. 4. Prioritized Correlated Alerts by IOC Category (non-zero categories only).

4.3 Comparison with Static Approaches and Prior Literature

While several prior works address alert fatigue through either static rule refinement, standalone enrichment, or isolated correlation mechanisms, they typically operate in a non-adaptive manner and do not integrate real-time CTI, deduplication, and dynamic severity recalibration within a unified pipeline. Static approaches generally rely on signature tuning, thresholding, or rule-based suppression to limit redundant alerts (e.g., filtering based on frequency or time-based grouping). These methods can reduce noise but are inherently limited: they do not incorporate indicator freshness, do not adapt to adversary activity over time, and often fail to promote low-severity alerts that should be elevated when linked to high-confidence threat intelligence. Prior efforts such as [3, 5, 8] emphasise alert prioritisation and triage criteria, while correlation frameworks [11, 20, 21] typically focus on merging alerts across sources or detecting multi-step attack sequences. However, these largely static or batch-oriented processes lack the ability to apply IOC-driven contextual recalibration as threats evolve in real time.

To highlight the difference in practice, we compared our pipeline's reduction behaviour with what a purely static deduplication mechanism would achieve. A standard static deduplication model one that collapses identical alerts based solely on repeated signatures or timestamps would reduce our 1,584 correlated alerts to approximately 663 (a 58.16% reduction). In contrast, our full pipeline first applies real-time CTI correlation, reducing the initial 69,029,689 raw alerts by over 99.99% before deduplication is even applied, and then further reduces these correlated alerts by 58% through cross-sensor aggregation. Static systems generally operate only on the latter layer, missing the CTI-driven suppression of low-value alerts and the promotion of high-signal ones. Moreover, our dynamic severity recalibration ensures that indicators tied to active campaigns, fresh sightings, and high-confidence sources are elevated even when associated baseline NIDS severity is low something traditional systems cannot achieve.

This operationally meaningful distinction positions our model closer to adaptive and intelligence-driven paradigms described in [3, 8, 11], while extending them with real-time IOC scoring, freshness weighting, and cross-sensor aggregation. The comparative results illustrate that the proposed pipeline provides a more holistic and context-aware reduction mechanism that aligns with modern SOC requirements for workload reduction without compromising detection fidelity.

5 Conclusions

This work demonstrated that combining real-time CTI correlation, with alert grouping/deduplication and IOC prioritization, can substantially reduce the volume of notifications presented to SOC analysts, while preserving and in targeted cases improving detection fidelity. Across our 24-hour time frame evaluation, correlation suppressed most low-value events (near-total reductions for severities 1 and 3, and ~99.8% for severity 2), and deduplication further decreased workload by ~58% when comparing raw versus deduplicated totals. Prioritizing the remaining, correlated alerts by IOC threat type concentrated analyst attention on high-signal, but lower priority activity (e.g., Scanning/Reconnaissance and Spam Infrastructure), while still surfacing smaller counts from mission-critical IOC categories such as C2, malware and exploitation. Together, these results indicate that a layered pipeline (i) normalize and group, (ii) correlate with verified CTI, (iii) reprioritize by IOC semantics offers a principled path to combat alert fatigue in production SOCs. Further granular prioritization within the same IOC category can be further achieved based on the confidence level assigned to each alert.

A key novelty of the proposed model is that it moves beyond static or rule-based SOC processes by combining real-time CTI correlation, and cross-sensor deduplication within a single operational pipeline. Unlike static alert-reduction methods, our approach uses IOC freshness and campaign context to adaptively elevate low-severity alerts when they are associated with high-confidence intelligence, thereby reducing the risk of missed detections. At the same time, redundant events across distributed sensors collapsed to minimise analyst workload without sacrificing visibility. This unified, intelligence-driven design differentiates our work from prior static approaches and provides a more robust foundation for practical SOC fatigue mitigation.

The proposed approach is practical and adaptive since severity can be recalibrated by indicator freshness, corroboration, and campaign context. Limitations include dependence on CTI coverage/quality and potential bias introduced by heterogeneous data sources. Future work will (1) extend correlation across host, identity, and cloud telemetry for multi-signal promotion; (2) incorporate feedback-driven learning; and (3) evaluate analyst-centric outcomes (MTTD/MTTR, missed-alert rates, and cognitive load) in larger, multi-tenant deployments.

Acknowledgments. This work has received funding from the European Union's Digital Europe Pro-gramme (DIGITAL) under the Grant Agreement No. 101128017 (CY-TRUST project). Views and opinions expressed are, however, those of the authors only and do not necessarily reflect those of the European Union or the granting authorities. Neither the European Union nor the granting authorities can be held responsible for them.

Disclosure of Interests. The authors have no competing interests to declare that are relevant to the content of this article.

References

1. Tellache, A., Korba, A.A., Mokhtari, A., Moldovan, H., Ghamri-Doudane, Y.: Advancing autonomous incident response: leveraging LLMs and cyber threat intelligence. https://doi.org/10.48550/arXiv.2508.10677 (2025)
2. Sun, N., et al.: Cyber threat intelligence mining for proactive cybersecurity defense: a survey and new perspectives. IEEE Commun. Surv. Tutor. **25**(3), 1748 (2023). https://doi.org/10.1109/COMST.2023.3273282
3. Gelman, B., Taoufiq, S., Vörös, T., Berlin, K.: That escalated quickly: an ML framework for alert prioritization. https://doi.org/10.48550/arXiv.2302.06648 (2023)
4. Maosa, H., Ouazzane, K., Ghanem, M.C.: A hierarchical security events correlation model for real-time threat detection and response. Res. Sq. (2023). https://doi.org/10.21203/rs.3.rs-3698487/v1
5. Tariq, S., Chhetri, M.B., Nepal, S., Paris, C.: Alert fatigue in security operations centres: research challenges and opportunities. ACM Comput. Surv. (2025). https://doi.org/10.1145/3723158
6. Rafiey, P., Namadchian, A.: Using LLMs as AI agents to identify false positive alerts in a security operation center. Res. Sq. (2024). https://doi.org/10.21203/rs.3.rs-5420741/v1
7. Tseng, P., Yeh, Z., Dai, X., Liu, P.: Using LLMs to automate threat intelligence analysis workflows in security operation centers. https://doi.org/10.48550/arXiv.2407.13093 (2024)
8. Jalalvand, F., Chhetri, M.B., Nepal, S., Paris, C.: Alert prioritisation in security operations centres: a systematic survey on criteria and methods. ACM Comput. Surv. (2024). https://doi.org/10.1145/3695462
9. Jalalvand, F., Chhetri, M.B., Nepal, S., Paris, C.: Adaptive alert prioritisation in Security Operations Centres via learning to defer with human feedback. https://doi.org/10.48550/arXiv.2506.18462 (2025)
10. Ismail, I., et al.: Toward robust SOAR in SOCs with hyper-automation using agentic AI. Information **16**(5), 365 (2025). https://doi.org/10.3390/info16050365
11. Shah, A., Ganesan, R., Jajodia, S., Samarati, P., Çam, H.: Adaptive alert management for balancing optimal performance among distributed CSOCs using reinforcement learning. IEEE Trans. Parallel Distrib. Syst. **31**(1), 16 (2019). https://doi.org/10.1109/TPDS.2019.2927977
12. Freitas, S., Gharib, A.: GraphWeaver: billion-scale cybersecurity incident correlation. https://doi.org/10.48550/arXiv.2406.01842 (2024)
13. Ghadermazi, J., Shah, A., Jajodia, S.: A machine learning and optimization framework for efficient alert management in a cybersecurity operations center. Digit. Threats Res. Pract. **5**(2), 1 (2024). https://doi.org/10.1145/3644393
14. Kearney, P., Abdelsamea, M.M., Schmoor, X., Shah, F., Vickers, I.: Combating alert fatigue in the security operations centre. SSRN (2023). https://doi.org/10.2139/ssrn.4633965
15. Louca, A., Peratikou, A., Stavrou, S.: 802.11 man-in-the-middle attack using channel switch announcement (2021)
16. Peratikou, A., Stavrou, S.: On corporate resilience in the face of data breaches and the preventative power of awareness training (2025)
17. Charalambous, A., Piki, A., Stavrou, E.: Redesigning cybersecurity awareness-raising and training programs: insights from professionals on knowledge, skills and educational practices. Inf. Comput. Secur. (2025). https://doi.org/10.1108/ICS-04-2025-0163

18. Potamos, G., Stavrou, E., Stavrou, S.: Enhancing maritime cybersecurity through operational technology sensor data fusion: a comprehensive survey and analysis. Sensors **24**(11), 3458 (2024)
19. Floros, E., et al.: Towards the design of cyber range training programs for enhanced preparedness: Investigating the training needs in critical infrastructures. In: 2025 IEEE Global Engineering Education Conference (EDUCON), pp. 1–10 (2025)
20. Guarascio, M., Cassavia, N., Pisani, F.S., Manco, G.: Boosting cyber-threat intelligence via collaborative intrusion detection. Future Gener. Comput. Syst. **135**, 30 (2022). https://doi.org/10.1016/j.future.2022.04.028
21. Albasheer, H., et al.: Cyber-attack prediction based on NIDS for alert correlation techniques: a survey. Sensors **22**(4), 1494 (2022). https://doi.org/10.3390/s22041494
22. Alturkistani, H., Chuprat, S.: Artificial intelligence and large language models in advancing cyber threat intelligence: a systematic literature review. Res. Sq. (2024). https://doi.org/10.21203/rs.3.rs-5423193/v1
23. Alevizos, L., Dekker, M.: Towards an AI-enhanced cyber threat intelligence processing pipeline. Electronics **13**(11) (2024). https://doi.org/10.3390/electronics13112021
24. Peratikou, A., Charalambous, E., Smyrli, P., Stavrou, S.: ATHENA: a federated architecture for cross-border cybersecurity operations and situational awareness (2025)
25. Nguyen, H., Tariq, S., Chhetri, M.B., Vo, Q.B.: Towards effective identification of attack techniques in CTI reports using large language models (2025). https://doi.org/10.1145/3701716.3715469
26. Fieblinger, R., Alam, T., Rastogi, N.: Actionable cyber threat intelligence using knowledge graphs and large language models. In: 2024 IEEE EuroS&P Workshops, p. 100 (2024). https://doi.org/10.1109/EuroSPW61312.2024.00018
27. Mavroeidis, V., Bromander, S.: Cyber threat intelligence model: evaluation of taxonomies, sharing standards, and ontologies within CTI. In: Proceedings of the EISIC, p. 91 (2017). https://doi.org/10.1109/EISIC.2017.20
28. Ovabor, K., Sule-Odu, I.O., Atkison, T., Fabusoro, A.T., Benedict, J.O.: AI-driven threat intelligence for real-time cybersecurity: frameworks, tools, and future directions. Open Access Res. J. Sci. Technol. **12**(2), 40 (2024). https://doi.org/10.53022/oarjst.2024.12.2.0135
29. Preuveneers, D., Joosen, W.: Sharing machine learning models as indicators of compromise for cyber threat intelligence. J. Cybersecur. Priv. **1**(1), 140 (2021). https://doi.org/10.3390/jcp1010008
30. Rahman, M.R., Mahdavi-Hezaveh, R., Williams, L.: What are the attackers doing now? Automating CTI extraction from text on pace with the changing threat landscape: a survey. ACM Comput. Surv. **55**(12), 1 (2022). https://doi.org/10.1145/3571726
31. Saeed, S., Suayyid, S.A., Al-Ghamdi, M.S., Almuhaisen, H.A., Almuhaideb, A.M.: A systematic literature review on cyber threat intelligence for organizational cybersecurity resilience. Sensors **23**(16), 7273 (2023). https://doi.org/10.3390/s23167273

Power Grids

Human and Organizational Factors in Smart Grid Cybersecurity: A Systematic Literature Review

Ronak Tejas Shah[1(✉)], Michel van Eeten[1], Wolter Pieters[2], and Simon Parkin[1]

[1] Faculty of Technology, Policy and Management, Delft University of Technology, Delft, The Netherlands
{R.T.Shah,M.J.G.vanEeten,S.E.Parkin}@tudelft.nl
[2] Behavioural Science Institute, Radboud University, Nijmegen, The Netherlands
wolter.pieters@ru.nl

Abstract. The increasing digitalization of power systems into "smart grids" has introduced complex cybersecurity challenges. Although technical solutions dominate research in this area, non-technical factors crucial to smart grid cybersecurity remain unknown. This paper presents a systematic review of 27 studies examining how human and organizational factors are addressed in the smart grid cybersecurity literature. Our analysis reveals three key limitations: (1) a disconnect between proposed solutions and real-world challenges; (2) an overemphasis on individual operator decision-making during cyber incidents, despite empirical evidence supporting collaborative approaches; and (3) the imprecise use of concepts like "cybersecurity awareness" and "security culture", neglecting established human factors literature developed around these concepts. Future research should ground interventions in real-world operational complexities, ensuring alignment between empirical and methodological approaches.

Keywords: human factors · organizational factors · smart grids · cybersecurity · systematic literature review

1 Introduction

The shift to sustainable energy transition relies on integrating renewable sources into the power grid, which requires advanced controls, real-time monitoring, and intelligent electricity management to ensure stability and reliability [3,5,61]. To support this transition, power systems are adopting digital technologies, evolving into modern digitized infrastructures, also called smart grids. While these advancements improve operational efficiency, they also introduce cybersecurity challenges, making power systems more vulnerable to cyber threats [10,17,43].

Recent cyberattacks on energy infrastructure have demonstrated the severe economic and societal consequences that these attacks can have on a national

E. Bergström et al. (Eds.): CRITIS 2025, LNCS 16291, pp. 39–57, 2026.
https://doi.org/10.1007/978-3-032-19540-1_3

level. For example, cyberattacks on power systems in Ukraine, 2015 [66], 2016 [55], and 2022 [49] which involved coordinated cyberattacks using Industroyer malware to breach critical control systems and disrupt grid operations, eventually causing severe power outages. In 2023, SektorCERT [51], Denmark's cybersecurity center for critical infrastructures, reported a major cyberattack on the energy sector, affecting at least 22 companies. In this attack, SCADA control systems were compromised with malware, leading to disruption of power system operations.

How can smart grids be protected against cyber threats? While significant advances in cybersecurity research for smart grids have been made, these efforts have primarily focused on securing the technology [2,9,12,18,23,25,35]. But the abovementioned incidents have revealed challenges that extend well beyond purely technical factors. For instance, the 2015 Ukraine attack involved spear-phishing emails targeting employees of multiple grid operators, suggesting a lack of cybersecurity awareness and training as a contributing factor. Similarly, the SektorCERT 2023 report describes how the scale of the cyberattacks exceeded incident response capacities, linking this failure to shortcomings in organizational preparedness and coordination. Hence, in studying cyberattacks on modern power systems it is essential to also look at human and organizational factors. However, our understanding of human and organizational factors in the cybersecurity of smart grids remains unclear. The number of studies is limited, and they are fragmented across various academic communities. We lack a coherent view of the state of the art and of potential gaps. This hinders this critical work from advancing.

In this paper, we aim at providing such a coherent view. Our primary research question is: What is the current state of research on human and organizational factors in the cybersecurity of smart grids, and what insights can guide future studies? Synthesizing the existing academic discourse on this topic can provide a foundation for social science scholars in the energy and cybersecurity domain to engage with the fragmented research landscape, addressing the lack of a consistent understanding of human and organizational factors in smart grid cybersecurity and advancing the maturity of research in this field.

To identify relevant papers, we developed a comprehensive search query covering key concepts from (i) smart grids, (ii) cybersecurity, and (iii) human and organizational factors. Our focus was on papers at the intersection of these three areas. After filtering 2000 initial matches from Google Scholar and Scopus, we examined 76 full-text peer-reviewed papers. Only 27 papers met the criteria for inclusion in the final review, revealing a striking scarcity of research in this area and signaling a clear need for deeper academic engagement.

The findings of this review highlight three key arguments. First, there is a misalignment between empirical findings and proposed solutions, leading to many studies operating in isolated silos. Second, a lot of cybersecurity solutions are often targeted at improving system operators' decision-making in managing cyber incidents, despite empirical evidence emphasizing the need for collaborative efforts across roles. Third, terms like cybersecurity awareness and security culture are used abstractly, without drawing on well-established conceptual understanding from broader cybersecurity literature. These findings reflect critical gaps in existing research surrounding beyond-technical aspects of cybersecurity in smart grids.

This review starts by outlining the scope of cybersecurity in smart grids and the concept of human and organizational factors. It then details the methodology used to select papers for review and concludes with a discussion based on the studies included.

2 Cybersecurity in Smart Grids

In the existing literature, digitized power systems are discussed using various terminologies. The most commonly used term is "smart grids," but terms like "cyber-physical power systems," "power grid operations," and "modern power systems" are also prevalent [12,59,67]. Although these terms differ in some nuances, they generally refer to the same concept. Hence, for this review, we will adopt the popular term "smart grids". We use a well-established definition for "smart grids" from the European context. The European Commission defines smart grids as: "An electricity network that can cost efficiently integrate the behavior and actions of all users connected to it—generators, consumers, and those that do both—in order to ensure an economically efficient, sustainable power system with low losses and high levels of quality, security of supply, and safety" [1]. This definition highlights several key objectives: economic efficiency, low losses, high levels of quality, security of supply, and safety, all aimed at optimizing the current value chain of the electricity network from generation to delivery. Digitization is meant to bring the capabilities to fulfill these objectives, transforming traditional power systems into "smart grids" [17,25].

With the advent of digitalization, cybersecurity has naturally become a critical concern. Given the relatively recent emergence of cybersecurity challenges in this domain, policy makers, industry, and the scientific community have been exploring various perspectives [3,34,42]. Among these efforts, non-technical factors have gained recent attention as essential components of cybersecurity for smart grids [34,37,43,52,53]. To provide clarity for this review, we categorize these non-technical considerations under the term "human and organizational factors", appreciating its connotation in capturing individual and organizational dimensions within the rather ambiguous scope of non-technical factors.

3 Human and Organizational Factors

Defining "human factors" in the context of cybersecurity for smart grids presents significant challenges. Even within the computer science community studying cybersecurity, the conceptualization of the term "human factors" remains underdeveloped [11]. For instance, Kaur et al. [32] conducted a systematic review of "human factors" research in cybersecurity within computer science, covering literature from 2008 to 2018. The review distinguished between humans involved in the development and operation of technical systems, and those humans who were end-users of a technical system. This distinction not only highlights the role of humans in technical environments, but also that there can be dependencies between different groups of users (in this case, professionals) who rely on each other. It suggests that "human factors" extend beyond just individual considerations to include the interdependencies that shape their interactions.

Concepts beyond focusing on individuals, like team dynamics and organizational culture, are also loosely grouped under the umbrella of "human factors" in existing cybersecurity literature. For example, Ioannou et al. [30] studied cybersecurity culture in incident response teams, focusing on factors of communication and coordination. Steinke et al. [57] conducted research on team dynamics in situations of cybersecurity incident response. The "Cyber-Security Culture" (CSC) framework proposed by Georgiadou et al. [22] incorporates both individual factors—such as individual awareness, attitudes, and skills—and organizational factors, including organizational policies and practices, emphasizing the importance of addressing organizational and individual factors together. These studies demonstrate that addressing both human (individual) and organizational factors (collective) in combination is essential, as a strong cybersecurity posture relies on the dynamic interaction between individual and organizational elements [11].

Hence, to clarify our approach, we adopt the concept of "human factors" from the computer science community and expand it to include collective factors, such as teams and organizations, thereby framing our review under the broader term "human and organizational factors." The following section details the methodology adopted in this review.

4 Methodology

The methodology of this literature review adheres to the guidelines set forth by the Preferred Reporting Items for Systematic Reviews and Meta-Analyses (PRISMA) framework [45]. The PRISMA framework was selected for its widespread adoption in systematic literature reviews and its ability to ensure transparency, reproducibility, and methodological rigor in study selection and reporting. The strategy was to collect the relevant peer-reviewed papers, without limiting the search to a specific time range and see how far back relevant papers meeting the set criteria could be found. We used a combination of two databases: Google Scholar and Scopus. Google Scholar is known for its ability to retrieve a broad range of relevant papers [24], while Scopus offers a more curated database of peer-reviewed articles [8]. This combination of Google Scholar and Scopus ensured both relevance and reliability, while avoiding redundancy with databases such as IEEE Xplore, ACM, and Springer, which are largely indexed in Scopus. Our choice to use Scopus and Google Scholar was also informed by empirical comparisons of bibliographic databases: Scopus offers broader journal coverage and more reliable citation indexing, while Google Scholar provides greater recall across grey literature and preprints. Using both maximizes retrieval breadth without sacrificing citation traceability [36,48].

4.1 Data Collection

The scope of this review is the intersection of three areas. To represent this, we developed keywords using a snowballing technique. We began with some pertinent papers that intersected the three domains like Scholtz et al. [52], Scholtz et al. [53], Le Blanc et al. [37], then scanned their references to find additional relevant research. This iterative process led to broad concepts derived from a collection of a few relevant papers, from which specific keywords and closely related terms were identified in Table 1.

Table 1. *List of keywords and synonyms derived from three overarching concepts*

Concepts	Keywords and Synonyms
Cyber security	cyber security; cybersecurity; cyber-attack; information security
Human factors	human factors; awareness; training; exercise; team; situational awareness; sensemaking; organization; risk; resilience; behavior; coordination; communication; collaboration; incident response; crisis
Power systems	power grid; smart grid; cyber-physical power systems; power systems; TSO (Transmission System Operator); DSO (Distribution System Operator); energy; electric power industry

We developed a search query for the keywords from Table 1 that uses Boolean operators (AND, OR) in combination with wildcards (e.g., "*" and "?") to include written variations of the keywords. Special attention was given to the different ways in which similar concepts are typically expressed in scientific discourse, such as "cyber security" and "cybersecurity," or "power grids" and "power grid," to ensure thorough coverage of potential results. The search query employed in this study is:

> (("cyber secur*" OR cybersecurity OR "cyber-attack*" OR "information security") AND ("human factor*" OR awareness OR training OR exercise OR team OR "situational awareness" OR sensemak* OR organisation* OR risk OR resili* OR behavio* OR coordination OR communication OR collaboration OR "incident response" OR crisis) AND ("power grid" OR "smart grid" OR "cyber-physical power system*" OR "power system*" OR TSO OR "Transmission System Operator" OR DSO OR "Distribution System Operator" OR energy OR "electric power industry"))

4.2 Eligibility

Figure 1 outlines the step-by-step selection process for this review. The search query produced 7,430 results on Google Scholar and 6,521 on Scopus. Given the large volume of papers retrieved, the initial results were ordered by relevance, leveraging the algorithmic capabilities of both platforms [16,63]. This ensured the most pertinent studies were prioritized, and the large volume of search results was managed effectively [46]. From these ordered results, the first 1000 papers from each database were selected, totaling 2000 papers. These 2000 papers were exported as BIBTeX files to Zotero, where duplicates, books, book sections, and thesis were removed, resulting in 1,746 unique papers.

This set of papers was assessed using defined inclusion and exclusion criteria. During the title and metadata screening, papers explicitly addressing all three core concepts—human and organizational factors, cybersecurity, and smart grids—or closely related terminologies were included for further review. Inclusion criteria also required papers to be peer-reviewed, written in English, and have full-text availability, narrowing the selection to 96 papers for abstract screening. Abstract screening applied exclusion criteria to remove papers lacking meaningful discussion of the intersection of these core concepts. For example, Gajanan et al. [18]—cyberattacks in smart grids systems, a review—was initially considered in the title and metadata screening, due to its broad scope but excluded after abstract review revealed no substantive discussion of non-technical aspects or human and organizational factors. Abstract screening excluded 20 papers, reducing the selection to 76 papers for full-text review.

The full-text review further excluded papers where human or organizational factors were mentioned only superficially or in passing. For instance, Alfiah and Prastiwi [2] briefly mention human factors in their conclusion as a potential challenge but did not integrate the concept into the main argument or analysis. Ultimately, 27 papers were selected for detailed review. This systematic process ensured that the final selection fully addressed the interplay between the three core concepts, aligning with the defined scope of this review.

4.3 Limitations

Despite the systematic methodology employed in this study, several limitations must be acknowledged:

1. **Scope of databases:** While Google Scholar and Scopus were chosen for their extensive, yet different, coverage of academic literature, relying solely on these databases may have excluded relevant studies only available in other databases or grey literature sources.

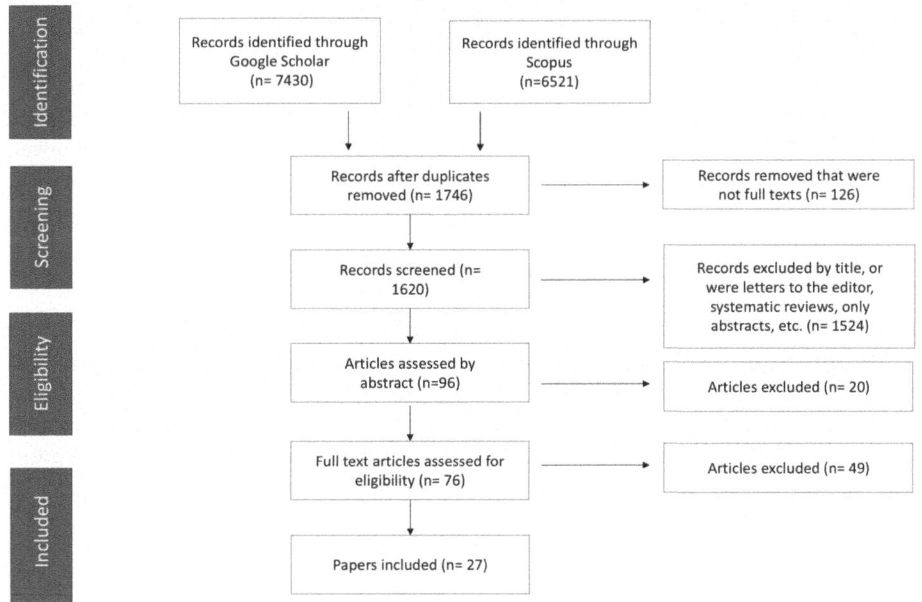

Fig. 1. Flowchart depicting the PRISMA process for study selection.

2. **Choice of only considering top results:** The search query produced over 10,000 results combined from both databases. Due to practical constraints in terms of time and resources, only the first 2000 papers filtered by relevance were selected for initial screening. Consequently, some potentially relevant studies might have been overlooked.
3. **Filtered by relevance:** On both databases, the results were filtered by relevance, which relies on the algorithms of the individual databases. While this approach theoretically increases the likelihood of retrieving a broader range of relevant papers, there is no transparency on how the "filtered by relevance" function works exactly for each database.
4. **Screening and selection process:** The initial screening process involved title and abstract reviews, which might have resulted in the exclusion of relevant studies that did not explicitly mention key terms in their titles or abstracts. Full-text reviews were only conducted on a subset of papers.
5. **Geographical and cultural bias:** The study may have a bias towards research conducted in Western and other countries that publish scientific research predominantly in English. This could result in an underrepresentation of perspectives and findings from non-Western regions—a challenge commonly observed in usable security research [26].
6. **Manual processes:** The process of manually selecting and screening papers introduces the possibility of human error and subjectivity. While efforts were made to standardize the selection criteria, inconsistencies may still arise.

The systematic methodology employed in this review ensured a thorough and structured approach to identifying the most relevant papers across all three domains. While acknowledging inherent limitations, this study aims to provide a comprehensive overview, contributing to this evolving field and guiding future research. The next section delves into synthesizing the findings from the reviewed literature.

5 Synthesizing the Existing Literature

The synthesis of the 27 reviewed papers was structured around eight criteria: (1) whether the paper has an empirical or methodological focus; (2) if it was an empirical paper, what population was studied; (3) what problem is being addressed or explored; (4) the research objective; (5) which theories or frameworks were adopted; (6) which human factors are identified; (7) which organizational factors are identified; and (8) which interventions are proposed. The findings are summarized in Table 2.

5.1 Empirical Versus Methodological Focus

Table 2 highlights an almost equal division between empirical (13 out of 27) and methodological (14 out of 27) studies, each pursuing distinct research objectives. Among the 13 empirical papers, 10 studies the population of practitioners—individuals actively working within power system organizations—while two studies subject matter experts. An exception is Krkoleva Mateska et al. [34], which examines how organizations implement cybersecurity compliance, specifically focusing on transmission system operators (TSOs) in Southeast Europe. Most empirical studies (9 out of 13) utilize qualitative methods, such as interviews and exercise observations, with a common research objective of exploring cybersecurity challenges within smart grids. The remaining four empirical studies employ quantitative methods to validate specific factors like cybersecurity awareness, workforce competency [20,21,28], and cybersecurity compliance [34]. The research objective of validation in this case involves evaluating how cybersecurity-related factors are operationalized within power system organizations [21].

Methodological studies primarily center on providing solutions as their main research objective, with a few notable exceptions. Chowdhury & Gkioulos [13] conducted a systematic literature review to explore optimal cybersecurity training methods for critical infrastructure, including the energy sector. Wallis & Leszczyna [65] applied a cybersecurity applicability framework [38] to validate the practical adaptability of the European Energy Information Sharing and Analysis Center (EE-ISAC) [39]. Some methodological studies incorporate stakeholder engagement to improve the practical relevance of their solutions. For example, Teufel & Teufel [60] consulted experts to develop information security guidelines, and Boroomand et al. [7] for designing automation strategies. However, in both cases, the studies argue for a solution—training in one, automation

Table 2. Dissecting the findings from the literature (Part 1). Column 3: E = Empirical, M = Methodological

Year	Ref.	Type	Population Studied	Problem Being Addressed	Research Objective	Theory/Framework Adopted	Human Factors	Organizational Factors	Proposed Intervention
2024	[19]	E	Practitioners	Risk assessment	Exploratory	N/A	Interdisciplinary knowledge	Common understanding	Collaboration across domains
2024	[47]	M	Experts	Capability development	Solution	Design science methodology	Individual skills	N/A	Curriculum design
2024	[62]	M	N/A	Risk assessment	Solution	Network theory	Decision making	N/A	Modeling human actions
2023	[20]	E	Practitioners	Capability development	Validation	Cyber-Security Culture (CSC)	Cybersecurity awareness	Workforce competency	Improving security culture
2023	[14]	M	N/A	Information management	Solution	N/A	Decision making	N/A	Improving visualization for operators
2023	[43]	E	Experts	Risk assessment	Exploratory	Sociotechnical Imaginaries	Perspective	N/A	Vision driven by technical considerations
2022	[21]	E	Practitioners	Capability development	Validation	N/A	Cybersecurity awareness	Workforce competency	Improving security culture
2022	[42]	E	Practitioners	Capability development	Exploratory	N/A	Perspective	N/A	Non-aligned practitioner and academic perspectives
2022	[65]	M	N/A	Capability development	Validation	Cybersecurity applicability	N/A	N/A	Applicability of European Energy ISAC
2022	[41]	M	N/A	Information management	Solution	N/A	Decision making	N/A	Improving visualization for operators
2021	[34]	E	Organizations	Capability development	Exploratory	N/A	N/A	Compliance	Ensuring inter-organizational compliance
2021	[13]	M	N/A	Capability development	Exploratory	N/A	N/A	Training	No optimum training method
2021	[54]	E	Experts	Capability development	Exploratory	N/A	Individual skills	N/A	Curriculum design
2020	[56]	M	N/A	Risk assessment	Solution	Design Thinking	Decision making	N/A	Threat prioritization
2020	[58]	M	N/A	Risk assessment	Solution	CIRA Method	Decision making	N/A	SGAM-H with human layer
2019	[39]	M	N/A	Information management	Solution	N/A	N/A	Common understanding	European Energy ISAC
2018	[53]	M	Practitioners	Information management	Solution	UCD framework, Situational Awareness	Role specific information	Common understanding	Tool for improving collective SA
2017	[37]	E	Practitioners	Incident response	Exploratory	N/A	Role specific information	Common understanding	Collaboration across domains

(continued)

Table 2. (*continued*)

Year	Ref.	Type	Population Studied	Problem Being Addressed	Research Objective	Theory/Framework Adopted	Human Factors	Organizational Factors	Proposed Intervention
2016	[6]	E	Practitioners	Incident response	Exploratory	N/A	Perspective	Training	Collaboration across domains
2016	[31]	E	Practitioners	Incident response	Exploratory	N/A	Interdisciplinary knowledge	Common understanding	Collaboration across domains
2016	[52]	E	Practitioners	Incident response	Exploratory	N/A	Perspective	Common understanding	Collaboration across domains
2015	[60]	M	Experts	Risk assessment	Solution	OECD Standards	Cybersecurity awareness	N/A	Information security guidelines (CEIS)
2014	[40]	E	Practitioners	Incident response	Exploratory	N/A	Perspective	Training	Collaboration across domains
2014	[50]	M	N/A	Risk assessment	Solution	Routine Activities, Rational Choice	Decision making	N/A	PARE RISKS framework
2013	[4]	M	N/A	Risk assessment	Solution	Game theory	Decision making	N/A	Modeling attacker-operator interaction
2013	[28]	E	Practitioners	Capability development	Validation	N/A	Cybersecurity awareness	Workforce competency	Improving security culture
2010	[7]	M	Experts	Risk assessment	Solution	Human-Automation Interaction	Decision making	N/A	Human-automation framework

in the other—implicitly assuming what the problem is, without deriving it from practice.

With the exception of two studies that incorporate elements of real-world context, most methodological studies rely purely on assumptions to design interventions, overlooking the complexities that become visible when studying how problems are understood and experienced in actual practice. Gallardo et al. [19], for instance, surfaced needs expressed by OT practitioners—such as "make existing OT systems more usable"—emphasizing improvements to current systems rather than introducing completely new solutions. If such practitioner-informed concerns were considered, they could meaningfully shape the problem framings underlying methodological efforts. Hence, comparing the problems explored and addressed by empirical and methodological studies would provide insight into how the complexities of reality are represented in the literature and reveal the assumptions that shape methodological proposals. The next section examines this further by analyzing the alignment—or lack thereof—between the problems empirical and methodological approaches explore and address.

5.2 The Problems Explored Versus the Problems Addressed

When analyzing all the papers collectively, clear problem-focused themes begin to emerge, with empirical and methodological studies diverging in their areas of emphasis. Column 5 in Table 2 outlines these problem-focused themes. Risk assessment of cyber threats and capability development for incident response are central themes shared across both domains. Methodological studies predominantly focus on risk assessment, with half of them—Umunnakwe et al. [62], Snow et al. [56], Szekeres & Snekkenes [58], Rege [50], Backhaus et al. [4], Teufel & Teufel [60], and Boroomand et al. [7]—proposing frameworks to better assess cybersecurity risks in smart grids. These solutions, however, show minimal alignment with empirical studies, which focus on understanding the nature and scope of cybersecurity risks from real-world perspectives. For example, Gallardo et al. [19] analyzes how different disciplines, such as energy operations and information technology, approach cybersecurity as a risk to smart grids, based on interviews with energy operations teams and cybersecurity analysts, while Michalec et al. [43] captures expert perspectives on emerging cybersecurity risks and their potential evolution. Hence, empirical studies focus on contextual understanding by drawing insights from practitioners and experts, whereas methodological studies prioritize advancing risk assessment models grounded in technical frameworks, with human factors incorporated as an additional layer.

This misalignment is also evident in studies addressing capability development for incident response. Empirical studies, based on insights from practitioners and experts, identify key challenges such as cybersecurity skill gaps in the smart grid domain [54], overestimation of organizational capacities to manage cyber incidents [34,42], workforce incompetency in managing cyber incidents [20,21,28], lack of standardised training schedules [6,40], unclear documentation [40], and divergent practitioner views on cybersecurity in smart grids [6,40,42]. In contrast, methodological studies do not pick-up on this identified challenges, and have discussed solutions like the European Energy Information Sharing and Analysis Center (EE-ISAC) to enable information sharing across organizations [39,65], or, explore optimum training method for cybersecurity training in critical infrastructure [13].

The divide between empirical and methodological studies extends beyond the problems they address to justify the interventions they propose, as they often aim to achieve different objectives. Typically, methodological studies focus on tools designed specifically for system operators [7,14,41], arguing that enhancing their capabilities will improve overall cyber incident response. However, a key underlying assumption of these solutions is that system operators bear the major responsibility for managing cyber incidents [7,14,41]. This assumption is not fully supported by empirical findings, which instead emphasize that incident response is largely a collaborative effort involving multiple actors who interact, communicate, and collectively make sense of situations to devise appropriate responses [6,31,37,40,52,53]. Therefore, while interventions like improved operator visualizations may contribute to these collaborative efforts, it remains unclear (1) what roles and responsibilities operators actually hold and are expected to hold during cyber incidents and (2) how operators themselves would perceive these additional capabilities. Empowering operators with additional tools and technologies without understanding their perspectives could be counterintuitive, and potentially overload an already cognitively demanding task [44,64].

In summary, two key insights emerge when comparing empirical and methodological studies through the lens of the problems they address. First, a consistent misalignment exists between the challenges investigated in empirical studies and the interventions designed in methodological studies. This disconnect can be attributed to differing disciplinary incentives: methodological studies, frequently published in computer science or power engineering venues, prioritize artifact/tool design, while empirical studies, often found in other disciplines, focus on understanding real-world problems. Second, methodological studies exhibit a strong tendency to focus solutions on system operators, despite limited empirical evidence clearly defining their roles or responsibilities in managing cyber incidents. In Klein's work on decision-making [33], for instance, importance is given to the need for 'common ground' between professionals who have to coordinate; this includes how they collectively resolve ambiguous situations, but also address ambiguities between team members to reach a common understanding, and help each other in order to perform better as a team. This includes not only when each team member uses their own provisioned tools, but also how they coordinate meaningfully with each other when incidents arise.

The next section shifts focus from the problems these studies address to how they address them. It discusses the specific factors emphasized in empirical versus methodological studies and analyzes the proposed interventions to reflect on their broader implications and potential future research directions.

5.3 Human and Organizational Factors and Interventions

This review identifies ten factors—six human and four organizational—detailed in columns 8 and 9 of Table 2, along with corresponding interventions in column 10. This section analyzes how the literature consider these factors, comparing empirical findings with methodological approaches to demonstrate alignment or gaps.

A prominent organizational factor discussed in the literature is the need for establishing a common understanding of cybersecurity. Empirical studies highlight cross-departmental collaboration as the intervention to achieve common understanding, also emphasizing human factors such as interdisciplinary knowledge exchange, divergent practitioner perspectives, and role-specific information [19,31,37,52]. This collaboration is also pointed as an intervention in empirical studies addressing the organizational factor of training, to improve the outcomes of training exercises [6,40,42]. In contrast, methodological studies accounting for organizational factor of establishing common understanding and training prioritize inter-organizational information sharing [39,65], and finding an optimum medium of training [13]. An exception is Scholtz et al. [53], who design role-specific tools to improve intra-organizational collaboration by achieving common understanding of incidents, based on prior empirical work [52]. A second exception aligning empirical and methodological approaches is the work by Siemers et al. [54] and Pirta-Dreimane et al. [47], who address the human factor of individual skills and propose a curriculum design framework to address the cybersecurity skill gap in the smart grid industry.

Cybersecurity awareness and workforce competency are also addressed as a blend of human and organizational factors, specifically in the empirical papers [20,21,28]. However, these studies often lack engagement with established literature on concepts such as cybersecurity awareness—defined as an individual's understanding of cyber risks and their ability to act securely; security culture—the shared values, norms, and practices within an organization that shape security-related behavior; and human-centered cybersecurity—an approach that emphasizes practitioners' lived experiences, needs, and constraints in socio-technical environments [15,29,30,68]. This inconsistent use of terminology is not limited to empirical studies; methodological studies, such as Teufel & Teufel's [60] proposed guidelines for distributed grids, also exhibit ambiguity in interpreting cybersecurity awareness.

Such challenges are again not isolated to the smart grid domain, where sectors including energy and beyond define "security awareness" in different ways, but also have regulations which under-specify what security awareness (and in turn, "security culture") should include, thereby leaving practitioners – and their vendors – to decide this [27]. This extends to whether there is support for users who are not able to follow the training and thereby work securely, which would be key in critical domains such as energy provision. However, with the focus in the energy sector on incident response, there may be opportunities to hook user support into existing sectoral approaches. Further, assurance measures may be gathered, and woven into incident-planning procedures (e.g., logging user difficulties and addressing them, which is generally not a regular part of security awareness management).

Methodological studies further emphasize decision-making as a prominent human factor, addressing it from both defender and attacker perspectives. For defenders, proposed solutions focus on technical tools, such as improved visualizations, game-theoretic models, and automated detection processes [4,7,14, 41,58]. From the attacker's perspective, frameworks are developed to evaluate attack severity based on assumptions about attacker behavior [50,56,62]. This dominant focus on decision-making in methodological studies is entirely absent in empirical studies, further raising questions about the applicability of these interventions.

To summarize, the analysis of factors and proposed interventions reveals a consistent disconnect between the focus of empirical research and methodological approaches. Empirical studies address the factor of common understanding within the scope of an organization, while methodological studies focus on solutions that ensure inter-organizational information sharing to achieve common understanding. Additionally, decision-making emerges as a dominant human factor in methodological studies but is entirely absent in empirical studies. Another observation from this analysis of factors is that many empirical studies fail to engage with established literature on well-discussed human factors concepts like security culture and cybersecurity awareness, resulting in ambiguous interpretations across studies.

6 Conclusion and Future Research Directions

This systematic literature review analyzed the state-of-the-art on human and organizational factors in addressing cybersecurity challenges within smart grids. Examining 27 studies, we identified three key limitations in the current literature: (1) a significant disconnect between proposed solutions and the real-world cybersecurity complexities; (2) an overemphasis on system operators' decision-making in methodological studies, without a corresponding empirical understanding of their actual roles and responsibilities during cyber incidents; and (3) the imprecise and inconsistent use of concepts such as "cybersecurity awareness" and "security culture," without grounding them in the established literature surrounding these topics. While a substantial body of research exists on human and or organizational factors in cybersecurity of computer science domain, this review reveals a critical gap in its application within the smart grid context.

To improve the contribution of non-technical academic research to smart grid cybersecurity, future research should improve the alignment between real-world challenges highlighted by empirical studies and the proposed solutions. This integration requires methodological studies to be informed by the operational realities of smart grid environments, while empirical investigations should focus on addressing specific gaps in current practice to inform the design and assumptions of proposed methodologies. This integrated and collaborative approach will facilitate the development of targeted, actionable solutions, ultimately strengthening the resilience of smart grids.

Funding Acknowledgment. We wish to thank our participants for their contributions to the study. This work has been partially supported by the RESCUE project (Grant No. ESI.2019.006), funded by the Netherlands Organization for Scientific Research (NWO).

References

1. Commission staff working document: Definition, expected services, functionalities and benefits of smart grids. European Commission staff working document, European Commission, Brussels (2011)
2. Alfiah, F., Prastiwi, N.R.: Cyber security in smart grid technology: a systematic review. Int. J. Cyber IT Serv. Manage. **2**(1), 48–54 (2022). https://doi.org/10.34306/ijcitsm.v2i1.79
3. Alvarez-Alvarado, M., et al.: Cyber-physical power systems: a comprehensive review about technologies drivers, standards, and future perspectives. Comput. Electr. Eng. **116** (2024). https://doi.org/10.1016/j.compeleceng.2024.109149
4. Backhaus, S., et al.: Cyber-physical security: a game theory model of humans interacting over control systems. IEEE Trans. Smart Grid **4**(4), 2320–2327 (2013)
5. Badal, F., Sarker, S., Nayem, Z., Moyeen, S., Das, S.: Microgrid to smart grid's evolution: technical challenges, current solutions, and future scopes. Energy Sci. Eng. **11**(2), 874–928 (2023). https://doi.org/10.1002/ese3.1319
6. Bartnes, M., Moe, N.B., Heegaard, P.E.: The future of information security incident management training: a case study of electrical power companies. Comput. Secur. **61**, 32–45 (2016)
7. Boroomand, F., et al.: Cyber security for smart grid: a human-automation interaction framework. In: IEEE PES Innovative Smart Grid, pp. 1–6. IEEE (2010)
8. Burnham, J.F.: Scopus database: a review. Biomed. Digit. Libr. **3**(1), 1 (2006). https://doi.org/10.1186/1742-5581-3-1
9. Cai, J., Zheng, Y., Zhou, Z.: Review of cyber-security challenges and measures in smart substation. In: 2016 International Conference on Smart Grid and Clean Energy Technologies, ICSGCE 2016, pp. 65–69. Institute of Electrical and Electronics Engineers Inc. (2017). https://doi.org/10.1109/ICSGCE.2016.7876027
10. Cassotta, S., Sidortsov, R.: Sustainable cybersecurity? Rethinking approaches to protecting energy infrastructure in the European High North. Energy Res. Soc. Sci. **51**, 129–133 (2019). https://doi.org/10.1016/j.erss.2019.01.003
11. Ceesay, E., Myers, K., Watters, P.: Human-centered strategies for cyber-physical systems security. ICST Trans. Secur. Safety **4**(14), 154773 (2018). https://doi.org/10.4108/eai.15-5-2018.154773
12. Chatterjee, K., Padmini, V., Khaparde, S.: Review of cyber attacks on power system operations. In: 2017 IEEE Region 10 Symposium (TENSYMP), pp. 1–6 (2017). https://doi.org/10.1109/tenconspring.2017.8070085
13. Chowdhury, N., Gkioulos, V.: Cyber security training for critical infrastructure protection: a literature review. Comput. Sci. Rev. **40**, 100361 (2021). https://doi.org/10.1016/j.cosrev.2021.100361
14. Cobilean, V., et al.: A review of visualization methods for cyber-physical security: smart grid case study. IEEE Access **11**, 59788–59803 (2023). https://doi.org/10.1109/ACCESS.2023.3286304

15. de Bruijn, H., Janssen, M.: Building Cybersecurity Awareness: the need for evidence-based framing strategies. Gov. Inf. Q. **34**(1), 1–7 (2017). https://doi.org/10.1016/j.giq.2017.02.007
16. Elsevier Support Center: What content is included in scopus? (2025). https://service.elsevier.com/app/answers/detail/a_id/14182/supporthub/scopus/. Accessed 9 July 2025
17. Farhan, M., et al.: Towards next generation Internet of Energy system: framework and trends. Energy AI **14** (2023). https://doi.org/10.1016/j.egyai.2023.100306
18. Gajanan, L., Kirar, M., Raju, M.: Cyber-attacks on smart grid system: a review. In: 2022 IEEE 10th Power India International Conference, PIICON 2022. Institute of Electrical and Electronics Engineers Inc. (2022). https://doi.org/10.1109/PIICON56320.2022.10045208
19. Gallardo, A., Erbes, R., Le Blanc, K., Bauer, L., Cranor, L.F.: Interdisciplinary approaches to cybervulnerability impact assessment for energy critical infrastructure. In: Proceedings of the CHI Conference on Human Factors in Computing Systems, Honolulu HI USA, pp. 1–24. ACM (2024). https://doi.org/10.1145/3613904.3642493
20. Georgiadou, A., Michalitsi - Psarrou, A., Askounis, D.: A security awareness and competency evaluation in the energy sector. Comput. Secur. **129** (2023). https://doi.org/10.1016/j.cose.2023.103199
21. Georgiadou, A., Michalitsi-Psarrou, A., Askounis, D.: Evaluating the cyber-security culture of the EPES sector: applying a cyber-security culture framework to assess the EPES sector's resilience and readiness. In: ACM International Conference Proceeding Series. Association for Computing Machinery (2022). https://doi.org/10.1145/3538969.3543813
22. Georgiadou, A., Mouzakitis, S., Bounas, K., Askounis, D.: A cyber-security culture framework for assessing organization readiness. J. Comput. Inf. Syst. **62**(3), 452–462 (2022). https://doi.org/10.1080/08874417.2020.1845583
23. Ghiasi, M., Niknam, T., Wang, Z., Mehrandezh, M., Dehghani, M., Ghadimi, N.: A comprehensive review of cyber-attacks and defense mechanisms for improving security in smart grid energy systems: past, present and future. Electric Power Syst. Res. **215** (2023). https://doi.org/10.1016/j.epsr.2022.108975
24. Haddaway, N.R., Collins, A.M., Coughlin, D., Kirk, S.: The role of google scholar in evidence reviews and its applicability to grey literature searching. PLoS ONE **10**(9), e0138237 (2015). https://doi.org/10.1371/journal.pone.0138237
25. Hasan, M.K., Habib, A.A., Shukur, Z., Ibrahim, F., Islam, S., Razzaque, M.A.: Review on cyber-physical and cyber-security system in smart grid: standards, protocols, constraints, and recommendations. J. Netw. Comput. Appl. **209**, 103540 (2023). https://doi.org/10.1016/j.jnca.2022.103540
26. Hasegawa, A.A., Inoue, D., Akiyama, M.: How WEIRD is usable privacy and security research? In: 33rd USENIX Security Symposium (USENIX Security 2024), pp. 3241–3258 (2024)
27. Hielscher, J., Parkin, S.: "What keeps people secure is that they met the security team": deconstructing drivers and goals of organizational security awareness. In: 33rd USENIX Security Symposium (USENIX Security 2024), pp. 3295–3312 (2024)
28. Holm, H., Flores, W.R., Ericsson, G.: Cyber security for a Smart Grid - What about phishing? In: IEEE PES ISGT Europe 2013, pp. 1–5 (2013). https://doi.org/10.1109/ISGTEurope.2013.6695407
29. Hossain, M.N., Hassan, M.M., Monir, R.J., Sayeed, M.S., Wajiha, S., Ullah, S.W.: Cyber security and people: human nature, psychology, and training affect user

awareness, social engineering, and security professional education and preparedness. In: 2023 14th International Conference on Computing Communication and Networking Technologies (ICCCNT), pp. 1–5. IEEE (2023)
30. Ioannou, M., Stavrou, E., Bada, M.: Cybersecurity Culture in Computer Security Incident Response Teams: investigating difficulties in communication and coordination. In: 2019 International Conference on Cyber Security and Protection of Digital Services (Cyber Security), pp. 1–4 (2019). https://doi.org/10.1109/CyberSecPODS.2019.8885240
31. Jaatun, M.G., Bartnes, M., Tøndel, I.A.: Zebras and lions: better incident handling through improved cooperation. In: Fahrnberger, G., Eichler, G., Erfurth, C. (eds.) I4CS 2016. CCIS, vol. 648, pp. 129–139. Springer, Cham (2016). https://doi.org/10.1007/978-3-319-49466-1_9
32. Kaur, M., Eeten, M., Janssen, M., Borgolte, K., Fiebig, T.: Human factors in security research: lessons learned from 2008-2018. ACM SIGCAS Computers and Society (2021)
33. Klein, G.A.: Streetlights and Shadows: Searching for the Keys to Adaptive Decision Making. MIT Press (2011)
34. Krkoleva Mateska, A., Krstevski, P., Borozan, S.: Overview and improvement of procedures and practices of electricity transmission system operators in South East Europe to mitigate cybersecurity threats. Systems **9**(2), 39 (2021). https://doi.org/10.3390/systems9020039
35. Kumar, V., Prasad, J., Samikannu, R.: A critical review of cyber security and cyber terrorism - threats to critical infrastructure in the energy sector. Int. J. Crit. Infrastruct. **14**(2), 101–119 (2018). https://doi.org/10.1504/IJCIS.2018.091932
36. Lasda Bergman, E.M.: Finding citations to social work literature: the relative benefits of using web of science, scopus, or google scholar. J. Acad. Librariansh. **38**(6), 370–379 (2012). https://doi.org/10.1016/j.acalib.2012.08.002
37. Le Blanc, K., Ashok, A., Franklin, L., Scholtz, J., Andersen, E., Cassiadoro, M.: Characterizing cyber tools for monitoring power grid systems: what information is available and who needs it? In: 2017 IEEE International Conference on Systems, Man, and Cybernetics (SMC), pp. 3451–3456 (2017). https://doi.org/10.1109/SMC.2017.8123164
38. Leszczyna, R.: Aiming at methods' wider adoption: applicability determinants and metrics. Comput. Sci. Rev. **40**, 100387 (2021). https://doi.org/10.1016/j.cosrev.2021.100387
39. Leszczyna, R., Wallis, T., Wróbel, M.R.: Developing novel solutions to realise the European Energy – Information Sharing & Analysis Centre. Decis. Support Syst. **122**, 113067 (2019). https://doi.org/10.1016/j.dss.2019.05.007
40. Line, M.B., Tøndel, I.A., Jaatun, M.G.: Information security incident management: planning for failure. In: 2014 Eighth International Conference on IT Security Incident Management & IT Forensics, pp. 47–61 (2014). https://doi.org/10.1109/IMF.2014.10
41. Mawle, P.P., Dhomane, G., Narukullapati, B.K., Venkatesh, P., Chakravarthi, M.K., Kumar Shukla, S.: A novel framework for data visualization via power system monitoring control and protection based on wireless communication. In: 2022 2nd International Conference on Advance Computing and Innovative Technologies in Engineering (ICACITE), pp. 1056–1060 (2022). https://doi.org/10.1109/ICACITE53722.2022.9823492
42. Meyer, J., Apruzzese, G.: Cybersecurity in the smart grid: practitioners' perspective. In: Industrial Control Systems Security Workshop (ICSS). arXiv (2022). https://doi.org/10.48550/arXiv.2210.13119

43. Michalec, O., Shreeve, B., Rashid, A.: Who will keep the lights on? Expertise and inclusion in cyber security visions of future energy systems. Energy Res. Soc. Sci. **106**, 103327 (2023). https://doi.org/10.1016/j.erss.2023.103327
44. Obradovich, J.H.: Understanding cognitive and collaborative work: observations in an electric transmission operations control center. In: Proceedings of the Human Factors and Ergonomics Society Annual Meeting, vol. 55, no. 1, pp. 247–251 (2011). https://doi.org/10.1177/1071181311551051
45. Page, M.J., et al.: PRISMA 2020 explanation and elaboration: Updated guidance and exemplars for reporting systematic reviews. BMJ p. n160 (2021). https://doi.org/10.1136/bmj.n160
46. Petersen, H., Poon, J., Poon, S.K., Loy, C.: Increased workload for systematic review literature searches of diagnostic tests compared with treatments: challenges and opportunities. JMIR Med. Inform. **2**(1), e11 (2014). https://doi.org/10.2196/medinform.3037. https://www.ncbi.nlm.nih.gov/pmc/articles/PMC4288066/
47. Pirta-Dreimane, R., et al.: Enhancing smart grid resilience: an educational approach to smart grid cybersecurity skill gap mitigation. Energies **17**(8), 1876 (2024)
48. Pranckutė, R.: Web of science (WOS) and Scopus: the titans of bibliographic information in today's academic world. Publications **9**(1), 12 (2021). https://doi.org/10.3390/publications9010012. https://www.mdpi.com/2304-6775/9/1/12
49. Rattray, G., Brown, G.: The cyber defense assistance imperative: Lessons from Ukraine. Casestudy, The Aspen Institute (2023)
50. Rege, A.: A criminological perspective on power grid cyber attacks: using routine activities theory to rational choice perspective to explore adversarial decision-making. J. Homel. Secur. Emerg. Manage. **11**(4), 463–487 (2014)
51. Ribeiro, A.: SektorCERT reports cyber attack against Danish critical infrastructure, raises concerns of state involvement (2023)
52. Scholtz, J., Franklin, L., Le Blanc, K., Andersen, E.: Cybersecurity awareness in the power grid. In: Nicholson, D. (ed.) Advances in Human Factors in Cybersecurity. AISC, pp. 183–193. Springer, Cham (2016). https://doi.org/10.1007/978-3-319-41932-9_15
53. Scholtz, J.C., et al.: Employing a user-centered design process for cybersecurity awareness in the power grid. J. Hum. Perform. Extreme Environ. **14**(1) (2018). https://doi.org/10.7771/2327-2937.1094
54. Siemers, B., et al.: Modern trends and skill gaps of cyber security in smart grid. In: IEEE EUROCON 2021 - 19th International Conference on Smart Technologies, pp. 565–570 (2021). https://doi.org/10.1109/EUROCON52738.2021.9535632
55. Slowik, J.: CRASHOVERRIDE: Reassessing the 2016 Ukraine Electric Power Event as a Protection-Focused Attack. Forensics, Dragos Inc, USA (2019)
56. Snow, S., Happa, J., Horrocks, N., Glencross, M.: Using design thinking to understand cyber attack surfaces of future smart grids. Front. Energy Res. **8**, 591999 (2020). https://doi.org/10.3389/fenrg.2020.591999
57. Steinke, J., et al.: Improving cybersecurity incident response team effectiveness using teams-based research. IEEE Secur. Priv. **13**(4), 20–29 (2015). https://doi.org/10.1109/MSP.2015.71
58. Szekeres, A., Snekkenes, E.: Representing decision-makers in SGAM-H: the smart grid architecture model extended with the human layer. In: Eades III, H., Gadyatskaya, O. (eds.) GraMSec 2020. LNCS, vol. 12419, pp. 87–110. Springer, Cham (2020). https://doi.org/10.1007/978-3-030-62230-5_5
59. Tatipatri, N., Arun, S.: A comprehensive review on cyber-attacks in power systems: impact analysis, detection, and cyber security. IEEE Access **12**, 18147–18167 (2024). https://doi.org/10.1109/ACCESS.2024.3361039

60. Teufel, S., Teufel, B.: Crowd energy information security culture - security guidelines for smart environments. In: 2015 IEEE International Conference on Smart City/SocialCom/SustainCom (SmartCity), Chengdu, China, pp. 123–128. IEEE (2015). https://doi.org/10.1109/SmartCity.2015.58
61. Trahan, R.T., Hess, D.J.: Who controls electricity transitions? Digitization, decarbonization, and local power organizations. Energy Res. Soc. Sci. **80**, 102219 (2021). https://doi.org/10.1016/j.erss.2021.102219
62. Umunnakwe, A., Sun, S., Davis, K.: Toward proactive cyber-physical-human risk assessment in power systems. In: 2024 IEEE Texas Power and Energy Conference (TPEC), pp. 1–6 (2024). https://doi.org/10.1109/TPEC60005.2024.10472174
63. Utrecht University Library: What does relevance ranking mean on Google Scholar? (2023). https://libguides.library.uu.nl/googlescholar_en/find-out-more. Accessed 09 July 2025
64. von Meier, A.: Occupational cultures as a challenge to technological innovation. IEEE Trans. Eng. Manage. **46**(1), 101–114 (1999). https://doi.org/10.1109/17.740041
65. Wallis, T., Leszczyna, R.: EE-ISAC–practical cybersecurity solution for the energy sector. Energies **15**(6), 2170 (2022). https://doi.org/10.3390/en15062170
66. Whitehead, D.E., Owens, K., Gammel, D., Smith, J.: Ukraine cyber-induced power outage: analysis and practical mitigation strategies. In: Conference for Protective Relay Engineers, pp. 1–8 (2017). https://doi.org/10.1109/cpre.2017.8090056
67. Yohanandhan, R.V., Elavarasan, R.M., Manoharan, P., Mihet-Popa, L.: Cyber-Physical Power System (CPPS): a review on modeling, simulation, and analysis with cyber security applications. IEEE Access **8**, 151019–151064 (2020). https://doi.org/10.1109/ACCESS.2020.3016826
68. Zwilling, M., Klien, G., Lesjak, D., Wiechetek, Ł, Cetin, F., Basim, H.N.: Cyber security awareness, knowledge and behavior: a comparative study. J. Comput. Inf. Syst. **62**(1), 82–97 (2022). https://doi.org/10.1080/08874417.2020.1712269

The Dark Side of Flexibility: How Aggregated Cyberattacks Threaten the Power Grid

Daniel Myrén[1], Zeeshan Afzal[2](✉), and Mikael Asplund[2]

[1] Sectra Communications, Linköping, Sweden
[2] Linköping University, Linköping, Sweden
{zeeshan.afzal,mikael.asplund}@liu.se

Abstract. Flexible energy resources are increasingly becoming common in smart grids. These resources are typically managed and controlled by aggregators that coordinate many resources to provide flexibility services. However, these aggregators and flexible energy resources are vulnerable, which could allow attackers to remotely control flexible energy resources to launch large-scale attacks on the grid. This paper investigates and evaluates the potential attack strategies that can be used to manipulate flexible energy resources to challenge the effectiveness of traditional grid stability measures and disrupt the first-swing stability of the power grid. Our work shows that although a large amount of power is required, the current flexibility capacities could potentially be sufficient to disrupt the grid on a national level.

1 Introduction

The electric grid must always maintain a balance between demand and supply [19] to ensure continuous and efficient power delivery. This balance is typically measured through the frequency of alternating current (AC) and is set at 50 Hz in the EU (also called nominal frequency). Figure 1 illustrates this task of maintaining balance. When power production and consumption are perfectly balanced, the grid frequency stays at its nominal value. If consumption exceeds production, the frequency decreases. If production exceeds consumption, the frequency increases. Consequently, the grid operators continuously monitor the frequency to detect and mitigate any imbalances. If the frequency deviations are not promptly managed and counteracted, there is a risk of significant disruptions such as blackouts and damage to critical infrastructures such as generators [5].

The growing prevalence of renewable energy sources (RESs) such as solar and wind in the power grid makes power generation more variable and unpredictable, creating a challenge to maintain the balance between supply and demand [17]. This increased variability creates a need for flexible energy resources (FERs) such as energy storage systems and heat pumps which are increasingly utilized by grid operators as a solution to maintain the stability of the grid. These resources can quickly adapt their energy consumption or inject more energy into the grid to

E. Bergström et al. (Eds.): CRITIS 2025, LNCS 16291, pp. 58–81, 2026.
https://doi.org/10.1007/978-3-032-19540-1_4

restore balance when required, and are expected to grow significantly in numbers over the coming years [30]. Another significant challenge with a higher share of RESs and FERs is that most RESs do not inherently contribute to grid inertia. As a result, a grid with reduced inertia and higher variability in energy production becomes more sensitive and susceptible to fluctuations in demand and bidirectional energy flow, where certain FERs, such as batteries, can both consume power from the grid (charging) and supply energy back to it (discharging). Unfortunately, these factors introduce new risks and vulnerabilities to the power grid, increasing its exposure to both cyber and physical threats. Adversaries could manipulate FERs to increase their demand or inject energy into the grid, to execute large-scale distributed attacks with potentially catastrophic consequences [6]. Furthermore, the ability to remotely control these resources enables attackers to launch large scale attacks capable of impacting the stability of the power grid [19]. By targeting aggregators, attackers can potentially take control over and manage hundreds or thousands of distributed assets simultaneously.

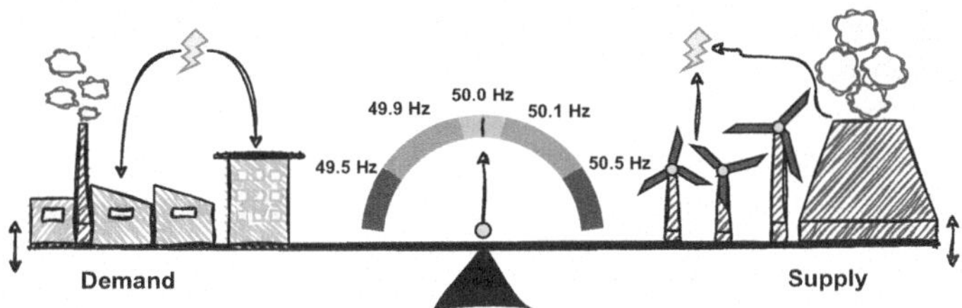

Fig. 1. Balance between supply and demand and its impact on frequency.

As the capacity, prevalence, and reliance on FERs continue to grow, they will likely draw increased attention from adversaries. It is therefore crucial to investigate the threats posed by adversaries who can control and manipulate multiple FERs within the power grid. In this work, we identify potential attack methods or strategies where adversaries can manipulate demand and bidirectional energy flow of aggregated FERs and assess the impact of these strategies on the grid frequency stability. Moreover, we evaluate the severity of these attacks in the context of both current and future capacities of FERs and analyze the effectiveness of existing frequency mitigation measures such as the Fast Frequency Reserve (FFR) and Frequency Containment Reserves (FCR) in countering such threats. By investigating potential attack strategies, their impact, and their severity, we aim to provide insights into how FERs can be manipulated to affect the frequency stability of the power grid. This knowledge is expected to inform the development of robust defensive strategies to protect the power grid against these emerging threats.

The remainder of this paper is structured as follows. Section 2 provides necessary background and related work. Section 3 defines aggregated attack strategies that adversaries could employ to destabilize the grid. Section 4 describes the simulation environment, grid model, and results from evaluating the impact of identified attacks on the stability of the grid. Section 5 provides a discussion on the results and outlines future research directions. Finally, Sect. 6 provides conclusions.

2 Background and Related Work

The frequency of the power grid directly influences the speed of generators and other rotating components connected to the power grid [5]. If the frequency falls below 49.5 Hz, it becomes necessary to start disconnecting specific loads to reduce demand. Should the frequency, despite these measures, fall below 47.5 Hz, large power stations are automatically disconnected, potentially cascading to total system collapse and widespread power blackouts. Conversely, an increase in frequency is also problematic and dangerous for the grid. If the frequency exceeds 52 Hz, the power stations are disconnected from the grid to prevent damaging vital components. Regardless of whether the frequency increases or decreases from the nominal frequency, exceeding these critical thresholds leads to the disconnection of loads and generators, potentially triggering a chain reaction that can ultimately cause the entire system to collapse. System-wide power blackouts would significantly disrupt and put enormous stress on society as critical infrastructure and essential services cease normal operations. This has been seen in several recent real-world incidents such as the cascading power outage in Puerto Rico, the major blackout in Spain and Portugal leaving millions without power for a half-day, and the attack against Ukraine's power grid [34].

To maintain grid balance and correct any deviations in frequency, constant coordination is required among many actors, including power grid operators (TSOs and DSOs), energy producers, and consumers [5]. In the Nordic countries, the power grids are tightly interconnected with bilateral connections [33]. The frequency is managed by coordinating the production and consumption within the Nordic synchronous grid, with each country incorporating frequency reserve resources that provide up and down regulation to minimize frequency fluctuations. Fluctuations in the power grid frequency are traditionally mitigated by two primary mechanisms: inertia provided by the large rotating masses such as turbines and frequency reserve resources [5]. The rotational masses in turbines and generators directly connected to the grid act as an initial buffer against changes in demand and generation. If the frequency decreases, the synchronous generators rotate slower, releasing some of their rotational energy to the power grid. Conversely, if the frequency increases, the generators rotate faster, absorbing some of the excess energy in the grid as rotational energy. As RESs increasingly constitute a larger share of power generation, the grid's inertia is decreasing since RESs are typically not connected via synchronous generators. Consequently, this buffer is slowly vanishing, making the grid more susceptible to sudden changes in demand and supply, and requiring larger capacities of frequency reserves and FERs to manage fluctuations in frequency.

2.1 The Swedish Power Grid

In Sweden, various frequency reserve resources are utilized to mitigate sudden frequency deviations and maintain the balance between demand and supply [5,33]. These resources must have sufficient capabilities, including capacity and responsiveness, to stabilize the power grid during sudden changes in demand and supply. There are currently six types of frequency reserve resources, as listed in Table 1, along with their activation range, response time, and capacity [32]. As soon as a frequency deviation is detected, automatic frequency reserves are activated to perform up- or down-regulation to keep the frequency within the normal operating range of 49.90–50.10 Hz [5]. According to a 2023 report [30], the estimated flexibility capacity of various FERs in Sweden is expected to reach 1747 MW in 2025 and increasing substantially to 8000 MW by 2030. Key contributors include large-scale battery systems (1200 MW by 2030), heat pumps (1300 MW), EV charging (500 MW), and hydrogen production via electrolysis, which is expected to grow from 120 MW in 2025 to a dominant 4400 MW in 2030. The increase reflects a strategic push to meet Sweden's forecasted power demand of 25800 MW by 2030 (up from 17800 MW in 2023).

Unfortunately, there have been several instances in Sweden and worldwide where the grid frequency has deviated significantly from the nominal value. In Sweden, during 2011, the sudden disconnection of the Oskarshamn 3 nuclear plant, which supplied 1400 MW, caused the grid frequency to drop to 49.36 Hz within approximately ten seconds. According to the Swedish TSO, this is one of the lowest frequencies recorded within the N-1 criterion, which requires the grid to withstand the loss of the largest single generator (up to 1450 MW) [28]. The grid is designed to handle disturbances up to this magnitude, and the frequency reserves are dimensioned to support this criterion. During this critical period,

Table 1. Frequency reserve and restoration products.

Reserve Type	Regulation Direction	Activation Range (Hz)	Response Time	Capacity (MW)
Fast Frequency Reserve (FFR)	Upwards	Below 49.7–49.5	0.7–1.3 s	Up to 100
Upward Frequency Containment Reserve (FCR) - Disturbance	Upwards	Below 49.9	Within seconds	Up to 567
Downward FCR - Disturbance	Downwards	Above 50.1	Within seconds	Up to 547
FCR - Normal	Both	Outside 50.0	Within seconds	235
Automatic Frequency Restoration Reserve (aFRR)	Both	Outside 50.0	Within 5 min	Up to 111
Manual Frequency Restoration Reserve (mFRR)	Both	Manual Activation	Within 15 min	Up to 300

frequency reserves were automatically activated, and the frequency recovered to 49.8 Hz within 25 s, successfully preventing a more severe grid failure. Another incident in February 2023, involved the Nordlink HVDC connection unexpectedly importing 300 MW instead of exporting 1375 MW, creating a 1675 MW imbalance within the power grid [33]. The frequency briefly dropped to 49.41 Hz before recovering to the normal operating range. This event underscored the increasing risk posed by modern interconnections, as the potential imbalance in such failures can exceed traditional design limits like the N-1 criterion. A more severe event occurred in April 2023, when maintenance failures caused voltage drops and automatic disconnection of multiple generators, including Forsmark 1 and 2, removing 2130 MW from the grid. The frequency quickly dropped to 49.3 Hz within eight seconds. Emergency injections through HVDC connections and activation of frequency reserves (600 MW and 700 MW, respectively) helped restore stability to 49.8 Hz. Over the next minutes, the frequency restoration reserve (mFRR) added 2431 MW, and full normalization was achieved. Backup measures, including 7600 MW of additional mFRR and automatic load disconnection at 48.8 Hz, were available but not needed. The Swedish TSO concluded that despite the severity, the system remained within operational limits and the response measures were effective.

2.2 Related Work

A significant amount of prior work exists on smart grid security, covering a wide range of vulnerabilities and mitigation strategies. Research has demonstrated that the attack surface on the grid is large, and includes utility operators, aggregators, communication networks, smart meters, inverters, and energy management systems that ultimately manage and control various energy resources [22].

One significant challenge is insecure communication between autonomous cyber-physical systems, such as batteries and EVs, and their control systems, which often relies on legacy protocols designed without robust security measures [9]. These protocols frequently lack encryption and authentication, making them vulnerable to attacks like eavesdropping and false message injection [10]. Such attacks can distort state estimations and disrupt grid operations [36], highlighting the critical need to ensure the integrity of measurement data and control commands for safe and reliable system performance. Another major vulnerability lies within the Advanced Metering Infrastructure (AMI) which depends on real-time measurements from producers and remote control commands over the AMI network [4]. These remote commands could potentially be exploited allowing attackers to disconnect millions of connected smart meters [4]. Similar concerns are raised by Parks [20] and Li et al. [11] who note that AMI components located in customer premises are susceptible to tampering, potentially allowing users to manipulate pricing data for personal gain.

Beyond AMI, vulnerabilities extend to surrounding infrastructure and control systems. Firewalls can be undermined by misconfigurations that permit unauthorized access [26]. Energy management systems and aggregators also present risks, as they often rely on insecure or outdated communication protocols and commercial off-the-shelf (COTS) components with internet-facing interfaces [9–11]. These systems, managing large numbers of distributed energy resources (DERs), become high-value targets for cyberattacks [22]. For example, Baumgart et al. [3] revealed vulnerabilities that allow remote access, eavesdropping, and unauthorized system changes [3]. Collectively, these vulnerabilities demonstrate that many systems within the smart grid could be exposed to large-scale coordinated attacks capable of disrupting numerous energy assets simultaneously.

Attacks on the power grid are increasingly sophisticated and target various components to disrupt the critical balance between supply and demand. False data injection (FDI) attacks could corrupt state estimation process by manipulating meter data, leading to wrong control decision and potential grid instability [12,13,25]. Load-altering attacks, such as those evaluated by Dabrowski et al. [6], statically or dynamically [2] change electricity demand of remotely controlled assets, such as air conditioning and electrical heating. [15]. These attacks can cause frequency deviations, trip tie lines, and even split grid zones. EVs and charging stations have also emerged as potential vectors for such attacks [1,23]. In addition, attackers can exploit bidirectional energy flow enabled by technologies like battery energy storage systems (BESSs) and Vehicle-to-Grid (V2G) to inject power into the grid at unscheduled times, causing frequency oscillations and generator disconnections [16,23]. Aggregated attacks further escalate the threat by coordinating malicious actions across multiple grid components, such as generators and transmission lines, to induce cascading failures and maximize disruption [22,37]. As grid digitalization expands, the integration of IT systems, IoT devices, and decentralized control mechanisms makes it increasingly feasible for attackers to coordinate large-scale cyber-physical attacks with potentially catastrophic consequences.

Despite extensive research, gaps remain in understanding how different aggregated attack strategies impact the grid frequency, particularly in the context of existing frequency mitigation measures. While static and dynamic load-altering attacks have been widely discussed, their definitions and implementations vary. This paper formalizes these attack types and introduces a structured classification that includes novel attacks that combine multiple attack strategies. Furthermore, existing research seldom evaluates attacks based on realistic flexibility capacities. This work evaluates attacks using different timings and aggregated attack sizes that reflect the current and future flexibility potential, identifying which FERs pose the highest risk based on their capacity.

3 Aggregated Attacks

Aggregated attacks involve load-altering attacks where attackers manipulate the demand or bidirectional energy flow of multiple FERs. By aggregating many FERs, attackers can execute large-scale attacks involving significant amounts of power. If a sufficient number of FERs are aggregated, the attack could violate frequency stability parameters discussed earlier. We build upon previously discussed concepts of static and dynamic load-altering attacks and formalize them into a structured classification. This classification introduces four aggregated attack categories: static, switching, periodic, and combination attacks, that could be used by adversaries to destabilize the grid. While the static, switching, and periodic attack concepts are loosely based on existing literature, the combination attacks are a novel contribution of this work.

3.1 Static Attacks

Static attacks aim to create a persistent imbalance between supply and demand through various attack strategies. These strategies can be further divided into four types:

- **Demand Increase (DI) Attack**: This attack targets unidirectional loads primarily drawing energy from the grid. By increasing the demand of controlled assets the frequency in the grid declines.
- **Demand Reduction (DR) Attack**: Similar to the DI attack, this type typically involves unidirectional loads. However, contrary to a DI attack, this type decreases the energy demand of controlled assets, resulting in an increased grid frequency.
- **Supply Increase (SI) Attack**: This attack typically involves assets capable of bidirectional energy flow, such as V2G and batteries. By simultaneously injecting additional power into the grid, the controlled assets cause the grid frequency to increase. This attack type is sometimes also referred to as a power injection attack.
- **Supply Reduction (SR) Attack**: Like the SI attack, this type primarily involves bidirectional energy resources. However, controlled assets either reduce their power output or completely disconnect from the grid, resulting in a drop in grid frequency.

These attacks require an attacker to have control over assets with sufficient capacity. The assets may either be concentrated in a specific grid location or distributed across a larger geographic area. Ultimately, once the attacker has achieved control over assets, they can execute a static attack. To do this, the attacker simultaneously executes one of the attack types described above at a predetermined start time, T_{start}, and sustains the attack indefinitely. This attack is relatively simple to execute since it only involves a single activation action. Figure 2 shows an illustration.

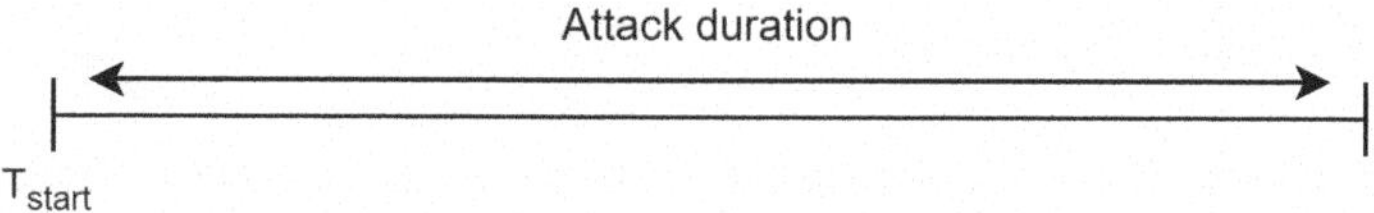

Fig. 2. Timeline of a static attack.

3.2 Switching Attacks

A switching attack, depicted in Fig. 3, is an extension of a static attack. Unlike static attacks, which maintain an increased or reduced demand or supply, switching attacks include a sudden reversion of the attack, restoring the balance between supply and demand to their original state. This restoration does not occur for static DI, DR, SI, and SR attacks. The switching attack begins with executing a static attack at T_{start}, followed by a reversion at T_1. Once the attack is reverted and the balance is restored, it is considered complete.

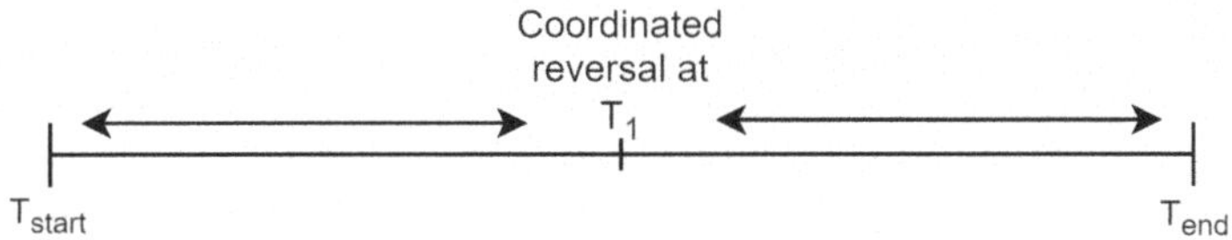

Fig. 3. Timeline of a switching attack.

3.3 Periodic Attacks

Periodic attacks involve repeatedly executing a series of switching attacks against the grid at certain intervals with the aim of achieving sustained destabilization. We define periodic attacks to only involve one static attack type (DI, DR, SI, or SR) to allow for a more targeted evaluation. The timing of the switching attacks could be either predetermined or dynamically selected based on real-time grid conditions. To dynamically determine this timing, an attack could, for example, continuously monitor the grid's frequency to launch subsequent attacks at moments that cause maximum disruptions. These subsequent attacks could have the largest impact if executed when the slope of the frequency deviation is the steepest.

Figure 4 illustrates a periodic attack consisting of five switching attacks. The first switching attack occurs between T_{start} and T_1, followed by subsequent switching attacks between the determined intervals. The periodic attack can continue as long as the assets remain connected to the grid, can adjust their energy demand, or have sufficient charge to execute the attacks effectively.

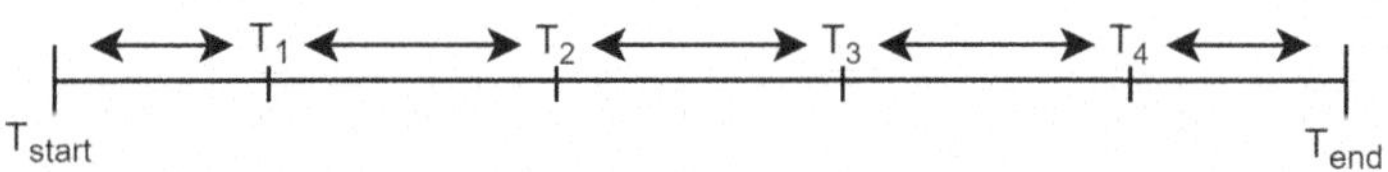

Fig. 4. Timeline of a periodic attack.

3.4 Combination Attacks

A combination attack builds upon the previously mentioned attacks and incorporates a combination of demand-based (increasing or decreasing) and supply-based (increasing or decreasing) attacks. By alternating between attack strategies that increase the frequency (e.g. DR and SI attacks) and those that decrease the frequency (e.g. DI and SR attacks), an attacker could take advantage of and leverage the frequency response in the grid to maximize the impact of the attack.

Particularly, if an attacker manages to activate the grid's frequency reserve, it can perform subsequent attacks that leverage the upward or downward regulation. For instance, an attacker could first execute a static DI attack to reduce the grid frequency, triggering the frequency reserve to compensate by increasing supply. Following this, the attacker could perform an SI attack, further increasing the supply and creating an even larger imbalance between supply and demand. This example is illustrated in Fig. 5, where the attacker executes the DI attack at T_{start}, followed by a SI at a strategically selected moment T_1, and then alternating between these.

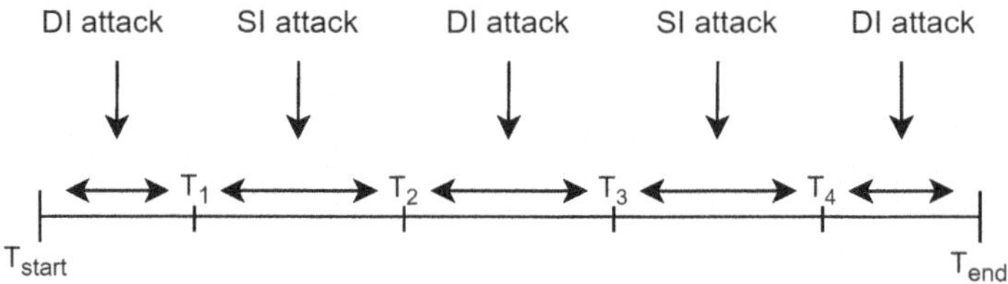

Fig. 5. Timeline of a combination DI and SI attack.

4 Evaluation

This section presents an evaluation of the impact of the aggregated attack strategies. We begin by describing the employed simulation environment and the grid model. The impact of the attacks on the first-swing stability of the power grid model is then assessed by measuring the grid's frequency response to the attacks. These results are then put in the context using the predicted flexibility potential and frequency reserves capacity.

4.1 Simulator and Model

Several simulators are used in the literature to simulate a grid. These include Matlab Simscape [14], Siemens Power System Simulation [24], Ge Vernova Steady State Power Flow [35], and PowerWorld Simulator [21]. While most offer free versions for research, these are often limited to models with fewer than 50 buses and may lack full features. In this work, we use the PowerWorld simulator, which meets the necessary technical and accessibility requirements. It supports up to 40 buses and includes essential tools for analyzing first-swing stability and executing predefined scenarios.

Apart from the simulator, the selection of the power grid model is also vital because it determines the grid's behavior, including its reaction to changes in demand and supply. There is a large body of works that are based on two grid models, the *WSCC 9-bus* [8], a literature-based model, and the *Hawaii 37-bus* [7], a synthetic model. The WSCC 9-bus model, consisting of three generators and nine buses, is a simplified theoretical model often used in research. Each bus is treated as a large substation, representing a broad geographical area. In contrast, the Hawaii 37-bus model, based on publicly available data from Oahu, includes 45 generators, 27 loads, and incorporates both conventional and renewable energy sources modeled with GENROU and REGC_A machine models. To assess model accuracy and select a model for our work, both models were tested using simulated attack scenarios involving an 8% increase in demand, designed to replicate the frequency response observed during the Oskarshamn 3 incident described in Sect. 2. Both models dropped below the 49.5 Hz frequency stability threshold, but the WSCC model stabilized more effectively and replicated the frequency response of the Swedish grid. The Hawaii model showed poorer stability and did not align with the observed data. Thus, due to its realistic and consistent frequency response, the WSCC 9-bus model is selected for this work. It offers a reliable platform for evaluating attack scenarios with reduced variability and dependence on specific load configurations.

Obviously, the WSCC 9-bus model cannot exactly represent the Swedish national grid in terms of complexity or magnitude. However, we use it as a proxy model in which both attacks and responses are scaled according to characteristics of the Swedish grid. The model behavior is also validated against real observed events to ensure that it is sufficiently representative. This allows us to gauge high-level system behavior and the potential impact of large-scale coordinated attacks.

4.2 Results

An evaluation of aggregated attack strategies using simulations conducted in the PowerWorld simulator with the WSCC 9-bus model is presented below.

Static Attacks

Static attacks are performed by executing a DI, DR, SI or SR attack on the grid and sustaining over a certain period of time. Although the controlled and manipulated assets can be distributed across many loads and injection points, we assume that they are concentrated on a single load. This assumption allows us to reduce model complexity and preserves the net power imbalance driving frequency changes, though it omits local network effects that would arise with geographically dispersed real attacks. The following assess the impact of static attacks on the grid frequency.

Demand Increase Attacks. Three DI attacks, where demand is increased by different amounts, are executed to evaluate the impact and behavior. The increments in demand are derived from past incidents described in Sect. 2. The incident at Oskarshamn 3 caused an imbalance of 1400 MW, the Nordlink incident caused an imbalance of 1675 MW, and the Forsmark 1 & 2 incident caused an imbalance of 2130 MW. When compared to the average annual generation for the respective years, these incidents correspond to 8%, 9.4%, and 12% of total generation in the grid, respectively. By applying the same demand changes observed in these previous incidents, we compare and benchmark the grid's frequency response based on the WSCC model against the actual incidents.

The results of the DI attacks with demand increases of 8%, 9.4%, and 12% are illustrated in Fig. 6. This clearly demonstrates that DI attacks that induce greater increases in demand lead to larger frequency deviations from the nominal frequency. A greater increase leads to a larger imbalance between supply and demand, resulting in a more significant frequency response.

Comparing these frequency responses observed in Fig. 6 against the actual incidents is important to assess how the frequency response in the model varies due to different demand increases. For the WSCC model, a static DI attack by 12% (Forsmark 1 & 2 incident) causes the grid's frequency to drop to 49.17 Hz before stabilizing at 49.8 Hz. In the actual incident, the lowest measured frequency was 49.3 Hz, stabilizing at 49.8 Hz. These results indicate that the WSCC model appears slightly more sensitive to DI attacks. However, this can be partly explained by the fact that, in the real incident, the frequency was 50.1 Hz before rapidly declining [29]. This difference results in a smaller frequency deviation from the nominal frequency (50 Hz), but when measured from the highest to lowest frequency, the frequency responses are similar. The frequency of the simulated grid in response to the other two DI attacks closely matches the frequency

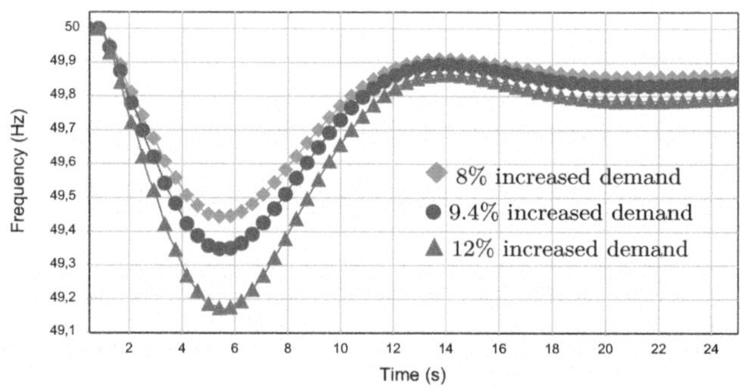

Fig. 6. Frequency response under three DI attack scenarios derived from real-world incidents.

responses observed in the real incidents, with similar first-swing stability. However, the time in which this plays out does not accurately reflect the reality. For example, the frequency responses in Fig. 6 stabilize after approximately 12 s, while in the actual incidents, the time it takes for the Swedish grid to stabilize is around 30 s. This suggests that the simulator underestimates the time aspect, and the attacks may take longer for an actual grid to recover from. However, the lowest frequency and first-swing stability of the WSCC model are very similar to the Swedish grid, which is the primary focus of this paper. These DI attacks are sufficient to activate upwards-regulating frequency reserves, including FCR-Normal, FFR, and upwards FCR, as the frequency falls below 49.5 Hz. In addition, certain loads can be automatically disconnected to return the frequency to acceptable operating ranges. Consequently, an attacker that has the capability to execute attacks of this magnitude would pose a significant threat to the stability of the grid. In this case, the grid returns to within the normal operating range (49.9–50.1 Hz) but the sudden frequency drop to under 49.5 Hz could still result in deterioration of frequency reserves, disconnection of loads, or even further cascading instabilities.

Furthermore, we note that the observed imbalances of 1400, 1675, and 2130 MW respectively were sufficient to cause a frequency drop below 49.5 Hz. Therefore, DI attacks replicating these incidents appear to be feasible in 2025 as they require control over a capacity of less than 1747 MW, which is the estimated flexibility potential of FERs in Sweden in 2025, as discussed in Sect. 2. Although such an attack would require considerable coordination and control of many FERs, the capacity and deployment of FERs is continuously growing, increasing the likelihood of an attacker controlling sufficient resources to perform such attacks in the coming years.

We conducted additional simulations with varying attack capacities to further analyze the impact of DI attacks on the grid. These are aimed to determine how different amounts of power impact the grid frequency. The results demonstrate a negative linear trend, indicating that the lowest frequency decreases as the attack capacity increases. Based on this data, a linear function ($Y = -0.06X + 49.92$) is derived where Y, represents the lowest achieved frequency in Hz, as a function of X, the attack capacity expressed as a share of the total average generation in Sweden. This function can be used to approximate the lowest frequency induced by a DI attack.

Demand Reduction and Supply Increase Attacks. In terms of frequency response, DR and SI attacks have the opposite effect of DI attacks. While DI attacks increase the power demand of FERs, DR attacks reduce the energy demand, and SI attacks inject additional power into the grid. Both DR and SI attacks create a similar imbalance between supply and demand, causing the frequency in the grid to increase. During the attack simulation, it is not possible to increase the generator's power output. Therefore, SI attacks are modeled by applying a negative demand to a load, which results in a similar frequency response. However, DR and SI attacks may differ in other aspects that could be important when analyzing, such as voltage or phase stability, two other important stability measurements for the grid. For simplicity, the paper will only refer to DR attacks in the following. However, it should be noted that SI attacks are also included in the analysis and are attacks that can cause the frequency to increase, similar to DR attacks.

Since DR attacks are the opposite of DI attacks, the frequency response of such attacks should be inverted. To compare the differences between these, the three DI attacks with capacities corresponding to real incidents, as presented in Fig. 6, are converted into DR attacks. The magnitudes of the DR attacks are thus 8%, 9.4%, and 12% of the total generation. The impact of these attacks on the grid's frequency is presented in Fig. 7.

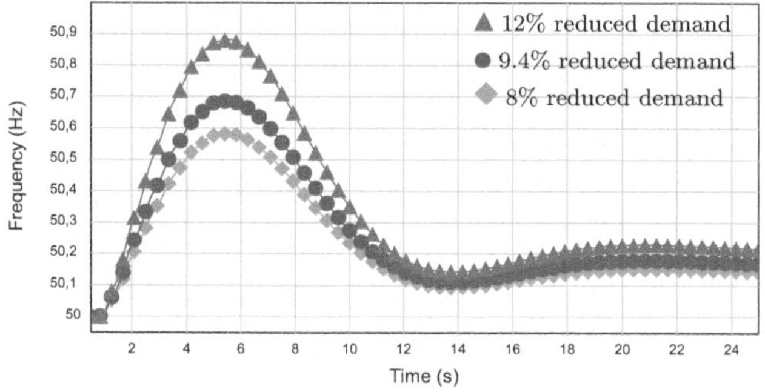

Fig. 7. Frequency response of three DR attack scenarios with varying demand reductions.

The incidents described in Sect. 2 involve a sudden decrease in power supply to the grid, making them valuable benchmarks for evaluating DI and SR attacks. However, there have been no incidents involving large power injections or sudden reductions in demand within the Swedish power grid. Thus, it is not possible to compare DR attacks with any actual incidents. Instead, comparisons between DI and DR attacks are performed.

The frequency response presented in Fig. 7 demonstrates that DR attacks have an inverted frequency response compared to DI attacks and that the magnitude of the frequency response for DR attacks is slightly larger than that of DI attacks. Reducing demand by 12% of the total generation in the grid results in a peak frequency of 50.88 Hz (a deviation of 0.88 Hz), while increasing demand by 12% caused the frequency to drop to 49.17 Hz (0.83 Hz deviation). This suggests that the grid is slightly more vulnerable and sensitive to DR attacks. This behavior aligns with Sweden's grid characteristics, where down-regulation reserves have less capacity and slower response times than reserves providing up-regulation, as presented in Table 1.

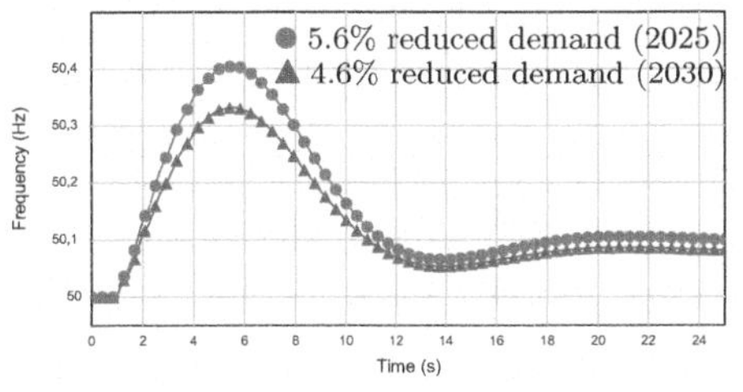

(a) Frequency response without FCR mitigation.

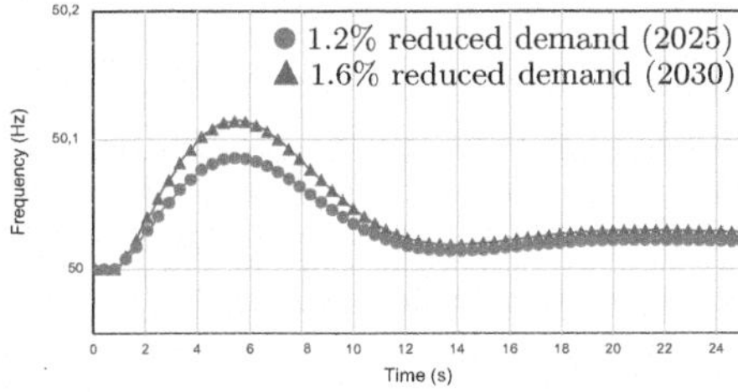

(b) Frequency response with FCR mitigation.

Fig. 8. Frequency response of two DR attacks.

It is unlikely that attackers manage to control all the FERs. Instead, controlling a subset of them is more probable. For instance, FERs such as large-scale battery systems, are estimated to provide 1000 MW of flexibility in 2025 and 1200 MW in 2030, corresponding to 5.6% and 4.6%, respectively. By 2030, large-scale battery systems will represent a smaller share of total generation due to predicted growth in overall generation. Both 1000 MW and 1200 MW exceed the downregulation frequency reserves of FCR-Normal and downward FCR. Therefore, these frequency reserves are not sufficient to completely mitigate a DR attack of this size. DR attacks with these magnitudes are executed and presented in Fig. 8a, which shows the frequency increasing to 50.40 Hz (2025) and 50.33 Hz (2030). Although these frequency deviations do not violate important frequency stability parameters, if these large-scale battery systems are concentrated within a small geographic area, their effect on the local grid could be more severe.

The combined capacity of FCR-Normal and downward FCR was 782 MW in 2024, which is not expected to increase significantly by 2026, as per the projections [31]. This paper assumes that the same capacities will be true for 2030, representing a worst-case scenario where the capacities of these frequency reserves are not increased. Assuming that these frequency reserves instantly and linearly respond to changes in demand and supply, the remaining magnitude of the 1000 MW DR attack is 218 MW and 418 MW for the 1200 MW DR attack. These remaining capacities correspond to 1.2% in 2025 and 1.6% in 2030 of the total generation. DR attacks of these magnitudes are executed and presented in Fig. 8b. The result shows that the frequency remains within the normal operating range, indicating that DR of this size should not pose a significant challenge to grid stability, provided all FFR-Normal and downward FCR products are activated.

Switching Attacks

Switching attacks are performed by executing a static DR, DI, SI, or SR attack followed by a sudden reversion to the original demand or supply at a predetermined time. Although relatively straightforward, this attack requires the attacker to have the capability to rapidly and synchronously change the power demand or supply of FERs. However, not all FERs can realistically change their demand or supply of energy quickly enough due to various limitations, such as ramp rates, that restrict the speed at which they can adjust their consumption or supply. In addition to the sudden imbalance caused by the switching attack, the activation of frequency reserves can be exploited to further amplify the imbalance between supply and demand. This is possible because frequency reserves respond to frequency deviations with a predictable delay. An attacker may alter the demand or supply of FERs so that they, during this time period, align with the frequency reserve's response.

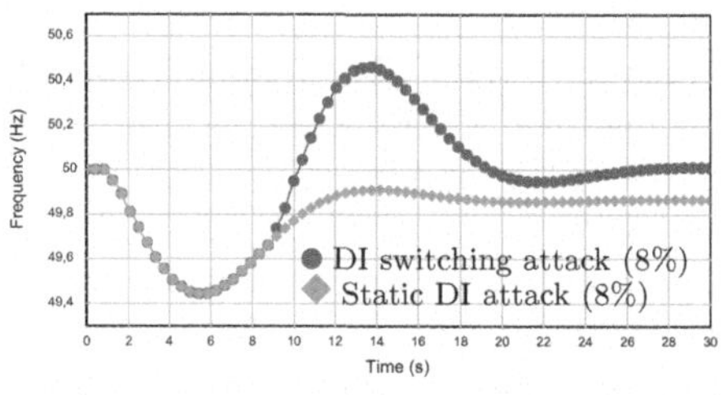

(a) Frequency response to a DI switching attack.

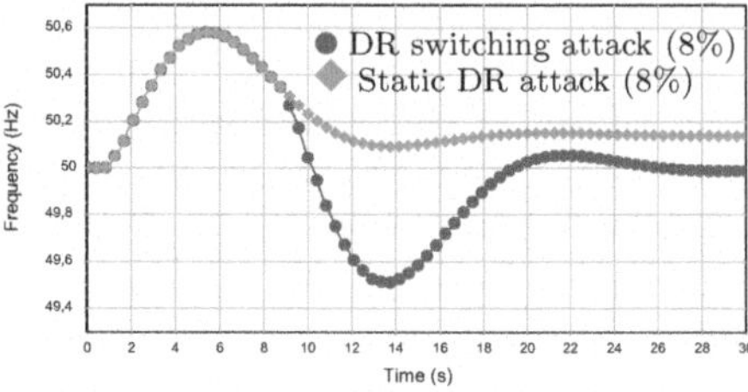

(b) Frequency response to a DR switching attack.

Fig. 9. Impact of switching attacks on grid frequency.

We examine two types of switching attacks. The first involves initially decreasing the frequency by performing a static DI or SR attack and then reverting it to the original demand or supply. The second type involves initially increasing the frequency through a DR or an SI attack, followed by the reversion. A DI-switching attack is executed and presented in Fig. 9a, while a DR attack is shown in Fig. 9b, where each switching attack increases or decreases demand by 8%. For comparison, static DI and DR attacks are also displayed in the respective figures. Each switching attack changes the demand by 8% of the initial total supply in the grid. The static attack is executed after one second and then continues for seven seconds, at which point the reversion occurs. The precise timing of the reversal is determined to be critical for maximizing the disturbance to grid stability.

The figures above illustrate the impact of switching attacks. The attacks are essentially static attacks with an additional reversion component, and are thus identical up to the point of the reversion to the original demand. Thereafter, the sudden reversion back to the original demand causes the frequency to rapidly increase in Fig. 9a while rapidly decreasing in Fig. 9b. Since the demand is returned to the original, the frequency ultimately stabilizes at the nominal frequency range. Comparing these results with their static counterparts, it is evident that these do not result in a higher or lower frequency than their equivalent static attacks. However, the quick change in frequency, from 49.4 to 50.4 Hz, causes oscillation and is very disruptive to the stability of the grid. It could also potentially impact voltage and phase stability of the grid.

The timing of the reversion in switching attacks, where the FERs revert back to the original demand, is critical for maximizing the disturbance to grid stability. This is because the grid's frequency reserves have a delayed response. To investigate this, several switching attacks with various reversion timings are executed. Four DI-switching attacks with reversion occurring at different times (3, 6, 9, and 12 s) are shown in Fig. 10a. Similarly, Fig. 10b illustrates DR-switching attacks with the same reversion times.

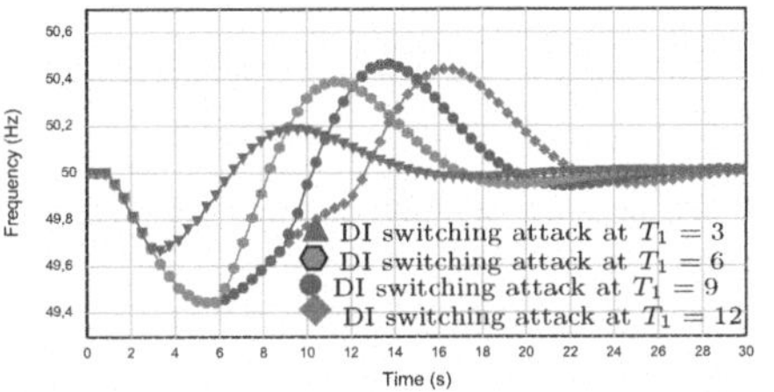

(a) Four DI switching attacks with reversal times at $T_1 = 3$, $T_1 = 6$, $T_1 = 9$, and $T_1 = 12$ (s).

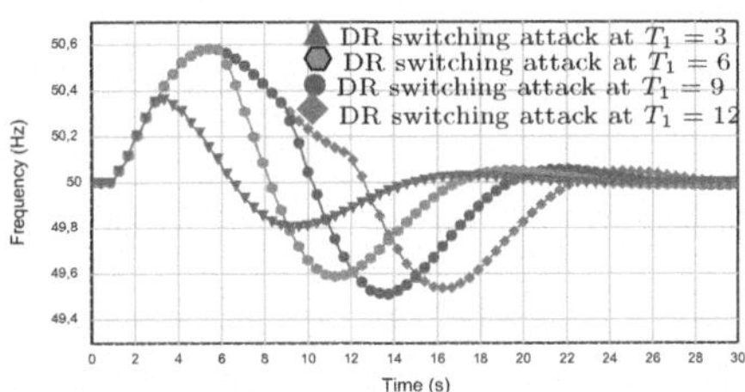

(b) Four DR switching attacks with reversal times at $T_1 = 3$, $T_1 = 6$, $T_1 = 9$, and $T_1 = 12$ (s).

Fig. 10. Impact of different reversal times (T_1) in switching attacks.

The presented DI and DR attacks illustrate how varying the reversal time (T_1) affects the grid's frequency response. In this grid model, the optimal time for the reversion component of the switching attack is about 8 s. These results indicate that switching attacks do not achieve larger deviations from the nominal frequency than achieved by executing static DI, DR, SI, and DR attacks. However, switching attacks that induce sudden changes in demand and supply could still disrupt the grid's stability as they can repeatedly swing the grid frequency and cause oscillations.

Periodic Attacks

Periodic attacks are executed by performing a series of switching attacks at specific intervals, with some duration between each attack. In this approach, once one switching attack is executed, the next switching attack is performed after a certain duration. This sequence creates a continuous chain of switching attacks that together form a periodic attack. As each switching attack involves a reversion, the grid is subjected to repeated fluctuations, leading to continuous changes in the demand or generation of FERs. Previous observations of switching attacks demonstrate that the duration between the switching attacks is important for maximizing their impact on grid stability. Thus, this timing has a profound effect on periodic attacks. To investigate this further, three periodic attacks are executed in total, each consisting of a series of four DI-switching (8% increase) attacks with varying durations between each attack. The frequency responses from periodic attacks with 4, 8, and 16 s between each switching attack are presented in the figures below.

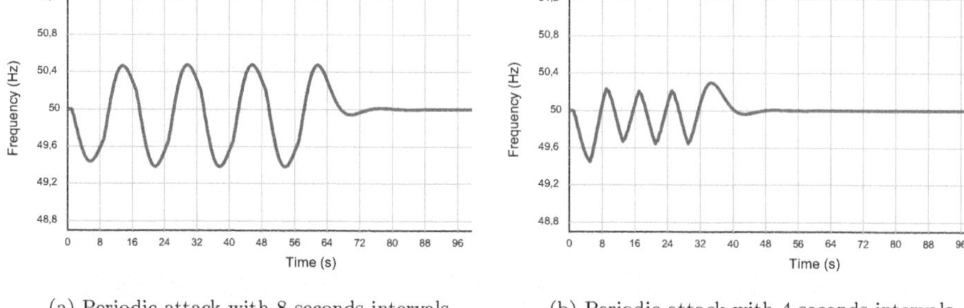

(a) Periodic attack with 8 seconds intervals.

(b) Periodic attack with 4 seconds intervals.

Fig. 11. Impact of periodic attacks on grid frequency.

A periodic attack with a duration of 8 s between the switching attacks is presented in Fig. 11a, which reflects the optimal timing for switching attacks as described earlier. The intervals of 4 and 16 s are chosen to explore both half and double the optimal timing, providing a broader understanding of how different durations between the switching attacks, in a periodic attack, affect grid stability. The frequency responses for periodic attacks with 4 and 16-s intervals are illustrated in Figs. 11b and 12a, respectively. The periodic attacks cause the frequency to oscillate around the nominal frequency. Comparing the frequency response, in Fig. 11a, of the periodic attack with 8 s between each switching attack with Figs. 11b and 12a, it is evident that 8 s between each switching attack induces the largest frequency deviation and is thus more effective from an attacker's perspective. In addition, periodic attacks do not induce a larger frequency deviation than regular switching attacks.

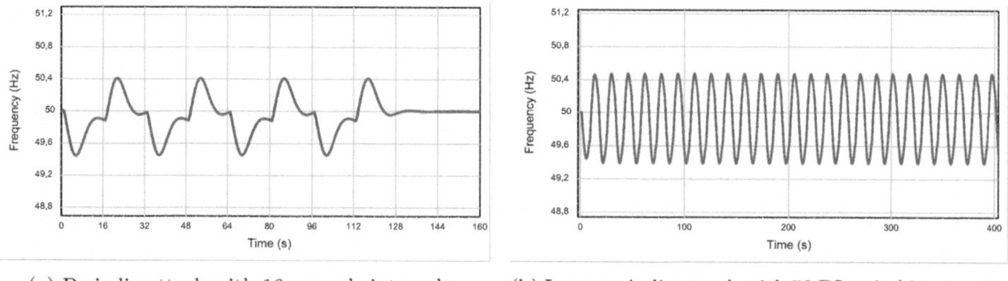

(a) Periodic attack with 16 seconds intervals.

(b) Long periodic attack with 50 DI-switching events.

Fig. 12. Impact of periodic attacks of varying duration and quantity.

Further examination of the frequency response in Fig. 11a indicates that the frequency deviation slightly increases over the entire attack duration. The highest achieved frequency during this periodic attack is 50.476 Hz at approximately 62 s, compared to 50.465 Hz in Fig. 9a at roughly 14 s. Building upon this observation, a longer periodic attack lasting 400 s and consisting of 50 switching attacks is executed and presented in Fig. 12b. For this periodic attack, an 8-s interval between each switching attack is chosen, as it has been identified as the most optimal duration for achieving the largest frequency deviation in this model. However, the results in Fig. 12b indicate that the frequency does not consistently grow over time, with the highest measured frequency being 50.476 Hz at 93 s. In addition, a similar attack performed over a duration of 10,000 s produced similar results, indicating that frequency deviations do not grow over time. This suggests that the periodic nature of the attacks does not lead to increasingly large deviations in frequency. Due to their continuous nature, periodic attacks might be more challenging to mitigate than static and switching attacks. Mitigating a periodic attack would involve continuously activating and deactivating the frequency reserves to counteract the imbalance. Without effective mitigation, periodic attacks sustained over time could significantly challenge the grid's ability to operate within normal operating ranges. The resulting frequency oscillations could place stress on critical grid infrastructure such as connected loads and generators, potentially leading to damage or causing them to disconnect from the grid. If such disconnection were to occur, there is an increased risk of cascading failures throughout the power grid as more generators or loads may need to be disconnected. Another challenge is identifying the assets involved, as many FERs are potentially distributed across a large geographical area, and each one only constitutes a small portion of the total attack.

Combination Attacks

The definition of combination attack allows for mixed directions of switching attacks, with the first attack increasing the frequency and the subsequent attack decreasing it, or vice versa. By evaluating this combined attack, this paper aims to investigate whether this attack has a worse impact on the grid's stability and if a more complex attack strategy is more successful in exploiting the frequency response pattern from a sequence of attacks. Three combination attacks that alternate between increasing demand by 8% and subsequently decreasing it by 8% are presented in the following figures. Each combination attack employs a different timing interval, specifically 4, 8, or 16 s, based on previous evaluations and to ease comparison. The results for these combination attacks are presented in Fig. 13a (4 s), Fig. 13b (8 s), and Fig. 14a (16 s).

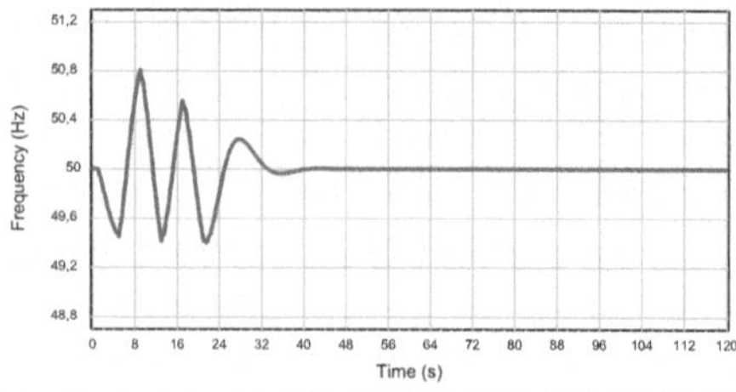

(a) Combination attack with 4 seconds interval.

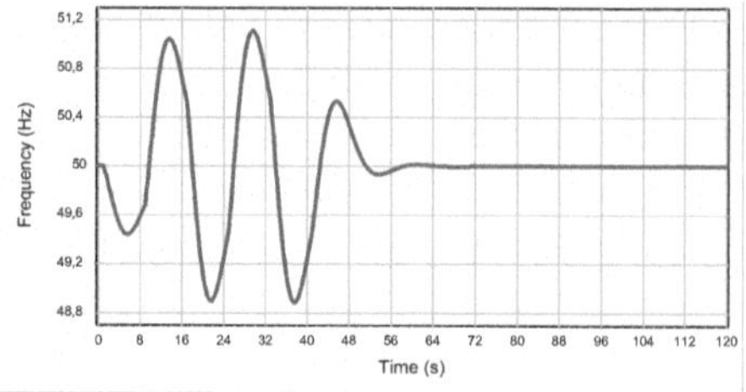

(b) Combination attack with 8 seconds interval.

Fig. 13. Impact of combination attacks on grid frequency.

The impact of the combined attacks as shown in figures is similar to previous periodic attacks, but the corresponding frequency deviation is more than twice as large from the nominal frequency compared to periodic attacks. The highest achieved frequency for combination attacks is 51.11 Hz, which can be observed in Fig. 13b , while the best periodic attack, from an attacker's perspective, achieved the highest frequency of 50.476 Hz. A larger impact for combination attacks is not surprising, as the alternating pattern effectively doubles the magnitude of the attack, first increasing demand by 8%, then returning it to the original demand, and finally decreasing it by 8%. Consequently, combination attacks that incorporate both DI and DR attacks are capable of causing larger frequency deviations and thus larger disturbances to first-swing stability than other attacks, that either increase or reduce demand, but not both simultaneously.

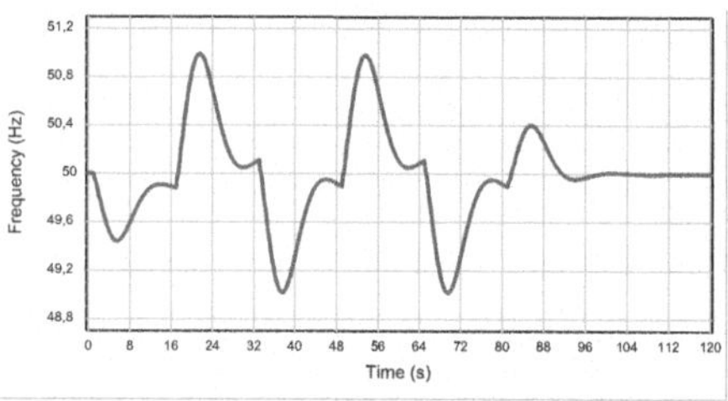

(a) Combination attack with 16 seconds interval.

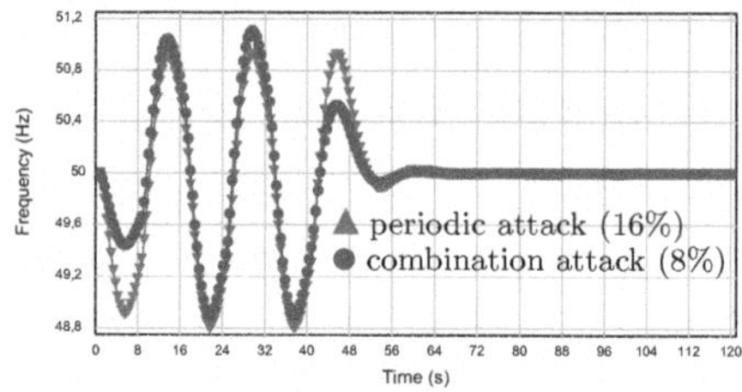

(b) Comparison of combination and periodic attack.

Fig. 14. Impact of combination attacks of varying intervals and equivalent periodic attack.

Since the combination attack effectively doubles the attack magnitude, it is also of interest to see how it compares to periodic attacks that increase demand by similar amounts. A period attack increasing demand by 16% (double that of previously evaluated periodic attacks) is presented in Fig. 14b, alongside the frequency response of the combination attack demonstrated in Fig. 13b (8-s interval). The periodic attack that increases demand by 16% achieves a similar frequency response as a combination attack that alternates between increasing and decreasing demand by 8%. Therefore, it can be concluded that combination attacks can achieve the same impact as periodic attacks while only requiring changes in demand by half the amount. This is particularly interesting because the total change (16%) for combination attacks remains the same as for periodic attacks. Moreover, the combination attack keeps the demand and supply levels closer to normal amounts which is likely to avoid tripping fuses, as well as voltage and current relays. From an attacker's perspective, a strategy that optimizes impact while evading detection and tripping of defenses is highly desirable. However, this strategy also comes with a caveat that the controlled FERs must be capable of executing both DI and DR switching attacks. This could be achieved by e.g., BESSs that first charge and then suddenly discharge, or through heat pumps that can initially increase their demand, restore it to original demand levels, and subsequently reduce demand by an equivalent amount. To conclude, combination attacks pose a greater risk to grid stability, while requiring fewer or smaller FERs to achieve the same impact as other attacks.

5 Interpretation of Results

The aim of this paper is to identify and assesses potential cyberattack strategies targeting FERs in order to assess their impact on the first-swing stability of the power grid. A detailed evaluation of the attack scenarios is presented in Sect. 4 where the necessary steps and parameters for each scenario, including various time intervals and attack sizes, are provided, to ensure applicability and reliability. However, the evaluated attacks are only a representative selection of possible attack strategies and there might be other attacks that are not evaluated in this work. The experiments demonstrate that the impact of the different attack scenarios on the frequency in the power grid follows a linear relationship with the size of the induced change. For the static DI, DR, SI, and SR attacks, results demonstrate a distinct linear correlation between the lowest respective highest frequency and the size of the static attacks. According to the Swedish TSO, the regulation provided by the frequency reserves should be linear to the frequency deviation [27]. This confirms the linear function derived in our results. Even though the attack scenarios' impact on the frequency follows a linear relationship, some are superior in other aspects. Periodic attacks, for example, can induce severe frequency oscillations that can potentially damage equipment and components connected to the grid while simultaneously disrupting grid stability. Whereas combination attacks that alternate between increasing and decreasing load can remain closer to normal operating values in terms of current and voltage while maximizing the frequency deviations, achieving a similar effect as periodic attacks but with half capacity. Other attacks, such as switching attacks, stand out due to being easy to execute, while still causing lots of disruption.

The timing of various attacks has also been shown to have a significant impact on the frequency stability of the power grid. To maximize frequency deviations, an attacker must identify the optimal timing of when to execute these attacks. For the simulated attacks, the optimal timing between attacks seems to be around eight seconds. However, the optimal timings identified in this paper are difficult to extrapolate to a real grid since the grid model recoups much faster than it would in reality. Nevertheless, the results suggest that the optimal timing for switching, periodic and combination attacks is when the frequency curve has the largest rate of change when approaching the nominal frequency. The power grid has shown some resilience to sudden and large static attacks, as demonstrated both in this work and in real-world incidents, where the grid remains stable and eventually returns to normal operating ranges. While the current capacities of FERs in 2025 pose a significant threat to the power grid on a national level they still require a substantial share of assets capable of providing flexibility. By 2030, the potential increase in FER capacities will allow attackers to more easily carry out attacks, both in terms of assets required and the potential attack surface. Moreover, the capacities of FERs are based on approximations of their flexibility potential, but an attacker could possibly take over other resources that could be remotely controlled but not currently used for flexibility, for example batteries in households.

The presented work has an extensive focus on Sweden, utilizing its grid conditions, FER capacity, and frequency reserves. This scope allows for an in-depth analysis of potential attacks against a grid with realistic characteristics and provides an opportunity to assess whether existing frequency mitigation mechanisms can defend against the attacks. Nevertheless, our findings should be generally applicable to any representative grid with similar characteristics. To support replicability, configuration files for the simulator and attacks, are openly published on GitHub [18]. While the presented work provides critical insights into aggregated attack strategies against the power grid using remotely connected FERs, several directions remain for future research. One idea could be to focus on enhancing the realism and complexity of the power grid model by incorporating geographically distributed generation and loads, line capacity constraints, frequency reserves, and protection mechanisms such as relays. These additions would allow for more accurate assessments of attack impacts, including cascading failures. Further research could also evaluate attack strategies under worst-case conditions, such as peak demand periods or adverse weather, where the grid is most vulnerable. Furthermore, the development of detection mechanisms remains critical. Future efforts could focus on identifying potential indicators of compromise within FER aggregators and applying frameworks like MITRE ATT&CK to design robust detection and mitigation strategies.

6 Conclusions

This paper investigates the threats posed by adversaries who can gain control over multiple FERs within the power grid. The paper focuses on identifying potential aggregated attack strategies, assessing their impact on the grid's frequency stability, and evaluating the effectiveness of existing frequency reserves in mitigating these impacts. The work also incorporates realistic estimations of FER capacities to assess the risk of severe consequences, both today and in the future. The results show that all explored attack strategies impact the first-swing stability of the power grid. However, combination attacks are the most severe, capable of causing the largest frequency deviations, while controlling the same amount of power. The work demonstrates that such attacks are already feasible today in 2025 based on the current capabilities of FERs and represent a significant threat to the power grid. As FERs continue to grow in both prevalence and capacity in the coming years, the associated risks and threats are expected to escalate, highlighting the urgent need for robust security measures and effective frequency mitigation strategies.

Acknowledgments. The work was conducted as part of the Cybersecurity for Resilient Energy Communities of the Future (CyREC) project, funded by the Swedish Innovation Agency (ref nr. 2023-02987).

References

1. Acharya, S., Dvorkin, Y., Karri, R.: Public plug-in electric vehicles + grid data: is a new cyberattack vector viable? IEEE Trans. Smart Grid **11**(6), 5099–5113 (2020)
2. Amini, S., Pasqualetti, F., Mohsenian-Rad, H.: Dynamic load altering attacks against power system stability: attack models and protection schemes. IEEE Trans. Smart Grid **9**(4) (2018)
3. Baumgart, I., Borsig, M., Goerke, N., Hackenjos, T., Rill, J., Wehmer, M.: Who controls your energy? On the (in)security of residential battery energy storage systems. In: IEEE International Conference on Communications, Control, and Computing Technologies for Smart Grids, pp. 1–6 (2019)
4. Cleveland, F.M.: Cyber security issues for advanced metering infrastructure (AMI). In: 2008 IEEE Power and Energy Society General Meeting - Conversion and Delivery of Electrical Energy in the 21st Century, pp. 1–5 (2008)
5. Karlsson, D., Power, G., Nordling, A.: Svängmassa i elsystemet. Tech. rep., Kungliga Ingenjörsvetenskapsakademien (2016)
6. Dabrowski, A., Ullrich, J., Weippl, E.R.: Grid shock: coordinated load-changing attacks on power grids: the non-smart power grid is vulnerable to cyber attacks as well. In: Proceedings of the 33rd Annual Computer Security Applications Conference, pp. 303–314. Association for Computing Machinery (2017)
7. Electric Grid Test Case Repository: Hawaii synthetic grid (2024). https://electricgrids.engr.tamu.edu/hawaii40/. Accessed 11 Nov 2025
8. Electric Grid Test Case Repository: WSCC 9-bus system (2024). https://electricgrids.engr.tamu.edu/electric-grid-test-cases/wscc-9-bus-system/. Accessed 11 Nov 2025
9. Gopstein, A., Nguyen, C., O'Fallon, C., Hastings, N., Wollman, D.A.: NIST framework and roadmap for smart grid interoperability standards, release 4.0 (2021-02-18 00:02:00) (2021)
10. Igure, V.M., Laughter, S.A., Williams, R.D.: Security issues in SCADA networks. Comput. Secur. **25**(7), 498–506 (2006)
11. Li, X., Liang, X., Lu, R., Shen, X., Lin, X., Zhu, H.: Securing smart grid: cyber attacks, countermeasures, and challenges. IEEE Commun. Mag. **50**(8), 38–45 (2012)

12. Lin, J., Yu, W., Yang, X., Xu, G., Zhao, W.: On false data injection attacks against distributed energy routing in smart grid. In: Third International Conference on Cyber-Physical Systems (2012)
13. Liu, Y., Ning, P., Reiter, M.K.: False data injection attacks against state estimation in electric power grids. ACM Trans. Inf. Syst. Secur. **14**(1) (2011)
14. MathWorks: Simscape. https://se.mathworks.com/products/simscape.html
15. Mohsenian-Rad, A.H., Leon-Garcia, A.: Distributed internet-based load altering attacks against smart power grids. IEEE Trans. Smart Grid **2**(4), 667–674 (2011)
16. Mojumder, M.R.H., Ahmed Antara, F., Hasanuzzaman, M., Alamri, B., Alsharef, M.: Electric vehicle-to-grid (V2G) technologies: impact on the power grid and battery. Sustainability **14**(21) (2022)
17. Moslehi, K., Kumar, R.: A reliability perspective of the smart grid. IEEE Trans. Smart Grid **1**(1), 57–64 (2010)
18. Myren, D.: The threat of aggregated cyberattacks on power grids (2025). https://github.com/danielmyren/the-threat-of-aggregated-cyberattacks-on-power-grids/
19. Öhrström, F., Oscarsson, J., Afzal, Z., Dani, J., Asplund, M.: From balance to breach: cyber threats to battery energy storage systems. Energy Inform. **8**(1), 39 (2025)
20. Parks, R.C.: Advanced metering infrastructure security considerations. Tech. rep., Sandia National Laboratories (2007). https://www.energy.gov/ceser/articles/advanced-metering-infrastructuresecurity-considerations
21. PowerWorld: Powerworld simulator. https://www.powerworld.com/products/simulator/overview
22. Qi, J., Hahn, A., Lu, X., Wang, J., Liu, C.C.: Cybersecurity for distributed energy resources and smart inverters. IET Cyber-Phys. Syst. Theor. Appl. **1**(1), 28–39 (2016)
23. Sayed, M.A., Atallah, R., Assi, C., Debbabi, M.: Electric vehicle attack impact on power grid operation. Int. J. Electr. Power Energy Syst. **137**, 107784 (2022)
24. Siemens: Power system simulation. https://www.siemens.com/global/en/products/energy/grid-software/planning/pss-software/pss-e.html
25. Soltan, S., Mittal, P., Poor, H.V.: BlackIoT: IoT botnet of high wattage devices can disrupt the power grid. In: 27th USENIX Security Symposium, pp. 15–32. USENIX Association (2018)
26. Sun, C.C., Hahn, A., Liu, C.C.: Cyber security of a power grid: state-of-the-art. Int. J. Electr. Power Energy Syst. **99**, 45–56 (2018)
27. Svenska kraftnät: Hur ska FCR-reglering ske i förhållande till frekvensen? https://www.svk.se/aktorsportalen/bidra-med-reserver/fragor-och-svar-om-reserver/fcr/hur-ska-fcr-reglering-ske-i-forhallande-till-frekvensen/. Accessed 11 Nov 2025
28. Svenska kraftnät: Integrering av vindkraft (2013). https://www.svk.se/siteassets/om-oss/rapporter/2015-och-aldre/20130313-integrering-av-vindkraft.pdf. Accessed 11 Nov 2025
29. Svenska kraftnät: Driftstörningen den 26 April 2023 (2023). https://www.svk.se/siteassets/om-oss/rapporter/2023/rapport-driftstorning-2023-04-26_slutversion.pdf. Accessed 11 Nov 2025
30. Svenska kraftnät: Främjandet av ett mer flexibielt elsystem (2023). https://www.svk.se/siteassets/om-oss/rapporter/2023/framjande-av-ett-mer-flexibelt-elsystem-deluppdrag-5-ei-r2023-18.pdf. Accessed 11 Nov 2025
31. Svenska kraftnät: Framtida volymbehov (2024). https://www.svk.se/aktorsportalen/bidra-med-reserver/behov-av-reserver-nu-och-i-framtiden/framtida-volymbehov. Accessed 11 Nov 2025

32. Svenska Kraftnät: Overview of requirements for reserves (2025). https://www.svk.se/495bac/siteassets/aktorsportalen/bidra-med-reserver/om-olika-reserver/oversiktlig-kravbild-for-reserver-sve-20250324.pdf. Accessed 11 Nov 2025
33. Svenska Kraftnät, Energinet, Fingrid, Statnett: Nordic grid development perspective (2024). https://www.svk.se/siteassets/om-oss/rapporter/2023/svk_ngpd2023.pdf. Accessed 11 Nov 2025
34. UN: Attacks on Ukraine's electricity infrastructure threaten key aspects of life. https://ukraine.un.org/en/278995-attacks-ukraine's-electricity-infrastructure-threaten-key-aspects-life-winter-approaches-. Accessed 11 Nov 2025
35. Vernova, G.: Steady state power flow. https://www.gevernova.com/consulting/planos/steady-state-power-flow. Accessed 11 Nov 2025
36. Wang, W., Xu, Y., Khanna, M.: A survey on the communication architectures in smart grid. Comput. Netw. **55**(15), 3604–3629 (2011)
37. Xiang, Y., Wang, L., Liu, N.: Coordinated attacks on electric power systems in a cyber-physical environment. Electr. Power Syst. Res. **149**, 156–168 (2017)

Optimal Pathways in Hierarchical Smart Distribution Grid Models with Large Scale Adversarial Attacks and Dynamic Adversaries

Nataša Gajić[1(✉)] and Stephen Dirk Bjørn Wolthusen[1,2]

[1] Department of Information Security and Communication Technology, NTNU, Trondheim, Norway
{natasa.gajic,stephen.wolthusen}@ntnu.no

[2] Department of Information Security, Royal Holloway University of London, Egham, UK

Abstract. The demands increasingly placed on distribution grids by moving from simple distribution to bidirectional flows of future smart distribution grids that must also be constrained to ensure robust operation require a substantial increase in instrumentation for distribution networks. This instrumentation represents a possible target for both isolated and coordinated attacks, given the large number of nodes and distribution. In this paper we therefore study mechanisms for enhanced resilience for the **control and communication** (C2) paths as the topology of the actual power network is assumed to involve greater cost in modification. We explore algorithms over a hierarchical multilayer graph model in which multiple distant adversaries can manipulate C2 paths and vertices in future smart distribution grids and study how the grid operator can retain full or partial control over the distribution network under these circumstances, discussing different scenarios under different adversarial capability assumptions, study both static and dynamic adversaries, as well as conservative and risk taking defense approaches a grid operator can take.

Keywords: Adversary Models · Dynamic Adversaries · Large Scale Attacks · Distribution Grid Control · Communication and Control Networks

1 Introduction

Future smart distribution grids (DGs in further text) will need to have more instrumentation. This is because society is changing towards smart infrastructures, such as smart DGs ([24] and smart cities [2]). Smart DGs inherently have many entry points in the grid (e.g. EVs, household water heaters, private solar panels, etc.). This multitude of entry points in future smart DGs is important because it provides flexibility in the grid. This flexibility is significant because

E. Bergström et al. (Eds.): CRITIS 2025, LNCS 16291, pp. 82–101, 2026.
https://doi.org/10.1007/978-3-032-19540-1_5

it makes the grid more resilient [7,11] in the sense of having temporary backup options in critical situations. As society is currently transitioning towards smart DGs, it means that there is bidirectional communication present in the DG, both of energy [22] and of information [26], which was not there before. Standard practice of DG protection is "cutting" contaminated or suspicious pathways; however, having these bidirectional flows means that it will be more dangerous to cut these connections in protection schemes, as they will be more critical components in a network. Therefore, securing DGs will need to be done with more care than ever and while taking into account the changing conditions of DGs that are transitioning toward smart design.

DGs need to have very high availability and it may be acceptable to reduce overall functionality in a critical situation (e.g. harsh adversarial attack, natural disasters) for the sake of maintaining core functionality of a DG.

Our previous work [19] posed the question of what happens in a smart DG when there are adversaries that are close enough to each other, that is, whose areas of influence (also called neighborhoods) overlap. In this work, the question that will be studied is: What happens if there are multiple adversaries in a future smart DG who are far away from each other, that is, their initial areas of influence *do not* overlap, but they collaborate and coordinate their attacks? Types of adversaries that will be looked into will be static, static with a special type of attack and dynamic. We consider an adversary model where adversaries can be placed in multiple locations across the grid and can compromise components at a distance from their initial location. The question of how the number of adversaries affects the problem and its solution will also be considered. Possible entry points for these adversaries will be considered and discussed, and strict boundaries on their initial locations will be set. Limitations on their capabilities will also be set.

The novelty in this work lies in the study of large scale and coordinated attacks on the future smart DGs, consideration of multiple adversarial entry points in it, as well as the study of specific type of attack and how it can be used to study and deal with the dynamic adversaries in such a system.

1.1 Structure of the Paper

The remainder of this paper is structured as follows: First, Problem Statement is presented in (Sect. 2), after which some Assumptions are made in (Sect. 2.1) which make the problem area more concrete. Then Related Work in presented in (Sect. 3), followed by the Problem Setup in (Sect. 4). After that, each Problem Case is considered separately in (Sect. 5) and Sect. 6. Next, the discussion on Dynamic Adversaries and how they are tied into this work is presented in Sect. 9 as well as the discussion on what happens if there are $n > 2$ adversaries in (Sect. 10). Following that is a discussion on what happens if there are both local and global adversaries (Sect. 11). Lastly, conclusions are presented (Sect. 12) as well as a brief description of the ongoing and future work in (Sect. 13).

2 Problem Statement

As defined in [19], a system contaminated by adversaries can be defined as follows:

$$f(multilayerModel, locations, radius) = compromisedModel, \quad (1)$$

where f is a function that represents the adversarial activity, *multilayerModel* is the original, contamination-free multilayered graph model used to model Future Smart Distribution Grid (see [18] and [17] for a detailed overview, short description in the following paragraph), *locations* are locations in the *multilayerModel* where the adversaries are and *radius* denotes the reach of each adversaries (for proof that it can be a single radius rather than having each adversary have their own radius, see [19]). The domain of this function will be a subset of the whole multilayer model, while its co-domain will be defined as the whole graph since adversarial actions in their respective areas of influence could potentially influence other parts of the graph. Therefore, we can see the action of contamination of the graph model as labeling a subset of the original graph model to now fall under the adversarial control. Thus, area of influence and area of contamination are used interchangeably in this work. It is important to note that the radius is an estimate, since in reality it is hard to know the precise reach of an adversary. To protect the grid, it is important to let a grid operator know that there is contamination in the grid, which in turn means finding an uncontaminated path from a neighbor of a contaminated area to the grid operator (which is assumed to be located in the top layer of Information Overlay). The task here, then, is to find an information path (or paths) from the Distribution Grid or the lowest layer of the Information Overlay (which can consist of one or more layers, see [17]) to the top layer of the Information Overlay. This path needs to be uncontaminated or, as uncontaminated as possible since the task is to make grid operator(s) aware that there is suspicious activity in the system and using contaminated nodes, or the nodes that are suspected to be contaminated, could be counterproductive since the information these nodes provide can be tampered with by adversaries.

The central problem of this work can then be defined as follows (for a visual representation of the problem, see Fig. 1).

Let us assume that there is a hierarchical multilayer graph model that approximates a future smart DG and is comprised of Distribution Grid, Information Overlay (which can consist of one or more layers) and Adaptive Layer (see [18] *and* [17] *for a detailed overview of this model). Additionally, lets assume that there are multiple adversaries located in the Distribution Grid or the lowest layer of the Information Overlay, each with a k - neighborhood (or area of influence), which is defined in our previous work* [19] *as a set of neighbors (which is a set of nodes and edges) that are not immediate neighbors (except in the case of* $k = 1$*, when they are), but are connected to their neighbor via* k*, or less, edges; and such that the intersection of their neighborhoods (or areas of influence) is an empty set. We want to find the shortest and least costly/risky path (or paths), if they exist, from a* $(k + 1)$ *neighbor of all adversaries located in the Distribution Grid or the lowest Information Overlay layer to the top layer in the Information Overlay.*

The path needs to be shortest and/or least risky because a grid operator needs to receive uncontaminated information about adversarial activity in the grid in a timely manner.

2.1 Assumptions

We will make the following assumptions:

- The hierarchical multilayer graph model will be used as a close approximation of future smart DGs (as shown in [18]).
- There will be n adversaries present in the graph, with the same reach of influence k and their neighborhoods *do not* intersect.
- Initial locations of adversaries are static but random (thus the adversaries are not able to choose where they are initially located), and those locations can only be in the Distribution Grid layer of the model or in the lowest layer of the Information Overlay.
- Adversaries use the same communication channels as grid operators and not any outside communication channels. Therefore, they have the same opportunities and restrictions as grid operators.
- Adversaries coordinate their attacks to achieve a specific goal.
- Adversaries do not specifically target the defense mechanisms of the model and are not aware of the defensive power of a grid.
- No new edges are allowed to be added in the Distribution Grid layer.
- New edges are allowed to be added in other parts of the model, in case that the edge budget is provided.
- In searching for the shortest/least weighty/least risky path, edges between the layers are preferred to edges that are on the same layer.

3 Related Work

3.1 Application Domain

Cyber security of a smart DG is an important question for which there have been different approaches throughout the years. A common current approach to cyber security of smart DGs has been to make a security and risk assessment of different specific network architectures. The authors in [20] do so by proposing an approach using convolutional neural networks and take into account node voltage, current, power, and the location of distributed power generation. [32] uses Bayesian attack graph on IEEE-39 node system simulation to model network attack success probability while [6] uses data from smart meters to propose a security assessment in real time. This security assessment they model by an iterative algorithm.

With their work from 1983 [14], Dolev and Yao had laid down not only the groundwork for research into adversaries, but also protocols regarding adversaries and adversarial behavior. Creation of such protocols is important because they present a set of rules for an adversary to abide by. Effectively, protocols define adversaries by assigning them things that they can and cannot do and setting up boundaries which makes it possible for researchers to study them.

An adversary can be defined as someone or something with the goal of disrupting the normal, expected state of a system or a network. The work in [25] presents a rough adversary classification. It separates adversaries into two categories: passive adversaries (also known as semi-honest or honest-but curious) and active (also known as malicious) adversaries. One of the earliest adversary models is the BellareRogaway Adversary Model [4] It allows for modeling of different types of adversaries, whether it is a passive or an active adversary. It also allows for an adversary to be benign as well as malign.

Adversary models with large-scale attack capabilities, or just large-scale attacks have been better studied in some other research areas, such as large-scale forest fires [9], flood modeling [31], or pandemic spreading [27] compared to the adversary models with specific large-scale attack capabilities in power grids or communication networks. There have been some, such as studying large-scale virus/worm attacks on computer networks [28], large-scale attacks where an adversary has the ability to inject large numbers of fake clients (e.g. spam bots) into the system [5], an adversary with large-scale attack where the adversary will compromise a small number of actual users, but then use their data to fabricate a large number of fake clients, or an adversary that can create a large-scale attack specifically using EV charging loads to disrupt the grid [21].

There has also been some study of different types of dynamic adversaries, with different approaches of what makes specific adversaries dynamic in their behavior. In 1993, the authors of [3] used adversaries that are dynamic because they can dynamically choose which set of clients to corrupt. In the work from 2014 [23], very powerful dynamic adversaries are considered. Their adversaries can generate graphs in the network, which makes the overview of the system by a network operator impossible, and therefore, the protection of the network not feasible. Dynamic adversary the authors of [8] present is different in the sense that it is more reactive than active, since it can choose a corruption strategy after seeing the cryptographic protocol used. Many studies on dynamic adversaries come from the area of cryptographic research.

An adversary can also be perceived as dynamic if it can coordinate and/or correlate an attack with other adversaries. In [16] the authors consider a sequential coordinated attack on cyber-physical systems (CPS) where the coordinated attack is done by having physical attack on the lines, by the way of cascading failure and cyber-attack by load redistribution (LR). The authors of [29] consider correlated attacks in IoT (Internet of Things) networks. In [30], a coordinated adaptive attack on the smart grid is considered. The attack is made up of steps and based on available local and global information.

3.2 Methods

The kind of problem setup where there are attackers and defenders in a system can be approached from another angle. Specifically, it could be approached from the game theory perspective. Setting it up as a game and then seeing who would reach their respective winning conditions first and, therefore, win the game.

One of the most famous examples is a game of cops and robbers on finite connected graphs [1] where a number of cops are trying to catch a robber in a finite connected graph. There have been many variations on this vertex-pursuit (also known as graph searching and good guys vs bad guys games) such as Zombies and Survivors [15] where the zombies are trying to catch all of the survivors but have limited intelligence and their only strategy is to move closer to a survivor; or firefighters vs fire on infinite grids [10]. Studying our problem in this context is interesting because multilayer graph model used in this work is tree-like, and [1] shows that (finite) tree graphs are a family of cop-win graphs, which is promising information for grid operators.

4 Problem Setup

With all that now in place, close examination of the problem can now be done, and some solutions and suggestions can be provided to grid operators and grid architects.

Let us suppose that there are $n = 2$ adversaries (for the proof that the problem solution is the same for any $n \in \mathbb{N}$, see Sect. 10, page 10). There are two possible scenarios:

1. The adversaries are working together to disrupt the system in some way, but their areas of influence remain separated.
2. The adversaries are working together *and* their areas of influence spread out to connect in one spanning and connected area of influence that contaminates a large part of the graph model.

5 CASE I: Distant and Separated Areas of Influence

In this first case, there are $n = 2$ adversaries whose areas of influence don't overlap and who don't use the special attack presented in Sect. 2.1, where they grow their respective areas of influence to merge into one huge area of influence but instead stay separated. It is still assumed that they coordinate their attacks to reach some specific goal. Since both adversaries stay isolated and don't have overlaps in their respective areas of influence, it is possible to separate the problem of finding optimal paths for each adversary into two distinct local problems and solve individually. To solve each, Optimal Path Algorithm (denoted with OPA from now on) from [19] is used. OPA is an algorithm inspired by Dijkstra's algorithm [13] that finds an optimal path from a neighborhood of an area of influence of an adversary in a multilayer graph model to the top layer of the Information Overlay which is a layer where a grid operator is located and, therefore, a layer with the decision power in a critical situation such as adversarial attack on the system in question. Using OPA twice, once for each of the adversaries, two information paths, in case they exist, will be created and each of them will give information about their respective adversaries.

Figure 1 showcases a visual representation of this case, with two possible, but not necessarily optimal, information paths from the neighborhood of contaminated ares to the top layer of the Information Overlay.

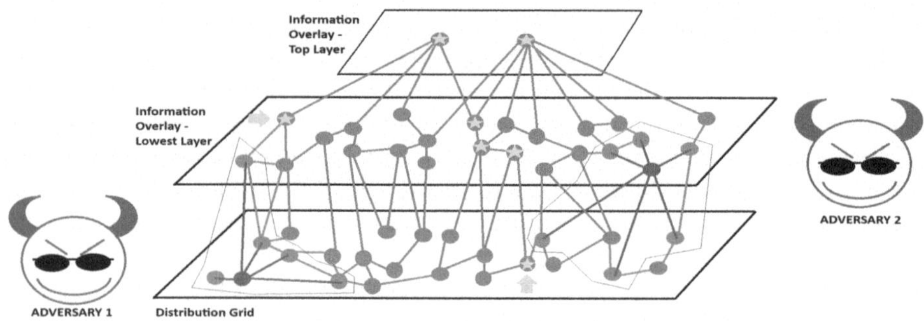

Fig. 1. This figure is a visual representation of Sect. 5 for $n = 2$, where the non-neighboring adversaries in the multilayer graph model stay separated while still coordinating their attacks. Red nodes represent locations of adversaries, orange nodes represent contaminated nodes while green nodes represent uncontaminated nodes. Using the same logic, red edges represent edges directly connected to the adversaries, orange edges represent edges that are in contaminated area but not directly connected to the adversarial nodes and therefore risky to use in any information paths, while green edges represent uncontaminated edges. Blue outlines visually showcase the respective area of influence of each of the adversaries. The picture also showcases two possible (although not necessarily optimal!) respective information paths from the immediate neighbors of contaminated areas to the top layer of the Information Overlay, where a grid operator is located. These paths are depicted by yellow stars.

6 CASE II: Distant but Merged Areas of Influence

This case will look into what happens if the adversaries whose initial areas of influence don't overlap use the special attack presented in Sect. 2.1 where they widen their respective areas of influence to create the overlap and create one spanning and connected area of influence that contaminates large area of the graph model. There are two possible outcomes: either the area of contamination is too large and there is no information path to be found by the OPA *or* there is still a possibility to find a path. Both of these cases will be considered, as well as whether there is anything grid operators and grid architects can do to salvage and/or de-escalate the situation.

7 Case A: Threshold Reached

Threshold Reached scenario will happen in case that the spanning and connected area of influence splits the graph in two disjoint subsets, or, in mathematical terms, if the spanning and connected area of influence is a *cut-set* that cuts the multilayer graph. In graph theory, a *cut* is defined as a partition of nodes of the given graph into two disjoint subsets, while a *cut-set* is defined as the set of nodes that have one endpoint in each subset of the partition (for more details, see [12]). This would be easily tested in a practical model by running the OPA [19] and seeing whether it finds a path or terminates without finding a path.

Figure 2 shows an example of this scenario.

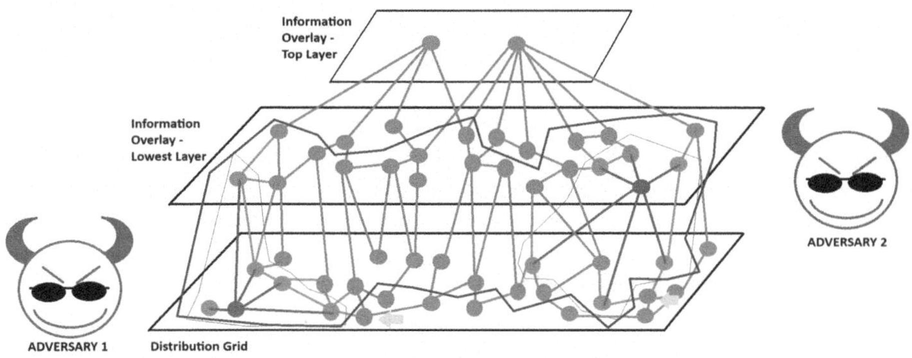

Fig. 2. This figure shows a visual representation of a Threshold Reached scenario Sect. 7 where the spanning and connected area contains a cut-set that cuts the shown multilayer graph model. Yellow arrows point to the only possible start points for a needed information path, but they have no way to connect to the top layer of the Information Overlay without stepping into the contaminated area. Therefore, it is a Threshold Reached scenario.

Salvage. There might be a possibility to salvage a Threshold Reached scenario. In [19], there is a recommendation to use an edge budget in case that an optimal path doesn't exist. Having an edge budget means that there exists a flexibility to add new edges in the multilayer graph model, specifically in the Adaptive (or Interconnecting) Layer and the Information Overlay layers. Because of the significant cost difference in adding a new edge in the Distribution Grid, which would entail putting down an actual cable in the ground compared to adding a virtual link in the "smart" part of the model (that is, Adaptive Layer and the Information Overlay), adding new edges exclusively in the "smart" part of the model is one of the constraints in [19] and this work will follow that logic, allowing for new edges only in those parts of the model as well.

By putting new edges in those layers, a new information path or paths from the needed location to the top layer of the Information Overlay might open up. This can be tested by using the OPA and checking whether it finds a path or not, based on the new edge or edges incorporated in the model. Success obviously depends on how large the given edge budget is.

If this salvage attempt fails as well, there is additional possibility of having not only an edge budget but also a node budget, meaning that both new nodes *and* new edges can be incorporated. New nodes will also be only allowed in the Adaptive Layer and Information Overlay. The edge budget and the node budget can be treated as separate things, but they could also be combined into one single budget for either of the new components. Either approach works and it only depends on what a grid, in this case, architect needs more. Components could, and likely should, have different costs since adding a new node in the information part of the network is more expensive than making a connection between two already existing nodes. If there is a need for that, the edges could also have different costs depending on where in the model they are, both because cost of connections can be different in different parts of the graph (e.g. long edges might be more costly than the local ones) or because there is a preference in the model (e.g. in Sect. 2.1 it is stated that there is a preference for edges between the layers while searching for an optimal information path compared to the edges that are on the same layer, therefore, preferred types of edges might be deemed cheaper and non-preferred types of edges might be deemed more expensive.

8 Case B: Under Threshold

In the case that the spanning and connected area of influence doesn't cut the graph, it means that the system isn't in the Threshold Reached scenario and that an optimal path does exist. Now, there are two options for how to approach finding this path. If a grid operator wants to completely avoid the spanning and connected area of influence, they might decide to take a longer way by going around the spanning and connected area, or otherwise, they might take a calculated risk and go through the spanning and connected area. Both options will be considered.

Case B1: Avoiding Contaminated Area. If a grid operator deems it too risky to use any of the nodes or edges that lie in the spanning and connected area of contamination for their information path, they might choose to completely avoid it and go around it. It is important to note here that it is crucial to have the starting node of the information path be a neighbor of the contaminated area, since the uncontaminated nodes that are neighbors to the contaminated ares are the only ones that will be able to transmit a true information about the discrepancy in their neighborhood. The uncontaminated nodes that are far away from the situation, that is, that are not neighbors to the contaminated area(s) won't be able to tell that something is wrong within the system, as their sensors will show normal information and it will be "business as usual" for them. Figure 3 shows an example of an information path that goes around the spanning and connected area of contamination.

While it is crucial that the starting point is carefully selected and close enough to the contaminated area, there isn't such a requirement for the rest of the nodes and edges in the information path. They are picked solely on their merit of being uncontaminated and optimal for the shortest path. OPA is used to find this path. Because of its setup (see [19], Sect. 5.1 Choosing Adversaries), the OPA allows for excluding nodes and edges from the pool of possible nodes and edges in the optimal information path. In the practical sense, this is easily done in the algorithm by setting the desired edges to have an ∞ or NaN value and that will tell the OPA to exclude them. And by excluding the spanning and connected area of adversarial influence, the OPA will find a path that will go around. The path will exist because we are considering the case where the spanning and connected area does *not* contain a cut-set.

Salvage method from Sect. 7 is also applicable here since it might give better results.

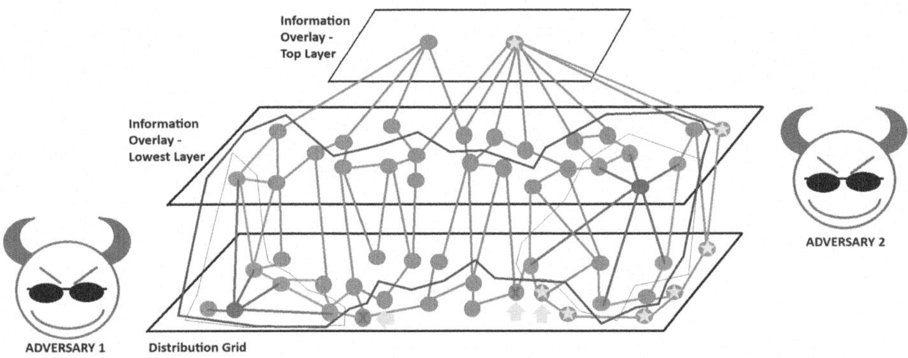

Fig. 3. This figure presents a visual representation of an information path from Sect. 8 where the spanning and connected area is completely avoided. Yellow arrows point to the only possible start points (they need to be neighbors to the initial contaminated areas, for a discussion on this point, see Sect. 8 on page 8) for the needed information path, but only one of them creates a valid information path from the neighbor of the initial contaminated area to the top layer of the Information Overlay. Valid path is marked with yellow stars, while the other two possible starting nodes are marked with red X-es, since any information path that uses either of them as a starting point cannot reach the top layer of the Information Overlay without going through the contaminated spanning and connected area.

Case B2: Utilizing Contaminated Area. In some cases it might be beneficial to take the risk and use the edges that are in the spanning and connected area of influence. One such possible situation is if the Threshold Reached scenario has occurred and there is no edge or node budget provided. Or if the given edge or node budget isn't sufficient to salvage the situation. Another case would be if a grid operator deems that the risk of using parts of the spanning and connected area of contamination is small enough. This, in some cases, could be argued to be true. As it has been stated in Sect. 2.1, this work assumes that the creation of such a large contaminated area is a special attack by the adversaries and not a usual adversarial behavior. This large area of influence could be achieved in different ways (more on this in Sect. 9). But because this is a special attack, not every node and edge in that spanning and connected area has to be equally influenced by the adversaries. Because of this, it is still important to choose a starting point such that its a neighbor of the initial area of influence of one of the adversaries, since if the chosen starting point is a neighbor of the spanning and connected area, but not a neighbor of one of the initial areas of adversarial influence, it is possible that such a path would not transfer the information that something is wrong with the system to the top layer of the Information Overlay. This is because, while the spanning and connected area is considered the "enemy" territory, not every part of it is necessarily under the full control of one of the adversaries. Therefore, for the same reason it might be possible, while still risky, to use nodes and edges that are in the spanning and connected area somewhere in the information path. It is not advisable to use a neighbor of the spanning and connected area (that is not also a neighbor of one of the initial areas of adversarial influence before the special attack) as a starting point for the necessary information path.

Figure 4 shows an example of two possible information paths that utilize the spanning and connected area and include possibly contaminated nodes in the information path.

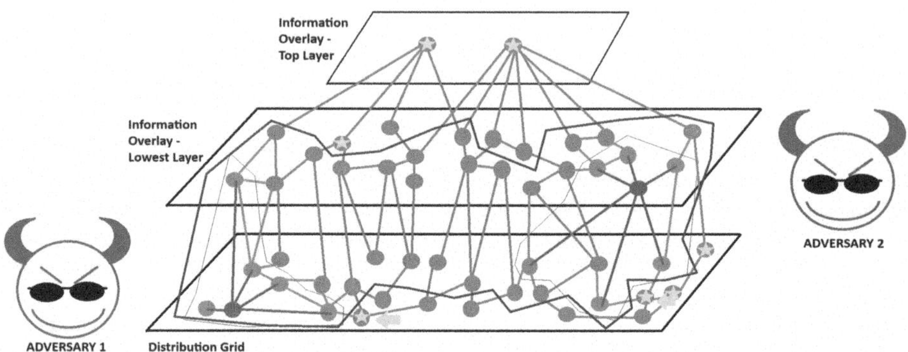

Fig. 4. This figure shows a visual representation of two possible information paths from Sect. 8 where the risk is taken and information paths go through the contaminated spanning and connected area. Yellow arrows point to the only possible start points for the needed information path(s). Possible valid (but not only) paths are marked with yellow stars outside of the spanning and connected area, denoting that those nodes send uncontaminated information, and orange stars inside the spanning and connected area, denoting that using those nodes in the information path bears the risk that the information those nodes send is contaminated.

In this case of using possibly contaminated nodes in the information path, rather than finding only a shortest path, finding an optimal path will mean finding the least risky shortest path from an immediate neighbor of the initial areas of adversarial influence to the top layer of the Information Overlay. Since the OPA has an inherent flexibility on how to treat different nodes, it is possible to approach this problem by tweaking the weights in the multilayer graph model. This inherent flexibility of the OPA stems from the edges being separated into different categories based on different things, such as node preference and risk edges can bear. Those categories are then denoted and differentiated by weights of different orders of magnitude. Edges closer, in a graph sense, to the adversaries are assigned weights with higher orders of magnitude, while preferred edges, such as edges between the layers that connect the top layer of the Information Overlay with the next layer in the Information Overlay, are assigned weights with low orders of magnitude (for more details on this, see [19], Sect. 5.1 Choosing Weights). Those orders of magnitude are used both as a tool for the algorithm while searching for the optimal path but also as an indicator to a grid operator which nodes and edges are used (meaning that the total weight of the path will indicate exactly whether the nodes and edges from the adversarial areas of influence are used or not).

For the sake of clarity and the ease of notation in the further text, let us define *Risky Area* or *RA*

$$RA = SA \setminus (AOI_1 \cup AOI_2), \tag{2}$$

where SA, AOI_1 and AOI_2 are subsets of *compromisedModel* from the definition of contaminated model 1 on page 2, such that AOI_1 denotes area of influence of the first adversary, AOI_2 denotes area of influence of the second adversary and SA denotes the whole spanning and connected area of influence created by the special attack from 2.1.

To use potentially less risky nodes and edges of the spanning and connected area in the information path is to use the nodes and edges from RA. That means that edges from RA need to given weights of specific orders of magnitude - such that they are of higher order of magnitude than uncontaminated nodes and edges but lower orders of magnitude than nodes and edges that lie in AOI_1 and AOI_2. These orders of magnitude also need to be selected in such a way so that when used, they would clearly indicate to a grid operator that they are being used in the information path.

Depending on the size (meaning total number of nodes and edges) of the multilayer model and the size of the spanning and connected area, it is possible to refine this idea further. If RA is much larger in size compared to the AOI_1 and AOI_2, there could be different orders of magnitude assigned to different edges depending on different factors. For example, one possible idea would be to assign weights of gradually lower orders of magnitude the farther away they are, in graph terms, from either of the initial areas of adversarial influence. And this while ensuring that they are staying in between of orders of magnitude of weights of the edges that are in AOI_1 and AOI_1 and orders of magnitude of the uncontaminated nodes and edges. An easy way to imagine and represent this gradual descent of orders of magnitude would be to use linear algebra. So, for example, if uncontaminated edges that are on the same layer are assigned a constant value grater than 1 and uncontaminated edges between the layers are assigned a value of 1 (to show the preferential treatment of vertical to edges that are on the same layer, see Sect. 2.1), edges that are directly connected to the adversarial nodes are assigned either a *NaN* or an ∞ value to showcase that they should not be used in any information paths, and edges in the initial areas of influence of respective adversaries but not directly connected to the adversarial node are assigned different exponential values depending on how close, in graph sense, they are to the adversaries. Next the edges in RA can be assigned different polynomials depending on different reasons. If, as it has been suggested, it only depends on how far an edge is from both initial adversarial areas of influence, then a linear function x can be assigned to those edges that are the farthest away from both AOI_1 and AOI_2, x^2 can be assigned to the next farthest edges from both AOI_1 and AOI_2, x^3 can be assigned to the next and so on. That way every edge category has a strict order of magnitude weight assigned to it that can be both used a tool for the OPA to use and to showcase to a grid operator which category of edges have been used in the found information path.

Other than this idea of nodes and edges that are more removed from the initial areas of adversarial influence being less risky to use, there could be other insights that grid operators and architects could use to assign weights to certain edges. Examples being geography or popularity of certain nodes and edges and thus, load burden of certain connections.

Additionally, salvage method from Sect. 7 can also be applied here due to the possibility of getting better results.

Finding an Optimal Path. In cases where it is possible, it might be beneficial to do both cases (avoiding and utilizing SA) and find two information paths, one that goes around the spanning and connected area and one that goes through it. Comparing the two might give a more optimal solution. This can be easily done by comparing the length or risk, which the OPA also provides, of the two found paths from Sect. 8 and Sect. 8. If there is an edge or node budget to use, that would allow for an additional possibility for better results. However, the budget needs to be used in each case separately, prior to comparing the paths. This is because if the edge or node budget is used after the path comparison, while it might improve the result of the chosen path, it would not consider the case of examining and possibly finding a better path in the case that was not chosen.

9 Dynamic Adversaries

So far in this work not much attention has been given to the thought of whether the adversaries are static or dynamic. For the most part, they were treated as static entities with fixed locations and initial areas of influence and one special attack that is dynamic in a very specific way. This section will present a more detailed discussion on this point.

If a static adversary is defined as one with a fixed location and a fixed area of influence, then a dynamic adversary might be defined as an adversary that can move from one location in the graph to another and widen its area of influence. When defining a dynamic adversary in such a way, there needs to be precaution taken not to give an adversary too much power, because it could lead to a permanent Threshold Reached Scenario, if an adversary can migrate around in the network wherever and however it wants to. Some concrete assumptions can be made:

- An adversary can only migrate to a node in a Distribution Grid or one of the lower layers in the Information Overlay. This assumption can be made more strict by allowing only specific layers where an adversary can be located.
- An adversary cannot migrate to any of the nodes in the top layer of the Information Overlay (as that would lead to a permanent Threshold Reached scenario).
- An adversary can only migrate to a location in its area of influence. This assumption can be relaxed or made more strict if necessary.

- An adversary can migrate more than once within its area of influence. This assumption can be made more strict if necessary.
- When it migrates, an adversary keeps its initial area of influence and it also contaminates new part of the model with its original reach k.

In a real setting, a grid operator does not have a true full overview of whole system in real time. That means that whenever an adversary migrates to a new location, it doesn't mean that its previous area of influence can be reclaimed as uncontaminated just because the adversary has migrated to another location. This is both because it can still have influence over that area (if it migrates only once and therefore has some of the initial area still in its influence) or because it has tampered with nodes or edges in its initial area of influence in some permanent way (e.g. by destroying them before leaving). This means that any time an adversary migrates, the area of the multilayer graph model that is considered uncontaminated gets smaller, while the total area of adversarial influence gets bigger. With enough migrations adversarial area of influence will turn into a spanning and connected area of influence. This also means that it is not necessary to have multiple adversaries in the system to create a large scale attack. Therefore, a dynamic adversary can be treated as a static one with a special attack that allows it to influence bigger part of the multilayer graph model. Dynamic adversaries whose dynamic behavior stems from being able to widen their area of influence can also be treated as static adversaries with a special attack. Both of these mentioned dynamic behaviors can be treated not as any random attack, but specifically the special attack assumed in Sect. 2.1 which allows for the creation of the spanning and connected area. Being able to treat dynamic adversaries, especially the ones that can migrate around as static makes it easier to get a better understanding of the system and it's easier to work with since if something is treated as a static element, a system can be observed without taking time into account, which can be of significant importance.

10 Having $n > 2$ Non-local Adversaries

Throughout this work, we have mainly looked at the case of $n = 2$ adversaries. In this section, it will be shown that everything that has been said so far works for any $n \in \mathbb{N}$ numbers of adversaries. The proof will be done by induction and each of the two cases in Sects. 5 and 6 respectively will be done separately. Lets first look at Case I.

Theorem 1 (Separated Areas of Influence). *If there are n distant and separated adversaries present in the multilayer graph model that stay separated, Case I (Sect. 5) holds for any $n \in \mathbb{N}$ number of adversaries.*

Proof. **Base Case:** $n = 2$
Section 5 is the base case, since it deals with $n = 2$ adversaries.
Induction Step: We suppose that the statement of the theorem holds true for $n = l, l \in \mathbf{N}$ as well as any n, such that $2 \leq n \leq l$. We shall prove then that the statement of the theorem also holds true for $n = l + 1$.
Let us now suppose that the statement of the theorem holds true for $n = l, l \in \mathbf{N}$. That means that theory presented in Sect. 5 holds for $n = l$. Next, let us add another adversary with its own area of influence that stays separated from the rest and which area of influence doesn't overlap with any of the previous l adversaries. Because it stays isolated from the rest and its area of influence doesn't overlap with any other areas of influence of any of the other l adversaries, we can treat it as a local problem and find an information path that involves just that adversary using the OPA from [19]. Therefore, it is possible to search for information paths for $l+1$ adversaries as well which means the theory presented in Sect. 5 is valid for $l + 1$ adversaries as well.

Since we showed that the theory presented in Sect. 5 is valid for both the Base Case and Induction Step, that means that the theory is valid for any $n \in \mathbf{N}$ number of adversaries. ∎

Next, lets look at the Case II.

Theorem 2 (Spanning and Connected Area of Influence). *If there are n distant and separated adversaries present in the multilayer graph model that use the special attack to create the spanning and connected area of influence, Case II (Sect. 6) holds for any $n \in \mathbb{N}$ number of adversaries.*

Proof. **Base Case:** $n = 2$
Section 6 is base case, since it deals with $n = 2$ adversaries.
Induction Step: We suppose that the statement of the theorem holds true for $n = l, l \in \mathbf{N}$ as well as any n, such that $2 \leq n \leq l$. We shall prove then that the statement of the theorem also holds true for $n = l + 1$.
Let us now suppose that the statement of the theorem holds true for $n = l, l \in \mathbf{N}$. That means that the theory from Sect. 6 holds for every $n \in \mathbb{N}$, such that $n \leq l$. Lets suppose now that there are $l + 1$ adversaries in the multilayer graph model and their respective areas of influence don't overlap. Let us also assume that each one of them can use the special attack from Sect. 2.1. Because of the Induction Step assumption, we know that l of them can create a spanning and connected area of influence using that special attack. However, since the leftover adversary also has that special attack, it can widen its own area of influence to connect with the spanning and connected area made by the other l adversaries. Lets denote that new spanning and connected area with SA^+. Lets at now look at what happens with each of the cases of Case II:

- **Case A - Threshold Reached:** In the Threshold Reached scenario we know that the spanning and connected area has already cut the graph and adding nodes and edges from the newly introduced adversary won't change the scenario. Therefore, a Threshold Reached scenario won't change by adding more adversaries. A salvage can be attempted for the whole SA^+ area in the same manner as it can be done for the spanning and connected area.

- **Case B1 - Avoiding Contaminated Area:** The approach for the case of Avoiding Contaminated Area is completely same for spanning and connected and SA^+ area. The only difference in this case is that SA^+ is bigger, in terms of size, but that doesn't change the approach of trying to find a path around it.
- **Case B2 - Utilizing Contaminated Area:** This case is also the same for SA^+ and spanning and connected area, but not because of size, but instead because their initial areas of adversarial influence are isolated. Which means that in the new SA^+ area there still exists Risky Area $RA = SA^+ \setminus \bigcup_{i=1}^{l+1} AOI_i$, where weights of different orders of magnitude approach can be employed.

Therefore, the theory from Sect. 6 is valid for $l+1$ adversaries.

Since we showed that theory from Sect. 6 is valid for both the Base Case and Induction Step, that means that theory from Sect. 6 is valid for any $n \in \mathbf{N}$ number of adversaries. ■

11 Existence of Local and Non-Local Adversaries in the Same Multilayer Graph Model

Throughout all of this work, this study was solely focused on what happens in a situation when there are multiple adversaries in a multilayer graph model who are isolated, that is, whose respective areas of influence don't overlap as well as how to deal with such a situation. And our previous work in [19] was solely focused on what happens if there are local adversaries, that is, adversaries whose areas of influence do overlap. This section will examine what happens if there are both in the same system.

Lets then assume that there are $n+k$ adversaries in a multilayer graph model, such that $n, k \in \mathbb{N}$ and that every one of the n adversaries have at least 1 other adversary with which they have a non-empty intersection and every one one of the k adversaries is completely isolated. Since those n adversaries are local, they can be treated as a single adversary (for proof of this, see [19] Sect. 6 Having More than 2 Adversaries). Lets denote it as N. Next, N will be isolated from the other k adversaries. This means that the problem has turned into the core problem of this work and can be solved as such.

But what if there are $n_1, n_2, \ldots, n_m$ clusters of local adversaries in the system? Lets assume that the cluster are such that n_1 has l_1 local adversaries, that is, such that none of the l_1 adversaries in that cluster are isolated, n_2 has l_2 local adversaries and so on until the cluster n_m, which has l_m local adversaries, where $n_1, n_2, \ldots, n_m, 1_1, n_2, \ldots, l_m, m \in \mathbb{N}$. Let us also assume that clusters are isolated in regard to each other (otherwise they would be contained in the same cluster). And that there are additionally k isolated adversaries in it. In such a scenario, each of those m clusters of local adversaries can be treated of single adversaries, denoted by $N_1, N_2, \ldots, N_M$. Due to the assumption that those clusters are isolated in regard to each other, $N_1, N_2, \ldots, N_M$ are then also isolated adversaries in regard to each other. Then there exist $m + k$ isolated adversaries, which in turn means that the problem has turned into the core problem of this work and can be solved as such.

It is important to note here that the more adversaries with many or large areas of influence there are in the system, the greater the risk that the OPA won't find any paths, even with the edge and node budget.

12 Conclusions

Due to their inherent vulnerability of having a large amount of entry points for information, future smart grids will need protection from different types of attacks and adversaries. In this work we considered what happens when there are multiple isolated non-local adversaries with a special large-scale attack in a future smart DG, modeled with a hierarchical multilayer graph. Different scenarios have been considered, including a Threshold Reached scenario and Under Threshold scenarios with both conservative and risk taking approaches. For each case a suggestion to a grid architect and operator is presented. Next, we looked into what happens if adversaries are dynamic and concluded that a dynamic adversary can be treated as an adversary with a special large-scale attack presented in this work. Lastly, we have considered a scenario where there are both local and non-local adversaries present in a multilayer graph model.

13 Future Work

This work has been done under the assumption that adversaries work together in attacking a multilayer smart network, represented here by a multilayer graph model. However, adversaries could have different or opposing goals or even openly work against each other. These are the problems that will be looked into in future work.

Also, throughout this work, it has become obvious that dynamic adversaries that can migrate around in the system or that have special attacks have the obvious advantage compared to the grid operators since they can contaminate more of the network with every migration and special attack they make. However, this work also showcases that not every part of the spanning and connected area of adversarial influence necessarily bears equal risk in using it for information transfer. "Abandoned" parts of the network, that is, those areas of the network where an adversary has previously been located at but has since left are of particular interest as well as the Risky Areas of the spanning and connected areas. The question of whether some of the areas "abandoned" by the adversaries could be reclaimed is an important question that will be examined in future work.

This work focused on what happens in the network when there is already an attack and how adversarial influence can be alleviated or dealt with. Future smart grid defense mechanisms can be additionally augmented by studying boundary conditions for the Threshold Reached case. This study could provide better insight into what properties the Information Overlay layers need to satisfy in order to withstand an adversary that has specific capabilities.

Additionally, updating the OPA so that isolated critical paths, that is, paths without much redundancy will be focused on first since they could be targets of particular interest for adversaries, will be studied in future work. Creating adversaries that specifically target those weak links and/or defense mechanisms of the grid presents an interesting research problem.

References

1. Aigner, M., Fromme, M.: A game of cops and robbers. Discret. Appl. Math. **8**(1), 1–12 (1984). https://doi.org/10.1016/0166-218X(84)90073-8
2. Bakirci, M., Bayraktar, I.: Improving coastal and port management in smart cities with UAVs and deep learning. In: 2024 Mediterranean Smart Cities Conference (MSCC), pp. 1–6 (2024). https://doi.org/10.1109/MSCC62288.2024.10697069
3. Beaver, D., Haber, S.: Cryptographic protocols provably secure against dynamic adversaries. In: Rueppel, R.A. (ed.) EUROCRYPT 1992. LNCS, vol. 658, pp. 307–323. Springer, Heidelberg (1993). https://doi.org/10.1007/3-540-47555-9_26
4. Bellare, M., Rogaway, P.: Entity authentication and key distribution. In: Stinson, D.R. (ed.) CRYPTO 1993. LNCS, vol. 773, pp. 232–249. Springer, Heidelberg (1994). https://doi.org/10.1007/3-540-48329-2_21
5. Cao, X., Gong, N.Z.: MPAF: model poisoning attacks to federated learning based on fake clients (2022). https://arxiv.org/abs/2203.08669
6. Chen, J., Roald, L.A.: Real-time assessment of distribution grid security through adaptive smart meter measurements. In: 2024 IEEE 63rd Conference on Decision and Control (CDC), pp. 6493–6500 (2024). https://doi.org/10.1109/CDC56724.2024.10885867
7. Churchill, M., Monroe, J., Bristow, D., Crawford, C.: Using electric vehicles to enhance power outage resilience – an agent-based modeling approach. Heliyon **10**(11), e32104 (2024). https://doi.org/10.1016/j.heliyon.2024.e32104
8. Damgård, I., Escudero, D., Ravi, D.: Information-theoretically secure MPC against mixed dynamic adversaries. In: Nissim, K., Waters, B. (eds.) TCC 2021. LNCS, vol. 13042, pp. 591–622. Springer, Cham (2021). https://doi.org/10.1007/978-3-030-90459-3_20
9. Darwish Ahmad, A., et al.: Large-scale fire whirl and forest fire disasters: awareness, implications, and the need for developing preventative methods. Front. Mech. Eng. **9** (2023). https://doi.org/10.3389/fmech.2023.1045542, https://www.frontiersin.org/journals/mechanical-engineering/articles/10.3389/fmech.2023.1045542
10. Dean, A., et al.: Firefighting on the hexagonal grid and on infinite trees (2021). https://arxiv.org/abs/2010.05060
11. Di Silvestre, M., Riva Sanseverino, E., Telaretti, E., Zizzo, G.: Flexibility of grid interactive water heaters. the situation in the us. Renew. Sustain. Energy Rev. **182**, 113425 (2023). https://doi.org/10.1016/j.rser.2023.113425
12. Diestel, R.: Graph Theory, 6th edn. Springer, Heidelberg (2025). https://doi.org/10.1007/978-3-662-70107-2
13. Dijkstra, E.W.: A note on two problems in connexion with graphs. Numer. Math. **1**(1), 269–271 (1959). https://doi.org/10.1007/BF01386390

14. Dolev, D., Yao, A.: On the security of public key protocols. IEEE Trans. Inf. Theor. **29**(2), 198–208 (1983). https://doi.org/10.1109/TIT.1983.1056650
15. Fitzpatrick, S., Howell, J., Messinger, M., Pike, D.: A deterministic version of the game of zombies and survivors on graphs. Discret. Appl. Math. **213**, 1–12 (2016). https://doi.org/10.1016/j.dam.2016.06.019
16. Fu, J., Wang, L., Hu, B., Xie, K., Chao, H., Zhou, P.: A sequential coordinated attack model for cyber-physical system considering cascading failure and load redistribution. In: 2018 2nd IEEE Conference on Energy Internet and Energy System Integration (EI2), pp. 1–6 (2018). https://doi.org/10.1109/EI2.2018.8582135
17. Gajić, N., Wolthusen, S.: Improved distribution network topology generation with hierarchical information overlay. In: Staggs, J., Shenoi, S. (eds.) Critical Infrastructure Protection XVIII, pp. 179–190. Springer, Cham (2025a). https://doi.org/10.1007/978-3-031-81888-2_9
18. Gajić, N., Wolthusen, S.D.B.: Adaptable smart distribution grid topology generation for enhanced resilience. In: Pickl, S., Hämmerli, B., Mattila, P., Sevillano, A. (eds.) Critical Information Infrastructures Security, pp. 100–119. Springer, Cham (2024). https://doi.org/10.1007/978-3-031-62139-0_6
19. Gajić, N., Wolthusen, S.D.B.: Locally optimal information pathways in the presence of static adversaries for a hierarchical smart distribution grid model. In: Oliva, G., Panzieri, S., Hämmerli, B., Pascucci, F., Faramondi, L. (eds.) Critical Information Infrastructures Security, pp. 151–170. Springer, Cham (2025b)
20. Ge, J., Wu, D.: A novel intelligence analysis method based on graph convolutional neural networks for online security of power distribution networks. In: 2024 11th International Forum on Electrical Engineering and Automation (IFEEA), pp. 550–554 (2024). https://doi.org/10.1109/IFEEA64237.2024.10878514
21. Kern, D., Krauß, C., Hollick, M.: Anomaly detection and mitigation for electric vehicle charging-based attacks on the power grid. In: Proceedings of the 40th ACM/SIGAPP Symposium on Applied Computing, SAC '25, pp. 1790–1799. Association for Computing Machinery, New York, NY, USA (2025). https://doi.org/10.1145/3672608.3707802
22. Kim, B.G., Ren, S., van der Schaar, M., Lee, J.W.: Bidirectional energy trading and residential load scheduling with electric vehicles in the smart grid. IEEE J. Sel. Areas Commun. **31**(7), 1219–1234 (2013). https://doi.org/10.1109/JSAC.2013.130706
23. Luna, G.A.D., Baldoni, R., Bonomi, S., Chatzigiannakis, I.: Counting in anonymous dynamic networks under worst-case adversary. In: 2014 IEEE 34th International Conference on Distributed Computing Systems, pp. 338–347 (2014). https://doi.org/10.1109/ICDCS.2014.42
24. Nickahdar, F.A., Khalifa, F.A.A.: Smart sustainable neighbourhood design: a prototype for Bahrain. In: 2nd Smart Cities Symposium, SCS 2019, pp. 1–6 (2019). https://doi.org/10.1049/cp.2019.0197
25. Oded, G.: Foundations of Cryptography, Volume II Basic Applications, 1st edn. Cambridge University Press, USA (2009)
26. Paverd, A., Martin, A., Brown, I.: Privacy-enhanced bi-directional communication in the smart grid using trusted computing. In: 2014 IEEE International Conference on Smart Grid Communications (SmartGridComm), pp. 872–877 (2014). https://doi.org/10.1109/SmartGridComm.2014.7007758
27. Pujante-Otalora, L., Canovas-Segura, B., Campos, M., Juarez, J.M.: The use of networks in spatial and temporal computational models for outbreak spread in epidemiology: a systematic review. J. Biomed. Inform. **143**, 104422 (2023). https://doi.org/10.1016/j.jbi.2023.104422

28. Staniford, S., Paxson, V., Weaver, N.: How to own the internet in your spare time. In: 11th USENIX Security Symposium (USENIX Security 02) (2002)
29. Sudheera, K.L.K., Divakaran, D.M., Singh, R.P., Gurusamy, M.: ADEPT: detection and identification of correlated attack stages in IoT networks. IEEE Internet Things J. **8**(8), 6591–6607 (2021). https://doi.org/10.1109/JIOT.2021.3055937
30. Tian, Q.H., Sun, L.W., Dong, J.H., Li, H.S., Guo, N.N.: Coordinated cyber attack of multiple step based on local and global information. In: 2023 IEEE 2nd Industrial Electronics Society Annual On-Line Conference (ONCON), pp. 1–6 (2023). https://doi.org/10.1109/ONCON60463.2023.10430807
31. Xu, Q., Shi, Y., Bamber, J.L., Ouyang, C., Zhu, X.X.: Large-scale flood modeling and forecasting with FloodCast. Water Res. **264**, 122162 (2024). https://doi.org/10.1016/j.watres.2024.122162
32. Zeng, C., Fan, S., Liu, D.: Modeling and risk assessment of cyber attacks in distribution grid cyber-physical systems. In: 2023 5th International Conference on Electrical Engineering and Control Technologies (CEECT), pp. 257–262 (2023). https://doi.org/10.1109/CEECT59667.2023.10420626

Security and Safety Large and Small

Risk Assessment of Wind Power Accidents: Safety and Health Impacts

Peter Burgherr[1,2](✉) and Adolfo Alejandro Uribe Poblete[1]

[1] Laboratory for Energy Systems Analysis (LEA), PSI Centers for Nuclear Engineering and Sciences and for Energy and Environmental Sciences, Paul Scherrer Institute (PSI), Villigen PSI, Switzerland
peter.burgherr@psi.ch

[2] Chair of Energy Systems Analysis, Institute of Energy and Process Engineering, Department of Mechanical and Process Engineering, ETH Zurich, Zurich, Switzerland

Abstract. This study presents a spatially resolved risk assessment of onshore wind power accidents in Europe from 2000 to 2023. A harmonized dataset of 1244 accidents was compiled from publicly available information sources, serving as the basis for estimating human health impacts. First, normalized risk indicators (i.e., fatality rates) were calculated for different country groups. Second, Disability-Adjusted Life Years (DALY) were used as a composite indicator of fatalities, injuries, and disamenities. The total DALY comprised the sum of Years of Life Lost (YLL), Years Lived with Disability (YLD), and Years with Anxiety Disorder (YAD). A lognormal Hierarchical Bayesian Model (HBM) was developed to estimate DALY rates for individual countries (i.e., means and 95% credible intervals). In a second step, DALY rates were downscaled to the NUTS2 level using a capacity-based approach, and a risk map was generated for the EU 27, EFTA, UK, and candidate countries. The developed framework advances comparative risk assessment by integrating DALY metrics and geographic disaggregation, providing a robust empirical foundation for targeted safety interventions, policy formulation, and transparent stakeholder dialogue in the rapidly growing wind-energy sector.

Keywords: Wind Power · Risk Assessment · Health Impacts

1 Wind Power Development

1.1 Impacts and Social Acceptance

Wind and solar photovoltaic (PV) energy accounted for 97% of global renewable capacity additions in 2023, reaching 3870 GW [1]. Furthermore, wind (17%) and solar PV (18%) were the fastest-growing electricity generation technologies, achieving 7.6% and 4.5% shares, respectively, in the global electricity mix [2]. Despite its tremendous growth during the last two decades, wind power, like any other energy technology, affects the environment, economy, and society in multiple ways.

E. Bergström et al. (Eds.): CRITIS 2025, LNCS 16291, pp. 105–122, 2026.
https://doi.org/10.1007/978-3-032-19540-1_6

Recently, a comprehensive review by McKenna et al. identified 14 impacts of wind power across four categories [3]. Among these, safety and health impacts, the focus of the present study, represent a critical but often underexplored dimension. Specifically, this paper addresses accident risk, including direct health impacts from fatalities and injuries. To contextualize our work within the broader literature and clarify the scope of the Wind Energy Accident Database (WEAD) developed in this study, we briefly review related impact categories before focusing on risk assessment.

While our study focuses on human safety impacts from accidents, the WEAD database also captures environmental incidents. Among environmental impacts documented in the literature, biodiversity concerns predominate, particularly impacts on birds and bats, while other animal groups (e.g., insects) have rarely been studied [4, 5]. Furthermore, there is a need to address trade-offs between global impacts (i.e., climate change) and more localized disamenities and environmental concerns (e.g., noise, landscape aesthetics, biodiversity) [6], a topic that has been recognized for a long time [7, 8] but often receives insufficient attention. We note these briefly because the WEAD enables qualitative analysis of reported environmental incidents, though quantitative biodiversity assessment is beyond the present scope.

Accident risk is relevant to public acceptance of wind energy because it is a key societal concern. While acceptance itself is not our focus, understanding risk perceptions requires transparent accident data. Local acceptance comprises concerns about disamenities (e.g., noise, shadow flicker, visual impact) and safety (i.e., accident risk) [7], which our DALY-based framework can help quantify. Finally, the WEAD can provide qualitative insights on the spread of misinformation related to wind power impacts and lack of transparency (e.g., government, industry), which can lower acceptance and impede behavior ranging from more critical attitudes to opposition and even protests [9, 10].

1.2 Risk Assessment and Health Issues

Generally, direct health impacts from wind power (e.g., noise, shadow flicker, fatalities, and injuries from accidents) are predominantly negative and tend to affect people in the neighborhood (workers and the public) [11]. In contrast, indirect impacts can affect a region or a country, including themes like clean energy production (e.g., reduced atmospheric pollutants) and socio-economic aspects (e.g., job creation) [11].

The public's concerns about human health risks often focus on impacts during a wind farm's normal operation [12], whereas accidental events are more of an issue for the industry and authorities [13, 14]. Nevertheless, comparative risk assessment of energy accidents is well-established and covers a broad spectrum of fossil, nuclear, large hydropower, and new renewable technologies, making this information available to diverse stakeholders as well as decision-makers and policymakers [15, 16]. Examples of topical risk assessment studies include occupational risk [17, 18], turbine and component reliability [19–22], data mining approaches [23, 24], and societal risk [25, 26].

Despite the growing body of literature on wind power safety, significant gaps remain. First, existing accident risk assessments typically report only fatality counts, which underestimate total health impacts by excluding injuries and disamenity effects. Second, country-level aggregates obscure regional variations critical for targeted safety interventions. Third, sparse accident data in many countries limits the reliability of conventional statistical estimates. To address these gaps, this study poses the following research questions (RQ):

- RQ1: How can diverse health impacts from wind power accidents (fatalities, injuries, disamenities) be integrated into a single, comparable metric?
- RQ2: What are the spatial patterns of accident risk across European regions at the NUTS2 level?
- RQ3: How can Bayesian methods improve risk estimation for countries with limited accident data?

Building upon prior work [26], this study makes four novel contributions: (1) development of a Bayesian Hierarchical Model (HBM) to calculate risk indicators at the country level; (2) downscaling of risk indicators to the NUTS2 level; (3) computation of Disability Adjusted Life Years (DALY) as an aggregated indicator; and (4) generation of a DALY risk map.

Section 2 provides a detailed description of the approach and methodological developments. Section 3 presents and discusses the main results, while Sect. 4 summarizes the key insights and outlines future directions and extensions.

2 Approach and Methods

2.1 Accident Database

Compiling a comprehensive, global database of accidents in the wind power sector requires combining and harmonizing information from various sources. Examples of accident statistics by authorities include the UK Health and Safety Executive (HSE) for offshore accidents[1], the French database Analysis, Research and Information on Accidents (ARIA)[2], the European Agency for Safety and Health at Work (EU-OSHA) [27], the US Occupational Safety and Health Administration (OHSA)[3], and the US Bureau of Labor Statistics (BLS)[4]. In contrast, data from industry organizations often do not provide information on individual accidents but only report summary statistics, e.g., G + Global Offshore Wind [28], SafetyOn[5] for onshore wind, and Renewable UK (coverage 2006–2010)[6]. The most extensive, open-access data set has been developed and is regularly updated by the independent alliance Scotland against Spin (SaS)[7]. Other publicly available datasets include Ertek et al. [29].

This study used the SaS dataset as the primary source for European accidents. To ensure completeness and accuracy, we cross-referenced accident reports with EU-OSHA data and, where available, national regulatory databases (e.g., UK HSE, French ARIA).

[1] https://www.hse.gov.uk/offshore/statistics/index.htm.

[2] https://www.aria.developpement-durable.gouv.fr/the-barpi/the-aria-database/?lang=en.

[3] https://www.osha.gov/ords/imis/accidentsearch.html.

[4] https://www.bls.gov/iif/.

[5] https://safetyon.com/work-programme/statistics.

[6] https://www.firetrace.com/fire-protection-blog/wind-turbine-fire-statistics.

[7] https://scotlandagainstspin.org/turbine-accident-statistics/.

Note that while US sources (OSHA, BLS) were mentioned earlier as examples of authoritative accident databases globally, they were not used for the European analysis presented here. Direct internet searches provided supplementary information for event verification and harmonization.

The compiled dataset comprised 3335 entries but was reduced through several filtering steps for the present study. First, generic entries that could not be assigned to a specific event and location were removed. Second, events from 1980 to 1999 were excluded because of rapid capacity growth since 2000, driven by massive R&D efforts and policy support, along with falling costs [30]. This is also reflected in a more than 8-fold increase in reported accidents between the 1990s and 2000s (decade average). The year 2024 was also excluded because data were not available for the entire year when preparing this analysis. Third, this study only evaluates onshore accidents. Fourth, the geographic focus is on Europe, so the European Union (EU27), the UK, the European Free Trade Association (EFTA), and EU candidate countries were considered. Therefore, the final accident database included 1244 events for the years 2000–2023 and the abovementioned countries.

2.2 Risk Indicators

Aggregated risk indicators, such as fatality and injury rates, provide measures of the human health impacts of energy technologies. Normalizing performance per unit of electricity production (e.g., fatalities per kWh) enables direct comparisons between different technologies, geographic areas, and time periods. Using the compiled accident dataset and IRENA capacity data, we calculated updated fatality rates for three broad country groups, including the Organization for Economic Cooperation and Development (OECD), the European Union (EU27), and non-OECD countries [26]. It follows the general approach described in [31]. Data from the IRENASTAT[8] tool of the International Renewable Energy Agency (IRENA) were used to normalize fatality rates per Gigawatt-electric-year (GWeyr), allowing for direct comparisons between geographic units. Fatality rates were computed for all fatal accidents (≥1 fatality), and the so-called severe fatality rates were also calculated, which only included accidents with at least five fatalities [32]. The latter is an essential measure if a diverse set of energy technologies (e.g., fossil, renewable, nuclear) is to be compared [15].

2.3 Summary Measures of Health

Accidents can result in a range of consequences, including fatalities, injuries, and disamenities. In contrast to the normalized aggregated risk indicators presented earlier, a composite indicator that combines different impacts can facilitate broader comparisons across disciplines. Previous studies (a) used the Value of Statistical Life (VSL) to calculate external costs [33]; (b) compared impacts between Life Cycle Assessment (LCA), Comparative Risk Assessment (CRA), and terrorist threat assessment based on Years of Life Lost (YOLL) [34], and monetized composite indicators used in National Risk Assessment (NRA) [35]. In this study, Disability-Adjusted Life Years (DALY)

[8] https://www.irena.org/data/downloads/irenastat.

are utilized. This approach builds upon the Global Burden of Disease (GBD)[9] database, which assesses health losses from diseases, injuries, and other risk factors. The approach involves the following steps. For this purpose, a subset of the WEAD comprising the 1244 accidents described in Sect. 2.1 was used to calculate DALY values for individual accidents that occurred in the European Union (EU 27), the UK, the European Free Trade Association (EFTA), and candidate (CAND) countries[10]. The proposed DALY calculation method is visualized in Fig. 1.

Step 1A: The Years of Life Lost (YLL) per country and year were estimated using data from the World Health Organization (WHO) and the International Labor Organization (ILO). The Global Health Observatory of the WHO provides data on life expectancy at birth, expressed in years, by country, and by year[11]. The ILOSTAT database[12], provided by the ILO, offers information on the working-age population by sex and age (in thousands) per country and year. The difference between the two values is considered a suitable proxy for the YLL due to a fatality in an accident. This simplification follows a similar discussion to that in [34, 36]. This is, of course, a conservative (maximum) estimate. However, the actual age of workers and/or public persons affected by an accident is usually not known, as it is not provided in the available reports. However, it can be justified because wind power faces acceptance issues [3]. In this way, it counters potential criticism that DALY estimates are on the lower end, a typical argument raised in comparative risk assessments of accidents in the energy sector [15, 37].

Step 1B: The Years Lived with Disability (YLD) provides the DALY estimate for injuries. Data obtained from the study «Disability Weights for the Global Burden of Disease 2013» was used [38]. In particular, injury-related terms from Table 2 in this publication were selected, including "injury" or "musculoskeletal disorders," while "untreated" or "without treatment" conditions were excluded. This resulted in 37 of the 235 unique health states reported in this table being selected. For each of them, the mean DW and 95% uncertainty interval were extracted. The average of these 37 health states corresponds to a DW value of 0.161 (0.108–0.222). The YLD of an accident with injuries is calculated by multiplying the country- and year-specific YLL by the average disability weight (DW).

Step 1C: For accidents with no fatalities or injuries, it was assumed that unique traumatic aspects might occur, which interact with the variable perceptions of each person involved in the accident, a phenomenon that has been extensively researched among workers in high-risk environments [39]. Similarly to YLD, data from the Global Burden of Disease (GBD) study, reported in Table 1 by Santomauro et al. [40] was used. An average DW was calculated for anxiety disorders, weighted by category (asymptomatic, mild, moderate, severe). An optimal treatment was assumed as EU 27, UK, EFTA and CAND represent developed countries. Furthermore, a duration of one year was considered because either the treatment is effective, or a worker will not continue in the

[9] https://www.healthdata.org/research-analysis/gbd.

[10] Albania, Bosnia and Herzegovina, Kosovo, Montenegro, North Macedonia, Serbia, and Turkey were considered, whereas Georgia, Moldova, and Ukraine were excluded.

[11] https://data.worldbank.org/indicator/SP.DYN.LE00.IN.

[12] https://ilostat.ilo.org/.

same profession. The weighted anxiety disorder DW has a value of 0.060. Finally, the number of persons working at a wind farm using a Full-Time Equivalent per Capacity (FTE/cap) relationship was based on an NREL study [41]. The DALY of the Years with Anxiety Disorder (YAD) for each accident corresponds to the following multiplication: windfarm capacity x FTE/cap x DW x duration (1 year).

Step 1D: For each accident, the total DALY equals:

- YLL summed across all fatalities in that accident (YLL × number of fatalities).
- YLD summed across all injuries (YLD × number of injuries).
- YAD based on estimated workforce exposure.

Subsequently, the country values were downscaled to the NUTS2 level (see Step 3).

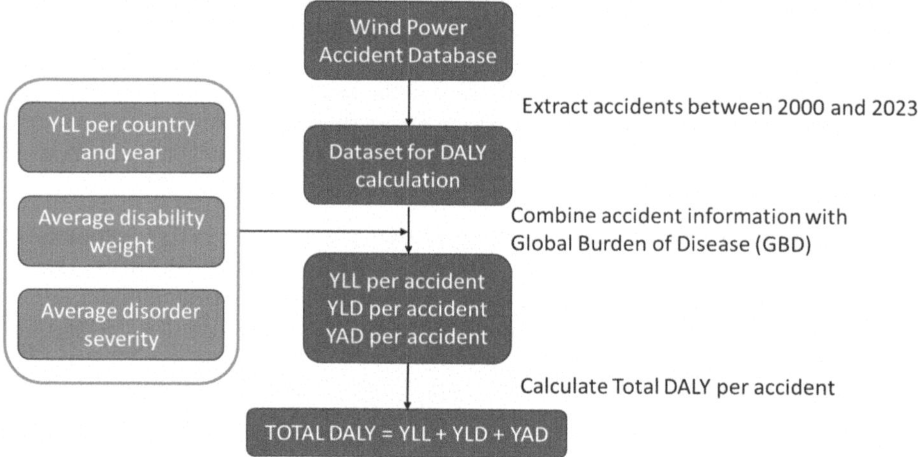

Fig. 1. Approach to estimate Disability-Adjusted Life Years (DALY) for all accidents considered in the years 2000–2023 across European countries.

Step 2: For the DALY rate calculations at the country and NUTS2 levels, the entire dataset can be used, while fatality rates were based on fatal accidents only. A Bayesian Hierarchical Model (HBM) was developed to estimate country-specific DALY rates with proper uncertainty quantification. The model employs a four-level hierarchical structure (Global → Cluster → Country → Observation), which enables partial pooling of information across 5 geographic clusters and 23 countries based on 1244 accident observations. This structure offers several advantages compared to direct calculation methods:

- Handling of complex, nested data structures through hierarchical modeling with partial pooling.
- Incorporation of prior information using tightened exponential priors to regularize variance parameters and prevent overfitting to sparse data.

- Improved parameter estimation through shrinkage, where countries with sparse data borrow strength from cluster- and global-level estimates, leading to more stable and accurate estimates.
- Full uncertainty quantification through posterior distributions, yielding 95% credible intervals in addition to point estimates.
- Flexibility to accommodate different prior specifications and model variants, allowing sensitivity analyses to assess robustness of results.
- Robustness to outliers through winsorization at the 95th percentile and use of a log-normal likelihood, which naturally handles the positive, right-skewed distribution of DALY values.

Bayesian models for risk assessment of energy accidents have been previously used, but not for DALY estimation or geographic downscaling. Several recent publications provide further information on the technical implementation and application cases [42, 43]. For a general overview of Bayesian modeling, numerous textbooks can be consulted, for example [44].

The HBM developed and applied in this study can be summarized by the pseudocode below. It was written and executed using R version 4.4.3 and RStudio 2024.12.1 Build 563.

```
Start
1.  Setup:
      a. input file
      b. likelihood type (lognormal selected based on
         diagnostic comparison)
      c. fitting method (adaptive, manual)
      d. prior specification (tightened exponential
         priors for variance parameters)
      e. MCMC parameters (4 chains, 4000 iterations, 2000
         warmup, adapt_delta=0.95)
2.  Load required libraries
3.  Data preprocessing
4.  Define Stan model code templates
5.  Fit the chosen model
6.  Convergence diagnostics (R-hat < 1.01, ESS > 400),
    posterior predictive checks
7.  Country-specific posterior effects (mean, 95%
    credible interval)
8.  Print/plot and export results (e.g., PNG, Excel)
9.  Print a message indicating the results have been
    saved
End
```

Two likelihood specifications were evaluated: Gaussian and lognormal. The lognormal model was selected based on superior diagnostic performance, as it naturally accommodates the positive, right-skewed distribution of DALY values while ensuring physical validity (i.e., strictly positive predictions). Model convergence was assessed using standard criteria: the Gelman-Rubin statistic (R-hat < 1.01), the effective sample size (ESS > 400), and absence of divergent transitions. The code can be expanded to include additional model types and automatically select the best-performing specification.

The MCMC sampling employed 4 parallel chains with 4000 iterations each (2000 warmup), using an adapt_delta of 0.95 and a maximum tree depth of 12 to ensure efficient exploration of the posterior distribution. The tightened exponential priors on variance parameters help prevent the well-known issue of poorly identified variance components in hierarchical models, while still allowing the data to inform the estimates. For the current analysis, we used a mixed approach combining adaptive tuning with manual verification to iteratively optimize the sampler settings.

Stan for R (accessed via the RStan package, version 2.32.7) is a powerful tool that allows users to fit complex Bayesian models using the Stan programming language directly from R. The package provides functionalities for posterior inference, including sampling from posterior distributions using Hamiltonian Monte Carlo with the No-U-Turn Sampler (NUTS). This integration enables advanced statistical analyses and model fitting in the R environment, with comprehensive diagnostics including trace plots, posterior predictive checks, and shrinkage visualizations.

Step 3: The country-specific DALY values were disaggregated to the NUTS2 level using a capacity scaling approach, i.e., installed wind power capacity in Megawatts (MW) per NUTS2 unit of a country. This follows the general ideas described in [31]. Similarly to fatality rates, data from the IRENASTAT tool were used to normalize DALY rates per Gigawatt-electric-year (GWeyr). For countries with no reported accidents, the aggregated DALY rate for the EU27, EFTA, or CAND countries was used as a proxy to downscale to the NUTS2 level.

Step 4: In the final step, a risk map was produced in QGIS Desktop 3.42.1 - Münster. For this purpose, several layers were selected and combined.

- NUTS 1–3 layer, 2024 (source: GISCO data distribution)[13]
- Bosnia and Herzegovina was not included in the NUTS layer, so it was sourced from GADM[14]
- The United Kingdom uses, after Brexit, the International Territorial Level (ITL) Geography Hierarchy Boundaries available from the Open Geography Portal of the National Statistical Office[15]
- DALY values at the NUTS2 level were imported as an Excel file and then merged with the abovementioned shapefiles.
- Locations of wind farm accidents were imported as a CSV file.
- Individual wind turbine locations were provided as a CSV file by DTU.
- OpenStreetMap was used as a standard background[16]

[13] https://gisco-services.ec.europa.eu/distribution/v1/nuts-2024.html.

[14] https://gadm.org/.

[15] https://geoportal.statistics.gov.uk/.

[16] https://tile.openstreetmap.de/.

The generated DALY risk map was then stored as a GeoPackage, which is an open, standards-based format for storing geospatial data. This format supports various types of spatial data, including points, lines, polygons, and raster images, making it versatile for diverse geospatial applications. Additionally, a GeoPackage is platform-independent and can be used across various software environments, thereby enhancing interoperability and data sharing within the geospatial community[17].

3 Results and Discussion

3.1 Overview of Accident Dataset

The final dataset analyzed in this study comprises 1244 wind power accidents for the years 2000–2023 in Europe (EU 27, UK, EFTA, and candidate (CAND) countries), see Sect. 2.1. Liechtenstein and Albania were excluded from the analysis because neither country had any operating wind farms at the end of 2023. The majority of accidents occurred in four countries, namely Germany (35%), and the UK (29%), followed distantly by Denmark (7%) and Ireland (5%), while the remaining countries had shares of 1.2% and below. This uneven distribution highlights the need to calculate normalized risk indicators as described in Sect. 2.2 and Sect. 2.3.

Among the 1244 accidents, 106 resulted in human casualties. Specifically, 53 accidents resulted in at least one fatality, 62 in at least one injury, and 9 involved both fatalities and injuries. These 106 events resulted in 54 fatalities and 95 injuries in total. The most severe accident in terms of fatalities occurred in the Netherlands (2013), in which two workers were killed in a turbine fire during maintenance. Regarding injuries, notable events include HSE safety breaches at a blade manufacturer (Scotland, UK, 2005, 13 workers with ill-health effects), a protest (Romania, 2010, 5 injuries), a blade transport accident (Germany, 2017, 3 injuries), a crane accident while lifting the nacelle (Sweden, 2017, 3 injuries), and an accident at a wind tower fabrication factory (Denmark, 2023, 3 injuries). For a more detailed characterization, see Burgherr et al. [26].

3.2 Risk Indicators

This section presents a global perspective on wind power accidents by country group, including the Organization for Economic Cooperation and Development (OECD), the European Union (EU 27), and non-OECD countries. For this purpose, normalized fatality rates are provided, i.e., fatalities per GWeyr for the years 2000–2023 (Fig. 2).

For all accidents (with $\geq$1 fatality), the fatality rate in non-OECD countries is comparable to that of the OECD and EU27. This contrasts with expectations and the general notion that less developed countries are more accident-prone [15]. However, in the case of wind power, two factors could contribute to this finding. The large scale capacity growth in non-OECD countries began later, when technologies were more mature. Additionally, the reporting in some countries may be less comprehensive, particularly if public information sources are used as in this study.

[17] https://www.geopackage.org/

Regarding severe accidents (with ≥5 fatalities), the expected pattern is confirmed, i.e., OECD and EU27 countries outperform non-OECD countries, resulting in fatality rates about one order of magnitude lower. This is likely an indication of differences between country groups in legal and regulatory frameworks that the industry has to comply with, as well as resulting differences in the safety cultures and their implementation in daily operations [15].

In the OECD and EU 27, the fatality rates of severe accidents are about 25 times lower compared to all accidents, while for non-OECD countries, the difference is only threefold. This discrepancy is driven by a few severe accidents in non-OECD countries, providing evidence that the maturity of HSE safety culture is a crucial aspect in reducing accident risk. However, it cannot exclude the possibility that a high-impact, low-probability (HILP) event may occur in the future in the OECD or the EU 27.

The differences in severe accident fatality rates between country groups may also reflect variations in healthcare infrastructure and emergency response capabilities [45]. Rapid emergency response and advanced trauma care in OECD and EU 27 countries could reduce fatalities in severe accidents, whereas rural wind power sites with longer response times may experience worse outcomes [46]. However, since the WEAD captures only fatality counts rather than medical outcomes or disability, the current analysis cannot fully assess these healthcare-related factors. Future research integrating healthcare access indicators could help distinguish between accident prevention (safety culture) and outcome mitigation (emergency response) to explain geographic patterns.

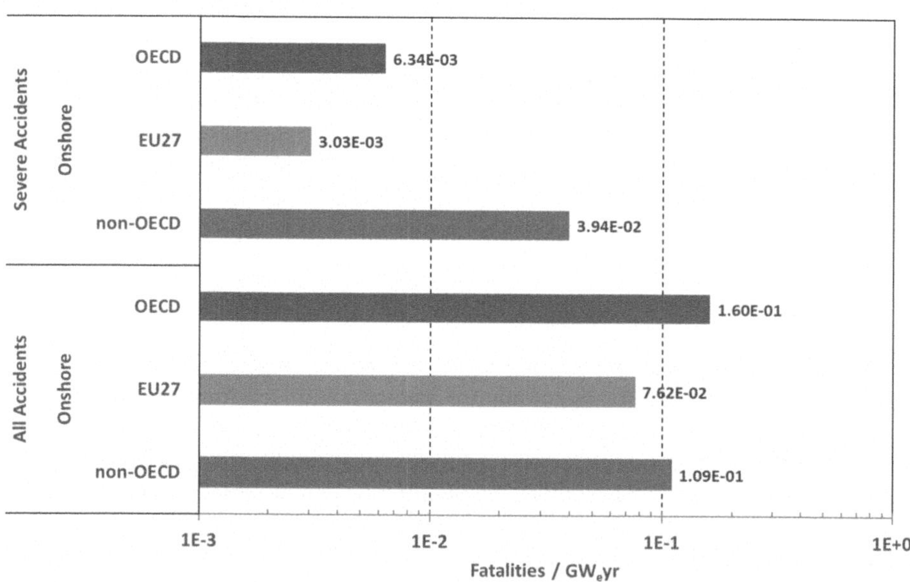

Fig. 2. Onshore fatality rates for all accidents (with ≥1 fatality) and severe accidents (with ≥5 fatalities) in OECD, EU27, and non-OECD countries (updated from Burgherr et al. [26]).

3.3 DALY Risk Map

A compound risk indicator, such as Disability-Adjusted Life Years (DALY), that integrates different health impacts (i.e., fatalities, injuries, and disamenities), provides several advantages. First, it can overcome issues related to limited data availability, as, for example, only a part of all accidents results in fatalities. Second, it provides a more comprehensive estimate of various types of impacts (e.g., fatalities and injuries). Third, it enables a direct comparison with other impact categories (e.g., noise and Life Cycle Assessment, LCA) because a standard metric (e.g., DALY) is applied. Consequently, the DALY risk indicator and derived risk map use the complete dataset of 1244 wind power accidents in Europe for the years 2000–2023, as previously characterized.

The violin plot in Fig. 3 reveals distinct distributional characteristics across the five risk categories. The VERY LOW category shows extreme right skewing with a median near 1E-5 DALY/GWeyr. This category includes only regions with installed wind capacity, while an additional 71 NUTS2 regions with zero DALY rates (no installed capacity) were excluded from the analysis. The right-skewed distribution justifies the use of an absolute threshold (1E-4) rather than a logarithmic subdivision, as values below this level represent a negligible risk that is practically indistinguishable for policy purposes.

The LOW and MEDIUM categories exhibit good within-class homogeneity (CVs of 0.58 and 0.69, respectively), as shown by their violin plots, which show controlled spread around their central values. The logarithmic progression of category boundaries (1E−4, 1E−3, 1E−2) appropriately captures the multiplicative scaling of risk across intermediate levels. The HIGH category shows a greater spread (CV = 1.34), reflecting its broader range from 1E−2 to 1E+0 DALY/GWeyr. This deliberate choice extends this category across two orders of magnitude to the empirically determined outlier threshold. While this represents increased heterogeneity compared to lower categories, it remains acceptable given that this category captures significantly elevated risks that nonetheless fall below the exceptional outlier threshold where qualitatively different risk factors emerge.

The VERY HIGH category represents a tight cluster at the upper extreme ($\geq$1.0 DALY/GWeyr), visually separated from the HIGH category by a substantial gap. This corresponds to the natural break between 0.71 and 1.72 DALY/GWeyr observed in the data. The exceptional homogeneity of this category (CV = 0.32) and its geographic coherence (all four regions are Western Balkans countries: North Macedonia, Kosovo, Bosnia and Herzegovina, and Montenegro) justify treating these as true statistical outliers requiring special investigation rather than grouping them with moderately elevated risks.

The applied classification maintains mathematical consistency through logarithmic progression in intermediate categories, while the final threshold at 1.0 preserves this multiplicative principle and adapts to the empirical data structure. This is consistent with established frameworks (e.g., EPA risk characterization, ICRP radiation protection, Richter scale), which enhance policy clarity by creating distinct actionable categories: VERY LOW (negligible risk), LOW through HIGH (graduated responses), and VERY HIGH (exceptional risk). The approach balances mathematical rigor with practical utility for evidence-based decision-making.

Finally, the reference lines marking the «Noise» and «LCA» DALY thresholds provide context for how accident impacts compare with noise and LCA health impacts. The majority of NUTS2 accident DALY values is below the «Noise» threshold, and all values except the VERY HIGH category have DALY values below the typical Life Cycle Assessment estimates. This confirms that the impacts from normal operation are substantially higher than those from accidents. However, despite this difference in absolute values, accidents play a crucial role in societal risk acceptance and the reduction of occupational health risks [34].

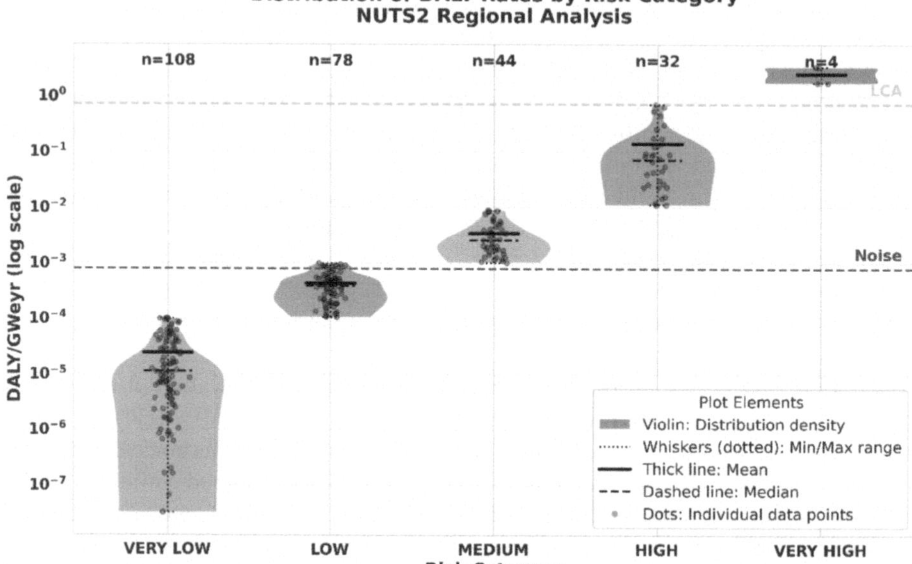

Fig. 3. Distribution of DALY rates by risk category at the NUTS2 level.

Figure 4 shows the spatial distribution of DALY rates across Europe at the NUTS2 level, using 9 logarithmic categories. The map reveals distinct geographic patterns that complement the statistical distributions shown in the violin plot (Fig. 3) and highlight regional variations not immediately apparent from summary statistics alone.

A substantial proportion of NUTS2 regions (21.8%, n = 74) have no DALY rates due to the absence of operational wind farms (NOIC - No Installed Capacity). These regions span 23 countries and are predominantly located in Turkey (approximately one-third of NOIC regions), Eastern and Southeastern European countries, special territories of EU member states (only partially shown on the map), and regions with low-wind potential or other constraints.

The remaining 266 NUTS2 regions with installed wind capacity display marked geographic clustering across the nine DALY categories. The lowest four categories (1E−8 to 1E−4 DALY/GWeyr) collectively encompass 108 NUTS2 regions (31.8%), predominantly in Western Europe (i.e., Germany, UK, France, Italy, and Spain), representing areas where wind energy deployment has occurred with minimal recorded accident impact.

The middle range categories show broader geographic distribution: 1E−4 to 1E−3 (n = 78, 22.9%) spans 16 countries across Western and Northern Europe; 1E−3 to 1E−2 (n = 44, 12.9%) encompasses 16 countries with increasing representation from Central and Eastern Europe; and 1E−2 to 1E−1 (n = 22, 6.5%) includes 11 countries with notable concentrations in Switzerland, Czech Republic, Portugal, Hungary, and parts of the Balkans. Together, these three middle categories account for 42.3% of all NUTS2 regions, representing mostly established wind operations with moderate accident risk profiles.

The 1E−1 to 1E+0 category (n = 10, 2.9%) represents an elevated risk tier spanning 9 countries, including Baltic states (Latvia, Estonia), Central Europe (Slovakia, Romania), Switzerland, and individual regions in Cyprus, Luxembourg, Bosnia and Herzegovina, and Serbia. This category exhibits considerable geographic diversity, representing a transition zone between typical operational risk and the exceptional outliers found in the highest category. Most strikingly, the 1E+0 to 4E+0 category (n = 4, 1.2%) exhibits complete geographic coherence, exclusively comprising the Western Balkan countries of Montenegro, Bosnia and Herzegovina, Kosovo, and North Macedonia. This represents the only category limited to CAND countries (excluding Turkey), suggesting region-specific risk factors. These potentially include data quality issues, regulatory differences, or distinct operational conditions requiring further investigation.

Overall, the geographic distribution reveals systematic spatial patterns rather than random variation. Western and Northern European regions predominantly occupy lower risk categories, Central European regions cluster in middle categories, and elevated to high rates appear primarily in Eastern Europe and the Balkans.

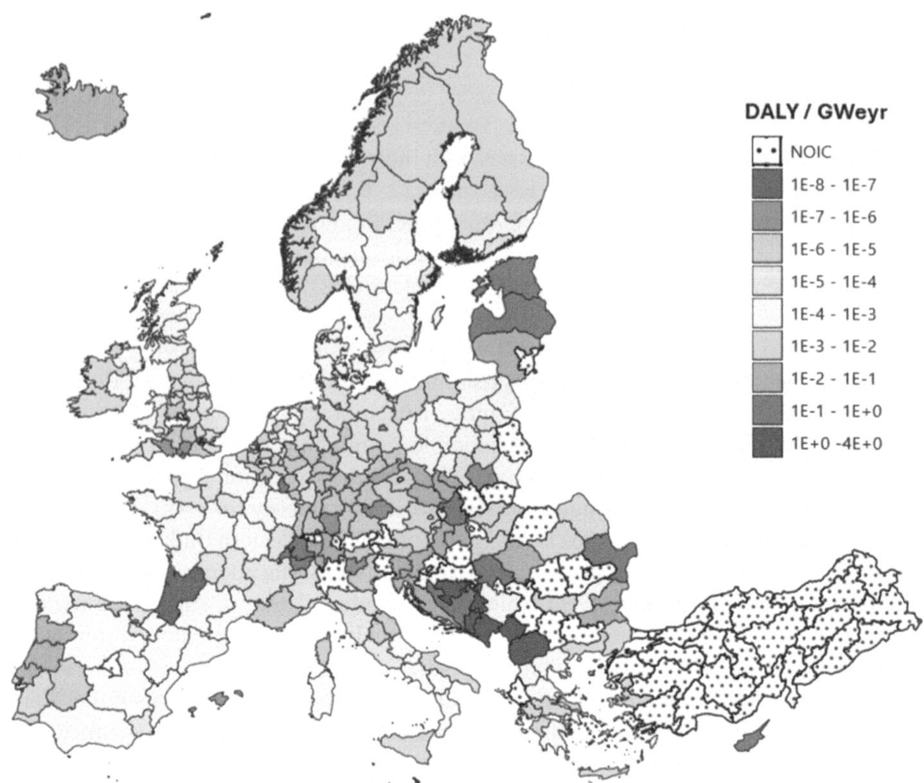

Fig. 4. DALY rates (DALY/GWeyr) at the NUTS2 level for 39 European countries. NUTS2 units filled in white with black dots indicate that no DALY rates are available based on the current dataset (i.e., NO Installed Capacity, NOIC).

4 Final Remarks and Outlook

A novel approach has been developed to assess the accident risk of wind power in Europe, allowing downscaling to the NUTS2 level, aggregating different types of health impacts, and calculating Disability-Adjusted Life Years (DALY) using a first-of-its-kind method not previously applied in accident risk assessment. This substantially improves the accuracy and spatial resolution of accident risk indicators. Furthermore, such a quantitative assessment is beneficial for providing transparent, fact-based input into controversial discussions on risk perception and acceptance, as well as for supporting evidence- and risk-informed decision-making.

The practical implications of this work are threefold. First, the DALY risk map enables regulators and industry stakeholders to identify high-risk regions warranting enhanced safety measures or inspections. Second, the Bayesian approach provides more reliable risk estimates for countries with sparse data, supporting evidence-based policy-making even where accident records are limited. Third, by expressing accident impacts in

DALY, a metric also used in noise assessments and LCA, this framework facilitates integrated impact assessments across multiple wind power effects, supporting more holistic decision-making in energy planning.

Future efforts could further improve the estimation of health impacts expressed as DALY. Stricter and more detailed reporting could reduce limitations in data availability and the number of assumptions necessary, ultimately leading to estimates with higher accuracy and lower uncertainties. However, this requires a joint effort from authorities, regulators, and industry, as this cannot be overcome by simply increasing the effort devoted to data collection.

From a methodological point of view, the applied methods and models could be improved by incorporating more aspects and greater complexity. However, this is partially dependent on data quality and completeness because otherwise the effects would not fully translate into the actual results.

Finally, a comparative perspective is needed. This applies to the technology portfolio considered (i.e., fossil, large hydro, nuclear, and various new renewables), the geographic coverage (i.e., beyond Europe), and the potential future changes in health impacts from accidents (i.e., long-term energy transition scenarios).

Acknowledgments. This work has been funded by the HE Project WIMBY [grant number 101083460]. P.B. acknowledges the financial support of the State Secretariat for Education, Research and Innovation (SERI) of the Swiss Confederation, SERI No. 22.00340.

Disclosure of Interests. The authors have no competing interests to declare that are relevant to the content of this article.

References

1. REN21: Renewables 2024 - Global Status Report Collection, Global Overview. Renewables Now, Paris, France (2024)
2. EMBER: Global Electricity Review 2023. EMBER, London, UK (2023)
3. McKenna, R., et al.: System impacts of wind energy developments: key research challenges and opportunities. Joule **9**, 101799 (2025). https://doi.org/10.1016/j.joule.2024.11.016
4. Froidevaux, J.S.P., Le Viol, I., Barré, K., Bas, Y., Kerbiriou, C.: A modeling framework for biodiversity assessment in renewable energy development: a case study on European bats and wind turbines. Renew. Sustain. Energy Rev. **211**, 115323 (2025). https://doi.org/10.1016/j.rser.2024.115323
5. Voigt, C.C.: Insect fatalities at wind turbines as biodiversity sinks. Conserv. Sci. Pract. **3** (2021). https://doi.org/10.1111/csp2.366
6. Grimsrud, K., Hagem, C., Haaskjold, K., Lindhjem, H., Nowell, M.: Spatial trade-offs in national land-based wind power production in times of biodiversity and climate crises. Environ. Resour. Econ. **87**, 401–436 (2024). https://doi.org/10.1007/s10640-023-00764-8
7. Tsani, T., Weinand, J.M., Linßen, J., Stolten, D.: Quantifying social factors for onshore wind planning – a systematic review. Renew. Sustain. Energy Rev. **203**, 114762 (2024). https://doi.org/10.1016/j.rser.2024.114762
8. Stadelmann-Steffen, I., Dermont, C.: Acceptance through inclusion? Political and economic participation and the acceptance of local renewable energy projects in Switzerland. Energy Res. Soc. Sci. **71**, 101818 (2021). https://doi.org/10.1016/j.erss.2020.101818

9. Caporale, D., Sangiorgio, V., Amodio, A., De Lucia, C.: Multi-criteria and focus group analysis for social acceptance of wind energy. Energy Policy **140** (2020). https://doi.org/10.1016/j.enpol.2020.111387
10. Winter, K., Hornsey, M.J., Pummerer, L., Sassenberg, K.: Anticipating and defusing the role of conspiracy beliefs in shaping opposition to wind farms. Nat. Energy **7**, 1200–1207 (2022). https://doi.org/10.1038/s41560-022-01164-w
11. Simos, J., Cantoreggi, N., Christie, D., Forbat, J.: Wind turbines and health: a review with suggested recommendations. Environnement Risques et Sante **18**, 149–159 (2019). https://doi.org/10.1684/ers.2019.1281
12. Freiberg, A., Schefter, C., Girbig, M., Murta, V.C., Seidler, A.: Health effects of wind turbines on humans in residential settings: results of a scoping review. Environ. Res. **169**, 446–463 (2019). https://doi.org/10.1016/j.envres.2018.11.032
13. Cunha, L., Silva, D., Macedo, M.: Different shades of green: an analysis of the occupational health and safety risks faced by wind farm workers. Sustainability **16** (2024). https://doi.org/10.3390/su16073012
14. Fischer, S.L., Koltun, S., Lee, J.: A cross-sectional survey of musculoskeletal disorder hazard exposures and self-reported discomfort among on-shore wind turbine service technicians. Ergonomics **64**, 383–395 (2021). https://doi.org/10.1080/00140139.2020.1831079
15. Burgherr, P., Hirschberg, S.: Comparative risk assessment of severe accidents in the energy sector. Energy Policy **74**, S45–S56 (2014). https://doi.org/10.1016/j.enpol.2014.01.035
16. Spada, M., Burgherr, P.: Comparative accident risk assessment of energy system technologies for the energy transition in OECD countries. In: Brito, M.P., Aven, T., Baraldi, P., Čepin, M., Zio, E. (eds.) Proceedings of the 33rd European Safety and Reliability Conference. Research Publishing, Singapore, SG (2023)
17. Aneziris, O.N., Papazoglou, I.A., Psinias, A.: Occupational risk for an onshore wind farm. Saf. Sci. **88**, 188–198 (2014). https://doi.org/10.1016/j.ssci.2016.02.021
18. Karanikas, N., et al.: Occupational health hazards and risks in the wind industry. Energy Rep. **7**, 3750–3759 (2021). https://doi.org/10.1016/j.egyr.2021.06.066
19. Sheng, S., O'Connor, R.: Reliability of wind turbines. In: Wind Energy Engineering: A Handbook for Onshore and Offshore Wind Turbines, pp. 195–211. Elsevier (2023). https://doi.org/10.1016/B978-0-323-99353-1.00016-5
20. Sanchez-Fernandez, A.J., González-Sánchez, J.L., Luna Rodríguez, Í., Rodríguez, F.R., Sanchez-Rivero, J.: Reliability of onshore wind turbines based on linking power curves to failure and maintenance records: a case study in central Spain. Wind Energy **26**, 349–364 (2023). https://doi.org/10.1002/we.2793
21. Li, H., Peng, W., Huang, C.G., Guedes Soares, C.: Failure rate assessment for onshore and floating offshore wind turbines. J. Mar. Sci. Eng. **10**, 1–28 (2022). https://doi.org/10.3390/jmse10121965
22. Ferrari, L., Soldi, G., Bianchini, A., Dalpane, E.: Statistical analysis of component failures: a 16 year survey on more than 550 wind turbines. J. Eng. Gas Turbine Power **140** (2018). https://doi.org/10.1115/1.4041131
23. Ertek, G., Kailas, L.: Analyzing a decade of wind turbine accident news with topic modeling. Sustainability **13** (2021). https://doi.org/10.3390/su132212757
24. Asian, S., Ertek, G., Haksoz, C., Pakter, S., Ulun, S.: Wind turbine accidents: a data mining study. IEEE Syst. J. **11**, 1567–1578 (2017). https://doi.org/10.1109/JSYST.2016.2565818
25. Moura Carneiro, F.O., Barbosa Rocha, H.H., Costa Rocha, P.A.: Investigation of possible societal risk associated with wind power generation systems. Renew. Sustain. Energy Rev. **19**, 30–36 (2013). https://doi.org/10.1016/j.rser.2012.11.006

26. Burgherr, P., Siskos, E., McKenna, R., Spada, M., Lordan-Perret, R.: Comparative risk assessment of wind turbine accidents from a societal perspective. In: Brito, M.P., Aven, T., Baraldi, P., Cepin, M., Zio, E. (eds.) Proceedings of the 33rd European Safety and Reliability Conference (ESREL 2023). Research Publishing Services, Singapore, SG (2023)
27. European Agency for Safety and Health at Work: Occupational safety and health in the wind energy sector. European Risk Observatory Report, Brussels, Belgium (2013). https://doi.org/10.2802/86555
28. G+ Global Offshore Wind: 2021 Incident Data Report. G+ Global Offshore Wind Health & Safety Organisation, London, UK (2022)
29. Ertek, G., Asian, S., Haksoz, C., Pakter, S., Ulun, S.: Wind turbine accident news (1980–2013). Mendeley Data, V1. https://doi.org/10.17632/jkjvmn9tz3.1
30. IRENA: Future of wind: Deployment, investment, technology, grid integration and socio-economic aspects (A Global Energy Transformation paper), Abu Dhabi, UAE (2019)
31. Hidalgo Gonzalez, I., Uihlein, A.: High-resolution energy atlas. Methodology and data. Publications Office of the European Union, Luxembourg (2023). https://doi.org/10.2760/83784
32. Burgherr, P., Spada, M., Kalinina, A., Vandepaer, L., Lustenberger, P., Kim, W.: Comparative risk assessment of accidents in the energy sector within different long-term scenarios and marginal electricity supply mixes. In: Proceedings of the 29th European Safety and Reliability Conference, ESREL 2019, pp. 1525–1532 (2019). https://doi.org/10.3850/978-981-11-2724-3_0674-cd
33. Burgherr, P., Hirschberg, S., Spada, M.: Comparative assessment of accident risks in the energy sector. In: Kovacevic, R., Pflug, G., Vespucci, M. (eds.) Handbook of Risk Management in Energy Production and Trading. ISORMS, vol. 199, pp. 475–501. Springer, Boston (2013). https://doi.org/10.1007/978-1-4614-9035-7_18
34. Hirschberg, S., et al.: Health effects of technologies for power generation: Contributions from normal operation, severe accidents and terrorist threat. Reliab. Eng. Syst. Saf. **145**, (2016). https://doi.org/10.1016/j.ress.2015.09.013
35. Spada, M., Burgherr, P., Hohl, M.: Toward the validation of a national risk assessment against historical observations using a Bayesian approach: application to the Swiss case. J. Risk Res. **22**, 1323–1342 (2019). https://doi.org/10.1080/13669877.2018.1459794
36. Spada, M., Burgherr, P.: Comparative risk assessment and external costs of accidents for passenger transportation in Switzerland. In: Castanier, B., Cepin, M., Bigaud, D., Berenguer, C. (eds.) Proceedings of the 31st European Safety and Reliability Conference (ESREL 2021). Research Publishing, Switzerland, SG (2021). https://doi.org/10.3850/978-981-18-2016-8354-cd644
37. Burgherr, P., Hirschberg, S.: A comparative analysis of accident risks in fossil, nuclear, and hydro energy chains. Hum. Ecol. Risk Assess. **14**, 947–973 (2008). https://doi.org/10.1080/10807030802387556
38. Salomon, J.A., et al.: Disability weights for the global burden of disease 2013 study. Lancet Glob. Health **3**, e712–e723 (2015). https://doi.org/10.1016/S2214-109X(15)00069-8
39. Carey, M.G., et al.: The prevalence of PTSD, major depression and anxiety symptoms among high-risk public transportation workers. Int. Arch. Occup. Environ. Health **94**, 867–875 (2021). https://doi.org/10.1007/s00420-020-01631-5
40. Santomauro, D.F., Purcell, C., Whiteford, H.A., Ferrari, A.J., Vos, T.: Grading disorder severity and averted burden by access to treatment within the GBD framework: a case study with anxiety disorders. Lancet Psychiatry **10**, 272–281 (2023). https://doi.org/10.1016/S2215-0366(23)00037-8
41. Kotarbinski, M., Keyser, D., Stefek, J.: Workforce and economic development considerations from the operations and maintenance of wind power plants. Technical report NREL/TP-5000-76957. National Renewable Energy Laboratory (NREL), Golden, CO, USA (2020)

42. Spada, M., Burgherr, P.: A hierarchical approximate Bayesian computation (HABC) for accident risk in the energy sector triggered by natural events. In: Proceedings of the 29th European Safety and Reliability Conference, ESREL 2019 (2020). https://doi.org/10.3850/978-981-11-2724-30758-cd
43. Kalinina, A., Spada, M., Burgherr, P.: Application of a Bayesian hierarchical modeling for risk assessment of accidents at hydropower dams. Saf. Sci. **110** (2018). https://doi.org/10.1016/j.ssci.2018.08.006
44. Gelman, A., Carlin, J.B., Stern, H.S., Rubin, D.B.: Bayesian Data Analysis. Chapman and Hall/CRC (2003). https://doi.org/10.1201/9780429258480
45. Tin, D., Cheng, L., Hata, R., Hertelendy, A.J., Hart, A., Ciottone, G.: Descriptive analysis of the healthcare aspects of industrial disasters around the world. Disaster Med. Public Health Prep. **17**, e400 (2023). https://doi.org/10.1017/dmp.2023.64
46. Hernandez, N., et al.: Factors contributing to disparities in trauma care between urban vs rural trauma centers: towards improving trauma care access and quality of care delivery. Injury **55**, 112017 (2024). https://doi.org/10.1016/j.injury.2024.112017

Designing Cyber Security Communities of Support to Improve SME Cyber Hygiene and Resilience

Neeshe Khan[1(✉)], Ram Herkanaidu[1], Steven Furnell[1], Jason R. C. Nurse[2], Maria Bada[3], and Matthew Rand[3]

[1] School of Computer Science, University of Nottingham, Nottingham, UK
neeshe.khan1@nottingham.ac.uk
[2] School of Computing, University of Kent, Canterbury, UK
[3] School of Biological and Behavioural Sciences, Queen Mary University of London, London, UK

Abstract. Small-to-Medium-sized Enterprises (SMEs) represent the vast majority of businesses in the UK and many other countries. At the same time, however, SMEs can often lack preparedness in relation to cyber security. This becomes problematic for SMEs in their own right, as well as in the context of supply-chains for larger organisations. Despite the availability of information and resources many SMEs are challenged by a lack of understanding and skills to help address questions and enact advice. Based upon ongoing research into the support available to SMEs, this paper proposes the concept of Cyber Security Communities of Support. The discussion presents the principles of the communities, as well as various practical considerations to be accounted for in operationalizing the approach (including the provision of an online Support Broker platform as an enabler for community dialogue). Finally, attention is given towards the planning for a series of pilot communities, from which it is intended that the findings will help to provide the basis for an ongoing and replicable model of support.

Keywords: Cyber security · SMEs · Small Businesses · Communities · Cyber Security Support · networks · collaborative learning · shared expertise

1 Introduction

It is widely recognized that Small-to-Medium-sized Enterprises (SMEs) can find themselves challenged by cyber security. In the UK, the most recent Cyber Security Breaches Survey suggests that half of small businesses have experienced a cyber security breach or attack in the last 12 months, while at the same time showing that such organisations are much less likely to have relevant controls in place than their larger counterparts [1]. At the same time, SMEs represent a significant provider of employment and account for a significant proportion of the economic value in many countries [2]. Again, using the UK as a specific example, the 5.5 million SMEs collectively account for 99.8% of businesses and three fifths of employment (16.6 million people), and half of the turnover (£2.8 trillion) in the private sector [3]. As such, they collectively represent a critical national asset that merits appropriate protection.

E. Bergström et al. (Eds.): CRITIS 2025, LNCS 16291, pp. 123–139, 2026.
https://doi.org/10.1007/978-3-032-19540-1_7

The need to support SME engagement with cyber security is well-known, and there are various routes through which support can be sought, including online guidance and via third-party service providers. However, what is less clear is whether these are recognized and utilized appropriately by the target audience (e.g. do SMEs know who to contact and how easily can they establish the correct route), and whether resulting guidance is considered sufficient and effective. These are critical factors that impact the resulting cyber security provision in SMEs. Moreover, in addition to representing a large segment of the economy, SMEs are embedded within key and critical supply chains. Vulnerabilities emerging from SMEs, when successfully leveraged by malicious actors, result in headline breaches of large organisations, such as the National Health Service [4] and Transport for London [5], due to 3rd party compromises. However, by default, many are not positioned to play their part in this context and so need support to do so. Indeed, SMEs can be positioned very differently in terms of familiarity with cyber security and ability to act upon it. This can vary from those that feel they know little or nothing about it, through to those that know they need something but are unclear about what, or those that know what they want but not how to get there. All require a level of support, and access to related skills and expertise to provide it.

Efforts are being made at a governmental level to secure SMEs. This includes a range of local and regional initiative representatives aiding to improve their baseline cyber hygiene and resilience through grass-root efforts for awareness raising and engagement. However, little attention has been paid to the creation of peer-to-peer cyber support communities. Additionally, there is limited literature examining the design of communities in such specialized contexts that go beyond sociological or business management thought (discussed in further detail the Background section).

In parallel with the concerns on the SME side, those providing frontline support can receive queries that they are not confident or competent to address. For example, a prior survey of technology retailers had revealed a third to have less awareness around ransomware and cloud breaches [6], meaning that they must either decline or pass on the query or make a (potentially flawed) best effort attempt to help. Meanwhile, those with the technical capabilities to assist have the potential to be overwhelmed by the volume of enquiries or the extent of support required.

In response to these concerns, the authors are involved in a project that has sought to both characterise the current cyber security support landscape and then design a new approach that seeks to complement it. The resulting Cyber Security Communities of Support (CyCOS) project is a two-and-a-half-year initiative funded by the UK's Engineering and Physical Sciences Research Council (EPSRC) and linked to the Research Institute for Socio-technical Cyber Security (RISCS). It is a collaborative project led by the University of Nottingham, in partnership with Queen Mary University of London and the University of Kent, and supported by additional organisations including the Chartered Institute of Information Security, the Federation of Small Business, the Home Office, IASME, ISC2 and three regional Cyber Resilience Centres (covering the Eastern, East Midlands, and London regions of the UK).

The early phases of the work focused upon data collection from SMEs and cyber security support providers in order to assess the existing landscape, as well as to assess the coverage and clarity of existing online support materials. This work, which has been documented in prior publications [7–9] served to confirm some of the existing challenges, and provided further justification for the idea of providing an additional form of support via the community-based approach suggested in the project title. There are two related objectives for this aspect of the work:

1. To design and establish the foundations for Cyber Security Communities of Support, enabling collaborations that enhance the level and availability of specialist support available to SMEs.
2. To evaluate and refine the communities initiative via a series of pilot activities, ensuring an effective, repeatable and sustainable model for wider use.

The aim of this paper is to explain the basis of the approach that has been designed, including the concept of the communities, how they are anticipated to operate, and the related mechanisms that are provided to enable them. The discussion begins with some further consideration of the importance of SMEs in the national context, and the basis on which a community-based approach is considered suitable to reach them. This then leads into specific attention to the community approach in a cyber security context, drawing upon supporting evidence from earlier data collection and consideration of the different factors that could inform community formation. From this, the more detailed operational considerations are examined, including the roles of SME and cyber providers as community participants, and the factors that need to be addressed in terms of initiating and maintaining their engagement. Finally, attention is given to how SMEs within the communities will be supported via a Support Broker (i.e. an online platform) that enables them to socialise their questions, concerns, and other contributions. The paper concludes with thoughts on how these foundations will be used to inform a series of operational pilot communities, in order to evaluate the approach in practice.

2 Background

As already indicated, SMEs account for the vast majority of businesses in many countries and make an important economic contribution. A significant amount of research explores routes to improve cyber security practices and resilience of SMEs in the UK including their barriers to adopting cyber security [10], SME constraints [11], information transparency in supply-chains [12], and the role of service providers for SMEs to improve cyber security practices of SMEs [13]. At the same time, SMEs are playing a growing role in providing various services that can be linked to the Critical National Infrastructure (CNI). However, depending on the country and its strategic priorities, sectors that qualify as CNI are variable [14]. Perhaps consequently, the cyber security advice and guidance offered by authorities to supply-chains also varies between countries for instance, between UK, US and the European regions [15, 16]. Many countries – including the US [17], Canada [18], and Nigeria [19] - are recognizing the importance of securing SMEs to protect their CNI.

For SMEs to improve their cyber defenses or become resilient in the first instance, it is of interest to examine the sources that they are likely to interact with when trying to do so. One route within their journey is potentially through using the Internet as their first recourse. This choice is likely as it offers SMEs a wide array of information, presents them with solutions that might feel closely aligned to their challenge and, it can offer accessibility to knowledge in a technically inclined domain. To understand the information SMEs might encounter as part of this endeavor, a critical analysis was carried out to examine the coverage, completeness and clarity of online guidance documents offered by UK-based sources [7]. The findings revealed that guidance is dated and there is significant diversity in the content SMEs are presented with. This varied guidance can subsequently result in inconsistent and potentially ill-informed decision making when trying to implement organizational cyber security controls. Additionally, findings showed guidance documents in many cases provided limited information, for instance often lacking actionable steps or demonstratable successful outcomes, which can result in confusion and queries being left unresolved for the reader. Subsequent research findings within this project [8] highlighted the magnified impact from these guidance documents when SMEs are implementing advice which is amplified by their reactive needs (i.e. SMEs reaching out to advisory sources *after* an incident or a breach), limited resources and a lack of cyber security awareness and knowledge. These findings informed the design within CyCOS through the Support Broker which offers 'resources' tab to established guidance documents and affords SMEs opportunities to communicate with other members in various ways (discussed in further detail later in this section).

Further insights about SMEs' reactive needs, and the barriers to their efforts, were discovered in subsequent in-depth conversations with providers of cyber security advice [9]. The general views are that cyber hygiene amongst SMEs remains low despite efforts being made at a national level, that SMEs are considered unlikely to proactively engage with the cyber security domain, and their efforts are further hampered by aspects such as comprehension, capability, attitudes, and resources. Having said this, various activities undertaken by providers such as, interactive sessions, outreach initiatives, in-person events and regionally focused events etcetera, had been found to have a positive impact. These activities primarily include two main elements:

- **Building rapport with SMEs**. Considerations here can include various criteria such as, catering to different forms of learning, offering relatable examples, simplifying technical language, identifying relevant guidance documents that are appropriate for their queries, and capturing feedback.
- **Face-to-face interactions**. Examples include training and cyber security related events, which can have a positive impact in helping SMEs improve their baseline hygiene and resilience. Successful outcomes were noted by providers when they deliver bespoke trainings catering to SME needs.

To determine context-specific needs, organisations must be recognized with a more detailed lens than that offered by the broad term of 'SME'. Additionally, long-term exposure between SMEs and providers was believed to nurture strong relationships between the two parties and encourage active engagement through dialogue (i.e. opportunities to directly ask questions, request help, seek guidance etcetera).

In addition to existing findings from various studies conducted in the overarching project, informal discussions were held with relevant external stakeholders who have been involved with, or lead other types of, communities in their professional careers. These discussions were held with the aim to deepen authors' understanding of designing communities (in virtual and/or real-world settings), to learn and replicate aspects that worked well, and to identify challenge areas.

Research from Johnson [20] examined online communities to define key characteristics. These include a varying level of expertise present within the group, progression in knowledge within community members and authentic tasks and communications occurring within the group's interactions. Distinctions are made within this work between designed communities (i.e. purpose based communities that exist online) and 'communities of practice' which emerge from within designed communities due to the affordances offered to users in their use (for instance, the emergence of specialized interest groups within a broader category of interest). Within the design of Cyber Security Communities of Support (CyCOS), groups are initiated by shared remits of interest for instance, in topic areas or regions (discussed in greater depth in Sect. 4). However, it is possible that additional groupings or specialized communities emerge from within the ones initially designed by the authors and discussed in this writing. Johnson [20] also makes a case for the various advantages and disadvantages that emerge from exclusively virtual communities that include encouragement for introvert members to participate equally to their extrovert counterparts. Good facilitation techniques can limit member withdrawal and attrition.

A study by Schou and Adarkwah [21] discussed peer-to-peer communities to develop entrepreneurial opportunities through social engagement. Findings showed online communities provide relevant developmental opportunities for individuals by providing meaningful feedback, emotional support and aspects that reduce uncertainty amongst its members. In instances investigated by them, community members were responsive (due to internet capabilities) to assist other members with sense-making when they were confused or unsure. Members also provided each other with emotional support and offered vicarious learnings which helped others when faced with ambiguity. Findings from another study [22] revealed that bonds within group members are strengthened by shared interpersonal similarities and social interactions.

Prior studies have established various design principles when creating information systems which are relevant in this writing in the context of the Support Broker (discussed in further detail in subsequent sections). For instance, authors considered the adoption of Action Research (AR) commonly used in the design of information systems [29]. Whilst data was informally captured from target audience groups at public engagements (casting votes to show preferences for various designs), AR was inappropriate due to the time resource it requires within its five research phases.

When considering the design for the Support Broker, Mansell's human capabilities [30] i.e. divergence in people's capabilities which include knowledge, habits, skills etcetera which can be developed through interactions with technologies, were also considered as part of design discussions with stakeholders. Additionally, the 'four value-rational questions' [31] were discussed and argued by the authors as part of design meetings for the Support Broker until consensus was reached. These rationale questions are listed as follows:

- Where are we going?
- Is it desirable?
- What can be done?

- Who gains and who loses, and by which mechanism of power?

Understanding about human capabilities and the use of rationale questions which are utilized as part of information systems design, resulted in supportive evidence for the design principles discussed above to empower SMEs and segment environments within the Support Broker (and in further detail in Sect. 4 and 5).

3 Cyber Security Communities of Support

Part of the early work in the CyCOS project focused upon data collection from SMEs and existing support providers, in order to better understand and characterise the SMEs' needs and assess how well they are currently being served. The data collection included a series of survey and interview activities, which are already documented in prior publications [7–9]. One of the key findings from this was a clear level of concern amongst both groups that SMEs currently lack opportunities to share and discuss cyber security issues with a peer community. The following are some illustrative quotes from different participants to show these perspectives:

> *"It's very difficult to find peers that have a similar mindset to your own of a similar size that then you can have a conversation with" (SME)*
>
> *"What we don't know of ... is a network of people that you can share best practices with ... But there's nobody around" (SME)*
>
> *"One of the things I've struggled to find is like a community really ... I've looked in various places and I think because my role isn't necessarily deeply technical ... it has been difficult to do" (SME)*
>
> *"In terms of who would I go to talk about this, I wouldn't know" (SME)*
>
> *"For businesses in regions that are not specialised, it can be hard ... They don't have access to the people, they don't have the funding to pay for people, they don't have the funding to pay for the tools, that's what causes a lot of the problems" (Provider)*
>
> *"I see it as almost like self-help groups between businesses, where actual competition is not even factoring in there, it's just a place where everyone can get on a level pegging" (Provider)*
>
> *"This idea of having some sort of bridge, where SMEs are able to find us, and likewise we can find them ... being more collaborative with others is something I wish was a bit better" (Provider)*

Interestingly the quotes not only suggest an appetite from the SMEs, but also a recognition from those already supporting them that they would benefit from further routes. Indeed, the final quote also suggests that the providers themselves could also draw benefit from being linked together in a community context.

Another key finding from the data collection was that smaller organisations tend to seek information reactively and can be overwhelmed by what they find. While a myriad of resources is available, this does not equate to them being discovered, understood or used by those that need them. Again, referring to the findings from the Cyber Security

Breaches Survey, the fact that only 12% of micro and small firms had heard of the *Small Business Guide* on cyber security [1] which has been available since 2018 from the National Cyber Security Centre [23], and is specifically written for this target community, demonstrates that availability does not equate to uptake. As such, having a further route through which relevant resources can be promoted and discussed would be a potentially useful means of spreading good practice.

In response to these needs, we propose the novel concept of Cyber Security Communities of Support, with the aim of guiding SMEs in understanding the need for security, how it relates to their business, and how to achieve it, while also progressively increasing the capability of the SMEs themselves and sharing the support provision across the community members. The communities are seen as a means of being able to socialize cyber security discussions within a trusted context. They deliver potential for more distributed, peer-based support, with the aim of progressively increasing the capability of the SMEs themselves and sharing the support provision across the community members. As such, participation in a community would ultimately provide a behaviour transformation mechanism for the participant SMEs.

Founded by this understanding above and considering the research findings [9] discussed earlier about the main elements that have a positive impact from activities conducted by providers, community members will share similar interests and common goals, leading to a stronger community sense and trust in sharing information and receiving advice. In practice it is envisaged that communities may be formed around different characteristics of the participating SMEs. It is important to note that whilst providers will also be part of the communities, they are there in a supporting role and thus, it is the nature of the SMEs that remains the driving factor. Thus, potential characteristics of communities considered within the project to improve cohesion are:

- **Location** – The primary option would be to group SMEs based upon their physical location. This has the advantage of then enabling community members to meet and interact in face-to-face contexts rather than just online, which is less likely to happen if they are physical disparate.
- **Sector** – SMEs may also wish to come together with others working in a common domain (e.g. construction, retail, technology), as this would give more of a shared sense of what their specific cyber security needs might be, and a common basis on which to discuss specific threats that may affect their area of business.
- **SME size** – Given that the term SME may encompass anything from 1 to 249 people, there is potential for organizations to prefer to establish dialogue with others of a similar size. Indeed, the issues, experiences and constraints facing a sole-trader or micro business are likely to differ from those at the high-end of the medium size group. As such, size groupings based on the UK/EU standard of micro (headcount of <10), small (<50) and medium (<250) classifications would be a potential basis on which to distinguish them [24].
- **SME maturity** – This option is proposed on the basis that more established SMEs will potentially be at a different stage of their business development journey than start-ups, which in term may shape attitudes, appetite and prior experiences in relation to cyber security. As such, the nature of resulting community discussions could be quite different as their journeys continue.

- **Supply Chain** – Commonality here would be based upon SMEs being partners in the same supply chain (e.g. of a larger organization). The large business could then act as the primary source of (initial) cyber expertise to inform the community members, from which it would then benefit having raised cyber security awareness and practices amongst the businesses it depends upon. This approach links to the notion of larger organizations signing up to a Cyber Charter, as proposed in 2024's McPartland Review of cyber security in the UK [25].

The planned activity includes the establishment of a series of community pilots in order to trial the operation in practice and enable comparison of resulting experiences. Where possible, the project will facilitate face-to-face meetings to support the community building, monitor progress, and gain feedback on the outcomes and experience. The communities will be underpinned by an ethos of digital responsibility amongst the participants, and this will be emphasized in the core messaging at their formation. It is expected that SMEs will then benefit from the communities by:

- accessing community knowledge of cyber security
- receiving impartial advice and guidance from contributing security professionals
- discovering relevant resources recommended by community members
- joining (or initiating) community activities tailored to their needs and interests
- learning from other SMEs' cyber security experiences and sharing their own experiences to help others

Having outlined the concept and intent of the communities, the next section provides a more detailed examination of the underlying design and operational considerations. This involves defining operational parameters and metrics, and the baseline skills and resource requirements needed in each community.

4 Design and Implementation of the Communities

Fundamentally, the community design should offer SMEs a platform whereby they can access authentic cyber security support, guidance and resources that are in line with current national guidance to support effective decision making. Additionally, these designed communities should offer opportunities for individuals to query information that they encounter in order to assist SMEs in their efforts to improve their cyber hygiene and resilience.

4.1 Overall Principles

Given the intent to create a trusted and safe environment, community membership is not just a case of letting anyone in. Community formation will commence with member self-assessments informing an initial map of support provision (e.g. which source can offer what content or experience in relation to which issue). Maps will be progressively enriched as new experiences are gained within the community. Each community will incorporate SMEs alongside participants offering expertise for frontline advisory support and more specialised response capabilities.

To safeguard all community members, members who are not adhering to the code of conduct, shared at the time of signing up to the broker, will be removed by CyCOS team members who initially act as moderators within this context. The code of conduct contains general house-keeping rules which encourage members to act respectfully, honestly and ethically within their respective communities and aims to discourage disruptive behaviour which can negatively impact community wellbeing.

4.2 SME Participation

Whilst CyCOS project team members will regulate the content on the Support Broker platform (with users being able to 'flag' suspicious activity or conduct), only a small proportion of the community will be providers (i.e. approximately each group will contain a 1:4 ratio e.g. 20 SMEs to 5 Providers). This also aims to empower SMEs as a majority grouping within each community.

To implement aspects of trust and safety, SME status will be checked by CyCOS team members at the time of sign-up. This includes SME's listing and status on the 'Companies House' [26] website (UK's registrar of companies) to verify company identities. Additionally, through the Support Broker (discussed in greater detail below), email account verification of users will take place when users join the community.

4.3 Provider Participation

Providers will also be asked to declare their areas of expertise and share any supporting credentials at the sign-up stage which will subsequently be verified by CyCOS team members. Providers will also be requested to select a suitable role within the community as either a provider or an SME i.e. if they are representing their organization or are acting in an independent or volunteer capacity. This will limit any assumptions being made on behalf of members since individuals who might be in a cyber security or IT related role within their organization can be representing the interests of their SME organization.

Preliminary efforts when engaging target audiences for pilots, for instance a CyCOS exhibition stand at the SME XPO 2025, has generated a healthy interest from providers who have been eager to share their expression of interest. This appetite amongst providers, i.e. to network with SMEs and other providers, was also garnered from findings from earlier research conducted by the authors [9]. This enthusiasm demonstrated by providers initially serves as a predominant motivator for them to participate and engage with the designed pilots. One insight from informal discussions with stakeholders indicated the need to crystallize the role providers play within communities. Providers, who can potentially come from organisations that provide commercial cyber security services to SMEs, can rapidly become a majority population within the user base. Thus, any providers being accepted into CyCOS must adhere to providing impartial, independent advice at the time of their admittance to the community. Additionally, provider roles are voluntary in their nature and thus must be performed ethically (i.e. providing impartial, independent and non-competing advice).

4.4 Provisioning Communities and Maintaining Engagement

Based on insights discussed in the Background section above, CyCOS are designed to offer a hybrid approach (i.e., virtual and in-person events) to realize these benefits and encourage active engagement. Face-to-face events in real-world settings will be offered to SMEs participating in the pilots with various objectives such as those that offer to raise awareness and knowledge about cyber security for example, an 'Exercise in a Box' activity offered by affiliated partner NCSC [27], to those that celebrate national seasonal festivities. These sessions will also capture feedback from pilot participants about individual experiences to highlight areas that can replicate success or identify learning opportunities. Simultaneously, the Support Broker can cater to individual needs of learning, and facilitate dialogue (between providers and SMEs, and within peer-to-peer groups amongst SME groups) and up-skilling incentives will continue to be offered to participants through affiliated project partners such as, 'Certified in Cybersecurity' online certification offered by affiliated partner ISC2 [28].

The presence of cyber security professionals (or 'providers') within these communities is also designed to provide SMEs with a medium to ask questions, assist in simplifying technical language and concepts, and provide help with identifying relevant guidance documents that are best suited to their needs – resulting in potentially establishing strong inter-relations within and across the two parties. Prior to joining the pilots, SME members will be given the opportunity to express interest in the type of community they would prefer to join (e.g. regional or sectorial communities, SME maturity, and/or if they are supply-chain entities, all aspects that they most identify with to offer them a group which resonates with their own organizational identity). Furthermore, discussions initiated by SMEs about their lived experiences or challenges will provide organic examples that are relatable to other members within their respective group.

Our preliminary findings suggested that in addition to individual learning needs (including independent learning) and establishing the relevance of security advice to their contexts, SMEs can be further supported in their cyber security pursuit through incentivization. Thus, CyCOS are designed to offer participants cyber security materials, courses and events that upskill existing talent within organisations. For instance, through our affiliated partner, ISC2, as part of this project participants are offered a free 'Certified in Cybersecurity' course for their early-career employees as part of their professional development within this domain. This up-skilling will also provide each community with a varying level of expertise amongst SMEs to supplement providers who are qualified and/or experienced cyber security professionals.

The approach discussed above is founded by the project's published and preliminary findings and shown in Fig. 1 below.

Informal discussions with stakeholders highlighted the importance of autonomous, self-regulating communities to achieve successful outcomes. Consequently, the SME role will be designed to encourage them to be proactive for instance, through identifying communities they would like to join at the time of signing up (discussed above), requesting them to identify cyber security topics they would like to learn more about, ask questions or share their daily experiences. To supplement this effort, CyCOS team members will share information relevant to each community (for instance, with relevant

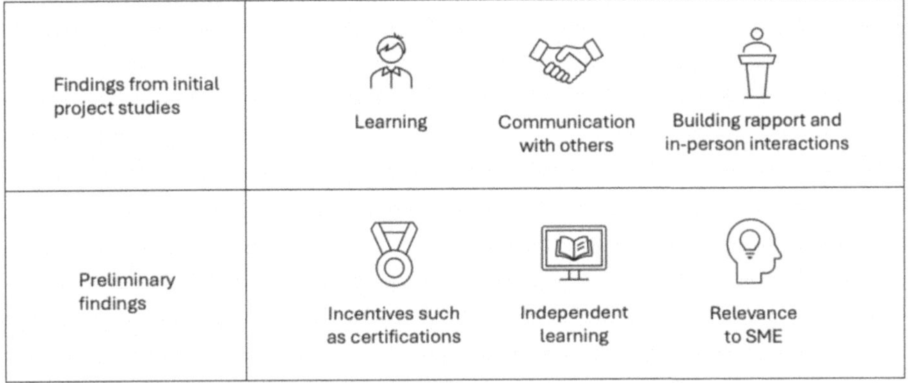

Fig. 1. Findings from earlier research studies to inform the design of CyCOS

news stories, regional initiatives, relevant research findings, domain developments etc.) and remind inactive members to engage within their groups.

In addition to the role of providers and SMEs, equal thought was paid in discussions to the role of the community itself, which is to facilitate cyber security discussions with an aim to improve SMEs' baseline hygiene and resilience. CyCOS is designed to enable discussions to achieve stated aims but is not a creator of advice. Instead, the communities can act as a channel to promote existing good practice, such as the guidance offered by National Cyber Security Centre. As an enabler, it provides a platform through which different voices within the community are sources of advice to varying degrees i.e. CyCOS team members facilitating workshops and events with recognized professionals from partners, independent providers within the communities acting as volunteers, and the SMEs themselves through sharing information and their experiences.

Finally, discussions highlighted 'outreach activities' as foundational work to create successful communities. A main aspect of this outreach is through affiliated partners. Leveraging existing partnerships were believed to improve recognition of an initiative and stimulate participation from target groups. CyCOS aims to utilize relevant partnerships and its affiliations with regional bodies and those who operate in specific sectors to initially promote its emergence. Outreach activities can also assist in gaining initial momentum and traction to engage relevant SME audiences in the first instance. CyCOS has initially leveraged public expositions and existing partners to organize the delivery of the first piloting communities. Once pilots commence, CyCOS team members are designed to play an assistive role to further this aspect through propositioning community discussions and scheduling period emails.

Based on extant literature, findings from our overarching project's research studies and insights gained from discussions with various stakeholders, Fig. 2 inspired from [20, 21] below, depicts the principles underpinning communities of support. Members are able to operate with feelings of safety and trust within the designated community, and the overarching expectation is that community knowledge is greater than individual knowledge.

Fig. 2. Underpinning principles used to design CyCOS

Communities have three main features which are dynamic and responsive to each other i.e. they exhibit authentic tasks and communications, there is a varying level of expertise within the community, and there is implicit progression in learning amongst members. Varying level of expertise available to support tasks and communications within communities will provide support (technical and emotional) to improve self-efficacy amongst members. This is supplemented by CyCOS team members' efforts (discussed above). For instance, members requesting assistance or reading about others' experience might subsequently improve their self-belief and confidence in their own abilities. Communications in virtual and physical settings with peer-to-peer groups and providers will implicitly contribute to members' knowledge and learnings. This can potentially be demonstrated via analytical tools for the Support Broker to reflect ill-structured problems, collaboration and engagement between members, and posts that provide feedback to proposed solutions. Similarly, a varying level of expertise within a community can potentially allow members at varying knowledge levels and with individual forms of learning to improve their cyber security understandings. This understanding, knowledge and awareness can reduce uncertainty experienced by SMEs when they are trying to improve their cyber hygiene or resilience. At any given point, for the community to function effectively, the overall knowledge within the group must be larger than that held by one individual within the same group to facilitate equal learning opportunities and interactions.

Since cyber security domain contains sensitive data and SMEs sharing specific organizational challenges can risk exposure, communities must be safe and deemed trustworthy by its members. To instill safety and trust amongst members (i.e. people are who they say they are and are presenting their skills accurately), the CyCOS team members will perform initial manual checks via public domains prior to admitting members and verify user accounts via automated emails through the Support Broker. Members will not be able to change key information such as their names or email IDs after the verification check is complete. Data documenting user activity will also be securely held as part of back-ups to keep activity logs in case information is removed from the Support Broker.

In keeping with earlier findings, face-to-face events will also be periodically facilitated by CyCOS team members to promote strong rapport amongst community members and foster trust. The Support Broker platform supporting the virtual aspects of the communities is enabled by the Internet.

5 Support Broker Platform

One of the key foundations for the communities is the creation of an online Support Broker, enabling the SMEs to identify support needs and contact advisory sources positioned to help them (which, as the community develops and grows in experience, may include peer support from other SMEs). The Support Broker is an online platform enabling SMEs to submit support requests and other members to provide responses (ranging from direct advice to facilitating linkage to specialized support).

The original plan was for the project to develop a fully bespoke tool that would enable access to online support, and some initial exploratory work was undertaken in this direction. However, it was realised that the development effort required would outweigh the likely benefits when compared to using an existing online forum and discussion platforms. A bespoke tool would require ongoing maintenance that would then require commitment and support beyond the initial funded period of the project, whereas the selection of a suitable third-party platform would ensure this happened naturally, and there would be a wider community of platform users to help encourage longevity of support.

The resulting Support Broker is based on the open-source community building and discussion platform, Discourse, shown in Fig. 3 below.

There will be two primary user groups initially to start the communities (i.e. SMEs and Providers) with an option to create more user groups later on. Sign-ups to the community will be by invitation only. CyCOS team members will initially act as the administrators and moderators of the platform. They will designate users to their correct group and give them the appropriate role-based permissions and tags, e.g. SME or Provider. Upon signing up users will be directed to the CyCOS welcome message, a general introduction on how to navigate the forum, and the community's code of conduct.

The Support Broker, enabled via Discourse platform, will be segmented – potentially into at least three environments –with groupings based on distinct and potentially collegial features such as location, sector, SME size, SME maturity and supply-chain. These decisions will be determined by users at the time of sign-up as discussed earlier. Each of these groups informing their respective community will be architecturally identical with an announcement category (for the CyCOS team members), security news, general discussions and support. As pilots progress, new features to support community activities and engagement can be added. SMEs will be able to raise topics of interest or respond to an existing discussion. Providers, who are professional cyber security experts, can then share relevant advice or ask SME users for further information. This can help foster a

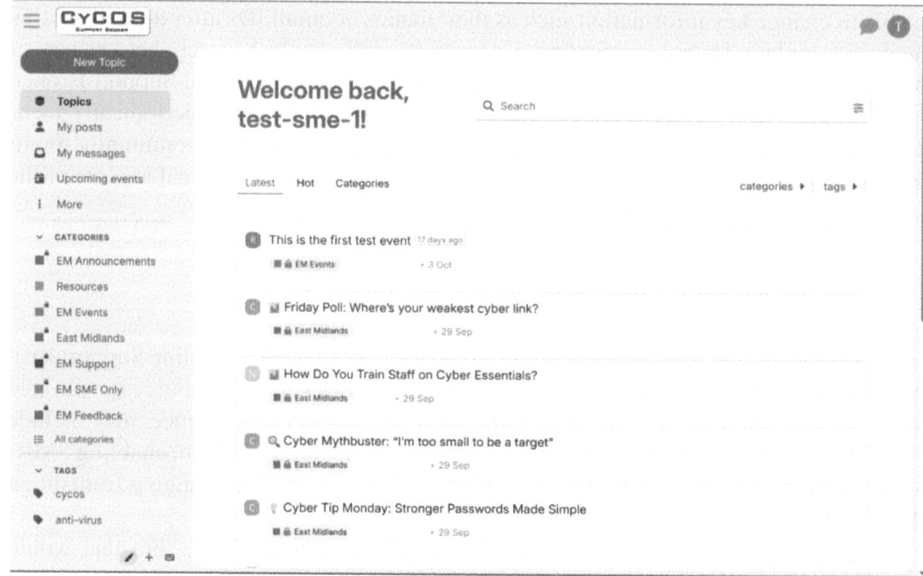

Fig. 3. An image of the Support Broker as viewed by a participant within a community

gradual building of SMEs' cyber security capability. For the experts the platform will offer networking opportunities within focussed communities.

SME users will be able to interact with and access targeted expertise within their community of support. They will also have the ability to provide peer-to-peer support to others. For example, if they are in a regional community they will be able share local threat intelligence and discuss their region's infrastructure. In an industry-focused community, they will be able to discuss sector-specific cyber security challenge and regulatory and compliance issues. For a supply-chain community, discussions can involve vendor-client cyber security requirements or risk assessments.

The Support Broker platform is designed to be a scalable model and will be able to support multiple community types. These community types can become self-sustaining communities of support with minimal oversight needed in line with the earlier discussion about autonomous, self-regulating communities to achieve successful outcomes. There is also a Data Explorer module which will allow team members to make custom SQL queries against the live database. At the same time, it should be noted that the Support Broker, and indeed the wider community approach, will give participants control over what level of information they share and to whom it is available, in order to respect the business sensitivity that may be linked to some support requirements.

6 Evaluation of the Communities

As discussed in Sects. 4 and 5 above, the communities are designed to be in a hybrid format which utilises in-person engagements as well as online interactions facilitated by the Support Broker. To analyse and reflect on the pilots' delivery, data will be collected and evaluated to support conclusions.

Various metrics will be captured from in-person events metrics such as, attendance, qualitative feedback, and audience participation. Additionally, through self-assessment forms participants will be asked to share their experiences at three specific points: 1) Prior to the commencing of pilots, 2) at the midway point and, 3) at the end of pilots. Feedback forms will contain qualitative and quantitative questions which seek to capture their motivations for being part these communities, any perceived benefits or challenges they have encountered, change in their cyber security knowledge, and perceived variance in organisational security levels. These qualitative self-assessment forms can provide impact generated from these designed communities and offer insights to potential challenges for them to be autonomous and self-regulated when being scaled up.

Additionally, during pilots CyCOS team members will be able to collect analytical data from the Support Broker. These data points can include a range of activity related metrics such as, topics discussed by users, views to a post, likes, replies etcetera. This quantitative dataset can provide further evidence of engagement amongst participants when seeking support to improve their security or resilience and provide insights to responsiveness amongst the community when SMEs endeavour to do so.

7 Conclusions and Future Plans

The next stage of the work is to test the community approach in practice, via a series of pilot groups, with the aim of running at least three communities and monitoring their operation for a period of at least three months. While addressing SMEs in general, the research is particularly interested in small and micro firms, where there is greatest likelihood of needing additional support combined with the least potential to have the resources to enable security to be outsourced.

During the operational period, communities are expected to interact largely via online communications, including the use of the Support Broker to enable and maintain activity. The project team will maintain oversight and engage as necessary throughout the period, including initially providing the role of community moderators as needed. It is anticipated that one of the key findings from the pilots will be to expose the challenges around achieving initial and sustained engagement from the community members.

The conduct of the community pilots will lead to analysis and reflection, considering both the operational metrics (e.g. queries submitted and resolved) and participants' feedback on their pilot experience (captured during reflection meetings). Both aspects will feed into an evaluation of the pilots, and the refinement and finalization of the operational guidance to support the establishment, operation and sustainability of such communities beyond. As part of future plans for the communities to be autonomous and self-regulating, providers and SME users will be enabled to act as leaders and champions of the Support Broker platform. This can include aspects such as members being selected to perform administrator or moderator roles within their respective communities or members contributing nominal monetary amounts to sustain the operational costs such as those associated to the broker. It is hoped that this will inform the potential for wider uptake of the Community of Support concept, providing a replicable model with applicability beyond the initial UK context.

Acknowledgments. The research is conducted as part of the project 'Enhancing Cyber Resilience of Small and Medium-sized Enterprises through Cyber Security Communities of Support', funded by the Engineering and Physical Sciences Research Council (grant reference EP/X037282/1) and linked to the Research Institute for Sociotechnical Cyber Security.

Disclosure of Interests. The authors have no competing interests to declare that are relevant to the content of this article.

References

1. DSIT: Cyber Security Breaches Survey 2025. Department for Science, Innovation and Technology, 10 April 2025 (2025). https://www.gov.uk/government/statistics/cyber-security-breaches-survey-2025/cyber-security-breaches-survey-2025
2. OECD: SMEs and entrepreneurship. Organisation for Economic Co-operation and Development (2022). https://www.oecd.org/en/topics/policy-issues/smes-and-entrepreneurship.html. Accessed 24 Aug 2025
3. FSB: UK Small Business Statistics. National Federation of Self Employed & Small Businesses Limited (2025). https://www.fsb.org.uk/media-centre/uk-small-business-statistics
4. NHS Homepage. https://www.england.nhs.uk/2024/06/synnovis-cyber-attack-statement-from-nhs-england/. Accessed 27 Aug 2025
5. Transport for London Homepage. https://tfl.gov.uk/fares/free-and-discounted-travel/cyber-security-incident. Accessed 27 Aug 2025
6. Koshnaw, B., Furnell, S.: Assessing cyber security consumer support from technology retailers. Comput. Fraud Secur. (2022). https://doi.org/10.12968/S1361-3723(22)70560-X
7. Khan, N., Furnell, S., Bada, M., Nurse, J.R.C., Rand, M.: Assessing cyber security support for small and medium-sized enterprises. In: Clarke, N., Furnell, S. (eds.) HAISA 2024. IFIPAICT, vol. 721, pp. 148–162. Springer, Cham (2025). https://doi.org/10.1007/978-3-031-72559-3_11
8. Khan, N., Furnell, S., Bada, M., Nurse, J.R.C., Rand, M.: The hidden barriers to cyber security adoption amongst small and medium-sized enterprises. Inf. Comput. Secur. (2025)
9. Khan, N., Furnell, S., Bada, M., Rand, M., Nurse, J.R.C.: Investigating the experiences of providing cyber security support to small-and medium-sized enterprises. Comput. Secur. **154**, 104448 (2025)
10. Arroyabe, M.F., Arranz, C.F., De Arroyabe, I.F., de Arroyabe, J.C.F.: Exploring the economic role of cybersecurity in SMEs: a case study of the UK. Technol. Soc. **78**, 102670 (2024)
11. Osborn, E., Simpson, A.: Risk and the small-scale cyber security decision making dialogue—a UK case study. Comput. J. **61**(4), 472–495 (2018)
12. Lewis, R., Louvieris, P., Abbott, P., Clewley, N., Jones, K.: Cybersecurity information sharing: a framework for information security management in UK SME supply chains (2014)
13. Cartwright, A., Cartwright, E., Edun, E.S.: Cascading information on best practice: cyber security risk management in UK micro and small businesses and the role of IT companies. Comput. Secur. **131**, 103288 (2023)
14. Mbanaso, U.M., Makinde, J.A., Kulugh, V.E.: A methodological approach for characterisation of critical national infrastructure. Int. J. Crit. Infrastruct. **19**(2), 172–197 (2023)
15. Pemmasani, P.K.: National cybersecurity frameworks for critical infrastructure: lessons from governmental cyber resilience initiatives. Int. J. Acta Informatica **2**(1), 209–218 (2023)
16. Topping, C., Dwyer, A., Michalec, O., Craggs, B., Rashid, A.: Beware suppliers bearing gifts!: Analysing coverage of supply chain cyber security in critical national infrastructure sectorial and cross-sectorial frameworks. Comput. Secur. **108**, 102324 (2021)

17. Melnyk, S.A., Schoenherr, T., Verter, V., Evans, C., Shanley, C.: The pandemic and SME supply chains: Learning from early experiences of SME suppliers in the US defense industry. J. Purch. Supply Manag. **27**(4), 100714 (2021)
18. Quigley, K.: "Man plans, God laughs": Canada's national strategy for protecting critical infrastructure. Can. Public Adm. **56**(1), 142–164 (2013)
19. Obokoh, L.O., Goldman, G.: Infrastructure deficiency and the performance of small-and medium-sized enterprises in Nigeria's liberalised economy. Acta Commercii **16**(1), 1–10 (2016)
20. Johnson, C.M.: A survey of current research on online communities of practice. Internet High. Educ. **4**(1), 45–60 (2001)
21. Schou, P.K., Adarkwah, G.K.: Digital communities of inquiry: how online communities support entrepreneurial opportunity development. J. Small Bus. Manag. **62**(5), 2364–2395 (2024)
22. Fiedler, M., Sarstedt, M.: Influence of community design on user behaviors in online communities. J. Bus. Res. **67**(11), 2258–2268 (2014)
23. NCSC: Small Business Guide: Cyber Security, National Cyber Security Centre, 15 November 2018 (2018). https://www.ncsc.gov.uk/collection/small-business-guide. Accessed 24 Aug 2025
24. Government Commercial Function: Supplementary information: Small and Medium-sized Enterprises definition, 11 April 2025 (2023). https://www.gov.uk/government/publications/procurement-act-2023-short-guides/supplementary-information-small-and-medium-sized-enterprises-definition-html. Accessed 24 Aug 2025
25. DSIT: "McPartland review of cyber security and economic growth", Department for Science, Innovation and Technology, 6 February 2024 (2024). https://www.gov.uk/government/publications/mcpartland-review-of-cyber-security-and-economic-growth. Accessed 24 Aug 2025
26. Companies House. https://www.gov.uk/government/organisations/companies-house/about. Crown copyright
27. National Cyber Security Centre Homepage. https://www.ncsc.gov.uk/section/exercise-in-a-box/. Accessed 27 Aug 2025
28. ISC2 Homepage. https://www.isc2.org/certifications/cc. Accessed 27 Aug 2025
29. Lau, F.: A review on the use of action research in information systems studies. In: Lee, A.S., Liebenau, J., DeGross, J.I. (eds.) Information Systems and Qualitative Research. IFIPAICT, pp. 31–68. Springer, Boston (1997). https://doi.org/10.1007/978-0-387-35309-8_4
30. Mansell, R.E., Silverstone, R.: Communication by Design, pp. 15–43. Oxford University Press, Oxford (1996)
31. Flyvbjerg, B.: Making Social Science Matter: Why Social Inquiry Fails and How it Can Succeed Again. Cambridge University Press, Cambridge (2001)

Vehicles

Towards a Holistic and Multi-modal Vehicle Security Monitoring

Ali Recai Yekta[1](✉), Dominik Spychalski[2], Cenk Yekta[1], Markus Heinrich[2], Christoph Krauß[2], and Stefan Katzenbeisser[3]

[1] Yekta IT GmbH, Ruhrallee 9, 44139 Dortmund, Germany
{ali,cenk}@yekta-it.de
[2] INCYDE GmbH, Unter den Linden 21, 10117 Berlin, Germany
{dominik.spychalski,markus.heinrich,christoph.krauss}@incyde.com
[3] Chair of Computer Engineering, University of Passau, Passau, Germany
stefan.katzenbeisser@uni-passau.de

Abstract. As connectivity increases in automotive and rail transport, operators need comprehensive security monitoring solutions. This paper presents a multi modal Vehicle Security Operations Center architecture that covers automotive and rail systems across vendors and integrates the VATT&EK framework for standardized attack classification. It implements a five step data processing model from raw data collection through Electronic Control Unit and domain monitoring to vehicle and fleet specific analysis. The model uses intelligent sensors, a Vehicle Security Event Center and a central VSOC. New cross vendor security event and alert formats extend existing AUTOSAR standards with forensic fields such as rule_id, severity and confidence to enable GDPR compliant resource and data efficient monitoring. Scenario-based evaluations demonstrate that the architecture meets defined VSOC requirements. The solution provides a scalable foundation for future autonomous transport applications.

Keywords: Vehicle Security Operations Center · VSOC · Automotive VSOC · Rail VSOC · Security Monitoring

1 Introduction and Related Work

Rapid digitalization and connectivity offer significant efficiency gains in road and rail transport but also greatly amplify cybersecurity risks. Notable examples include Miller & Valasek's remote compromise of a Jeep Cherokee via its Uconnect telematics system [16] and security vulnerabilities in Polish Electric Multiple Units (EMUs) [19]. These cases illustrate the critical need for robust, specialized security-monitoring solutions.

Vehicle architectures in the automotive and rail sectors have evolved from purely mechanical designs to software-defined, distributed systems. The automotive industry, for instance, transitioned through basic electronics in the 1970s, digital control via Electronic Control Unit (ECU) in the 1980s, and

E. Bergström et al. (Eds.): CRITIS 2025, LNCS 16291, pp. 143–162, 2026.
https://doi.org/10.1007/978-3-032-19540-1_8

standardized infrastructures enabled by Automotive Open System Architecture (AUTOSAR) from 2003 onwards. Current automotive trends highlight software-defined, Service-oriented architecture (SOA) with cloud integration. Rail systems have followed a parallel path, adopting distributed control systems and increasingly embracing IP-based protocols, reflecting developments in the automotive domain.

Despite regulatory efforts such as UN R155 [17], UN R156 [18], and ISO/SAE 21434, cybersecurity frameworks in the transportation sector remain fragmented and domain-specific. AUTOSAR standardizes Intrusion Detection System (IDS) within automotive vehicles [2–5], yet integration into backend platforms like Vehicle Security Operations Center (VSOC) remains largely undefined.

Vehicle networks have grown more sophisticated over time: from Controller Area Network (CAN) in cars and Multifunction Vehicle Bus (MVB) in trains to Ethernet-based systems with protocols such as Scalable Service-Oriented Middleware over IP (SOME/IP) and Train Real Time Data Protocol (TRDP), alongside SOA approaches [21]. This evolution brings common challenges across both industries, including managing cybersecurity under Operational Technology (OT) constraints (limited bandwidth, intermittent connectivity) and the lack of unified monitoring across multi-vendor fleets.

1.1 Background

This section contrasts traditional Security Operations Center (SOC) with VSOCs, briefly reviews existing standards, introduces the VATT&EK [25] framework.

IDS: Intrusion detection in vehicles has been intensively studied, with a primary focus on CAN-based communication. Surveys include [1,14,22,26], and numerous machine learning approaches have been proposed [6,7,13,15]. Other techniques exploit clock skews [9] or physical signal properties such as voltage levels [10].

Traditional SOC vs. VSOC: A classic SOC monitors IT infrastructure servers, clients via IDS and SIEM, allowing infected machines to be isolated. A VSOC, by contrast, oversees vehicle fleets. It must handle automotive and rail protocols (CAN, Unified Diagnostic Services (UDS), MVB, TRDP) and proprietary vendor protocols. While cloud backends can scale arbitrarily, in-vehicle ECUs impose real-time and resource constraints, and cannot be quarantined. Requirements for a VSOC appear in Sect. 2. Recent work has analyzed these operational differences [11,12].

AUTOSAR IDS and Standardization Gap: AUTOSAR defines the Intrusion Detection System Manager (IdsM) and event formats: Security Event (SEv) and Qualified Security Event (QSEv)). Detected anomalies are reported as QSEv, enabling cross-manufacturer monitoring. Rail vehicles, however, lack comparable standardization.

VATT&EK Framework. Vehicle Adversarial Tactics, Techniques, and Expert Knowledge (VATT&EK) [25] adapts MITRE ATT&CK to the transport domain, formalizing attack techniques across 14 tactic classes, ranging from function manipulation and CAN injection to GNSS spoofing, to support structured threat analysis.

Research and Technology Gaps. Despite AUTOSAR formats, comprehensive solutions that combine real-time processing, hierarchical data handling, and cross-fleet analysis are scarce. Existing SEv/QSEv lack forensic fields (rule IDs, severity, confidence). The railway domain remains underserved. Our multi-modal VSOC architecture fills these gaps with enhanced formats and domain-specific smart sensors.

1.2 Contributions

We make four key contributions:

- **Multi-Modal VSOC Architecture**: We present a unified monitoring architecture for automotive and rail fleets that uses standardized and adaptable components.
- **Hierarchical Data-Processing Framework**: We introduce a five-level structure that transforms raw sensor data into actionable insights by progressively aggregating information from individual bits to ECU level, then to domain, vehicle, and finally fleet level.
- **Security Event Center (SEC) Design**: We propose a vehicle-level analysis node that balances local response capabilities with fleet-wide situational awareness.
- **Enhanced Security Event Formats**: We extend the SEv and QSEv formats with rule identifiers, severity levels, and confidence scores to improve forensic readiness, and introduce new event formats specifically designed for rail transport.

1.3 Paper Organization

The remainder of this paper is organized as follows. Section 2 presents our systematic requirements analysis. Section 3 details the proposed VSOC architecture and hierarchical processing framework. Section 4 presents the security event formats. Section 5 evaluates the architecture through scenario-based analyses. Section 6 discusses limitations and future work.

2 System Model and Requirements

In our approach to requirements engineering for Vehicle Security Monitoring (VSM) in the automotive and rail sectors, we began with a systematic review of scientific and non-scientific literature to understand the current state of VSM and to derive appropriate requirements. In [20] the authors conducted a bibliographic survey and systematic literature review to understand the requirements engineering context for autonomous vehicles. We also engaged with different stakeholders like Original Equipment Manufacturers (OEMs), operators, and suppliers to gather industry specific insights.

2.1 Definition of Multi-modal and Holistic VSM

Our multi-modal approach addresses common security challenges across automotive and railway domains, including protocol modernization (e.g., CAN to Automotive Ethernet/SOME/IP, MVB to TRDP/Ethernet-based systems), security under OT constraints, and the lack of standardized cross-vendor monitoring approaches. Instead of isolated domain-specific solutions, we propose unified design principles adaptable to different transportation contexts.

Multi-modal refers to standardized architectural patterns applicable to various domains (automotive and railway), enabling hierarchical data processing, standardized event formats, and distributed correlation. Our architecture is designed to be adaptable by automotive OEMs, railway operators, and integrated multi-modal transport providers.

Our holistic approach integrates diverse data sources (in-vehicle sensors, vehicle-level correlation, fleet-wide analytics) into actionable security insights. This systematic hierarchical approach ensures robust, scalable, and adaptable security monitoring, addressing bandwidth limitations, intermittent connectivity, and real-time requirements.

2.2 Requirements

Based on the insights gathered in requirements engineering, we categorized the requirements into the following classes: *(I) Vehicle Safety:* Ensuring that the VSM system does not negatively impact the safety of the vehicle. *(II) Vehicle Security:* Ensuring that the VSM system does not adversely affect deployed security solutions. *(III) VSM Security:* Defining security requirements specific to the VSM system itself. *(IV) Privacy and Data Protection:* Addressing concerns related to data privacy and ensuring compliance with data protection regulations. *(V) Operational and Financial:* Considering the operational feasibility and financial constraints of implementing the VSM system. *(VI) VSM Functional:* Defining the core functionalities that the VSM system should offer.

Vehicle Safety (I)

I_1 The vehicles safety and its safety-relevant components must not be at risk at any time. This also includes no loss of safety relevant data and no effect on the performance of these systems.

I_2 False positive alerts shall be minimized to prevent safety-compromising incident response actions and driver behavior.

Vehicle Security (II)

II_1 The Vehicle Security Monitoring (VSM) must not impair the effectiveness of other security functions at any time.

VSM Security (III)

III_1 *Resilience:* The VSM System should be resilient to attacks, including those specifically designed to disable or mislead it.

- $III_{1,1}$ *Event Data Security:* Since event data is the foundation of attack detection, its integrity and authenticity has to be ensured end-to-end.
- $III_{1,2}$ *Event Data Freshness:* The IDS must ensure the timeliness of event data to prevent replay attacks or outdated information being used in decision-making. This also implies protocols for time synchronisation between the different VSM components within the same system boundaries. This is necessary to prevent time drifts or attacks on time synchronisation and thus SEv correlation.
- $III_{1,3}$ *Component Authentication:* All VSM components must authenticate each other before exchanging data to prevent spoofing or Man-in-the-Middle (MitM) attacks.
- $III_{1,4}$ *Secure Attack Detection:* The VSM should be capable of reliably detecting attacks without being susceptible to evasion or Denial of Service (DoS) attacks. This requires robust detection algorithms, regular updates to these algorithms to keep up with emerging threats, and protective measures to ensure the VSM itself is resistent against attacks. The VSM should also be designed to function even under partial failure, limiting the impact of an attack on a single component.

III_2 *State Coupling:* VSM can not be shut down or switched in maintenance state while vehicle in operational state.

III_3 *Auditability:* The VSM should maintain logs of security-relevant events in a secure and tamper-proof manner, to facilitate later analysis and forensic investigation. The logs should be regularly audited for signs of potential security incidents.

Privacy and Data Protection (IV)

IV_1 No transmission of private data and Personally Identifiable Information (PII) to other systems without permission.

IV_2 The system must not track passengers or the driver.

IV_3 When PII is processed, the processing must be based on the key principles of §5 General Data Protection Regulation (GDPR):

- $IV_{3,1}$ *Lawfulness, fairness and transparency:* PII must be processed lawfully, fairly, and in a transparent manner concerning the data subject. This means the VSM must have a legitimate reason to process the data and must be open with the data subject about how their data is used.

$IV_{3,2}$ *Purpose limitation:* PII should be collected for specific, explicit, and legitimate purposes, and not further processed in a way that is incompatible with those purposes.

$IV_{3,3}$ *Data minimisation:* The VSM should only collect and process PII that is adequate, relevant, and limited to what is necessary for the intended purpose.

$IV_{3,4}$ *Accuracy:* PII must be accurate and, where necessary, kept up to date. The VSM must take reasonable steps to ensure that inaccurate or outdated data is erased or rectified without delay.

$IV_{3,5}$ *Storage limitation:* PII should be kept in a form that permits identification of data subjects for no longer than it is necessary for the purposes for which the data was collected. The VSM should securely delete or anonymize PII when it is no longer needed.

$IV_{3,6}$ *Integrity and confidentiality:* The VSM must process PII in a manner that ensures its security, including protection against unauthorized or unlawful processing, accidental loss, destruction, or damage

$IV_{3,7}$ *Accountability:* The VSM must be able to demonstrate compliance with the GDPR principles, taking responsibility for their data processing activities and implementing measures to ensure adherence to the regulation.

Operational and Financial (V)

V_2 *Connectivity & Data Economy:* Due to the characteristics of vehicle operation, there are fluctuations in their connectivity. While maintaining connectivity, the IDS should be designed to minimize the data it transmits. Especially for vehicles relying on cellular data for connectivity, there can be significant costs associated with transmitting data. An IDS must balance the need for connectivity with the need to minimize data transmission costs.

V_3 *Resource limitation:* Unlike common servers in enterprise Information Technology (IT), vehicle systems are subject to significant resource constraints. They can have limited processing power, memory, and battery life, all of which can limit the amount of connectivity and computation complexity they can maintain.

VSM Functional (VI)

VI_1 *Integrability:* The VSM System should be fully integrable in a sufficiently digitized vehicle's existing systems/architecture and should not interfere with normal vehicle operations.

VI_2 *Updating and Scalability:* The VSM System should be capable of receiving updates to its software, threat detection algorithms, and rule sets to cope with evolving threats. It should also be scalable to accommodate the growing complexity of vehicle systems.

VI_3 *Network visibility:* The IDS should be capable of monitoring all network traffic within the vehicle, across different bus systems like CAN and LIN or Ethernet. It should also monitor any external communication interfaces such as V2V, V2I, or connectivity to mobile devices.

VI_4 *Continuous monitoring:* The VSM System should provide continuous monitoring to rapidly detect and respond to potential security threats.

VI_5 *Anomaly detection & Intrusion detection:* The IDS should be capable of detecting deviations from normal vehicle operation, which could signify potential attacks or intrusion. Furthermore, the system should be capable of detecting specific already known attack patterns. Additionally, the system should be designed to detect techniques from the VATT&EK framework, enabling structured categorization of identified threats according to standardized tactics and techniques.

VI_6 *Low false-positive and false-negative rate:* To effectively safeguard against cyber threats, Vehicle Intrusion Detection System (VIDS) have to keep their false-{positive,negative} rates low. A low false-negative rate ensures the IDS captures and reports the maximum number of threats, enhancing the VSM protective capabilities. A low false-positive rate minimizes unnecessary alerts to obtain operational efficiency

VI_7 *Reporting and Alerting:* In the event of a potential security threat, the system should generate detailed reports and alerts to notify relevant stakeholders, such as the driver, vehicle manufacturer, or fleet operator.

VI_8 *Rapid response:* The VSM System should be capable of triggering appropriate responses upon detection of potential threats. This could range from simple notifications to more active or complex responses like isolating affected systems.

VI_9 *Manageability:* The VSM should provide interfaces for administrators to configure the system, monitor its status, and respond to security incidents. This interfaces should be secured and should provide all necessary functionality in a user-friendly manner.

3 System Architecture and Data Hierarchy

3.1 Hierarchical Architecture

Our VSOC architecture adopts a five-level hierarchical structure based on the DIKW framework, systematically converting raw sensor data into actionable fleet-level security insights. Figure 1 illustrates this data processing pipeline with standardized components adaptable to automotive and railway contexts.

The hierarchy consists of five clearly defined levels:

- **Level 0 (Bits)** represents raw computational and communication activities on ECUs without direct security monitoring.
- **Level 1 (ECU)** implements host-based intrusion detection on individual ECUs, detecting anomalous behavior at the component level.

- **Level 2 (Domain)** provides network-based intrusion detection for specific vehicle domains, parsing protocols and identifying suspicious traffic patterns.
- **Level 3 (Vehicle/SEC)** aggregates and correlates ECU and domain-specific events in a vehicle-level Security Event Center, enabling immediate local security responses.
- **Level 4 (Fleet/VSOC)** performs cross-vehicle analysis, integrating data from multiple vehicles, OEM backends, and external threat intelligence to support comprehensive incident response and long-term security strategies.

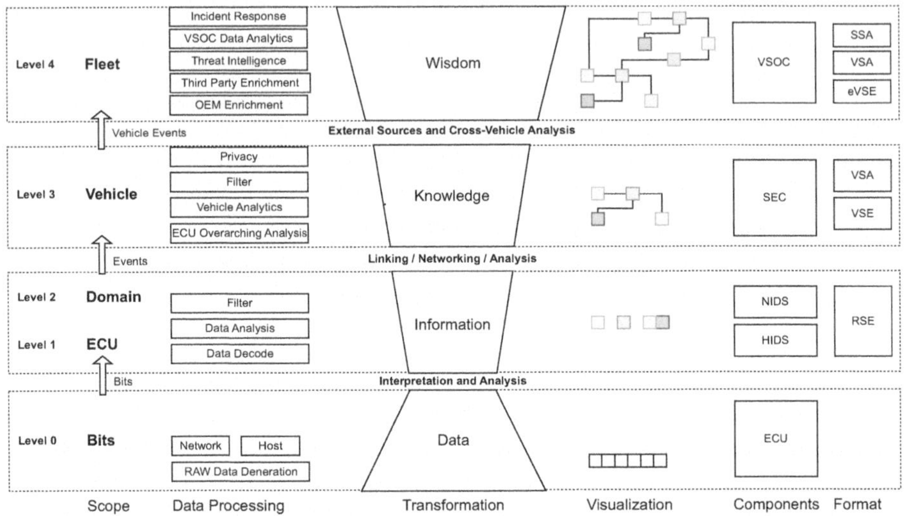

Fig. 1. Hierarchical data processing pipeline across VSOC architecture levels.

3.2 Multi-modal Adaptation

The architecture supports automotive and railway domains through a standardized event processing pipeline (RSE→VSE→eVSE, detailed in Sect. 4). Protocol-agnostic smart sensors capture domain-specific context data, while SEC and VSOC components use unified, configurable analysis logic.

3.3 Key Component Descriptions

Smart Sensors (Levels 1–2). Smart Sensors provide foundational security monitoring by generating Raw Security Events (RSE). As depicted in Fig. 2, these sensors employ hardware-based Trust Anchors for event authenticity and local intelligence to classify and filter security events before forwarding them to the SEC.

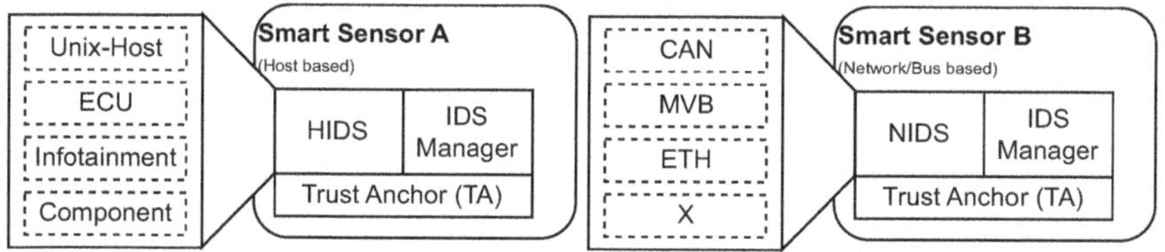

Fig. 2. Smart Sensors secured by hardware-based Trust Anchors.

Security Event Center (SEC Level 3). The SEC acts as a centralized vehicle-level analysis unit, correlating RSEs across ECUs and domains. It ensures real-time responses such as immediate driver notifications and automated defensive actions. The SEC further enriches RSEs into meaningful Vehicle Security Events (VSE) for fleet-wide analysis (see Fig. 3).

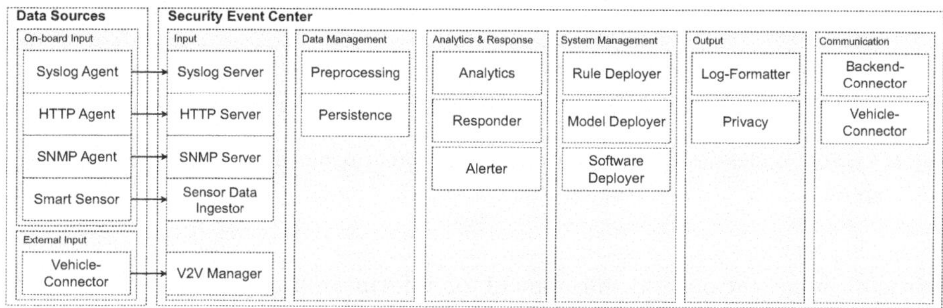

Fig. 3. Functional overview of the SEC architecture.

Vehicle Security Operations Center (VSOC Level 4). The VSOC aggregates and enriches VSEs from multiple vehicles into Enhanced Vehicle Security Events (eVSE). It employs standardized attack classification using the VATT&EK framework to facilitate effective incident response. Integration with SIEM systems, Threat Intelligence Platforms (TIP), and SOAR platforms ensures coordinated, fleet-wide security management (see Fig. 4).

Detailed technical specifications, sensor hardware configurations, precise event format definitions, and additional implementation details are provided in the appendix for clarity and readability.

4 Security Event Formats

To implement the proposed hierarchical architecture, we have defined multiple security event formats that build upon each other and are distinguished by

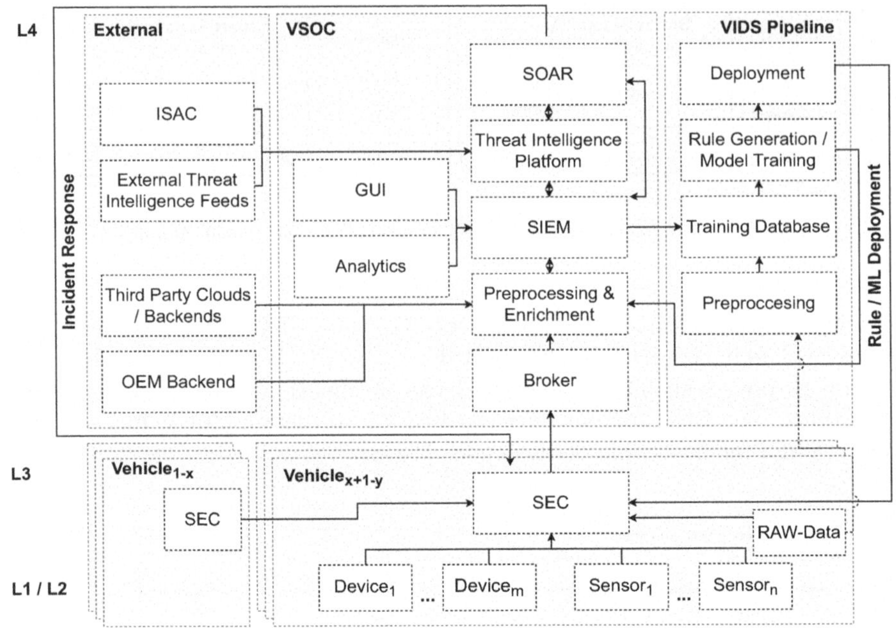

Fig. 4. Overall multi-modal VSOC architecture integrating threat intelligence and incident response.

increasing aggregation and enrichment of information. These formats help to make the data hierarchy from sensors through SEC to VSOC comprehensible, interoperable, and efficient, while providing a systematic approach to security event processing across different transportation domains.

4.1 Raw Security Events (RSE)

Raw Security Events extend the AUTOSAR standard (SEv/QSEv) with additional security relevant fields including `rule_id`, `rule_version`, `severity`, and `context_data_version`.

Context Data Architecture: The format employs a hybrid design separating standardized processing fields from protocol-specific context data, enabling unified correlation while preserving domain expertise. As illustrated in Fig. 5, CAN-based RSE include specific information such as CAN-ID, Data Length Code (DLC), and frame data in the structured context_data field, while railway-specific RSE include MVB-specific identifiers and TRDP context information. This separation enables both protocol-agnostic processing and domain-specific analysis.

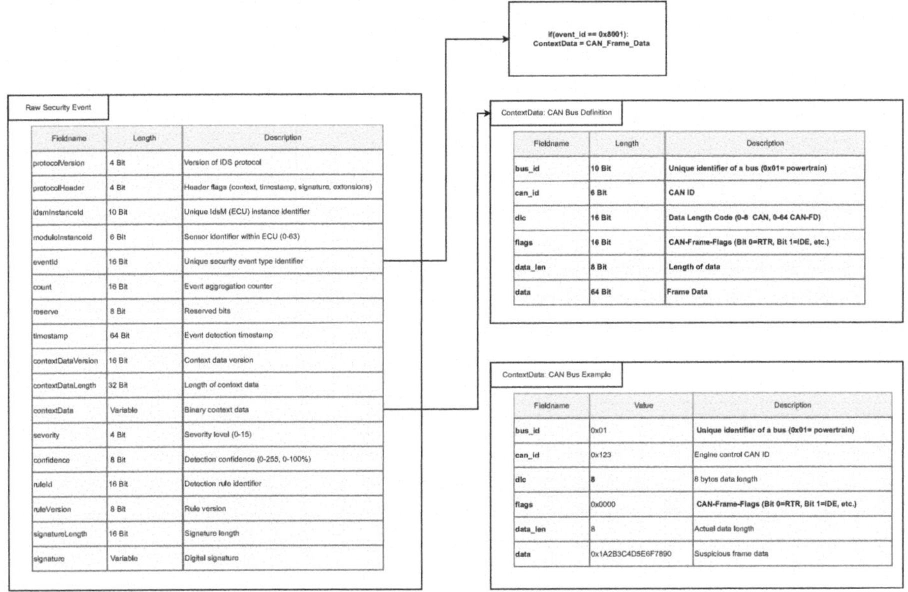

Fig. 5. Raw Security Event with Context Data.

4.2 Vehicle Security Events (VSE) and Enhanced Vehicle Security Events (eVSE)

At the SEC level, aggregation and correlation of RSE creates Vehicle Security Events (VSE). Additional information is incorporated, such as vehicle state data (speed, operational mode) or affected ECU domains. These VSE provide the necessary context for understanding security events within the broader vehicle operational context, whether in automotive or railway environments.

In the VSOC, these VSE are further enriched and converted into Enhanced Vehicle Security Events (eVSE). Comprehensive information is added, including precise assignments to VATT&EK techniques, vehicle variants, OEM-specific data, and external threat intelligence. This enrichment enables more sophisticated analysis and response planning across different transportation modalities.

4.3 Vehicle Security Alerts (VSA) and SOC Security Alerts (SSA)

Aggregated security events are provided in the form of alerts optimized for different response scenarios. Vehicle Security Alerts (VSA) are generated immediately at the vehicle level in the SEC, enabling rapid responses such as driver warnings or automated defensive actions. SOC Security Alerts (SSA) are generated in the VSOC, aggregating events from multiple vehicles or extended time periods to support comprehensive incident response measures and strategic fleet security management across automotive and railway operations (Fig. 6).

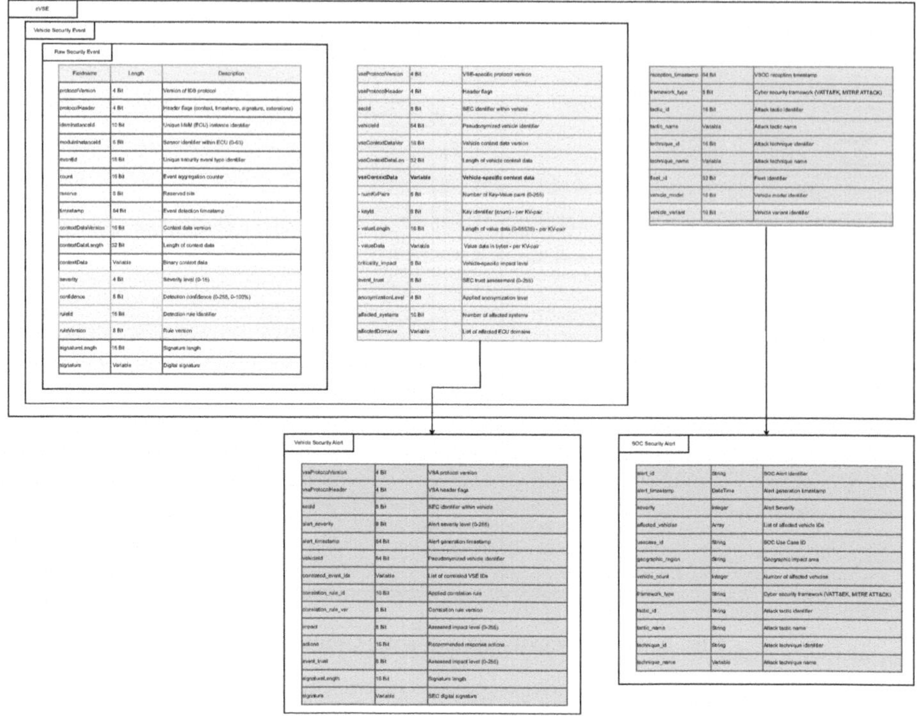

Fig. 6. Advanced Security Alert Formats (VSA/SSA).

5 Evaluation

This section evaluates the proposed multi-layer VSOC architecture against the six requirements defined in Sect. 2.2 and demonstrates its effectiveness through three real-world scenarios:

1. Systematic validation of the requirements (Table 1)
2. Detection flow for the **CAN injection attack** (Sect. 5.1)
3. Detection flow for **MVB message spoofing** (Sect. 5.1)
4. Extended kill-chain analysis illustrated by the **2018 BMW hack** (Sect. 5.2)

By mapping each requirement to specific detection and correlation components within these scenarios, we illustrate the architecture's end-to-end capability for classifying complex attacks.

Table 1 shows how the proposed VSOC architecture addresses the requirements defined in Sect. 2. For each requirement, the corresponding implementation approach is described.

Table 1. Requirement satisfaction overview: Implementation of VSM architecture requirements

Req.	Implementation
	Vehicle Safety (I)
I1	SEC provides information and alerts only, without interfering with safety-critical ECU operations.
I2	Multi-layer verification improves detection accuracy through VSOC's consolidated data foundation. Requires empirical validation.
	Vehicle Security (II)
II1	Smart Sensors, SEC, and VSOC provide an additional security layer complementing existing mechanisms without interference.
	VSM Security (III)
III1	Hierarchical architecture with distributed detection reduces complete system compromise risk through isolated security layers.
III1.1	RSE formats include cryptographic signatures via Hardware Trust Anchors ensuring data integrity and authenticity.
III1.2	Synchronized timestamps between system components prevent replay attacks and ensure event data freshness.
III1.3	Hardware Trust Anchors in Smart Sensors enable mutual authentication between all system components.
III1.4	Distributed Smart Sensors with SEC-level correlation minimize detection blind spots and enable secure attack detection.
III2	SEC is designed to maintain continuous monitoring capabilities during vehicle operation without requiring shutdown.
III3	SEC and VSOC provide tamper-protected event storage, enabling comprehensive forensic analysis and auditability.
	Privacy & Data Protection (IV)
IV1	SEC Privacy Component anonymizes all data before external transmission to VSOC, preventing unauthorized PII transmission.
IV2	Event formats exclusively capture technical security events without including personal tracking data, preventing passenger or driver tracking.
IV3.1	System design supports GDPR-compliant data processing with built-in consent mechanisms, ensuring lawfulness and transparency.
IV3.2	Event data is exclusively used for security monitoring purposes, adhering to the principle of purpose limitation.
IV3.3	Event formats contain only security-relevant data, with hierarchical filtering mechanisms ensuring data minimization.
IV3.4	Automated timestamping and data validation mechanisms ensure the accuracy of all event data.
IV3.5	Architecture supports configurable retention periods with automatic data deletion, implementing storage limitation.
IV3.6	Cryptographic signatures and encrypted transmission throughout the system hierarchy ensure data integrity and confidentiality.
IV3.7	Complete event logging across all system levels enables accountability and GDPR compliance demonstration.

(*continued*)

Table 1. (*continued*)

Req.	Implementation
	Operational & Financial (V)
V1	Multi-level filtering (Smart Sensors, SEC, VSOC) with efficient transmission protocols ensures connectivity and data economy.
V2	Event-driven processing with hierarchical load distribution across system levels addresses resource limitations effectively.
	VSM Functional (VI)
VI1	RSE format extends AUTOSAR SEv/QSEv standards, ensuring backward compatibility and seamless integration with existing systems.
VI2	SEC Rule Deployer and Model Deployer enable remote updates to Smart Sensors, supporting system updating and scalability.
VI3	Smart Sensors support monitoring of CAN, Ethernet, TRDP, MVB, and V2X protocols, providing comprehensive network visibility.
VI4	Continuous monitoring with rapid local detection (seconds); VSOC correlation takes longer for cross-vehicle processing.
VI5	VATT&EK framework integration at VSOC level enables standardized threat classification and anomaly detection.
VI6	Hierarchical correlation with confidence scoring mechanisms is designed to minimize false-positive rates.
VI7	VSA/SSA alert formats provide structured notifications to relevant stakeholders, enabling effective reporting and alerting.
VI8	SEC enables immediate local response capabilities, while VSOC coordinates fleet-wide actions for rapid response.
VI9	SEC management components and VSOC GUI provide comprehensive system administration and management interfaces.

5.1 VATT&EK Scenario Examples

We highlight two representative VATT&EK techniques to illustrate end-to-end detection and response:

CAN Injection Attack - Example Flow. This example demonstrates the hierarchical event processing pipeline using a CAN injection attack scenario. A Smart Sensor detects an impossible speed acceleration (20→100 km/h in 15 ms) on the powertrain bus, indicating malicious frame injection. Table 2 shows the progressive event enrichment across the system hierarchy.

The hierarchical processing enables local detection (RSE), contextual validation (VSE), and fleet-wide threat intelligence correlation (eVSE), demonstrating the system's ability to identify and classify sophisticated attacks.

MVB Message Spoofing Attack - Example Flow. This example demonstrates the hierarchical event processing pipeline using an MVB message spoofing attack on a railway vehicle. A Smart Sensor detects a physically impossible

Table 2. Progressive event enrichment in CAN injection attack scenario

Level	Event Enhancement
RSE	Smart Sensor detects CAN timing anomaly (Rule 0x4A2B): Speed jump from 20 to 100 km/h in 15 ms on bus 0x01, CAN-ID 0x3B4. Severity: 12/15 (High), Confidence: 84%.
VSE	SEC enriches event with vehicle context: VIN (pseudonymized), actual vehicle speed (20 km/h), operational mode (normal driving), engine state (running). Criticality impact: 8/10 (High).
eVSE	VSOC enriches event with VATT&EK classification: Tactic ATA13 (Affect Vehicle Function), Technique ATE14 (Message Injection).

brake pressure jump indicating message injection on the train control bus. Table 3 shows the progressive event enrichment across the system hierarchy.

Table 3. Progressive event enrichment in MVB message spoofing attack scenario

Level	Event Enhancement
RSE	Smart Sensor detects MVB message injection anomaly (Rule 0x5C1A): Physically impossible brake pressure jump on Brake Control Port 0x12. Severity: 14/15 (Critical), Confidence: 96%.
VSE	SEC enriches event with train operational context: Train ID (pseudonymized), current speed (120 km/h), passenger service mode, legitimate brake state (released/0 bar), track section (0x2A4), passenger load (85%). Criticality impact: 10/10 (Critical).
eVSE	VSOC enriches event with VATT&EK classification: Tactic ATA13 (Affect Vehicle Function), Technique ATE14 (Message Injection). Fleet correlation identifies coordinated attack pattern on regional railway fleet (ICE 4 trains) in Munich-Berlin corridor.

The hierarchical processing enables rapid detection of safety-critical attacks on railway brake systems through physical plausibility checks, demonstrating the system's applicability beyond automotive to multi-vehicle transportation domains.

Attack Analysis: The MVB Message Validation Rule detected a physically impossible brake pressure transition (0→8 bar in 256 µs) on the Brake Control Port. This instantaneous value change indicates malicious message injection targeting the critical brake control system while the train was operating at 120 km/h with 85% passenger load. VSOC classification maps this to VATT&EK technique ATE14 (Message Injection) under tactic ATA13 (Affect Vehicle Function), with critical safety implications for high-speed passenger rail operations.

5.2 Detection of 2018 BMW Hack

In [8] the authors demonstrated multiple local and remote attack kill chains to compromise BMW vehicles. In [25] the authors formalized the attack in distinct attack phases suitable for improved attack analysis and thus better attack detection modeling. Due to the variety of attack vectors of modern vehicles a multi-leveled and distributed IDS sensor architecture, like proposed in this work, is needed to detect such more sophisticated attacks. Figure 7 illustrates the architectural subset and systems of the targeted vehicles and the Smart Sensors necessary to detect this attack.

To detect attack vector AV_1 and AV_2 under our paradigm following components are necessary: (1) Host-based Smart Sensor to detect malicious or abnormal behavior on the vehicles most connected Headunit, (2) Ethernet Smart Sensor to detect Ethernet-based discovery activities such as port scans or application level attacks on plain text traffic, (3) CAN Smart Sensor to detect suspicious CAN messages and Unified Diagnostic Services (UDS) commands including unauthorized diagnostic access and message injection attempts(for a comprehensive taxonomy of UDS attacks see [24] and detection strategies in [23]). All relevant L1 data, L2 information, and L3 knowledge is aggregated and further analyzed by the (4) Security Event Center (SEC), before shipping to the (5) VSOC.

Due to our VSM paradigm, the SEC has a sophisticated view on the vehicles architecture, state, and system behaviour. To gain wisdom and thus a more comprehensive view on the security of vehicles, fleets, or a mobility ecosystem, the SEC sends generated alerts and logs to the (5) VSOC for further correlation and analysis.

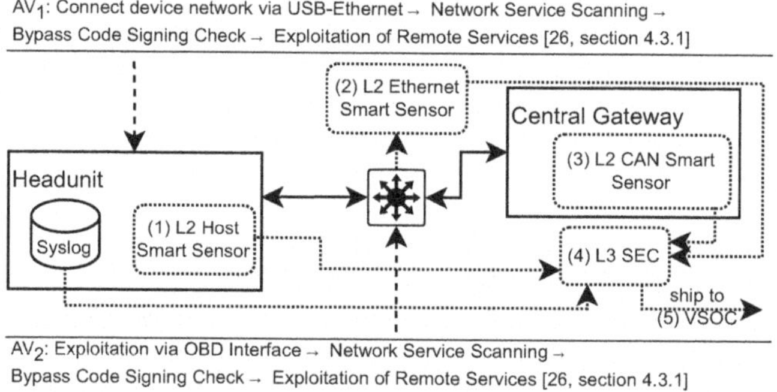

Fig. 7. Local attack chain of 2018 BMW hack [8] via Headunit and OBD-2/USB interface.

6 Discussion

This section discusses the core innovations of our multi-modal VSOC architecture and their practical implications for vehicle security monitoring.

6.1 Extended Security Event Format

Our extended RSE format addresses critical limitations of current AUTOSAR SEv/QSEv by adding essential fields for operational security management. The `rule_id` and `rule_version` fields enable tracking of which detection rules triggered alerts and ensure vehicles use current detection rules. This helps reduce false positives by providing rule context and enables validation of detection rule deployment across fleets.

The `confidence` field enables threshold-based incident response based on detection certainty. Confidence scores reflect sensor detection reliability: signature-based systems provide high confidence for exact matches, while ML-based systems report variable scores. This enables informed correlation and response decisions at SEC and VSOC levels. The `context_data` field captures protocol-specific attack details that current AUTOSAR formats support but railway systems lack entirely.

Beyond RSE extensions, our architecture introduces entirely new event types absent from current AUTOSAR: Vehicle Security Events (VSE), Vehicle Security Alerts (VSA), enhanced Vehicle Security Events (eVSE), and SOC Security Alerts (SSA). These provide concrete proposals for vehicle-level correlation and fleet-wide security management that AUTOSAR currently does not address.

At the VSOC level, `rule_id` enables automated mapping to VATT&EK attack techniques during eVSE enrichment, eliminating manual threat classification by analysts while providing standardized threat categorization across automotive and railway domains.

6.2 Hierarchical Response Architecture for Compromised Vehicles

Smart sensors provide localized detection but lack broader context for coordinated response. Our hierarchical architecture addresses this through specialized capabilities at each level.

SEC enables rapid first response by notifying drivers or operators and correlating events across multiple sensors to assess attack scope. For current vehicles, SEC provides information-only responses maintaining safety independence. For future autonomous vehicles, SEC can implement defensive measures under safety-certified conditions.

VSOC enables fleet-wide coordination including software updates, security policy distribution, and threat intelligence sharing to prevent attack propagation. The architecture also supports recovery: isolated components enable partial operation under compromise, while VSOC coordinates restoration without complete system shutdown.

6.3 Multi-modal Cross-Domain Intelligence

Our unified approach enables unprecedented cross-manufacturer and cross-domain security monitoring. Railway operators can achieve consistent security visibility across heterogeneous fleets from different manufacturers (Siemens,

Alstom, Bombardier), while automotive OEMs can enforce standardized logging requirements throughout their supply chains including diverse Tier 1 and Tier 2 suppliers.

The VATT&EK integration facilitates cross-domain threat intelligence where attack patterns from automotive CAN injection can inform railway MVB manipulation detection, and railway signaling interference patterns enhance automotive V2X security monitoring. This cross-pollination of threat knowledge provides security benefits impossible with domain-isolated approaches.

6.4 SEC Advanced Capabilities Beyond AUTOSAR IDSR

While AUTOSAR defines basic Intrusion Detection System Reporting (IDSR) for event transport, our SEC provides significantly enhanced capabilities beyond simple event forwarding. SEC implements comprehensive sensor management including rule deployment and machine learning model distribution to smart sensors across vehicle domains.

Cross-sensor correlation enables detection of sophisticated attack patterns spanning multiple ECUs and domains, providing threat visibility impossible with isolated sensor monitoring. SEC serves as a central coordination point for security policy enforcement, sensor configuration management, and local threat intelligence processing, representing a substantial advancement over current AUTOSAR IDSR capabilities.

6.5 Implementation Readiness and Evolutionary Deployment

Our architecture supports practical deployment through evolutionary design that respects current operational constraints while enabling future capabilities. The dual-mode SEC operation (information-only for current systems, control-capable for autonomous vehicles) reduces safety certification complexity for initial deployments by minimizing direct interference with safety-critical systems, while providing clear migration paths.

The hierarchical processing approach distributes computational load across sensor, vehicle, and fleet levels, addressing scalability concerns through bandwidth-efficient event filtering and correlation. This design enables deployment while supporting future autonomous vehicle security requirements.

6.6 Limitations and Future Validation

Our evaluation demonstrates architectural feasibility through theoretical analysis but requires empirical validation with real vehicle fleets to prove performance characteristics under operational conditions. The approach addresses network-based and host-based detection but provides limited coverage for sophisticated physical attacks or supply chain compromises at manufacturing level.

Future work should focus on large-scale pilot programs with automotive and railway operators to validate scalability assumptions and advanced correlation algorithms for cross-domain threat detection that can identify subtle attack patterns spanning multiple transportation domains.

Acknowledgments. This research is accomplished within the project "FINESSE" (FKZ 16KIS1584K). We acknowledge the financial support for the project by the Federal Ministry of Research, Technology and Space (BMFTR).

References

1. Al-Jarrah, O.Y., Maple, C., Dianati, M., Oxtoby, D., Mouzakitis, A.: Intrusion detection systems for intra-vehicle networks: a review. IEEE Access **7**, 21266–21289 (2019)
2. AUTOSAR: Requirements on Intrusion Detection System - R22-11. Tech. rep., AUTOSAR (2022). https://www.autosar.org/fileadmin/standards/R22-11/FO/AUTOSAR_RS_IntrusionDetectionSystem.pdf
3. AUTOSAR: Specification of Intrusion Detection System Manager - R22-11. Tech. rep., AUTOSAR (2022). https://www.autosar.org/fileadmin/standards/R22-11/CP/AUTOSAR_SWS_IntrusionDetectionSystemManager.pdf
4. AUTOSAR: Specification of Intrusion Detection System Manager for Adaptive Platform - R22-11. Tech. rep., AUTOSAR (2022). https://www.autosar.org/fileadmin/standards/R22-11/AP/AUTOSAR_SWS_AdaptiveIntrusionDetectionSystemManager.pdf
5. AUTOSAR: Specification of Intrusion Detection System Protocol - R22-11. Tech. rep., AUTOSAR (2022). https://www.autosar.org/fileadmin/standards/R22-11/FO/AUTOSAR_PRS_IntrusionDetectionSystem.pdf
6. Berger, I., Rieke, R., Kolomeets, M., Chechulin, A., Kotenko, I.: Comparative study of machine learning methods for in-vehicle intrusion detection. In: Katsikas, S.K., et al. (eds.) SECPRE/CyberICPS -2018. LNCS, vol. 11387, pp. 85–101. Springer, Cham (2019). https://doi.org/10.1007/978-3-030-12786-2_6
7. Buschlinger, L., Rieke, R., Sarda, S., Krauß, C.: Decision tree-based rule derivation for intrusion detection in safety-critical automotive systems. In: 2022 30th Euromicro International Conference on Parallel, Distributed and Network-based Processing (PDP), pp. 246–254 (2022). https://doi.org/10.1109/PDP55904.2022.00046
8. Cai, Z., Wang, A., Zhang, W., Gruffke, M., Schweppe, H.: 0-days & mitigations: roadways to exploit and secure connected BMW cars. Black Hat USA **2019**(39), 6 (2019)
9. Cho, K.T., Shin, K.G.: Fingerprinting electronic control units for vehicle intrusion detection. In: Proceedings of the 25th USENIX Conference on Security Symposium, SEC'16, pp. 911–927. USENIX Association, USA (2016)
10. Choi, W., Joo, K., Jo, H.J., Park, M.C., Lee, D.H.: VoltageIDS: low-level communication characteristics for automotive intrusion detection system. IEEE Trans. Inf. Forensics Secur. **13**(8), 2114–2129 (2018)
11. Grimm, D., Zink, M., Schindewolf, M., Sax, E.: Cyber situational awareness in vehicle security operations: holistic monitoring and a data model. In: 2024 20th International Conference on Network and Service Management (CNSM), pp. 1–7 (2024). https://doi.org/10.23919/CNSM62983.2024.10814319

12. Hofbauer, J., Gomez Buquerin, K., Hof, H.J.: From SOC to VSOC: transferring key requirements for efficient vehicle security operations (2023). https://doi.org/10.5281/zenodo.10182821
13. Kang, M.J., Kang, J.W.: Intrusion detection system using deep neural network for in-vehicle network security. PLOS ONE **11**(6), 1–17 (2016). https://doi.org/10.1371/journal.pone.0155781
14. Lampe, B., Meng, W.: A survey of deep learning-based intrusion detection in automotive applications. Exp. Syst. Appl. **221**, 119771 (2023). https://doi.org/10.1016/j.eswa.2023.119771
15. Markovitz, M., Wool, A.: Field classification, modeling and anomaly detection in unknown can bus networks. Veh. Commun. **9**, 43–52 (2017). https://doi.org/10.1016/j.vehcom.2017.02.005
16. Miller, C., Valasek, C.: Remote exploitation of an unaltered passenger vehicle. Black Hat USA **2015**(S 91), 1–91 (2015)
17. No, U.R.: 155 [uniform provisions concerning the approval of vehicles with regards to cyber security and cyber security management system] (2021)
18. No, U.R.: 156: Uniform provisions concerning the approval of vehicles with regards to software update and software updates management system (2021)
19. Redford, q3k, MrTick: Breaking "DRM" in Polish trains: Reverse engineering a train to analyze a suspicious malfunction. In: Proceedings of the 37th Chaos Communication Congress (37C3). Hamburg, Germany, December 2023. Recorded session, 61 min. https://media.ccc.de/v/37c3-12142-breaking_drm_in_polish_trains
20. Ribeiro, Q.A.D.S., Castro, J.: Safety & security alignment in requirements engineering process for autonomous vehicles (2022). https://dblp.org/rec/conf/wer/RibeiroC22.html
21. Rumez, M., Grimm, D., Kriesten, R., Sax, E.: An overview of automotive service-oriented architectures and implications for security countermeasures. IEEE Access **8**, 221852–221870 (2020)
22. Wu, W.: A survey of intrusion detection for in-vehicle networks. IEEE Trans. Intell. Transp. Syst. **21**(3), 919–933 (2020)
23. Yekta, A.R., Loza, N., Gramm, J., Schneider, M.P., Katzenbeisser, S.: From ECU to VSOC: UDS security monitoring strategies. In: Proceedings of the Nineteenth International Conference on Emerging Security Information, Systems and Technologies, SECURWARE 2025, pp. 1–6. IARIA (2025)
24. Yekta, A.R., Loza, N., Gramm, J., Schneider, M.P., Katzenbeisser, S.: UDS attack taxonomy: Systematic classification of vehicle diagnostic threats. In: 2025 IEEE Conference on Communications and Network Security (CNS), pp. 1–8. IEEE (2025)
25. Yekta, A.R., Spychalski, D., Yekta, E., Yekta, C., Katzenbeisser, S.: Vatt&ek: formalization of cyber attacks on intelligent transport systems - a TTP based approach for automotive and rail. In: Proceedings of the 7th ACM Computer Science in Cars Symposium, CSCS '23, Association for Computing Machinery, New York, NY, USA (2023). https://doi.org/10.1145/3631204.3631867
26. Young, C., Zambreno, J., Olufowobi, H., Bloom, G.: Survey of automotive controller area network intrusion detection systems. IEEE Des. Test **36**(6), 48–55 (2019)

A Systematic Literature Review on Cybersecurity in Autonomous Vehicles

Issa Morad, Yousef Yako, and Görkem Kılınç Soylu(✉)

Department of Computer Science and Informatics, School of Engineering, Jönköping University, Jönköping, Sweden
{mois19hm,yayo20gt}@student.ju.se, gorkem.kilinc.soylu@ju.se

Abstract. Autonomous vehicles (AVs) rely on interconnected sensing and communication systems to support navigation, coordination, and decision-making. While this connectivity enhances safety and efficiency, it also broadens the attack surface, exposing AVs to cyber threats that can compromise operational reliability. Among these threats, message spoofing, i.e., injection of falsified or manipulated data into in-vehicle or Vehicle-to-Vehicle (V2V) communication channels—poses a critical risk, as it can mislead vehicle perception, disrupt cooperative behavior, and undermine traffic safety. This systematic literature review analyzes studies published between 2015 and 2025, examining spoofing attacks targeting AV communication layers and surveying the full range of detection and mitigation mechanisms proposed in the literature. The review considers both traditional security techniques and emerging artificial intelligence (AI)–driven approaches, assessing how AI is being incorporated alongside conventional methods. Through a structured review process, the study synthesizes attack vectors, defense strategies, and technological trends, highlighting the growing role of AI in enhancing AV resilience. The review aims to consolidate current knowledge and outline key considerations for designing robust, multi-layered cybersecurity frameworks that support the safe integration of autonomous vehicles into connected transportation ecosystems.

Keywords: Autonomous Vehicles (AVs) · Cybersecurity · Vehicle-to-Vehicle (V2V) Communication · Message Spoofing · Artificial Intelligence (AI) · Anomaly Detection · Systematic Literature Review (SLR)

1 Introduction

This systematic literature review analyzes studies published between 2015 and 2025 that address spoofing attacks threatening Connected and Autonomous Vehicles (CAVs) and the corresponding detection and mitigation mechanisms. Rather than focusing on a single communication channel, the review considers spoofing across multiple layers, including V2X/V2V communication, in-vehicle networks (CAN/LIN), GPS-based localization, and perception sensors. Both traditional techniques and emerging artificial intelligence (AI)–driven approaches

E. Bergström et al. (Eds.): CRITIS 2025, LNCS 16291, pp. 163–181, 2026.
https://doi.org/10.1007/978-3-032-19540-1_9

are examined, with AI treated as one category among several rather than as the sole solution.

Cybersecurity in autonomous and connected vehicles is a rapidly evolving field. Attacks such as message spoofing, denial-of-service (DoS), and sensor manipulation pose serious risks to vehicles and road users. Adversaries can exploit vulnerabilities to manipulate behavior, disrupt traffic, or endanger lives [6]. The complexity of CAV systems demands robust security to ensure data integrity, system resilience, and passenger safety; without it, large-scale deployment and public acceptance may be hindered [30].

Even if a vehicle's internal networks are secured, attackers may still target external signals. GPS spoofing attacks, for example, can broadcast counterfeit satellite-like signals to mislead an AV's navigation system. Experimental work has shown that AV trajectories can be diverted or degraded without any compromise of the in-vehicle network itself [1,32]. These risks illustrate that both in-vehicle and environmental attack vectors require attention.

The motivation for this study stems from growing reliance on V2X communication and automation in CAVs. Demonstrations like the Jeep Cherokee hack [19] have exposed the fragility of automotive networks when security is not systematically engineered. Meanwhile, standards such as ISO/SAE 21434 [11,12] stress structured cybersecurity practices but do not specify technical solutions for spoofing. There is a need to consolidate knowledge on spoofing types, impacts, and defenses, including, but not limited to, AI-based methods.

Ensuring that communication and sensing in CAVs is trustworthy is critical to their safe operation. One major threat is message spoofing in V2V/V2X communication, where malicious actors inject falsified beacons or cooperative awareness messages [9,31]. Similarly, GPS spoofing can mislead localization, and in-vehicle CAN/LIN spoofing can inject falsified control signals. Together, these attacks can trigger incorrect maneuvers, unsafe braking or acceleration, and systemic traffic disruption.

Recent work highlights AI-based anomaly detection as a promising component in future defenses. Studies like [28] explore how AI can analyze communication and sensor streams to detect suspicious behavior in near real time. However, cryptographic and protocol-level protections remain central for message integrity at scale.

This review investigates: (i) what types of spoofing attacks affect AVs, (ii) what detection and mitigation strategies are proposed across communication, localization, and in-vehicle layers, and (iii) how AI-based techniques are applied for spoofing detection. Conducted as a systematic literature review (SLR) [17], it surveys the state of the art, identifies trends and gaps, and examines how AI is being integrated into broader CAV security architectures.

The cybersecurity of CAVs has become a critical concern as reliance on V2X communication, GPS-based localization, and in-vehicle electronic control units (ECUs) continues to grow. These components enable real-time data exchange and automated decision-making, but they also introduce attack surfaces that can be exploited by malicious actors [31].

Spoofing is one of the most serious families of threats in this space. In V2V/V2X communication, attackers can inject false traffic or safety messages; on CAN/LIN buses, they can forge internal control frames; in GPS, they can falsify position and timing; and at the perception layer, they can manipulate inputs to sensors such as cameras or LiDAR. These spoofed signals may mislead AVs into making unsafe decisions, disrupt traffic flow, and undermine trust in autonomous driving systems [6,32].

AI offers a promising approach to strengthening CAV cybersecurity, particularly in the context of anomaly detection. AI-driven models can analyze patterns in communication, network, and sensor data to detect deviations from expected behavior [1]. However, AI must be understood and evaluated alongside more classical defenses such as cryptographic authentication and secure architectures.

To guide this study, the following research questions are addressed:

RQ1 What types of spoofing attacks threaten AVs and what are their impacts?
RQ2 What detection and mitigation strategies have been proposed to counter spoofing attacks?
RQ3 How are AI-based techniques applied to detect spoofing anomalies across AV layers?

To answer the above defined research questions, this review investigates spoofing related cybersecurity threats in CAVs, focusing on V2V/V2X communication, GPS-based localization, in-vehicle networks (CAN/LIN), and, where applicable, perception sensors. It explores three main aspects: (i) the types and impacts of spoofing attacks, (ii) the range of proposed detection and mitigation strategies, and (iii) the application of AI techniques in spoofing detection across these layers.

2 Background

The integration of CAVs into modern transportation systems represents a significant technological shift. These vehicles rely on advanced software, AI, and cyber-physical systems to enhance mobility, safety, and efficiency. A key enabler is Vehicle-to-Everything (V2X) communication, which allows vehicles to exchange real-time data with other vehicles, infrastructure, and road users. At the same time, this connectivity introduces critical cybersecurity challenges, requiring robust protection mechanisms to ensure the reliability and safety of CAV networks.

2.1 Vehicle-to-Everything (V2X) Communication and Its Importance

V2X communication is fundamental to autonomous mobility, enabling vehicles to exchange information such as speed, position, direction, and road conditions. The four primary modes of V2X communication, i.e., Vehicle-to-Vehicle (V2V),

Vehicle-to-Pedestrian (V2P), Vehicle-to-Infrastructure (V2I), and Vehicle-to-Network (V2N), work together to create a connected transportation ecosystem that supports real-time decision-making and automation. Among these, V2V communication plays a central role in enhancing road safety by allowing vehicles to share real-time data about their movements and intentions. Other modes, such as V2I and V2N, support cooperative traffic management and cloud-assisted services, while V2P communication improves pedestrian safety by enabling vehicles to detect and communicate with vulnerable road users. However, all of these rely on wireless protocols such as DSRC and C-V2X, which are exposed to cyber attacks if not adequately secured [15].

2.2 Cybersecurity Threats in CAV Communication

The increasing connectivity of CAVs introduces multiple attack surfaces. Common threats include message spoofing, replay and Sybil attacks, man-in-the-middle attacks, and denial-of-service. At the in-vehicle level, internal networks such as CAN and LIN lack built-in authentication and encryption, making them susceptible to message injection and spoofing [15,27]. At the external level, V2X channels and GPS/GNSS signals can be forged, delayed, or replayed [13].

Message and Signal Spoofing. Spoofing occurs when an attacker injects or forges data to mislead the system about the state of the environment or the vehicle. Examples include:

- **V2V/V2X message spoofing**: false congestion notifications, fake emergency vehicle messages, or forged beacons that misrepresent position or speed.
- **In-vehicle network spoofing**: falsified CAN or LIN frames that manipulate RPM, gear, or braking signals.
- **GPS/GNSS spoofing**: counterfeit satellite-like signals which cause position drift or abrupt jumps.
- **Perception-layer spoofing**: crafted scenes or signals targeting LiDAR, radar, or cameras to create phantom obstacles or hide real ones.

These attacks can mislead AV perception and decision-making, potentially resulting in unsafe maneuvers or systemic traffic impacts.

2.3 Real-World Cybersecurity Incidents in AVs

Demonstrated attacks and real-world incidents reveal the risks posed by insecure automotive systems. The Jeep Cherokee hack in 2015 exposed how remote attackers could exploit connectivity to take control of steering and braking functions [19]. Other research has shown that GPS spoofing can mislead navigation systems without breaching in-vehicle components, underscoring the need to secure both internal networks and external signals.

2.4 Cybersecurity Solutions in Autonomous Vehicles

Multiple classes of security mechanisms have been proposed to address vulnerabilities in CAV communication and control:

- **Cryptographic security protocols**: Digital signatures, PKI, and lightweight authentication schemes help ensure message integrity and origin, especially in V2X communication.
- **AI-based intrusion detection systems (IDS)**: Machine learning–driven IDS can flag suspicious behavior in network or sensor data, complementing cryptographic safeguards.
- **Sensor and message fusion**: Cross-validating data from GPS, IMU, odometry, and V2X channels can detect inconsistencies and spoofing attempts.
- **Blockchain and secure logging**: Tamper-resistant logs support traceability and strengthen trust in distributed systems.
- **Regulation and standardization**: Frameworks such as ISO/SAE 21434 promote structured cybersecurity processes and security-by-design in CAV development.

Hybrid security architectures increasingly combine these techniques to provide layered defenses against evolving threats.

3 Method

This research employs a systematic literature review (SLR) to analyze spoofing-related vulnerabilities and defenses in CAVs. An SLR was chosen because it provides a structured and replicable way to identify recurring threat patterns, consolidate knowledge on detection and mitigation techniques, and reveal gaps in the current body of work [17,24].

3.1 Systematic Literature Review Process

The SLR follows established guidelines proposed by [17] and [25]. The process consists of: (i) defining research questions, (ii) designing and executing search strategies, (iii) applying inclusion and exclusion criteria, (iv) assessing study quality, and (v) extracting and synthesizing data.

The research questions in Sect. 1 define the scope of the review. RQ1 targets the classification of spoofing attack types and their impacts; RQ2 focuses on detection and mitigation strategies across communication, localization, and in-vehicle layers; and RQ3 investigates how AI-based techniques are applied within these defenses.

Inclusion and Exclusion Criteria. To maintain relevance and quality, the following inclusion criteria were applied:

- Peer-reviewed journal articles or conference papers.

- Published between 2015 and 2025.
- Explicitly address spoofing attacks (e.g., falsified messages, GPS spoofing, in-vehicle signal spoofing, perception spoofing) in the context of connected or autonomous vehicles.
- Describe or analyze at least one detection, mitigation, or protection mechanism (AI-based or non-AI).

Excluded were:

- Non-English or non-peer-reviewed sources.
- Studies focusing exclusively on non-spoofing threats (e.g., only DoS or only privacy) without a clear connection to spoofing or spoofing-aware defenses.
- Work unrelated to vehicular or transportation systems.

Search Strategy. A systematic search was conducted in major digital libraries, primarily IEEE Xplore, SpringerLink, and Scopus. Additional relevant papers were identified via citation chasing and snowballing from reference lists and citing articles.

A representative search string used in the main databases was:

("autonomous vehicle" OR "connected vehicle" OR "CAV" OR "V2X" OR "vehicular communication") AND ("spoofing" OR "falsified message" OR "GNSS spoofing" OR "GPS spoofing") AND ("security" OR "cybersecurity" OR "attack" OR "intrusion detection")

Search strings were adapted slightly to match the syntax of each database, but all maintained the focus on spoofing in CAV contexts.

Data Extraction and Synthesis. For each included study, the following key data items were extracted:

- Bibliographic information (year, venue, and type of contribution).
- Spoofing attack type(s) considered (e.g., V2X, CAN/LIN, GPS, perception, cross-layer).
- AV layer(s) targeted (communication, in-vehicle network, localization, perception).
- Detection or mitigation strategy (e.g., cryptographic/authentication, AI-based IDS, sensor fusion, hybrid or architectural approaches).
- For AI-based approaches: model type, evaluation environment (simulation, testbed, real vehicle, conceptual only), effectiveness metrics, and real-time feasibility.

The data were synthesized using a narrative synthesis approach [25], supported by tabular summaries. First, a conceptual framework was established to map spoofing threats to AV layers and defense mechanisms. Second, preliminary synthesis was produced via tables (e.g., Tables 1 and 2) and descriptive statistics (e.g., distribution of spoofing types, yearly trends). Third, relationships between threat types, defenses, AI usage, evaluation environments, and real-time capability were explored. Finally, the robustness of the synthesis was assessed by examining consistency of evidence and acknowledging limitations such as the dominance of simulation-based studies.

Quality Assessment. To ensure the reliability and relevance of the selected studies, a quality assessment checklist adapted from [17] was used. Each paper was evaluated against the following points:

- **QA1: Clarity of research objectives** – The study clearly states its goals in relation to CAV security or spoofing threats.
- **QA2: Methodological rigor** – The study uses a sound and transparent methodology (e.g., well-defined experiments, threat analysis, or architectural reasoning).
- **QA3: Relevance to the research questions** – The work contributes to understanding spoofing attacks in CAVs and/or corresponding detection and mitigation strategies, including AI-based techniques.
- **QA4: Transparency of findings** – The paper reports sufficient detail on assumptions, data, and metrics to support its conclusions.

Studies that did not satisfy the minimum thresholds for these criteria were excluded from the final synthesis. The resulting set of 21 studies forms the basis for the analysis presented in the Results and Discussion chapters.

4 Results

Table 1 provides a consolidated overview of all 21 primary studies, summarizing their focus areas, targeted spoofing threats, use of AI-based techniques, and key findings.

4.1 Spoofing Attack Types and Impacts

Our analysis of 21 primary studies identified four main categories of spoofing threats in CAVs: vehicle-to-everything (V2X) message spoofing, in-vehicle bus (CAN/LIN) spoofing, GPS signal spoofing, and sensor signal spoofing. Figure 1 illustrates the frequency of these attack types in the selected studies. The identified categories align with previous review studies by Kim *et al.* [16] and Rathore *et al.* [27], which also describe attacks at the network level versus the sensor level. These categories reflect whether an attacker injects falsified messages into vehicle communications, spoofs GPS reception, or manipulates sensor readings.

For example, V2X spoofing involves forging or replaying messages between vehicles and infrastructure [9,28], whereas CAN/LIN bus spoofing entails injecting malicious control messages on the vehicle's internal network [14]. GPS spoofing refers to falsifying the vehicle's perceived location; it is addressed by Vitale *et al.* [32], Dasgupta *et al.* [6], and Abrar *et al.* [1]. Sensor spoofing (e.g. LiDAR

Table 1. Summary of Spoofing-related Studies

	Focus Area	Cybersecurity Threat	AI-based Approach	Key Findings
[5]	V2X & in-vehicle security	Spoofing across V2X and in-vehicle comms	No	Analyzes major threat vectors including spoofing; emphasizes need for robust authentication and layered security approaches
[7]	Vehicular communication security	Spoofing/falsified data on CAN/LIN and V2X links	No	Shows that unauthenticated frames enable falsified data injection; motivates cryptographic message authentication and IDS.
[13]	V2X cybersecurity	V2X spoofing, jamming, DDoS, misbehavior	No	Identifies spoofing as a recurring V2X threat and advocates layered defenses combining crypto and IDS.
[10]	CAV security	Message & sensor spoofing in CAVs	No	Provides a CAV threat taxonomy; recommends encryption, authentication, and intrusion detection for spoofing mitigation.
[2]	ML & blockchain for CAV security	Message spoofing and data manipulation	Conceptual ML	Proposes ML-based IDS integrated with blockchain logging to improve integrity and spoofing resilience; no empirical evaluation.
[4]	Zero-trust for connected vehicles	Spoofing among multiple CAV threats	No	Promotes Zero-Trust principles with continuous verification; suggests AI-driven anomaly detection as complement to cryptography.
[8]	Autonomous driving security	GPS/sensor spoofing, V2X spoofing	Conceptual ML/RL	Highlights GPS spoofing as particularly dangerous; discusses LSTM/RL-style defenses but notes lack of real-world validation.
[18]	CAV attack detection	Spoofing, DoS, Sybil and other attacks	No	Analyzes detection/prevention schemes; hybrid approaches (e.g., RF fingerprinting + challenge–response) reach very high spoofing detection rates.
[23]	ITS/CPS perception security	Sensor/perception spoofing (camera/LiDAR)	No	Analyzes attacks and countermeasures in ITS perception; shows that securing sensor data channels can block simple spoofing attempts.
[1]	GPS-IDS for AVs	GPS/GNSS spoofing	Yes	Anomaly-based GPS IDS reliably detects sudden spoofing; slow-drift attacks are harder and benefit from sensor fusion.
[6]	Slow-drift GPS spoofing	Stealthy gradual GPS spoofing	No	Demonstrates that slow-drift spoofing can evade simple detectors; recommends cross-checking GPS with IMU/odometry to spot subtle drifts.
[32]	CARAMEL secure AV architecture	GPS spoofing & cross-layer inconsistencies	Fusion logic + ML	Implements architecture that fuses GNSS with wheel/IMU/V2X data; detects spoofed locations with low false alarms in trials.
[20]	VANET tolling security	Spoofed/malicious VANET messages	No	Veins-based tolling scenario shows spoofed messages can distort cost and traffic; motivates plausibility checks and secure payment messaging.
[31]	CAV congestion-impact	Spoofed congestion/traffic messages	No	Shows that a small share of vehicles sending false congestion alerts can trigger gridlock; argues for filtering and validating V2V congestion reports.
[14]	CAN-bus intrusion detection	CAN message injection/spoofing	Yes (RF, ANN, ensembles)	Trains ML models on CAN traffic; spoofed signals exhibit patterns enabling near-perfect detection in experiments.
[22]	Neurocomputing-based IVN IDS	CAN/LIN spoofing and anomalies	Yes (DCNN, SNN)	Reports very high accuracy for DCNN and strong results for SNNs, with SNNs promising for energy-efficient ECU deployment.
[26]	Automotive network security	Spoofing in CAN, LIN, Ethernet	Conceptual AI-based IDS	Analyzes threats and countermeasures; recommends lightweight crypto plus adaptive, AI-based IDS to handle evolving spoofing patterns.
[21]	Mini-AV real testbed	V2V/V2X message attacks (incl. spoofing)	Yes (Random Forest)	On a mini-AV platform, RF-based IDS detects network attacks with ≈96% accuracy and low false positives, showing feasibility in practice.
[29]	VANET wireless security	Beacon spoofing and DoS	Yes (Kalman/Particle filters)	Context-Adaptive Beacon Verification uses predictive filters to selectively verify beacons, blocking spoofed/DoS traffic with low overhead.
[3]	Lightweight IoAV authentication	Message spoofing/impersonation	No (crypto)	Designs lightweight authentication for IoAV; analysis shows resistance to spoofing with minimal latency/overhead.
[9]	Secure V2X message implementation	V2X message spoofing/impersonation	No (crypto)	Implements signed V2X messages over 802.11p; experiments indicate spoofed beacons are effectively rejected with small latency penalty.

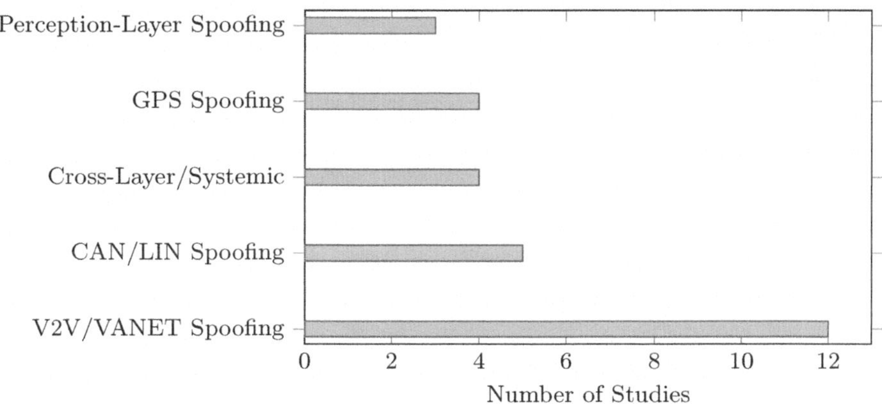

Fig. 1. Distribution of spoofing threat categories across the reviewed studies.

or camera inputs) causes false environmental data and is mentioned by Onur *et al.* [21], though it is less commonly studied. Each of these attack vectors is explored by multiple works in our sample, reflecting a broad interest in different threat surfaces.

In terms of impacts, spoofing attacks can directly compromise vehicle safety and operation. False CAN or V2X messages may trigger unintended control actions: Kim *et al.* [16] observe that bogus actuator commands could engage brakes or steering improperly, and Sedar *et al.* [28] note that false traffic alerts could cause dangerous reactions. GPS spoofing can cause significant route errors; for instance, Tzoannos *et al.* [31] demonstrate that under congested conditions even small GPS deviations lead to increased collision risk. Similarly, Vitale *et al.* [32] show that spoofed GPS data can undermine autonomous path planning. Sensor spoofing may result in misidentified obstacles or phantom detections [21]. These impacts illustrate the severe risks that spoofing poses to CAV reliability and safety.

Figure 2 shows the publication trend over time for the reviewed studies. A notable acceleration occurs in 2021–2024, indicating growing research interest. It is seen that the majority have been published since 2022.

4.2 Detection and Mitigation Strategies

For RQ2, the proposed defenses were grouped into four categories: (i) AI-based detection, (ii) cryptographic or trust-based schemes, (iii) hybrid approaches combining multiple techniques, and (iv) non-AI classical methods. A substantial portion of the reviewed studies employ AI and machine learning. For example, Onur *et al.* [21] apply a Random Forest classifier on a real mini-vehicle testbed to detect V2V/V2X message spoofing (achieving approximately 96% accuracy), while Abrar *et al.* [1] develop an anomaly-based detector capable of identifying abrupt GPS/GNSS spoofing attacks in real time. Dasgupta *et al.* [6] focus on

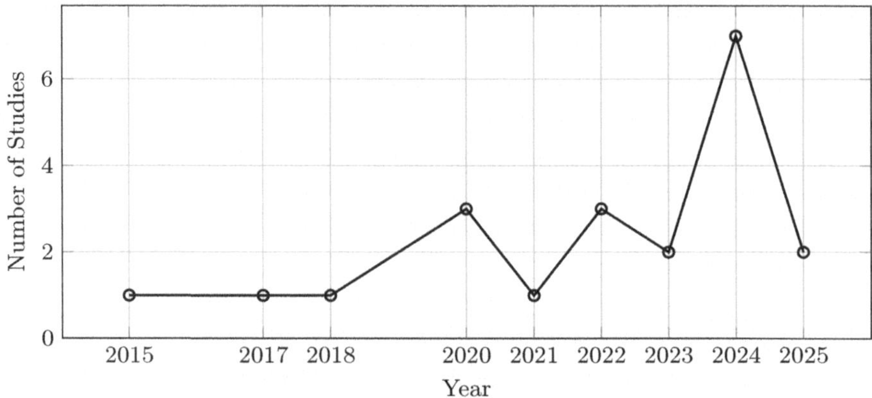

Fig. 2. Yearly trend of spoofing-related studies.

slow-drift GPS spoofing and show how gradual manipulations can evade simple threshold-based detectors, motivating more sophisticated validation mechanisms.

Cryptographic or trust-based defenses aim to ensure message integrity and authenticity in V2X communication. Giaccaglini *et al.* [9] implement signed and authenticated V2X messages over IEEE 802.11p and demonstrate that properly verified beacons can effectively block spoofed or impersonated messages with minimal latency overhead. Sedar *et al.* [28] emphasize that public-key infrastructure (PKI), certificate-based message signing, and secure session establishment remain fundamental building blocks for protecting V2X channels.

Several studies employ hybrid strategies that combine cryptographic assurances with anomaly detection or cross-layer consistency checks. Vitale *et al.* [32] present the CARAMEL architecture, which detects GPS spoofing through multi-sensor fusion (GNSS, wheel-speed, IMU, V2X Signals of Opportunity) without relying on cryptographic GPS authentication. Their system demonstrates low false-alarm rates on a prototype autonomous vehicle platform. Similarly, Sedar *et al.* [28] discuss how authenticated V2X channels can be complemented with behavioral verification to improve resilience against sophisticated spoofers.

Non-AI classical approaches include plausibility and consistency checks, redundant sensor cross-validation, and rule-based decision logic. Prior analyses such as [15] and [27] highlight the effectiveness of sanity checks, physical-model validation, and redundant sensing (e.g., GPS+IMU) as lightweight mechanisms that can filter implausible data before it reaches safety-critical modules.

Overall, the reviewed studies show that V2X spoofing is typically mitigated using cryptographic message authentication combined with network intrusion detection [9,28], while GPS spoofing countermeasures rely on anomaly detection and sensor-fusion-based validation [1,6,32]. Sensor-level spoofing is addressed primarily through AI-based perception checks [21]. Although AI-driven detection forms a significant portion of the literature, the most robust protection strategies integrate multiple defenses—combining cryptographic trust anchors, multi-sensor consistency checks, and data-driven anomaly detection methods.

4.3 AI-Based Anomaly Detection

AI-based anomaly detection represents one of the most active and technically diverse approaches to mitigating spoofing attacks in Connected and Autonomous Vehicles (CAVs). While Table 1 maps all 21 studies to their respective spoofing categories, only nine of these works incorporate AI as part of their proposed defense strategy. Among them, six papers present measurable AI-based detection results, whereas three offer conceptual or architectural proposals without empirical evaluation. Table 2 summarizes the nine AI-related studies, describing the applied techniques, targeted attack vectors, evaluation setups, and real-time feasibility.

Figures 3a and 3b visualizes the distribution of evaluation environments and real-time capabilities. These figures show that most AI models are assessed exclusively in simulation environments (55.6%), around one-third are evaluated on real-world vehicular platforms (33.3%), and only a single study provides no concrete evaluation (11.1%). Similarly, 44.4% of the AI techniques demonstrate explicit real-time feasibility, while 55.6% remain non-real-time or conceptual. These trends reveal that, despite promising algorithmic results, real-world readiness remains limited.

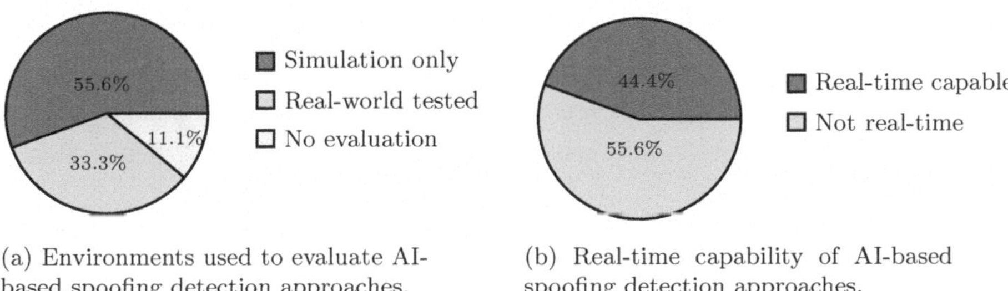

(a) Environments used to evaluate AI-based spoofing detection approaches.

(b) Real-time capability of AI-based spoofing detection approaches.

Fig. 3. Overview of evaluation environments and real-time capability among AI-based spoofing detection studies.

CAN Bus and In-Vehicle Network Detection. The strongest concentration of AI-based spoofing research lies in detecting message injection attacks on in-vehicle networks, particularly CAN and LIN buses. These buses lack authentication and are highly vulnerable to low-level spoofing. Three studies in Table 2 directly address these threats. Kalkan and Sahingoz [14] show that traditional machine learning methods such as Random Forest, AdaBoost, and ANN can detect CAN-bus signal spoofing with near-perfect accuracy in simulation. Parandkar *et al.* [22] extend this line of work using DCNNs and energy-efficient

Table 2. AI-Based Anomaly Detection Techniques in Spoofing Mitigation

	AI Technique	Targeted Threat	Effectiveness	Evaluation Environment	Advantages/Limitations	Real-Time?
[21]	Random Forest	V2V/V2X message spoofing	96.1% detection; 93.6% benign accuracy	Real-world mini autonomous vehicle platform	Demonstrated in real-world driving; increased false positives in dense traffic	Yes
[14]	Random Forest, AdaBoost, ANN	CAN-bus RPM/Gear spoofing	≈100% accuracy, precision, recall	Simulated CAN bus traffic	Computationally light; strong performance but no hardware validation	No
[22]	DCNN, SNN	CAN/LIN spoofing and anomalies	>90% detection; SNN low-power inference	Simulated IVN datasets (not specified)	SNNs energy-efficient and real-time capable; training complexity high	Yes
[8]	LSTM, Reinforcement Learning	GPS spoofing + adaptive response strategies	Detects sequential anomalies; RL adapts over time (qualitative)	Synthetic GPS datasets; conceptual design	Adaptive and robust, but computationally heavy; no timing guarantees	No
[29]	Context-Adaptive Beacon Verification (CABV)	VANET beacon spoofing	76% spoof detection; 86.5% overhead reduction	SUMO + OMNeT++ (Veins) simulation	Lightweight and designed for real-time use; may miss rare outlier attacks	Yes
[26]	Adaptive ML-based IDS	Behavioral spoofing in CAN/LIN/Ethernet	~85% (with message authentication); ~70% IDS-only	Automotive network testbed (experimental)	Adapts to evolving attacks; risk of model drift; high computational cost	No
[1]	Statistical anomaly-based ML (GPS-IDS)	Abrupt GPS/GNSS spoofing	High detection for sudden deviations; weak against slow-drift attacks	CARLA + synthetic GPS data	Lightweight and low-latency; requires pairing with drift-aware methods	Yes
[32]	ML-supported sensor fusion (CARAMEL)	GPS spoofing + cross-layer inconsistencies	Low false-alarm rate; robust fused-position estimates	Prototype AV system; on-vehicle V2X + inertial fusion	Strong robustness through multi-sensor AI fusion; limited benchmark comparability	Yes
[2]	Conceptual ML + Blockchain IDS architecture	V2X spoofing and data manipulation	No empirical metrics (architectural proposal)	Conceptual framework	Tamper-resistant logging + ML detection; lacks empirical evaluation	No

Spiking Neural Networks (SNNs), demonstrating high accuracy with architectural advantages for embedded real-time execution. Raghavan [26] further introduces adaptive IDS models capable of tracking evolving behavioral anomalies across CAN, LIN, and Ethernet; however, their approach incurs higher computational cost and has not been validated in real-time or on physical ECUs. Across these three studies, detection performance is consistently high, yet practical on-vehicle deployment remains underexplored.

GPS and Positioning System Detection. GPS spoofing requires analyzing long-term sequential dependencies in position data. Gao *et al.* [8] and Abrar *et al.* [1], explore the use of AI for this purpose. Gao et al. investigate LSTM-based models and reinforcement learning to identify anomalous trajectories and develop adaptive responses. While their approach is conceptually advanced, it remains entirely simulation-based and lacks real-time validation. In comparison, Abrar et al. propose a lightweight anomaly detection system that operates in real time and demonstrates strong performance against abrupt spoofing attacks. However, their method is less effective in identifying gradual or slow-drift spoofing scenarios. These contributions highlight the potential of AI in enhancing GPS spoofing detection, though the lack of real-world deployment continues to be a critical limitation for both approaches.

V2X and V2V Communication-Level Detection. AI-based spoofing detection at the communication layer extends beyond vehicle-to-vehicle (V2V) beacons to encompass broader vehicle-to-everything (V2X) message exchanges, including interactions with roadside infrastructure and cloud-connected services. Two empirical studies focus specifically on V2V beacon integrity. Sharma *et al.* [29] introduce the Context-Adaptive Beacon Verification (CABV) method, which uses predictive filtering to detect inconsistencies in mobility-related beacon parameters, achieving lightweight real-time operation with significantly reduced communication overhead. Onur *et al.* [21] evaluate Random Forest classifiers on a physical mini-autonomous vehicle platform, providing one of the few real-world demonstrations of AI-based V2X spoofing detection; although effective, their results show increased false positives under dynamic conditions.

Beyond V2V communication, several studies address spoofing across V2X channels more broadly. Vitale *et al.* [32] incorporate machine-learning-supported sensor and message fusion as part of the CARAMEL security architecture, enabling cross-layer detection of GPS and V2X inconsistencies with low false-alarm rates on a prototype autonomous vehicle. Ahmad *et al.* [2] propose a conceptual AI-enhanced intrusion detection framework integrated with blockchain-based integrity verification for V2X data flows, highlighting how AI can strengthen trust and resilience across heterogeneous communication links. Collectively, these works demonstrate that AI techniques are increasingly applied not only to V2V message validation but also to cross-layer and infrastructure-supported V2X security. However, empirical validation across diverse environments remains limited, and robustness under real-world communication variability continues to be an open challenge.

Summary. AI-based anomaly detection techniques are applied across several layers of the CAV ecosystem, including in-vehicle CAN/LIN networks, GPS-based localization, V2V/VANET communication, and broader V2X message validation. Ensemble learning and deep neural networks dominate CAN-focused research, where structured signal patterns make injected messages comparatively easier to detect. Sequential models such as LSTMs and reinforcement learning are explored for GPS spoofing, while context-aware filtering methods and Random Forest classifiers are used for detecting V2V and V2X communication-level anomalies. More advanced architectures, such as ML-supported sensor fusion [32] and conceptual ML–blockchain hybrids [2], illustrate how AI is increasingly being integrated into cross-layer security frameworks.

The synthesis presented in Table 2 and the distributions in Figs. 3a–3b highlight several key trends. First, AI techniques show strong promise, but real-time capability is demonstrated in only about half of the reviewed approaches. Second, evaluation environments remain uneven: while some methods are validated on physical autonomous vehicle platforms or prototype systems, many rely exclusively on simulation or do not specify their testing setup. Although most studies report high accuracy in controlled environments, the lack of large-scale real-world testing, standardized benchmarks, and integration into production-grade AV stacks limits the maturity of current solutions. Addressing these gaps—particularly robustness under real driving conditions—is an important direction for future research on AI-based spoofing mitigation.

5 Discussion

This study investigated spoofing attacks in Connected and Autonomous Vehicles (CAVs) and examined the extent to which AI-based anomaly detection can mitigate these threats. The reviewed literature reveals a diverse threat surface—spanning in-vehicle networks, GPS-based localization, V2V/V2X communication, and cross-layer inconsistencies—and highlights both the promise and current limitations of AI-driven defenses.

5.1 Message Spoofing Threats in V2X Communication

Spoofing emerged as a pervasive threat across multiple layers of CAV operation. Reviewed works consistently show that falsified messages—whether on CAN/LIN buses, GPS, or V2X links—can mislead decision-making and compromise safety. Prior analyses such as [13] and [7] emphasize how injected falsified data can propagate across internal and external communication paths, reinforcing the need for resilient message validation and fallback logic.

The evidence shows some subsystems are more frequently targeted. CAN/LIN spoofing is well-documented, with [14] and [22] demonstrating how malicious signals can manipulate RPM or gear state. GPS spoofing remains a major concern due to GNSS signal weaknesses, as highlighted in [8] and [1], especially given their direct impact on vehicle control and navigation.

Spoofing also appears at higher communication layers. V2V and V2X manipulation—from false congestion alerts to forged beacons—can influence cooperative behavior and network stability. Studies such as [31] and [9] show how modest levels of falsified data degrade traffic flow or disrupt awareness functions.

Perception-layer spoofing is comparatively underexplored. Although [10] and others describe LiDAR or camera deception, few studies offer concrete detection mechanisms. This imbalance suggests that not all critical threat surfaces are equally addressed.

5.2 Effectiveness of AI-Based Anomaly Detection

AI-based anomaly detection plays a growing role in identifying spoofed messages. The reviewed works cover a range of techniques—ensemble learning, deep learning, sequential models, and context-aware filtering—applied across various spoofing domains.

For in-vehicle networks, traditional ML remains effective. [14] show that Random Forest, AdaBoost, and ANN can detect CAN-bus spoofing with near-perfect accuracy in simulation. [22] extend this with DCNNs and energy-efficient Spiking Neural Networks, demonstrating high accuracy and suitability for embedded real-time use. [26] introduce adaptive IDS models for CAN/LIN/Ethernet, though with computational costs and no real-time validation.

In GPS spoofing detection, AI focuses on temporal modeling. [8] explore LSTM-based anomaly detection and reinforcement learning for adaptive response, while [1] demonstrate a lightweight GPS-IDS capable of real-time detection of abrupt spoofing. Slow-drift spoofing remains difficult to detect, underscoring the need for drift-aware methods.

At the communication layer, [29] propose Context-Adaptive Beacon Verification (CABV) for detecting inconsistent beacons with low overhead, and [21] provide one of the few real-world evaluations of AI-based V2X spoofing detection. Their results show promising accuracy but also elevated false positives under dynamic conditions, reflecting the sensitivity of detection to environmental variation.

Overall, AI techniques show strong potential but remain unevenly validated. Many results rely on controlled simulations, and the leap from algorithmic capability to vehicle-grade robustness is still developing.

5.3 Real-World Relevance and Limitations

Several limitations emerge. Most AI models are evaluated only in simulations, and few demonstrate testing on physical vehicles. Real-time feasibility is inconsistent: less than half of the AI approaches explicitly prove timing guarantees for CAV use.

Further issues include data scarcity, ECU constraints, and vulnerability to adversarial manipulation. Hybrid methods—such as combining AI with blockchain [2] or lightweight authentication—are promising but mostly conceptual. The lack of shared benchmarks also complicates evaluation and comparison.

Finally, this SLR faces limits common to secondary research, such as database scope, language coverage, and simulation-heavy primary sources. These constraints underscore the need for stronger collaboration among academia, industry, and integrators to advance empirical validation.

5.4 Validity and Reliability

To ensure methodological rigor, this review followed established SLR guidelines [17], including predefined research questions, systematic search strategies, and transparent inclusion and exclusion criteria. Reliability was strengthened through structured data extraction and the use of a quality assessment checklist.

Nevertheless, external validity is constrained by the dominance of simulation-based studies and the exclusion of non-English or non-peer-reviewed sources. Some subjectivity in assessing relevance and quality is unavoidable, although predefined criteria mitigated this risk. Despite these limitations, the methodology provides a consistent and replicable foundation for analyzing spoofing threats and AI-based defenses in CAVs.

5.5 Future Work

Future research should prioritize integrating AI-based anomaly detection with lightweight cryptographic mechanisms to jointly ensure message integrity and behavioral consistency. Blockchain-assisted logging and trust mechanisms offer potential for tamper resistance, though practical deployment challenges remain.

Bridging the gap between controlled simulations and real-world evaluation is essential. Spoofing detection techniques must be tested under diverse environmental conditions, including varying traffic density, weather, and sensor noise, to ensure robustness. Underexplored attack vectors, particularly perception-layer spoofing, merit greater attention to develop more comprehensive defenses.

Another pressing need is the establishment of shared benchmarks and standardized datasets. Consistent evaluation metrics, covering accuracy, false-positive rates, latency, and resource consumption, would enable meaningful comparison across detection techniques and accelerate progress in the field.

Finally, research should further explore energy-efficient AI approaches, such as SNNs, lightweight deep models, and hardware-aware optimization, to ensure that detection mechanisms are feasible for deployment on commercial AV platforms.

6 Conclusions

This study examined spoofing threats in Connected and Autonomous Vehicles (CAVs), with a particular focus on communication, positioning, and in-vehicle network vulnerabilities. The review shows that spoofing remains a significant cybersecurity risk across multiple layers of the CAV ecosystem, affecting

CAN/LIN buses, GPS-based localization, and V2V/V2X message exchanges. These attacks can mislead vehicle perception and decision-making, underscoring the need for reliable and adaptive defense mechanisms.

AI-based anomaly detection has emerged as a promising approach, with ensemble learning, deep learning, sequential models, and context-aware filters demonstrating strong potential for identifying spoofed inputs. However, the majority of AI-based solutions are validated only in simulation, and less than half provide evidence of real-time feasibility. This highlights a critical gap between algorithmic capability and operational deployment.

Effective spoofing mitigation will require combining multiple strategy types, including lightweight authentication, sensor and message fusion, and AI-enhanced intrusion detection. Strengthening empirical evaluation—particularly through real-world testing on physical vehicles and shared benchmark datasets—remains essential for advancing the field.

Continued interdisciplinary collaboration between researchers, industry, and standards bodies is vital for developing secure and resilient CAV systems. By prioritizing robust security architectures and practical validation efforts, the community can help ensure safer integration of autonomous vehicles into future transportation infrastructure.

References

1. Abrar, M.M., et al.: GPS-IDS: an anomaly-based GPS spoofing attack detection framework for autonomous vehicles, December 2024. https://doi.org/10.48550/arXiv.2405.08359, arXiv:2405.08359
2. Ahmad, J.: Machine learning and blockchain technologies for cybersecurity in connected vehicles. WIREs Data Min. Knowl. Discov. **14**(1), e1515 (2024). https://doi.org/10.1002/widm.1515
3. Ali, H.I., Kurunathan, H., Eldefrawy, M.H., Gruian, F., Jonsson, M.: Navigating the challenges and opportunities of securing internet of autonomous vehicles with lightweight authentication. IEEE Access **13**, 24207–24222 (2025). https://doi.org/10.1109/ACCESS.2025.3537800
4. Annabi, M., Zeroual, A., Messai, N.: Towards zero trust security in connected vehicles: a comprehensive survey. Comput. Secur. **145**, 104018 (2024). https://doi.org/10.1016/j.cose.2024.104018
5. Bharati, S., Podder, P., Mondal, M.R.H., Robel, M.R.A.: Threats and countermeasures of cyber security in direct and remote vehicle communication systems (2020)
6. Dasgupta, S., Ahmed, A., Rahman, M., Bandi, T.N.: Unveiling the stealthy threat: analyzing slow drift GPS spoofing attacks for autonomous vehicles in urban environments and enabling the resilience, January 2024. https://doi.org/10.48550/arXiv.2401.01394
7. El-Rewini, Z., Sadatsharan, K., Selvaraj, D.F., Plathottam, S.J., Ranganathan, P.: Cybersecurity challenges in vehicular communications. Veh. Commun. **23**, 100214 (2020). https://doi.org/10.1016/j.vehcom.2019.100214
8. Gao, C., Wang, G., Shi, W., Wang, Z., Chen, Y.: Autonomous driving security: state of the art and challenges. IEEE Internet Things J. **9**(10), 7572–7595 (2022). https://doi.org/10.1109/JIOT.2021.3130054

9. Giaccaglini, A.: Implementing secured messages for V2X communication. Laurea, Politecnico di Torino, December 2024
10. Gozubuyuk, B., Bailey, W., Everson, D., Dong, Z., Cheng, L., Pesé, M.D.: An overview of security in connected and autonomous vehicles. In: 2023 International Conference on Artificial Intelligence of Things and Systems (AIoTSys), pp. 206–213 (2023). https://doi.org/10.1109/AIoTSys58602.2023.00052
11. Grimm, D., Lautenbach, A., Almgren, M., Olovsson, T., Sax, E.: Gap analysis of ISO/SAE 21434 - improving the automotive cybersecurity engineering life cycle. In: 26th IEEE International Conference on Intelligent Transportation Systems, ITSC 2023, Bilbao, Spain, 24–28 September 2023, pp. 1904–1911. IEEE (2023). https://doi.org/10.1109/ITSC57777.2023.10422100
12. Henle, J., Otten, S., Sax, E.: Systems engineering approach for compliant over-the-air update development. In: 2024 IEEE International Conference on Recent Advances in Systems Science and Engineering (RASSE), pp. 1–9 (2024). https://doi.org/10.1109/RASSE64357.2024.10773922
13. Herman Muraro Gularte, K., et al.: Safeguarding the V2X pathways: exploring the cybersecurity landscape through systematic review. IEEE Access **12**, 72871–72895 (2024). https://doi.org/10.1109/ACCESS.2024.3402946
14. Kalkan, S.C., Sahingoz, O.K.: In-vehicle intrusion detection system on controller area network with machine learning models. In: 2020 11th International Conference on Computing, Communication and Networking Technologies (ICCCNT), pp. 1–6 (2020). https://doi.org/10.1109/ICCCNT49239.2020.9225442
15. Khan, S.K., Shiwakoti, N., Stasinopoulos, P., Chen, Y.: Cyber-attacks in the next-generation cars, mitigation techniques, anticipated readiness and future directions. Accid. Anal. Prev. **148**, 105837 (2020). https://doi.org/10.1016/j.aap.2020.105837
16. Kim, K., Kim, J.S., Jeong, S., Park, J.H., Kim, H.K.: Cybersecurity for autonomous vehicles: review of attacks and defense. Comput. Secur. **103**, 102150 (2021). https://doi.org/10.1016/j.cose.2020.102150
17. Kitchenham, B., Charters, S.: Guidelines for performing systematic literature reviews in software engineering. EBSE Technical Report (2007)
18. Limbasiya, T., Teng, K.Z., Chattopadhyay, S., Zhou, J.: A systematic survey of attack detection and prevention in connected and autonomous vehicles. Veh. Commun. **37**, 100515 (2022). https://doi.org/10.1016/j.vehcom.2022.100515
19. Miller, C., Valasek, C.: Remote exploitation of an unaltered passenger vehicle. Tech. rep., Black Hat USA, Las Vegas, NV (2015)
20. Ming, L., et al.: A general testing framework based on veins for securing vanet applications. In: 2018 IEEE SmartWorld, Ubiquitous Intelligence & Computing, Advanced & Trusted Computing, Scalable Computing & Communications, Cloud & Big Data Computing, Internet of People and Smart City Innovation (SmartWorld/SCALCOM/UIC/ATC/CBDCom/IOP/SCI), pp. 2068–2073 (2018). https://doi.org/10.1109/SmartWorld.2018.00347
21. Onur, F., Gönen, S., Barısçkan, M.A., Kubat, C., Tunay, M., Yılmaz, E.N.: Machine learning-based identification of cybersecurity threats affecting autonomous vehicle systems. Comput. Ind. Eng. **190**, 110088 (2024). https://doi.org/10.1016/j.cie.2024.110088
22. Parandkar, P., Suresh, D., Joshi, P.V., Sudharshan, K.M.: Intrusion detection in in-vehicle networks using neuro computing. SSRN Electron. J. (2024). https://doi.org/10.2139/ssrn.4917843
23. Pavithra, R., Kaliappan, V.K., Rajendar, S.: Security algorithm for intelligent transport system in cyber-physical systems perceptive: attacks, vulnerabilities,

and countermeasures. SN Comput. Sci. **4**(5), 544 (2023). https://doi.org/10.1007/s42979-023-01897-9

24. Petersen, K., Vakkalanka, S., Kuzniarz, L.: Guidelines for conducting systematic mapping studies in software engineering: an update. Inf. Softw. Technol. **64**, 1–18 (2015). https://doi.org/10.1016/j.infsof.2015.03.007
25. Petticrew, M., Roberts, H.: Systematic Reviews in the Social Sciences: A Practical Guide. Blackwell Publishing (2006). https://doi.org/10.1002/9780470754887
26. Raghavan, S.S.: Cybersecurity in automotive networks: mitigating threats in CAN, LIN and automotive ethernet systems. Int. J. Comput. Sci. Eng. Res. Develop. (IJCSERD) (2025). https://doi.org/10.5281/ZENODO.14892660
27. Rathore, R.S., Hewage, C., Kaiwartya, O., Lloret, J.: In-vehicle communication cyber security: challenges and solutions. Sensors **22**(17) (2022). https://doi.org/10.3390/s22176679
28. Sedar, R., Kalalas, C., Vazquez-Gallego, F., Alonso, L., Alonso-Zarate, J.: A comprehensive survey of V2X cybersecurity mechanisms and future research paths. IEEE Open J. Commun. Soc. **4**, 325–391 (2023). https://doi.org/10.1109/OJCOMS.2023.3239115
29. Sharma, P., Liu, H., Wang, H., Zhang, S.: Securing wireless communications of connected vehicles with artificial intelligence. In: 2017 IEEE International Symposium on Technologies for Homeland Security (HST), pp. 1–7 (2017). https://doi.org/10.1109/THS.2017.7943477
30. Stubler, T., Amodei, A., Capriglione, D., Tomasso, G., Bonnotte, N., Mohammed, S.: An investigation of denial of service attacks on autonomous driving software and hardware in operation. In: 2024 IEEE 20th International Conference on Automation Science and Engineering (CASE), pp. 3051–3056 (2024). https://doi.org/10.1109/CASE59546.2024.10711339
31. Tzoannos, Z.R., Kosmanos, D., Xenakis, A., Chaikalis, C.: The impact of spoofing attacks in connected autonomous vehicles under traffic congestion conditions. Telecom **5**(3), 747–759 (2024). https://doi.org/10.3390/telecom5030037
32. Vitale, C., et al.: CARAMEL: results on a secure architecture for connected and autonomous vehicles detecting GPS spoofing attacks. EURASIP J. Wirel. Commun. Netw. **2021**(1), 1–28 (2021). https://doi.org/10.1186/s13638-021-01971-x

Methods

A Workflow for Secure and Tamper Resistant Software Test Reporting

Jakob Rechberger(✉) and Steffen Heinzl

Faculty of Computer Science and Business Information Systems, Technical University of Applied Sciences Würzburg-Schweinfurt, Würzburg, Germany
jakob.rechberger@gmx.de, steffen.heinzl@thws.de

Abstract. This paper proposes a novel workflow to prevent software and test report tampering. This plays a crucial role in industries operating in critical infrastructures where special emphasis is placed on the reliability of these reports for audits. Looking at the state-of-the-art, we identify tampering with test code, pseudo-accountability, and error-prone manual testing as problems that need to be dealt with. Our proposed workflow can be regularly initiated by a supervisor. It identifies every contributor to a project in a set time and asks them to verify their contributions and ultimately sign off on these contributions. This allows for straightforward and thorough reviews of a release and leads to enhanced tamper resistance, protecting the project against malicious alterations.

Keywords: Test Reporting · Workflow · Tamper Resistance · Digital Signatures

1 Introduction

Data tampering has been a persistent issue, intensified by the digital era, where attacks increasingly focus on intercepting and modifying data in transit. Traditionally, these threats came from external actors, but insider tampering has emerged as a growing concern. The Boeing 737 Max crashes in 2018 and 2019, which claimed 346 lives, exposed severe flaws in the aircraft's Maneuvering Characteristics Augmentation System (MCAS). Investigations revealed that Boeing deliberately withheld critical MCAS details from pilots to avoid costly retraining. This omission played a significant role in the accidents, as pilots were unaware of the system's behavior and lacked the necessary training to counteract its effects [1]. Further inspections uncovered systemic quality assurance failures within Boeing. [2] reports that the company manipulated test results and falsified records, raising serious concerns about its commitment to safety. Despite the initial backlash and regulatory actions, [3] highlights that these issues persisted even in 2024, with evidence of ongoing documentation falsification and compromised safety standards.

But corporate tampering is not unique to Boeing. The Volkswagen emissions scandal involved software designed to cheat pollution tests, resulting in major

E. Bergström et al. (Eds.): CRITIS 2025, LNCS 16291, pp. 185–199, 2026.
https://doi.org/10.1007/978-3-032-19540-1_10

fines and loss of trust [4]. Financial institutions have also faced insider tampering, with employees selling sensitive data or altering software test results for financial gain or sabotage [5]. Insider threats pose significant risks, from regulatory penalties to operational disruptions, particularly in critical sectors like finance, healthcare, and utilities. Given their authorized access, insiders can bypass security measures, making detection difficult. These cases underscore the need for tamper resistance and traceability in software test reports, which are vital for audits and quality assurance.

This paper introduces a novel approach where supervisors initiate reviews, and contributors digitally sign their work, ensuring transparency, traceability, immutability, and auditability. Section 2 reviews existing research and technologies. Section 3 shows a number of problems not addressed by the State of the Art. Section 4 introduces our proposed workflow. Section 5 presents a prototypical implementation of our proposed workflow. Section 6 evaluates our chosen approach in regard to the previously identified problems. Section 7 summarizes the key findings.

2 Related Work

Several studies have explored countermeasures against tampering from a systems perspective. For instance, [6] proposes a blockchain-based approach to secure and archive drug trial reports, ensuring their integrity and long-term availability. Similarly, other works such as [7,8] advocates for blockchain solutions to prevent data manipulation. The key advantage of these approaches lies in blockchain's decentralized nature, which minimizes the risk of unauthorized alterations.

However, while blockchain ensures data immutability once a block is added, it does not inherently verify the accuracy of the data before inclusion. If manipulated data is submitted, the blockchain will preserve it without validation. Another limiting factor is the high computational cost required to operate the nodes of the blockchain, which becomes especially hard when dealing with large files. Instead, digital signatures have been increasingly adopted across industries to enhance data integrity and security. As described by [9], these signatures leverage cryptographic mechanisms such as public key cryptography and hashing to achieve a high level of tamper resistance. By ensuring accountability and traceability, digital signatures discourage tampering attempts and enforce greater scrutiny, as any unauthorized modification is immediately detectable. Although [10] mentions that digital signatures convey less trust in the signed document than handwritten signatures, they are an essential part in the era of digitization and have the same legal binding as handwritten signatures in official documents in many parts of the world, such as the EU and the United States.

For enhanced tamper resistance and long-term verifiability, [11] introduces a blockchain system that preserves digitally signed records, allowing verification even after the original digital signature certificate has expired. Another complementary approach is User Entity and Behavior Analytics (UEBA), as discussed by [12]. UEBA continuously monitors user activities to detect anomalies that may indicate malicious intent or security threats, thus further strengthening system integrity. But this comes at the cost of interference with the privacy of the employees and requires high operating costs.

3 State of the Art

In many organizations, periodic reviews of software development projects are conducted to ensure compliance with internal policies, regulatory requirements, and industry standards. Among these reviews, audits play a crucial role in verifying that both the development process and the team are following the organization's established strategies and procedures. Software test reports serve as essential records for both the verification of individual software components and the validation of system requirements. Tracing test results to the tests and to the corresponding requirements is one key element in those audits. Tests can usually be split up into two categories: automated tests and manual tests.

To be able to use automated tests in an automated way some sort of configuration management, such as Chef[1], GitHub[2], or GitLab[3], along with a Version Control System (VCS), such as Git[4] is used. First, the source code, test code, manual test procedures, and documentation in general belonging to the next release are tagged in the VCS. Second, the tests are executed by the configuration management tool, and the test reports are committed to the VCS or stored separately in the configuration management tool. Depending on industry standards (e.g. ASPICE[5]), the applied software development model (e.g. the V-Model[6]), or other relevant factors, an automatic release or deployment of the software might be possible, but usually accountable persons for certain parts of the development need to sign off that the release works as stated in the requirements. This can even be possible if not all tests passed. After automated tests are completed, manual tests often need to be performed and documented to verify whether a requirement has been fulfilled. Manual tests are executed by a human being, usually adhering to a list of previously documented steps.

However, this procedure suffers from several issues that compromise its reliability. These problems include:

- **Tampering with test code:** Tests for software component verification could be tampered with to automatically succeed regardless of the state of the software component. This can largely be circumvented by using continuous integration/development (CI/CD) tools, which automatically execute tests and

[1] https://www.chef.io/.
[2] https://github.com/.
[3] https://gitlab.com.
[4] https://git-scm.com/.
[5] https://vda-qmc.de/en/automotive-spice/automotive-spice-veroeffentlichungen/.
[6] https://www.cio.bund.de/Webs/CIO/DE/digitaler-wandel/Achitekturen_und_Standards/V_modell_xt/v_modell_xt-node.html.

create test reports for a release (e.g. a tagged version in a VCS). Theoretically, there is still a chance that an internal attacker changes checked-out test code before its execution.
- **Pseudo-accountability:** In many cases, one or two individuals are designated as the accountable signatories for the final release, i.e. they provide their official approval by signing off on the test reports. However, these individuals did not necessarily execute the verification or validation tests and, in most cases, did not write the test cases themselves. This creates a critical responsibility gap, as these signatories are held accountable for the integrity of the test reports despite not being directly involved in the testing process.
- **Error-prone manual testing:** Validation of requirements is often (at least partially) done by manual testing. The workflow that leads to testing whether a requirement is fulfilled is often executed by a software tester, and then the results are documented by him/her. Sometimes the steps described in the manual tests are outdated due to changes during the release and this may lead to unexpected results in the documentation. The tester might not fully understand the requirement and, by mistake, document a wrong result. Or the tester might even intentionally document the wrong test result.

4 Our Proposed Workflow

The problems mentioned above highlight the need for a specialized solution that ensures the integrity, traceability, and auditability of test reports while integrating into software development workflows. While the approaches mentioned in Sect. 2 address various aspects of document tamper resistance and improve traceability, they are not specifically tailored to the unique requirements of software test reports. For example, the approach proposed by [7] uses a blockchain to ensure immutable software test records, preventing unauthorized modifications. However, it does not ensure that contributors who have participated in the project's development are identified and, therefore, can be held responsible. The same limitation applies to the methods proposed by [6,8].

To counteract tampering with test results, test reports must be secured while ensuring clear evidence and log trails for future investigations. We achieve this by leveraging digital signatures for authenticity, hash values to verify project integrity throughout the review cycle, and a timestamp authority to validate signatures and support long-term archival. Furthermore, a modern Version Control System (VCS), such as Git, is used, and a testing environment, such as a Continuous Integration (CI) pipeline, is required.

4.1 Roles

For our approach, we define two simple roles:

- supervisors, who initiate and verify the process,
- contributors, who made changes to the project.

Both roles act as clients to a web server, which manages all communications between the clients and a database.

4.2 Database Design

The database operates on three different entities: Project, User, and Link. To ensure the security and integrity of the workflow, the database must meet the minimal requirements by including the mentioned essential data fields. These fields are necessary to maintain a secure and verifiable system. However, during implementation, additional fields can be added as needed to improve usability, such as extra name fields for users or other customization options that enhance functionality while preserving security standards. When a review is initiated, a project entry is created in the Project table, storing the project's data, its hash value, and the project's name. Contributors are linked to the project, initially identified by email. The Link table connects users to projects using $project\_id$ and $user\_id$ as foreign keys, along with an expiry timestamp and a unique token. This setup allows users to participate in multiple projects while maintaining distinct associations. Figure 1 illustrates an exemplary database structure.

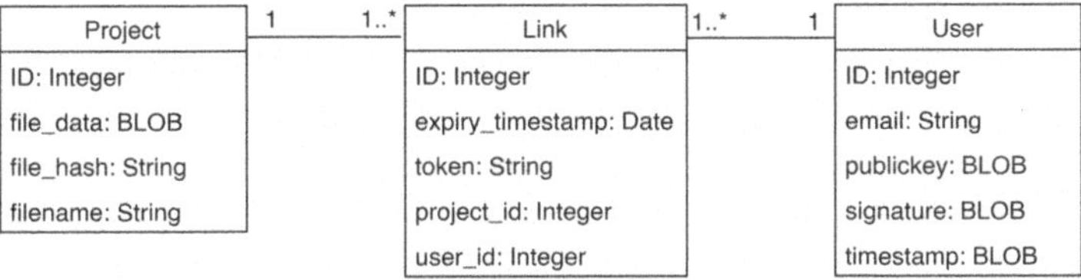

Fig. 1. Database design.

4.3 Workflow Design

A supervisor can obtain a comprehensive, verifiable record of all project contributions and changes over a specified timeframe. Each contribution is securely logged and confirmed by digital signatures and timestamps, providing a robust audit trail. Digital signatures use public-key encryption, where a signer generates the signature with their private key, and others verify it using the corresponding public key. To enhance security and trust, digital signatures are often backed by a Certificate Authority (CA), which issues digital certificates to confirm the signer's identity. A timestamped certificate issued by a Timestamp Authority (TSA) serves as proof that the submitted signature (or any other file sent) remained unchanged at the exact time of submission so that even if the signature certificate expires, the timestamp ensures that signatures were valid at the time of signing.

The steps (as illustrated in Fig. 2) describe how the proposed workflow works in detail.

1. **Supervisor Initiates the Workflow:** The supervisor begins the workflow by providing repository link to a project in a VCS and specifying the relevant timeframe (for example, from January 1, 2024, to June 1, 2024) to the

server (e.g. through a web interface). The server automatically identifies all contributors who have committed changes to the project within the specified timeframe and records their information as users in the database. The subsequent steps are carried out automatically, reducing additional input and room to interfere with the process.
2. **Automatic Project Retrieval from Repository:** Upon submission, the workflow automatically clones the specified repository from version control and temporarily stores it as a directory object in the database.
3. **Test Execution and Report Generation:** All test cases located in the project's test directory are executed using the company's designated testing environment. A decompiler can be used alongside the test results to extract and integrate the corresponding test code directly into the report. The resulting test reports are then added to a temporary directory on the server.
4. **Archiving and Generating a Unique Hash:** The entire directory, comprising project files and test reports, is compressed (zipped). A hash value is generated for the zipped file, and both the file and its hash are stored in the database.
5. **Contributor Notification and Secure Access Token Distribution:** Each identified contributor from Step 1 receives an email containing:
   - A link to the compressed file (containing the project and test reports directory) that includes a unique token in the UUID format
   - The previously generated hash value of the project
6. **Hash Verification and Download:** When a contributor accesses the link, they must enter the emailed hash value to verify the project's integrity. If the provided hash matches the stored value, the system confirms that the link and project have not been tampered with. This verification step ensures that no intermediary has altered any information related to the link or the project, as the hash must match the one calculated and stored in the database at the start of the process. Once verified, the contributor can download the project files for a local review of their contributions.
7. **Contributor Approval of Their Work:** After verifying the project data and ensuring their contributions are accurately reflected, the contributor submits an approval response through the web interface.
8. **Digital Signature Appending:** As soon as a contributor approves, the system automatically appends their digital signature, along with the corresponding public key and a timestamp from the Timestamping Authority, to the respective user in the database. The timestamp serves as proof of validity that the signature was valid at the time of signing even if the signature certificate has already expired.
9. **Supervisor Oversight and Progress Monitoring:** The supervisor can monitor which contributors have signed off on the project (e.g. through a web interface again). Optional reminder emails can be sent to any users who have not yet provided their signatures.
10. **Secure Long-Term Storage with Blockchain Archiving:** Once the supervisor approves all signed contributions, a container containing the entire project data, along with the associated signatures and timestamps, is securely

stored in a database. To ensure optimal long-term archival, it is recommended to adopt a Blockchain-based approach. Given the critical nature of these data containers, a Proof of Authority (PoA) consensus mechanism is advised, allowing only authorized entities to append blocks to the chain. This significantly enhances data integrity and prevents future unauthorized modifications, reinforcing the reliability and security of stored test reports.

This workflow ensures that every contribution is captured in a tamper-resistant manner, providing a clear audit trail and guaranteeing compliance with rigorous security or regulatory requirements.

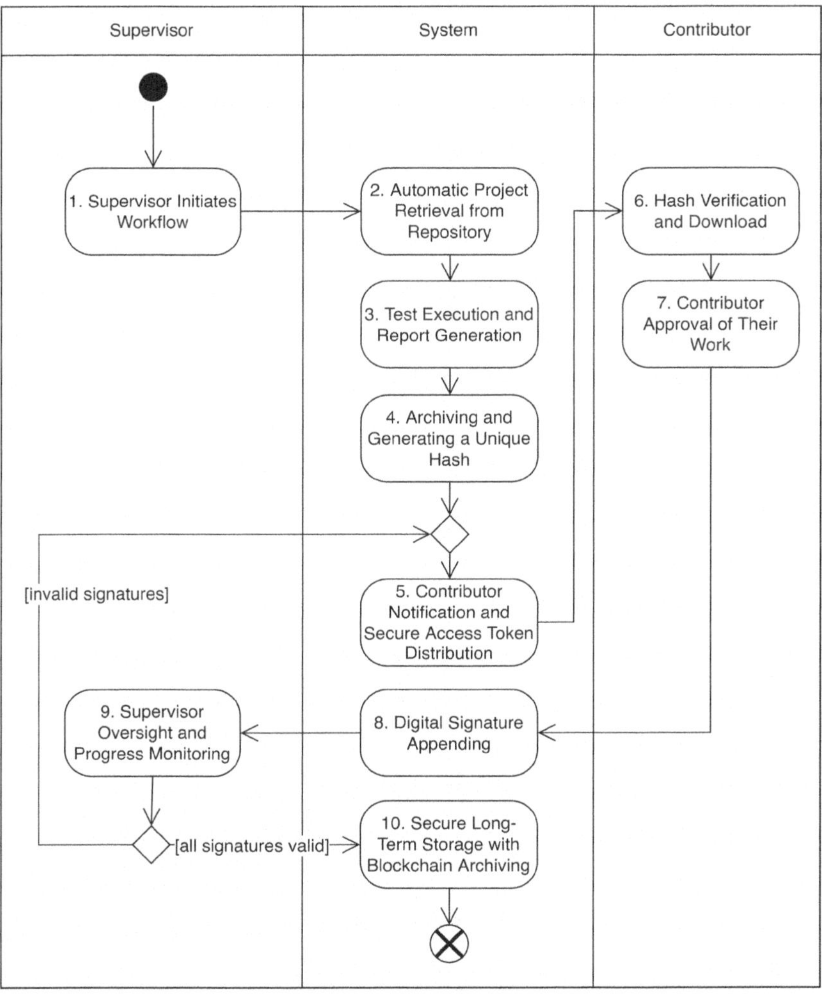

Fig. 2. Workflow as a UML Activity Diagram.

5 Implementation

Using the database structure and the steps mentioned above, an initial implementation was developed in Java to demonstrate the system's benefits[7]. This implementation integrates Git-based contributor tracking, email notifications, test report generation, digital signature verification, and a web-based interface to ease workflow management.

The backend was developed using the Spring framework[8], along with a MySQL database. To simplify interaction with the Web API endpoints developed in Spring, a simple frontend was implemented using React[9]. This frontend provides an exemplary interface for managing and visualizing all actions within the workflow.

Supervisors can initiate the process by specifying the Git repository's URL and defining the timeframe for the review. Figure 3 displays the view for the supervisor. Using Git, all contributors associated with a given project are retrieved and notified via individual emails. This notification process is handled using the Java Mail API and Gmail. When entering the project name into the field below, a table is displayed listing all contributors alongside their respective signing status, allowing supervisors to send reminder emails.

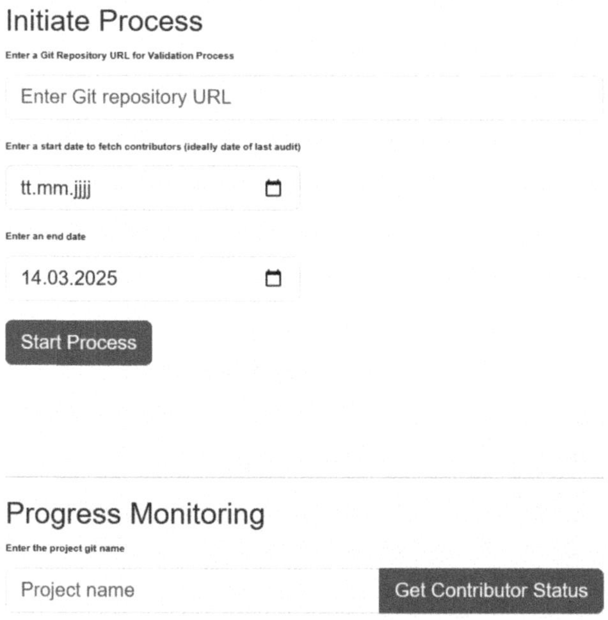

Fig. 3. Frontend for the supervisor.

[7] https://doi.org/10.5281/zenodo.17455932.
[8] https://spring.io/projects/spring-framework.
[9] https://react.dev/.

For test report generation, the Maven Surefire Plugin was used to produce fast and reliable test reports immediately after the build process. To enhance traceability in test reporting, a decompiler was used alongside the Surefire test execution data to extract and display the actual test case code in a separate column within the test report. This addition significantly improves auditability, as it allows users to easily

- check whether the actually executed test code matches the code from the repository
- correlate test results with the exact test case code that produced them, along with all referenced methods from the development code.

It is important to note that the decompiled code is not meant to verify the authenticity of contributions. Instead, it serves as a helpful reference to clarify any misunderstandings that may arise. Figure 4 and 5 illustrate how the test code is integrated into the test report using the decompiler.

```
public class TestReport {
    @Test
    void UnitTestTrue(){
        int x = 0;
        int y = 0;
        for(int i = 0; i < 100; i++){
            y = i;
            for(int j = 0; j < 100; j++){
                x = j;
            }
        }
        assertEquals(x, actual: 99);
        assertEquals(y, actual: 99);
    }
    @Test
    void testNull() {
        Object obj = null;
        assertNull(obj, message: "Object should be null");
    }
    @Test
    void testDivisionByZero() {
        Exception exception = assertThrows(ArithmeticException.class, () -> {
            int result = 1 / 0;
        });
        assertEquals( expected: "/ by zero", exception.getMessage());
    }
    @Test
    void UnitTestFalse(){
        int x = 0;
        int y = 0;
        for(int i = 0; i < 100; i++){
            y = i;
            for(int j = 0; j < 100; j++){
                x = j;
            }
        }
        assertEquals(x, actual: 10);
        assertEquals(y, actual: 10);
    }

}
```

Fig. 4. Basic JUnit test code example.

Test Report

Test Suite: TestReport

Report created: 11-03-2025 17:08:13

Test Case	Class	Time	Result	Message	Code

UnitTestTrue	TestReport	0s	[illegible]		@Test
					void UnitTestTrue() {
					int x = 0;
					int y = 0;
					for (int i = 0; i < 100; ++i) {
					y = i;
					int j = 0;
					while (j < 100) {
					x = j++;
					}
					}
					Assertions.assertEquals((int)x, (int)99);
					Assertions.assertEquals((int)y, (int)99);
					}

testNull	TestReport	0s	[illegible]		@Test
					void testNull() {
					Object obj = null;
					Assertions.assertNull(obj, (String)"Object should be null");
					}

testDivisionByZero	TestReport	0s	[illegible]		@Test
					void testDivisionByZero() {
					Exception exception = (Exception)Assertions.assertThrows(ArithmeticException.class, () -> {
					int result = 1 / 0;
					});
					Assertions.assertEquals((Object)"/ by zero", (Object)exception.getMessage());
					}

UnitTestFalse	TestReport	0.001s	Failed	org.opentest4j.AssertionFailedError: expected: <99> but was: <10> at TestReport.UnitTestFalse(TestReport.java:29)	@Test
					void UnitTestFalse() {
					int x = 0;
					int y = 0;
					for (int i = 0; i < 100; ++i) {
					y = i;
					int j = 0;
					while (j < 100) {
					x = j++;
					}
					}
					Assertions.assertEquals((int)x, (int)10);
					Assertions.assertEquals((int)y, (int)10);
					}

Fig. 5. Test report with decompiled test code from Fig. 4.

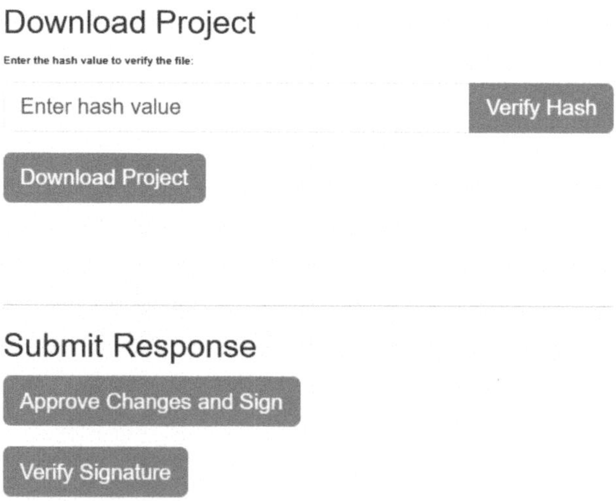

Fig. 6. Frontend for the contributor.

Contributors receive an access link via email. Upon clicking this link, the system automatically validates the link and its associated token. If both are valid, contributors are prompted to enter the hash value, which is also provided by email. A correct hash value grants access to download the project for local review. When a contributor approves the changes, a digital signature is generated using the Java Security package. This signature, along with the contributor's public key and a timestamp retrieved from the timestamping service FreeTSA[10], is added to the database. The additional button allows contributors to verify that their approval was successfully recorded and that their signature remains valid. This is illustrated in Fig. 6. While minimal in scope, it effectively demonstrates the core functionalities and user experience of our approach. However, since both the decompiler and the Surefire plugin are specifically designed for Java projects using Maven, the current implementation is limited to this setup. If applied to a real-world system, this restriction would necessitate additional development efforts to support other programming languages and build environments. However, for the purposes of this proof of concept, universal adaptability to all project structures was considered non-essential. The focus was instead on demonstrating the feasibility and advantages of the proposed workflow within a controlled environment. As a side note, access to the web interface should be restricted, requiring users to log in with company-issued credentials before accessing any resources.

6 Qualitative Evaluation

In Sect. 3, several problems have been identified. In this section, we evaluate for each problem how using our workflow helps.

- **Tampering with test code:** The code that is actually executed has to be copied and stored. In script languages, the (test) scripts can simply be copied. When executing compiled code, a decompiler can be used, for instance, to identify the actual executed code. In our workflow, this is done in steps 2 (Automatic Project Retrieval) and 3 (Test Execution and Report Generation). These steps strengthen traceability, and thus auditability.
- **Pseudo-accountability and Contributor Identification:** Our approach leverages the Git commit history of the specific project to accurately identify the contributors responsible for both the development code and the test cases (Step 1: Process Initiation). These contributors are then directly included in the verification process (Step 5: Contributor Notification to Step 7: Contributor Approval of Their Work). By integrating commit history tracking into the workflow, every modification to the codebase or test code is automatically logged and attributed to the respective contributor. This ensures that all responsible parties are actively involved in the verification and approval process and reinforces accountability.

[10] https://freetsa.org.

- **Error-prone manual testing:** If it is possible to replace manual testing with automated testing in a reasonable manner, this should be a first step, as human errors can usually be reduced in this way. But not every test (especially acceptance tests) can be replaced by automated tests. Having contributors sign off that their tests work correctly ensures that the manual test procedures are up-to-date, thus reducing the number of errors that originate from wrongly understanding outdated test descriptions during manual testing. The problem of documenting results incorrectly could be solved by applying the four-eyes principle. The four-eyes principle is not part of our workflow, but can easily be used additionally.

6.1 Advantages

Implementing our workflow offers multiple benefits, particularly in environments requiring strict traceability and auditability. The key advantages include:

- **Automation:** Since most of the workflow is automated, there is minimal opportunity for interference once the workflow is initiated. This ensures that no party, whether a supervisor or a contributor, can modify the process undetected, including altering test code or tampering with results. Any modifications made, such as changes to the test code, are automatically captured.
- **Enhanced Auditability:** By creating a snapshot of the project at a predetermined point in time, our workflow enables a thorough and verifiable audit process. In the event of a regulatory review, both the complete test results and the exact version of the code that generated those results (i.e. the decompiled/copied code can be examined). This provides a robust foundation for compliance, ensuring that any investigation can be conducted transparently and in full detail.
- **Tamper-Proof Data Exchange and Security:** Multiple safeguards, such as continuous hash value verification, secure distribution of the project, and authentication via a secondary channel (e.g., an email containing the unique token and the corresponding hash value) protect against unauthorized alterations. Even if an outside party intercepts the communication, malicious alterations are prevented because, at this stage, all participants maintain only read access to the archived codebase. Furthermore, to even gain read access, an intermediary would need to acquire both the unique access link and the corresponding project hash, making unauthorized access highly unlikely. This structure significantly reduces the risk of external attacks and preserves the integrity of the data.
- **Traceability and Contributor Accountability:** All contributors are mandated to follow a clearly defined process that involves regularly verifying their work and the corresponding test results, followed by digitally signing off on their changes. By requiring each contributor to sign their modifications within the predetermined timeframe, the workflow promotes a heightened sense of accountability among team members. This structured approach ensures that

every change in the development code is directly linked to a specific contributor, making it possible to trace modifications with full transparency. As a result, any instance of malpractice, unauthorized alterations, or errors can be accurately allocated to the responsible individual. This reinforces accountability, strengthens trust in the integrity of the project, and enhances overall reliability in both development and audit processes.

6.2 Drawbacks of the Proposed Workflow

One drawback of the proposed workflow is that it does not help with tracking contributions made by multiple people or handling cases where one person's changes are overwritten by another person's changes. There is no way to automatically verify who made which contribution. A possible solution is to integrate pair programming, which allows two contributors to share responsibility for the work, making authorship clearer and more collaborative. Another concern is the risk of excessive review work for contributors if the workflow is not followed regularly by the supervisors. To prevent the review process from becoming too extensive and placing too much verification responsibility on contributors, it is recommended to adopt more frequent review cycles and software releases. This helps keep the workload manageable and ensures a smoother development process.

This workflow is most appropriate for organizations operating within critical infrastructure or heavily regulated environments, such as those in the aerospace or automotive industries (e.g., Boeing or Volkswagen). In such contexts, the cost and complexity of the system can be justified by the need for extensive audit trails and tamper-proof records. However, for other companies, the resource requirements may be perceived as disproportionate to the benefits. Specifically:

- **High Implementation and Maintenance Costs:** Introducing and maintaining this approach, complete with databases, blockchain, servers, and various security features, can be expensive, both in terms of hardware and personnel. Some organizations may conclude that these expenses outweigh the anticipated benefits, especially if they have not experienced tampering incidents in the past.
- **Potential Overhead for Non-Critical Industries:** While strict process controls are dominant in industries where safety and compliance are essential, the overhead involved might be impractical for smaller companies or those without stringent regulatory mandates. The additional time and effort needed to manage this system may be seen as restrictive in environments that prioritize flexibility and rapid development cycles.

7 Conclusion

The objective of this research was to enhance the tamper resistance and auditability of test reports, a critical requirement in safety-sensitive industries and critical infrastructures. Numerous real-world incidents demonstrate how faulty documentation and unverified changes have led to severe consequences, many of which could have been mitigated through a robust tamper resistance strategy. This paper proposes a workflow that strengthens tamper resistance by continuously monitoring employee contributions and requiring digital signatures for all modifications. This approach ensures that project changes are securely archived in the database within a predefined timeframe, creating a comprehensive and verifiable audit trail. A key advantage is the seamless integration of digital signatures, requiring minimal additional effort from users while significantly improving data integrity. However, large-scale implementation may introduce some operational overhead for companies that do not operate under strict regulatory requirements. Overall, this workflow provides a practical and effective solution for improving the integrity, transparency, traceability, and auditability of test reports, making it particularly valuable for organizations where compliance and security are paramount.

Disclosure of Interests. The authors have no competing interests to declare that are relevant to the content of this article.

References

1. U.S. Department of Justice, January 2021. https://www.justice.gov/opa/pr/boeing-charged-737-max-fraud-conspiracy-and-agrees-pay-over-25-billion. Accessed 09 Aug 2024
2. Jasrotia, S.S., Kamila, M.K., Sinha, P.: Boeing: reclaiming the lost ground? J. Inf. Technol. Teach. Cases (2024). https://doi.org/10.1177/20438869241255960
3. Gates, D.: Boeing 787 employees falsified inspection records; FAA opens probe. Seattle Times, May 2024. https://www.seattletimes.com/business/boeing-aerospace/faa-opens-new-investigation-into-boeing-787-wing-to-body-join-work. Accessed 04 Sept 2024
4. Schiermeier, Q.: The science behind the Volkswagen emissions scandal. Nature (2015). https://doi.org/10.1038/nature.2015.18426
5. Whitelaw, F., Riley, J., Elmrabit, N.: A review of the insider threat, a practitioner perspective within the U.K. financial services. IEEE Access **12**, 34752–34768 (2024). https://doi.org/10.1109/ACCESS.2024.3373265
6. Wong, D.R., Bhattacharya, S., Butte, A.J.: Prototype of running clinical trials in an untrustworthy environment using blockchain. Nat. Commun. **10**(917), 1–8 (2019). https://doi.org/10.1038/s41467-019-08874-y
7. Yau, S.S., Patel, J.S.: A blockchain-based testing approach for collaborative software development. In: 2020 IEEE International Conference on Blockchain (Blockchain), pp. 98–105 (2020). https://doi.org/10.1109/Blockchain50366.2020.00020
8. Chowdhury, M.J.M., Colman, A., Kabir, M.A., Han, J., Sarda, P.: Blockchain as a notarization service for data sharing with personal data store. In: 2018 17th IEEE International Conference on Trust, Security And Privacy in Computing and Communications/12th IEEE International Conference on Big Data Science and Engineering (TrustCom/BigDataSE), pp. 1330–1335 (2018). https://doi.org/10.1109/TrustCom/BigDataSE.2018.00183

9. Katz, J.: Digital Signatures, vol. 1. Springer, Heidelberg (2010). https://doi.org/10.1007/978-0-387-27712-7
10. Tzelios, K., Williams, L.A.: The psychological impact of digital signatures: a multistudy replication. Technol. Mind Behav. **1**(2) (2020). https://doi.org/10.1037/tmb0000019
11. Bralić, V., Stančić, H., Stengård, M.: A blockchain approach to digital archiving: digital signature certification chain preservation. Rec. Manag. J. **30**(3), 345–362 (2020). https://doi.org/10.1108/RMJ-08-2019-0043
12. Khaliq, S., Abideen Tariq, Z.U., Masood, A.: Role of user and entity behavior analytics in detecting insider attacks. In: 2020 International Conference on Cyber Warfare and Security (ICCWS), pp. 1–6 (2020). https://doi.org/10.1109/ICCWS48432.2020.9292394

Breaking the Android Code: A Decade of Methods, Tools and Trends in Mobile Forensics

José María Gil-Delgado del Pozo, Lander Aguirregomezcorta Belinchon, and Görkem Kılınç Soylu(✉)

Department of Computer Science and Informatics, School of Engineering, Jönköping University, Jönköping, Sweden
{gajo24dk,agla24tq}@student.ju.se, gorkem.kilinc.soylu@ju.se

Abstract. The exponential growth of Android smartphone usage has elevated the relevance of Android-focused mobile forensics in both criminal investigations and cybersecurity domains. This paper presents a systematic literature review (SLR) of methodologies, tools, and challenges associated with forensic investigations of Android applications. The review synthesizes current practices in data acquisition and evaluates the performance of widely used forensic tools, while also discussing emerging trends and critical limitations. This study aims to provide a comprehensive reference for practitioners and researchers, to highlight best practices, and to propose future directions to enhance reliability, reproducibility, and legal defensibility in Android forensic investigations.

Keywords: Android digital forensics · forensic acquisition techniques · forensic analysis tools · anti-forensic techniques · encrypted data extraction · forensic tool evaluation · hybrid acquisition methods · forensic soundness · systematic literature review

1 Introduction

Mobile forensics is a subfield of digital forensics that focuses on the recovery, analysis, and preservation of digital evidence from mobile devices [15]. With the widespread adoption of smartphones, mobile forensics has become increasingly relevant in various fields, including criminal investigations, cybersecurity, and critical infrastructure protection. Modern cyber-physical systems often rely on mobile devices as interfaces or control units, making Android forensic capabilities vital for security incident response in these domains.

The role of mobile forensics extends across multiple domains, such as law enforcement, fraud detection, cybercrime investigation, and corporate data protection. However, forensic analysis of mobile devices is often more complex than traditional computer forensics due to frequent software updates, diverse hardware configurations, and security features, including end-to-end encryption in

E. Bergström et al. (Eds.): CRITIS 2025, LNCS 16291, pp. 200–223, 2026.
https://doi.org/10.1007/978-3-032-19540-1_11

messaging applications [7,57]. Additionally, cloud-based storage further complicates data extraction, as much of the digital evidence is no longer stored solely on the device but on remote servers, requiring legal procedures for access [48]. Mobile forensics also faces significant challenges due to anti-forensic techniques. Malicious actors employ obfuscation tools, secure deletion applications, and encrypted communication platforms to erase or conceal their activities. Obfuscation tools manipulate or obscure data to make forensic analysis more difficult. Some malware applications use polymorphic code, which changes its structure upon each execution, making detection more difficult [21]. These evolving threats require forensic methodologies to adapt in order to maintain the integrity and reliability of collected evidence.

Smartphones operate on different platforms, with Android and iOS being the most prevalent. Each platform presents unique forensic challenges due to its security mechanisms, encryption techniques, and proprietary architectures. While this study acknowledges the broader landscape of mobile forensics, a focused examination of Android forensic methodologies is conducted due to Android's significant global market share and its open-source nature, which allows for more extensive forensic research. As of July 2025, Android holds approximately 74.26% of the global smartphone market, significantly surpassing iOS's 25.39% share [53]. This widespread adoption makes Android devices a frequent subject in forensic investigations. Additionally, Android's open-source nature provides researchers access to its source code, facilitating the development of specialized forensic tools and methodologies, which is less feasible with proprietary systems like iOS [5]. Furthermore, Android powers a vast array of devices across different manufacturers, leading to a variety of hardware configurations and customizations. This diversity presents unique challenges in forensic analysis, requiring research efforts to develop adaptable solutions.

The evolving landscape of mobile security and digital privacy introduces various challenges for forensic investigations. Many traditional forensic tools and methodologies face difficulties when extracting and analyzing data from Android devices. The complexity of forensic data acquisition has led to ongoing discussions about forensic methodologies, tools, and emerging trends. Conducting a systematic literature review (SLR) following established guidelines may provide insights into current methods, their applications, and the limitations that forensic practitioners encounter [31]. Reviewing existing literature may also highlight aspects of forensic methodologies that require further study and refinement.

This research aims to review the methodologies and tools used in mobile forensic investigations, with a specific focus on Android forensics. By narrowing the scope to Android, the study enables a more in-depth examination of platform-specific forensic techniques, tools, challenges, and limitations. To address these aspects, the study considers the following research questions:

- RQ1: What are the most commonly used methodologies and tools for forensic investigations of Android applications?
- RQ2: What are the key challenges and limitations in Android application forensics?

- RQ3: How do commonly used forensic tools perform in terms of data acquisition, analysis, and data recovery in Android application forensics?

2 Background

Mobile forensics involves not only the technical aspects of acquiring and analyzing data but also the theoretical frameworks and procedural models that guide digital investigations. Accordingly, this section offers a broad overview of foundational concepts and specialized methods used throughout the forensics process, focusing on the unique challenges posed by Android platforms. In particular, this section explores established process models, data acquisition techniques, and the diverse security issues that investigators encounter when performing forensic analysis on mobile devices.

2.1 Digital Forensics and Mobile Forensics Foundations

Digital forensics involves methodical processes for retrieving, examining, and presenting electronic information. Subdisciplines include computer forensics, network forensics, cloud forensics, and mobile forensics (each with its own specialized tools and procedures). In the mobile arena, investigators target artifacts ranging from text messages and call logs to application-specific data, such as chat histories, images, and metadata [4]. For instance, messaging platforms often store user content in databases that require decryption or reverse engineering of proprietary formats, posing unique challenges for analysts [7,9].

Although approaches differ among these subdisciplines, the broader methodology typically spans four central phases [14,15]:

- **Identification**: Potential data sources are located, documented, and preserved. On mobile devices, these sources often include device-internal flash memory, removable storage (e.g., SD cards), synchronized cloud repositories, and logs generated by apps.
- **Acquisition**: Practitioners extract data in a manner that maintains evidentiary integrity. Methods include logical or physical imaging, with the choice depending on factors like encryption level, software version, and the capability of available forensic tools.
- **Analysis**: Collected data undergoes thorough examination for relevant evidence. Investigators parse call histories, SMS/MMS messages, installed applications, network connections, and location logs, among other elements. Decryption keys and tool plugins are often required to interpret app databases or recover deleted items.
- **Presentation**: Findings are compiled in a legally admissible format. Reports detail the tools and techniques used, the chain of custody, and the significance of any discovered artifacts, enabling courts or organizational stakeholders to assess the evidence's credibility.

These stages underscore the need for structured, repeatable procedures, particularly in mobile forensics, where device-specific factors like encryption schemes and proprietary file systems can complicate the process. Successfully navigating these hurdles ensures that digital evidence remains credible, accurate, and supportive of legal or organizational decision-making [15].

2.2 Forensic Frameworks and Methodologies for Mobile Investigations

Owing to the intricate hardware configurations, encryption schemes, and data storage methods of modern mobile devices, various forensic frameworks have emerged to guide and standardize investigative practices. In addition to general guidelines from organizations such as the National Institute of Standards and Technology (NIST), specialized process models have been formulated to address the unique challenges posed by smartphones and tablets [20].

Several process models originally developed for digital forensics have been adapted for mobile environments. *The McKemmish model* is one of the earliest structured approaches, outlining four key phases: identification, collection, analysis, and presentation. Although designed for traditional computer forensics, this model provides a foundational framework that is still relevant to mobile investigations [38]. *The Integrated Digital Investigation Process* (IDIP) model builds upon this by including earlier stages such as incident detection and initial response. This proactive focus is particularly valuable in mobile contexts, where rapid reaction to emerging threats is crucial [14]. *The Enhanced Digital Investigation Process* (EDIP) model further extends these frameworks by emphasizing the preservation of volatile evidence and the mitigation of anti-forensic techniques [10]. Applied to mobile forensics, EDIP may involve capturing live memory or monitoring running applications before data is lost due to shutdown or reset.

2.3 Data Acquisition Techniques in Android Forensics

Android's popularity stems from its open-source nature and dominant position in the global smartphone market. However, this diversity results in a fragmented ecosystem, with vendors implementing different bootloaders, chipsets, and security mechanisms. Consequently, forensic methods that work on one device may be ineffective on another, requiring flexible and device-specific approaches. In mobile forensics, four primary data acquisition techniques are commonly used, each offering varying levels of access to system and user data [15,28].

Physical acquisition is the most comprehensive method, involving the creation of a bit-by-bit copy of the device's entire storage. This allows recovery of deleted files, unallocated space, and hidden partitions. While it offers the most complete data set, it often requires bypassing advanced security features, which can be difficult on modern devices.

Logical acquisition uses standard interfaces such as Android Debug Bridge (ADB) or forensic tools like Magnet AXIOM and Cellebrite UFED to extract accessible files and user data from the file system. It is less invasive but cannot recover deleted or encrypted content.

File system acquisition focuses on the structure of files and directories, enabling the extraction of metadata, application-specific folders, and databases such as SQLite files used by many apps [34]. Although more detailed than logical acquisition, it may still be limited by device-level encryption.

Cloud-based acquisition targets data stored in remote services. This method often requires legal authorization and faces obstacles such as multi-factor authentication or remote wipe capabilities [48], but it can reveal valuable synced data and backups unavailable on the device itself.

2.4 Challenges in Android Forensics

Android's fragmented ecosystem, strong encryption mechanisms, and user modifications present several challenges to forensic investigators. These obstacles require adaptable and often device-specific analysis methods. A broader survey by [18] underscores that such challenges are persistent across multiple domains of mobile forensics, from device-level encryption and volatile memory artifacts to the need for standardized acquisition procedures.

Modern Android devices typically integrate *Advanced Encryption Standard* (AES) with hardware-backed key management to protect user data [8]. Messaging applications like WhatsApp and Signal utilize *end-to-end encryption* (E2EE), ensuring messages remain cryptographically protected from sender to recipient [57]. Consequently, digital examiners often rely on recovered artifacts, such as locally cached database files or temporary memory dumps, to gain insight into encrypted communications. As app developers refine encryption implementations and secure ephemeral storage, these remnants become increasingly difficult to identify and interpret.

Malicious actors can turn to *anti-forensic* measures to hide or destroy incriminating evidence. *Secure deletion tools* are designed to overwrite deleted data repeatedly with random or specific patterns, rendering it irrecoverable by standard forensic techniques [24]. By sanitizing the disk or flash storage thoroughly, attackers can purge sensitive files in a manner that circumvents typical data recovery methods. *Obfuscation methods* such as steganography, XOR encoding, and layered encryption can conceal data within seemingly benign files [27,46]. Steganography, for instance, embeds hidden information inside images or audio, while XOR-based schemes may encrypt or randomize file content to evade detection by conventional scanning tools. *Hidden partitions or containers* can be used to store encrypted data in volumes mounted to obscure system paths or in partitions that do not appear in standard file system scans [28]. This technique makes automated forensic analysis more difficult and requires investigators to apply more targeted methods. To combat these tactics, analysts employ memory forensics and live acquisition methods to capture ephemeral encryption keys or decrypted message content that persists only in RAM [2] [58]. Decompiling or reverse engineering suspicious applications can also reveal how they implement custom obfuscation or data-wiping routines.

Rooted devices and *custom ROMs* present additional challenges for forensic analysis. Gaining root privileges on an Android device provides elevated access to system areas, logs, and configurations, allowing malicious users to delete or modify evidence [11]. Similarly, custom ROMs (e.g., LineageOS) replace stock firmware, potentially altering the file system layout or disabling default security checks. These factors often demand that investigators adopt specialized or device-specific methods to ensure data is acquired accurately and preserved in a legally defensible manner.

2.5 Emerging Trends in Mobile Forensics

Recent advancements in mobile forensics involve the integration of artificial intelligence, blockchain, and Internet of Things (IoT) technologies. As highlighted in [18], these emerging techniques represent not only opportunities for more robust investigations but also introduce new layers of complexity that require ongoing methodological development. AI techniques such as machine learning and natural language processing improve the speed and accuracy of analyzing large volumes of mobile data, though expert oversight remains essential [41]. Blockchain offers a secure method for maintaining the chain of custody and ensuring evidence integrity [30].

The rise of IoT devices presents both challenges and opportunities, requiring forensic tools to adapt to diverse data sources and environments [1]. Notable trends in IoT forensics include blockchain-based logging, fog computing, and video-based evidence extraction, all of which aim to address the complexity and scale of investigations in connected ecosystems [40].

3 Method

This section outlines the research approach adopted for this study, detailing the systematic literature review process, search strategy, selection criteria, and quality assessment measures. The methodology ensures a structured and rigorous approach to reviewing existing literature, minimizing bias, and enhancing the reliability of findings.

3.1 Research Method

The review follows the SLR guidelines by Kitchenham and Charters [31], ensuring rigor, transparency, and replicability. The process consists of three phases: (i) **planning** the review by defining research questions, concepts, and a search strategy; (ii) **conducting** the review through database searches, study selection, and data extraction; and (iii) **reporting** the findings via synthesis and analysis to identify trends, challenges, and gaps.

The searches were performed in IEEE Xplore, ACM Digital Library, Elsevier ScienceDirect, SpringerLink, and Scopus. Keywords and Boolean operators (e.g., "*Android forensics*", "*mobile forensic tools*", and "*data acquisition in Android*") were combined with filters for publication year, language, and file type. Additional sources were identified via backward and forward snowballing.

3.2 Selection Criteria and Quality Assessment

To ensure the inclusion of high-quality and relevant research, specific selection criteria were established.

Inclusion criteria:

- Peer-reviewed journal articles and conference papers published between 2015 and 2025.
- Studies focusing on Android mobile forensics, tools, techniques, and challenges.

Non-peer-reviewed sources, unrelated topics, duplicates, papers without significant forensic contributions, and non-English works were excluded. Quality assessment considered (i) relevance to Android forensic investigations, (ii) methodological rigor, and (iii) transparency in reporting limitations and data sources.

A total of 33 high-quality studies meeting the selection and quality assessment criteria were included in the review and analyzed in depth.

3.3 Data Extraction and Analysis

For each study, structured data extraction captured metadata, research objectives, forensic techniques (e.g., acquisition methods, tools, evaluation approaches), key findings, and recommendations. Comparative synthesis grouped findings by methodological focus, tool usage, and reported challenges, highlighting recurring approaches, device-specific issues, and aspects of forensic soundness. This process ensured consistency and supported evidence triangulation for the subsequent discussion.

4 Results

This section presents the key findings derived from the analysis of selected studies in the field of Android application forensics. Each research question (RQ) is addressed in its own subsection, covering distinct but interconnected themes: methodologies and tools (RQ1), challenges and limitations (RQ2), and forensic tool performance (RQ3). By systematically organizing and synthesizing insights from the literature, the section aims to offer a comprehensive understanding of the current landscape, prevailing practices, and emerging trends in Android forensic investigations.

4.1 Forensic Methodologies and Tools for Android Application Investigations (RQ1)

4.1.1 Overview of Methodologies in Android Forensics

Android forensic investigations involve the acquisition, preservation, and analysis of data stored on Android devices. Given the heterogeneity and rapid evolution

Table 1. Android forensic acquisition methodologies and the studies that discuss them.

Category	Methodology	Description	Key references
Primary acquisition techniques	Manual acquisition	Direct interaction with the device UI (often photographed); useful for quick triage when tools fail or when no root/debug access is available.	[12,51]
	Logical acquisition	Extracts files via standard Android APIs; non-invasive and dominant on un-rooted devices, but cannot recover deleted content.	[3,12,16,42,44,45,49,51,52]
	Physical acquisition	Bit-for-bit copy of device storage; enables recovery of deleted/hidden data; requires root or low-level access and may pose legal/technical risks.	[3,12,16,29,42,44,45,51,52]
Complementary specialised techniques	Memory imaging	Captures volatile RAM to reveal active processes and transient data.	[12,50–52]
	Dynamic file monitoring	Tracks file-system changes during app execution to link user actions to data modifications (e.g., *Argus* tool).	[13,35]
	Dynamic black-box simulation	Simulates user actions in an emulated Android environment to correlate artifacts with behaviour (e.g., *AnForA* framework).	[6]
	Network traffic analysis	Intercepts and analyzes app network communications to capture evidence not stored on device (e.g. message content in transit).	[57]

of the Android ecosystem, methodologies have evolved in parallel, resulting in both standardized and case-specific approaches. Across the reviewed literature, three primary categories of acquisition techniques consistently emerge: manual, logical, and physical acquisition, along with several complementary strategies. The techniques, their descriptions, and the papers that discuss them are summarized in Table 1.

Furthermore, several papers will advocate aligning Android investigations with well-established forensic frameworks such as the NIST model (Preservation, Acquisition, Examination, Analysis, and Reporting) and the DFRWS model (Identification, Preservation, Collection, Examination, Analysis, and Presentation) to guarantee methodological consistency, defensibility, and legal soundness.

4.1.2 Tool Comparison and Integration Practices

A significant number of tools, both commercial and open-source, are employed in Android application forensics. These tools can be categorized based on their primary capabilities: acquisition, analysis, and specialized investigation. Tables 2 and 3 summarize the key tools in each category, highlighting their type and main functionalities.

Many studies converge on a clear finding: no single tool can acquire all the evidential data stored on an Android device. Commercial 'all-in-one' suites, such as Cellebrite UFED and MOBILedit Forensic, are the most frequently cited tools. They typically bypass screen locks, retrieve encrypted artifacts, and generate well-structured courtroom reports. However, these suites are expensive and limited to the devices they explicitly support [36,43,44,49]. Free, open-source alternatives such as Autopsy and AFLogical are readily available and run on a wider range of handsets, yet they prove far less effective when the evidence is encrypted [51] or resides in cloud services [17,56]. To bridge these gaps, several authors show that combining rapid logical extraction with a deeper physical image yields substantially broader coverage: application-level traces can be correlated with device-level files, and loss of artifacts is markedly reduced [36,42,49].

4.1.3 Recent Trends and Innovations

New methodologies and tools are addressing long-standing limitations in coverage, depth, and precision. The trend is shifting toward automation, behavioral analysis, and dynamic monitoring.

Argus captures file modifications caused by user actions and creates snapshots of the device's file system state. This enables precise correlation of user actions to data changes [13]. Fordroid achieves 98% accuracy in identifying the storage locations of sensitive data and complete schema extraction from APKs, highlighting the effectiveness of static approaches when dynamic analysis is unfeasible [35]. AnForA introduces a new dimension of forensic soundness by maintaining fidelity and repeatability, using emulator-based testing to track artifacts in response to emulated behaviors [6].

AI-driven tools are emerging as a complementary layer, applying machine learning to automatically classify and triage artifacts (especially multimedia and messaging data) while NLP models can surface entity mentions and contextual cues from app logs for hypothesis generation. These models enhance prioritization of artifact review and reduce human effort in initial triage.

In parallel, cloud-focused methodologies have been gaining traction as mobile users increasingly rely on cloud-backed apps. Researchers have demonstrated effective techniques for detecting forensic artifacts from cloud services on both internal storage and volatile memory. [19] proposes an automated approach to recover residual data (e.g., logins, uploads, file sharing) even after deletion. Runtime memory dumps recover credentials and metadata from apps like Baidu Cloud and 360 Cloud [17], while a comparative evaluation shows notable variability among commercial forensic suites [16].

Overall, Android forensics is evolving toward hybrid methodologies integrating static and dynamic analysis, automation, and robust validation. While ADB, Andriller, and UFED remain foundational, innovations like Fordroid, AnForA, and Argus are expanding the scope of reliable forensic extraction.

4.1.4 RQ1 Synthesis

The reviewed literature on Android forensic methodologies and tools reveals a dynamic field shaped by technological diversity and ongoing innovation. Logical and physical acquisition remain foundational, with logical methods favored for non-invasiveness and physical methods valued for completeness. Manual and environmental approaches are still used in specific field scenarios.

Tool use is highly contextual, influenced by device state, OS version, and investigation scope. Andriller, Cellebrite UFED, and AFLogical form the core of acquisition, while platforms like Fordroid, AnForA, and Argus increasingly support analysis and recovery. Static tools excel in schema extraction, dynamic tools in behavioral analysis, and GUI-based platforms in visualization and reporting.

The complexity of modern Android ecosystems calls for multi-tool workflows and hybrid methodologies spanning static, dynamic, and memory-based techniques. Forensic soundness, reproducibility, and interoperability remain central, with automation and dynamic monitoring poised to enhance precision and coverage.

4.2 Key Challenges and Limitations in Android Application Forensics (RQ2)

As Android forensic practices mature, researchers and practitioners continue to face a wide range of obstacles that hinder the effectiveness and reliability of investigations. These challenges stem from both technical constraints such as platform diversity and encryption and broader issues related to forensic soundness, legal admissibility, and evolving anti-forensic tactics. The following subsections outline the most significant limitations identified across the reviewed literature.

4.2.1 Device and OS Fragmentation

The vast heterogeneity of Android devices is one of the most pervasive obstacles to forensic consistency and tool reliability. Devices differ in chipset architecture, file systems (e.g., YAFFS2, Ext4), bootloaders, and security patches. [23] empirically shows OEM-specific customizations and preinstalled app ecosystems across more than 200 vendors, underscoring how firmware divergence and supply-chain variability yield inconsistent artifacts and behaviors that complicate repeatable acquisition and parsing.

Likewise, [37] reports version and model-dependent extraction success rates of MOBILedit (including issues on devices with newer boot chains and encryption), illustrating how each model often requires device-specific profiles, cables, and workflows, effectively prohibiting a universal toolkit.

4.2.2 Built-In Security and Access Limitations

Android's default security features severely limit evidence access. Features such as file-based encryption (FBE), secure boot, and sandboxing prevent forensic tools from acquiring data unless privileged access (e.g., root or custom recovery) is achieved. [26] shows that even when data at rest is protected, unencrypted metadata leakage is limited, while content remains shielded, practically blocking straightforward file-level acquisition in many workflows.

Complementing this, [22] analyzes secure boot and bootloader controls and proposes a legally-aware extraction model; they note that locked bootloaders and modern storage (e.g., UFS) can thwart physical imaging and even chip-level approaches unless a validated vulnerability or vendor cooperation is available.

4.2.3 Evidence Volatility and Ephemerality

Mobile evidence is highly volatile—application caches, logs, and RAM artifacts can be overwritten or lost on shutdown, remote wipe, OS clean-up, or app updates. Live RAM capture methods (e.g., device-specific modes such as Odin) are possible [58] but must be conducted quickly to avoid altering the system state.

Volatile evidence of inter-app messaging can be recovered [55], though persistence is short-lived and reconstruction requires rapid, minimally intrusive acquisition. Live acquisitions may also fail due to power constraints or process interruptions in field conditions [51].

4.2.4 Anti-forensics and Malicious Countermeasures

A growing challenge in Android forensics is the proliferation of anti-forensic strategies. [33] empirically shows that malware abusing accessibility services can execute "living-off-the-land" actions (e.g., UI-driven operations) that minimize on-disk artifacts, hindering both live and post-mortem analysis.

At a data-manipulation level, [47] demonstrates how timestamp tampering and artifact manipulation can be performed and detected, evidencing that trail obfuscation and selective wiping can degrade examiner confidence and tool output if not specifically validated against such attacks. Similarly, [42] observed that certain recovery tools produced corrupted or padded files, illustrating how artifact manipulation—whether intentional or incidental—can compromise evidentiary integrity. In addition, [57] highlight that encrypted and ephemeral messaging functions act as built-in anti-forensic barriers, leaving investigators with incomplete or non-reproducible evidence trails.

4.2.5 Tool Immaturity and Validation Gaps

Tool limitations are a recurring theme across studies. [32] experimentally compares ADB-based and commercial suites (e.g., Magnet, Belkasoft, Autopsy), finding inconsistent artifact coverage and output across devices/OS versions for common evidence types.

Further, [25] shows that even platform-provided backup mechanisms (often treated as "forensically friendly") can diverge from ground truth in corner cases (e.g., databases with pending writes), underscoring the need for standardized validation before courtroom use.

4.2.6 Cloud and Network Complexity

With mobile applications increasingly reliant on cloud services, forensic practitioners face challenges accessing off-device data. [56] outlines a tamper-evident, HSM-backed approach to controlled cloud acquisitions and stresses the hurdles of provider APIs, jurisdiction, and chain-of-custody when evidence resides off-device.

For app ecosystems, [54] details Android Telegram artifacts, emphasizing encryption, replication, and volatility of cloud-synchronized data; often, only partial, decontextualized sync remnants are available on-device without provider cooperation.

4.2.7 Legal and Ethical Constraints

Forensic analysis of Android devices is deeply entangled with privacy and legal considerations. [22] emphasizes that rooting or bypassing device security to defeat encryption can jeopardize forensic soundness unless the method is transparent, validated, and proportional to the investigative need (and jurisdictionally authorized).

In parallel, [59] discusses using custom recovery as a controlled pathway for physical imaging on locked devices, while noting the evidentiary risks (partition modification, logs) and the necessity of documenting all changes to maintain admissibility.

4.2.8 RQ2 Synthesis

[37] stresses that Android's handset and OS fragmentation (different chipsets, boot chains, file systems, and update cadences) means every model "speaks its own dialect," forcing device-specific exploits and cabling instead of a universal toolkit. Building on that, [26] shows how full-disk/file-based encryption and locked bootloaders can block even chip-off imaging, while [22] warns that rooting

or flashing a custom recovery to bypass those safeguards may overwrite system partitions and compromise forensic soundness.

Volatility is another recurring limitation: [57] highlights that encrypted and ephemeral messaging functions in social apps can erase evidence after brief retention windows, leaving only incomplete traces in memory or network captures. Likewise, [42] observed that certain recovery tools produced corrupted or padded files after factory resets, illustrating how fragile data can vanish or degrade if not acquired immediately. [13] further emphasizes that obfuscation and encryption techniques in modern apps restrict investigators to volatile logs and caches that can be purged automatically by the OS.

At the same time, [33,47] catalogue a rising tide of anti-forensic tactics: secure-wipe utilities, timestamp tampering, trail obfuscation, and even attacks that crash forensic software, all designed to hide or destroy incriminating traces before an examiner powers on the phone.

Tool maturity remains uneven: [25,32] find that commercial and open-source suites often disagree on what they can extract, lack thorough documentation, and are rarely validated, raising admissibility concerns in court. Finally, [54,56] note that key artifacts now live in cloud back-ends protected by provider-specific APIs and multi-jurisdictional privacy laws; access tokens discovered on the device may expire within hours, and existing tools offer only partial, app-by-app coverage, leaving investigators to piece together incomplete, legally sensitive remnants.

4.3 Performance of Commonly Used Forensic Tools in Data Acquisition, Analysis, and Recovery (RQ3)

4.3.1 Performance in Data Acquisition

Forensic tools vary widely in their ability to acquire data from Android devices, with trade-offs between speed, depth, and technical requirements. Logical acquisition tools like ADB Backup and Magnet Acquire are praised for their accessibility and non-invasiveness, but fall short in extracting deleted or encrypted content. The study in [36] highlights that ADB Backup, while scriptable and free, provided fewer artifacts and required over 3 h for logical extraction.

By contrast, physical acquisition methods such as DD Imaging, FTK Imager, and Andriller allow deeper access to device memory and the potential to recover deleted data. [42] found that while AccessData FTK Imager could retrieve deleted artifacts, including pictures, audio, and video, it failed to recover contacts, SMS, or call logs, and also exhibited low throughput, recovering only about 14% of the device's storage in some cases. [43] confirms that FTK Imager could not extract deleted contacts or SMS, although it did recover some media. However, recovery was inconsistent across different device models, and processing times remained high. Andriller has shown moderate success in recovering browser history, Wi-Fi credentials, and some encrypted databases, but these findings remain anecdotal and require further validation in controlled experiments.

High-performing hybrid tools like Belkasoft Acquisition and Magnet Acquire combine logical and physical capabilities. In the same comparative study [36],

Belkasoft completed logical acquisition in just 10 min and yielded the highest number of artifacts when paired with Belkasoft Evidence Center.

4.3.2 Artifact Detection and Recovery Capabilities

Artifact recovery is a primary metric for assessing a mobile forensics suite. A controlled comparison [49] on a factory-reset Nexus 6P found that Paraben E3:DS reconstructed all tested Facebook, Twitter, and WhatsApp artifacts with reliable timestamps, whereas Autopsy recovered none for Facebook and Twitter and retrieved WhatsApp items without temporal metadata.

A broader evaluation [39] examined a 196 MB Android-10 logical image using three modern forensic suites. Magnet AXIOM achieved the highest multimedia recovery, extracting 61.9k images—about 10% more than Autopsy—and carving roughly 11k open-format documents. Belkasoft X proved the strongest in encryption-aware analysis, identifying 278 encrypted containers missed by the other tools and leading in app-inventory and chat artifact counts. Autopsy retrieved 3.6k open documents but recovered less than half the installed-app artifacts obtained by its commercial competitors.

4.3.3 Recovery of Deleted and Hidden Data

The ability to recover deleted files is a key factor distinguishing higher-tier forensic solutions. An evaluation [42] found that DiskDigger recovered the highest number of files (20,145), particularly multimedia formats such as .jpeg and .mp3, while Recover My Files extracted the largest total data size (7.37 GB) and even recovered some uncommon file formats like .myob and .spss. Foremost was especially effective in slack space recovery, retrieving deleted graphical content from memory remnants. In contrast, tools such as AFLogical and AccessData FTK performed poorly on factory-reset or encrypted devices; for example, AFLogical produced empty outputs after a reset, confirming that logical-only acquisition is ineffective on reformatted devices. Similar results in [43] showed that AFLogical could not recover even basic user data such as contacts, SMS, or MMS after a reset, underscoring the need for physical or hybrid acquisition methods for meaningful recovery.

4.3.4 Tool Integration and Comparative Strengths

A recurring conclusion across studies is that no single forensic tool offers complete coverage, and a multi-tool strategy is often necessary to combine complementary strengths and offset individual weaknesses. Magnet Acquire is frequently noted for rapid GUI-based logical acquisition, while DD Imaging remains a practical option for physical extraction in cost-sensitive environments, and Belkasoft is recognized for its detailed analysis and handling of encrypted artifacts [36]. The effectiveness of any tool is also influenced by factors such as device model, OS version, and app-level encryption [39]. Overall, forensic tools vary widely in acquisition depth, artifact scope, and recovery capabilities. Table 3 consolidates these observations, summarizing the performance characteristics of commonly used tools based on insights from multiple comparative evaluations.

Table 2. Acquisition and recovery tools in Android forensics.

Tool	Type	Artifact Coverage	Deleted Data Recovery	Strengths	Limitations
ADB Backup/AFLogical	Logical	SMS, MMS, contacts	No	Free, low-level access not needed	Cannot recover deleted/encrypted data
FTK Imager	Logical/Phys.	SMS, contacts, images	Yes	Good for deleted contacts	GUI-only; slow
Andriller	Partial phys.	Browser, Wi-Fi, chats	Yes	Encrypted DB cracking	No cloud; Android-only
Dr.Fone	Phys. (soft)	Media, app data	Yes	Rich app/media recovery	Slow; some data types missed
Magnet Acquire	Log./Phys.	Broad (with analysis)	Yes	Fast, GUI-based	Large outputs; needs license
Cellebrite UFED	Log./Phys.	Wide app/device scope	Yes	Locks bypass; reliable extractions	Expensive; selective app support
XRY, Oxygen, MOBILedit	Log./Phys.	Enterprise range	Yes	Broad support; scalable	Win-only; proprietary format
Magnet AXIOM	Log./Phys.	Extensive apps/media	Yes	Integrated carving/analysis	Heavy; licensed
Belkasoft X	Log./Phys.	Encrypted app data	Yes	Most artifacts; encrypted DBs	Commercial only
DiskDigger	File-level	Media files	Yes	Large total file recovery	Fewer rare formats
Recover My Files	File-level	Broad file types	Yes	Recovers rare formats (.spss)	Slightly lower total recovery

Table 3. Analysis and specialized tools in Android forensics.

Tool	Type	Artifact Coverage	Deleted Data Recovery	Strengths	Limitations
Autopsy (Sleuth Kit)	Analysis	FS artifacts, timelines	Partial	GUI; open-source	Limited encrypted recovery
SQLite Browser, Meld	Manual analysis	Raw DBs, hex	N/A	Direct binary view	Manual; no automation
Volatility Framework	Memory analysis	RAM (live data)	N/A	Deep RAM insight	Needs RAM dump; plug-in issues
ForDroid	Static analysis	DB schema, flow	N/A	Taint analysis; APK logic	No runtime or obfuscation
AnForA	Dynamic analysis	File changes	N/A	Behavior simulation in VM	Misses pre-sim. artifacts
Argus	Dyn. monitoring	File modification logs	N/A	Tracks user-file interaction	Misses startup traces

4.3.5 Key Considerations in Forensic Tool Selection

Performance metrics such as acquisition time, artifact quantity, format coverage, and ability to process encrypted or deleted data are all critical when selecting forensic tools. Tools must also be evaluated on their:

- **Forensic soundness**: Whether the tool alters the target system during acquisition.
- **Usability and automation**: Execution time, interface design, and report generation.
- **Legal admissibility**: Audit trails, logging mechanisms, and validation standards.

Given these variables, practitioners are advised to test toolchains in their specific environments and to use layered analysis workflows, as supported by findings in [42] and in [36].

4.3.6 RQ3 Synthesis

Belkasoft X's 10-minute logical acquisition is 18 times faster than ADB Backup's 3 h. Physical or file-level tools outperform logical ones for deleted content: DiskDigger's 20145 carved files were around 2.7 times the file count of the next best tool in [42]. Across three cross-tool evaluations, Belkasoft X succeeded against all tested AES-encrypted app databases, whereas Autopsy failed on more than 40% of the same datasets. Logical acquisition is referenced in 65% of the papers for its safety and ease, yet those same studies acknowledge its inability to recover post-reset or encrypted artifacts, a gap physical methods fill at the cost of soundness.

No single Android forensic tool delivers complete, fastest, and most reliable acquisition, analysis, and recovery. Commercial hybrid suites such as Belkasoft X and Magnet Axiom offer the best all-around performance, combining rapid logical extraction, superior encrypted-data handling, and courtroom-ready audit logs. Utilities focused on a single task dominate niche metrics: DiskDigger and

Table 4. Key considerations across tools.

Tool	Forensic soundness	Usability/automation	Legal admissibility
ADB Backup	Logical and non-invasive	Scriptable, free, but slow (around 3 h)	Low risk (no root)
Magnet Acquire	Logical and non-invasive	GUI-based; fast logical extraction	Low risk (no root)
FTK Imager	Physical mode; may alter system	GUI-dependent; time-consuming	Potential risk (system alteration)
Andriller	Partial physical; often root-dependent	Mid-level runtime; CLI/GUI options	Risk (root may compromise evidence)
Belkasoft X	Least-intrusive acquisition first; chain-of-custody hashing	Very fast (around 10 min) commercial UI	Built-in hash and task logs for courtroom chain-of-custody
Dr.Fone	Requires device root for deep recovery (system modified)	Wizard UI; step-by-step export and recovery	Vendor claims data remains admissible in court
DiskDigger	Full scan needs root; risk to integrity	Basic scan seconds; deep scan minutes	No documented courtroom validation
Recover My Files	Forensic Imager creates sector-level DD/AFF/E01 with hashes	Wizard workflow; event log and progress	E01 format widely accepted as evidence
Autopsy (Sleuth Kit)	Post-acquisition analysis (no device alteration)	Free GUI suite; moderate automation (slower parsing)	Standard reports; widely accepted output
Cellebrite UFED	Physical extraction via exploit (device state altered)	Dedicated hardware; rapid full extraction	Detailed logs; widely accepted in court
Oxygen Forensic Suite	Logical (no root) or rooted physical (system modified)	GUI tool; broad device/app support	Comprehensive reports; accepted with proper procedure

Recover My Files remain unmatched for bulk deleted-file carving. Conversely, ADB Backup and similar logical-only tools are indispensable when forensic soundness or device warranty constraints forbid rooting, despite their limited depth and slower runtimes.

Consequently, multi-tool, multi-layer workflows are essential: practitioners routinely pair a fast logical acquisition (e.g., Magnet Acquire) with at least one deep-recovery tool (e.g., DiskDigger) and a rich analysis suite (e.g., Belkasoft X) to cross-validate findings and mitigate the weaknesses inherent to any single method.

5 Discussion

This systematic review addressed three interlocking research questions: RQ1 mapped the tools and methodological approaches currently used to acquire and analyze Android applications; RQ2 examined the technical, procedural, and legal challenges that constrain those approaches; and RQ3 assessed how well the principal tools perform when benchmarked on representative datasets. Taken together, the results show investigators moving toward hybrid static-and-dynamic workflows that combine logical and physical acquisition, emulator-based analysis, and memory forensics. Tools like Belkasoft X, Magnet Axiom, and Argus demonstrate the value of integrating rapid logical extraction, encrypted data handling, and behavioral monitoring, while AI-driven triage and NLP log analysis are beginning to reduce manual review burdens. Cloud-hosted artifacts (recoverable via storage and memory-level techniques from apps such as Baidu Cloud and 360 Cloud) are increasingly critical for bypassing on-device encryption.

Persistent tensions remain: suites with broad platform coverage often sacrifice granular artifact recovery, and frameworks maximising forensic soundness can slow or limit acquisitions. No single tool offers complete coverage: for example, AFLogical fails on post-reset devices, FTK Imager recovers media but not contacts/SMS, and DiskDigger carves around 20,145 deleted files (2.7 times more than its nearest rival) yet misses rare formats that Recover My Files can extract. These contradictions underscore the need for shared validation corpora, modular toolchains capable of adapting to Android's security evolution, and closer coordination between technical and legal stakeholders to ensure evidentiary requirements shape tool development.

5.1 Implications and Benefits of This Review

For researchers, the categorised methodologies in Tables 1, 2 and 3 (ranging from manual triage to dynamic black-box simulation) highlight innovations such as Fordroid's 98% schema extraction, AnForA's emulator-based behavioural mapping, and Argus's file-change correlation. For practitioners, the comparative tool data in Table 4 show that Belkasoft X's 10-min logical acquisition outpaces ADB Backupy's 3 h while also succeeding against all tested AES-encrypted app databases; Magnet Axiom dominates raw multimedia recovery; and DiskDigger excels in bulk deleted-file carving. These concrete benchmarks, together with evidence of vendor and OS-specific variability, allow investigators to design multi-tool workflows that balance acquisition depth, forensic soundness, and admissibility.

The review also consolidates key constraints: device fragmentation across 200 OEMs, inconsistent artifacts, encryption (FBE, locked bootloaders), volatile evidence losses, and anti-forensic tactics such as timestamp tampering, selective wiping, and tool-crashing malware. By understanding these patterns, practitioners can better prioritize live acquisition, memory imaging, or cloud artifact recovery according to case urgency and technical feasibility.

5.2 Limitations and Potential Threats to Validity

Although inclusion and exclusion criteria ensured relevance and quality, restricting the search to English academic sources may have omitted valuable gray literature. The fast-paced evolution of Android and its tools means that some recent developments may not be captured. Performance findings rely on existing comparative studies, which differ in experimental setup; nevertheless, cross-study patterns (e.g., safety of logical methods but inability to recover post-reset or encrypted artifacts) were consistent.

The methodology was documented, cross-checked, and supported by snowballing across multiple databases, but the conclusions largely reflect laboratory-based contexts. Operational, legal, or geographic differences could impact tool efficacy in the field. Future work should extend standardized validation protocols, expand real-world testing, and refine hybrid workflows that integrate static, dynamic, memory, and cloud analysis (particularly for volatile or encrypted environments) while maintaining forensic soundness and legal defensibility.

6 Conclusions and Future Work

This systematic literature review has examined methodologies, tools, challenges, and performance considerations within the field of Android mobile forensics, synthesizing key insights into the current forensic landscape. The analysis highlighted that while logical and physical acquisition methods remain central, there is a clear trend toward hybrid approaches that integrate dynamic and behavior-based analyses. This shift responds to increasing forensic complexity driven by device fragmentation, robust encryption, evolving software ecosystems, and sophisticated anti-forensic techniques.

Commercial tools such as Magnet Axiom and Belkasoft X offer advanced capabilities, particularly in handling encrypted and deleted data. In contrast, open-source tools like Autopsy and Andriller continue to provide essential functionality, particularly suited to academic research or resource-constrained environments. However, the review underscores that no single forensic tool currently achieves comprehensive coverage across all data types, device conditions, or investigation contexts. Consequently, multi-tool workflows have become a pragmatic necessity, leveraging complementary strengths to mitigate the inherent limitations of individual tools.

Significant challenges persist in acquiring data from encrypted and cloud-based sources, effectively countering anti-forensic methods, and ensuring evidence admissibility. Recent works demonstrate that automated analysis of cloud client applications can reveal residual data such as usernames, passwords, and file activity on Android devices—even when applications attempt to hide or delete these traces. Meanwhile, research on volatile memory analysis shows that runtime memory dumps can expose user identities, timestamps, and file operation logs from cloud apps like Baidu Cloud and 360 Cloud. These findings point to the increasing importance of cloud-specific forensic workflows that incorporate both storage- and memory-level analysis.

Simultaneously, artificial intelligence is beginning to influence forensic methodologies. It has been shown that AI-driven systems can assist with triaging forensic artifacts using facial recognition and natural language processing, enabling scalable person-of-interest detection within large volumes of messaging and multimedia data [41]. These techniques help reduce manual workloads and offer new pathways for integrating behavioral and semantic context into forensic analysis pipelines.

Future research must therefore prioritize the development of standardized validation protocols, improve resistance to anti-forensic measures, and enhance the utility and integration of emerging analysis methodologies such as emulator-based frameworks (e.g., AnForA, Fordroid), AI-based triage models, and automated cloud forensics. In particular, there is a need for robust toolsets that can intelligently correlate artifacts across volatile memory, cloud services, and encrypted containers, while remaining forensically sound and legally admissible. Furthermore, expanding the role of reinforcement learning and adaptive analysis agents, as explored in AI-guided forensic collection models, may enable more responsive and autonomous investigations in the face of growing data complexity.

In summary, this review provides a valuable foundation for practitioners and researchers alike by underscoring the importance of tool interoperability, regular updates, and rigorous validation in meeting the evolving demands of Android forensic investigations.

References

1. Acquah, M.: Integration of cloud in mobile forensics. In: Research Nexus in IT, Law, Cyber Security & Forensics, pp. 125–130. AIMS Research Nexus/iSTEAMS (2022). https://doi.org/10.22624/AIMS/CRP-BK3-P21
2. Adelstein, F.: Live forensics: diagnosing your system without killing it first. Commun. ACM **49**(2), 63–66 (2006). https://doi.org/10.1145/1113034.1113070
3. Al-Mousa, M.R., et al.: Examining digital forensic evidence for android applications. In: 2022 International Arab Conference on Information Technology (ACIT), pp. 1–8 (2022). https://doi.org/10.1109/ACIT57182.2022.9994221

4. Al Mutawa, N., Baggili, I., Marrington, A.: Forensic analysis of social networking applications on mobile devices. Digit. Investig. **9**, S24–S33 (2012). https://doi.org/10.1016/j.diin.2012.05.007, the Proceedings of the Twelfth Annual DFRWS Conference
5. Almuqren, A., Alsuwaelim, H., Hafizur Rahman, M.M., Ibrahim, A.A.: A systematic literature review on digital forensic investigation on android devices. Procedia Comput. Sci. **235**, 1332–1352 (2024). https://doi.org/10.1016/j.procs.2024.04.126, international Conference on Machine Learning and Data Engineering (ICMLDE 2023)
6. Anglano, C., Canonico, M., Guazzone, M.: The android forensics automator (anfora): A tool for the automated forensic analysis of android applications. Comput. Secur. **88**, 101650 (2020). https://doi.org/10.1016/j.cose.2019.101650
7. Anglano, C.: Forensic analysis of whatsapp messenger on android smartphones. Digit. Investig. **11**(3), 201–213 (2014). https://doi.org/10.1016/j.diin.2014.04.003, special Issue: Embedded Forensics
8. (AOSP): Android open source project, Full-Disk Encryption (2023). https://source.android.com/security/encryption
9. Barmpatsalou, K., Damopoulos, D., Kambourakis, G., Katos, V.: A critical review of 7 years of mobile device forensics. Digit. Investig. **10**(4), 323–349 (2013)
10. Baryamureeba, V., Tushabe, F.: The enhanced digital investigation process model. Digital Investigation (2004). https://api.semanticscholar.org/CorpusID:18623260
11. Bennett, D.: The challenges facing computer forensics investigators in obtaining information from mobile devices for use in criminal investigations. Forensic Sci. Int. **231**(1–3), 130–135 (2012)
12. Bernardo, B.M.V., Mamede, H.S., Barroso, J.M.P., dos Santos, V.M.P.D.: Mobile device forensics framework: a toolbox to support and enhance this process. Emerging Sci. J. **8**(3), 972–998 (2024)
13. Boztas, A., De Jong, J., Hadjigeorghiou, C.: Argus: A new approach for forensic analysis of apps on mobile devices. Forensic Sci. Int. Digital Investigation **53**, 301938 (2025). https://doi.org/10.1016/j.fsidi.2025.301938
14. Carrier, B., Spafford, E.H.: Getting physical with the digital investigation process. Int. J. Digital Evidence **2**(2) (2003)
15. Casey, E.: Digital evidence and computer crime: Forensic science, computers, and the internet. Academic Press (2011)
16. Chauhan, P., Jaitly, T., Agrawal, A.K.: Comparative analysis of mobile forensic proprietary tools: an application in forensic investigation. J. Forensic Sci. Res. **6**, 077–082 (2022). https://doi.org/10.29328/journal.jfsr.1001039
17. Chen, L., Zhao, H.: Forensic analysis of cloud storage on android volatile memory. In: Proceedings of the 12th International Conference on Latest Trends in Engineering and Technology (ICLTET). pp. 20–23. Kuala Lumpur, Malaysia, May 2017. https://doi.org/10.15242/IIE.E0517012
18. Chernyshev, M., Zeadally, S., Baig, Z., Woodward, A.: Mobile forensics: advances, challenges, and research opportunities. IEEE Secur. Privacy **15**(6), 42–51 (2017). https://doi.org/10.1109/msp.2017.4251107
19. Daryabar, F., Tadayon, M.H., Parsi, A., Sadjadi, H.: Automated analysis method for forensic investigation of cloud applications on android. In: 2016 8th International Symposium on Telecommunications (IST), pp. 145–150 (2016). https://doi.org/10.1109/ISTEL.2016.7881799
20. on Digital Evidence (SWGDE), S.W.G.: Swgde best practices for mobile device forensic analysis. Tech. rep., Scientific Working Group on Digital Evidence / National Institute of Standards and Technology (2020)

21. Faruki, P., Bharmal, A., Laxmi, V., Ganmoor, V., Gaur, M.S., Conti, M., Rajarajan, M.: Android security: a survey of issues, malware penetration, and defenses. IEEE Commun. Surv. Tutorials **17**(2), 998–1022 (2015)
22. Fukami, A., Stoykova, R., Geradts, Z.: A new model for forensic data extraction from encrypted mobile devices. Forensic Sci. Int. Digital Investigation **38**, 301169 (2021). https://doi.org/10.1016/j.fsidi.2021.301169
23. Gamba, J., Rashed, M., Razaghpanah, A., Tapiador, J., Vallina-Rodriguez, N.: An analysis of pre-installed android software. In: 2020 IEEE Symposium on Security and Privacy (SP), pp. 1039–1055 (2020). https://doi.org/10.1109/SP40000.2020.00013
24. Garfinkel, S., Shelat, A.: Remembrance of data passed: a study of disk sanitization practices. IEEE Secur. Privacy **1**(1), 17–27 (2003). https://doi.org/10.1109/MSECP.2003.1176992
25. Geus, J., Ottmann, J., Freiling, F.: Systematic evaluation of forensic data acquisition using smartphone local backup. In: Proceedings of the Digital Forensics Research Conference USA (DFRWS USA) (2023)
26. Groß, T., Ahmadova, M., Müller, T.: Analyzing android's file-based encryption: Information leakage through unencrypted metadata. In: Proceedings of the 14th International Conference on Availability, Reliability and Security (ARES 2019), pp. 1–7. ACM (2019). https://doi.org/10.1145/3339252.3340340
27. Harris, R.: Arriving at an anti-forensics consensus: Examining how to define and control the anti-forensics problem. Digit. Investig. **3**, 44–49 (2006). https://doi.org/10.1016/j.diin.2006.06.005, the Proceedings of the 6th Annual Digital Forensic Research Workshop (DFRWS '06)
28. Hoog, A.: Android Forensics: Investigation. Elsevier, Analysis and Mobile Security for Google Android (2011)
29. Jeyaseeli, J.A.M., Shanthi, C.: A smart techniques to extract the deleted data form the android application. International Journal of Health Sciences **6**(S1), 2864–2871 (2022). https://doi.org/10.53730/ijhs.v6nS1.5284
30. Khubrani, M.: Mobile device forensics, challenges and blockchain-based solution. In: Proceedings of the 2nd International Conference on Smart Technologies for Smart Nation (2023)
31. Kitchenham, B., Charters, S.M.: Guidelines for performing systematic literature reviews in software engineering. Tech. rep, Technical Report (2007)
32. Kumar, P., Rashid, E., Narayan, R.: A comparative study of mobile forensic tools for android devices. In: Proceedings of the International Conference on Recent Advances in Artificial Intelligence for Sustainable Development (RAISD 2025). Advances in Intelligent Systems Research, vol. 196, pp. 750–757. Atlantis Press (2025). https://doi.org/10.2991/978-94-6463-787-8_56
33. Leguesse, Y., Vella, M., Colombo, C., Hernandez-Castro, J.: Reducing the forensic footprint with android accessibility attacks. In: Markantonakis, K., Petrocchi, M. (eds.) STM 2020. LNCS, vol. 12386, pp. 22–38. Springer, Cham (2020). https://doi.org/10.1007/978-3-030-59817-4_2
34. Lessard, J., Kessler, G.: Android forensics: simplifying cell phone examinations. Small Scale Digital Device Forensics J. **4**(1), 1–12 (2010)
35. Lin, X., Chen, T., Zhu, T., Yang, K., Wei, F.: Automated forensic analysis of mobile applications on android devices. Digit. Investig. **26**, S59–S66 (2018). https://doi.org/10.1016/j.diin.2018.04.012
36. Lwin, H.H., Aung, W.P., Lin, K.K.: Comparative analysis of android mobile forensics tools. In: 2020 IEEE Conference on Computer Applications (ICCA), pp. 1–6 (2020). https://doi.org/10.1109/ICCA49400.2020.9022838

37. Maheshwari, K.D., Kumar, P., Ali, N.I., Brohi, I.A., Agha, D.: Digital forensics across multiple android versions using the mobiledit forensic tool. In: 2024 26th International Multi-Topic Conference (INMIC), pp. 1–6 (2024). https://doi.org/10.1109/INMIC64792.2024.11004410
38. McKemmish, R., of Criminology, A.I.: What is Forensic Computing? Trends & issues in crime and criminal justice, Australian Institute of Criminology (1999)
39. Mehta, J., Bhadania, Y., Shah, P., Prajapati, P.: Comparative study of mobile forensics tools: Autopsy, belkasoft x and magnet axiom. In: Proc. 5th Int. Conf. Electron. Sustain. Commun. Syst. (ICESC), pp. 1257–1263 (2024). https://doi.org/10.1109/icesc60852.2024.10689971
40. Musa, N.S., Mirza, N.M., Ali, A.: Current trends in internet of things forensics. In: 2022 International Arab Conference on Information Technology (ACIT), pp. 1–5 (2022). https://doi.org/10.1109/ACIT57182.2022.9994213
41. Mykhaylova, O., Fedynyshyn, T., Sokolov, V., Kyrychok, R.: Person-of-interest detection on mobile forensics data - AI-driven roadmap. In: Proceedings of the Workshop Cybersecurity Providing in Information and Telecommunication Systems (CPITS 2024), Kyiv, Ukraine, February 28, 2024. CEUR Workshop Proceedings, vol. 3654, pp. 239–251. CEUR-WS.org (2024)
42. Ogazi-Onyemaechi, B.C., Dehghantanha, A., Choo, K.K.R.: Performance of Android Forensics Data Recovery Tools, pp. 91–110. Elsevier (2017). https://doi.org/10.1016/b978-0-12-805303-4.00007-1
43. Osho, O., Ohida, S.O.: Comparative evaluation of mobile forensic tools. Int. J. Inf. Technol. Comput. Sci. **8**(1), 74–83 (2016). https://doi.org/10.5815/ijitcs.2016.01.09
44. Padmanabhan, R., Lobo, K., Ghelani, M., Sujan, D., Shirole, M.: Comparative analysis of commercial and open source mobile device forensic tools. In: Proceedings of the IEEE Conference, pp. 1–6 (2016)
45. Patel, A., Sharma, P., Dholariya, D.: A forensic evidence recovery from android device applications. Int. J. Sci. Res. Sci. Eng. Technol. (IJSRSET) **8**(3), 135–140 (2021). https://doi.org/10.32628/IJSRSET218321
46. Petitcolas, F., Anderson, R., Kuhn, M.: Information hiding-a survey. Proc. IEEE **87**(7), 1062–1078 (1999). https://doi.org/10.1109/5.771065
47. Pieterse, H., Olivier, M., van Heerden, R.: Evaluation framework for detecting manipulated smartphone data. SAIEE Africa Res. J. **110**(2), 67–76 (2019). https://doi.org/10.23919/SAIEE.2019.8732797
48. Quick, D., Choo, K.K.R.: Google drive: Forensic analysis of data remnants. J. Netw. Comput. Appl. **40**, 179–193 (2014). https://doi.org/10.1016/j.jnca.2013.09.016
49. Raji, M., Wimmer, H., Haddad, R.J.: Analyzing data from an android smartphone while comparing between two forensic tools. In: SoutheastCon 2018, pp. 1–6 (2018). https://doi.org/10.1109/SECON.2018.8478851
50. Rao, V.V., Chakravarthy, A.: Forensic analysis of android mobile devices. In: 2016 International Conference on Recent Advances and Innovations in Engineering (ICRAIE). pp. 1–6 (2016). https://doi.org/10.1109/ICRAIE.2016.7939540
51. Roy, N.R., Khanna, A.K., Aneja, L.: Android phone forensic: Tools and techniques. In: 2016 International Conference on Computing, Communication and Automation (ICCCA), pp. 605–610 (2016). https://doi.org/10.1109/CCAA.2016.7813792
52. da Silveira, C.M., et al.: Methodology for forensics data reconstruction on mobile devices with android operating system applying in-system programming and combination firmware. Appl. Sci. **10**(12), 4231 (2020). https://doi.org/10.3390/app10124231

53. Stats, S.G.: Mobile operating system market share worldwide. https://gs.statcounter.com/os-market-share/mobile/worldwide (2025). Accessed 17 June 2025
54. Vasilaras, A., Dosis, D., Kotsis, M., Rizomiliotis, P.: Retrieving deleted records from telegram. Forensic Sci. Int. Digital Investigation **43**, 301447 (2022). https://doi.org/10.1016/j.fsidi.2022.301447
55. Vella, M., Cilia, R.: Memory forensics of insecure android inter-app communications. In: Proceedings of the 3rd International Conference on Information Systems Security and Privacy (ICISSP 2017), pp. 481–486. SCITEPRESS – Science and Technology Publications (2017). https://doi.org/10.5220/0006215504810486
56. Vella, M., Colombo, C.: D-cloud-collector: Admissible forensic evidence from mobile cloud storage. In: Proceedings of the IFIP International Conference on ICT Systems Security and Privacy Protection (SEC 2022). IFIP Advances in Information and Communication Technology, vol. 648, pp. 161–178. Springer (2022). https://doi.org/10.1007/978-3-031-06975-8_10
57. Walnycky, D., Baggili, I., Marrington, A., Moore, J., Breitinger, F.: Network and device forensic analysis of android social-messaging applications. Digit. Investig. **14**, S77–S84 (2015)
58. Yang, S.J., Choi, J.H., Kim, K.B., Bhatia, R., Saltaformaggio, B., Xu, D.: Live acquisition of main memory data from android smartphones and smartwatches. Digit. Investig. **23**, 50–62 (2017). https://doi.org/10.1016/j.diin.2017.09.003
59. Yudha, F., Ramadhani, E., Sudyana, D., Hamzah, W.N.: A custom recovery approach for physical forensic imaging of android devices. In: Proceedings of the International Conference on Information Technology and Digital Applications 2021 (ICITDA 2021). AIP Conference Proceedings, vol. 2508, p. 020011. AIP Publishing, Yogyakarta, Indonesia (2023). https://doi.org/10.1063/5.0114894

Operational Technology Network Anomaly Detection Using N-Grams

Jack Nunnelee, Alex Howe(✉), and Mauricio Papa

Tandy School of Computer Science, The University of Tulsa, Tulsa, OK, USA
{jen2603,alex-howe,mauricio-papa}@utulsa.edu

Abstract. This paper proposes the use of n-grams to enhance anomaly detection in operational technology (OT) networks using byte-histograms. Byte histograms are highly effective at detecting anomalies but they often require domain-specific optimization techniques for reliable performance without an abundance of false alarms. The proposed technique does not require deep-packet inspection or protocol-specific information (beyond the physical and datalink layer), making the approach transferable and generalizable. Five different weighting schemes are used with similarity scores to fine tune n-gram evaluation and optimize anomaly detection. Furthermore, experimental results using an OT network traffic dataset show that it is possible to achieve good anomaly detection rates without any protocol-specific knowledge. Testing our generalized approach against this dataset shows an F1 score of 93.9% and an F2 score of 91.4%.

Keywords: Operational Technology · Network Security · Anomaly Detection

1 Introduction

Operational Technology (OT) networks interconnect physical devices within industrial control systems, enabling remote monitoring and automation. However, these networks often rely on communication protocols, e.g. Modbus, which may lack protection mechanisms such as encryption and authentication. In addition, due to their critical nature, many OT deployments have been operating for a long time and now rely on legacy systems. [12]. As a result, these networks are particularly vulnerable to zero-day attacks and other novel cyber threats.

Anomaly-based Intrusion Detection Systems (IDSs) offer a promising solution for detecting both zero-day and known attacks in OT environments. These detection systems construct a model of normal operational network behavior and flag deviations as anomalies or potential intrusions. Given that OT network traffic consists mostly of machine-to-machine communication, operational patterns of behavior are well-defined, allowing for accurate models representing normal communications.

E. Bergström et al. (Eds.): CRITIS 2025, LNCS 16291, pp. 224–242, 2026.
https://doi.org/10.1007/978-3-032-19540-1_12

Prior work has applied machine learning [1,3] and statistical methods [16] for anomaly detection in OT networks. However, these approaches often rely on extensive, domain-specific feature engineering to transform network traffic into variables suitable for learning algorithms. These features are heavily reliant on network environment/configurations which limit their potential for generalization across different OT domains.

To address these limitations, recent efforts have explored byte-level anomaly detection, which operates directly on the raw bytes of each packet. This approach is more general, as it operates using the fundamental representation of all network traffic and does not rely on protocol knowledge. However, traditional ML models struggle with such data due to the lack of structure and the high dimensionality of byte sequences, where semantically meaningful fields (i.e. IP addresses) span over multiple bytes.

Byte histograms are a recent technique that incorporates a rule-based approach for the detection of anomalies in OT network traffic [6]. These approaches model the expected values for each byte position in a network packet using histograms and flag packets when incoming bytes deviate from the expected set of values. However, this approach assumes that all bytes are equivalent which makes them susceptible to noise generated from fields that may have values that vary widely across several byte positions (i.e. TCP acknowledgment numbers and checksums), leading to high false positive rates. Tuning techniques can be used to prune noisy fields from the histogram, but these methods often rely on domain-specific knowledge that may limit generalization.

To overcome this limitation, this work proposes a novel n-gram comparison approach for Byte Histogram-based anomaly detection. Rather than comparing individual bytes independently, sequences of bytes (n-grams) are analyzed, capturing higher-level semantic structures within packets. This approach allows the system to capture anomalies in multi-byte fields such as IP addresses or function codes.

In addition, four weighting schemes are proposed to dynamically quantify the relative importance of bytes positions based on their frequency and distributional stability. During inference, the similarity between incoming and baseline histograms is computed using these weights; positions with higher weights (higher importance) have more impact on the overall similarity score. This similarity-based approach reduces the fragility of strict position-to-position matching and improves tolerance to data drift.

In summary, this work presents a generalizable, low-overhead method for detecting anomalous OT network traffic using only raw packet bytes. By combining n-gram analysis with adaptive byte-position weighting, the proposed method achieves high detection accuracy without requiring extensive tuning or domain-specific knowledge. This makes the approach generalizable across different domains and enhances the robustness of byte-level intrusion detection for OT systems.

Section 2 reviews related works leveraging the use of N-gram structures. Section 3 describes byte histograms and their novelty, with the following Sect. 4

describing N-gram structures and the proposed weighting scheme. Section 5 reviews the dataset used in the experimental results. Section 6 provides experimental results and evaluation for the proposed technique and Sect. 7 offers concluding remarks.

2 Related Work

Prior work has explored the performance of intrusion detection systems that use byte-level data. A wide variety of these solutions leverage the fine-grained information found in raw bytes to construct meaningful anomaly detection and classification systems. While many of these approaches operate directly on raw network packet bytes to detect anomalies, they often overlook the comparative power and generalizability offered by n-grams. n-grams have been successfully used in host-based systems to evaluate file similarity and have more recently been used in NIDS. Systems that use n-grams in NIDS often limit their detection scope to only payloads or specific protocols (e.g., HTTP or FTP), which restricts their generalizability and applicability.

In contrast, our work combines the modeling capabilities of byte histograms enhanced with n-gram comparisons across the full packet structure and layers of the protocol stack. This protocol-agnostic NIDS architecture is generalizable and transferable, allowing for it to be adopted across a wide range of OT network domains.

2.1 Byte-Level Network Intrusion Detection

Several works have explored the potential of byte-level network intrusion detection, developing techniques that can extract semantically meaningful patterns without relying on protocol-specific features. In [9], a one-class convolutional autoencoder is trained on fixed-length byte arrays extracted from raw packet payloads. This unsupervised approach leverages the reconstructed error to detect anomalies, enabling protocol-agnostic detection of abnormal traffic patterns. Similarly, the approach in [14] analyzes byte-normalized payloads of network packets using a deep neural network, treating each packet as a raw byte vector and performing classification without any handcrafted features or protocol-level parsing.

These methods demonstrate the potential for detecting network-level anomalies using only raw packet bytes. However, important semantic information is often encoded in protocol fields that span multiple bytes; pure machine learning techniques may lack the representational capacity to capture these multi-byte relationships. Alternatively, n-gram modeling enables comparison across multiple adjacent byte values, offering a richer representation of packet structure and facilitating more expressive anomaly detection.

2.2 N-Gram Malware Detection

Prior work has explored the effectiveness of n-grams in capturing multi-byte relationships over a relatively large sequence of bytes. For example, [5] applies association rule mining to 4-gram byte patterns extracted from PE (portable executable) files. The approach generates a set of rules capable of identifying malicious binaries in local executable files. Similarly, [2] relies on static analysis and disassembly to perform Android malware detection by extracting opcode n-gram frequency vectors and using them to train a time-aware Transformer. In [15], a comparative analysis of byte-level n-grams for malware detection (both anomaly detection and classification) is provided. Overall, this work leverages the effectiveness of n-gram detection for local files, with 3 to 5-gram patterns offering the best tradeoff for accuracy and efficiency.

Although powerful for file-based malware detection, these techniques assume structured binary formats and have not been widely used in packet-level network intrusion detection.

2.3 N-Gram Network Intrusion Detection

Recently, solutions that apply n-grams to detect anomalies using raw packet bytes have been proposed. For example, [10] applies n-gram frequency modeling to detect worm traffic based on payload content. Specifically, their approach builds statistical signatures of known malicious content using byte-level 3-grams extracted from the payload of the packet. Additionally, in [8], the authors introduce a technique that models the expected frequency range of byte-level n-grams in HTTP payloads; anomalies are detected based on the n-gram values that exceed the nominal range. In [13], the authors extract character-level n-grams from raw packet payloads and use Bloom filters to detect anomalous network behavior. Similarly, [11] extracts character-level n-grams from HTTP requests which are used to classify network traffic using an ensemble learning approach.

These techniques show promise for the use of n-gram modeling in detecting network traffic anomaly anomalies. However, they are generally limited to analyzing only payload content and are designed around structured application-layer traffic such as HTTP or FTP. As a result, they are less effective for identifying anomalies in other layers of the protocol stack, and struggle to generalize to the diverse domain of OT network environments.

In contrast, this work expands the scope of n-gram-based detection by including all layers of the packet structure. By combining byte histograms with n-gram comparison, we develop a protocol-agnostic anomaly detection system capable of capturing multi-byte dependencies throughout the entire packet. Specifically, a novel n-gram histogram testing method is proposed that leverages novel byte position weighting schemes to create dynamic and protocol-agnostic tuning methods that reduce false positive rates caused by entropic positions. This greatly improves the efficiency and generalizability of the approach, reducing the need for context-specific tuning required by earlier byte histogram methods.

3 Byte Histograms

A byte histogram is a data structure designed to model statistical byte-level values in packets sent over the network. Specifically, a byte histogram D contains a set of keys i that correspond to each byte position in a network packet; for Ethernet packets, the maximum packet length is 1514 bytes, thus $i \in [0, 1513]$. The values of each key d_i represent the byte values that were observed at that position and their frequency, i.e., each d_i is a dictionary where the keys are the recorded byte values and the values are the number of packets that were observed with that value at position i. As an example, consider $d_{54} = \{(0, 440), (1, 505), (2, 512), (3, 2636), (4, 4413)\}$ (Fig. 1), a dictionary showing distinct byte values in byte position 54 and the number of times each value appears in the dataset. This key in the histogram shows that at position 54, the observed byte values are 1,2,3 and 4, with value 4 (appearing 4,413 times) being the most frequently observed value.

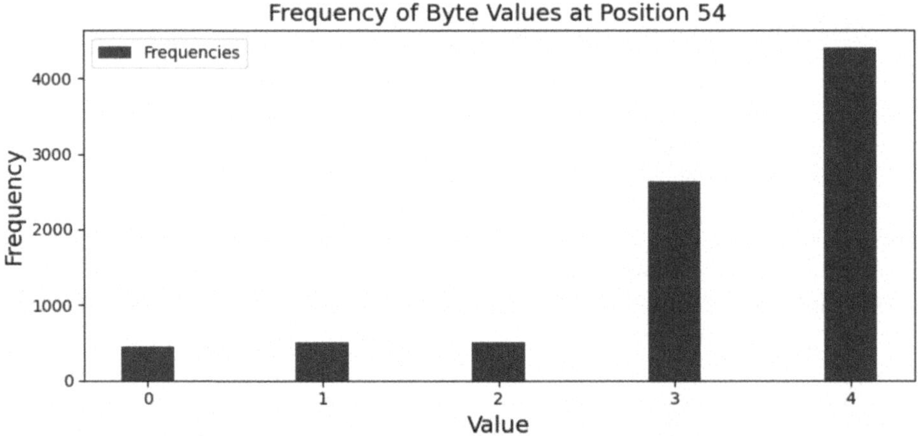

Fig. 1. Frequency Distribution for Position 54

A byte histogram captures the nominal behavior of raw packet bytes over a set of packets; while a global histogram is capable of capturing general network-wide nominal behavior, one powerful aspect of the byte histogram method is its flexibility in generating additional criteria to help identify abnormal packets. For example, device-specific histograms can capture the fine-grained traffic behavior unique to a certain device; further, histograms can be built for each unique conversation between two devices. This work considers four different byte histograms, each with increasing specificity in the information they use to construct the histograms:

1. **Global:** one histogram over the entire set of packets.
2. **Ethernet source:** one histogram for each observed *eth_src*

3. **Ethernet source-destination:** one histogram for each observed *(eth_src, eth_dst)* tuple.
4. **Ethernet source-destination-type:** one histogram for each observed *(eth_src, eth_dst, eth_type)* triple.

Each histogram is constructed, possibly offline, using network traffic that fully characterizes normal behavior. Once constructed, incoming network traffic can then be compared against a particular histogram using the histogram test.

3.1 Byte Histogram Tests

Since byte histograms record expected byte values at each byte index, strictly speaking, anomalies can be defined as a byte value at a particular position of a packet that was not observed in the training data. This can be easily done by determining whether a byte value in an incoming packet is in the set of observed values stored in the histogram.

Although effective in capturing low-level anomalies, this strict style of histogram testing requires that each byte value match directly with the information recorded during training. However, over time data drift will subtly and naturally shift the distribution of normal network behavior, resulting in a large number of false positives.

Further, this testing scheme makes the assumption that each byte position holds the same semantic importance. However, this is inherently not true, as some positions (i.e. TCP sequence numbers) are randomly generated, while other positions (i.e. function codes or addresses) contain vital information for anomaly detection. Subtle and natural shifts in these randomly generated positions can reduce the overall efficiency and accuracy of the entire anomaly detection scheme. To improve accuracy and efficiency, optimizations are proposed to prune these values and eliminate unnecessary false positives.

3.2 Optimizations

One limitation of the strict byte histogram test is the assumption that all positions are equivalently meaningful. However, some byte positions offer little to no information that can be used to model normal network behavior. These positions, often related to packet fields that are noisy or randomly generated (i.e. TCP sequence numbers or ephemeral ports), can skew nominal behavioral modeling resulting in a large false positive rate.

Consider a full histogram for device with Ethernet address `00:0c:29:3c:11:3f` (Fig. 2), with unique value counts on the y-axis scaled logarithmically for visibility. As shown, numerous byte positions are naturally entropic and are observed to have substantially more unique values than more predictable positions (i.e. address fields or function codes). Subsequently, these fields produce noisy value distributions and can degrade anomaly discriminability due to their variability. Protocol-variant fields, where the normal values are ephemeral, incremental, or randomly generated, can mimic anomalies and are infeasible to model as the encountered byte values have no nominal behavioral pattern.

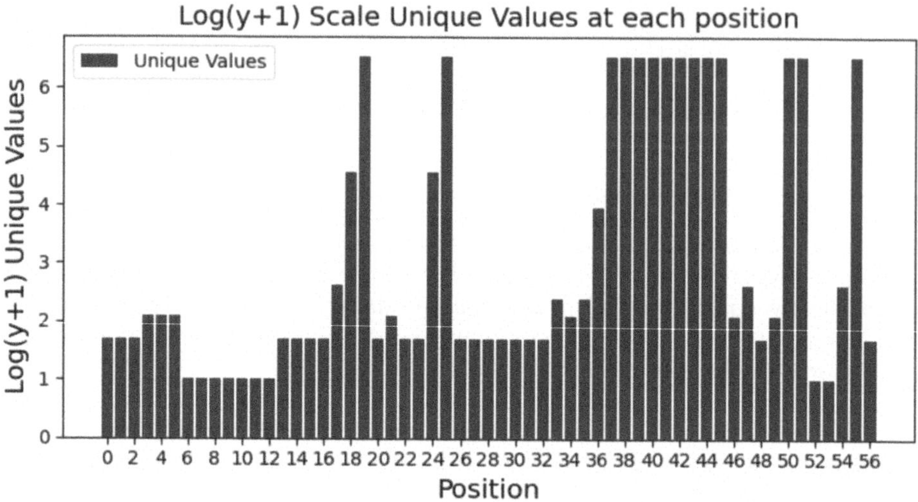

Fig. 2. Histogram for Source `00:0c:29:3c:11:3f`

Three optimization techniques are introduced to reduce the false positive rate of these positions:

- **Threshold**: This technique involved removing any specific byte position which contained numerous byte values. Specifically, any byte position b_i is pruned if the number of values is greater than or equal to threshold t. This is a simple optimization, however, it requires testing different values of t or thorough histogram analysis to determine the most effective value of t.
- **Field Mask**: This technique introduces an initial pre-processing step in packet evaluation to map each byte position in the packet to its corresponding field. Using the map, any byte position b_i is skipped during testing if it corresponds to any user-defined ignored field. This technique was implemented in order to reduce false flags from fields that contain no potential for anomalous data. This is a more intrusive optimization, requiring knowledge about each protocol used in the network to evaluate which fields should be ignored during testing.
- **Conditional-Masking**: This technique was introduced only for UDP and TCP packets. Using the ephemeral port range defined by the network, if any port value is in the ephemeral port range, the bytes for that field are skipped during histogram testing. This was done in order to reduce false positives from flagging irregular bytes in the destination port fields. While less intrusive than the previous optimizations, conditional masking requires knowledge of ephemeral port value ranges being used.

While these optimization techniques greatly increased the accuracy and efficiency of byte histogram anomaly detection, they require significant network context to fully define them. As such, the resulting generalizability of the byte histograms may be somewhat reduced. Thus, other histogram testing methods that complement the natural protocol-agnostic nature of byte histograms are required to create truly transferable detection systems.

4 N-Gram Byte Histogram Testing

Traditional byte histogram testing requires context-specific tuning, limiting its applicability. Additionally, comparisons between individual byte positions overlook important dependencies that span across multiple bytes. To address these limitations, this work introduces a novel n-gram-based approach to testing byte histograms for anomaly detection.

N-grams are sequences of n consecutive items; this is a commonly used technique in Natural Language Processing to model word co-dependencies in a sentence. Similarly, n-grams can be applied to the raw-bytes in a packet to collect them into groups of size n. This extends histogram comparison from individual bytes to multi-byte groups, allowing for the modeling of packet fields.

Applying n-grams to byte histograms involves iterating over each position in the histogram, creating groups of bytes, or grams, each of size n. Formally, given a packet with m bytes, each position $i \in [0, m - n - 1]$ defines an n-gram window consisting of consecutive bytes $(b_i, b_{i+1}, \cdots, b_{i+n-1})$. Grouping bytes into n-grams enables the identification of meaningful multi-byte patterns without prior protocol knowledge, essential for anomaly detection in network packets.

However, this scheme still maintains the assumption that all positions are semantically equivalent, allowing entropic positions to negatively impact the anomaly detection performance. Previous methods applied context-sensitive tuning techniques to remove these positions. Conversely, this work introduces a novel histogram weighting scheme which dynamically assigns weights to each byte value based on its importance. The only requirement to selecting a weighting scheme is understanding the distribution of byte values and frequencies.

4.1 Weighting Scheme

A key innovation of the proposed approach is the configurable weighting scheme, designed to dynamically assign weights to byte positions based on their importance to anomaly detection. This approach enables efficient adaptation to diverse OT domains without requiring extensive prior knowledge of the structure of the network.

After training, each byte position $i \in [0, 1513]$ is assigned a weight w_i reflecting its relevance for anomaly detection. Higher weights indicate greater importance for discriminating between normal and anomalous network traffic. This work examines five different weighting schemes which can be used to assign importance values to byte positions: uniform, inverse-entropy, count, inverse-frequency, and inverse-variance.

Uniform. Each byte position is assigned an equal weight of 1.0. This baseline treats all positions uniformly without considering semantic differences.

Inverse-Entropy. Each byte position is weighted inversely proportional to its Shannon entropy [7]. The weight for position i is calculated as:

$$p(k) = \frac{t_k}{T_i},\ w_i = \frac{1}{-\sum_{k=0}^{j} p(k) log_2 p(k)}$$

where j represents the total number unique values at byte position i, T_i represents the total sum of frequencies at position i, and t represents the frequency of byte value k at position i. This scheme favors highly predictable byte positions that have a small number of imbalanced values; for instance, positions that have very few recorded entries will be weighted highly. While effective, this scheme can be sensitive to small training data.

Count-Based each position is weighted based on the inverse count of unique byte values observed. Formally:

$$w_i = \frac{255}{j}$$

Positions with fewer unique values (more consistent fields) receive higher weights, effectively penalizing noisy byte positions. However, low-frequency, or rarely seen byte positions, can skew results if the training data is insufficient. For example, byte position 1500 is rarely seen in OT network traffic as packets tend to be relatively small, if the training data contains 1 packet that extends to the 1500th position then that w_{1500} will be artificially deemed to be high as it has a very small number of unique values.

Inverse-Frequency-Based. Positions are weighted based on how infrequently the occur across packets:

$$w_i = \frac{1}{\sum_{k=0}^{j} freq_k}$$

where $freq_k$ is the frequency of each byte value. This scheme favors rarely used, or infrequent byte positions which could potentially highlight anomalous data. However, this field could inadvertently prioritize noisier fields (i.e. IP identifiers or checksums) as the values seen at these fields occur infrequently.

Inverse-Variance-Based. Positions are weighted inversely to their variance:

$$w_i = \frac{1}{\sigma^2}, \sigma^2 = \frac{\sum_{k=0}^{j}(b_k - \bar{x})^2}{j-1}$$

where b_k are byte values at position i and $\bar{x}$ is the mean of those values. This scheme favors positions that are frequently used which have consistently close byte values.

4.2 N-Gram Evaluation

Classification for an incoming packet is divided into two main steps: histogram validation and byte validation. In the histogram validation step, incoming packets generate the following three keys using their Ethernet attributes: eth_{src}, (eth_{src}, eth_{dst}), and $(eth_{src}, eth_{dst}, eth_{type})$. A corresponding histogram must exist for these keys, if none are found that packet is labeled anomalous. For instance, if a histogram does not exist for the key eth_{src}, then the incoming packet was sent from an address that was not observed in the training data that fully characterizes normal network behavior and is therefore anomalous.

In the byte validation step, four similarity scores are generated between the incoming packet and the four relevant histograms: global, eth_{src}, (eth_{src}, eth_{dst}), and $(eth_{src}, eth_{dst}, eth_{type})$. Immediately after training each histogram generates a set of associated weights w_i using the chosen weighting scheme; these weights are used to calculate the similarity score S between an incoming packet and the four relevant histograms.

The classification of a new packet p with bytes b_i can be formally described in four steps:

1. Partition incoming packet bytes into n-grams ng_i, where $ng_i = (b_i, b_{i+1}, ...b_{n+i-1})$.
2. For each histogram, compare all ng_i of the incoming packets to the corresponding n-grams of histogram keys, i.e. $(d_i, d_{i+1}, ...d_{n+i-1})$, which contain all nominal byte values observed during training. We can define the total weight for each n-gram in the histogram key as:

$$TW_i = \sum_{j=i}^{i+1n-1} w^j$$

   Where TW_i is the summation of the weights generated for histograms within the current n-gram window.
3. For each n-gram window comparison an indicator function can be defined as:

$$v_i(b_i) = \begin{cases} 1, & \text{if } b_j \in V_j, j \in [i, i+n-1] \\ -1, & \text{otherwise} \end{cases}$$

   where V_j is the set of observed nominal values recorded in d_j during training. More specifically, the indicator function equates to 1 if the incoming byte values in the n-gram window are found in the corresponding histogram n-gram.

4. The final similarity score S can be calculated using:

$$S = \sum_{i=0}^{B-n} TW_i \cdot v_i(b_i)$$

where B represents the total length of the incoming packet. This score describes the similarity between an incoming packet and a corresponding byte histogram.

Once S has been calculated between the incoming packet and the four relevant histograms, the optimal threshold for classification is selected by evaluating multiple thresholds within the observers score range Specifically, the F1 score is observed across 1000 evenly spaced thresholds, the one resulting in the highest score is chosen. Packets which fall below the similarity threshold are labeled as anomalous and the final detection performance is assessed using the F1 and F2 scores as well as precision and recall.

To demonstrate this process, consider an n-gram ($n = 3$) derived from the Ethernet source histogram corresponding to `00:0c:29:58:97:2a`. Suppose the first n-gram for this histogram (positions $0 - 2$) contains values: $\{0 \rightarrow \{255, 0\}, 1 \rightarrow \{255, 12\}, 2 \rightarrow \{255, 41\}\}$, indicating that at $i = 0$, the expected nominal byte value could either be 255 or 0. Furthermore, consider weights generated using the count-based weighting scheme: $w = (127.5, 127.5, 127.5)$, which represents the weights of the first three positions respectively.

Then, given some incoming packet p_1 sent from `00:0c:29:58:97:2a` whose first n-gram is $ng_0 = (0, 12, 41)$. This n-gram matches the expected n-gram for the corresponding histogram; thus, the total weight of all three positions (i.e. $TW_0 = 382.5$) in the n-gram will be added to S. Conversely, consider a second incoming packet p_2 which is also sent from `00:0c:29:58:97:2a` whose first n-gram is $ng_0 = (255, 255, 0)$. While the first two values match the corresponding set of nominal values in the histogram n-gram, the final value 0 is not present in d_3. As such, the total weight for that n-gram will be subtracted from the similarity score (i.e. $S = -382.5$). This process creates a similarity comparison technique which is heavily dependent on the weighting scheme; important byte positions will have a large impact both in the positive (if the incoming n-gram values match the expected nominal values) or negative (if the n-gram does not fully match) capacity.

Overall, the proposed configurable weighting and n-gram scheme significantly reduces the manual tuning required in prior byte histogram efforts. The method leverages statistical properties of network traffic data, balancing detection accuracy with computational efficiency. By focusing on multi-byte relationships without explicit protocol knowledge, the proposed n-gram-based byte histogram approach achieves high generalizability across various OT network environments.

5 Dataset

The dataset used in this work consists of a simulated electrical substation operating over Modbus/TCP traffic [4]. Raw network traffic files (pcap files) were captured between an HMI and a set of PLCs; several capture files were evaluated, each containing a different attack scenario (Table 1 depicts detailed analysis of the five attack files evaluated in this work).

In each attack scenario, all packets were sent over the Ethernet protocol. A large majority of the traffic was sent using the IPv4 networking protocol, however, 21 packets were sent over IPv6 while 41 were sent over the ARP protocol. Furthermore, a majority of IPv4 traffic was sent using the TCP transport-layer protocol with 19 packets sent over UDP.

Finally, the *run1_6rtu* pcap file was chosen for training to generate the normal histograms; this file contains one hour of strictly normal network traffic.

Table 1. Modbus/TCP Dataset Attack Scenarios

File	Packet Count	Anomalous Packets	Description
characterization	12296	6743	Compromised RTU sends READ commands to other RTUs
exploit_ms08	1856	1205	Attacker takes control of a PLC using the netapi MS08 exploit
moving_two_files	3319	75	Compromised RTU uploads files to two other RTUs
send_fake_command	11166	53	Forged write commands sent from a compromised RTU
CnC_uploading_exe	1426	121	Malware delivered to another RTU from compromised RTU

6 Experimental Results

The proposed n-gram byte-histogram anomaly detection method is evaluated with different parameter tuning techniques and against state-of-the-art techniques. Initial evaluation is considered by investigating the impact of varying the n-gram size as well as the applied weighting scheme to find the values that produce the best classification results. Finally, the performance of the proposed technique is validated by comparing the most effective n-gram configuration (found by fine tuning parameters) against other established OT network anomaly detection approaches.

6.1 Parameter Sensitivity Analysis

Preliminary analysis involved exploring how critical parameters, mainly the n-gram size and chosen weighting scheme, influences the effectiveness of the histogram-based technique.

N-Gram Size Analysis. To evaluate how the size of the n-gram influences performance n values of 2 through 20 were considered. Figures 4, 5 and 6 illustrate how the F1 scores vary for different n-gram sizes for each of the five weighting schemes (Figs. 3 and 7).

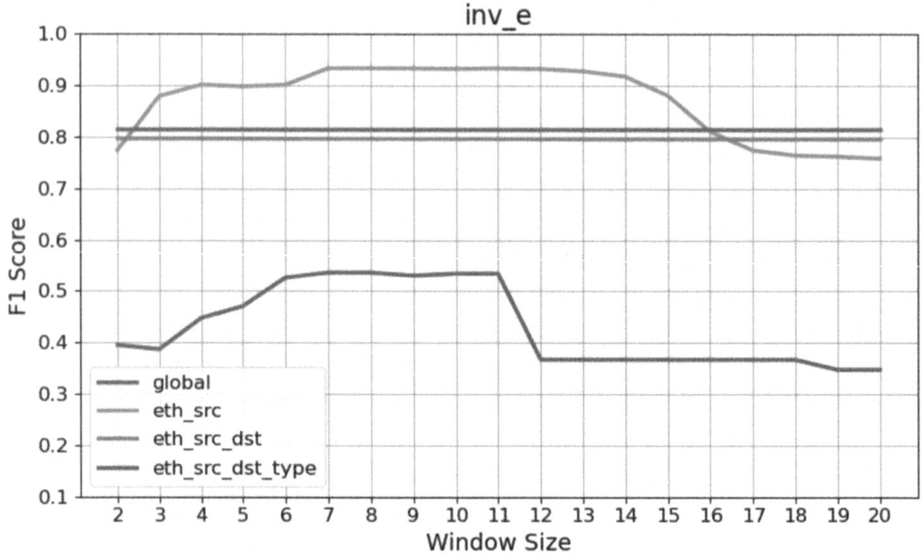

Fig. 3. Inverse Entropy F1 score across $n \in [2, 20]$

Results show that the global histogram achieves poor detection results while the (eth_{src}, eth_{dst}) and $(eth_{src}, eth_{dst}, eth_{type})$ histograms are not affected by window size. This demonstrates that general histograms prevent the n-gram from extracting field-level information, most likely due to the large amount of protocol variation captured by the histogram. Further, more specific histograms are unaffected by differing window sizes due to the small amount of recorded data. The eth_{src} histogram strikes a fine tradeoff between the amount of data observed in the global histogram and the specificity of the more unique histograms, allowing n-grams to fully capture field-level packet information.

Furthermore, results indicate that smaller values of n are capable of capturing basic byte-level features but can miss important multi-byte and multi-field relationships. On the other hand, large values of n could capture broader semantic structures but risk introducing irrelevant or noisy data (i.e. mixing fixed addresses with random identifiers).

More specifically, these results show that as n increases, the F1 score increases until approximately $n = 12$. Beyond $n = 12$, performance gradually degrades, suggesting an optimal tradeoff at $n = 12$. These results are consistent throughout

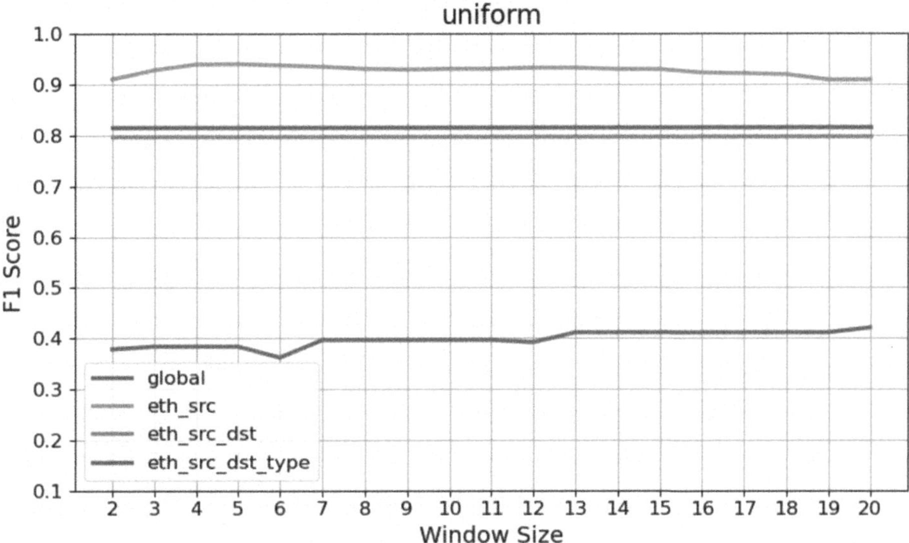

Fig. 4. Uniform F1 score across $n \in [2, 20]$

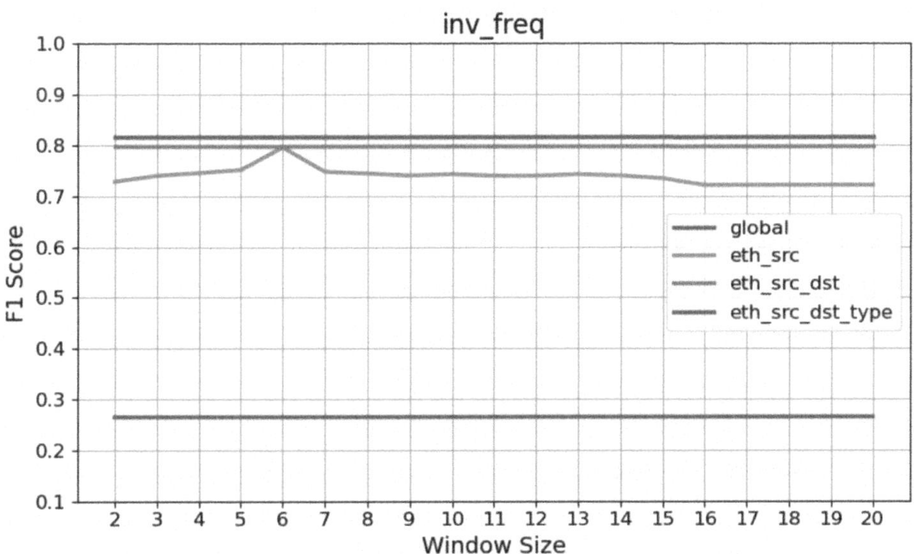

Fig. 5. Inverse Frequency F1 score across $n \in [2, 20]$

the varying weighting schemes, indicating the robust performance of 12-byte n-grams for capturing multi-byte semantic patterns prevalent in Modbus/TCP OT Network traffic.

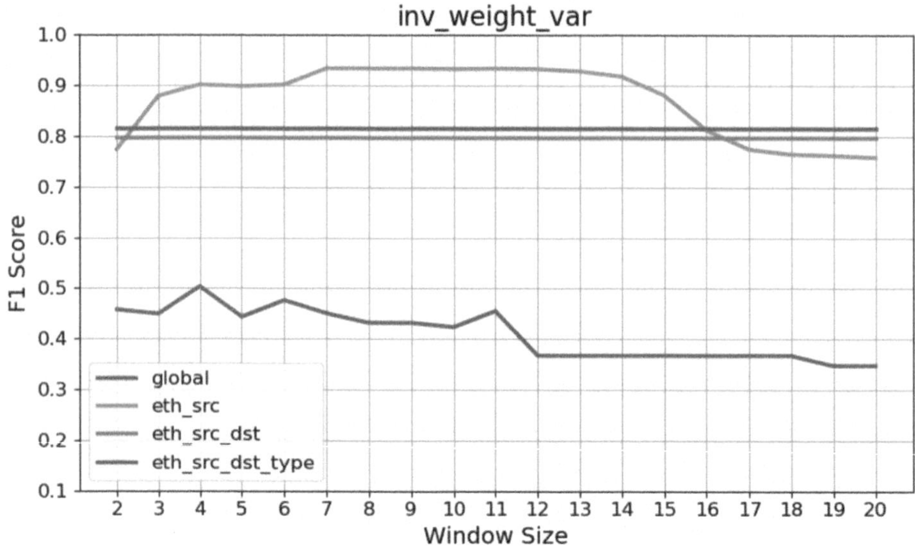

Fig. 6. Inverse Weighted Variance F1 score across $n \in [2, 20]$

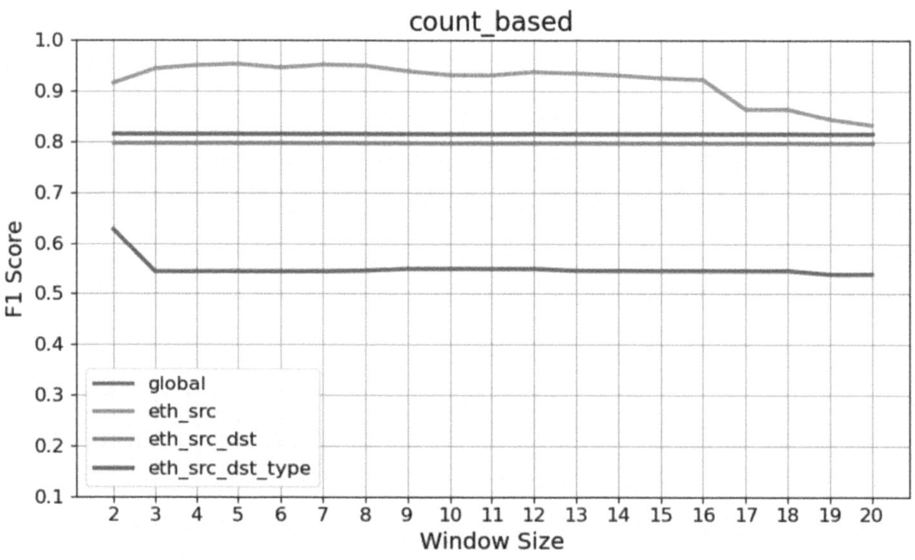

Fig. 7. Count Based F1 score across $n \in [2, 20]$

Weighting Scheme Analysis. Five weighting schemes were evaluated, each assigning varying degrees of importance to byte positions based on different statistical properties of byte distributions:

1. **Uniform**: Assigns even weights to each position.
2. **Inverse-Entropy**: Favors byte positions with high predictability, or low noise.
3. **Count-based**: Favors byte positions with a lower number of unique values.
4. **Inverse-Frequency**: Favors byte positions that occur rarely.
5. **Inverse-Variance**: Favors high frequency positions with numerically close values.

Table 2 summarizes the performance of each weighting scheme for the optimal window size ($n = 12$) using the eth_{src} histograms.

Table 2. Comparison of different weighting schemes with $n = 12$

Weight Scheme	F1	F2	Precision	Recall
Inverse-Entropy	0.933	0.900	1.0	0.880
Uniform	0.932	0.911	0.972	0.898
Count-based	**0.937**	**0.914**	**0.982**	**0.899**
Inverse-Frequency	0.739	0.692	0.911	0.678
Inverse-Variance	0.933	0.900	1.0	0.880

The Count-based weighting scheme achieves the highest F1 and F2 scores, effectively balancing anomaly detection accuracy while reducing false-positive rates. This method assigns higher weights to byte positions that are frequently observed in packets but have fewer unique values, proving to be particularly effective in identifying anomalies within stable packet-level fields.

6.2 Final Evaluation

To demonstrate the performance of the proposed technique, it is compared against several state-of-the-art byte-level anomaly detection techniques:

1. 1D CNN Autoencoder: 1 Dimensional Convolutional Neural Network (CNN) capture local byte-level relationships using a convolution kernel.
2. 1D CNN-LSTM Autoencoder: Includes the Long Short-Term Memory network to append time-series anomaly detection to the spatial feature extraction of the CNN autoencoder.
3. Linear Autoencoder: Deep Neural Network based autoencoder.
4. Linear Autoencoder with PCA reduction: Deep Neural Network based autoencoder with Principal Component Analysis to reduce the 1514 byte input space to 20 core components.

Each algorithm was trained using only the raw bytes of each packet (input vectors were padded to 1514 for consistent sizing).

The proposed Count-based n-gram method significantly outperforms other models in terms of F1 and F2 scores, demonstrating the superior precision and recall. The method's advantage lies in its ability to dynamically weigh byte positions based on their informational relevant, greatly reducing false alarms while maintaining high recall. Furthermore, the explainability of the proposed technique is significantly greater than the machine learning-based methods, which is ideal for critical network security.

Notably, the proposed n-gram comparison technique for byte histograms offers several practical advantages when compared to previous byte histogram and machine learning efforts:

- No protocol-specific knowledge or deep packet inspection is required which makes it a highly generalizable technique
- Feasible for real-time deployment as inferences can be made simply by calculating the difference between two distributions
- Use of n-grams and dynamic weighting reduces false-positive rates (Table 3)

Table 3. Final comparison against state-of-the-art byte-based OT network anomaly detection techniques

Model	F1	F2	Precision	Recall
N-Gram Byte Histogram	**0.937**	**0.914**	**0.982**	**0.899**
1-D CNN-LSTM	0.924	0.908	0.954	0.897
1-D CNN-Autoencoder	0.788	0.704	0.980	0.658
Linear Autoencoder	0.775	0.691	0.971	0.645
Linear Autoencoder + PCA	0.775	0.709	0.921	0.670

Overall, these results validate that the proposed n-gram-based byte histogram anomaly detection approach, paired with a count-based weighting scheme and an optimal n-gram size of 12, significantly improves upon the generalization and effectiveness of byte-level anomaly detection methods previously used in OT environments. The method demonstrates highly accurate and efficient network intrusion detection performance without requiring extensive tuning or protocol-specific knowledge.

7 Conclusion

This work introduces a novel, protocol-agnostic anomaly detection approach that effectively eliminates the need for deep packet inspection or domain specific feature engineering. While optimized byte histograms slightly outperform n-grams in anomaly detection rates by leveraging capture-specific patterns, they require significant manual tuning and static traffic structures to reliably detect anomalies. In contrast, n-gram based methods achieve a high 93.7% F1 and 91.4% F2 scores with no protocol assumptions, parsing logic, or reliance on consistent packet structures.

More importantly, the n-gram method significantly reduces false positives. This is important for real-world deployments since evaluating false positives can potentially involve system downtime and waste system analysts' time. Its domain-agnostic nature makes it well-suited for environments with frequent topology changes, encrypted traffic, or network traffic that includes proprietary protocols with limited public documentation available.

The configurable weighting scheme component allows for varying prioritization of byte patterns depending on communication flows. When benchmarked against state-of-the-art generalizable baselines, including PCA, linear autoencoders, and 1-D CNNs, our approach demonstrates superior performance without requiring any protocol knowledge. Taken together, these results highlight the proposed method as a highly practical alternative and low-friction solution for building strong intrusion detection systems.

References

1. Anton, S.D., Kanoor, S., Fraunholz, D., Schotten, H.D.: Evaluation of machine learning-based anomaly detection algorithms on an industrial modbus/tcp data set. In: Proceedings of the 13th International Conference on Availability, Reliability and Security, pp. 1–9 (2018)
2. Han, X., Cui, S., Liu, S., Zhang, C., Jiang, B., Zhigang, L.: Network intrusion detection based on n-gram frequency and time-aware transformer. Comput. Secur. **128**, 103171 (2023)
3. Howe, A., Papa, M.: Feature engineering in machine learning-based intrusion detection systems for ot networks. In: 2023 IEEE International Conference on Smart Computing (SMARTCOMP), pp. 361–366 (2023)
4. Lemay, A., Fernandez, J.M.: Providing SCADA network data sets for intrusion detection research. In: 9th Workshop on Cyber Security Experimentation and Test (CSET 16) (2016)
5. Li, B., Zhang, Y., Yao, J., Yin, T.: Mdba: detecting malware based on bytes n-gram with association mining. In: 2019 26th International Conference on Telecommunications (ICT), pages 227–232. IEEE, 2019
6. Rahal, P., Nunnelee, J., Howe, A., Papa, M.: Using heuristics and byte histograms to detect anomalies in ot network traffic. In: World Congress in Computer Science, Computer Engineering & Applied Computing, pp. 282–298. Springer (2024)
7. Shannon, C.E.: A mathematical theory of communication. Bell Syst. Tech. J. **27**(3), 379–423 (1948)
8. Swarnkar, M., Hubballi, N.: Rangegram: a novel payload based anomaly detection technique against web traffic. In: 2015 IEEE International Conference on Advanced Networks and Telecommuncations Systems (ANTS), pp. 1–6. IEEE (2015)
9. Swarnkar, M., Hubballi, N.: Ocpad: One class naive bayes classifier for payload based anomaly detection. Expert Syst. Appl. **64**, 330–339 (2016)
10. Tang, Y., Chen, S.: An automated signature-based approach against polymorphic internet worms. IEEE Trans. Parallel Distrib. Syst. **18**(7), 879–892 (2007)
11. Tyagi, R., Paul, T., Manoj, B.S., et al.: A novel http botnet traffic detection method. In: 2015 Annual IEEE India Conference (INDICON), pp. 1–6. IEEE (2015)

12. Upadhyay, D., Sampalli, S.: Scada (supervisory control and data acquisition) systems: vulnerability assessment and security recommendations. Comput. Secur. **89**, 101666 (2020)
13. Wang, K., Parekh, J.J., Stolfo, S.J.: Anagram: a content anomaly detector resistant to mimicry attack. In: International Workshop on Recent Advances in Intrusion Detection, pp. 226–248. Springer (2006)
14. Wang, K., Stolfo, S.J.: Anomalous payload-based network intrusion detection. In: International Workshop on Recent Advances in Intrusion Detection, pp. 203–222. Springer (2004)
15. Wressnegger, C., Schwenk, G., Arp, D., Rieck, K.: A close look on n-grams in intrusion detection: anomaly detection vs. classification. In: Proceedings of the 2013 ACM Workshop on Artificial Intelligence and Security, pp. 67–76 (2013)
16. Yang, Y., et al.: Multiattribute scada-specific intrusion detection system for power networks. IEEE Trans. Power Delivery **29**(3), 1092–1102 (2014)

Knowledge, Skills and Education

Blueprint for K-12 Cybersecurity Education: Integrating Cybersecurity Throughout All K-12 Subjects

Timothy Crisp(✉) and John Hale

The University of Tulsa, Tulsa, OK 74104, USA
Tim-Crisp@utulsa.edu

Abstract. The increase in cyber attacks impacting critical infrastructure and the economy motivates a focus on cybersecurity defense and awareness. However, a knowledge gap exists in both the technical and non-technical understanding of cybersecurity, creating a weakness in the global and US cybersecurity workforce. Closing this gap requires a multi-faceted approach, but of extreme importance is education. We use the NICE Workforce Framework TKS statements to develop a model of the most generalizable requirements needed to work in cybersecurity. We seek to apply this model to increase the Cybersecurity Language use in all K-12 subjects, walking educators and content developers through a process incorporating cybersecurity into their lessons.

Keywords: Cybersecurity Education · K-12 · Primary Education · Secondary Education · Cybersecurity language · NICE Workforce Framework

1 Introduction

Cybersecurity vulnerabilities pose ever-growing threats to our critical infrastructure and economy [1–4]. With the rise in attacks, a solution must be found to tackle the shortcomings of a diminished workforce. To address these challenges, the world needs more professionals working in cybersecurity, and also a global workforce with common knowledge of cyber hygiene and early-detection warning signs. The conversation of increasing cybersecurity education is expansive, yet no clear pathway exists for accomplishing these goals. What is known is that the United States suffers from a growing need for cyber professionals; a gap exists in those prepared to be in the cyber workforce with a shortfall of around 4 million people as of 2023 [5–7]. To help close this gap, this study aims to establish a model and curricular solution for the US equivalent of primary and secondary "K-12" education space using the state of Oklahoma as a model.

K-12 Schools educate and prepare future workforces—cybersecurity education is now an essential component of this preparation. Increasing the number of technically educated students in this area is a national priority. However, the cyber workforce is not only based on technical skills but also on improving the general cyber hygiene of individuals. Accordingly, the proposed K-12 curriculum development methodology focuses on

E. Bergström et al. (Eds.): CRITIS 2025, LNCS 16291, pp. 245–264, 2026.
https://doi.org/10.1007/978-3-032-19540-1_13

closing the cyber workforce gap with employees that have better cyber hygiene for operating securely in their future work environments, detect early-warning signs of attacks, and understand how to protect our critical infrastructure.

The rest of the paper is organized as follows: Sect. 2 outlines the cybersecurity problem and need for education, describing the current K-12 cybersecurity education policy landscape. Section 3 presents the primary national cybersecurity standards. Section 4 gives a presentation of the current national (NICE) objectives for cybersecurity education and the workforce alongside an analysis of the NICE Framework presenting a model for use as a blueprint for Cybersecurity education. Section 5 presents our method for integrating Cybersecurity into all K-12 subjects—where subjects are classified as categories of topical content around which a class is organized, e.g. "Writing," or "Chemistry"—and provides some preliminary results. Section 6 outlines the future work of the research.

2 The Need for Cybersecurity Education

Cybercrime and cybersecurity are not new issues in the computer science uniqueness debate, which contemplates whether technology creates new crimes or merely expands the way criminals commit already known crimes. Crimes of all types are now propagated using computers, making old crimes happen in new ways [8]. Cyberattacks are on the rise and the individual's ability to protect themselves is increasingly difficult. Many of these attacks are increasing in the critical infrastructure sector, which requires a higher degree of focus for protection. Many are victims of social engineering tactics which are evolving and escalating. Most lack the skills needed to protect themselves [1, 9]. Research indicates a need to understand how to navigate the landscape of cyber threats and protect oneself, companies, and organizations from experiencing the effects of an attack [3, 10–12]. At the same time, a gap exists in the workforce's ability to protect critical infrastructures because programs for preparation in IT and computing industries do not focus on cybersecurity education. This is manifested by the lack of focused coursework [13, 14]. Additionally, the employees responsible for maintaining our critical infrastructures are not IT nor Cybersecurity professionals with educational training. Thus, it is important that all employees in the critical infrastructure space are aware of cyber threat landscape to the industry with a deeper knowledge of cyber terminology. The literature agrees on these two points and on the need to increase both cyber hygiene and technical skills of the US workforce.

Yet, the literature is conflicted on where we should implement this cybersecurity education and on what educational targets we should concentrate investment. Cybersecurity education separates into two categories - the technical and the non-technical (encompassing the managerial and psychological) [15]. Technical education focuses on the skills that prevent, detect, and mitigate the effects of attacks by assailants. These training targets focus on producing employees with the hard skills needed to keep systems secure. Managerial and psychological education focuses on developing an individual's ability to recognize signs of attacks on personal and business devices [15]. The literature is divided as to which area education we should focus investment. Should we devote resources to teach students in the technical manner to close the cyber workforce gap or to the managerial and psychological aspects, increasing the cyber hygiene of general users?

This research aims to address the dichotomy of technical and non-technical (managerial and psychological) K-12 cybersecurity education programming at the state level.

There are three categories in which literature discusses education on cybersecurity: K-12, college, and on-the-job training [9, 16, 17]. Each requires unique parameters to educate its target population. The space for education and training is very diverse in need, as on-the-job training focuses on those who are already in the workforce, while college and K-12 are focused on preparing those aspiring to future careers. Some argue that on-the-job training is most needed to strengthen the skills of employees already at organizations, as they pose the greatest immediate risk to an organization's security [18, 19]. Others argue that universities need to implement more cybersecurity curriculum into their courses of study for students to grow a cyber workforce skilled to handle emerging challenges [20, 21]. Other literature explains how cyber education should be included in K-12 curriculum in order to build the cyber hygiene skills of youth to keep them safe and cultivate a cyber-savvy workforce [16, 21, 22].

3 Cybersecurity Education Standards

Standards are integral to our objective, centered around curriculum for K-12 schools. K-12 institutions are required to offer courses based on their state's graduation requirements and align them to the set of standards established by the state's Department of Education. However, often there are courses schools offer which do not have a set of standards from the state. These are generally elective courses, cybersecurity included. When states lack a set of standards for courses being offered, academic organizations and curriculum companies generally create standards that schools can use to build and structure their courses. Research exploring the current standards for K-12 cyber education is lacking as there is only one state currently with a claimed dedicated set of standards for cybersecurity, and only a few major K-12 curricula designed with standards for cybersecurity education. North Dakota (ND) has implemented a cybersecurity K-12 set of standards for the entire state and required it to be implemented by the year 2026 [23]. These standards were created by ND House Bill (HB) 1398 and were established as a part of their "North Dakota Computer Science and Cybersecurity Standards" [23, 24]. These standards, however, are not explicitly for cybersecurity but, as with other states, are incorporated in the computer science standards as a Digital Citizenship component. While specific state standards may not presently exist for cybersecurity, many Computer Science standards have a section which covers cybersecurity topics. Oklahoma's Academic Standards for Computer Science (OASCS) have a cybersecurity component for grades K-10 but are only covered as short units rather than full course subject matter [25]. Oklahoma's Computer Science Standards were published in 2023 and implemented in the 2024–2025 school year. These standards focus on Computer Science but include one singular sub-concept for Cybersecurity. This sub-concept relates predominantly to the non-technical side of cybersecurity education, the managerial and psychological, focusing on being better digital citizens with good cyber hygiene.

3.1 Professional Organizations

Academic organizations such as colleges, universities, curriculum companies, professional organizations, and accreditation institutions have engaged in the development of guidelines which cybersecurity courses at a college level are encouraged to follow in order to award a degree in Cybersecurity. One of the first instances of these cybersecurity guidelines occurred when four major international computing societies began creating guidelines for universities. In 2015, these societies established a Joint Task Force on Cybersecurity Education; the Association for Computing Machinery (ACM), Institute of Electrical and Electronics Engineers (IEEE), Association for Information Systems (AIS), and the International Federation for Information Processing (IFIP). Of note are the Cybersecurity Curricular Guidelines of 2017 (CSEC 2017), and a current working group developing a Supplement to CSEC 2017: Content for a Foundational Cybersecurity Degree Course (Supplement to CSEC) [20, 21].

The CSEC 2017 established a set of knowledge areas which "define a structure for the cybersecurity discipline… and develops curricular guidance that is grounded in fundamental principles that provide stability yet is structured to provide flexibility to support evolving program needs" [20]. The CSEC defines eight Knowledge Areas that all graduates "of a cybersecurity program of study should" know: Data Security, Software Security, Component Security, Connection Security, System Security, Human Security, Organizational Security, Societal Security [20]. Knowledge Areas are "made up of critical knowledge with broad importance within and across multiple computing-based disciplines" [20]. These eight Knowledge Areas (KAs) break down into individual Knowledge Units (KUs): eight each for Data Security, Software Security, and Connection Security; four for Component Security; seven each for System Security and Human Security; nine for Organizational Security; and five for Societal Security. Every Knowledge Unit separates into individual lesson topics with a description and curricular guidance on what courses should cover when teaching in a Knowledge Area. These units are designed as "thematic groupings that encompass multiple, related topics… [covering] the required curricular content for each KU" [20]. The CSEC's guidelines have given universities and educators a baseline for curriculum for four-year and graduate degrees in cybersecurity.

The CSEC guidelines recognize that professional practices and workforce development programs must be considered in the creation of courses and Knowledge Areas. Thus, the CSEC maps out how KAs and KUs connect to the most recognized framework used for the cybersecurity workforce, the NICE Cybersecurity Workforce Framework [20]. Each learning objective from the CSEC's KUs is correlated to the NICE Framework Knowledge, Skill, and Abilities (KSA) statements. The KSA statements are individual objectives that correlate to a specific task an individual would be responsible for in a specific work role function. The working group uses the KSA Statements to provide "a frame of reference for students embarking on the course of study…[explaining] the relationship between the knowledge and the specific work role" a student will be employed to do after graduation [20]. It should be noted that these guidelines were published in 2017 and updates to the NICE framework have been made, the latest in November 2020. In this revision, NICE changed KSA to Tasks, Knowledge, and Skills Statements

(TKS Statements) and added more work roles. An updated CSEC has not been released currently.

The supplement to CSEC 2017 is a working document established by a committee to review the CSEC 2017 and other Cybersecurity education canonical documents to produce a set of Knowledge Units best suited for a foundational course in cybersecurity. This supplement asserts that the CSEC 2017 creates a "Comprehensive body of knowledge for cybersecurity degree programs, [but does] not explicitly identify the essential topics to be covered in foundational courses" [21]. The audience targets high schools, community colleges, universities, and states, as the document outlines the basic areas and competencies an introduction to cybersecurity course should include. The supplement keeps five of the Knowledge Units from the CSES 2017: Data Security, System Security, Software Security, Organizational Security, and Societal Security. The authors added one additional Knowledge Unit to the supplement, Network Security, to cover the deep connection between cybersecurity and networks. This working draft concluded its public comment period on November 10th, 2024, and was presented to the ACM Education Committee in January 2025 [21]. Ultimately, it aims to provide a structure scraping the curricular guidelines for the material which would best suit an introductory class for cybersecurity.

3.2 Government Agencies

Additionally, government agencies such as the National Security Agency (NSA), Department of Homeland Security (DHS), the Central Security Services (CSS), National Institute of Standards and Technology (NIST) influence the cybersecurity education space through research grants and designations for institutions meeting certain academic criteria. Of note are the National Security Agency (NSA) and Department of Homeland Security's (DHS) National Centers of Academic Excellence in Cybersecurity (NCAE-C) programs. There are three institutional NCAE designations: Cyber Defense (CAE-CD), Cyber Operations (CAE-CO), and Research (CAE-R). The CAE-CD is a designation recognizing that an institution is "helping reduce threats to [the US] national infrastructure by promoting higher education and research in cyber defense as well as provide the nation with a pipeline of qualified cybersecurity professionals" [26, 27]. CAE-CO designates that an institution's program is in support of the President's National Initiative for Cybersecurity Education (NICE) [27]. These programs promote a workforce prepared to work in support of a cyber-secure nation. If an institution receives a CAE-R designation it indicates an "institution increases the understanding of robust cyber defense technology, policy, and practices that will enable [the US] to prevent and respond to a catastrophic event" [27]. The CAE-R intuitions must offer doctorate degrees in one of the three classifications of the Carnegie Foundation Basic Classification system or other independent bodies. To maintain the CAE-CD and CAE-R designation, an institution must apply for re-designation every five years [27].

To qualify for these designations an institution must meet the requirements outlined by the NCAE-C application guidelines. Both the CAE-CD and the CAE-CO designations have a set of general knowledge units required to be taught in a higher education program [28, 29]. Additionally, an institution must meet a certain number of optional knowledge units for each designation. These knowledge units span a variety of topics in cybersecurity and are a basis for courses and pathways an institution should offer. Each of these KU sets the learning outcomes an institution must prove a course covers and provides a description and reasoning for the required KU. The structure, materials, and methods of instruction are left to the institution's preferences and needs; all that is required is that these units are covered, and that the outcomes are met. These KUs are integral to understanding what a comprehensive cybersecurity education should entail and are an additional resource to institutions offering cybersecurity as a degree option. These designations' KUs are helpful to establish a common ground for the topics a learner should know to work in cybersecurity. Therefore, understanding them is imperative to establish a basis for developing a curriculum for K-12 cybersecurity education in Oklahoma or any state.

The general required knowledge units for the CAE-CD designation can be deployed in two ways, a technical program and a non-technical program. There are three foundational knowledge units for both technical and non-technical to qualify for the CAE-CD: Cybersecurity Fundamentals, Cybersecurity Principles, and IT Systems Components [28]. Additionally, they both have five separate Core KUs they must cover to qualify. An institution focusing in the technical area must teach the following Core-Technical KUs: Basic Cryptography, Basic Networking, Basic Scripting and Programming, Network Defense, and Operating System Concepts. To obtain the CAE-CD designation as a non-technical program, an institution must cover the following five KUs: Cyber Threats; Cybersecurity Planning and Management; Policy, legal, Ethics, and Compliance; Security Program Management; and Security Risk Analysis. Once an institution offers these basic courses, there are 60 optional KUs an institution may offer to specialize in certain areas of cybersecurity.

Cyber Operations is focused on increasing the cybersecurity workforce through practical education covering a broad spectrum of topics. These organizations must comply with the 2008 Presidential National Initiative for Cybersecurity Education (NICE), to better prepare the cybersecurity workforce to handle cybersecurity challenges. Institutions obtaining the CAE-CO designation are required to cover ten Mandatory Knowledge units which must be included in core classes at an institution. Additionally, the institution must cover four of the eleven optional knowledge units to qualify for this designation. The ten mandatory knowledge units span the following topics: Cyber Policy, Law, and Ethics; Computer Science Foundations; Operating Systems; Computer Networks; System Programming; Cybersecurity Foundations; Applied Cryptography; Software Reverse Engineering; Defensive Cyber Operations; and Offensive Cyber Operations. These KUs are not required to be covered fully in one course and may span courses to address the information [29].

The CAE-R designation does not outline specific KUs for institutions to cover and is focused exclusively on higher education institutions offering doctorate programs. These requirements focus on the type of doctorate program and its designation/classification, the faculty members and their produced research material, the types and amounts of grant/research funding brought into an institution, and the research accomplishments of students and faculty [30]. These requirements are not in the scope of K-12 education and are therefore not considered here.

The community of institutions with a NCAE-C designation extends to all 50 states, the District of Columbia, and Puerto Rico [31]. These designations are an important step in receiving funding from DHS and the NSA. There are currently 474 institutions with a NCAE designation in the US and its territory of Puerto Rico [31]. Of these there are currently 427 institutions with a CAE-CD, 23 with a CAE-CO, and 93 institutions with a CAE-R designation [31]. 56 of the 474 NCAE-C institutions have received multiple designations. Eleven hold all three [31]. These numbers showcase the importance of the NCAE-C designations and their KU's influence on the cybersecurity education objectives landscape.

3.3 Accrediting Bodies

Due to the Veterans Readjustment Act of 1952, colleges and universities are required to obtain accreditation to participate in federal financial aid programs [32]. These accrediting organizations have, since 1952, increasingly become a symbol of a university degree having merit. Accreditation bodies like the Accreditation Board for Engineering and Technology (ABET) are of importance to cybersecurity and have established criteria for accreditation for Computer Science, Engineering, and Cybersecurity programs and many more. Cybersecurity education for ABET accreditation falls under two commissions: the Computing Accreditation Commission and the Engineering Accreditation Commission. These commissions focus on accrediting Computing Programs and Engineering Programs, respectively. Computing programs prepare graduates for careers in computing, encompassing areas like computer science, information technology, cybersecurity, and related fields [33]. Engineering programs prepare graduates for careers encompassing the engineering profession, within which is a Cybersecurity Engineering path [34].

ABET accreditation for cybersecurity and similarly named *Computing* programs can be awarded at two levels, Associate and Bachelor's. All ABET accredited programs must meet a standard set of criteria for students, program educational objectives, student outcomes, continuous improvement, curriculum, and faculty. Of importance here are the student outcomes and curriculum criteria. The student outcomes requirements are expressed as five key statements that must be documented and publicly stated for all graduates [33]. The only difference between the associate and bachelor's level cybersecurity requirements is the number of semester credit hours and one curricular requirement for each. ABET requires Associate level degrees to have a minimum of 30 semester credit hours and bachelor's to have 45 related to the field of study. Engineering Programs accredited by ABET for a Bachelors in Cybersecurity Engineering and similarly named Engineering programs also must meet a standard set of criteria for students, program educational objectives, student outcomes, continuous improvement, curriculum, faculty, facilities, and institutional support. And again, the student outcomes and curriculum criteria are relevant. The student outcomes requirements are expressed in seven key statements [34]. For Cybersecurity Engineering and similarly named *Engineering* programs there are six specific additional curricular guidelines that must provide breadth and depth across engineering topics. Like accreditation in Computing Programs, Engineering Programs from ABET are also given the liberty to determine the methods, structure, and schedule defining their cybersecurity engineering programs.

ABET Computing Programs and Engineering Programs are awarded across 42 countries with over 930 institutions [35]. There are 4,773 programs accredited across these 930 institutions of which (as of 2020) 548 have a Computing Program accreditation [35]. Currently 45 institutions are registered with a Cybersecurity program and 10 with a Cybersecurity Engineering program through ABET. It must also be noted that institutions can have a cybersecurity accreditation awarded through their computer science or computer engineering programs, so a detailed account might be skewed in these numbers through ABET.

Ultimately, these accrediting bodies play a large part in shaping the academic structure of degree programs in cybersecurity, as institutions are legally required to obtain accreditation for federal funding. Using these guidelines, requirements, and criteria to establish a baseline of material that should be covered in a cybersecurity degree program of all levels of higher education is correspondingly beneficial in creating a structure for an introduction to cybersecurity course for K-12. As seen in the supplement to the CSES 2017, there is a movement to segment the field of cybersecurity into topics suitable for an introductory class for institutions from High School, Technical Schools, 2-year institutions, and colleges and universities.

These developments have a unique benefit of positioning K-12 to produce cybersecurity coursework aligned with the requirements of colleges and universities, government agencies and programs, and federal and cultural requirements for accreditation. As seen in the guidelines and program requirements above, standards for a cybersecurity course diverge drastically from those of cyber standards as additions to the current computer science standards. Cybersecurity standards focus more on the concepts and application of security whereas computer science focuses on how cybersecurity pertains to computer science topics such as data and code [23, 36]. The creation of core cybersecurity objectives will be integral in the production of a cybersecurity curriculum for the state of Oklahoma. However, it is important to fill in the gap of the current literature by not only applying content objectives for an introduction to cybersecurity in the K-12 educational system, but also to provide guidance on the order in which the objectives should be covered in courses.

4 NIST NICE Framework

In 2014, the National Institute of Standards and Technology (NIST) established an initiative for cybersecurity education. This National Initiative for Cybersecurity Education (NICE) began to be developed in 2008 when the Comprehensive National Cybersecurity Initiative was established [37]. However, NICE fully formed under Title IV "National cybersecurity awareness and education program" of the Cybersecurity Enhancement Act of 2014 [38]. As of 2023, NICE was no longer referred to as an "initiative" and is now simply referred to as NICE [4]. It is designed to "energize, promote, and coordinate a robust community working together to advance an integrated ecosystem of cybersecurity education, training, and workforce development" [39]. As a part of this effort the NICE Workforce Framework or Cybersecurity (NICE Framework) was "established to provide a standard approach and common language for describing cybersecurity work and learner capabilities … seeking to improve communication around stakeholders throughout the cybersecurity ecosystem about how to identify, recruit, develop, and retain talent" [40].

4.1 Definition

The NICE Framework was originally established by Special Publication (SP) 800-181 in 2017 and updated with its first revision SP 800-181r1 in 2024 [40, 41]. In this publication, NICE conducted research of DHS's "IT Essential Body of Knowledge," the Federal Chief of Information Officer's "National Cybersecurity Workforce Framework," and in the employees in the field of cybersecurity, collaborating with academics, institutions, industry professionals, and companies [4]. Upon the first revision, NICE established the Framework with seven work role categories which outline the seven areas of work available for cybersecurity professionals (see Fig. 1). Work roles are individual tasks that an employee might complete as a part of their job and each job can be responsible for more than one work role. Every job is a part of an occupation inside the cybersecurity workforce, where multiple jobs make up the occupation. Ultimately, the Framework breaks these seven categories into 52 individual work roles. Figure 1 shows the number of work roles in each of the seven categories. The Framework establishes a modular approach to the cybersecurity workforce using Task, Knowledge, and Skill (TKS) Statements. Each Task Statement describes the work an individual will conduct as a part of their job requirements. Each task requires a set of skills and prior knowledge in order for an individual to complete the task. The current Framework version has 2,280 individual TKS Statements.

16 Work Roles | 8 Work Roles | 7 Work Roles | 7 Work Roles | 2 Work Roles | 5 Work Roles | 7 Work Roles

Fig. 1. NICE Framework Work Role Categories and Number of Work Roles

4.2 TKS Statement Frequency Analysis

We analyze the NICE Framework, yielding a model using the framework to support cybersecurity education. This Framework is beneficial for K-12 education, as it provides a basis for the tasks, knowledge, and skills a future cybersecurity workforce employee will need to possess, execute, and maintain. Using the framework, instructors and curriculum developers can establish lessons and assignments to teach learners. As seen above, there are many curricula, guidelines, and objectives which have used these TKS statements to develop their content. Using these TKS statements alone, without any analysis, an instructor or content creator would focus on educating students solely based on a job role in the framework and a personal understanding of the connections between job roles in the cybersecurity workforce landscape. Lacking is a strategic, sustainable model suitable for curriculum and content creation.

The NICE Framework lacks an organization of the TKS statements which would enable an instructor to start from a standardized introductory baseline. The current framework does not categorize the TKS statements based on a generalizability into all work roles. Thus, it is difficult to begin curriculum development for new or re-skilled learners, as these individuals do not yet have or know the work role they will fulfill. We identify a model to utilize this framework as a method to establish guidelines, objectives, and a roadmap for educating students on an Introduction to Cybersecurity. It is important to establish these guidelines as a living and breathing model. The model should evolve as revisions of the NICE Framework are released. Such a model enables updates not only to the content, but also to the order in which it is taught. The benefit herein is in being in harmony with the ever-changing cybersecurity landscape. For the purpose of this study, we will adopt the NICE SP-800-181-r1 and its supplemental documentation of the TKS Statements. Currently, NICE is in the process of releasing Version 2.0.0; the community awaits revised supplemental documents, specifically the Special Publication Revision 2 to be released [4, 42].

We propose a model which will enable educators, especially those in the K12 space, to create educational content based on TKS Statements that are most generalizable to all work role categories for cybersecurity. This model relies on the frequency in which TKS Statements appear in the seven individual work role categories and, more specifically, the individual work roles of each category. We separated the 2,280 TKS Statements into a frequency of appearance model for each work role and its respective category (See Fig. 2). Each of the 52 work roles forms enumerate the TKS statements from the 2,280 which are required for that specific role. Only 20 TKS statements were found in all seven work role categories and 36 TKS statements were found in six of the seven work role categories.

This frequency analysis shows 20 items an individual must know to fulfill any job role inside all cybersecurity careers. It would be impossible to cover all 2,280 TKS statements in one course. Therefore, we determined that the cutoff would be any TKS statement which appeared in at least six out of the seven categories. This left 57 total TKS statements. Using these most generalizable task, knowledge, and skills (20 in all seven categories and 37 more in six of the seven categories), we establish the basis of the remaining work presented here, integrating Cybersecurity into all K-12 subjects, a comprehensive "Introduction to Cybersecurity" Curriculum, and a potential cybersecurity curriculum solution for the State of Oklahoma.

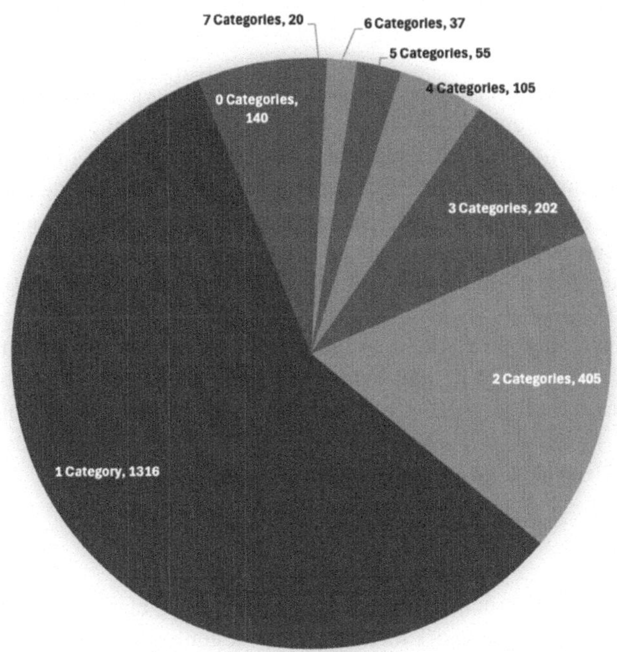

K0674	Knowledge of computer networking protocols
K0675	Knowledge of risk management processes
K0676	Knowledge of cybersecurity laws and regulations
K0677	Knowledge of cybersecurity policies and procedures
K0678	Knowledge of privacy laws and regulations
K0679	Knowledge of privacy policies and procedures
K0680	Knowledge of cybersecurity principles and practices
K0681	Knowledge of privacy principles and practices
K0682	Knowledge of cybersecurity threats
K0683	Knowledge of cybersecurity vulnerabilities
K0684	Knowledge of cybersecurity threat characteristics
K0710	Knowledge of enterprise cybersecurity architecture principles and practices
K0751	Knowledge of system threats
K0752	Knowledge of system vulnerabilities
K0791	Knowledge of defense-in-depth principles and practices
K0812	Knowledge of digital communication systems and software
K0915	Knowledge of network architecture principles and practices
K0983	Knowledge of computer networking principles and practices
K1014	Knowledge of network security principles and practices
T1020	Determine the operational and safety impacts of cybersecurity lapses

Fig. 2. NICE Framework TKS Statement Frequencies and 20 Most Generalizable Statements

5 Integrating Cybersecurity into All K-12 Subjects

Non-technical (the managerial and psychological/cyber hygiene) cybersecurity education is extremely important for increasing the cyber resilience of everyday people who do not work in the technical realm of cybersecurity. One component of our approach is the integration of a common cybersecurity language into every classroom. Science, Technology, Engineering, and Math (STEM) education is a prime example of a path educational institutions can increase the general cybersecurity knowledge through instruction. STEM education is integrated throughout all subjects, using STEM Languages (terminology) to develop a robust understanding of STEM ideas in school [43]. This practice has increased the STEM understanding of students and promoted a STEM-based attainment goal from students across the world [43]. This same practice can be done with cybersecurity languages to increase the cybersecurity knowledge and attainment goals of learners. This section presents the method and process to teach teachers how to integrate cybersecurity topics into their lessons using the NICE Framework TKS Statements.

5.1 Method

In order to increase cybersecurity language use in all K-12 classrooms, we have created a model educators can use to work through the most generalizable 20 TKS statements to learn what terms should be included in their lessons to increase the awareness of terms used in cybersecurity. The model has three components: (1) a Worksheet, (2) a Critical Thinking Guidance Sheet, and (3) the most generalizable 20 TKS Statements. The main part of the model is an eight-step approach using a guided worksheet to complete the steps necessary to develop classroom statements which include terms generalizable to cybersecurity. This model, using the worksheet can be exercised by an individual, but was designed to be given in a professional development guided presentation. As an instructor becomes more familiar with cybersecurity language, this process will become natural, and the frequency of cybersecurity terminology used in their classroom will increase. (1) The first step in this process is simple for teachers to complete: identify the subject. In this step, the instructor names the course subject (e.g., math or science) for which they will be developing classroom statements. (2) In step two, the teacher considers the unit or lesson they will teach next in their classroom. For instance, a teacher in math may be moving on to two-step equations, or an English teacher might be starting a unit on literary elements. Figure 3 shows steps 1 and 2 completed using an example of an English teacher planning classroom statements on cybersecurity for literary elements.

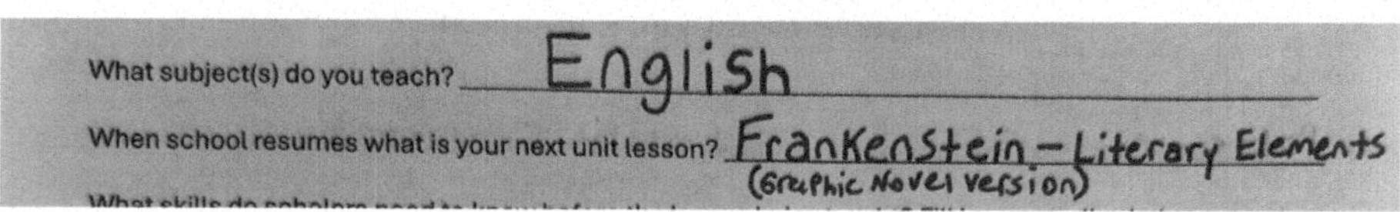
What subject(s) do you teach? English

When school resumes what is your next unit lesson? Frankenstein – Literary Elements (Graphic Novel version)

Fig. 3. Step 1 and 2 in the Integrating NICE Framework throughout all K-12 Subjects

(3) The third step of this process is to consider and write out the answer to the following question: what skills do scholars need to know before the lesson being taught next? In this step, an instructor must analyze the knowledge and skills that a student has learned previously in other classes/grade levels or units in the current curriculum. This step helps shape the instructor's frame of mind towards the actual topics they will cover in the lesson and which items are already assumed to be known. To develop classroom statements including cybersecurity language, an instructor must understand the difference between information they will cover, and knowledge students already know (see Fig. 4).

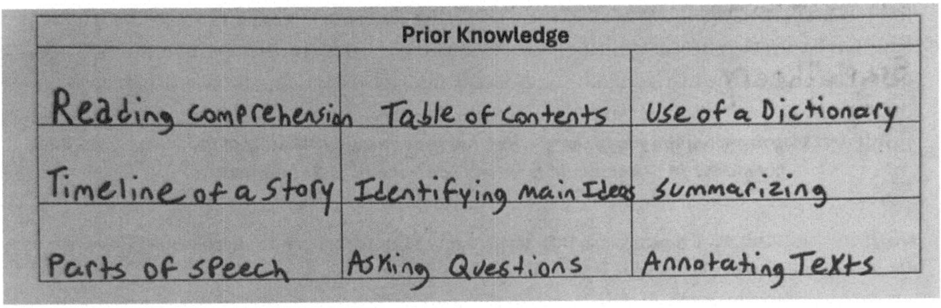

Prior Knowledge		
Reading comprehension	Table of contents	Use of a Dictionary
Timeline of a Story	Identifying main Ideas	Summarizing
Parts of Speech	Asking Questions	Annotating Texts

Fig. 4. Step 3 in the Integrating NICE Framework throughout all K-12 Subjects

(4) In the fourth step, the instructor conducts an analysis of the new skills/knowledge a student will learn in the lesson. Here a teacher will look through the objectives and standards from their curriculum or lesson plan writing them down or analyzing them for their curriculum. The goal of this step allows an instructor to frame the remaining steps towards the goals of the unit/lesson they will be teaching. An example of this step as completed can be seen in Fig. 5.

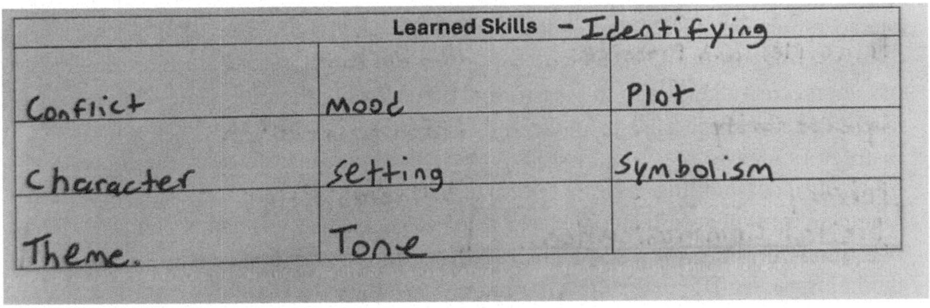

Learned Skills - Identifying		
Conflict	Mood	Plot
Character	Setting	Symbolism
Theme.	Tone	

Fig. 5. Step 4 in the Integrating NICE Framework throughout all K-12 Subjects

(5) The fifth step of this process asks teachers to characterize the implicit skills or underlying competencies scholars will learn during the lesson. This step is often quite difficult, as it engages the instructor to think outside of the lesson plan and the inherent skills they will be teaching throughout the lesson. When a lesson is created, it is designed to assist students with retaining and succeeding at the standards. However, every lesson has what is considered to be hidden curriculum by the education community, which is the idea that teachers teach students skills without knowing. Often this hidden curriculum is generalized to be more from the social/psychological area, but this concept can also be applied to underlying competencies a lesson gives students from the academic content [3, 44, 45]. Ultimately, students are learning objectives not explicitly called out in the classroom. These are often gained from the teacher describing or answering questions about content. Figure 6 continues the English example showing hidden curriculum and underlying competencies students gain from classroom discussions of reading. To assist teachers in this process, a document was created to guide instructors through this process, discussing common implicit skills/underlying competencies from major subjects and elective courses.

Implicit Skills/Underlying Competencies	
Pattern Recognition	Symbolic Intepretation
Understanding Authorial Intent	Organization
Graph Theory	

Fig. 6. Step 5 in the Integrating NICE Framework throughout all K-12 Subjects

(6) The sixth step of this process asks the teachers to engage with the NICE Workforce Framework TKS Statement Frequencies, specifically the 20 which appear in all work roles from the framework. The goal of this process is to increase the use of cybersecurity language in classrooms that are not geared towards cybersecurity. Therefore, the researcher provides only the most generalizable TKS statements to instructors for two reasons: First is to not overwhelm instructors with the responsibility of understanding 2,280 TKS Statements. Second, is to use the cybersecurity language most generalizable to every role in cybersecurity. Teachers are asked to do two things in the sixth step of this model to integrate cybersecurity language into their classroom. The first step is to read through the 20 TKS statements and analyze them for emerging words. Once teachers have read through these TKS statements, they are asked to document these terms in the worksheet. Working in a Professional Development (PD) session or with other participants is encouraged in this moment, as each individual will recognize different emerging words (Fig. 7). The second part

of using the TKS Statements is step 7 of the Integrating NICE Framework throughout all K-12 subjects' worksheet.

Emerging Words...	
Principles and Practices	Networking
Cybersecurity	Defense-in-Depth
Privacy	Vulnerabilities
Digital Communication	

Fig. 7. Step 6 in the Integrating NICE Framework throughout all K-12 Subjects

(7) Step 7 of the model asks the participants to research the words which emerged in the sixth step. Participants are encouraged to use the words "in cybersecurity" while researching the emerging words guiding them to the most effective definition of the term. The main portion of this process is to increase the use of cybersecurity language in the classroom. Thus, it is imperative that the participants using this model research what the terms used in the most generalizable 20 TKS statements mean for the field of cybersecurity. Understanding these common cybersecurity terms helps participants comprehend and grasp the objective of the model – including cybersecurity language into their class. Figure 8 shows this step continuing with the English example.

Word Meanings...	
Principles and Practices are the foundational concepts used in a line of work, field of study, ... various contexts	Networking is the Practice of connecting and securing multiple systems, Devices, and networks to Communicate and Share Data.
Cybersecurity is the Practice of CIA, IAAA and "Protection and Defense."	Defense-in-Depth is the Practice of establishing redundancy and resilience with multiple Defenses/Protections for threats
Privacy is the Protection of information and systems from unauthorized access or use	Vulnerabilities are weaknesses or flaws that can be exploited in a system, app, or net.
Digital communication Transmitting Data and ensuring it is secure with: encryption, authentication, secure protocols, non-repudiation, etc.	

Fig. 8. Step 7 in the Integrating NICE Framework throughout all K-12 Subjects

(8) The final step in the model prepares the teacher to use the terms which they have researched into the lesson they analyzed at the beginning of the process. This asks the teacher to consider phrases they would use in their classroom to teach the upcoming unit or lesson and incorporate these phrases by adapting their normal verbiage to

incorporate the emerging words. An example is talking about "errors," "holes," or "gaps" as "vulnerabilities" instead. Such minor shifts have proven effective in the incorporation of STEM languages and can be effective here as well [43] (Fig. 9).

As you Identify the vulnerabilities in the Plot, think about ways you could fix the flaws. Lets write those Down.	When setting out the timeline of the Plot, think about cybersecurity and Privacy using a timeline of Hackers events to tell the story.
What Patterns did you recognize in this Chapter? How could [illegible] network between the Patterns?	

Fig. 9. Step 8 in the Integrating NICE Framework throughout all K-12 Subjects

As instructors and curriculum designers alike begin to engage in this process, an increase in the usage of cybersecurity language will occur. Hearing the same terminology used in cybersecurity throughout other contents and in different contexts will help students better understand concepts related to cybersecurity.

5.2 Preliminary Experiences and Results

The model *Integrate NICE Framework throughout all K-12 Subjects* was presented at the 2024 NICE K-12 Cybersecurity Education Conference and tested before two groups of participants. The first group was a practice run in preparation for the conference. This was conducted at a local Oklahoma high school and middle school where one of the co-authors currently teaches courses in Cybersecurity Basics and Computer Science Principles. The teachers participating in this presentation were from different subjects and levels of administration. Teachers who participated discussed how beneficial this model was in increasing their understanding of Cybersecurity. When speaking with the teachers a few weeks later, they expressed how they had utilized some of these phrases in their classroom. In the future, we will conduct a study to analyze students' understanding of cybersecurity language both before and after their instructor has participated in using this model for their lessons. Key takeaways from this experience include:

- The structured model helped instructors have a better understanding of cybersecurity terminology
- Instructors felt more confident in understanding cybersecurity.
- The model assisted in thinking about the implicit skills their lessons taught.

The second presentation was conducted at the NICE K-12 Cybersecurity Education Conference in San Antonio, Texas. This presentation was attended by directors and administrators of NICE and the NICE K-12 division, teachers, curriculum developers, administrators, cybersecurity professionals, and higher education employees. The response from this presentation was an overwhelming appreciation and engagement in the process. Teachers were excited to return to their schools to use the phrases they had developed by walking through the model in the presentation. Others were eager to obtain copies of the presentation and model to use in their districts to encourage teacher's support in increasing Cybersecurity Languages in their school. Administrators from NICE were very eager to see where the rest of the research concluded, and how it would align with the forthcoming release of NICE Framework version 2.0.0. In an effort to collect more results from this model, an IRB protocol for a study will be submitted and more data will be collected. As a consequence of this engagement:

- Participants in the session asked for the model so they could take it back to their schools and administer a PD session using the model.
- NIST NICE Director and K-12 director complemented the work and asked questions about when this would be available to send out to their community.
- Curriculum designers were interested in learning more about the future of the model and the curriculum being built.

6 Conclusions and Future Work

The increase in attacks affecting critical infrastructure and the economy creates a need for a focus on cybersecurity defense and awareness. However, a knowledge gap exists in both the technical and non-technical domains of cybersecurity, creating a weakness in the global and US cybersecurity workforce. Decreasing the workforce gap that exists in cybersecurity must be addressed through many avenues, but of extreme importance is education. Educational objectives and standards for cybersecurity education are numerous through NICE, ABET, and NCAE-C. However, initiatives in the technical and non-technical camps do not offer much outside higher education, leaving a gap in K-12. Addressing K-12 education is important in tackling the workforce gap to prepare the next generation of students. To address the gap, we developed a model with which to structure and organize cybersecurity objectives for an Introduction to Cybersecurity course using the NICE Workforce Framework.

The NICE Workforce Framework consists of 2,280 Task, Knowledge, and Skill Statements (TKS Statements) which outline the information and functions an individual will need for certain work roles in cybersecurity. We found that 20 TKS Statements appeared in all work role categories from the NICE Framework, lending a model of the most generalizable requirements needed to work in cybersecurity. The first use of this model is increasing the Cybersecurity Language use in all K-12 subjects. The model walks educators and content developers through a process which incorporates cybersecurity terms from the 20 most generalizable TKS Statements into their lessons. Following this model will increase both the instructors and content creators' knowledge of cybersecurity languages, as well as those of the students.

In the future, we will use these TKS statements to develop a yearlong K-12 focused Introduction to Cybersecurity course. We will test the efficacy of the curriculum with student data and have analysis by industry and academic professionals on the content of the curriculum. We will conduct train-the-trainer sessions to prepare instructors for utilizing the curriculum. From these sessions, data will be collected using models that collect quantitative and qualitative data from the instructors. Moreover, we will conduct data collection steps of revisions for the curriculum throughout the school year with these instructors. Research will need to be conducted on the best models to follow in order to obtain these data points. Finally, we will collect data from students enrolled in an introductory cybersecurity course using the curriculum we designed. We anticipate these efforts will help us better understand the potential of this approach for closing the cybersecurity workforce gap.

Acknowledgments. This project was supported in part by federal award number ARPAYY001807 awarded to the State of Oklahoma and administered by OCAST and OMES, by the U.S. Department of the Treasury. Matching funds were provided for this project by the George Kaiser Family Foundation.

Disclosure of Interests. The authors have no competing interests to declare that are relevant to the content of this article.

References

1. Garfinkel, S.L.: The cybersecurity risk. Commun. ACM **55**, 29–32 (2012). https://doi.org/10.1145/2184319.2184330
2. Gracy, M., Jeyavadhanam, B.R., Babu, P.K., Karthick, S.H., Chandru, R.: Growing threats of cyber security: protecting yourself in a digital world. In: 2023 International Conference on Networking and Communications (ICNWC), pp. 1–5 (2023). https://doi.org/10.1109/ICNWC57852.2023.10127398
3. Moffitt, T.: 2020's Most (and Least) Cyber-Secure States | Webroot. https://www.webroot.com/blog/2020/04/03/2020s-most-and-least-cyber-secure-states/. Accessed 10 Nov 2022
4. NICE Framework History. NIST (2024)
5. Frost, A.: 2017 Global Information Security Workforce Study, p. 8 (2017)
6. 2024 Cybersecurity Statistics: The Ultimate List Of Stats, Data & Trends. https://purplesec.us/resources/cybersecurity-statistics/. Accessed 13 Apr 2025
7. 2022 Cyber Security Statistics Trends & Data. https://purplesec.us/resources/cyber-security-statistics/. Accessed 11 Nov 2022
8. Tavani, H.T.: The uniqueness debate in computer ethics: what exactly is at issue, and why does it matter? Ethics Inf. Technol. **4**, 37–54 (2002). https://doi.org/10.1023/A:1015283808882
9. Jacob, J., Wei, W., Sha, K., Davari, S., Yang, T.A.: Is the nice cybersecurity workforce framework (NCWF) effective for a workforce comprising of interdisciplinary majors? In: Proceedings of the 16th International Conference on Scientific Computing (CSC 2018), Las Vegas, USA (2018)
10. Cain, A.A., Edwards, M.E., Still, J.D.: An exploratory study of cyber hygiene behaviors and knowledge. J. Inf. Secur. Appl. **42**, 36–45 (2018). https://doi.org/10.1016/j.jisa.2018.08.002
11. $(ISC)^2$ 2022 Cybersecurity Workforce Study. https://www.isc2.org:443/Research/Workforce-Study. Accessed 10 Nov 2022
12. 2024 ISC2 Cybersecurity Workforce Study. https://www.isc2.org/Insights/2024/10/ISC2-2024-Cybersecurity-Workforce-Study. Accessed 13 Apr 2025
13. Schulte, C., et al.: What we talk about when we talk about k-12 computing education. In: 2024 Working Group Reports on Innovation and Technology in Computer Science Education, New York, NY, USA, pp. 226–257. Association for Computing Machinery (2025). https://doi.org/10.1145/3689187.3709612
14. Chiosea, F.: The State of Cybersecurity Education in K-12 Schools. 12

15. Kocsis, D., Segal, D.: Cyber hygiene, cyberpsychology, and impacting the future workforce. In: AMCIS 2022 TREOs (2022)
16. Alrabaee, S., Al-Kfairy, M., Barka, E.: Efforts and suggestions for improving cybersecurity education. In: 2022 IEEE Global Engineering Education Conference (EDUCON), pp. 1161–1168 (2022). https://doi.org/10.1109/EDUCON52537.2022.9766653
17. Cyber Security for Everyone: An Introductory Course for Non-Technical Majors. JCERP
18. Baker, M.: Striving for effective cyber workforce development, p. 26
19. Kaspersky Security Bulletin 2021. Statistics. https://securelist.com/kaspersky-security-bulletin-2021-statistics/105205/. Accessed 10 Nov 2022
20. Joint Task Force on Cybersecurity Education: Cybersecurity Curricula 2017: Curriculum Guidelines for Post-Secondary Degree Programs in Cybersecurity, New York, NY, USA. ACM (2018). https://doi.org/10.1145/3184594
21. ACM Supplement to CSEC 2017: Content for a Foundational Cybersecurity Degree Course. https://learning-outcomes.csec-foundations.org/. Accessed 13 Apr 2025
22. Javidi, G., Sheybani, E.: K-12 cybersecurity education, research, and outreach. In: 2018 IEEE Frontiers in Education Conference (FIE), pp. 1–5 (2018). https://doi.org/10.1109/FIE.2018.8659021
23. Dempsey, K.: North Dakota Computer Science and Cybersecurity Standards
24. HB1398. https://ndlegis.gov/assembly/68-2023/regular/documents/23-0970-03000.pdf
25. 2023 Computer Science Standards_0.pdf. https://sde.ok.gov/sites/default/files/documents/files/2023%20Computer%20Science%20Standards_0.pdf
26. Becker, A., et al.: National Centers of Academic Excellence in Cybersecurity (NCAE-C) – Cyber Defense (CAE-CD) Knowledge Units (KUs) (2024)
27. What is a CAE in Cybersecurity? | CAE Community. https://caecommunity.org/about-us/what-cae-cybersecurity. Accessed 08 Apr 2025
28. unclass-cae-cd_designation_requirements.pdf. https://dl.dod.cyber.mil/wp-content/uploads/cae/pdf/unclass-cae-cd_designation_requirements.pdf
29. unclass-cae-co_knowledge_units.pdf. https://dl.dod.cyber.mil/wp-content/uploads/cae/pdf/unclass-cae-co_knowledge_units.pdf
30. unclass-cae-r_proposed_designation_requirement.pdf. https://dl.dod.cyber.mil/wp-content/uploads/cae/pdf/unclass-cae-r_proposed_designation_requirement.pdf
31. CAE Institution Map | CAE Community. https://www.caecommunity.org/cae-map. Accessed 22 Apr 2025
32. Hegji, A.: An Overview of Accreditation of Higher Education in the United States
33. Criteria for Accrediting Computing Programs, 2025 - 2026 – ABET. https://www.abet.org/accreditation/accreditation-criteria/criteria-for-accrediting-computing-programs-2025-2026/. Accessed 13 Apr 2025
34. Criteria for Accrediting Engineering Programs, 2025 - 2026 – ABET. https://www.abet.org/accreditation/accreditation-criteria/criteria-for-accrediting-engineering-programs-2025-2026/. Accessed 13 Apr 2025
35. Accreditation. https://www.abet.org/accreditation/. Accessed 22 Apr 2025
36. Cybersecurity 2023 Legislation. https://www.ncsl.org/technology-and-communication/cybersecurity-2023-legislation. Accessed 22 Apr 2024
37. NIST. (2017). https://www.nist.gov/itl/applied-cybersecurity/nice/nice-framework-resource-center/about/nice-framework-history
38. Sen. Rockefeller, J.D.: Cybersecurity Enhancement Act of 2014. https://www.congress.gov/bill/113th-congress/senate-bill/1353/text. Accessed 16 Jan 2025
39. NICE. NIST (2016)
40. Getting Started with the NICE Framework. NIST (2023)

41. Newhouse, W., Keith, S., Scribner, B., Witte, G.: National Initiative for Cybersecurity Education (NICE) Cybersecurity Workforce Framework. National Institute of Stand-ards and Technology, Gaithersburg, MD (2017). https://doi.org/10.6028/NIST.SP.800-181
42. NICE Framework: Current Versions. NIST (2019)
43. Kelley, T.R., Knowles, J.G.: A conceptual framework for integrated STEM education. Int. J. STEM Educ. **3**, 1–11 (2016). https://doi.org/10.1186/s40594-016-0046-z
44. Jackson, P.W.: Life in Classrooms. Holt, Rinehart and Winston, New York (1968)
45. Good education in an age of measurement: on the need to reconnect with the question of purpose in education - ProQuest. https://www.proquest.com/docview/201488249/fulltextPDF/581F4ED02F5A4398PQ/1?accountid=14676&sourcetype=Scholarly%20Journals. Accessed 15 Apr 2025

Joining the Dots Between Cybersecurity Career Roles, Skills and Knowledge

Eliana Stavrou[1](✉) and Steven Furnell[2]

[1] Faculty of Pure and Applied Sciences, Open University of Cyprus, Nicosia, Cyprus
eliana.stavrou@ouc.ac.cy

[2] School of Computer Science, University of Nottingham, Nottingham, UK
steven.furnell@nottingham.ac.uk

Abstract. The increasing complexity of cyber threats, particularly in critical infrastructure sectors, has amplified the need for a skilled and adaptable cybersecurity workforce. While frameworks such as the European Cybersecurity Skills Framework (ECSF) and the Cyber Security Body of Knowledge (CyBOK) offer structured representations of professional cyber career roles, skills and foundational knowledge areas, practical guidance on how to use them together for designing industry-aligned training programs remains limited. This paper addresses this gap by demonstrating how the compatibility between ECSF and CyBOK can inform the development of targeted, role-based training programs aimed at accelerating the upskilling of the cybersecurity workforce. Building on our recent compatibility study that mapped ECSF career role profiles to CyBOK knowledge areas, we present a practical use case focused on the Cyber Threat Intelligence Specialist career role. We detail a methodology for translating ECSF-CyBOK mappings into a modular training program, showcasing the design approach and the practical value of "joining the dots" between career roles, skills and knowledge. The proposed approach offers a replicable methodology to be applied to other roles and sectors, supporting the systematic design of tailored training programs aligned with evolving industry needs and regulatory requirements.

Keywords: Cyber Threat Intelligence · ECSF · CyBOK · Cybersecurity · Curricula design · Skills · CTI

1 Introduction

While the need for cybersecurity practitioners is now widely recognised, individuals and organisations can remain challenged in understanding the available skills and how they may map to the needs of a given cyber role. Similarly, ensuring that people can be suitably prepared for a role can be problematic if the knowledge and skills requirements of the role, and how to address them, are not clearly established. As evidence of a resulting problem, the latest Workforce Study from ISC2 (based on responses from over 15,800 individuals responsible for workplace cybersecurity) estimates the global cybersecurity workforce at 5.5 million employees [1]. At the same time, the findings suggest that two-thirds of

E. Bergström et al. (Eds.): CRITIS 2025, LNCS 16291, pp. 265–283, 2026.
https://doi.org/10.1007/978-3-032-19540-1_14

respondents reported a cyber-related staffing shortage, with the overall workforce gap estimated at 4.8 million. This highlights an urgent need to accelerate the upskilling of the cybersecurity workforce. However, achieving this is far from straightforward. Skills development in cybersecurity requires more than fragmented or ad hoc initiatives. Rather, it demands structured, credible learning programs grounded in recognised standards and aligned with industry needs.

Designing cybersecurity training programs is a complex task. Educators, training providers, and policymakers must first identify which competences are required and how they map to the needs of specific cybersecurity roles. There are different resources such as skills frameworks and knowledge bases that can support the design process of training curricula, with notable contributions being the European Cybersecurity Skills Framework (ECSF) [2], and the Cyber Security Body of Knowledge (CyBOK) [3]. ECSF provides high level specification of 12 core cybersecurity roles, and the knowledge and skills requirements associated with them. More recently ENISA has released a document that links ECSF roles to the obligations of essential and important entities under the NIS2 Directive [4]. This evidences the importance of role-based competence development in critical areas such as healthcare, energy, telecom and maritime, and highlights the need to gain an understanding of how roles are required and applied in practice. While ECSF profiles the key aspects of each role, additional resources can be utilized to complement and operationalize the role descriptions into actionable training curricula. CyBOK offers such complementary, providing a comprehensive body of knowledge structured across 21 domains, offering the depth and detail needed to contextualize and enrich the knowledge needs defined within ECSF roles. Currently, there is a lack of practical examples showing how to use these frameworks together. The integration of such resources should not be made on an ad hoc basis but rather performed in a systematic way to develop coherent training programs that are tailored to specific roles' competences. The benefit of such integration is the complementary of resources in a structured approach that leverages their strengths while bridging their potential limitations.

The objective of this paper is to demonstrate how ECSF and CyBOK can be systematically integrated to "join the dots" between career roles, skills, and knowledge. We present a replicable methodology that illustrates how ECSF–CyBOK compatibility can inform the design of targeted, role-based training programs. To demonstrate the approach, the paper focuses on the Cyber Threat Intelligence (CTI) Specialist role as a use case. This "skills-first" perspective is critical to accelerating workforce development and fostering a competent cybersecurity workforce that can keep up with the emerging technologies and the dynamics of the cyber threat landscape. The need to consider a skills-based approach in the training process aligns with policy priorities to create flexible learning pathways and enable learners to upskill based on their career stage and long-term career goals. A key design principle to achieve flexibility in a learning pathway is modularity in the learning units undertaken by learners. Such modularity can be achieved through structured, role-based training programs which focus on cultivating specific competences, and which can be mapped to stand-alone syllabus topics. This work demonstrates how ECSF-CyBOK can be mapped to syllabus topics in a systematic approach and create flexible learning pathways. From a policy perspective this is highly beneficial. By operationalizing the ECSF in combination with knowledge bases such as

CyBOK, the proposed methodology provides a practical mechanism to translate career role needs into tangible training programs that are grounded in recognized resources. Embedding such approaches into national strategies can accelerate the design of tailored curricula for critical sectors and support compliance with regulatory frameworks such as NIS2.

2 Background

The ECSF was released by the European Agency for Cybersecurity (ENISA) in 2022 and aims to provide "an open European tool to build a common understanding of the cybersecurity professional role profiles and common mappings with the appropriate skills and competences required" [5]. The result is a set of 12 role profiles, as listed below, spanning a range of cybersecurity activities and responsibilities, as well as varying in terms of their areas of technical focus and specialisation.

- Chief Information Security Officer
- Cyber Incident Responder
- Cyber Legal, Policy & Compliance Officer
- Cyber Threat Intelligence Specialist
- Cybersecurity Architect
- Cybersecurity Auditor
- Cybersecurity Educator
- Cybersecurity Implementer
- Cybersecurity Researcher
- Cybersecurity Risk Manager
- Digital Forensics Investigator
- Penetration Tester

These roles clearly vary in terms of scope and requirements, and the profiles are specified in terms of tasks, knowledge and skills that a related role-holder would be expected to need and undertake. The tasks, knowledge and skills draw from a common base set, which are then mapped to each 12 roles as appropriate. The ECSF User Manual indicates that "*the framework is designed to be suitably general to ensure that it may be easily understood and applied by a wider audience*" [5]. The profiles are described at a high-level to be applicable in different use cases such as in writing job advertisements, specifying training curricula, informing policy-making decisions, specifying role responsibilities, etc. For example, a typical Knowledge item is "Cyber Threat Actors", while an example Skill is "Identify threat actors TTPs and campaigns". Depending on the use case and whether the user of the framework is already well-versed in cyber security, then such indicators might be sufficient to provide direction and guidance. However, in some cases it is likely that they will need further amplification, thus the need to utilize external resources to enhance the ECSF profiles. Drawing from the ECSF User Manual, it is suggested that:

> "*The skills, knowledge and competences sections of the ECSF are neither exhaustive nor restrictive, allowing the user to enrich them by also including external resources e.g., the Cyber Security Body Of Knowledge (CyBOK), JRC Classification*" [5].

The highlighting of CyBOK is relevant, as it provides a potentially complementary resource that can provide supporting detail that the ECSF roles need. Indeed, one of the drivers for the creation of CyBOK was the need for a comprehensive reference that distills the key knowledge required as the foundations for the topic area. As a result, the UK's National Cyber Security Programme commissioned a project starting in 2017 to produce a 'guide to the body of knowledge in cyber security'. The resulting initiative involved subject expert authors from the international community, supported by further expert review and public comment, leading to the creation of a 1000+ pages resource collectively described as 'CyBOK'. The core content is framed around 21 Knowledge Areas (KAs), as depicted in Fig. 1. As the diagram shows, these are grouped into five higher level categories, which are largely technically-focused, but with clear emphasis on other perspectives (e.g. human and social factors) in some areas. Note that the acronyms used in the figure are used as the shorthand for referring to the individual KAs at later points in the discussion.

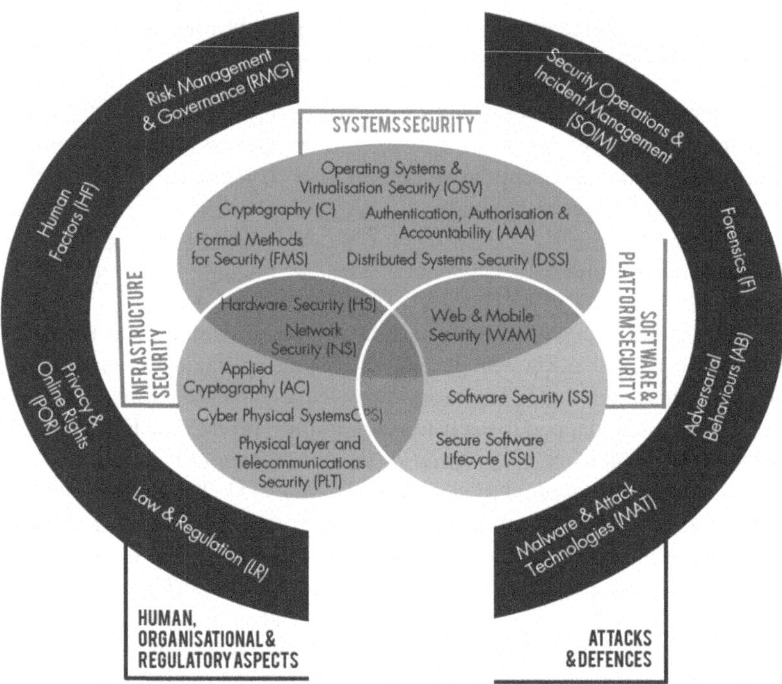

Fig. 1. CyBOK categories and Knowledge Areas [3]

With CyBOK having been specifically identified as a potential reference point for supporting the ECSF profiles, the authors undertook a study to determine the extent to which it could serve as an accompanying reference point, examining whether it provides coverage of the issues and topics that the ECSF profiles suggest [6].

3 Mapping ECSF Roles to CyBOK

This section outlines the approach taken to identify the key coverage within ECSF role profiles, and then map this to the Knowledge Base offered by CyBOK. This was somewhat aided by the fact that the CyBOK project already has a process and related resources that are intended to support mapping activities. These resources include an overall framework description [7], a detailed mapping reference list [8], and brief knowledge area summary in tabular form [9]. Additionally, each KA has an accompanying 'Knowledge Tree', showing the related Keywords and Phrases (KWoPs) in a layered structure.

A fundamental part of the CyBOK process is to identify KWoPs from the source material that can then be cross-referenced to the CyBOK Knowledge Base. The 'source material' in this case is the ECSF role profiles, and having examined the way in which they are presented, it was considered that drawing solely from the Knowledge statements for a given role could limit the potential for identifying sufficient KWoPs to properly characterise the roles. As such, the process also considered the text from the list of Skills and Tasks associated with each role.

The KWoP identification process involved independent assessment of the 250+ ECSF statements by each of the investigators. Those identified by both parties were directly included, and others were discussed prior to inclusion or exclusion. The KWoP identification process was performed independently for the Task, Knowledge and Skills statement sets, and the resulting KWoPs were then consolidated into a single list (removing duplicates) before performing the mapping over to CyBOK. The resulting list, across the role profiles, was 118 distinct KWoPs [6].

The mapping process used the full CyBOK Knowledge Base v1.1 as the basis for assessing coverage of the resulting KWoPs. Because it was necessary to consider the extent of the content/coverage, the process followed a bottom-up approach, directly searching within the Knowledge Base text, and then cross-referencing matches to the CyBOK Knowledge Trees. As such, the key steps for each KWoP were then as follows:

- Search for the KWoP text, or a characteristic element of it (e.g. for the KWoP "cybersecurity policies" a search would be made for "security polic", in order to also return any hits for 'information security policy', etc.).
- Assess how much material is included for each match in the knowledge base and determine the level of coverage provided (see below).
- Where a qualifying level of coverage was found within a given Knowledge Area, consult the accompanying Knowledge Tree for that KA to determine if the KWoPs are also matched there. If so, record the level and path within the tree to where the match is found.

For CyBOK to be a *useful* knowledge reference for topics raised in the ECSF, it needs to include something of substance about the KWoPs concerned. For example, simply encountering a mention of a term or concept would be unlikely to be sufficiently informative, whereas a definition, a description or a related discussion (especially if supported by references to the wider body of knowledge) would be expected to be more helpful. As such, the mapping process involved assessing the level of coverage that CyBOK provided for a given KWoP. For this purpose, three categorisations were used:

- Passing mention (i.e. the words appear but there is little or no content to further explain them)
- Basic coverage (e.g. a sentence or two of description or mention in an explanatory context)
- Detailed coverage (e.g. reflecting a dedicated paragraph / sub-section, typically supported by references)

In practice it typically proved straightforward to determine the difference and classify the KWoP occurrences accordingly. It should be noted that even for 'detailed coverage', readers would not necessarily expect to find exhaustive material on a given topic. This is in line with CyBOK's intended role as a *guide* to the body of knowledge (i.e. using it as a meaningful reference point to learn something about the topic or be pointed towards a further source for doing so).

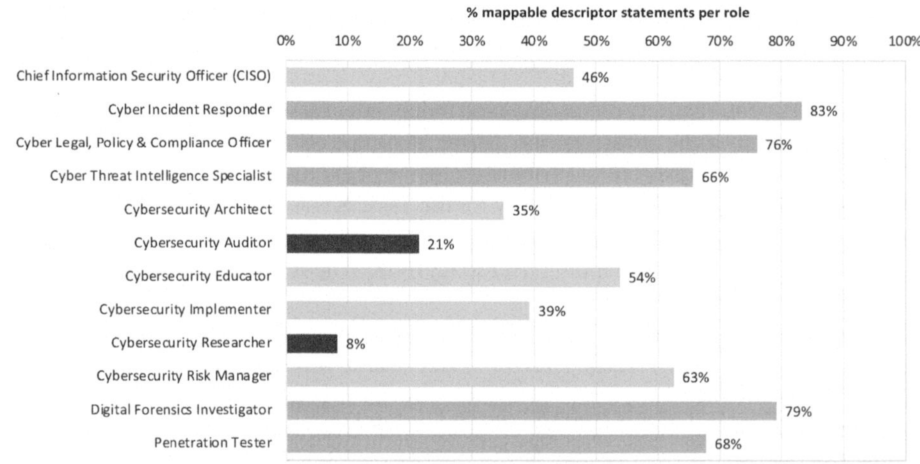

Fig. 2. Extent of KWoP mappings for the overall set of ECSF roles

For the CyBOK content to be considered suitable as a knowledge reference for the ECSF, it was necessary for at least Basic Coverage to be offered within at least one Knowledge Area (i.e. KWoP was not counted as mapped/covered if it only received passing mention(s) in the CyBOK text). The outcome of the process varied depending upon the role profile concerned, with some roles proving to be highly mappable, while there were others for which CyBOK had relatively little to offer. This is illustrated in Fig. 2, which shows the percentage of identified KWoPs that could be mapped for each of the ECSF roles. The chart is colour coded for easier reference, with green bars for those roles were two thirds or more of the KWoPs could be mapped, amber for those between a third and two thirds, and red for the two remaining cases where less than a third of candidate KWoPs were mappable. While it is clear that the results are not unform, CyBOK appears to fare particularly well in relation to the mapping of the more technical roles, as well as the legal and compliance role, where the majority of the KWoPs could be mapped to the Law and Regulation KAs.

4 Applying the ECSF-CyBOK Mapping to a Specialist Role

As an example, we focus on the role of Cyber Threat Intelligence Specialist, which is relevant in the context of recent regulations such as NIS2, and with CTI itself being important as an activity, both in its own right and as a key informant in support of other roles. The ECSF description of the role is as follow:

> "*Manages cyber threat intelligence life cycle including cyber threat information collection, analysis and production of actionable intelligence and dissemination to security stakeholders and the CTI community, at a tactical, operational and strategic level. Identifies and monitors the Tactics, Techniques and Procedures (TTPs) used by cyber threat actors and their trends, track threat actors' activities and observe how non-cyber events can influence cyber-related actions.*" [2]

As illustrated in Fig. 2, this was one of the roles for which the greater proportion of identified KWoPs could be mapped to CyBOK content, and as such CyBOK represents a good knowledge reference for this role.

It can be observed that for many of the ECSF roles there is often one CyBOK Knowledge Area that would clearly be relevant as the primary reference point. In the case of Cyber Threat Intelligence Specialist this is Security Operations and Incident Management (SOIM). However, examination of the necessary knowledge, tasks and skills quickly reveals that this is not the only Knowledge Area of relevance and as such a more granular evaluation is needed. As such, Table 1 presents the details of the mapping for the Cyber Threat Intelligence Specialist role, listing all of the Task, Knowledge and Skills statements associated with the role (as specified in the ECSF role profile) and then indicating in bold the KWoPs that were identified from them. The rightmost column then indicates which CyBOK Knowledge Area(s) were found to have relevant content in relation to those KWoPs. Figure 1 illustrates all CyBOK KAs and lists the relevant acronyms. It can be seen from the table that some of the statements were considered too general for meaningful KWoPs to be identified, and therefore these have a dash (-) in the righthand column. There are, however, also two instances ('Cybersecurity controls and solutions' and 'Responsible information disclosure') where KWoPs were identified, but then a suitable mapping within the CyBOK KAs could not be found. In these cases the mapping is indicated as N/A to signify that it was not achieved.

It is clear from Table 1 that where KWoP mappings could be achieved, they led to coverage being identified across a broad range of Knowledge Areas (nine in total). However, it is also clear that they do not apply in equal measure, and as can be seen from Fig. 3, the resulting cross-mapping to CyBOK helps to more fully understand the topic areas that contribute towards the role, and while SOIM is indeed the most prominent KA, it is far from the only with relevance. So, from a practical perspective, the CTI Specialist role holder can now be guided towards the KAs that are most relevant for them to understand.

For the purposes of contrast, we can consider how this compares to the breakdown for one of the other ECSF roles. Again, picking a candidate that was well represented in the overall proportion of KWoPs that could be mapped, Fig. 4 presents the result for the Penetration Tester role. Here we can see a very different range and distribution of

Table 1. CyBOK mapping of KWoPs from the Task, Knowledge and Skills statements for the Cyber Threat Intelligence Specialist role

Source	Statement	KA mappings
Tasks	Articulate and communicate intelligence openly and publicly at all levels	–
	Convey the proper security severity by explaining the **risk exposure** and its consequences to non-technical stakeholders	RMG, SSL
	Coordinate with stakeholders to share and consume intelligence on relevant cyber **threats**	CI, RMG
	Develop plans and procedures to manage **threat intelligence**	SOIM
	Develop, implement and manage the organisation's **cyber threat intelligence strategy**	SOIM
	Elaborate and advise on **mitigation plans** at the tactical, operational and strategic level	RMG
	Identify and assess **cyber threat actors** targeting the organisation	AB
	Identify, monitor and assess the **Tactics, Techniques and Procedures (TTPs)** used by **cyber threat actors** by analysing open-source and proprietary data, information and intelligence	AB, SOIM
	Implement **threat intelligence** collection, analysis and production of actionable intelligence and dissemination to security stakeholders	SOIM
	Leverage intelligence data to support and assist with **threat modelling**, recommendations for **Risk Mitigation** and cyber **threat hunting**	RMG, SSL
	Produce actionable reports based on **threat intelligence** data	SOIM
	Translate business requirements into **Intelligence** Requirements	SOIM
Knowledge	**Advanced and persistent cyber threats (APT)**	MAT
	Computer **networks security**	NS
	Computer programming	–
	Cross-domain and border-domain knowledge related to cybersecurity	–
	Cyber **threat actors**	AB

(*continued*)

Table 1. (*continued*)

Source	Statement	KA mappings
	Cyber Threat Intelligence (CTI) sharing **standards, methodologies** and **frameworks**	SOIM
	Cyber **threats**	CI, RMG
	Cybersecurity attack procedures	–
	Cybersecurity controls and solutions	N/A
	Cybersecurity-related **certifications**	LR
	Operating systems security	OSV
	Responsible information disclosure procedures	N/A
	Threat actors Tactics, Techniques and Procedures (TTPs)	AB, SOIM
Skills	Automate **threat intelligence** management procedures	SOIM
	Collaborate with other team members and colleagues	–
	Collect, analyse and correlate **cyber threat information** originating from multiple sources	SOIM
	Communicate, coordinate and cooperate with internal and external stakeholders	–
	Communicate, present and report to relevant stakeholders	–
	Conduct technical analysis and reporting	–
	Identify non-cyber events with implications on cyber-related activities	–
	Identify **threat actors TTPs** and campaigns	AB, SOIM
	Model threats, actors and TTPs	AB, RMG, SOIM, SSL
	Use and apply **CTI** platforms and tools	SOIM

topic coverage coming through. While there are some KAs in common, such as Risk Management and Governance (RMG), the role is more clearly dominated by topics drawn from the Secure Software Lifecycle (SSL) and Software Security (SS) KAs.

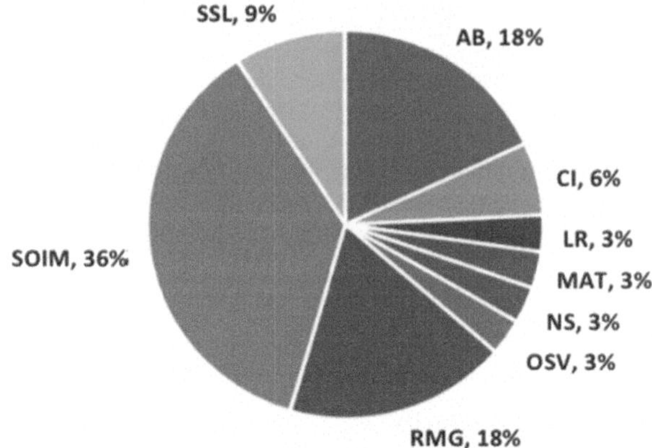

Fig. 3. CyBOK KA mapping for the ECSF Cyber Threat Intelligence Specialist role.

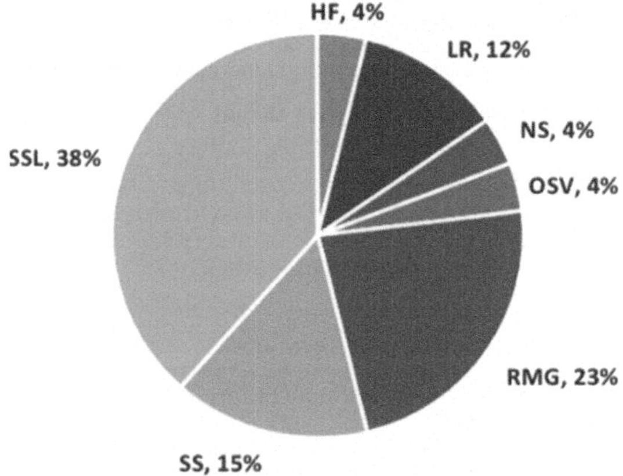

Fig. 4. CyBOK KA mapping for the ECSF Penetration Tester role.

5 Using the Mappings for Syllabus Design

Based on the mapping approach, the ECSF-CyBOK combination can also be utilized by educators and training providers to structure role-based training programs. With ECSF having been utilised to identify the relevant knowledge, skill and task requirements, CyBOK can be referenced to assist in the development of learning material. Figure 5 illustrates how ECSF and CyBOK can work together to facilitate the process of structuring and developing role-based training programs.

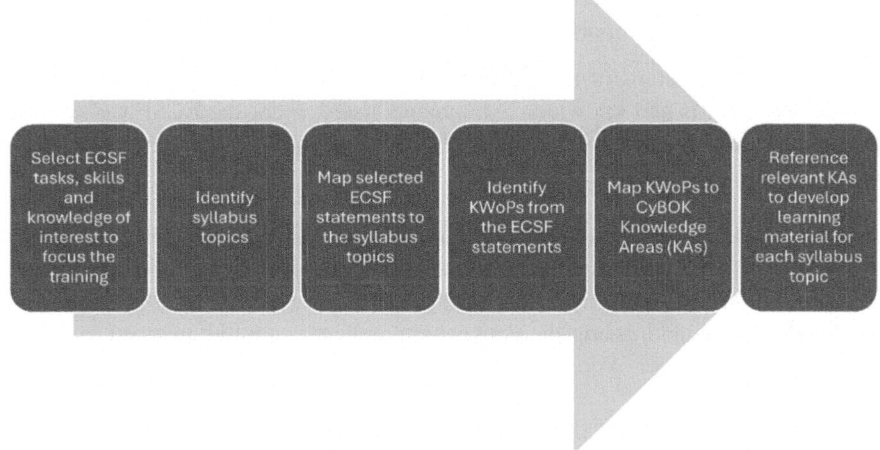

Fig. 5. ECSF-CyBOK mapping process to syllabus topics

In the case of ECSF CTI career role, the tasks, skills and knowledge listed under the relevant profile can be analysed to extract core thematic topics that should be included in the training syllabus to foster relevant CTI competences. Considering the ECSF CTI profile description, 8 core topics have been identified to build the training's syllabus:

1. *Introduction to Cyber Threat Intelligence.* This topic introduces the foundational concepts of CTI and its overarching mission within an organization.
2. *Building a CTI program.* This topic focuses on establishing, developing, and managing the CTI strategy within an organization.
3. *Cyber Threat Landscape & Actors.* A core aspect of CTI is to be able to profile cyber threats. Therefore, a solid understanding of the cyber threat landscape and actors is imperative. This topic aims to develop a solid understanding of adversaries' Tactics, Techniques and Procedures (TTP).
4. *Technical foundations for CTI.* This topic covers the underlying technical knowledge required to effectively perform CTI tasks.
5. *Legal and ethical aspects in CTI.* Given the sensitive nature of the CTI tasks, professionals are essential to be able to address the legal and ethical considerations pertinent to CTI operations. ECSF CTI Specialist profile mainly focuses on "Responsible information disclosure procedures". The syllabus can also consider broader legal and ethical aspects to ensure that CTI specialists are equipped to handle issues such as cross-border data sharing, privacy and data protection obligations, regulatory compliance, intellectual property concerns, and the ethical implications of intelligence use and dissemination within both public and private sector contexts.
6. *Threat information sources and data collection.* This topic focuses on identifying, accessing, and gathering raw data for intelligence purposes.
7. *Data analysis and threat profiling.* This topic covers the techniques and knowledge required to transform raw data into actionable insights and to understand adversary profiles.

8. *Intelligence production and dissemination.* Finally, this topic focuses on producing actionable intelligence reports and disseminating them to target stakeholders.

Table 2 presents details of the ECSF-CyBOK mapping to the syllabus topics. Initially, the tasks, skills and knowledge statements listed under the ECSF Cyber Threat Intelligence Specialist role, have been mapped to the relevant syllabus topic. Each statement indicates in bold the KWoPs that were identified from them. The rightmost column then indicates which CyBOK KAs were found to have relevant content in relation to those KWoPs. The KAs can be referenced to facilitate the development of the learning material. It should be highlighted that, where appropriate, other resources are expected to be utilized alongside CyBOK to facilitate the learning content development process, which would help in addressing the gaps where content cannot be mapped to CyBOK or where a sufficient level of coverage is not provided.

Table 2. ECSF-CyBOK mapping to the syllabus topics

Mapped ECSF Tasks/Skills/Knowledge	Related KWoPs	Relevant CyBOK KA (s)
Syllabus topic: *Introduction to Cyber Threat Intelligence*		
(T) Implement **threat intelligence** collection, analysis and production of actionable intelligence and dissemination to security stakeholders (K) Cybersecurity-related **certifications** (K) Cross-domain and border-domain knowledge related to cybersecurity (K) **Cyber Threat Intelligence (CTI)** sharing **standards, methodologies** and **frameworks**	threat intelligence certifications Cyber Threat Intelligence (CTI) standards, methodologies and frameworks	SOIM LR SOIM SOIM
Syllabus topic: *Building a CTI program*		
(T) Develop, implement and manage the organisation's **cyber threat intelligence strategy** (T) Develop plans and procedures to manage **threat intelligence** (T) Translate business requirements into **Intelligence** Requirements (S) Automate **threat intelligence** management procedures	cyber threat intelligence strategy threat intelligence Intelligence threat intelligence	SOIM SOIM SOIM SOIM
Syllabus topic: *Cyber Threat Landscape & Actors*		

(*continued*)

Table 2. (*continued*)

Mapped ECSF Tasks/Skills/Knowledge	Related KWoPs	Relevant CyBOK KA (s)
(K) Cyber **threats** (K) Cyber **threat actors** (K) **Advanced and persistent cyber threats (APT)** (K) **Threat actors Tactics, Techniques and Procedures (TTPs)** (K) Cybersecurity attack procedures	threats threat actors Advanced and persistent cyber threats (APT) Threat actors Tactics, Techniques and Procedures (TTPs)	CI, RMG AB MAT AB, SOIM
Syllabus topic: *Technical foundations for CTI*		
(K) **Operating systems security** (K) Computer **networks security** (K) Computer programming (K) **Cybersecurity controls and solutions**	Operating systems security networks security Cybersecurity controls and solutions	OSV NS N/A
Syllabus topic: *Legal and ethical aspects in CTI*		
(K) **Responsible information disclosure** procedures	Responsible information disclosure	N/A
Syllabus topic: *Threat information sources and data collection*		
(S) Collect, analyse and correlate **cyber threat information** originating from multiple sources	cyber threat information	SOIM
Syllabus topic: *Data analysis and threat profiling*		

(*continued*)

Table 2. (*continued*)

Mapped ECSF Tasks/Skills/Knowledge	Related KWoPs	Relevant CyBOK KA (s)
(T) Identify and assess **cyber threat actors** targeting the organisation (T) Leverage intelligence data to support and assist with **threat modelling […]** (S) Conduct technical analysis and reporting (S) Identify non-cyber events with implications on cyber-related activities (S) Identify **threat actors TTPs** and campaigns (S) **Model threats, actors and TTPs** (S) Collaborate with other team members and colleagues (T) Identify, monitor and assess the **Tactics, Techniques and Procedures (TTPs)** used by **cyber threat actors** by analysing open-source and proprietary data, information and intelligence	cyber threat actors threat modelling threat actors TTPs Model threats, actors and TTPs Tactics, Techniques and Procedures (TTPs)	AB RMG, SSL AB, SOIM AB, RMG, SOIM, SSL AB, SOIM
Syllabus topic: *Intelligence production and dissemination*		

(*continued*)

Table 2. (*continued*)

Mapped ECSF Tasks/Skills/Knowledge	Related KWoPs	Relevant CyBOK KA (s)
(T) Produce actionable reports based on **threat intelligence** data (T) Leverage intelligence data to support and assist with [...] recommendations for **Risk Mitigation** and cyber **threat hunting** (T) Convey the proper security severity by explaining the **risk exposure** and its consequences to non-technical stakeholders (T) Articulate and communicate intelligence openly and publicly at all levels (T) Coordinate with stakeholders to share and consume intelligence on relevant cyber **threats** (T) Elaborate and advise on **mitigation plans** at the tactical, operational and strategic level (S) Communicate, coordinate and cooperate with internal and external stakeholders (S) Communicate, present and report to relevant stakeholders	threat intelligence Risk Mitigation threat hunting risk exposure threats mitigation plans	SOIM RMG, SSL RMG, SSL CI, RMG RMG

6 Discussion

This study has provided a practical illustration of how the ECSF profiles can be supported and applied in practice, while also demonstrating the validity of CyBOK as a reference point in supporting their use [6]. This section reflects on the contributions and acknowledges some associated limitations.

6.1 Linking Roles, Skills and Knowledge

A core contribution of this research lies in demonstrating the benefits of "joining the dots" between prominent resources such as ECSF and CyBOK, creating a strong basis for effective training program design. Identifying how such resources can complement each other is fundamental in achieving this objective [10]. In the case of ECSF, the framework provides structured role profiles, outlining expected tasks, skills and knowledge [2]. Such frameworks assist in realizing what is expected when working in specific cybersecurity roles, and which competences are required [10, 11]. CyBOK [3] on the other hand, offers a comprehensive reference of core cybersecurity knowledge domains, educating about fundamental topics covered under each domain and which a professional is expected to be aware of. When applied in isolation, each resource provides a partial perspective, for example ECSF outlines a career role at a high-level, while CyBOK elaborates on cybersecurity domains without explicitly connecting them to professional roles. Joining the dots between these two resources enables a stronger bridge between what professionals are expected to do in practice and the knowledge base that supports their competences development [6, 10, 11].

Linking roles, skills and knowledge at a more granular level, provides benefits for both educators and learners. In the case of educators and training providers, the integration of established resources enables them to design learning programs that are grounded in widely recognised role profiles while drawing upon authoritative knowledge sources. Learners on the other hand, can realize how the expectations of a specific role connect to concrete knowledge areas and pursue targeted upskilling [12]. It is also notable that leveraging widely recognized resources carries a significant weight in terms of recognition and employability, ensuring that learners gain skills that are both valued by industry and directly applicable to professional practice.

An additional strength of the proposed mapping methodology is its replicability. The process developed in the context of the CTI Specialist role to facilitate the curriculum design of CTI training programs demonstrates a systematic approach that can be applied across all ECSF roles. Moreover, this replicability supports long-term sustainability of the designed curricula when utilized resources are updated. Specifically, the same process can be re-applied to ensure that the training programs stay up to date with technological and regulatory advances.

6.2 From ECSF–CyBOK Mapping to Micro-credentials and Flexible Learning Pathways

The ECSF–CyBOK mapping to syllabus topics provides a solid foundation for designing modular training programs. Such modularity is particularly valuable at a time when industry and policy alike are placing increasing emphasis on micro-credentials as a means for creating flexible learning pathways [13]. Micro-credentials allow learners to acquire clearly defined competences in short, focused learning units that can be accumulated, or "stacked," into broader qualifications over time [14]. This approach aligns closely with the shifting demands of the cybersecurity workforce, where professionals must continually update their knowledge and skills in response to evolving threats, technologies, and regulatory requirements.

By structuring training into micro-credentials, learners can engage in targeted upskilling that directly addresses their role-specific needs [12]. At the same time, this approach offers the flexibility to explore additional competency areas, opening pathways to new employability opportunities. This flexibility is highly beneficial for accommodating different entry points into programs and supporting diverse progression routes, as both novice learners and experienced professionals can tailor their learning journeys according to their individual needs and career goals. This approach contributes to personalizing education and empowering learners for lifelong learning. The EADTU report

[15] further reinforces this perspective, emphasizing that personalized and flexible learning pathways, supported by digital and AI-enhanced environments, are key enablers for inclusive, learner-centred, and sustainable higher education. Such pathways allow individuals to progress at their own pace, connect learning experiences across disciplines, and continuously update their competencies in response to evolving professional and societal demands. In this context, by considering the ECSF role profiles, specifically, in this study, the CTI Specialist role, discrete thematic units emerged such as "*Threat Information Sources and Data Collection*" and "*Legal and Ethical Aspects in CTI.*" These units can form the basis for standalone micro-credentials, each addressing a clearly defined set of skills and knowledge. Learners can therefore select the micro-credentials most relevant to their career stage or immediate workplace needs, while retaining the option to stack them into larger, cross-role qualifications. Ultimately, curricula that connect the dots between established resources such as ECSF and CyBOK provide a robust foundation for flexible, personalized, and industry-relevant learning pathways [12].

6.3 Limitations

While this study demonstrates the practical value of integrating ECSF and CyBOK for curriculum design, empirical validation has not yet been undertaken. Future work will seek feedback from educators, training providers, and policymakers to assess the usefulness and applicability of the methodology and to refine the approach accordingly. Another limitation relates to the scope of coverage provided by ECSF and CyBOK when translated into syllabus topics. The high-level design of ECSF ensures accessibility and broad applicability, while CyBOK offers detailed content structured around 21 knowledge areas. However, given the rapidly evolving nature of cybersecurity, reliance on these two resources alone may not fully capture emerging domains and competences. To address this, additional frameworks and knowledge bases should be incorporated into the "joining the dots" process, ensuring that curricula remain current and aligned with new challenges and technological developments.

7 Conclusions

This paper has illustrated how the integration of ECSF role profiles with CyBOK knowledge areas can provide a systematic approach and practical foundation for the design of cybersecurity training programs. The use case of the Cyber Threat Intelligence Specialist role demonstrates how the proposed methodology can be applied in practice, showing its potential to guide the development of modular industry-aligned curricula. Moreover, the contribution of this study goes beyond designing modular training programs, providing a replicable methodology that can be applied across ECSF roles or extended to other frameworks and knowledge bases. By "joining the dots" between widely adopted resources, the approach strengthens the coherence between professional role expectations and the underlying body of knowledge. This enables the creation of flexible and stackable learning pathways that can contribute to lifelong learning and ensure workforce readiness in safeguarding critical infrastructures against evolving cyber threats.

Acknowledgments. This work has received funding from the European Union's Digital Europe Programme (DIGITAL) under the Grant Agreement No. 101128017 (CY-TRUST project). Views and opinions expressed are, however, those of the authors only and do not necessarily reflect those of the European Union or the granting authorities. Neither the European Union nor the granting authorities can be held responsible for them. The work referenced in the paper relating to the ECSF-CyBOK mapping study was funded by the CyBOK project. Fig. 1 is adapted from [3]: the original is Crown Copyright 2021, used under the terms of the UK Open Government Licence v3.0.

Disclosure of Interests. Steven Furnell is a member of the Steering Group for the Cyber Security Body of Knowledge (CyBOK).

References

1. ISC2: Global Cybersecurity Workforce Prepares for an AI-Driven World. ISC2 Cybersecurity Workforce Study 2024, October 2024 (2024). https://www.isc2.org/Insights/2024/10/ISC2-2024-Cybersecurity-Workforce-Study
2. ENISA: European Cybersecurity Skills Framework (ECSF). European Union Agency for Cybersecurity, September 2022 (2022). https://www.enisa.europa.eu/sites/default/files/publications/European%20Cybersecurity%20Skills%20Framework%20Role%20Profiles.pdf. Accessed 22 Aug 2025
3. Rashid, A., Chivers, H., Lupu, E., Martin, A., Schneider, S.: CyBOK - The Cyber Security Body of Knowledge. Version 1.1.0, 31 July 2021 (2021). https://www.cybok.org/media/downloads/CyBOK_v1.1.0.pdf
4. ENISA: Cybersecurity Roles and Skills for NIS2 Essential and Important Entities: Mapping NIS2 obligations to ECSF, European Union Agency for Cybersecurity, June 2025 (2025). https://www.enisa.europa.eu/sites/default/files/2025-06/Mapping%20NIS%202%20obligations%20with%20ECSF%20role%20profiles.pdf. Accessed 22 Aug 2025
5. ENISA: User Manual - European Cybersecurity Skills Framework (ECSF). European Union Agency for Cybersecurity, September 2022 (2022). https://www.enisa.europa.eu/sites/default/files/publications/European%20Cybersecurity%20Skills%20Framework%20User%20Manual.pdf. Accessed 22 Aug 2025
6. Furnell, S., Stavrou, E.: Assessing the compatibility of CyBOK and the European Cybersecurity Skills Framework (ECSF), CyBOK Project Resources, July 2025 (2025). https://www.cybok.org/media/downloads/Assessing_the_compatibility_of_CyBOK_and_the_European_CybersecurityFramework_E_Khsz71X.pdf. Accessed 22 Aug 2025
7. Rashid, A., Nautiyal, L., Hallett, J., Shreeve, B.: CyBOK Mapping Framework - How to map concepts in academic and professional programmes to the Cyber Security Body of Knowledge. Version 1.0, 22 February 2021 (2021). https://www.cybok.org/media/downloads/CyBOK_Mapping_Framework_academic_professional_progs_Feb21.pdf. Accessed 22 Aug 2025
8. Nautiyal, L., Hallett, J., Clements, J., Shreeve, B., Rashid, A.: CyBOK Mapping Reference - Issue 1.3.0, July 2021 (2021). https://www.cybok.org/media/downloads/CyBOK_Mapping_Reference_v1.3.0.pdf. Accessed 22 Aug 2025
9. CyBOK: The Cyber Security Body of Knowledge - Tabular representation of CyBOK Broad Categories, Knowledge Areas and their descriptions, July 2021 (2021). https://www.cybok.org/media/downloads/CyBOK_Tabular_Representation_1_1_July_2021.pdf. Accessed 22 Aug 2025

10. Almeida, F.: Comparative analysis of EU-based cybersecurity skills frameworks. Comput. Secur. **151** (2025)
11. Dkaidek, Z., Rashid, A.: Bridging the cybersecurity skills gap: knowledge framework comparative study. IEEE Secur. Priv. **22**(5), 88–95 (2024)
12. Kallonas, C., Stavrou, S., Stavrou, E.: Multidisciplinary pathways into cyber threat intelligence roles: mapping knowledge areas and transferable skills. In: Furnell, S., Clarke, N. (eds.) HAISA 2025. IFIP AICT, vol. 761, pp. 135–151. Springer, Cham (2026). https://doi.org/10.1007/978-3-032-02504-3_10
13. Alenezi, M., Akour, M., Alfawzan, L.: Evolving microcredential strategies for enhancing employability and lifelong learning. Educ. Sci. **14**(12), 1307 (2024)
14. Ngoc Ha, N.T., Van Dyke, N., Spittle, M.: Micro-credentials in higher education: perceived benefits for graduate employability and interest levels in micro-credentials for training employability skills. Stud. High. Educ., 1–13 (2025)
15. EADTU: Personalised Education: Towards Flexible, Inclusive and AI-Enhanced Learning Pathways in Higher Education. European Association of Distance Teaching Universities, October 2025 (2025). https://zenodo.org/records/17279059. Accessed 07 Nov 2025

Phase-Driven Transitions in Cyber-Physical Incident Command Systems: Communication Dynamics from Tabletop Exercises

Kenta Nakayama[1,2](✉), Kenji Watanabe[1], and Ichiro Koshijima[1]

[1] Nagoya Institute of Technology, Gokiso-cho, Showa-ku, Nagoya, Aichi 466-8555, Japan
c210036@c21.icscoe.jp

[2] NEC Corporation, 7-1, Shiba 5-chome Minato-ku, Tokyo 108-8001, Japan

Abstract. Structural shifts in the Incident Command System (ICS) and communication networks during cyber incidents were analyzed through six Tabletop Exercises (TTXs) simulating a scenario with evolving priorities, from cybersecurity to operational safety. The early phase featured centralized coordination by the Computer Security Incident Response Team (CSIRT), while later phases exhibited a transition toward field-led, decentralized responses as safety threats emerged.

Analysis of communication logs and participant surveys indicated that tools such as organizational charts and predefined workflows, although effective for cybersecurity phases, may become bottlenecks in safety-critical situations. Exercises involving culturally neutral, mixed-role participants enabled observation of ideal ICS transitions, free from organizational bias or authority constraints.

Findings suggest that adaptive ICS frameworks, incorporating clear authority-transfer triggers and flexible communication patterns, are essential for timely incident response. Emphasis is also placed on psychological safety, which supports effective leadership transitions in high-stress scenarios. These insights contribute to the design of cyber-physical incident training and enhance resilience through phase-specific coordination models and human-centered preparedness strategies.

Keywords: Cyber Resilience · Tabletop Exercise (TTX) · Incident Command System (ICS) · Human Factor · Communication Network Analysis

1 Introduction

1.1 Cybersecurity Landscape of Critical Infrastructure

In recent years, cyberattacks have been increasing globally and becoming more sophisticated. Particularly, amid rising geopolitical tensions and the expansion

E. Bergström et al. (Eds.): CRITIS 2025, LNCS 16291, pp. 284–302, 2026.
https://doi.org/10.1007/978-3-032-19540-1_15

of hybrid warfare, critical infrastructure has become a frequent target of such attacks [1,2]. This has raised international concerns regarding the cybersecurity of essential systems supporting daily life, such as electricity, gas, water, and transportation [3,4]. For example, in 2015, a large-scale power outage occurred in Ukraine due to a disruption of the industrial control systems at a power company [5]. Similarly, in Norway, a ransomware attack crippled the OT (Operational Technology) network of an aluminum refining plant, resulting in a temporary halt to production activities [6]. In Japan as well, ransomware attacks have led to operational shutdowns at local medical institutions [7] and disruptions at major ports [8], demonstrating the growing impact of multi-layered damage, including to control systems.

Under such threat conditions, it has become increasingly urgent for organizations to strengthen their ability to maintain operations even during cyber incidents—that is, to enhance their cyber resilience [9]. Cyber resilience is shaped by a complex interplay of technical, human, and procedural factors [10]. Among these, international reports and academic studies emphasize that human factors play a critical role in determining the effectiveness of cyber resilience [11].

1.2 Human Factor in Cyber Resilience

Human factors have been increasingly recognized as a central component of cyber resilience. In particular, human behavior and decision-making significantly influence both organizational vulnerability and the capacity to recover from cyberattacks [12]. Organizational culture and open communication serve as foundational elements that enhance an organization's ability to respond effectively during incidents [13]. During times of crisis, maintaining a balance between stress and regulatory constraints is also crucial, as excessive stress or overly rigid rules can impair sound decision-making [14]. Moreover, the psychological impact of incidents and the employee's individual mental resilience are critical human aspects that contribute to an organization's overall resilience [15]. Therefore, beyond technical controls, strengthening organizational efforts to address these human dimensions is essential to achieving true cyber resilience.

Understanding how decisions are made and how communication unfolds during cyber incidents is especially important for improving resilience in organizations, including those operating critical infrastructure. Notably, delays in initial response decisions, insufficient communication structures, and ambiguous accountability are common challenges observed during incidents. Such breakdowns in internal coordination and communication represent additional human factors that can degrade resilience.

This issue is particularly pronounced in OT environments, where "availability" and "safety" are prioritized over confidentiality, unlike in traditional IT systems. In these settings, immediate actions such as network shutdowns or reboots are often restricted. Consequently, the situational judgment and coordinated efforts of on-site personnel become critical to the organization's ability to manage and recover from cyber incidents.

1.3 Initiatives to Enhance Cyber Resilience

To strengthen cyber resilience through human factors, critical infrastructure organizations are increasingly implementing cross-organizational training programs aimed at developing collaborative response capabilities [9,16]. These efforts include enhancing decision-making and coordination skills during the initial phase of incident response and institutionalizing security culture through practical cybersecurity exercises that allow for the evaluation and visualization of situational response capabilities [17,18].

Such initiatives help reinforce interdepartmental and interorganizational coordination during normal operations and enable the identification and improvement of current weaknesses through exercises. Among these methods, Tabletop Exercises (TTXs) have recently gained significant attention for their effectiveness in enhancing cyber resilience at both the organizational and community levels [19]. TTX is a cost-effective and impactful training approach for incident response [20]. By simulating realistic scenarios, it facilitates collaborative decision-making among stakeholders and has thus become a valuable method for both academic research and practical implementation [21].

2 Research Background and Questions

While Sect. 1.3 outlined various organizational initiatives for enhancing cyber resilience, critical challenges remain in practical implementation. In particular, the formation of an appropriate command structure, the demonstration of leadership, and smooth communication and decision-making among on-site teams are essential elements that can determine the success or failure of incident response. Despite the recognized effectiveness of TTX discussed earlier, specific challenges arise when applying these exercises to IT/OT systems. Notably, differences in culture between IT and OT environments, as well as conflicting priorities between security and safety, often have a complex impact on command structures and team performance.

Based on these challenges, this study addresses the following research questions:

1. Can Communication Network Analysis (CNA) serve as a quantitative evaluation metric for TTXs?
2. Do Incident Command System (ICS) changes similar to those observed during natural disasters occur when subjected to incident response exercises in IT/OT environments?

This section reviews previous studies and policy efforts related to these issues, clarifying the position and contribution of the present research in enhancing human-centered cyber resilience.

2.1 Previous Research

Recent studies have analyzed logs from cybersecurity exercises to better understand participant behavior [22,23]. In hands-on training, command-line data is mined to identify common problem-solving patterns and difficulties. These insights support the design of more effective training and learning strategies [24].

In addition, some studies have begun analyzing communication networks in organizational cybersecurity exercises. For example, Kokkonen et al., 2018 have analyzed team communication during large-scale cybersecurity exercises, showing that real-time communication patterns can support situational awareness and performance evaluation [25]. However, differences in data quality and collection methods remain, and few studies have quantitatively analyzed participant interactions in TTX. This study addresses that gap by examining communication networks in TTX in detail.

Studies on Communication Structures Across Crisis Phases. In crisis response, organizational communication networks often undergo dynamic shifts over time. While traditional emergency management divides events into "response/recovery" phases, recent studies highlight a mismatch between these formal phases and actual behavior in the field. Brown et al., 2021 proposed a three-phase model, "response/resolve/recovery" based on a terrorism simulation, showing it better reflects real communication patterns [26]. Their findings also suggest that communication becomes more decentralized as a crisis evolves, improving interagency coordination. Similarly, Bharosa et al., 2010 emphasized the need for flexible, phase-specific communication strategies [27]. These insights support the time-based network analysis used in this study to better understand communication changes during cyber incidents.

Research on Command Structures and Leadership Formation. A clear command and control system, such as the ICS, is essential for effective crisis response [28]. ICS standardizes roles, communication, and coordination to address past failures related to leadership and information flow. However, crises often require more than formal structures. In high-pressure situations, frontline actors may demonstrate spontaneous leadership by sharing situational awareness, as seen during the Haiti earthquake and the Great East Japan Earthquake [29]. Studies also warn that strict adherence to command charts in training can limit flexibility and inter-organizational learning [30]. Therefore, effective crisis management requires both structured command and the flexibility to adapt through emergent leadership and collaboration.

2.2 Research Gap and Contribution

Based on the prior literature, this study aims to clarify the research gap and define its academic contribution. While existing studies have made some progress in visualizing communication logs during technical or large-scale exercises, very few have quantitatively examined how command systems evolve across multiple phases in cyber exercises, especially through multiple cases. In particular, although Brown et al., 2021 highlighted the shift from centralized to decentralized communication structures in disaster response contexts, no prior research has empirically captured such patterns in cyber-related TTXs.

Moreover, most existing studies rely on single-case exercises or post-exercise interviews, lacking cross-exercise comparisons that verify the reproducibility of patterns.

To address these gaps, this study conducts a comprehensive analysis of communication logs from six TTX sessions simulating cyber incident responses. By tracking changes in network structure and leadership formation over time, the study offers a quantitative view of who becomes the communication hub, and when and how command structures evolve during the response process.

This approach provides insights not captured by earlier studies and contributes to the development of more effective team formation and training strategies for cyber incident response. Furthermore, the findings help bridge traditional disaster response research (such as phase-based coordination, ICS effectiveness, and leadership dynamics) with cybersecurity contexts, promoting interdisciplinary knowledge integration. In this sense, the study offers both academic and practical value.

3 Methods of this Study

3.1 Incident Response Exercise Scenario

The exercise was structured into four consecutive sessions spanning a single day (Table 1). It began with a lecture introducing the international incident response standard NIST SP 800-61 [31], followed by a scenario-based exercise. In the afternoon, participants engaged in a review workshop and a final debriefing session to reflect on their actions and share key insights.

Table 1. Schedule of the cybersecurity exercise

Session	Time	Content
1st Period	10:00–11:30	Lecture: Overview of NIST SP 800–61
2nd Period	11:45–13:15	Cybersecurity Incident Response TTX
3rd Period	14:15–15:45	Review Workshop (Reflection and Analysis)
4th Period	16:00–17:30	Group Debriefing (Sharing of Key Insights)

Cybersecurity incident response TTX was conducted using a simulated environment designed to provide participants with a shared operational context. A virtual company was created, consisting of two plants and an industrial control system, which delivered heat supply services to neighboring facilities. The scenario assumed that a plant shutdown would directly impact business operations, and a loss of control over the industrial control system could pose a threat to human safety. Participants referred to a pre-defined network diagram of the virtual company throughout the exercise (Fig. 1).

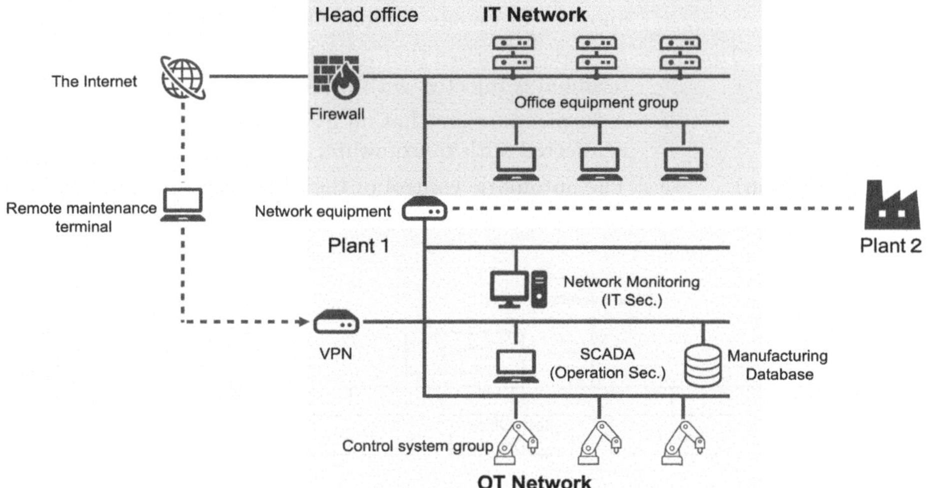

Fig. 1. Virtual company's network diagram

The scenarios used in this exercise are shown in Table 2. Based on the scenario information provided by the facilitator at appropriate times, participants discussed their response strategies according to their assigned roles and recorded their decisions and actions accordingly.

Participants engaged in discussions and decision-making from the perspective of the roles assigned to them, as illustrated in the organizational structure diagram (Fig. 2) and Table 3. They were expected to consider and carry out the most appropriate actions based on their assigned roles.

To evaluate whether the TTX conducted in this study was beneficial for participants, a post-exercise survey was used to assess overall satisfaction and changes in participants' perspectives on what they consider important in incident response before and after the exercise (shown in Table 4). Additionally, the survey gathered participants' thoughts on what information should be known or documented in advance to facilitate faster incident response. These responses were also used to support further analysis of communication frequency and changes in the command system during the exercise.

The questionnaire was administered digitally via an online survey platform immediately following the group debriefing session (Table 1). This timing was strategically selected to allow participants to reflect upon the entire collective learning experience, including the post-exercise discussions. The aim was to capture how participants' awareness and perceptions had potentially changed or

Table 2. Cybersecurity incident response TTX scenarios

Phase	No.	Scenario Description	Priority
Predictive(10 min)	1	A customer reports an anomaly in the service provided via the operational site.	Safety
	1'	The Operation Sec. (Fieldman) confirms the anomaly at on-site equipment.	
Emergency (30 min)	2	A suspicion arises that a back-office terminal is infected with ransomware.	Security
	2'	A suspicion arises that an SCADA terminal is infected with ransomware.	
Crisis (30 min)	3	The automatic control of the site's control system becomes non-functional.	Safety

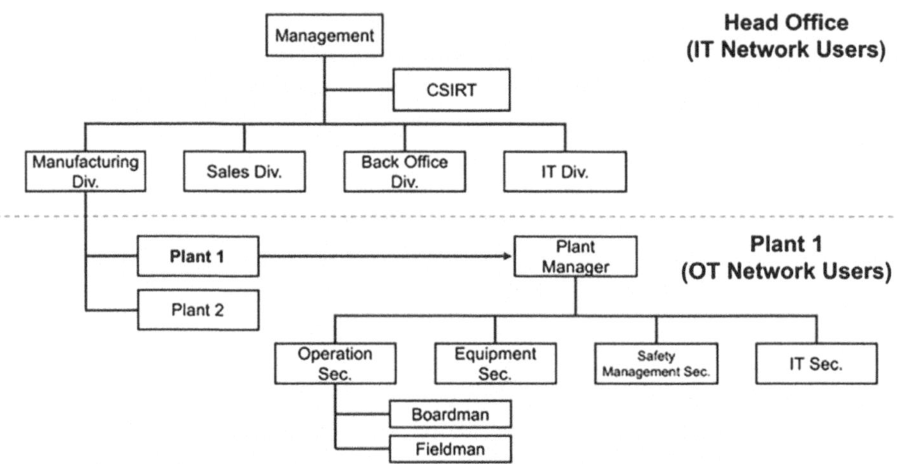

Fig. 2. The organizational structure diagram

been consolidated through the group dynamics and collaborative construction of understanding during the workshop. All 119 participants completed the online survey, resulting in a 100% response rate.

3.2 Exercise Participants

The participants of this exercise were trainees in the "Core Human Resource Development Program" offered by the IPA Industrial Cybersecurity Center [32]. Eligibility for this program requires either holding an IT Passport certification or having at least one year of experience in the IT or OT fields. During the first two months of the program, all participants receive foundational lectures on both IT and OT to ensure a consistent baseline of knowledge.

Table 3. Roles in the TTX

Location	Role	Role details
Head Office	Management	Make management-related decisions and represent the organization, including accountability
	CSIRT (Computer Security Incident Response Team)	Performs system security duties and has a role in planning, implementation, response, etc.
	Sales Div.	Performs operations for customers
	Back Office Div.	Perform tasks related to public relations, general affairs, accounting, and human resources
	IT Div.	Performs construction, operation, and maintenance of internal information systems and infrastructure
	Manufacturing Div.	Operates and maintains the plant to provide services
Plant1	Plant Manager	Head of plant management
	Operation Sec. (Boardman)	Monitors and operates Supervisory Control And Data Acquisition (SCADA)
	Operation Sec. (Fieldman)	Checks and operates on-site equipment
	Equipment Sec.	Manages maintenance of plant instrumentation and equipment
	Safety Management Sec.	Designs accident prevention for process safety, occupational safety, etc.
	IT Sec.	Management and operation of the network in the plant
Others	Others	Set up as necessary in the exercise

As a result, participants in this exercise had a minimum level of technical competency. Furthermore, the trainees were dispatched from critical infrastructure sectors such as electric power and railway companies, as well as from manufacturers, and had relevant practical experience. Therefore, the outcomes of the exercise are expected to reflect real-world operational contexts and offer a high degree of reliability.

Although the participants came from different companies and thus had diverse organizational cultures, they did not have direct hierarchical relationships or conflicting interests, such as supervisor-subordinate dynamics. This neutral relationship helped create an environment suitable for open communication and unbiased collaboration during the exercise.

3.3 Logging the Exercise

In addition, chronology, which is also used at disaster sites [33], was adopted as a recording method to allow participants to review the incident response process. Based on the recorded chronology, the frequency of communication and changes in the command system were analyzed across different scenario phases.

An example of the chronology format is shown in Fig. 3. In this example, a record is made when "at 12:18, senior management instructed the plant manager to report the plant's operating status every hour," followed by "at 13:19, the plant manager reported the status." This style of recording helps visualize how decisions and communications unfold over time.

Table 4. Content of post-exercise questionnaire

No.	Question	Answer format
1	Overall satisfaction with the incident response exercise (Unsatisfy: 1 - Satisfy: 5)	5-point rating
2	Please tell us the reason for the above	Free text
3	What types of information or indicators do you think would help accelerate incident response?	Free text
4	Please tell us what you thought was important in incident response "before" this exercise.	Free text
5	Please tell us what, if any, changes you have made to your thoughts on Q4 "after" this exercise.	Free text
6	Please tell us what you learned and realized through this exercise.	Free text
7	Please tell us what could be improved for the exercise (e.g., what was difficult to understand)	Free text

Phase	Time	From	To	Message or Instruction
1	12:18	Management	Plant Manager	Instructed to report the plant's operating status every hour.
	13:19	Plant Manager	Management	Reported that production was proceeding as scheduled.
		...	...	...

Fig. 3. Example of a chronology entry

4 Results

4.1 Quality of Exercise Delivery

The results of the exercises are summarized in Table 5. A total of 119 participants took part in six separate tabletop exercises conducted throughout the study.

The questionnaire results indicate that the exercises consistently provided participants with meaningful and high-quality learning experiences. Across all six sessions, average satisfaction scores remained stable, ranging from 4.00 to 4.39 out of 5.00, with an overall average of 4.22. This suggests that the program successfully maintained a reliable standard of delivery throughout.

In addition to satisfaction, the perceived change in participants' awareness, specifically, their understanding of incident response, showed notable variation, with response rates ranging from 41.0% to 84.2%. These awareness change rates represent the percentage of participants who reported a change in their understanding of incident response priorities when comparing their responses to questionnaire items Q4 (pre-exercise) and Q5 (post-exercise). The exercises successfully captured participants' evolving perspectives on incident response priorities.

For example, participants frequently reported shifting from an initial focus solely on rapid response to recognizing the critical importance of effective communication. As one participant noted, "I initially thought speed was everything in incident response, but through the TTX, I realized that clear communication among team members is equally crucial for successful incident management." A clear upward trend was observed over time, indicating improved learning impact in the later sessions. One likely contributing factor is that the same instructor facilitated all six exercises. As the facilitator gained experience, the precision and effectiveness of facilitation likely improved, resulting in higher participant engagement and understanding in the later sessions.

It is also noteworthy that satisfaction and awareness change did not always correlate. For instance, in December 2023, satisfaction was relatively high at 4.24 with an awareness change rate of 81.0%, while in December 2024, the awareness rate rose to 84.2% despite a lower satisfaction score of 4.00. This divergence suggests that even when participants experience greater cognitive challenge or effortful learning, the perceived enjoyment may not increase proportionally. This aligns with the educational concept of Desirable Difficulty [34], which posits that demanding learning experiences, while subjectively more difficult, often lead to deeper comprehension and long-term retention.

Overall, these findings confirm that the tabletop exercises offered both high-quality engagement and significant learning outcomes, while also highlighting the importance of continuous improvement in facilitation techniques.

Table 5. Summary of TTX: Schedule, number of participants, and session evaluations

No.	Date	Participants	Evauation (average)	Awareness Change Rates
1	October 4, 2023	20	4.20/5.00	11/20 (55.0%)
2	November 8, 2023	22	4.14/5.00	9/22 (41.0%)
3	December 18, 2023	21	4.24/5.00	17/21 (81.0%)
4	October 3, 2024	18	4.39/5.00	14/18 (77.8%)
5	November 6, 2024	19	4.37/5.00	14/19 (73.3%)
6	December 5, 2024	19	4.00/5.00	16/19 (84.2%)
-	Total	119	4.22/5.00	81/119 (68.1%)

4.2 Shifts in Communication Patterns and Command Systems over Different Incident Phases

This study analyzed communication logs from six cyber incident response TTXs based on chronology records to quantitatively visualize how command structures and information flows evolve. The exercise scenarios were designed to gradually shift from a focus on security to a greater emphasis on safety. By extracting the changes in "who communicated with whom" in each phase, this research aims to clarify the structural transitions of the ICS and the formation and transition of information hubs.

The analysis is based on data from all 119 participants across the six TTX sessions listed in Table 5. During each exercise, participants recorded their actions and communication content, including the sender, receiver, time-stamp, and communication phase. Table 6 presents the aggregated communication records from all six TTX sessions combined, not from a single exercise. This aggregation approach was chosen to identify consistent communication patterns across multiple exercises and different participant groups, rather than focusing on session-specific variations. The total dataset comprises 1,324 communication records distributed across the three phases, providing a robust foundation for the network analysis that follows.

Table 6. The number of data records of each phase

No.	Date	Predictive Phase	Emergency Phase	Crisis Phase	Total
1	October 4, 2023	28	47	25	100
2	November 8, 2023	45	140	117	302
3	December 18, 2023	51	144	115	310
4	October 3, 2024	43	100	76	219
5	November 6, 2024	37	113	49	199
6	December 5, 2024	45	78	71	194
-	Total	249	622	453	1,324

While existing studies have made some progress in visualizing communication logs during technical or large-scale exercises, very few have quantitatively examined how command systems evolve across multiple phases in cyber exercises, especially through multiple cases. In particular, although Brown et al., 2021 highlighted the shift from centralized to decentralized communication structures in disaster response contexts, no prior research has empirically captured such patterns in cyber-related TTXs.

To fill this gap, this study first divides the chronology-based communication records into three key phases defined in the exercises: predictive phase, emergency phase, and crisis phase. It then analyzes how network structures and the center of gravity within the command system change over time. Through this, the study seeks to identify how leadership emerges and roles shift during cyber crises, based on a time-series structural analysis.

Predictive Phase. Figure 4 shows the summary of communication frequency during Phase 1 (predictive phase). In this phase, participants began their response activities after receiving reports from customers about service disruptions and observing physical anomalies on-site. These observations were primarily recognized as safety-related issues, not immediately linked to cybersecurity.

Accordingly, the communication logs show active exchanges mainly among field-oriented departments such as the Sales Div. and Operation Sec., indicating that initial responses were concentrated at the operational level.

At this stage, however, it remained unclear whether the anomaly was cyber-related. Participants were required to make judgments under uncertain conditions. While communication reached the plant manager level, there were no signs of escalation to the executive level. This suggests that the issue was not yet perceived as critical or organization-wide, and that priority was placed on safety rather than security in the early response.

From \ To	Management	CSIRT	Sales Div.	Back Office Div.	IT Div.	Manufacturing Div.	Plant Manager	Operation Sec. (Boardman)	Operation Sec. (Fieldman)	Equipment Sec.	Safety Management Sec.	IT Sec.	Others	Total
Management														0
CSIRT														0
Sales Div.				2	1	21	1	2					9	36
Back Office Div.														0
IT Div.		1												1
Manufacturing Div.			8				14	8		1			1	32
Plant Manager			3			7		17	3	7	3			40
Operation Sec. (Boardman)			1			6	20		21	10	4		5	67
Operation Sec. (Fieldman)							4	27		1			1	33
Equipment Sec.						1	7	4	1		2		2	17
Safety Management Sec.							1	1		2				4
IT Sec.														0
Others			12				2	2	1	1	1			19
Total	0	1	24	2	1	35	49	61	26	22	10	0	18	249

1~10
11~20
21~30
31~40
41~

Fig. 4. Communication logs in Predictive Phase (Priority: Safety)

Emergency Phase. In Phase 2 (emergency phase), a ransomware infection was first detected in the office department, which triggered a shift to a security-prioritized incident response mode. The communication logs show that interactions became more active between the CSIRT, the IT Division, and executive management, indicating that a centralized command structure was established with the CSIRT functioning clearly as the commander (shown in Fig. 5).

At this stage, the incident was recognized as a cyberattack, and decision-making focused on technical and strategic aspects. Greater emphasis was placed on executive-level decisions and visualizing the overall scope of the incident. The logs also show an increasing number of communications with external parties such as vendors, legal departments, and affiliated companies. This suggests that collaboration with external stakeholders is essential in dealing with visible cybersecurity incidents like ransomware attacks.

Furthermore, in the latter part of this phase, the infection spread to devices within the plant department. However, no independent communication or proactive response from the field side was observed. The command system continued to be centered around the CSIRT. This implies that, in security-focused incidents, even if the infection spreads to physical sites, the central team (CSIRT) tends to retain control over the response. It also suggests the existence of a structure in which field teams lack informational leadership in such scenarios.

To / From	Management	CSIRT	Sales Div.	Back Office Div.	IT Div.	Manufacturing Div.	Plant Manager	Operation Sec. (Boardman)	Operation Sec. (Fieldman)	Equipment Sec.	Safety Management Sec.	IT Sec.	Others	Total
Management		29	1	5	2	1	3						3	44
CSIRT	48		5	25	48	12	10	2		1		9	39	199
Sales Div.		1		1		1							4	7
Back Office Div.	2	17	1		26								9	55
IT Div.	2	59		10		2	2	1				5	3	84
Manufacturing Div.	1	6	2	1	2		14	1			1			28
Plant Manager	6	7	1		4	10		11	3	8	4	8	10	72
Operation Sec. (Boardman)		6			6	2	13		6	7	1	8	1	50
Operation Sec. (Fieldman)							4	4		1	1			10
Equipment Sec.		4					6	4	1			2	1	18
Safety Management Sec.		1					2	1						4
IT Sec.		6		1	5		8	3		4			3	30
Others		3	2	6	2	1	4	2	1					21
Total	59	139	12	49	95	29	66	29	11	21	7	32	73	622

Legend
1~10
11~20
21~30
31~40
41~

Fig. 5. Communication logs in Emergency Phase (Priority: Security)

Crisis Phase. Phase 3 was designed as a critical situation in which the control systems became inoperable, and safety became the top priority. As a result, the focus of the response shifted significantly from cybersecurity to the protection of human life and equipment. This shift also led to a change in the command structure, moving away from the centralized CSIRT-led model seen in earlier phases toward a more field-driven response system.

Communication logs (Fig. 6) show that the plant manager played a central role, with an increase in messages exchanged among field departments. This indicates that on-site decision-making became more important during this phase. On the other hand, the CSIRT continued to communicate with external stakeholders but was no longer visibly involved in frontline coordination. Its role as a central commander diminished. Similarly, communication with executive management dropped sharply, suggesting that the involvement of upper management in the command chain had become minimal.

This decentralized structure is consistent with prior research (Brown et al., 2021), which suggests that in safety-critical situations, rapid and adaptive decision-making led by field units is more effective. Therefore, the shift in the command structure observed in this phase demonstrates that even in cybersecurity incidents, the command system must flexibly transition from a centralized to a decentralized model depending on the nature of the crisis. This finding was empirically confirmed through the tabletop exercise.

From \ To	Management	CSIRT	Sales Div.	Back Office Div.	IT Div.	Manufacturing Div.	Plant Manager	Operation Sec.(Boardman)	Operation Sec. (Fieldman)	Equipment Sec.	Safety Management Sec.	IT Sec.	Others	Total
Management		3	2	3		7	4						1	20
CSIRT	10		1	2	17	4	18			5		4	29	90
Sales Div.						1		1					12	14
Back Office Div.	2		1			1							10	14
IT Div.		9					1					4	4	18
Manufacturing Div.	6	1	3	2	1		14	1					3	31
Plant Manager	5	13	2		1	20		18	9	21	7	4	7	107
Operation Sec. (Boardman)		2	1		1	1	19		12	1	1	3	6	47
Operation Sec. (Fieldman)							7	9			1	1	1	19
Equipment Sec.		2					14		1		3	2	8	30
Safety Management Sec.							7	1	1					9
IT Sec.		3			2		1	1	1	3			5	16
Others	2	7	4	4	4		6	3	2	2		4		38
Total	25	40	14	11	26	34	91	34	26	32	12	22	86	453

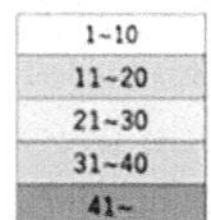

Fig. 6. Communication logs in Crisis Phase (Priority: Safety)

5 Discussion

In this study, we visualized the dynamic transformation of command structures in cyber incident response as the scenario progressed through different phases, shifting from centralized to decentralized models. Specifically, in Phase 1, safety became the priority due to equipment anomalies, resulting in field-led responses. In Phase 2, the CSIRT took a central role, and command shifted to a more centralized, security-driven model. In Phase 3, the situation again emphasized field discretion, prioritizing safety. This section examines key findings based on responses to a post-exercise survey question: "What types of information or indicators are necessary to accelerate incident response?" The results are summarized in Table 7.

Table 7. Survey Q3: Summary of responses on useful information/indicators for accelerating incident response

Rank	Item	Count
1	Organization Structures	40
2	Response flow diagram	32
3	Contact tree	30
4	Decision-making criteria	29
5	Contact format/template	14

5.1 Organizational Culture and Flexible Structure Design

Survey responses highlighted the importance of organizational structures (40 counts), response flow diagrams (32), and communication trees (30) as useful tools in incident response. However, some participants' open-ended comments pointed out that "in safety-critical situations, the formal structure may not function properly and can become a bottleneck." While this represents subjective perceptions from the exercise participants, it aligns with the objective communication pattern data showing increased decentralization in Phase 3 (as evidenced in Fig. 6), thus triangulating both quantitative and qualitative findings. This reflects Brown et al., 2021 who emphasized the need for decentralized command structures during crises. When frontline decision-making is prioritized, rigid hierarchical models may not be effective. Therefore, while centralized structures may be appropriate during security-focused phases, flexible and adaptive structures should be considered for safety-critical phases.

5.2 Dynamic Management of Command and Clarification of Decision Criteria

While the observed command structure transitions between phases were consistent with theoretical models like the ICS, such transitions do not always occur naturally in practice. "Decision-making criteria" (29 counts) were also frequently cited in the survey, suggesting concerns about the ambiguity of authority delegation and priority decisions. According to Multi-Team System (MTS) theory [35], teams must coordinate flexibly to achieve shared goals. In complex scenarios like those involving both cybersecurity and safety concerns, dynamic command restructuring is essential. Therefore, future training and Business Continuity Plans (BCPs) should include explicit decision criteria, delegation triggers, and role transition points.

5.3 External Collaboration Design and Transformation Into Educational Resources

In the later phases of the exercises, CSIRT increasingly communicated with external stakeholders (vendors, legal, government), while communication with on-site factory staff became limited. This temporary disconnect suggests the need for improved coordination. The CISA's incident response playbook recommends pre-defined protocols and timing for external collaboration, and this study supports that necessity [36]. Furthermore, as highlighted by HSEEP [37] and ISO 22398 [38], it is crucial to transform the lessons learned from exercises into formal knowledge and educational resources. Given that the necessary information and command structure differ by phase, the staged design of training materials and structured learning assessments will be essential for developing future cyber resilience.

6 Conclusion

This study empirically visualized how command structures evolve during cyber incident response, especially as priorities shift from security to safety across different phases of the scenario. Through the analysis of communication logs and participant actions across six TTXs, the results identified a clear transition from a centralized, CSIRT-led structure in the security-focused phase to a more decentralized, field-driven structure in the safety-critical phase. The shift in command actors, information hubs, and decision-making centers was found to occur dynamically in response to the scenario's changing demands.

The research questions posed at the outset of this study have been substantively addressed through our empirical analysis. Regarding the first question—whether Communication Network Analysis (CNA) can serve as a quantitative evaluation metric for TTX—our findings provide qualified support. The visualization of decentralized organizational communication successfully identified potential personnel bottlenecks and key coordination points during incidents. Since these behavioral patterns emerged under conditions of psychological safety and comprehensive participant training, they likely represent near-optimal response models that can serve as benchmarks for organizational maturity assessment and improvement initiatives.

For the second question—whether ICS changes similar to natural disaster responses occur in IT/OT incident exercises—the evidence strongly supports this parallel. The communication patterns observed across our TTX sessions demonstrated phase-based structural transitions remarkably similar to those documented in traditional emergency management contexts, providing empirical validation that cyber-physical incident response follows comparable organizational dynamics.

These findings suggest that effective cyber incident response requires more than strict adherence to formal hierarchies or static command structures. Instead, organizations need a flexible command system that supports adaptive leadership and situational decision-making. Crucially, this study marks a significant step forward by being the first to empirically apply and validate the organizational dynamics established in prior disaster response research (e.g., Brown et al., 2021) to the context of cyber-physical incidents in IT/OT environments, utilizing multi-session tabletop exercises. The demonstrated applicability of CNA as an assessment tool, combined with the verified similarity to established disaster response patterns, offers organizations practical frameworks for enhancing their cyber resilience capabilities. The results reaffirm prior disaster studies, which emphasized decentralized coordination in high-stakes, real-time environments. Integrating a Multi-Team System (MTS) perspective into the traditional ICS may provide a more realistic model for such dynamic crises.

Furthermore, survey responses revealed the need for clear authority transfer triggers, flexible organizational design, and timely external collaboration protocols, especially during transitions between security and safety phases. Participants also indicated that rigid structures can become bottlenecks under safety-priority conditions, underscoring the importance of design flexibility in command systems. Based on these insights, we propose a systematic approach to exercise design that incorporates phase-specific information flows, dynamic leadership development, and continuous knowledge transfer from training to practice. Regular implementation of such exercises can enhance human resilience and readiness in critical infrastructure sectors.

Acknowledgments. This research was made possible through the support of the IPA Industrial Cyber Security Center, which kindly facilitated the implementation of the cyber exercise. We extend our deepest appreciation for their cooperation and valuable contributions.

References

1. Hadri, A.R.: Hybrid warfare in the 21st century: a threat beyond the battlefield. Magna Carta Contemp. Soc. Sci. **4**(1), 14–25 (2025)
2. Stodolnik, M.: Cyber threats as hybrid activity against the European Union in light of the current geopolitical situation. Terroryzm - studia, analizy, prewencja, pp. 225–248 (2025). https://doi.org/10.4467/27204383TER.25.021.21524
3. World Economic Forum: Global Cybersecurity Outlook 2025. World Economic Forum, Geneva (2025). https://reports.weforum.org/docs/WEF_Global_Cybersecurity_Outlook_2025.pdf
4. NEC: Cyberattacks on industrial control systems and security countermeasures (in Japanese). NEC Technical J. **17**(2) (2017). https://jpn.nec.com/techrep/journal/g17/n02/170204.html
5. CISA: Cyber-Attack Against Ukrainian Critical Infrastructure. https://www.cisa.gov/news-events/ics-alerts/ir-alert-h-16-056-01
6. Hydro: Cyber-attack on Hydro. https://www.hydro.com/en/global/media/on-the-agenda/cyber-attack/
7. Handa Hospital: Expert Panel Report on the Computer Virus Incident at Handa Hospital. https://www.handa-hospital.jp/topics/2022/0616/index.html
8. Japan Construction Information Center: Report on the NUTS System Failure Incident. https://meikoukyo.com/wp-content/uploads/2023/07/0bb9d9907568e832da8f400e529efc99.pdf
9. NISC (National center of Incident readiness and Strategy for Cybersecurity): Cybersecurity 2024: Annual Report FY2023 and Annual Plan FY2024. Cabinet Secretariat, Japan (2024). https://www.nisc.go.jp/pdf/policy/kihon
10. World Economic Forum: Cyber Resilience Index 2022. World Economic Forum, Geneva (2022). https://www3.weforum.org/docs/WEF_Cyber_Resilience_Index_2022.pdf
11. Khadka, K., Ullah, A.B.: Human factors in cybersecurity: an interdisciplinary review and framework proposal. Int. J. Inf. Secur. **24**, 119 (2025). https://doi.org/10.1007/s10207-025-01032-0
12. Kadena, E., Gupi, M.: Human factors in cybersecurity: risks and impacts. Secur. Sci. J. **2**(2), 51–64 (2021)
13. Georgiadou, A., Mouzakitis, S., Bounas, K., Askounis, D.: A cyber-security culture framework for assessing organization readiness. J. Comput. Inf. Syst. **62**(3), 452–462 (2022). https://doi.org/10.1080/08874417.2020.1845583

14. Chamkar, S.A., Maleh, Y., Gherabi, N.: The human factor capabilities in security operation center (SOC). Edpacs **66**(1), 1–14 (2022). https://doi.org/10.1080/07366981.2021.1977026
15. Burton, S.L., Burrell, D.N., Nobles, C., Jones, L.A.: Exploring the nexus of cybersecurity leadership, human factors, emotional intelligence, innovative work behavior, and critical leadership traits. Sci. Bull. **28**(2), 162–175 (2023). https://doi.org/10.2478/bsaft-2023-0016
16. Security Magazine: 5 Key Elements of Cyber Simulation Exercises to Boost Cyber Resilience. https://www.securitymagazine.com/articles/100762-5-key-elements-of-cyber-simulation-exercises-to-boost-cyber-resilience
17. Aoyama, T., Nakano, T., Koshijima, I., Hashimoto, Y., Watanabe, K.: On the complexity of cybersecurity exercises proportional to preparedness. J. Disaster Res. **12**(5), 1081–1090 (2017). https://doi.org/10.20965/jdr.2017.p1081
18. U.S. Department of Energy, CESER: Exercises and Training. https://www.energy.gov/ceser/exercises-and-training
19. Vykopal, J., Celeda, P., Svabensky, V., Hofbauer, M., Horak, M.: Research and practice of delivering tabletop exercises. In: Proceedings of the 29th Annual ACM Conference on Innovation and Technology in Computer Science Education (ITiCSE'24), pp. 220–226 (2024). https://doi.org/10.1145/3649217.3653642
20. Angafor, G.N., Yevseyeva, I., He, Y.: Game-based learning: A review of tabletop exercises for cybersecurity incident response training. Security Privacy **3**(6), e126 (2020). https://doi.org/10.1002/spy2.126
21. Haddouch, R., Clouse, S.F., Wright, R.T., Floyd, T., Perry, P.: Strengthening incident response: lessons from cybersecurity tabletop exercises for rural critical infrastructure. In: Proceedings of the ISCAP Conference, vol. 10, no. 6201 (2024)
22. Abbott, G.R., Mcclain, J., Anderson, B., Nauer, K., Silva, A., Forsythe, C.: Log analysis of cyber security training exercises. Procedia Manuf. **3** (2015). https://doi.org/10.1016/j.promfg.2015.07.523
23. Veksler, V.D., Buchler, N., LaFleur, C.G., Yu, M.S., Lebiere, C., Gonzalez, C.: Cognitive models in cybersecurity: learning from expert analysts and predicting attacker behavior. Front. Psychol. **11** (2020). https://doi.org/10.3389/fpsyg.2020.01049
24. Ur Rehman, M., Bahsi, H., Bukauskas, L., Knox, B.: Exploring trainees' behaviour in hands-on cybersecurity exercises through data mining. In: Proceedings of the 23rd European Conference on Cyber Warfare and Security (ECCWS), pp. 585–593 (2024). https://doi.org/10.34190/eccws.23.1.2141
25. Kokkonen, T., Puuska, S.: Blue team communication and reporting for enhancing situational awareness from white team perspective in cyber security exercises. In: Galinina, O., Andreev, S., Balandin, S., Koucheryavy, Y. (eds.) NEW2AN/ruSMART -2018. LNCS, vol. 11118, pp. 277–288. Springer, Cham (2018). https://doi.org/10.1007/978-3-030-01168-0_26
26. Brown, O., Power, N., Conchie, S.M.: Communication and coordination across event phases: a multi-team system emergency response. J. Occupat. Organiz. Psychol. **94**, 591–615 (2021). https://doi.org/10.1111/joop.12349
27. Bharosa, N., Lee, J., Janssen, M.: Challenges and obstacles in sharing and coordinating information during multi-agency disaster response: Propositions from field exercises. Inf. Syst. Front. **12**(1), 49–65 (2010)
28. Buck, D., Aguirre, B.: A critical evaluation of the Incident Command System and NIMS. J. Homel. Secur. Emerg. Manag. **3** (2006). https://doi.org/10.2202/1547-7355.1252

29. Comfort, L.K., Okada, A.: Emergent leadership in extreme events: a knowledge commons for sustainable communities. Int. Rev. Public Adm. **18**(1), 61–77 (2013). https://doi.org/10.1080/12294659.2013.10805240
30. Berlin, J.M., Carlstrom, E.D.: Collaboration exercises-the lack of collaborative benefits. Int. J. Disaster Risk Sci. **5**, 192–205 (2014)
31. Cichonski, P., Millar, T., Grance, T., Scarfone, K.: Computer security incident handling guide. NIST Special Publication 800–61 Revision 2 (2012). https://doi.org/10.6028/NIST.SP.800-61r2
32. Information-technology Promotion Agency, Japan.: Industrial Cyber Security Center of Excellence (ICSCoE). https://www.ipa.go.jp/en/about/org/icscoe/index.html
33. Nakayama, K., Koshijima, I., Watanabe, K.: Analyzing important factors in cybersecurity incidents using table-top exercise. In: Moallem, A. (ed.) Human Factors in Cybersecurity. AHFE (2024) International Conference. AHFE Open Access, vol. 127. AHFE International, USA (2024). https://doi.org/10.54941/ahfe1004770
34. Bjork, R.A., Bjork, E.L.: Desirable difficulties in theory and practice. J. Appl. Res. Mem. Cogn. **9**(4), 475–479 (2020)
35. DeChurch, L.A., Marks, M.A.: Leadership in multi-team systems. J. Appl. Psychol. **91**(2), 311–329 (2006). https://doi.org/10.1037/0021-9010.91.2.311
36. CISA: Cybersecurity Incident & Vulnerability Response Playbooks (2021). https://www.cisa.gov/sites/default/files/2024-08/Federal_Government_Cybersecurity_Incident_and_Vulnerability_Response_Playbooks_508C.pdf
37. FEMA.: Homeland Security Exercise and Evaluation Program (HSEEP). FEMA/National Preparedness (2020). https://www.fema.gov/emergency-managers/national-preparedness/exercises/hseep
38. International Organization for Standardization (ISO): ISO 22398:2013 - Societal security - Guidelines for exercises. ISO (2013)

AI and Critical Infrastructures

AI-Augmented Scenario Design: Experiences from a National Cybersecurity Exercise

Lenhard Reuter[1,2(✉)], Paul Smith[2], and Florian Skopik[1]

[1] AIT Austrian Institute of Technology, Vienna, Austria
{lenhard.reuter,florian.skopik}@ait.ac.at
[2] Lancaster University, Lancaster, UK
{lenhard.reuter,paul.smith}@lancaster.ac.uk

Abstract. Designing high-quality cyber exercises requires more than technical fidelity, it demands credible narratives, immersive scenarios and expert-driven coordination. In this paper, we present a case study from the 2024 Austrian National Cybersecurity Exercise, exploring how ChatGPT was integrated into scenario design, infrastructure development and content creation. We identify four core quality criteria for cyber exercises (credibility, immersion, technical fidelity and expertise) and examine how AI-supported workflows influenced each criterion.

Our findings show that ChatGPT can accelerate ideation, reduce drafting time and increase creative flexibility, particularly during early-stage design. At the same time, we highlight structural limitations, including hallucinations, lack of temporal state awareness and restricted utility in offensive simulation. We argue that AI does not replace human expertise but reshapes its application, moving expert input downstream into validation and strategic alignment.

The paper concludes with a set of practical observations derived from hands-on use, offering insights for practitioners seeking to integrate AI tools into complex simulation environments, such as gains in early-phase efficiency, improved change resilience but also above mentioned risks and the continued need for expert validation.

Keywords: ChatGPT · Cyber Exercise · Cyber Range · Scenario Design · Generative AI · AI Limitations

1 Introduction

The increasing complexity and interdependence of financial systems, energy grids and manufacturing networks has heightened their exposure to sophisticated cyber threats. Modern adversaries increasingly deploy hybrid tactics that blend cyberattacks with physical sabotage or disinformation, creating systemic risks that transcend organizational boundaries. Ensuring the resilience of critical information infrastructures has therefore become a strategic national priority.

E. Bergström et al. (Eds.): CRITIS 2025, LNCS 16291, pp. 305–325, 2026.
https://doi.org/10.1007/978-3-032-19540-1_16

Cybersecurity exercises (CSEs) are a key mechanism to strengthen operational preparedness. By simulating attack scenarios, they provide safe environments to test detection, response and recovery capabilities, while also fostering inter-organizational communication, leadership under pressure and adaptive decision-making—skills difficult to cultivate through conventional training. ISO and ECSO guidelines [1,2] conceive such exercises as holistic preparedness events designed to reinforce systemic resilience.

The Austrian National Cybersecurity Exercise, organized by the KSÖ (Austrian Security Competence Centre)[1], has been conducted regularly since 2011 and brings together stakeholders from critical infrastructure sectors. Since 2017, our team has provided both the technical platform and the narrative design. In 2021, we introduced a cyber range platform based on OpenStack, Terraform and Ansible, and have since led scenario development for three exercise cycles (2021, 2023, 2024), offering a longitudinal view on the integration of generative AI into scenario design workflows.

The 2024 scenario centred on a hybrid attack against the financial and industrial sectors in the DACH region. It depicted a fictional APT campaign targeting the tech supplier OptiTeq and its affiliated bank after journalists publicly disclosed critical supply-chain vulnerabilities. The attackers aimed to cause financial loss and reputational damage through combined cyber and physical actions. Institutional stakeholders such as the national CERT and relevant ministries were involved in planning and execution, and a live red team further increased realism. This co-created, multilayered storyline, developed in collaboration with ChatGPT, is the core subject of this study.

The results of this case study feed into the EU-funded *CyberUnity* project, which seeks to federate national and sectoral cyber ranges into a shared, interoperable ecosystem. Among its activities, the project explores an AI Assistant that supports instructors in accelerating scenario production and creating reusable, high-fidelity training content. Our analysis of ChatGPT's role in the 2024 Austrian National Cybersecurity Exercise provides insights into how large language models can augment ideation, drafting and technical prototyping in cyber exercise workflows and inform the design of such an assistant.

Background and Related Work

The effectiveness of cybersecurity exercises depends heavily on the plausibility and coherence of their scenarios [3–7]. Poorly designed scenarios risk undermining engagement and limiting learning outcomes [8]. Creating high-quality scenarios requires a demanding mix of expert input, creative writing and iterative validation [9], while balancing technical accuracy, narrative immersion, stakeholder expectations and operational constraints.

Recent advances in generative AI—especially large language models (LLMs) such as ChatGPT—offer new tools for scenario development. With capabilities in ideation, drafting, summarization and style imitation, LLMs are reshaping

[1] https://kompetenzzentrum-sicheres-oesterreich.at/.

creative workflows. Studies show that models like GPT-4 can match human performance on divergent thinking tasks [10–12] and that hybrid human–AI teams often outperform either component alone in content generation tasks [13]. Chen et al. [14] highlight how help-seeking behavior changes when interacting with ChatGPT—favouring pragmatic, task-driven queries over reflective inquiry. Yamin et al. [15] introduce CyExec, a dual-agent framework that generates scenario content through role-specific prompting, although such tools remain largely detached from real-world exercise workflows.

Contribution: This paper presents a case study of the 2024 Austrian National Cybersecurity Exercise and analyses how ChatGPT was integrated into the full scenario development cycle. Rather than replacing human creativity, we show how AI reshaped the process by accelerating drafting, reducing preparation overhead and redefining the role of expert input. Framed by help-seeking theory and experiential learning [16,17], we treat scenario design as a dynamic process of evaluation, negotiation and stakeholder alignment, and examine how ChatGPT affected this interplay. The study offers practical insights for integrating generative tools into collaborative training environments for critical infrastructure protection.

The remainder of this paper is structured as follows: Sect. 2 outlines the core criteria that define high-quality cyber exercises. Sections 3 through 6 analyse how ChatGPT influenced credibility, immersion, technical fidelity and expertise during the 2024 Austrian National Cybersecurity Exercise. Section 7 synthesizes key findings, and Sect. 8 concludes with reflections on the future role of generative AI in cybersecurity training.

2 Characterization of an Effective Cyber Exercise

Designing an effective cybersecurity exercise goes far beyond simulating technical attack vectors or validating response procedures. Our exercises fall into the category of full-scale operational simulations [5], in which participants engage with a realistic technical environment that mirrors everyday workflows and systems. These setups serve not only for technical interaction, but also as immersive stages where the narrative unfolds. Placing a strong emphasis on simulating the **experience** of a crisis, one that challenges participants not only technically, but cognitively and foremost communicatively.

Unlike theory-based formats such as tabletop exercises or serious games, full-scale exercises unfold in real time and involve live interaction with institutional actors like CERTs and regulators. Effectiveness is not measured by whether an incident is *solved*, but by the insights gained into organizational readiness, for example, discovering unclear responsibilities, communication breakdowns or misaligned escalation paths.

Rooted in experiential learning [18,19], our design philosophy emphasizes the immersive experience of a crisis. The narrative is central, not merely a backdrop, but a scaffold for decision-making, role engagement and cross-organizational collaboration under pressure.

Drawing on our experience designing national-level exercises and informed by theories of experiential and conceptual learning, we define four core dimensions that characterize a high-quality cybersecurity exercise:

1. **Credibility** – The scenario must be internally consistent and believable, resonating with the target audience and relevant stakeholders. In our 2024 exercise, the overarching storyline involved a hybrid attack targeting the financial and manufacturing sectors. A setup that is too generic or abstract risks disengagement and limits learning. Scenarios lacking relevant detail often provoke reactions like *"this would never happen."* Credibility activates participants' conceptual frameworks, improving their ability to perceive and respond to cyber crisis dynamics [19,20].
2. **Immersion** – A compelling narrative should offer both depth and coherence, enabling participants to identify with their assigned role and the fictitious organization. Immersion creates a meaningful context for learning and improves retention and transferability [21]. Emotional engagement is only possible when the scenario reflects the structure of human storytelling, including motivations and a believable causal chain of events.
3. **Technical fidelity** – To sustain immersion, the environment must plausibly support the narrative logic, even without one-to-one realism, as this fidelity enhances both engagement and adaptive problem-solving [21]. This includes abstracted but functional representations of organizational infrastructure and realistic threat scenarios based on credible TTPs (Tactics, Techniques and Procedures), even if specific attack vectors are fictionalized.
4. **Expertise** – The depth of an exercise depends on the expertise involved—from scenario designers to technical operators and facilitators. Expert input ensures alignment with real-world cognitive challenges, prompting participants to improvise and collaborate under pressure while developing non-technical skills like coordination and communication [22,23]. The ability to anticipate friction points, structure injects, support decision-making and conduct meaningful post-exercise analysis depends on deep domain knowledge, ranging from exercise design specialists to CISOs, red teamers and public-sector stakeholders.

To meet these criteria efficiently and systematically, we integrated a variety of supporting tools into our workflow, most notably in 2024 generative AI in the form of *ChatGPT*. In the following sections, we analyze how the integration of AI changed our approach to scenario development and implementation: where it added value, where limitations emerged and how it reshaped long-standing practices. Each of the aforementioned criteria will be revisited in detail highlighting the adoption of AI-assisted workflows.

3 Credibility

Before scenarios can be imaginative or exploratory, they must first be plausible. In simulation design, plausibility acts as a necessary foundation—ensuring that narratives are coherent, credible and grounded in the constraints of the systems they reflect. Without this grounding, even the most inventive scenarios risk being dismissed as unrealistic, undermining their utility in training, decision-making, or strategic analysis [19,24]. Plausibility ensures alignment with known mechanisms, causal logic and system dynamics.

3.1 Prerequisite: Domain Knowledge

Scenario development is typically centered on a specific topic that must be meaningfully addressed. In domains where prior expertise is limited, designers must conduct foundational research and analyze underlying principles to construct a realistic narrative. This challenge became particularly evident in our case, as we initially lacked familiarity with banking systems and their associated security architectures.

3.2 Help-Seeking Process

Acquiring domain knowledge thus became a core requirement. To better understand this process, we drew on the five-phase model proposed by Gall et al. [16]. Although originally developed to study children's academic behavior, its structured, help-seeker-centered perspective remains applicable to adult, self-directed learning in complex domains:

1. **Awareness of the Need for Help** – Individuals recognize their limitations or the complexity of a task and assess whether external assistance is needed.
2. **Decision to Seek Help** – The benefits and costs of seeking help are weighed, considering both goal attainment and potential impacts on perceived competence.
3. **Identification of a Potential Help Source** – A suitable help source is identified based on available resources and the ability to provide effective support.
4. **Employment of Strategies to Elicit Help** – Help is sought through indirect methods, such as requesting information, or direct approaches, like explicitly asking for solutions.
5. **Reactions to Help-Seeking Attempts** – The received help is evaluated, influencing self-perception, judgments about the help source and future interactions.

3.3 AI-Augmented Help-Seeking

In this iteration, instead of relying primarily on traditional research or expert interviews, we used ChatGPT as our main exploratory interface, iteratively prompting the model to build a conceptual understanding of the financial sector. This led to a noticeable shift in our help-seeking behavior compared to the classical five-phase model.

While the *first phase—awareness of the need for help*—remains foundational, its role becomes more diffuse when AI is involved. Traditionally, formulating a specific question requires some prior sense of what is known and what is missing. With AI, this can be inverted: users may start by requesting broad overviews (e.g. "What are relevant cyber threats in the financial sector?"), effectively outsourcing the identification of knowledge gaps and substituting internal reflection with external capability assessment.

The *second phase—decision to seek help*—is also altered. This decision is often shaped by perceived social costs, such as the fear of appearing incompetent [25,26], which can lead to avoidant behavior even when a knowledge gap is recognised [27]. In AI-mediated interactions, the perceived *social cost* of seeking help approaches zero, rendering much of this traditional cost–benefit analysis obsolete.

Phase three—identification of a suitable help source—is largely compressed. When a general-purpose AI system is readily available and perceived as broadly competent, the cognitive effort of source selection diminishes and the tool becomes the default resource, similar to a highly responsive search engine. Refining prompts with specific examples significantly enhances the quality and relevance of responses [28].

Phase four—employing strategies to elicit help—also changes. In conventional settings, strategies range from indirect probing to explicit requests. Interaction with ChatGPT, in contrast, is direct and iterative by default. Responses are not only solution-oriented but often include contextual explanations, merging support with instructional value.

Phase five—evaluation of the received help—gains particular importance in AI-mediated workflows. Due to limitations such as hallucinations [29] and shallow contextual understanding [30], users must critically assess AI responses before integrating them into downstream outputs. Expert consultation typically occurs later, once uncertainty is encountered or additional validation is required. Experts are thus repositioned as targeted validators rather than continuous collaborators. As with peer review, AI suggestions should be considered, not blindly accepted [28].

These shifts led us to observe a natural reconfiguration of help-seeking behavior, one that differs markedly from the classical five-phase model and reflects the structure of our own workflow (also see Fig. 1):

1. **Exploration of the problem space** – AI is engaged to surface relevant concepts and understand the scope of the problem, often without clearly defined knowledge gaps.
2. **Iterative Querying** – Refining prompts based on the responses, gradually shaping a more accurate or complete picture. This stage involves both acquiring facts and learning how to ask better questions, often informed by feedback from the model.
3. **Validation and Externalization** – AI responses are cross-checked against trusted sources or human experts and reformulated into structured artifacts such as narratives, injects, or configurations.

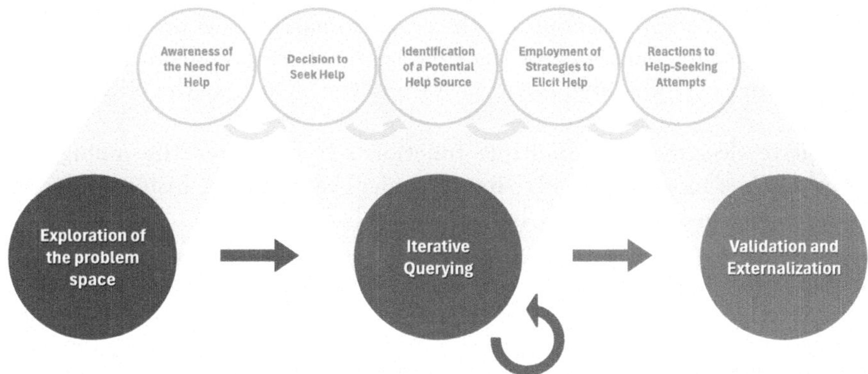

Fig. 1. Traditional vs AI-Augmented Help-Seeking Process

These stages are not strictly linear. Validation often reveals new gaps, prompting a return to exploratory querying. In this way, AI supports not just information access but also the development of increasingly precise inquiry strategies.

A key distinction between classical and AI-augmented help-seeking lies in where the process begins. Traditional approaches start with introspective gap identification, "What do I not know?", while AI-augmented workflows externalize this step, offloading it to the tool. Users often begin with loosely framed prompts, relying on the AI to define the contours of the problem space. This can accelerate onboarding but may also reduce reflective engagement, leading to surface-level fluency rather than deep comprehension. As Chen et al. [14] observe, AI-based help-seeking often promotes operational, task-oriented queries, whereas expert-guided consultation elicits more evaluative, conceptual engagement.

While tools like ChatGPT can serve as valuable ideation and drafting partners, they cannot replace the need for human expertise. Instead, they reshape how and when expert input is most effective—moving it downstream in the process, where it plays a critical role in validation, contextualization and refinement. A detailed discussion of this shift is presented in Sect. 6.

4 Immersion

The integration of generative AI into traditionally human domains, particularly those requiring imaginative judgment, has prompted a reassessment of long-held assumptions about machine capabilities. Creativity, often positioned as a uniquely human faculty, is now increasingly recognized as a domain in which hybrid human–AI systems can make meaningful contributions [10,12,17,31,32].

4.1 Narrative Design

This is particularly relevant in our training design, which emphasizes situational context, inter-organizational dynamics and the legal-regulatory dimensions of crisis response. Within this context, the scenario narrative is not peripheral—it forms the structural backbone of the exercise, anchoring realism, guiding escalation logic and enabling alignment with frameworks such as the NIS Directive[2] or DORA[3].

Narrative design serves multiple functions. It simulates the ambiguity of real-world crises more effectively than technical tasks alone, fostering decision-making under uncertainty [33]. It also scaffolds role interpretation across heterogeneous stakeholders (e.g., CSIRTs, legal teams, regulators), enabling shared situational awareness and cross-domain reasoning. Crucially, it supports participant engagement by fostering psychological plausibility, emotional resonance and immersion—factors shown to significantly enhance learning and retention [18,34].

A well-constructed scenario enables participants to identify with their roles and experience the incident as credible and consequential. This immersive quality shapes not only engagement but also the depth and durability of the learning experience.

4.2 ChatGPT as a Creative Collaborator

Given the creative and procedural complexity of scenario development, we used ChatGPT as an augmentative collaborator rather than aiming for full automation. The model acted as a high-capacity ideation partner, particularly effective in overcoming early-stage inertia, exploring attacker motivations or escalation paths and testing alternative framings. Single-line prompts rarely yielded directly usable material, but they helped surface unexpected perspectives and challenge narrative assumptions.

As drafts evolved, ChatGPT also supported iterative refinement. Through layered prompting and guided reworking, it helped align tone, narrative coherence and stylistic consistency. The model was most valuable when its outputs served as a foundation for targeted revision rather than as final products.

Finally, we frequently used the model as a conceptual mirror. Asking it to paraphrase, critique, or shift narrative perspectives often revealed latent inconsistencies or tonal mismatches, especially helpful during periods of creative fatigue, when critical self-editing became harder to maintain.

4.3 Model of Creative Collaboration

To structure our reflections, we draw on the three-stage model of creativity proposed by Wan et al. [17], which distinguishes between *ideation*, *illumination* and *implementation*. Adapted from the classical four-stage creativity framework, this model is tailored to AI-assisted writing contexts.

[2] https://eur-lex.europa.eu/eli/dir/2022/2555.

[3] https://eur-lex.europa.eu/eli/reg/2022/2554/oj.

1. **Ideation** – In early brainstorming, ChatGPT accelerated the generation of narrative premises, attacker profiles and threat dynamics. Minimal prompts—such as thematic anchors or scenario goals—often yielded structured narrative sketches. This reduced initial cognitive load and surfaced unconventional ideas, consistent with findings on cognitive blockage in co-creative systems [17,32,35].
2. **Illumination** – As ideas took shape, the model supported their expansion and recombination. It helped generate attacker motivations, escalation paths and interdisciplinary threat vectors. Knowing that linguistic precision could be deferred, we explored more freely—delegating stylistic polish to later AI-supported revisions.
3. **Implementation** – In final drafting, ChatGPT assisted with tone, consistency and clarity. While not a substitute for expert review, it served effectively as a first-pass editor and conceptual sparring partner.

Despite these benefits, human authorship remained essential. Scenario narratives are not merely stylistic—they must reflect threat models, target competencies and pedagogical intent. Prior work shows that LLMs often default to generic settings and oversimplified resolutions [36], underscoring the need for human oversight to ensure narrative depth and alignment. Furthermore, we emphasize that our use of AI was not aimed at reducing human creative labor, but at reallocating it more effectively, focusing human effort on judgment, integration and instructional design, while leveraging AI for rapid content generation and iterative refinement. Across all phases of the narrative design process, the most successful outcomes were achieved when we retained creative control and treated the AI as a high-capacity, fast-responding collaborator. Its outputs functioned as generative stimuli, inputs to be assessed, adapted or discarded based on human judgment, rather than as deterministic solutions.

Case Insight: Ideation Through Narrative Sketching. In the early ideation phase, one objective was to design an event requiring direct involvement from the Ministry of the Interior. We prompted ChatGPT to propose physical incidents severe enough to justify such intervention. Among the initial suggestions—a bomb threat at a data center, for example—none sufficiently integrated the cyber dimension.

We then asked for alternative physical threats aligned with the existing narrative. The model returned options ranging from hostage situations to drone attacks. One stood out: the risk of hazardous chemical release. This prompted further inquiry into which toxic substances are used in smart device manufacturing and whether an attack on such a facility could plausibly pose public danger.

ChatGPT listed several chemicals and their associated risks. From this, we developed a cyber-physical attack: a cyber intrusion disables surveillance at a battery storage facility, enabling arson that releases cadmium (Cd), a toxic substance used in battery production. This storyline not only introduced environmental and human health risks, but also expanded the set of engaged stakeholders to include civil protection, environmental agencies and public health authorities.

4.4 Narrative Realism Through Threat Modeling

To increase scenario plausibility and participant engagement, the attack storyline was grounded in detailed threat modeling conducted by the human exercise team. Drawing on well-documented real-world campaigns, including the JPMorgan Chase breach[4], the Bangladesh Bank heist[5] and the Carbanak campaign[6], we modeled an advanced persistent threat (APT) actor with financial motives, long dwell time and high operational maturity.

The scenario's backstory described a gradual compromise via spearphishing during a prior business relationship. From there, attackers moved laterally, established persistence and escalated access over time—mirroring behavioral patterns observed in real APT campaigns. This manual design effort aimed to ensure narrative plausibility and maintain control over key escalation dynamics.

5 Technical Fidelity

This section focuses on the technical environment provided to participants during the exercise, including simulated infrastructure, attack execution and inject development. It also examines how ChatGPT supported these processes as its role evolved over time.

As discussed previously, the aim of technical fidelity is not exact replication of real-world infrastructure, but internal consistency and plausibility from the participant's perspective. Excessive realism can hinder immersion—especially when participants begin to "fight" the scenario instead of engaging with it [20]. To counter this, our introductory briefings emphasize: *"Don't fight the scenario, fight the problem."*

Participants must rapidly familiarize themselves with a new environment, which limits how complex the infrastructure can be. It must support investigative depth (e.g., log analysis, anomaly detection) while remaining simple enough to learn quickly.

The same constraint applies to the simulation timeline. Real-world attack campaigns like APTs may span months, often averaging dwell times over 180 days [37], but in exercises, these must be compressed into hours. Without clear framing, such compression can undermine scenario credibility and learning impact [20].

---

[4] https://www.trendmicro.com/vinfo/us/security/news/cyber-attacks/jp-morgan-breach-affects-millions-shows-need-for-secure-web-apps.

[5] https://sk.sagepub.com/cases/the-soft-threat-the-story-of-the-bangladesh-bank-reserve-heist.

[6] https://media.kasperskycontenthub.com/wp-content/uploads/sites/43/\discretionary-2018/03/08064518/Carbanak_APT_eng.pdf.

Lacking detailed reference architectures for the banking sector, we adapted the Purdue Enterprise Reference Architecture [38]—originally designed for industrial control systems—to simulate a segmented environment. We reinterpreted the OT (Operational Technology) zone as the bank's most protected internal segment. This approach provided a clear security boundary structure without relying on institution-specific infrastructure details.

5.1 Application Prototyping with ChatGPT

To simulate transactional workflows, we developed a custom application incorporating standard security features such as multi-factor authentication and four-eyes approval for large transfers. Rather than exploiting software vulnerabilities, the narrative centered on the abuse of legitimate access: credentials were obtained via a keylogger (emulating long-term APT presence) and a second factor through social engineering and psychological manipulation. This allowed us to model realistic insider compromise without requiring intentionally flawed software.

We implemented a Flask-based client-server system comprising a cloud-facing service and a local terminal in the bank's secure zone. ChatGPT accelerated development by generating boilerplate code, simulating workflows and producing traceable logs and network traffic. Its strong Python performance, due to high training data representation, has been well documented [39].

With clearly scoped requirements, we built a usable prototype in under a week—without relying on senior developers [40–42]. However, ChatGPT's outputs often required manual debugging, especially for logic errors. This reflects a broader insight: while highly effective for rapid scaffolding and common tasks, AI-assisted coding still benefits from human oversight for correctness and refinement [42].

5.2 ChatGPT in Offensive Simulation

While participants were introduced to a pre-compromised environment, the offensive elements were implemented through a blend of automation and manual scripting. Attack orchestration relied on Sliver C2 agents[7], coordinated via the AttackMate framework [43].

While ChatGPT excelled in rapid prototyping of infrastructure and benign application logic, its utility in simulating offensive tools was limited. Even though recent studies demonstrate that LLMs can generate malicious code under certain conditions [44–47], we encountered significant restrictions. The model consistently refused to generate code when it inferred offensive intent, either from prompt phrasing or preceding dialogue context [48,49]. Some even suggest framing the request as part of a screenplay [50] in order to bypass restrictions. Attempts to clarify the educational intent of the request also proved inconsistent and unreliable. In practice, most offensive tooling, including malware stagers,

[7] https://github.com/BishopFox/sliver.

droppers and exfiltration scripts, was developed manually. However, ChatGPT remained helpful for standard coding questions throughout this process, supporting tasks like debugging or optimizing auxiliary scripts, in the same way it assisted with benign application development.

5.3 Infrastructure Provisioning and Automation

Our cyber range runs on OpenStack and is provisioned via Infrastructure-as-Code using Ansible and Terraform. Over time, our codebase has expanded to support extensive reuse and reduce manual setup. This time, ChatGPT contributed meaningfully in debugging misconfigurations, such as email server setups, but often hallucinated configuration options, especially in Ansible. These included nonexistent parameters or logically flawed solutions.

As our internal expertise grew, we shifted from relying on ChatGPT's suggestions to critically reviewing and correcting them, underscoring that its usefulness scales inversely with the user's domain proficiency.

Case Insight: Hallucination in Code Generation. Several hallucinations occurred during the development of technical artifacts, particularly in domains where we had prior expertise and could easily verify correctness, such as Ansible scripting. In these cases, ChatGPT sometimes produced highly plausible-looking solutions that ultimately relied on fabricated syntax or nonexistent task attributes: In one case, ChatGPT suggested looping over tasks in a `block` construct using `with_items`—a feature that does not exist in Ansible's execution model. Although the syntax appeared valid, it was functionally incorrect. When prompted, the model acknowledged the error and offered a workaround via task-level iteration.

Another instance involved the `pexpect` module. ChatGPT proposed a parameter for sending newline characters that exists in the Python module but is not available in Ansible's wrapper. These examples highlight a recurring risk: the model may conflate adjacent technologies or project logic across domains, producing outputs that seem credible but are subtly invalid.

5.4 Managing Injects

Inject creation was supported by structured pre-prompts that included scenario timeline, fictional personas and prior messages. This ensured consistency across injects and enabled tone modulation—for example, internal emails appeared procedural, while attacker messages were urgent and aggressive.

However, supplying full context introduced a new challenge: the model occasionally revealed future plot points in earlier injects, referencing attacker goals or responses not yet known to participants. This reflects a key limitation of long-context prompting: ChatGPT lacks persistent state awareness [51,52], making temporal consistency difficult to maintain. To avoid narrative leaks, we relied on careful prompt segmentation and manual oversight.

Despite these challenges, the resulting injects formed a coherent and emotionally engaging storyline that required minimal explanation. Participants noted that the scenario felt more realistic than in previous years.

Case Insight: Human Oversight in Inject Consistency. While ChatGPT generated coherent and stylistically aligned content, it occasionally introduced subtle but critical inconsistencies during inject development.

One recurring issue involved renaming a fictional organization mid-way through scenario design. Although the model applied the new name in subsequent prompts, it sometimes reverted to the old name when referencing earlier content, revealing that retroactive edits remain prompt-dependent and fragile across long sessions.

Another issue occurred during the generation of disinformation campaigns. Tasked with writing from the attacker's perspective, the model mistakenly targeted the attackers themselves rather than the intended journalist. This role inversion, though subtle, broke narrative logic and illustrates ChatGPT's limitations in maintaining consistent perspective across complex prompts.

These cases highlight the need for human oversight, not just for editing style or checking facts, but for preserving narrative coherence and identifying logical misalignments.

6 Expertise

High-quality cyber exercises rely not only on technical realism or narrative design, but also on human expertise. While ChatGPT enables rapid onboarding into unfamiliar domains and demonstrates surprisingly strong performance across diverse knowledge tasks [53], it does not replace expert input. Instead, it shifts the expert's role—from primary source to strategic validator. Experts are now consulted after an initial understanding has been shaped through AI, making their input more targeted and impactful. This section explores that evolving dynamic.

We observed this shift during our own scenario development. After building a preliminary threat model with ChatGPT, we consulted two Chief Information Security Officers (CISOs) to assess the plausibility of specific attack paths—such as whether an ATM compromise could realistically lead to internal access. Although both confirmed the general plausibility, their responses were intentionally vague, shaped by organizational and policy constraints.

This highlighted a parallel between AI and human experts: both limit disclosure, but for different reasons. ChatGPT is constrained by training data and system safeguards; human experts by context, ethics and institutional policy. The former is static and systemic, the latter situational and negotiable. Recognizing these boundaries is essential for deciding when and how to engage each type of knowledge source. To illustrate this comparison, we summarize key distinctions in Table 1.

Table 1. Comparison of expert consultation and ChatGPT-supported inquiry

Dimension	Human Expert	ChatGPT
Access and Availability	Limited, requires coordination	Constant, on-demand
Domain Knowledge	High (specialized)	Broad, varies by domain
Interaction Flexibility	Time-constrained, limited follow-up	Unrestricted, iterative
Level of Detail	Often selective or time-bound	User-defined depth
Accuracy	High, context-aware	Risk of hallucination
Effort to Engage	Finding the right expert takes effort	Single interface across topics
Perceived Social Cost	Can affect perceived competence	No social risk
Ethical Constraints	Shaped by organizational norms	Defined by system-level rules
Context Awareness	Deep, situationally adaptive	Limited, can miss nuance

ChatGPT offers several advantages as a first-line knowledge tool: it is available on demand, allows flexible and iterative interaction and adapts to varying levels of prior knowledge [28]. In contrast, expert consultations are often time-limited and require careful preparation—both technically and socially, due to concerns about reputation or perceived competence.

Access to experts can also be a structural barrier. While large institutions may maintain direct channels to industry experts, smaller organizations or students may not. In such cases, the choice between ChatGPT and expert input often never arises—AI becomes the default.

Rather than treating AI and expert consultation as competing modes, we found it more productive to see them as sequential and complementary. ChatGPT accelerates early exploration and ideation, while human experts refine depth, realism and contextual accuracy. In our exercise design, this dual-mode model proved highly effective: AI enabled breadth and speed, experts ensured strategic alignment and plausibility.

Critically, expertise provides more than just facts. Human experts bring lived experience, legal insight and organizational intuition—qualities essential for crafting credible crisis scenarios. In that sense, expertise is not just a resource; it is a design principle.

6.1 Human Experience During Exercise

While the execution phase lies outside the scope of this paper, human dynamics must still be anticipated during design. Institutional actors, participants and the control team introduce layers of realism, unpredictability and narrative richness that cannot be scripted—but can be planned for.

In our national exercise, key institutions such as the national CERT, regulators and crisis units were embedded directly into the scenario. Representing themselves, they responded dynamically to player actions and served as authentic contact points. This allowed participants to experience real reporting lines and support channels—adding procedural fidelity that scripted injects cannot match.

Participant behavior introduces further variation. Prior experience, personality and team culture shape how incidents unfold. Some teams improvise effectively under pressure; others rely on structure or anticipate escalation. These human patterns emerge naturally and enhance learning—but only if the exercise design leaves room for them.

The exercise control team plays a pivotal role in guiding these dynamics. We monitor engagement, detect friction and adapt the narrative in real time through clarifications, added injects, or live roleplay (e.g., messages from a fictional CEO or pressure from HR). These adjustments sustain immersion and emotional tension.

Such responsiveness is beyond the reach of AI. While ChatGPT supports content preparation, it lacks the contextual awareness and narrative intuition needed for live orchestration. Human presence, in this regard, is not just supportive—it is essential to authenticity.

7 Main Findings

In this section, we highlight key advantages and limitations that emerged from the integration of ChatGPT, into our cyber exercise design process. While some benefits, such as increased efficiency, were expected, several findings only became apparent through hands-on use. Below, we focus on selected, often underestimated, effects that significantly shaped our workflows and outcomes.

Efficiency and Evolution of Practice – Across three iterations of the national cybersecurity exercise (2021, 2023, 2024), we observed a clear shift in workflows and tool use. In 2021, scenario development was highly manual, with extensive domain research and early expert consultations driving the design process. By 2023, reusable infrastructure and maturing processes reduced technical overhead—but scenario content still relied heavily on human ideation.

In 2024, ChatGPT significantly accelerated early-stage work. The model supported narrative drafting, technical prototyping and ideation, reducing time-to-prototype and shortening iteration cycles. Experts remained essential, but their role shifted toward targeted validation and refinement. This repositioning allowed the team to reallocate time toward quality control and stakeholder alignment, without expanding staff or timeline.

Infrastructure preparation time dropped from four months and six FTEs in 2021 to 1.5 months and two FTEs in 2024. While accumulated experience played a role, the most transformative factor was the integration of ChatGPT in the design phase.

Creative Flexibility – ChatGPT also lowered the barrier for creative experimentation. Ideas previously discarded due to time or resource constraints—such as simulating social media noise or prototyping small interactive tools—became feasible. Rapid drafting enabled us to test alternative concepts without sunk-cost anxiety, encouraging a more iterative, exploratory mindset.

What once required extensive effort could now be quickly sketched, assessed and refined or discarded. This flexibility expanded our creative range without compromising planning discipline or narrative coherence.

Deliberative Querying – During development, we primarily used the free GPT-3.5 tier, with limited access to GPT-4. Despite this constraint, GPT-4's noticeably stronger performance [32,54] led us to reserve its use for high-impact prompts. In hindsight, this limitation proved valuable: it forced us to clarify our intent before asking, leading to more focused, efficient queries. Rather than relying on repetitive exploration, we engaged in more deliberate, goal-oriented prompting.

Emotional Neutrality – Particularly valuable was the model's emotionally neutral and non-possessive interaction style, an often underappreciated aspect of generative AI in collaborative contexts. In human teams, particularly when individuals have already invested significant effort into an idea, conflicting opinions can lead to friction or cognitive fixation. In contrast, ChatGPT can be instructed at any point to discard previous iterations and begin anew, without resistance or defensiveness. This low-friction, low-ego mode of interaction made it a uniquely effective brainstorming partner, especially in high-pressure creative environments, where iteration speed and emotional neutrality are critical.

Knowledge Gaps and Overconfidence – A significant challenge we encountered was the model's tendency to exhibit overconfidence in domains where its knowledge was limited. For example, when inquiring about the Austrian Directorate for State Security and Intelligence (DSN), the model produced plausible-sounding but ultimately inaccurate or unverifiable information, likely due to a lack of access to non-public sources.

Crucially, the model rarely admits uncertainty. Instead, it tends to generate confident answers even when its knowledge is thin, occasionally blending facts with hallucinated content. This behavior can be misleading and poses a risk in domains that demand high accuracy or trustworthiness.

Limitations in State and Context Management – While ChatGPT offered valuable support during scenario development, several limitations emerged around how it manages internal state, narrative context and temporal coherence.

- **Local vs. Global Adaptation:** The model handled local edits well—such as revising an attacker's goal or rephrasing specific passages—but struggled with persistent integration. In longer sessions, even small updates were sometimes forgotten or overwritten by earlier context. Change requests introduced late could require starting a new chat to avoid reversion to outdated assumptions.
- **Exploratory Branching and Contamination:** During creative drafting, attempts to explore alternate narrative paths and then return to the original often resulted in residual "contamination"—fragments from the detour that persisted despite clear instructions to discard them. While restarting a session helped, rebuilding prior context led to noticeable drops in consistency and output quality.
- **Temporal Inconsistencies:** The model also lacked temporal state awareness [51,52]. When building timeline-driven content (e.g., injects or event sequences), it occasionally referenced future events prematurely or failed to

reflect updates in earlier segments. Manual timeline management was necessary to ensure narrative logic.
- **Ethical Safeguards and System Lock-ins:** When working on attacker behavior or offensive tactics—common in cybersecurity exercises—ChatGPT sometimes refused to respond or reduced its output mid-conversation, interpreting the topic as unsafe. These refusals were often triggered by conversational context rather than specific prompts and could not reliably be undone. In many cases, starting fresh was the only workaround.

Together, these behaviors reflect a fundamental constraint: ChatGPT lacks structured memory, persistent internal state and timeline awareness. While powerful for short-form or modular writing, long-form scenario development still requires careful oversight, explicit prompt engineering and periodic resets to maintain consistency and creative control.

8 Conclusion

This paper examined how generative AI, in particular ChatGPT, reshaped the design and implementation of the 2024 Austrian National Cybersecurity Exercise. By analyzing four key quality dimensions: credibility, immersion, technical fidelity and expertise, we assessed both the benefits and limitations of integrating AI into a traditionally human-centric design process.

Our experience shows that AI can serve as a valuable creative collaborator, accelerating content generation, reducing the time to prototype and enabling more ambitious narrative structures. At the same time, it introduced new challenges, including hallucinated outputs, limitations in handling temporally structured content and ethical safeguards that complicate adversarial simulation. These constraints underscore the continuing need for expert oversight, particularly in validating scenario plausibility and supporting live facilitation.

Ultimately, we argue that the role of AI in cyber exercises is not to replace human input, but to reallocate it, shifting expert effort from foundational research toward higher-level refinement, quality assurance and strategic alignment. As generative models continue to evolve, their responsible use will depend not only on technical capabilities, but on clear boundaries, reflective integration and a continued emphasis on human judgment as a design principle.

As cybersecurity threats evolve and training environments grow in complexity, we argue that the future of scenario design will not be AI-driven or human-led, but hybrid by design.

9 Outlook and Future Work

Looking ahead, the rapid pace of generative AI development invites speculation about how current limitations may soon be overcome. While this study focused on the design and planning phase, future applications in live exercise execution appear increasingly plausible, ranging from adaptive storylines and AI-driven non-player characters to autonomous red teams.

We also foresee AI playing a greater role in pre- and post-exercise phases, supporting participant assessment, report generation and deriving meaningful insights from observed behaviors. However, when it comes to evaluating human behavior during complex, high-pressure situations, current models like ChatGPT still lack the depth, authenticity and contextual sensitivity required for qualitative judgment. For now, human experience remains irreplaceable in interpreting the human dimensions of crisis response.

It is also important to note that our findings are based exclusively on ChatGPT (GPT-4), and should therefore be interpreted in this specific context. Future work should extend this inquiry to other widely used LLMs in order to validate the observed patterns. Such comparisons may reveal whether the limitations and strengths identified here are model-specific or indicative of broader trends in AI-supported creative processes.

Acknowledgments. This work is conducted under the EU-funded project CyberUnity, Project Number 101128024, which aims to federate multiple Cyber Ranges across Europe.

References

1. ISO, I.O.f.S.: Societal security–Guidelines for exercises and testing. ISO 22398:2013, 1st edn. (2013)
2. Organisation, E.C.S.: Understanding cyber ranges: from hype to reality. Technical report (2020)
3. Dewar, R.S.: Cybersecurity and Cyberdefense Exercises. en. Technical report, 35 p. ETH Zurich (2018)
4. Stern, E.: Designing Crisis Management Training and Exercises for Strategic Leaders: A Swedish and United States Collaborative Project. National Defense College, Stockholm (2014)
5. Seker, E., Ozbenli, H.H.: The Concept of Cyber Defence Exercises (CDX): planning, execution, evaluation. In: 2018 International Conference on Cyber Security and Protection of Digital Services (Cyber Security), Glasgow, pp. 1–9. IEEE (2018)
6. Virág, C., O'Shea, D., Merialdo, M.: Cyber Exercise Scenario Development. Technical report, European Cyber Security Organisation (ECSO) (2024)
7. Ulsamer, P., et al.: Immersive Storytelling for Information Security Awareness Training in Virtual Reality (2021)
8. Ketelaars, E., Flandin, S., Poizat, G.: From 'normal exercises' to 'resilience training exercises'. A phenomenological study on participants' engagement with unforeseen situations. Cognition, Technology & Work (2025)
9. Buglova, E., et al.: Preparation, Conduct and Evaluation of Exercises to Test Preparedness for a Nuclear or Radiological Emergency. Technical report, IAEA, International Atomic Energy Agency (2005)
10. Haase, J., Hanel, P.H.: Artificial muses: generative artificial intelligence chatbots have risen to human-level creativity. J. Creativity **33**(3), 100066 (2023)

11. Koivisto, M., Grassini, S.: Best humans still outperform artificial intelligence in a creative divergent thinking task. Sci. Rep. **13**(1), 13601 (2023)
12. Guzik, E.E., Byrge, C., Gilde, C.: The originality of machines: AI takes the Torrance Test. J. Creativity **33**(3), 100065 (2023)
13. Vaccaro, M., Almaatouq, A., Malone, T.: When combinations of humans and AI are useful: a systematic review and meta-analysis. Nat. Hum. Behav. **8**(12), 2293–2303 (2024)
14. Chen, A., et al.: Unpacking help-seeking process through multimodal learning analytics: a comparative study of ChatGPT vs Human expert. Comput. Educ. **226**, 105198 (2025)
15. Yamin, M.M. et al.: Applications of LLMs for Generating Cyber Security Exercise Scenarios (2024)
16. Gall, S.N.-L.: Help-seeking: an understudied problem-solving skill in children. Dev. Rev. **1**(3), 224–246 (1981)
17. Wan, Q., et al.: "It Felt Like Having a Second Mind": investigating human-AI Co-creativity in prewriting with large language models. Proc. ACM Hum.-Comput. Interact. **8**(CSCW1), 1–26 (2024)
18. Kolb, A.Y., Kolb, D.A.: Experiential learning theory: a dynamic, holistic approach to management learning, education and development. In: The SAGE Handbook of Management Learning, Education and Development, vol. 7, no. 2, pp. 42–68 (2009)
19. Aaltola, K., Taitto, P.: Utilising experiential and organizational learning theories to improve human performance in cyber training. Inf. Secur. Int. J. **43**(2), 123–133 (2019)
20. Grunnan, T., Fridheim, H.: Planning and conducting crisis management exercises for decision-making: the do's and don'ts. EURO J. Dec. Processes **5**(1–4), 79–95 (2017)
21. Borell, J., Eriksson, K.: Learning effectiveness of discussion-based crisis management exercises. Int. J. Disaster Risk Reduct. **5**, 28–37 (2013)
22. Crichton, M., Flin, R.: Training for emergency management: tactical decision games. J. Hazard. Mater. **88**(2–3), 255–266 (2001)
23. Comfort, L.K.: Crisis management in hindsight: cognition, communication, coordination, and control. Public Adm. Rev. **67**(s1), 189–197 (2007)
24. Mases, S. et al.: Success factors for designing a cybersecurity exercise on the example of incident response. In: 2021 IEEE European Symposium on Security and Privacy Workshops (EuroS&PW), Vienna, Austria, pp. 259–268. IEEE (2021)
25. Karabenick, S.A., Gonida, E.N.: Academic help seeking as a self-regulated learning strategy. In: Schunk, D.H., Greene, J.A. (eds.) Handbook of Self-Regulation of Learning and Performance, pp. 421–433. Routledge (2017)
26. Leenknecht, M.J., Carless, D.: Students' feedback seeking behaviour in undergraduate education: a scoping review. Educ. Res. Rev. **40**, 100549 (2023)
27. Karabenick, S.A., Dembo, M.H.: Understanding and facilitating self-regulated help seeking. New Dir. Teach. Learn. **2011**(126), 33–43 (2011)
28. Steiss, J., et al.: Comparing the quality of human and ChatGPT feedback of students' writing. Learn. Instr. **91**, 101894 (2024)
29. Huang, L., et al.: A survey on hallucination in large language models: principles, taxonomy, challenges, and open questions. ACM Trans. Inf. Syst. **43**(2), 1–55 (2025)
30. Meşe, I., Kuzan, B., Kuzan, T.Y.: ChatGPT in medical writing: enhancing healthcare communication through artificial intelligence and human expertise. Anatolian Curr. Med. J. **6**(1), 97–104 (2024)

31. Bower, A.H., Steyvers, M.: Perceptions of AI engaging in human expression. Sci. Rep. **11**(1), 21181 (2021)
32. Hubert, K.F., Awa, K.N., Zabelina, D.L.: The current state of artificial intelligence generative language models is more creative than humans on divergent thinking tasks. Sci. Rep. **14**(1), 3440 (2024)
33. Yamin, M.M., Katt, B., Gkioulos, V.: Cyber ranges and security testbeds: scenarios, functions, tools and architecture. Comput. Secur. **88**, 101636 (2020)
34. Burch, G.F., et al.: A meta-analysis of the relationship between experiential learning and learning outcomes. Decis. Sci. J. Innov. Educ. **17**(3), 239–273 (2019)
35. Clark, E. et al.: Creative writing with a machine in the loop: case studies on slogans and stories. In: 23rd International Conference on Intelligent User Interfaces, Tokyo Japan, pp. 329–340. ACM (2018)
36. Beguš, N.: Experimental narratives: a comparison of human crowdsourced storytelling and AI storytelling. Hum. Soc. Sci. Commun. **11**(1), 1392 (2024)
37. Heming, J.: How to mitigate advanced persistent threats (APT) like Volt Typhoon (2024)
38. Williams, T.J.: The Purdue enterprise reference architecture. Comput. Ind. **24**(2–3), 141–158 (1994)
39. Feng, Y., et al.: Investigating code generation performance of ChatGPT with crowdsourcing social data. In: 2023 IEEE 47th Annual Computers. Software, and Applications Conference (COMPSAC), Torino, Italy, pp. 876–885. IEEE (2023)
40. Biswas, S.: Role of ChatGPT in computer programming. Mesopotamian J. Comput. Sci. **2023**, 9–15 (2023)
41. Liu, C. et al.: Improving ChatGPT Prompt for Code Generation (2023)
42. Coello, C.E.A., Alimam, M.N., Kouatly, R.: Effectiveness of ChatGPT in coding: a comparative analysis of popular large language models (2024)
43. Hotwagner, W.: AttackMate: Requirements for a research centric attack orchestration tool. MA thesis, University of Applied Sciences Technikum Wien (2024)
44. Pa Pa, Y.M. et al.: An attacker's dream? Exploring the capabilities of ChatGPT for developing malware. In: 2023 Cyber Security Experimentation and Test Workshop, Marina del Rey CA USA, pp. 10–18. ACM (2023)
45. McKee, F., Noever, D.: Chatbots in a Botnet World (2022)
46. Ben-Moshe, S., Gekker, G., Cohen, G.: OpwnAI: AI That Can Save the Day or HACK it Away (2022)
47. Gupta, M., et al.: From ChatGPT to ThreatGPT: impact of generative AI in cybersecurity and privacy. IEEE Access **11**, 80218–80245 (2023)
48. Al-Hawawreh, M., Aljuhani, A., Jararweh, Y.: Chatgpt for cybersecurity: practical applications, challenges, and future directions. Clust. Comput. **26**(6), 3421–3436 (2023)
49. Sebastian, G.: Do ChatGPT and other AI chatbots pose a cybersecurity risk?: An exploratory study. Int. J. Secur. Priv. Pervasive Comput. (IJSPPC) **15**(1), 1–11 (2023)
50. Iqbal, F., et al.: When ChatGPT goes rogue: exploring the potential cybersecurity threats of AI-powered conversational chatbots. Front. Commun. Networks **4**, 1220243 (2023)
51. Kim, J., Hwang, S.-W.: Counterfactual-Consistency Prompting for Relative Temporal Understanding in Large Language Models (2025)
52. Chen, M. et al.: Improving Large Language Models in Event Relation Logical Prediction (2023)

53. Revell, T., et al.: ChatGPT versus human essayists: an exploration of the impact of artificial intelligence for authorship and academic integrity in the humanities. Int. J. Educ. Integr. **20**(1), 18 (2024)
54. OpenAI, et al.: GPT-4 Technical Report (2023)

Sow Smarter, Not Harder: Evaluating LLM-Generated Seeds for Fuzzing Critical Infrastructure

Jorge Barredo[1,2](✉), Maialen Eceiza[1], Jose Luis Flores[3], and Mikel Iturbe[2]

[1] IKERLAN Technology Research Centre, 20500 Arrasate/Mondragón, Spain
jbarredo@ikerlan.es
[2] Mondragon Unibertsitatea, 20500 Arrasate/Mondragón, Spain
[3] University of the Basque Country, 20018 Donostia/San Sebastián, Spain

Abstract. Software vulnerabilities in critical infrastructure components can lead to severe disruptions. While fuzzing effectively identifies such weaknesses, the quality of initial seed inputs significantly impacts its effectiveness. This study evaluates how large language models (LLMs) can generate better fuzzing seeds for critical infrastructure software. We compared seven LLMs—ChatGPT-4-Turbo, Claude 3.0 Opus, Claude 3.7 Sonnet, DeepSeek-V3, Gemini 2.0 Flash, Grok 3, and Mistral 7B—with manual baselines across six programs, including industrial control libraries, routing components, and network firmware. Over 20 independent 24-h campaigns per model and program, LLM-generated seeds achieved 14.8% higher code coverage, detected 56.3% more unique crashes, and reached first crashes 373.9% faster than manual methods. Performance patterns emerged across different infrastructure protocols, with certain models excelling at complex SCADA data formats while others performed better for network security components. The 56.5% computational efficiency improvement benefits resource-constrained operational technology environments. These findings demonstrate that LLM-generated seeds can meaningfully enhance vulnerability detection in software underlying critical infrastructure systems, offering a practical approach to strengthening resilience against cyber threats.

Keywords: LLMs · Fuzzing · Vulnerability detection

1 Introduction

Critical infrastructure (CI) systems, such as power grids and healthcare facilities, depend on software, particularly embedded systems, to operate reliably [20]. Moreover, secure communication libraries like OpenSSL are essential for network servers supporting CI operations. However, software vulnerabilities can cause severe disruptions, as seen in the 2021 Colonial Pipeline attack, which interrupted fuel distribution, and the 2017 WannaCry ransomware attack, which

E. Bergström et al. (Eds.): CRITIS 2025, LNCS 16291, pp. 326–346, 2026.
https://doi.org/10.1007/978-3-032-19540-1_17

affected 200,000 healthcare systems across 150 countries [18]. Thus, detecting vulnerabilities during software development is essential to protect CI systems.

Fuzz testing, or fuzzing, stands out as an effective technique for identifying software vulnerabilities. By systematically providing programs with malformed inputs, fuzzing reveals errors that might otherwise remain hidden until exploitation [16]. This is highlighted by the discovery of the Heartbleed vulnerability in OpenSSL[1], which compromised secure communications. While recent advances have extended fuzzing's applicability to CI software, with ProphetFuzz [21] increasing code coverage by 18% in industrial control programs, Magneto [27] improving bug detection by 25% in SCADA systems, and Eom et al. [10] reporting 30% faster path exploration in power grid software, significant challenges persist. Comprehensive testing of complex protocols and firmware remains difficult [26], and fuzzing's effectiveness continues to depend heavily on the quality of initial seed inputs, which guide the exploration of code paths and potential vulnerabilities [5]. Manually crafted seeds often suffer from limited diversity due to time constraints, knowledge gaps, and human biases.

The remarkable evolution of large language models (LLMs) offers a promising new direction for addressing these limitations in fuzzing seed generation. Since 2023, models like ChatGPT (OpenAI) [8] and DeepSeek (DeepSeek AI) [7] have demonstrated strong capabilities in code generation and security analysis. These models, with architectures ranging from millions to trillions of parameters, can generate diverse and structured outputs, which could enhance the quality of fuzzing seeds for CI applications.

This study explores the use of LLMs to generate fuzzing seeds for CI software, focusing on energy, telecommunications, and industrial control systems. Through experimental evaluation, we address two research questions:

- **RQ1: How effectively can LLMs improve fuzzing seed generation for CI software in terms of code coverage, crash detection, and computational efficiency?** We compare LLM-generated seeds against manually crafted seeds, analyzing metrics such as error detection rates, code path coverage, and time to first failure.
- **RQ2: How do different LLMs perform in generating fuzzing seeds for CI software?** We evaluate multiple models to identify those best suited for specific CI domains.

2 Related Work

Prior research has investigated large language models (LLMs) and fuzzing for cybersecurity, including applications to CI systems. However, the use of LLMs for generating fuzzing seeds in CI software, particularly through multi-model comparisons and infrastructure-specific evaluations, remains unexplored.

LLMs have shown promise in cybersecurity tasks, but their application to CI fuzzing is limited. Jiang et al. reported that LLMs generated formatted inputs

[1] https://nvd.nist.gov/vuln/detail/cve-2014-0160.

with 58.47% accuracy across 10,000 tests, reducing generation time by 43% compared to traditional methods [15]. However, their study focused on general software, offering little insight into CI-specific challenges. While these results highlight LLMs' potential, they do not address fuzzing for CI software, where protocol-specific inputs and resource constraints are critical.

Fuzzing for CI systems has been widely studied, with recent work incorporating LLMs to enhance vulnerability detection. For instance, Zhang et al. [25] applied LLMs to detect 14 bugs in programmable logic controller (PLC) firmware, demonstrating their ability to target CI vulnerabilities. Similarly, Fuzz4ALL [23] used LLMs to improve bug detection by 21% across 1,000 open-source projects, including CI-related software, by generating diverse inputs. However, these studies typically evaluated a single LLM, limiting understanding of how different models perform across varied CI targets.

Seed generation, a key component of fuzzing, remains a challenge. Guan et al. [13] used an LLM to detect 17 errors in Internet of Things (IoT) devices, focusing on lightweight protocols. While effective for IoT, the approach was not tested on diverse CI systems like energy or telecommunications infrastructure, nor did it compare multiple LLMs. Similarly, the WhiteFox framework [24], which combines LLMs with dynamic analysis, identified 92 bugs in PyTorch by generating seeds for machine learning libraries. WhiteFox uses LLMs to create inputs targeting edge cases in tensor operations, refining seeds iteratively based on runtime feedback. However, its focus on machine learning limits its relevance to CI, where protocols like UPnP or SCADA require specialized inputs. A review by Zhang et al. [26] of 150 papers noted a 40% gap in seed diversity for fuzzing, with little emphasis on CI firmware or multi-LLM comparisons.

This study addresses these gaps by evaluating seven LLMs—ChatGPT-4-Turbo, Claude 3.0 Opus, Claude 3.7 Sonnet, DeepSeek-V3, Gemini 2.0 Flash, Grok 3, and Mistral 7B—against manual baselines across six CI programs, including industrial control libraries, routing components, and network firmware. Unlike Guan et al.'s IoT-focused study, this work spans multiple CI domains and protocols. In contrast to WhiteFox's machine learning focus, it tackles CI-specific challenges, such as generating seeds for complex, protocol-driven inputs in resource-constrained settings. Through 160 fuzzing campaigns per program, we analyze code coverage, crash detection, and computational efficiency, providing a detailed comparison of LLM performance to guide seed generation for CI security.

3 Evaluation Methodology

This section describes the large language models (LLMs), target programs, prompt engineering, and experimental setup used to address RQ1 (LLMs vs. manual seed generation) and RQ2 (inter-LLM differences). Following established fuzzing practices [5,16], we evaluate LLM-generated seeds for CI software, focusing on energy and telecommunication systems. Experiments were conducted from March to May 2025 to account for recent advancements in LLMs.

3.1 Evaluated LLMs

We selected seven general-purpose LLMs based on their capabilities in code generation, reasoning, and security analysis, which are essential for creating fuzzing seeds for CI software. Table 1 summarizes their characteristics, including support for direct file generation of fuzzing seeds and relevant references. These models span different sizes and providers to ensure a comprehensive comparison. For a baseline, we used manually crafted seeds developed by domain experts based on protocol specifications and known vulnerability patterns. To ensure consistency, we used prompts to generate seed creation scripts for all models, as some do not support direct file generation.

Table 1. Large Language Models Evaluated for Fuzzing Seed Generation

Model	Provider	Parameters	Focus	API Avail.	File Generation	Ref.
ChatGPT-4-Turbo	OpenAI	Large (~1T)	Code, text	✓	✓	[22]
Claude 3.0 Opus	Anthropic	Large	Code, safety	✓	×	[1]
Claude 3.7 Sonnet	Anthropic	Large	Code, efficiency	✓	Limited[a]	[1]
DeepSeek-V3	DeepSeek AI	Large (405B)	Reasoning, code	✓	✓	[7]
Gemini 2.0 Flash	Google	Medium	Structured data	✓	✓	[3]
Grok 3	xAI	Large	Reasoning	✓	✓	[6]
Mistral 7B	Mistral AI	Small	General text	✓	✓	[17]

[a]Experimental file generation only, e.g., via Claude Code feature.

3.2 Evaluated Software

This study evaluates software used in CI systems, divided into two categories: (1) libraries from the Google Fuzzer Test Suite [12] that support multiple CI systems, and (2) IoT firmware components from Firm-AFL [19]. Table 2 lists each program's characteristics and the CI systems they affect.

Table 2. Software and Firmware Evaluated for CI Vulnerabilities

Program	Type	System and Impact	Vulnerability	Fuzzer	Ref.
`libxml2 v2.9.2`	XML library	Industrial controls; data corruption in energy grids	CVE-2015-8317	AFL++	[12]
`openssl 1.0.1f`	SSL/TLS library	Network servers; data exposure in secure networks	CVE-2014-0160	AFL++	[12]
`jsonparser`	JSON parser	Cisco RV130 router; routing disruption in telecom	Not Indexed	AFL++	[4]
`hedwig.cgi`	CGI program	DLink DIR-815 router; command injection, RCE	EDB-ID-24926	Firm-AFL	[19]
`miniupnpd`	UPnP daemon	Trendnet TEW-632BRP router; buffer overflow, DoS	CVE-2013-0230	Firm-AFL	[19]
`httpd`	HTTP server	DLink DAP-2695 router; stack overflow, RCE	CVE-2016-1558	Firm-AFL	[19]

3.3 Prompt Design

We developed prompts to optimize LLM performance for generating fuzzing seeds, following established prompt engineering practices [14]. The process involved iterative refinement through the following steps:

1. **Initial design:** Prompts were created for each program, including its description, format requirements, and instructions to ensure seed diversity.
2. **Quality assessment:** Prompts were evaluated based on:
   - *Syntactic validity:* Whether the fuzzer accepted the seeds.
   - *Structural diversity:* Variation in protocol elements and input structures.
3. **Model-specific adjustments:** Prompts were tailored to account for model-specific behavior. For example, Claude models need explicit instructions for binary structure manipulation, while DeepSeek-V3 requires limits on seed quantity to avoid excessive outputs.
4. **Cross-validation:** Refined prompts were tested across all models to reduce model-specific biases and ensure consistent seed quality.
5. **Standardization:** Final prompts were standardized to enable fair comparisons, with minimal model-specific adjustments preserved.

This process produced prompts that effectively guided LLMs to generate diverse, high-quality fuzzing seeds tailored to CI software. The final prompt (Code 1.1) included: (1) program description and vulnerability details, (2) instructions for generating diverse inputs, including edge cases, and (3) protocol-specific format requirements. Standardization ensured that differences in seed quality reflected model capabilities rather than prompt variations.

Analysis of model outputs revealed distinct seed generation patterns:

- Claude models generated structured seeds targeting known vulnerabilities, aligning closely with specific test cases.
- DeepSeek-V3 produced seeds with high structural diversity, effectively covering complex nested input formats.
- Mistral 7B generated fewer seeds but prioritized quality.
- GPT-4-Turbo consistently followed instructions, producing reliable test cases.

Code 1.1. Example Final Prompt for `miniupnpd`

```
Given the miniupnpd program, a UPnP implementation in the Trendnet
TEW-632BRP router for critical infrastructure, generate a bash script
to create a seeds directory with initial fuzzing inputs. Seeds should
be valid or semi-valid UPnP messages (e.g., SOAP requests) to explore
diverse code paths.

Include the following types of inputs:
1. Well-formed requests that exercise standard functionality
2. Edge cases testing boundary conditions (e.g., extremely long fields
   )
3. Inputs exploring uncommon but valid parameter combinations
4. Messages targeting specific UPnP actions known to be error-prone

The script should create a file for each seed in a seeds/ directory.
```

4 Experimental Framework

This section outlines the environment and methodology for the fuzzing campaigns evaluating LLM-generated seeds in critical infrastructure (CI) software. It covers the computing setup, fuzzing tools, seed generation process, and evaluation metrics, ensuring reproducible experiments [2,9].

4.1 Experimental Setup

Experiments were conducted on a computing cluster with an AMD EPYC 7662 multi-core processor (128 logical CPUs). Each campaign ran in isolated Docker containers to ensure reproducibility. Campaigns had a 24-h timeout and targeted the six programs listed in Table 2.

4.2 Evaluation Procedure

Seven LLMs—ChatGPT-4-Turbo, Claude 3.0 Opus, Claude 3.7 Sonnet, DeepSeek-V3, Gemini 2.0 Flash, Grok 3, and Mistral 7B—were compared against a manual baseline to generate fuzzing seeds for the programs in Table 2. The process involved seed generation, fuzzing campaigns, and metrics analysis to evaluate LLM performance for CI security.

For software libraries (`libxml2`, `openssl`) and the JSON parser (`jsonparser`), we used `AFL++` [11], while IoT firmware components (`hedwig.cgi`, `miniupnpd`, `httpd`) were tested with `Firm-AFL` [19]. Seeds were generated using scripts created by the LLMs based on the standardized prompt in Sect. 3.3. These scripts were executed locally to ensure consistency across models, including those lacking direct file generation support (see Table 1). Manual seeds for `libxml2` and `openssl` came from the Google Fuzzer Test Suite [12], those for `jsonparser` from its reference [4], and those for IoT firmware components from `Firm-AFL`'s default seeds, targetting the vulnerabilities listed in Table 2.

Each program was subjected to 20 24-h fuzzing campaigns per LLM and manual baseline, totaling 160 campaigns per program, to ensure reliable results [9,16]. To account for fuzzing's randomness, we selected the median campaign based on efficiency for each LLM to minimize outlier bias [5].

Evaluation metrics included code coverage, crash detection, efficiency, and consistency, as described below, following established standards [16].

- **Code Coverage:**
  - *Edges Discovered* (`E`): Count of unique control-flow transitions found, correlating with code exploration breadth [5].
  - *Coverage* (`C%`): Edge coverage percentage relative to all edges, calculated as $\frac{\texttt{E}}{\texttt{total\_edges}} \times 100$, enabling normalized comparison [16].
  - *Growth* (`G`): Hourly coverage increase rate, indicating exploration speed, calculated as $\frac{\texttt{C\%}_{\text{final}} - \texttt{C\%}_{\text{initial}}}{\texttt{total\_time}}$, where $\texttt{C\%}_{\text{final}}$ and $\texttt{C\%}_{\text{initial}}$ represent coverage percentages at campaign end and start, respectively.

- **Crash Detection:**
  - *Unique Crashes* (`Cr`): Count of crashes with distinct stack traces, representing potential unique vulnerabilities [16].
  - *Time to First Crash* (T_C): Hours until initial crash detection, critical for time-constrained security assessments [5].
  - *Total Crashes* (`CrTot`): Aggregate crash count including duplicates, indicating fuzzing intensity.
- **Computational Performance:**
  - *Executions per Second* (`X/s`): Program execution frequency.
  - *Efficiency* (`Ef`): Edges discovered per million executions, computed as $\frac{\texttt{E}}{\texttt{total\_executions}} \times 10^6$.
  - *Time to Bug* (`TTB`): Median time (hours) to discover all unique crashes.
- **Consistency:**
  - *Edge Consistency* ($Cons_E$): Coefficient of variation measuring edge discovery reliability across campaigns, calculated as $\frac{\sigma_E}{\mu_E} \times 100$, where σ_E and μ_E represent standard deviation and mean of found edges. Values $< 10\%$ indicate high consistency, 10%–20% acceptable consistency, and $> 20\%$ low consistency.

5 Results

This section presents the evaluations of LLMs for fuzzing seed generation in CI software, addressing two research questions: (RQ1) the performance of LLM-generated seeds compared to manual seeds, and (RQ2) the differences among LLMs. Experiments were conducted on six programs described in Sect. 3.2, with results shown in Figs. 1, 2, 3, 4, 5, 6, 7, 8, 9, 10, 11 and 12 and listed in Tables 3, 4, 5, 6 and 7.

5.1 RQ1: LLM-Generated Seeds vs. Manual Seeds

Code Coverage and Edge Discovery

> **Finding 1:** LLM-generated seeds show comparable or higher exploration of program code paths compared to manual seeds, increasing the potential to detect vulnerabilities.

LLM-driven seeds outperformed manual seeds in code coverage metrics across most evaluated programs. The key improvements are summarized in Table 3.

Table 3. Comparison of LLM vs. Manual Seeds: Code Coverage

PROGRAM	MANUAL SEEDS			LLM SEEDS (MEDIAN)			GAIN (%)		
	E	C%	G	E	C%	G	E	C%	G
`libxml2`	$4.6k \pm 152$	9.18 ± 0.3	0.38	$5.2k \pm 205$	10.54 ± 0.4	0.44	**13.0**	**14.8**	**15.8**
`openssl`	$2.8k \pm 7$	7.65	0.32	$2.8k \pm 118$	7.66 ± 0.5	0.32	0	**0.1**	0
`jsonparser`	76	0.12	0.01	76	0.12	0.01	0	0	0
`hedwig.cgi`	56	0.01	0	60	0.01	0	**7.1**	0	0
`miniupnpd`	49	0.01	0	58	0.01	0	**18.4**	0	0
`httpd`	105	0.01	0	92	0.01	0	-12.4	0	0

For `libxml2`, LLMs achieved a 13.7% increase in edges, 14.8% higher coverage, and a 15.8% faster coverage growth rate. In `openssl`, improvements were minimal, with only 0.1% higher coverage. For IoT firmware components, `hedwig.cgi` showed a 7.1% increase in edges, while `miniupnpd` demonstrated an 18.4% improvement. However, for `httpd`, LLMs showed a 12.4% decrease in edge discovery, representing the only program where manual seeds outperformed LLMs in this metric.

Pattern analysis revealed distinct exploration behaviors across protocols. For data parsers like `libxml2`, LLMs maintained high discovery rates throughout campaigns. In `openssl`, while edge counts were nearly identical, LLMs sustained more consistent exploration. Figures 1 and 2 illustrate these patterns, demonstrating LLMs' ability to explore CI software more thoroughly in most scenarios.

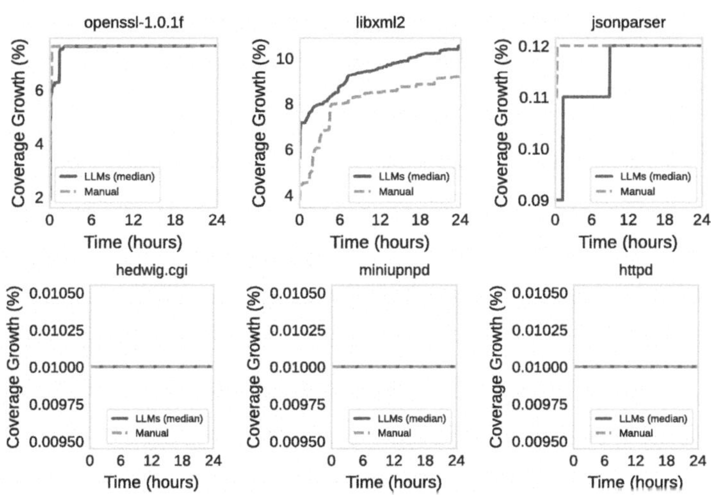

Fig. 1. Coverage Trends for the Evaluated Programs

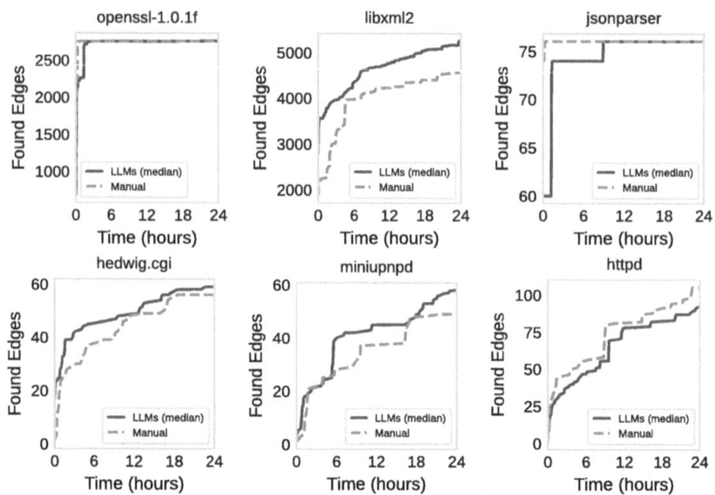

Fig. 2. Edge Discovery Trends for the Evaluated Programs

Vulnerability Detection

> **Finding 2:** LLM-generated seeds increase vulnerability detection rates, enabling faster and more effective security testing.

Our analysis of crash detection metrics revealed substantial improvements when using LLM-generated seeds as presented in Table 4. In `openssl`, unique crashes increased by 56.3% (25 vs. 16), and `jsonparser` showed a 50% increase (9 vs. 6). For `libxml2`, time-to-first-crash dropped from 774 s to 68 s (373.9% improvement), and total crashes rose by 20.5% (53,000 vs. 44,000).

Table 4. Comparison of LLM vs. Manual Seeds: Vulnerability Detection

PROGRAM	MANUAL SEEDS			LLM SEEDS (MEDIAN)			GAIN (%)		
	`Cr`	T_C	`CrTot`	`Cr`	T_C	`CrTot`	`Cr`	T_C	`CrTot`
`libxml2`	67 ± 14	00:12:54	$44k \pm 60k$	84 ± 26	01:01:08	$53k \pm 35k$	**25.4**	**373.9**	**20.5**
`openssl`	16 ± 7	00:00:04	$6k \pm 9k$	25 ± 7	00:00:01	$14k \pm 26k$	**56.3**	−75.0	**133.3**
`jsonparser`	6 ± 1	00:00:00	$43.6M \pm 1.7M$	9 ± 1	00:00:00	$39.4M \pm 1.1M$	**50.0**	0	−9.7
`hedwig.cgi`	0	None	0	0	None	0	0	N/A	0
`miniupnpd`	0	None	0	0	None	0	0	N/A	0
`httpd`	0	None	0	0	None	0	0	N/A	0

No crashes were detected in FIRM-AFL firmware components (`hedwig.cgi`, `miniupnpd`, and `httpd`) within our 24-h window, aligning with the original FIRM-AFL research [19] that reported longer campaigns are typically required. However, edge discovery improvements suggest higher potential for discovering previously unreached vulnerabilities in extended testing. Figure 3 illustrates these crash detection trends, highlighting the accelerated vulnerability identification capabilities of LLM-generated seeds.

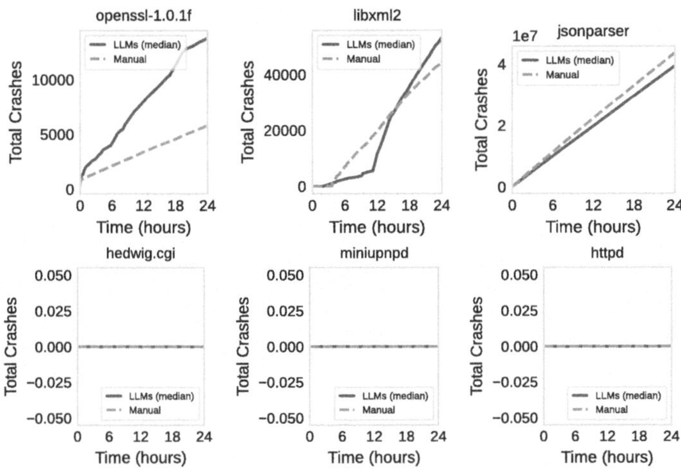

Fig. 3. Crash Detection Curves for the Evaluated Programs

Computational Efficiency

> **Finding 3:** LLM-generated seeds increase fuzzing efficiency, optimizing resource use for CI vulnerability testing.

Our analysis revealed significant improvements in computational efficiency metrics when using LLM-generated seeds compared to manual ones (Table 5).

Table 5. Comparison of LLM vs. Manual Seeds: Computational Efficiency

Program	Manual Seeds			LLM Seeds (Median)			Gain (%)		
	X/s	Ef	TTB	X/s	Ef	TTB	X/s	Ef	TTB
`libxml2`	$5k \pm 471$	10.8 ± 1	4.4 ± 3	$4k \pm 431$	16.9 ± 2	6.6 ± 3	-20.0	**56.5**	**50.0**
`openssl`	$6k \pm 607$	5.7 ± 1	1.0 ± 2	$6k \pm 1k$	7.0 ± 2	2.4 ± 4	0	**22.8**	**140.0**
`jsonparser`	550.9 ± 20.9	1.6 ± 0.1	0	484.3 ± 12.5	1.8 ± 0.0	0	-12.1	**12.5**	0
`hedwig.cgi`	2.6 ± 3.7	252.1 ± 210.8	None	2.5 ± 3.3	$331.9 \pm 19k$	None	-3.8	**31.7**	N/A
`miniupnpd`	1.8 ± 2.4	216.8 ± 115.1	None	2.8 ± 4.2	303.8 ± 147.7	None	**55.6**	**40.1**	N/A
`httpd`	0.5 ± 0.2	1494.1 ± 892.3	None	2.1 ± 1.9	1041.8 ± 298.1	None	**320.0**	-30.3	N/A

The efficiency improvements persist even when absolute code coverage gains are minimal. For example, `openssl` shows nearly identical coverage between LLM and manual seeds, yet efficiency is 22.8% higher with LLM seeds. This suggests LLM-generated seeds focus on exploring more valuable program paths in a structured manner, rather than exhaustively testing easily reached code segments.

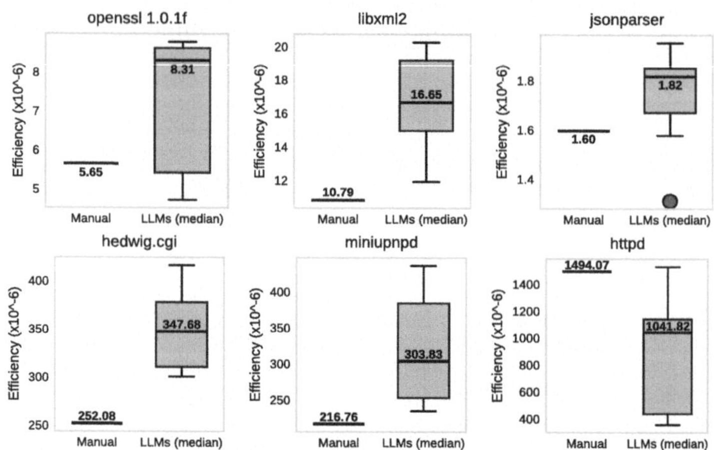

Fig. 4. Efficiency Boxplots for the Evaluated Programs

For resource-constrained environments, including operational technology settings with limited computing resources, these efficiency gains translate to more effective security testing within fixed computational budgets. This is particularly valuable in contexts where testing resources are limited and where operations often cannot be interrupted for extended periods.

Across different program types, LLM seeds consistently achieve 30–55% more exploration per computation unit (except for `httpd`). This pattern holds regardless of the specific infrastructure domain, suggesting the broad applicability of our approach. Figure 4 illustrates these efficiency improvements.

Variability and Reproducibility

> **Finding 4:** LLM-generated seeds show higher variability than manual seeds, enhancing exploration at the expense of reproducibility.

LLM seeds exhibit consistently greater variability in edge discovery than manual seeds across all tested programs, as shown in Table 6. For `openssl`, edge consistency ($Cons_E$) is 6.04% for LLMs versus 0.25% for manual seeds, a 24-fold increase in variability. This pattern persists in `hedwig.cgi` (30.11% vs. 21.66%, 39.0% higher), `miniupnpd` (42.73% vs. 29.34%, 45.6% higher) and `libxml2`, showing increased variability of 27.0% in LLM campaigns.

Table 6. Comparison of LLM vs. Manual Seeds: Consistency

PROGRAM	MANUAL SEEDS	LLM SEEDS (MEDIAN)	GAIN (%)
	$Cons_E$ (%)	$Cons_E$ (%)	
libxml2	3.33	4.23	27.0
openssl	0.25	6.04	2316.0
jsonparser	0	1.30	∞
hedwig.cgi	21.66	30.11	39.0
miniupnpd	29.34	42.73	45.6
httpd	21.55	26.69	23.9

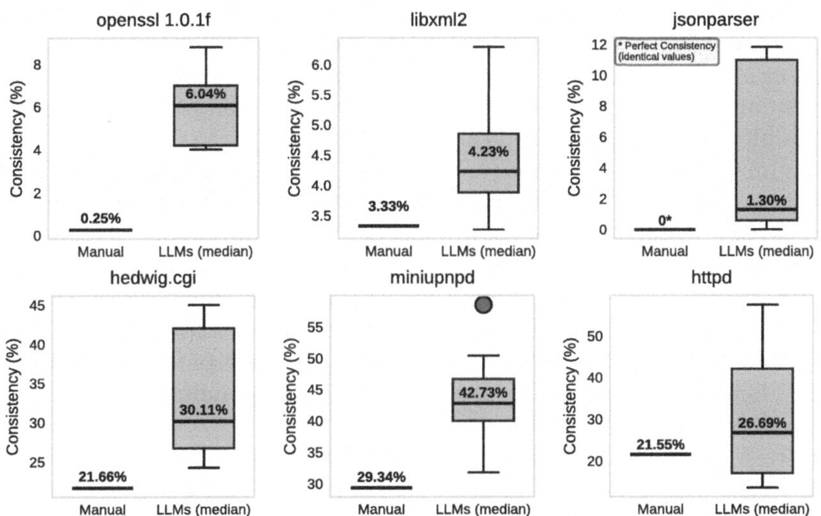

Fig. 5. Consistency Boxplots for the Evaluated Programs

Statistical analysis reveals this is not random noise but structured variation driven by the inherent probabilistic nature of LLM-generated seeds, which incorporate slight structural differences that guide the fuzzer toward different program regions. Security validation processes in CI often require deterministic test results for certification and compliance, which high-variability seeds complicate. Figure 5 illustrates these consistency differences, highlighting a trade-off between exploration breadth and reproducibility.

These results suggest LLMs are highly effective for initial exploratory testing phases but may require complementary approaches. Hybrid methodologies that combine probabilistic LLM seeds for discovery with deterministic manual seeds for verification could maximize benefits while addressing reproducibility requirements.

5.2 RQ2: Comparative Performance of LLMs in CI Fuzzing

Model Specialization and Training Effects

> **Finding 5:** LLMs exhibit domain-specific performance driven by their training focus rather than model size, with different models excelling in distinct protocols and demonstrating efficiency across CI applications.

Different LLMs excel in specific programs based on their training data content. In `libxml2`, DeepSeek-V3 achieves 10.67% coverage and 85 crashes, likely due to its training on structured data formats. For `miniupnpd`, Gemini 2.0 Flash leads with 66 edges and 401.9 edges per million executions, showing strength in protocol formats. Mistral 7B performs well in `openssl` (36 unique crashes) and `hedwig.cgi` (398.7 edges per million executions) despite its smaller size, indicating training data relevance outweighs model scale for protocol-based tasks. These results are summarized in Table 7.

Examining Table 7, we observe significant variation in consistency metrics ($Cons_E$) across models and programs—from DeepSeek-V3's perfect consistency in `jsonparser` to high variability in `hedwig.cgi`. Additionally, certain models demonstrate an inverse relationship between execution speed and edge discovery: GPT-4-Turbo executes `libxml2` faster (5k/s) but finds fewer edges than DeepSeek-V3 (3k/s), suggesting some models prioritize exploration depth over speed, valuable for complex CI protocols. The efficiency patterns across infrastructure domains indicate that model training focus influences vulnerability detection more than architecture size.

The case of `httpd` reveals a critical limitation in LLM application, where manual seeds outperformed LLM-generated ones with 12.4% higher edge discovery (105 vs. 92) and 30.3 better efficiency (1494.1 vs. 1041.8). This exception highlights that domain-specific knowledge encoded in manual seeds can surpass generalized AI approaches for specialized components with complex behaviors.

Figures 6 and 7 illustrate these model-specific strengths, suggesting that CI security assessments should carefully evaluate each component to determine the most appropriate seed generation approach.

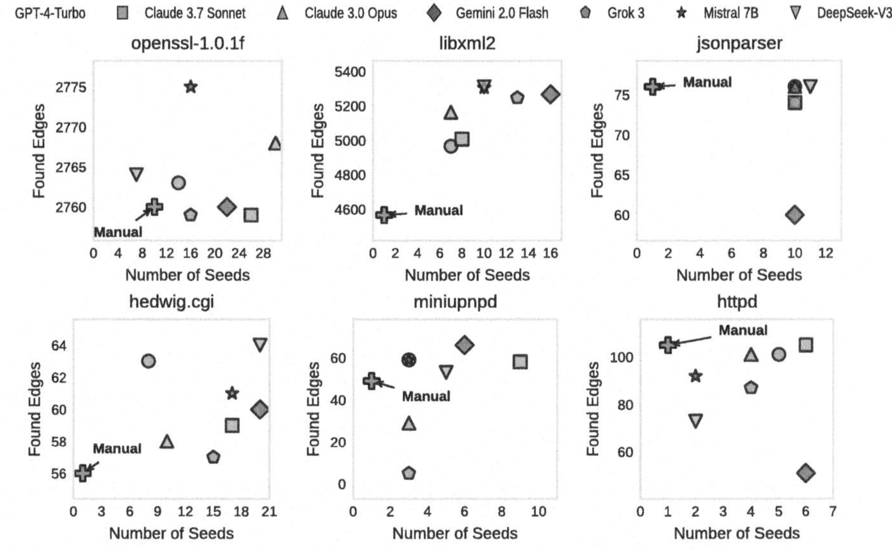

Fig. 6. Seed-to-edge Relationships for the Evaluated Programs

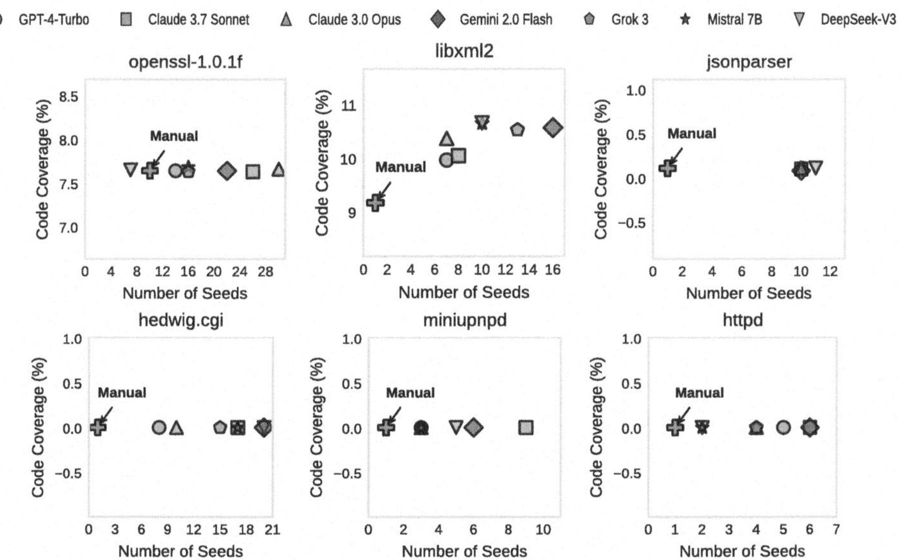

Fig. 7. Coverage Trends for the Evaluated Programs

Table 7. Performance Results by LLM Model Across All Programs

Program	Model	Code Coverage		Fault Detection		Comp. Performance		$Cons_E$ (%)
		E	C%	Cr	T_C	X/s	Ef	
libxml2	Claude 3.0	$5.2k \pm 232$	10.38 ± 0.5	84 ± 30	**00:00:00**	$4k \pm 327$	14 ± 2	4.58
	Claude 3.7	$5.0k \pm 253$	10.06 ± 0.5	55 ± 30	01:59:43	$4k \pm 360$	16 ± 1	5.11
	DeepSeek-V3	**5.3k ± 318**	**10.67 ± 0.6**	85 ± 32	02:03:06	$3k \pm 394$	**20 ± 3**	6.29
	Gemini 2.0	$5.3k \pm 172$	10.58 ± 0.3	100 ± 33	00:01:26	$4k \pm 431$	17 ± 2	**3.26**
	GPT-4-Turbo	$5.0k \pm 219$	9.98 ± 0.4	**105 ± 26**	01:01:08	**5k ± 576**	12 ± 2	4.23
	Grok 3	$5.2k \pm 204$	10.54 ± 0.4	77 ± 16	00:00:04	$3k \pm 337$	19 ± 2	4.04
	Mistral 7B	$5.3k \pm 190$	10.66 ± 0.4	72 ± 25	02:14:06	$3k \pm 513$	20 ± 4	3.71
	Manual	$4.6k \pm 152$	9.18 ± 0.3	67 ± 14	00:12:54	$5k \pm 471$	10.8 ± 1	3.33
openssl	Claude 3.0	$2.8k \pm 109$	7.67 ± 0.3	27 ± 8	00:00:01	$4k \pm 2k$	**9 ± 3**	**4.00**
	Claude 3.7	$2.8k \pm 232$	7.64 ± 0.6	8 ± 7	**00:00:00**	$4k \pm 1k$	8 ± 3	8.78
	DeepSeek-V3	$2.8k \pm 118$	7.66 ± 0.3	25 ± 8	00:00:01	**7k ± 757**	5 ± 1	4.35
	Gemini 2.0	$2.8k \pm 163$	7.65 ± 0.5	8 ± 6	00:00:04	$4k \pm 2k$	9 ± 2	6.04
	GPT-4-Turbo	$2.8k \pm 110$	7.65 ± 0.3	15 ± 7	**00:00:00**	$4k \pm 1k$	9 ± 2	4.03
	Grok 3	$2.8k \pm 200$	7.64 ± 0.6	14 ± 6	**00:00:00**	$6k \pm 1k$	5 ± 2	7.53
	Mistral 7B	$2.8k \pm 174$	**7.69 ± 0.5**	**36 ± 10**	00:00:04	$6k \pm 560$	6 ± 1	6.44
	Manual	$2.8k \pm 7$	7.65	16 ± 7	00:00:04	$6k \pm 607$	5.7 ± 1	0.25
jsonparser	Claude 3.0	76 ± 7	**0.12**	**10 ± 2**	00:00:00	470.0 ± 9.6	1.9 ± 0.2	10.50
	Claude 3.7	74	0.11	9 ± 1	00:00:00	485.9 ± 13.1	1.8 ± 0.1	1.18
	DeepSeek-V3	**76**	**0.12**	**10 ± 1**	00:00:00	**557.5 ± 18.6**	1.6 ± 0.1	**0**
	Gemini 2.0	60 ± 8	0.09	8 ± 1	00:00:00	529.8 ± 19.4	1.3 ± 0.2	11.83
	GPT-4-Turbo	**76**	**0.12**	**10**	00:00:00	450.2 ± 7.8	**2.0**	**0**
	Grok 3	74 ± 7	0.11	8 ± 1	00:00:00	468.3 ± 11.4	1.8 ± 0.2	11.48
	Mistral 7B	**76**	**0.12**	9 ± 1	00:00:00	484.3 ± 12.5	1.8	1.30
	Manual	76	0.12	6 ± 1	00:00:00	550.9 ± 20.9	1.6 ± 0.1	0
hedwig.cgi	Claude 3.0	58	0.01	0	None	2.5 ± 1.4	$300.8 \pm 6k$	24.63
	Claude 3.7	59	0.01	0	None	2.2 ± 2.1	**416.4 ± 21k**	**24.24**
	DeepSeek-V3	**64**	0.01	0	None	2.6 ± 4.4	$357.4 \pm 19k$	44.02
	Gemini 2.0	60	0.01	0	None	2.1 ± 7.2	$347.7 \pm 26k$	28.76
	GPT-4-Turbo	63	0.01	0	None	4.3 ± 3.3	$305.5 \pm 12k$	44.97
	Grok 3	57	0.01	0	None	**6.2 ± 4.8**	$316.2 \pm 28k$	30.11
	Mistral 7B	61	0.01	0	None	1.7 ± 4.0	$398.7 \pm 19k$	39.92
	Manual	56	0.01	0	None	2.6 ± 3.7	252.1 ± 210.8	21.66
miniupnpd	Claude 3.0	29	0.01	0	None	1.6 ± 1.4	234.8 ± 721.5	42.73
	Claude 3.7	58	0.01	0	None	**6.7 ± 2.6**	**436.1 ± 418.5**	50.30
	DeepSeek-V3	53	0.01	0	None	2.8 ± 7.9	303.8 ± 75.5	38.12
	Gemini 2.0	**66**	0.01	0	None	2.2 ± 7.1	401.9 ± 129.5	**31.76**
	GPT-4-Turbo	59	0.01	0	None	4.2 ± 4.2	366.7 ± 147.7	58.49
	Grok 3	5	0.01	0	None	0.0 ± 4.2	251.8 ± 161.5	42.82
	Mistral 7B	59	0.01	0	None	4.6 ± 2.5	254.2 ± 104.3	41.84
	Manual	49	0.01	0	None	1.8 ± 2.4	216.8 ± 115.1	29.34
httpd	Claude 3.0	101	0.01	0	None	2.4 ± 1.1	1082.6 ± 435.2	**13.60**
	Claude 3.7	**105**	0.01	0	None	2.1 ± 1.9	444.7 ± 91.5	40.82
	DeepSeek-V3	73	0.01	0	None	0.5 ± 1.0	356.5 ± 92.2	43.16
	Gemini 2.0	51	0.01	0	None	7.6 ± 5.7	429.9 ± 91.4	57.49
	GPT-4-Turbo	101	0.01	0	None	0.0 ± 1.3	1202.3 ± 505.2	26.69
	Grok 3	87	0.01	0	None	0.1 ± 2.9	**1528.5 ± 489.6**	16.96
	Mistral 7B	92	0.01	0	None	**13.6 ± 6.0**	1041.8 ± 298.1	17.12
	Manual	105	0.01	0	None	0.5 ± 0.2	1494.1 ± 892.3	21.55

Temporal Performance and Seed Quality Patterns

> **Finding 6:** LLMs show distinct temporal performance and seed generation patterns, affecting their suitability for different vulnerability detection timeframes.

Temporal analysis identifies three performance patterns among the LLMs. Claude models achieve rapid initial edge discovery but plateau (e.g., `miniupnpd`), where Claude 3.7 Sonnet discovers 58 edges early but shows limited sustained progress. DeepSeek-V3 maintains steady discovery over time, exploring state spaces without early convergence. GPT-4-Turbo and Grok 3 exhibit hybrid patterns, balancing early and sustained discovery, though Grok 3 struggles with the UPnP protocol in `miniupnpd` (only 5 edges). These patterns are consistent across programs despite varying domains.

Seed content analysis reveals distinct generation strategies. DeepSeek-V3 produces fewer seeds (average: 8.4) with high structural diversity, while ChatGPT-4-Turbo generates more seeds (average: 22.7) with systematic protocol variations. This results in different crash-to-seed ratios (DeepSeek-V3: 4.2 crashes/seed, ChatGPT-4-Turbo: 1.7 crashes/seed), reflecting a quality-versus-quantity trade-off. Seed similarity analysis indicates higher inter-model diversity than intra-model diversity, suggesting that different LLMs explore unique space regions. These patterns, shown in Figs. 8, 9, and 10, suggest that combining LLMs could enhance fuzzing coverage, improving vulnerability detection in CI systems.

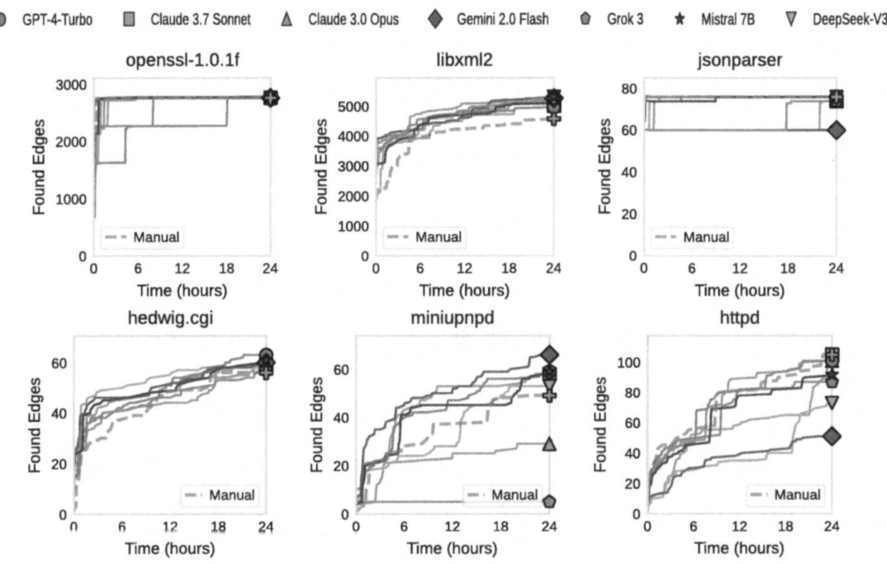

Fig. 8. Edge Discovery Trends for the Evaluated Programs

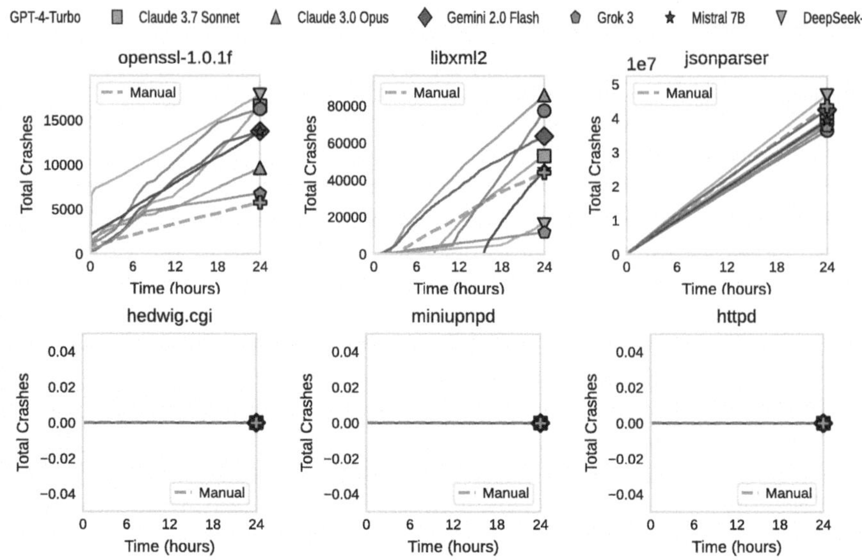

Fig. 9. Crash Detection Trends for the Evaluated Programs.

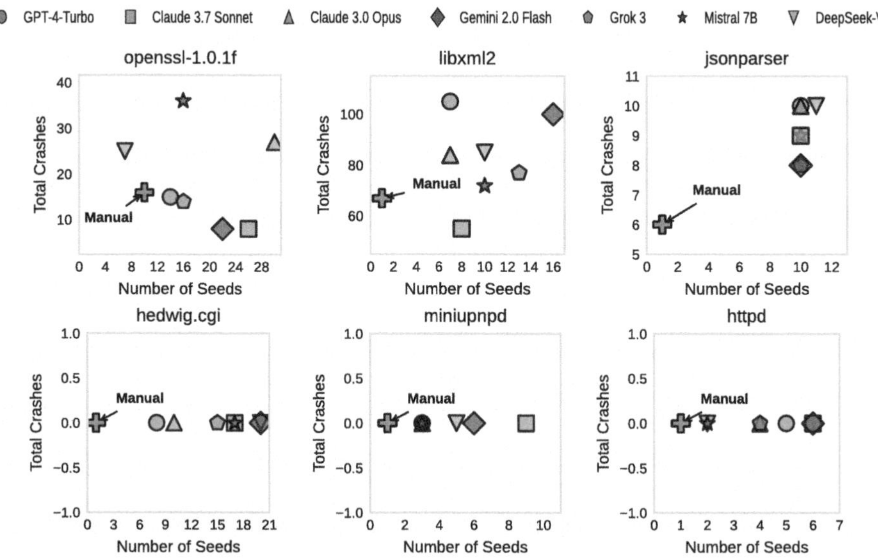

Fig. 10. Seed-to-crash Relationships for the Evaluated Programs

Resource Optimization and Practical Implications

> **Finding 7:** Smaller LLMs can achieve comparable efficiency to larger models in certain CI tasks, suggesting they are viable options in resource-constrained environments.

Efficiency analysis reveals interesting relationships between model size and fuzzing performance. While larger models generally achieve higher absolute discovery rates, efficiency metrics show varying returns based on parameter thresholds. ChatGPT-4-Turbo and DeepSeek-V3 achieve high throughput in `jsonparser` (450.2 and 557.5 executions/s, respectively), but Mistral 7B demonstrates comparable efficiency despite its significantly smaller size. Observation of response patterns suggests a potential relationship between generation time and seed quality in several models, raising interesting questions about computational efficiency in security applications.

Analysis of performance curves shows changes in marginal discovery rates after extended fuzzing periods, suggesting potential inflection points in testing efficiency. This pattern, observed across multiple models and programs, suggests considerations for resource allocation in software security testing. The consistency analysis further informs these decisions, with varying degrees of reproducibility across models as shown in Fig. 11.

These findings, illustrated in Fig. 12, indicate that optimal fuzzing performance may be achieved through strategic model selection and resource allocation based on specific infrastructure security requirements and constraints.

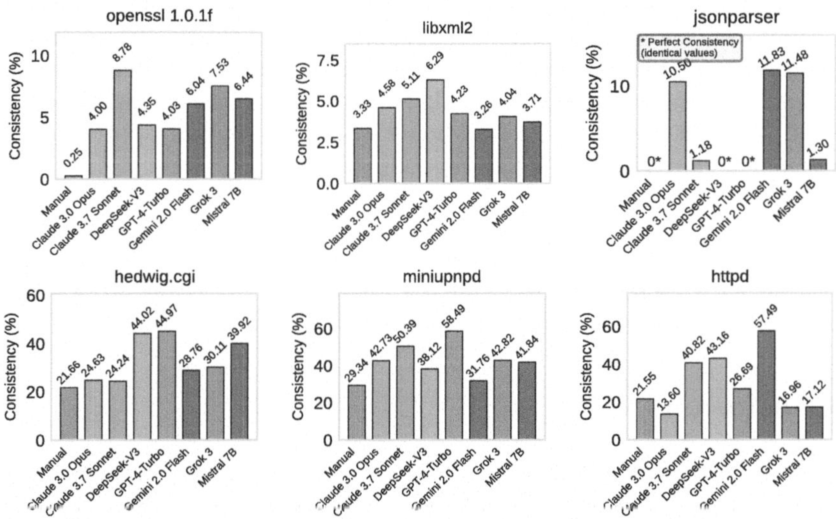

Fig. 11. Consistency Bar Charts for the Evaluated Programs

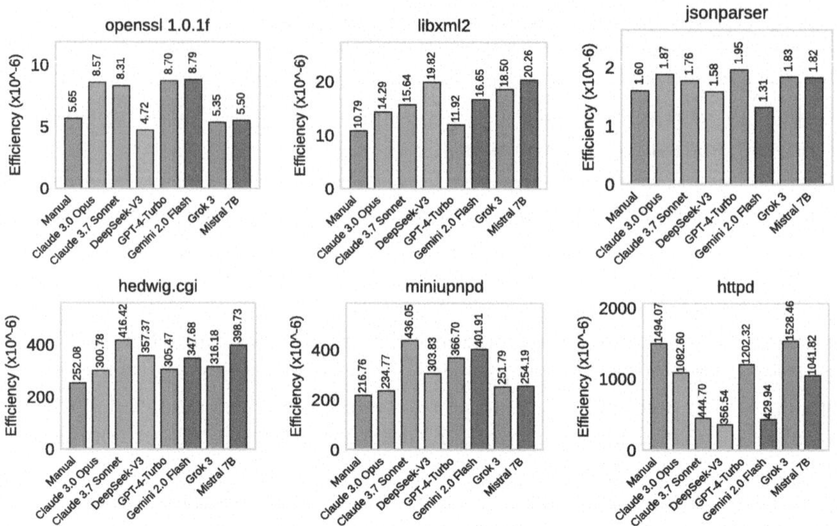

Fig. 12. Efficiency Bar Charts for the Evaluated Programs

6 Limitations and Future Work

This study has several limitations affecting its generalizability. First, evaluating only six programs does not fully represent CI system diversity. Second, despite prompt refinement, design variations still impact LLM performance.

The `httpd` results emphasize an important constraint: not all CI software components benefit equally from LLM-generated seeds. Programs with highly domain-specific protocols may require specialized knowledge that current LLMs lack. Future work should investigate characteristics that make programs amenable to LLM-based seed generation and develop hybrid approaches combining manual expertise with LLM capabilities.

Future research should pursue three directions: (1) model scaling analysis to examine how LLM size affects fuzzing performance, (2) hybrid approaches integrating LLMs with symbolic execution or grammar-based techniques to combine exploration with reproducibility, and (3) fine-tuning LLMs on proprietary CI protocols to improve performance in specialized contexts.

7 Conclusion

This study demonstrates that LLMs improve fuzzing seed generation for CI security. In five of six tested programs, LLM-generated seeds outperformed manual approaches, improving code coverage by up to 18.4% and accelerating crash detection by 373.9%. Different models show specialized strengths: DeepSeek-V3 excels in structured data parsing, Claude models in rapid crash detection, and ChatGPT-4-Turbo in consistent cross-domain performance.

While our 24-h testing window did not yield crashes in FIRM-AFL firmware components, the significant edge coverage improvements suggest strong potential for detecting previously unreached vulnerabilities in extended campaigns, particularly valuable for CI firmware. These findings support integrating LLM-based seed generation into CI security pipelines. The substantial efficiency gains justify adoption even in resource-constrained environments. Future work addressing identified limitations will enhance the practical utility of LLM-powered fuzzing for protecting CI systems.

Acknowledgments. CRITIC Project Grant PLEC2024-011222 funded by AEI/10.13039/501100011033, FEDER and UE. Mikel Iturbe is partially supported by the Basque Government, Spain (grant number IT1676-22).

Disclosure of Interests. The authors have no competing interests to declare.

References

1. Bae, J., Kwon, S., Myeong, S.: Enhancing software code vulnerability detection using GPT-4o and Claude-3.5 Sonnet: a study on prompt engineering techniques. Electronics **13**(13) (2024). https://doi.org/10.3390/electronics13132657
2. Barredo, J., et al.: GAFLERNA Ahoy! Integrating EM side-channel analysis into traditional fuzzing workflows. In: Proceedings of the 33rd ACM International Conference on the Foundations of Software Engineering, pp. 550–554. Association for Computing Machinery (2025). https://doi.org/10.1145/3696630.3728497
3. Black, G., Vaidyan, V.M., Comert, G.: Evaluating large language models for enhanced fuzzing: an analysis framework for LLM-driven seed generation. IEEE Access **12**, 156065–156081 (2024). https://doi.org/10.1109/ACCESS.2024.3484947
4. Blog, A.: Fuzzing IoT devices (2022). https://blog.attify.com/fuzzing-iot-devices-part-1/
5. Böhme, M., Pham, V.T., Nguyen, M.D., Roychoudhury, A.: Directed greybox fuzzing. In: Proceedings of the 2017 ACM SIGSAC Conference on Computer and Communications Security, pp. 2329–2344 (2017)
6. Chong, Z.K., Ohsaki, H., Ng, B.: LLM-net: democratizing LLMs-as-a-service through blockchain-based expert networks (2025)
7. DeepSeek-AI: DeepSeek-V3 Technical Report (2024)
8. Duarte, F.: Number of ChatGPT Users (2025). Accessed 13 Feb 2025
9. Eceiza, M.: Novel approaches for IoT and embedded device fuzzing and its evaluation. Ph.D. thesis, Mondragon Unibertsitatea (2022)
10. Eom, J., Jeong, S., Kwon, T.: Fuzzing JavaScript interpreters with coverage-guided reinforcement learning for LLM-based mutation, pp. 1656–1668 (2024). https://doi.org/10.1145/3650212.3680389
11. Fioraldi, A., Maier, D., Eißfeldt, H., Heuse, M.: AFL++: combining incremental steps of fuzzing research. In: 14th USENIX Workshop on Offensive Technologies (WOOT 2020) (2020)
12. Google: Fuzzer-test-suite (2018). https://github.com/google/fuzzer-test-suite
13. Guan, H., Bai, G., Liu, Y.: Large language models can connect the dots: exploring model optimization bugs with domain knowledge-aware prompts, pp. 1579–1591 (2024). https://doi.org/10.1145/3650212.3680383

14. Jha, S., Jha, S.K., Lincoln, P., Bastian, N.D., Velasquez, A., Neema, S.: Dehallucinating large language models using formal methods guided iterative prompting. In: 2023 IEEE International Conference on Assured Autonomy, pp. 149–152 (2023)
15. Jiang, Z., Wen, M., Cao, J., Shi, X., Jin, H.: Towards understanding the effectiveness of large language models on directed test input generation, pp. 1408–1420 (2024). https://doi.org/10.1145/3691620.3695513
16. Klees, G., Ruef, A., Cooper, B., Wei, S., Hicks, M.: Evaluating fuzz testing. In: Proceedings of the 2018 ACM SIGSAC Conference on Computer and Communications Security, pp. 2123–2138 (2018)
17. Samo, H., Ali, K., Memon, M., Abbasi, F.A., Koondhar, M.Y., Dahri, K.: Fine-tuning mistral 7b large language model for python query response and code generation: a parameter efficient approach. VAWKUM Trans. Comput. Sci. **12**(1), 205–217 (2024). https://doi.org/10.21015/vtcs.v12i1.1885
18. Schneier, B.: Click Here to Kill Everybody: Security and Survival in a Hyper-connected World. WW Norton & Company (2018)
19. Zheng, Y., Davanian, A., Yin, H., Song, C., Zhu, H., Sun, L.: FIRM-AFL: high-throughput Greybox Fuzzing of IoT Firmware via augmented process emulation. In: 28th USENIX Security Symposium (USENIX Security 2019), Santa Clara, CA, pp. 1099–1114. USENIX Association (2019). https://www.usenix.org/conference/usenixsecurity19/presentation/zheng
20. Siddiqui, F., Hagan, M., Sezer, S.: Establishing cyber resilience in embedded systems for securing next-generation critical infrastructure. In: 2019 32nd IEEE International System-on-Chip Conference (SOCC), pp. 218–223 (2019). https://doi.org/10.1109/SOCC46988.2019.1570548325
21. Wang, D., Zhou, G., Chen, L., Li, D., Miao, Y.: ProphetFuzz: fully automated prediction and fuzzing of high-risk option combinations with only documentation via large language model, pp. 735–749 (2024). https://doi.org/10.1145/3658644.3690231
22. Wu, F., et al.: Exploring the Limits of ChatGPT in Software Security Applications (2023)
23. Xia, C.S., Paltenghi, M., Tian, J.L., Pradel, M., Zhang, L.: Fuzz4ALL: universal fuzzing with large language models, pp. 1547–1559 (2024). https://doi.org/10.1145/3597503.3639121
24. Yang, C., et al.: WhiteFox: white-box compiler fuzzing empowered by large language models. Proc. ACM Program. Lang. **8** (2024). https://doi.org/10.1145/3689736
25. Zhang, C., et al.: How effective are they? Exploring large language model based fuzz driver generation, pp. 1223–1235 (2024). https://doi.org/10.1145/3650212.3680355
26. Zhang, J., et al.: When LLMs meet cybersecurity: a systematic literature review. Cybersecurity **8** (2025). https://doi.org/10.1186/s42400-025-00361-w
27. Zhou, Z., Yang, Y., Wu, S., Huang, Y., Chen, B., Peng, X.: Magneto: a step-wise approach to exploit vulnerabilities in dependent libraries via LLM-empowered directed fuzzing, pp. 1633–1644 (2024). https://doi.org/10.1145/3691620.3695531

A Multi-dimensional Cyber Range-Powered Scoring Framework for Evaluating Cyber Resilience of Critical Infrastructures

Savvas Theodoulou, Eliana Stavrou(✉), Adamantini Peratikou, and Stavros Stavrou

Faculty of Pure and Applied Sciences, Open University of Cyprus, Nicosia, Cyprus
{savvas.theodoulou1,eliana.stavrou,adamantini.peratikou, stavros.stavrou}@ouc.ac.cy

Abstract. As cyber threats targeting critical infrastructures grow in complexity and societal impact, the focus of cybersecurity must shift from mere protection to sustained resilience. This paper proposes a conceptual multi-dimensional scoring framework to be utilized by cyber ranges to assess and quantify the cyber resilience of critical infrastructure organizations. The framework is built upon seven interrelated cyber resilience dimensions across the technical, operational, and human spectrum. For each dimension, initial performance indicators are proposed to standardize the evaluation process and enable organizations to benchmark their cyber resilience, identify skill and coordination gaps, and align cybersecurity training with real-world mission continuity requirements. The proposed multi-dimensional approach provides a structured performance evaluation that is aligned with NIS2 regulation requirements, supporting compliance readiness and enabling tailored workforce development interventions. This contribution aims to enhance organizations' preparedness in safeguarding essential services under adverse conditions.

Keywords: Cyber Resilience · Critical Infrastructures · Cyber Ranges · Scoring · Cybersecurity · Skills Assessment · Compliance · Business Continuity

1 Introduction

In recent years, the increasing frequency, scale, and sophistication of cyber threats targeting critical infrastructures (CI) has emphasized the limitations of traditional cybersecurity approaches focused solely on protection. High-profile incidents impacting sectors such as energy, healthcare, maritime, and telecommunications have demonstrated that even highly secured systems can and will be compromised [1]. We are no longer in an era where mere protection through traditional perimeter defences is sufficient. The focus must shift from simply preventing breaches to building robust cyber resilience. According to the National Institute of Standards and Technology (NIST), cyber resilience is defined as "the ability to anticipate, withstand, recover from, and adapt to adverse conditions, stresses, attacks, or compromises on systems that use or are enabled by cyber

E. Bergström et al. (Eds.): CRITIS 2025, LNCS 16291, pp. 347–366, 2026.
https://doi.org/10.1007/978-3-032-19540-1_18

resources" [2], emphasizing the critical importance of sustaining an organization's core mission and service delivery even in the face of disruption.

Developing and sustaining cyber resilience is not merely a technical challenge; it is a human and organizational imperative [3]. The dynamic nature of the cyber threat landscape demands continuous skills development to cultivate capable professionals who can effectively navigate the complexities of modern cyber threat landscape. In the context of cyber resilience, it is crucial to foster competencies that enable teams to be prepared, anticipate emerging threats, respond decisively to unfolding incidents, and recover swiftly to maintain mission-critical operations. This involves not only technical proficiency but also business acumen, critical thinking, effective communication, and strategic decision-making under immense pressure [4, 5]. Cultivating such competencies is essential in high-stakes environments [6], where any disruption may lead to cascading consequences across economic, environmental, and public safety domains [7].

Cyber ranges have emerged as indispensable tools in this pursuit, offering safe, realistic, and dynamic environments for training cybersecurity professionals and enhancing preparedness [8]. These simulated platforms allow organizations to "learn by doing," providing hands-on experience with real-world attack scenarios without risking live critical systems. However, a significant gap persists in how these powerful tools are currently leveraged. Cyber ranges are largely utilized for Capture the Flag (CTF) exercises [9] focusing on individual skill challenges or for red versus blue team performance assessments which primarily emphasize assessment of isolated technical metrics (e.g., time to detection). This narrow focus fails to adequately capture the multi-faceted nature of cyber resilience. For regulated CI sectors, where performance is closely tied to public service obligations, regulatory compliance, and societal trust, there is a pressing need for a more holistic, measurable, and sector-sensitive approach to evaluating and improving cyber resilience. Thus, the complex interplay between human factors, technical systems, mission-centric objectives, and broader societal impacts need to be considered when assessing cyber resilience capabilities.

There is currently a notable lack of a holistic, measurable, and sector-driven approach to evaluating the cyber resilience level of CIs using cyber ranges. This paper addresses this critical gap by proposing a multi-dimensional scoring framework specifically designed to evaluate the cyber resilience level of CIs through cyber ranges. Section 2 reviews existing cyber range use cases and scoring approaches. Section 3 discusses the methodology utilised in this work and Sect. 4 details the proposed scoring framework. Section 5 reflects upon the conceptual proposed model, critically discusses implications for academia, industry and policy makers, identifies the limitations of this work and outlines future research directions for the proposed approach. Finally, Sect. 6 provides concluding remarks.

2 Related Work

2.1 Cyber Range Use Cases

Cyber range exercises represent a crucial element in contemporary cybersecurity education, training, and research, providing realistic, hands-on environments for participants to develop and hone their skills in defending against evolving cyber threats. For example, they allow professionals to evaluate the security posture of systems and networks, identifying and mitigating vulnerabilities before exploitation occurs [10]. These environments support both offensive and defensive skill development and serve as testbeds for operational readiness. Training programs increasingly leverage cyber ranges to deliver domain-specific knowledge tailored to industry needs [11]. These programs aim to equip the workforce with the practical and cognitive tools necessary to address evolving digital threats [12].

Cyber ranges are often paired with serious games and gamification-based learning models [13]. In [14], that concept was demonstrated through the design of a serious 3D game embedded in a cyber range, effectively combining immersive gamification with realistic cybersecurity scenarios. Moreover, authors in [15] illustrated how game mechanics can enhance both engagement and conceptual understanding, while the work performed in [16] showed how cyber-defense exercises reinforce team collaboration and problem-solving skills in undergraduate programs. Similarly, [17] introduced a model-driven approach for training that aligns exercises with cybersecurity assurance goals, ensuring strategic value in simulation design. This space was further expanded in [18], by integrating visual analytics into training, enabling instructors to assess learner behavior and identify pain points. Learning analytics are increasingly used to personalize training paths and improve curriculum design through data insights.

Beyond technical skills, cybersecurity awareness and education programs also focus on foundational concepts for non-expert users. These range from teaching basic cyber hygiene and phishing awareness to reinforcing software update practices and device safety protocols [12]. Programs that blend theoretical learning with simulated attacks and defenses provide comprehensive exposure, often augmenting classroom-based learning with real-time simulations [9, 19, 20].

To effectively leverage the capabilities of cyber ranges, it is essential to have access to multi-domain exercises, potentially integrating various infrastructures like ICT, naval, electrical grids, and telecommunications [20]. The design of such exercises needs to prioritize realism to provide valuable training experiences for cyber units, incorporating elements like realistic environments, adversaries, communications, tactics, and roles [21]. Given the intricate nature and substantial resource demands associated with multi-domain cyber ranges, collaborative partnerships and federated arrangements among diverse organizations are not merely beneficial but often indispensable for their successful implementation and widespread adoption [22].

2.2 Cyber Range Scoring Models

A fundamental aspect of cyber range exercises is the scoring mechanism, which serves to evaluate participant performance, provide feedback, and foster a competitive spirit that drives continuous improvement [9]. Effective scoring systems are transparent, fair, and aligned with the exercise's objectives. However, designing such systems is challenging, and different approaches have been proposed. One approach to performance evaluation involves the use of scoring systems that assess various aspects of a trainee's actions during an exercise [8] These scoring systems often consider factors such as the time taken to complete a task, the accuracy of the solution, and the efficiency of the approach used. The work performed in [8] introduces a dynamic Situational Awareness (SA) Scoring System designed to address this gap. Authors emphasize that SA assessment should account for the complexity and variability of simulated environments. Instead of solely focusing on overall performance, their approach focuses on extracting information from perception and comprehension.

Diakoumakos et al. [23] introduced a gamified, CR-agnostic scoring model designed for use across standalone and federated cyber ranges. The system evaluates user performance based on task difficulty, completion time, hints used, and steps taken, assigning normalized scores through weighted metrics. It supports various exercise types (CTFs, Red/Blue teaming, operational drills) and integrates via standardized messages (e.g., JSON), offering scalability, fairness, and adaptability across training setups.

Andreolini et al. [4] propose a novel scoring framework that uses graph operations to evaluate trainee performance. This approach models trainee activities as directed graphs, allowing for the assessment of speed and precision. Their algorithm can identify inefficiencies such as repeated trial and error or getting stuck in "rabbit holes". The graphs can also recognize users who follow intended paths, find all intended paths, or discover unintended paths. This method enables instructors to understand how a user is performing, not just whether they are succeeding.

Cautions against over-emphasizing scores are highlighted in [24], as it can lead to participants engaging in "evasive tactics" that prioritize score gains over genuine learning. They observed that participants might exploit weaknesses in the scoring system or adopt unrealistic strategies to maximize their scores. For example, in an availability-focused exercise, a blue team might shut down their systems to prevent red team attacks, even though this isn't a realistic response in a real-world scenario. This highlights the importance of designing scoring systems that incentivize realistic and effective behavior, rather than simply rewarding point accumulation [24].

3 Methodology

This study adopts a Design Science Research (DSR) methodology, which is commonly applied in cybersecurity and information systems research [25, 26] for developing innovative artefacts that address complex, real-world problems. The methodology further integrates principles of scenario-based cyber range simulation, performance-based assessment, and multi-dimensional scoring, enabling a comprehensive evaluation of resilience across technical, human, and organizational layers. The aim of this study is to conceptualize a cyber resilience scoring framework powered by cyber range simulations, addressing the problem of measuring resilience in CIs in a standardized, structured, and multi-dimensional way.

Consistent with the DSR paradigm, this research focuses on the initial stages of artefact development, including problem identification, objective definition, and design conceptualization. Initially, the design process was guided by a rigorous examination of established cybersecurity frameworks and regulations, notably the NIST Cybersecurity Framework [27], NIST SP 800.30, and the NIS2 Directive [28]. CSF specifies five functional areas (Identify, Protect, Detect, Respond, Recover) that directly contribute to resilience by structuring proactive and reactive capabilities across the cybersecurity lifecycle. NIST Special Publication 800-30 provides comprehensive guidance for performing risk assessments. Meanwhile, the NIS2 Directive introduces a broader regulatory scope and mandates essential and important entities to implement appropriate technical, operational, and organizational measures to ensure service continuity and manage cyber risks. These resources were analyzed to extract fundamental resilience principles, which were then translated into seven scoring dimensions: 1) Prevention & Preparedness Readiness, 2) Detection Capability, 3) Response Effectiveness, 4) Recovery & Restoration, 5) Mission Impact, 6) Communication & Reporting, and 7) Adherence to Protocols and Regulations.

The next phase of the research involved operationalizing each dimension by defining a set of performance indicators. These indicators are articulated in measurable terms to support both cyber range-based scoring and human-driven assessments where applicable. To ensure consistency in interpreting results, a dedicated scoring guide was developed for each dimension, taking inspiration from the approach utilized in NIST SP 800-30. These guides adopt a standardized 5-point scale, where each score reflects a specific level of maturity, ranging from minimal or absent capability (score 1) to optimized, well-documented, and resilient practices (score 5). This structured assessment model enhances transparency, reproducibility, and alignment with the demonstrated effectiveness of cyber resilience practices during simulated exercises.

For every dimension, performance indicators are scored individually. A score from 1 to 5 is assigned to each indicator, based on the criteria defined in the corresponding scoring guide. In exercises involving multiple participants, an average score per indicator is calculated to reflect collective performance. Subsequently, each dimension score is determined as the mean of its associated indicator scores. These averaged scores are then normalized by multiplying by 20, translating the 1–5 scale to a 20–100 range. This normalization facilitates more intuitive interpretation and enables seamless integration into dashboard visualizations and benchmarking tools, especially when presenting the overall cyber resilience level as a percentage.

Finally, the individual dimension scores are aggregated using a weighted average approach to derive a composite Cyber Resilience Score (CRS). The logic and rationale behind this weighting methodology are detailed in Sect. 4.3. Figure 1 illustrates the components of the proposed framework.

While this study does not include a practical implementation or empirical evaluation of the scoring framework, the design artefact is intended to be used in future research within cyber range environments, where it can be instantiated, tested, and refined. This aligns with the iterative nature of DSR, wherein artefacts are continuously improved based on real-world feedback and performance data.

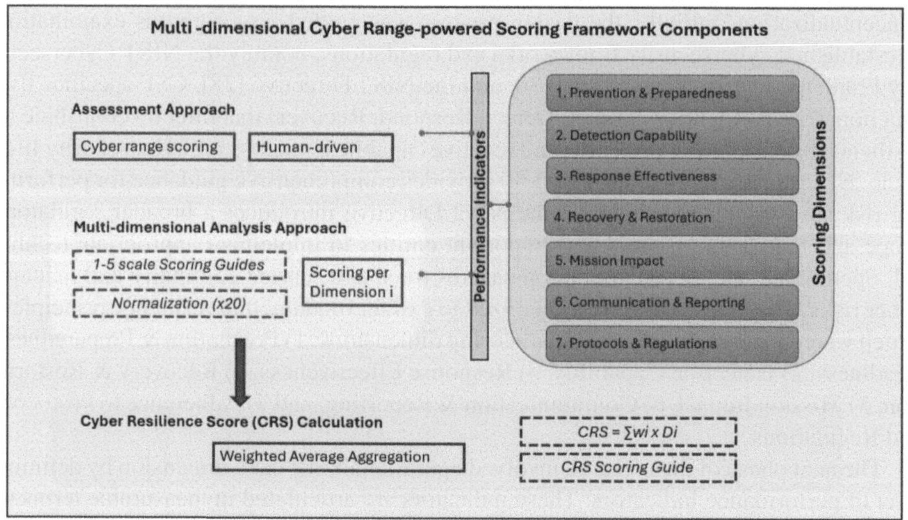

Fig. 1. Multi-dimensional Cyber Range-powered Scoring Framework Components

4 A Multi-dimensional Cyber Resilience Scoring Framework for Critical Infrastructures

4.1 Design Principles of the Scoring Framework

Quantifying cyber resilience in CIs demands a structured approach that integrates technical, operational, and human performance. Traditional cybersecurity metrics often emphasize protection and detection, but cyber resilience requires a broader, more systemic perspective. Specifically, it requires an approach that reflects how organizations anticipate, withstand, respond to, and recover from cyber disruptions while maintaining mission-critical operations. To enable such measurement, the proposed cyber range powered scoring framework is grounded in several core design principles that ensure its relevance and applicability across diverse CI environments.

Alignment with the Cyber Resilience Lifecycle. A foundational principle guiding the framework is alignment with the cyber resilience lifecycle. Rather than evaluating cybersecurity in isolation, the framework maps performance indicators to stages of resilience, including prevention, detection, response, recovery, impact mitigation, and post-incident communication. This lifecycle alignment allows stakeholders to assess readiness not just in terms of technological performance, but also in terms of how effectively teams manage continuity, restore functionality, and communicate under pressure.

Integration of Human, Technical and Organizational Indicators. The framework utilizes a holistic evaluation perspective by integrating human behavior (e.g., decision-making, communication, situational awareness), procedural adherence (e.g., escalation and reporting), and mission continuity (e.g., service degradation, stakeholder impact). By doing so, it links technical execution to organizational mission performance and societal-level outcomes. This evaluation approach goes beyond technical assessments, embracing public accountability and regulatory expectations [29]. By embedding this principle into its structure, the framework empowers CI operators, policymakers, and cyber trainers to assess, strengthen, and benchmark their resilience capabilities in a manner that is both operationally grounded and societally meaningful.

Cyber Range Interoperability. A critical enabling feature is the interoperability among cyber ranges. The scoring framework is platform-agnostic and can be integrated into diverse cyber range environments. By standardizing scoring indicators [30] and assessment logic, the framework supports comparative analysis across exercises, teams, and scenarios, enabling organizations or regulatory bodies to assess trends in performance and resilience maturity over time.

Flexibility. The framework offers flexibility across sectors, recognizing the diversity of operational architectures, regulatory requirements, and threat profiles in domains such as healthcare, transport, energy, and telecommunications. For example, the concept of mission impact differs significantly between a port authority and a national telecom operator. In the case of a port authority, cyber disruptions can halt cargo throughput, Operational Technology (OT) operations, and supply-chain continuity [31, 32], while a national telecom operator mission impact centers on maintaining network availability, service integrity, and data resilience [33]. The framework's structure allows each sector to reuse or adapt indicators and scoring weightings that reflect their own critical functions, service priorities, and resilience thresholds.

4.2 Scoring Model

This section presents the core of the proposed cyber resilience evaluation framework: a multi-dimensional scoring model designed to quantify the cyber resilience of CIs through structured cyber range performance indicators. The model is built upon seven interrelated dimensions, each reflecting a key component of organizational resilience across the technical, operational, and human spectrum. These dimensions include: Prevention and Preparedness Readiness, Detection Capability, Response Effectiveness, Recovery and Restoration, Mission Impact, Communication and Reporting, and Adherence to Protocols and Regulations. Each dimension captures a distinct aspect of resilience, from the implementation of proactive defenses to the ability to sustain operations and engage stakeholders during a crisis.

In the following subsections, each dimension is introduced with a brief rationale that explains its relevance to cyber resilience. A set of clearly defined performance indicators is specified to operationalize each dimension and guide both automated cyber range scoring and human driven scoring during cyber range exercises. Additionally, a dedicated scoring guide is provided per dimension to ensure consistent and meaningful evaluation across participants and scenarios. Together, these elements form the backbone of the proposed scoring framework that aims to enable organizations to benchmark, improve, and validate their cyber resilience capabilities.

Prevention and Preparedness Readiness. This dimension serves as the foundation of cyber resilience. It assesses an organization's ability to proactively minimize the likelihood and impact of cyber incidents by ensuring its systems are hardened, vulnerabilities are identified and mitigated, and secure configurations are maintained. In the context of CIs, where operational downtime can result in cascading disruptions, preparedness is not optional but essential. This dimension includes performance indicators to evaluate: 1) whether professionals are capable of conducting vulnerability assessments, 2) recognizing misconfigurations, 3) applying or confirming baseline hardening measures (e.g., disabling unused services, removing default credentials, updating configurations) and maintaining a security-first operational environment. In CI environments, where safety, reliability, and continuous service delivery are non-negotiable, preparedness serves not only as a proactive protection layer against threats but also as a resilience enabler that supports operational continuity in the face of emerging risks.

Scoring Guide. Table 1 can be utilized to map the scores related to the Prevention and Preparedness Readiness dimension.

Table 1. Scoring Guide for Prevention and Preparedness Readiness

Score	Description
5	Participants proactively identify vulnerabilities and demonstrate full mastery in applying hardening techniques. All critical assets are reviewed and secured before the incident scenario begins. Defensive preparations are aligned with maintaining system operability
4	Participants correctly identify most vulnerabilities and apply hardening measures to key assets. Preventive actions are taken early in the cyber range scenario and mostly maintain operational continuity. Some minor misconfigurations or overlooked elements may be present but do not significantly affect resilience
3	Participants take delayed preventive actions. Some vulnerabilities are detected, but hardening is incomplete or not prioritized by asset criticality. Operational continuity is affected by inconsistent preventive decisions
2	Participants demonstrate limited ability to detect or mitigate vulnerabilities. Hardening measures are missing or incorrectly applied. Some preventive actions conflict with operability, e.g., systems become inaccessible
1	No meaningful preventive readiness is demonstrated. Critical systems are left exposed or misconfigured, and participants show little awareness of baseline controls or vulnerability mitigation needs

Detection Capability. It refers to the organization's ability to accurately and promptly identify signs of malicious activity or system compromise. Within the context of critical infrastructure, where real-time awareness is essential to prevent cascading failures or operational paralysis, detection is a cornerstone of cyber resilience. Under this dimension, performance indicators should assess whether: 1) Indicators of Compromise (IoC) are correctly identified, 2) Attacks targeting multiple layers (e.g., phishing + lateral movement + command and control) are all identified, 3) The team adjusts SIEM filters to detect specific threats or integrates threat feeds, 4) A privilege escalation on a critical system was prioritized and escalated correctly to the incident response team, 5) Logs from different sources are integrated to detect lateral movement, and 6) How quickly a professional identifies unauthorized access to a critical system.

Scoring Guide. Table 2 presents the scoring guide related to the Detection Capability dimension.

Table 2. Scoring Guide – Detection Capability

Score	Description
5	Participants detect and correctly interpret all significant malicious activities or anomalies early in the simulation. Alerts are acted upon with precision, with no critical events missed. Situational awareness is maintained throughout the exercise
4	Most malicious activities or anomalies are detected in a timely manner. Minor misinterpretations or delays may occur, but key threats are addressed before escalation
3	Some threats are detected correctly, but others are either missed, detected too late, or misclassified. Response is triggered with delay or only partial understanding is demonstrated
2	Few threats are detected, and key indicators are missed or misunderstood. Detection occurs late, often after damage has begun. Awareness of system state is poor
1	No meaningful detection is demonstrated. Attacks proceed unnoticed, with participants showing little engagement with alerts or evidence of anomalous behaviour

Response Effectiveness. Response effectiveness refers to the organization's ability to contain, mitigate, and manage cyber incidents once they are detected. In the context of critical infrastructures, a rapid and well-coordinated response can mean the difference between minor disruption and systemic failure. This dimension assesses how effectively professionals identify appropriate countermeasures, apply them under pressure, and coordinate actions to contain damage and maintain essential services. Relevant performance indicators assess: 1) How quickly the team isolates a compromised system/segment of a network, 2) Whether actions, e.g. correct firewall blocks, account suspension, or network segmentation, were applied appropriately, 3) Whether safety-critical systems were prioritized over peripheral systems, 4) How well team members collaborate, delegate, and synchronize efforts under pressure, 5) Whether decision making and actions taken were effective to address the attacks, and 6) Whether an incident with external implications was escalated to appropriate authorities.

Scoring Guide. Response Effectiveness scores are mapped to an appropriate level according to Table 3.

Table 3. Scoring Guide – Response Effectiveness

Score	Description
5	Participants respond immediately and decisively with correct countermeasures. Systems isolated, threats neutralized, and continuity maintained. The team shows clear coordination and demonstrates adaptive decision-making under pressure

(*continued*)

Table 3. (*continued*)

Score	Description
4	Response is effective with minor delays or partial containment. Most critical systems are secured, and disruption is minimized. Coordination is good, though some communication gaps or tactical inefficiencies may occur
3	Participants react with moderate delays or apply countermeasures that are only partially effective. Some damage occurs before action is taken. Decision-making is somewhat fragmented or reactive rather than strategic
2	Response is disorganized or significantly delayed. Countermeasures are incomplete or misapplied, leading to avoidable escalation of the incident. Roles and responsibilities are unclear
1	No meaningful response is demonstrated. Systems remain vulnerable throughout the simulation. The team either fails to act or takes inappropriate actions that exacerbate the situation

Recovery and Restoration. Recovery and restoration reflect the organization's ability to bring systems, services, and operations back to a stable and fully functional state after a cyber incident. In CI environments, where prolonged downtime can have cascading economic, environmental, and safety consequences, the speed and effectiveness of recovery are essential to operational resilience. This dimension evaluates whether professionals can prioritize recovery efforts based on asset criticality, follow restoration procedures, validate system integrity, and restore full mission capability under time and resource constraints. Several performance indicators are specified to assess capabilities under the *Recovery and Restoration* dimension: 1) How quickly the team begins restoring systems after isolating an infected system/network segment, 2) Whether critical systems were prioritized before low-impact systems, 3) Whether recovery relied on verified backup sources or involved full reinstallation, and how data integrity was ensured, 4) Whether the restored data are validated before resuming operations, 5) Whether firewall rules, group policies, or endpoint settings were reinstated following restoration, 6) Whether systems were tested post-restoration to validate functionality and inter-system communication, 7) Whether actions taken during system recovery are logged and justified for audit or post-incident review, and 8) Whether appropriate stakeholders were updated in real time about system recovery status.

Scoring Guide. Table 4 specifies the scoring guide related to the Recovery and Restoration dimension.

Table 4. Scoring Guide – Recovery & Restoration

Score	Description
5	Recovery actions are initiated immediately after containment. Critical services are prioritized and restored in the correct sequence, with system integrity validated. Restoration is complete and aligns with mission objectives

(*continued*)

Table 4. (*continued*)

Score	Description
4	Most critical services are restored promptly and correctly. Recovery follows logical sequencing with minor deviations or delays. Integrity checks are performed with good operational results
3	Recovery is attempted with partial success. Some critical services are delayed, misprioritized, or restored without adequate validation. Recovery decisions are somewhat reactive or inconsistent
2	Restoration is slow, poorly coordinated, or incorrectly sequenced. Critical systems are left unavailable for extended periods, and validation is inconsistent or missing
1	No meaningful recovery actions are taken, or incorrect actions result in further degradation. Participants are unable to maintain operational continuity

Mission Impact. This dimension refers to the degree to which a cyber incident disrupts an organization's ability to perform its core functions and deliver critical services. In CI environments, resilience is not just measured by technical response, but by the extent to which operational capabilities and service continuity are preserved under cyber pressure. This dimension is divided into two interrelated subdimensions: *continuity of internal operations*, which assesses how well the organization maintains control over its internal systems and workflows, and *stakeholders impact*, which evaluates the external consequences of the disruption, including delays, reduced availability, and degraded service quality for stakeholders or the public. Together, these subdimensions provide a comprehensive view of the actual impact of an incident on the mission, moving beyond detection and response into the operational and societal consequences of cyber events.

Performance indicators related to *Continuity of Internal Operations* measure: 1) Whether core services continued without full shutdown during cyber disruptions, 2) How long the core services were inoperative, and 3) Whether operational workflows were maintained across collaborating departments. Regarding the *Stakeholders' Impact*, this can be measured by performance indicators considering: 1) How long users were unable to access services, 2) The proportion of users that were affected by the disruption, and 3) Whether the disruption caused delays or serious operational consequences for users.

Scoring Guide. This dimension utilized two scoring guides to provide scoring refinement between the two sub-dimensions. Table 5 maps the scores related to Continuity of Internal Operations, while Table 6 specifies the mapping related to Stakeholders' Impact scores.

Table 5. Scoring Guide – Continuity of Internal Operations

Score	Description
5	Internal systems and workflows remain fully operational. The organization sustains mission-critical functions with minimal degradation, despite the cyber incident

(*continued*)

Table 5. *(continued)*

Score	Description
4	Minor internal disruptions occur but are quickly mitigated. Most operational processes continue with negligible impact
3	Moderate disruption to internal operations. Some critical systems are slowed or partially offline but continue to function
2	Significant disruption to internal workflows. Multiple critical systems are down, affecting mission execution
1	Internal operations collapse. Critical systems fail, and the organization is unable to continue mission-relevant tasks

Table 6. Scoring Guide – Stakeholder Impact

Score	Description
5	External stakeholders experience no or negligible impact. Services remain available and stable
4	Minor service degradation is noticed by some users, but core service delivery is uninterrupted
3	Moderate disruptions affect a notable portion of users. Some delays or degraded services are observed
2	Significant impact on service delivery. Critical user-facing systems are offline or unreliable
1	Severe external impact. Most or all users are unable to access critical services. Substantial disruption to trust or safety

Communication and Reporting. Communication and reporting are critical to maintaining situational awareness, ensuring coordinated action, and preserving stakeholder trust during and after a cyber incident. In CI environments, the ability to share timely and accurate information, both internally among response teams and externally to stakeholders, regulators, service users, or the public can significantly influence the outcome of an incident. This dimension evaluates how effectively professionals convey the right information at the right time to the right recipients under pressure.

Performance indicators under the *Communication and Reporting* dimension include measuring whether: 1) The IT and other relevant personnel were alerted promptly after anomalous behaviour was detected, 2) The incident report clearly described the compromise, affected systems, and containment actions, 3) The technical team informed management, and legal/compliance in time about the breach of customer data, 4) Participants used the assigned communication channels/tools to coordinate incident response, 5) The organization notified collaborators about systems unavailability affecting operations, 6) Situational updates were issued to all involved parties during evolving attack scenarios, and 7) After-action reports were issued summarizing impact, actions, and lessons for future preparedness.

Scoring Guide. Table 7 presents the scoring guide related to the *Communication and Reporting* dimension.

Table 7. Scoring Guide – Communication and Reporting

Score	Description
5	Communication is timely, accurate, and well-targeted. All relevant internal and external stakeholders are informed proactively. Messages are clear and roles are well-coordinated. Situation updates are shared consistently
4	Most communication is effective and timely. Internal coordination is strong, and external communication occurs with minor delays or small gaps in clarity
3	Communication is functional but inconsistent. Some relevant stakeholders are informed late or not at all. Information may be incomplete or unclear at times
2	Communication is delayed, poorly structured, or reactive. Internal roles may be confused, and external reporting is insufficient or missing
1	No meaningful communication occurs. The team operates in silos or remains silent. Critical stakeholders are uninformed, leading to confusion or extended impact

Adherence to Protocols and Regulations. Adherence to protocols and sector-specific regulations (e.g., IMO, NIS2, GDPR, HIPAA) is a critical dimension of cyber resilience, especially in the context of regulated CI sectors. In highly regulated sectors such as transport, energy, healthcare, and telecom, compliance is not only a legal requirement but a resilience enabler, ensuring that systems and processes are aligned with safety, accountability, and operational continuity goals. Performance indicators under the *Adherence to Protocols and Regulation* dimension include measuring whether: 1) Staff followed the incident escalation and containment process outlined in their standard operating procedures, 2) The organization contacted authorities and submitted the required report on-time, 3) Contingency planning was initiated per company approved procedures, 4) Actions executed during containment and recovery were documented for review, 5) Participants avoided privilege escalation or sharing credentials during incident handling, and 6) Legal was consulted before notifying external entities about the incident.

Scoring Guide. Table 8 provides an exemplary guide to interpret scores related to *Adherence to Protocols and Regulation* dimension and maps them to an appropriate performance level.

Table 8. Scoring Guide – Adherence to Protocols and Regulations

Score	Description
5	All actions strictly align with predefined protocols, escalation paths, and regulatory requirements. Required reporting steps are completed correctly and on time. Documentation is thorough and properly submitted

(*continued*)

Table 8. (*continued*)

Score	Description
4	Most steps align with procedures and regulations. Minor deviations are observed, but do not affect compliance or response quality. Documentation and reporting are mostly complete
3	Participants show general awareness of protocols but apply them inconsistently. Some steps are skipped/ delayed. Documentation is incomplete or partially accurate
2	Protocols are poorly followed or misunderstood. Key procedures or reporting requirements are missed or delayed significantly. Limited compliance is evident
1	No adherence to protocols is observed. Participants improvise without referencing established procedures. Regulatory obligations are ignored or unknown

4.3 Cyber Resilience Score (CRS) Calculation

This section explains how the scoring methodology can be applied to assess the participants' performance for each proposed cyber resilience dimension and how to calculate a composite result reflecting a CI's cyber resilience maturity.

For each dimension, multiple indicators are evaluated during the cyber range simulation. These indicator scores are first averaged to produce a dimension-level score for each participant or team and then normalized by multiplying by 20 to express them on a 20–100 scale. The resulting dimension scores are then combined using a weighted average approach to generate a single composite Cyber Resilience Score (CRS), as shown in the formula below:

$$CRS = \sum wi \ x \, Di, \ i = 1\text{–}7 \quad (1)$$

Where:

- CRS is the overall Cyber Resilience Score (out of 100),
- D_i is the normalized averaged score (1–5) for the ith dimension,
- w_i is the weight assigned to the ith dimension,
- and $\sum \mathrm{w_i} = 1$.

Weighted Scoring Logic. Quantifying cyber resilience requires not only measuring performance across multiple dimensions but also recognizing that not all dimensions carry the same weight in sustaining cyber resilient operations. Some capabilities, such as timely recovery or effective detection, may have a more immediate and significant impact on the continuity of essential services in CI than others. To reflect this, the proposed framework incorporates a weighted scoring logic, allowing the final cyber resilience score to account for the relative importance of each dimension. This weighted and modular approach enables flexibility and relevance across different CI sectors. Weights can be uniform or sector-specific, depending on the intended use of the score:

- Uniform weights can be utilized to support cross-sector comparisons or generalized benchmarking in exercises that span multiple CI domains. This approach provides a consistent evaluation framework where each dimension contributes equally to the total resilience score. This is useful in early-stage assessments, pilot testing, or when aiming to establish a baseline understanding of resilience across infrastructures.
- Sector-specific weight profiles can be defined to reflect unique operational characteristics, risk tolerances, or regulatory obligations inherent to each CI sector. For example, in maritime or healthcare environments, where operational downtime can directly impact human safety and life-critical systems, greater emphasis may be assigned to *Recovery & Restoration* and *Mission Impact*. Conversely, in telecom or energy sectors, greater weight may be assigned to *Detection Capability*, given the critical need for service reliability. In these highly interconnected environments, rapid anomaly detection and early threat containment are essential to prevent cascading failures that could disrupt large-scale operations and societal functions. This ensures that the scoring model not only quantifies performance but does so in a way that aligns with the resilience priorities of each domain.

The modular weighted scoring logic also allows the scoring output to be adapted over time or recalibrated in response to emerging threat landscapes, sector reforms, or lessons learned from cyber range exercises.

Overall Cyber Resilience Interpretation Guide. The CRS reflects an organization's level of resilience. As presented in Table 9, five cyber resilience score ranges are specified to provide granularity and offer a clear interpretation of performance. These score ranges help classify an organization's resilience posture, from very low to high, enabling stakeholders to identify gaps, prioritize improvements, and benchmark progress over time.

Table 9. Overall Cyber Resilience Score (CRS) - Scoring Guide

CRS	Level	Interpretation
90–100	**Highly Resilient**	Organization demonstrates exceptional resilience across all dimensions. Strong preventive posture, effective coordination, and rapid recovery ensure operational continuity with minimal disruption
75–89	**Resilient**	Resilience capabilities are strong, with only minor areas requiring improvement. The organization can withstand and recover from cyber events with limited impact
60–74	**Moderately Resilient**	The organization has foundational resilience practices in place but demonstrates inconsistencies or vulnerabilities that could hinder its ability to respond to high-impact threats
40–59	**Low Resilience**	Key gaps exist in resilience capabilities. Incident response and recovery may be delayed, uncoordinated, or noncompliant. Operational and customer-facing disruptions are likely

(*continued*)

Table 9. (*continued*)

CRS	Level	Interpretation
<40	**Critically Vulnerable**	The organization lacks sufficient cyber resilience. Incidents are likely to cause major operational breakdowns and regulatory exposure. Immediate improvement is required

5 Discussion

5.1 Cyber Range Data Collection Mechanisms

Accurately measuring cyber resilience in cyber range environments requires a robust and structured approach to performance data collection. Performance data can be captured using a combination of automated and observational techniques: a) *Automated telemetry* forms the backbone of technical data collection. During the cyber range exercise, logs, alerts, system events, and timestamps can be captured automatically to track key activities such as threat detection, system isolation, service restoration, and communication flow [34]. These data are commonly collected through integrated SIEM platforms, packet capture tools, endpoint monitoring tools, and scenario-instrumented triggers. b) *Embedded scoring engines* within the cyber range platform track key simulation events, flag task completions, monitor command executions, and log compliance with expected actions in real time. This study proposed a range of performance indicators that are expected to be taken into consideration and integrated into the scoring engines to assess participants' performance across the proposed framework's cyber resilience dimensions. c) *Human observer evaluation* can be employed to assess qualitative performance, such as clarity of communication, interdepartmental coordination, or adherence to legal and reporting protocols. Observers may use structured rubrics, communication transcripts and checklists to ensure consistency.

This blended approach allows a multi-layer assessment, ensuring a comprehensive view of participant actions, decisions, and their impact across all seven dimensions of the proposed scoring model. Once scores are calculated, the results can be integrated into a composite cyber resilience score using the weighted logic described earlier. The output can be visualized on a sector-specific dashboard, included in post-exercise feedback reports, or used to benchmark performance across time, teams, or organizations. Results can enable CI operators to identify resilience gaps, plan targeted improvements, and demonstrate compliance with sectoral expectations.

5.2 Implications for Workforce Development and Training

The proposed multi-dimensional scoring framework holds significant potential to enhance workforce development, training programs, and competency assessment in the context of cyber resilience. By simulating realistic and high-fidelity cyber range scenarios and capturing both technical and non-technical dimensions of performance [30], the framework enables organizations to move beyond traditional security drills or checklists and toward measurable, mission-aligned skill development.

First and foremost, this approach directly supports the development of cyber resilience skills across a broad range of cybersecurity functions. By aligning scoring dimensions with core resilience capabilities such as detection, response, recovery, and communication, the framework ensures that cybersecurity teams are not only trained in attack mitigation but are also evaluated on their ability to sustain critical functions under stress. This shift from protection-centric to resilience-oriented training is especially crucial in CI sectors, where the continuity of services has direct implications for public safety and economic stability [35].

The scoring framework also facilitates compliance preparation. Regulations such as the NIS2 Directive [28] and IMO [36] cybersecurity guidelines (for the maritime sector) emphasize the importance of preparedness, incident response, and continuous improvement. By generating structured performance data mapped to specific resilience dimensions, the framework can serve as a pre-audit readiness tool, enabling organizations to assess and demonstrate capabilities in alignment with regulatory expectations.

Furthermore, organizations can use the framework for internal benchmarking, assessing the maturity and cohesion of their cybersecurity teams across scenarios and over time. The evaluation of technical execution, communication, and adherence to sectoral protocols provides insight into real-world readiness [8]. It helps identify specific skill gaps, breakdowns in team coordination, or decision-making bottlenecks that would not be observable through standard red-blue team assessments. This level of diagnostic capability is particularly valuable for team leads, SOC managers, and CISOs seeking to tailor their operational readiness plans based on concrete performance evidence across cyber resilience dimensions [4].

From a training design perspective, the framework opens the door for targeted and personalized interventions. Organizations and training providers can use performance data to inform the creation of role-specific training pathways [37, 38] or certification schemes that address weaknesses in specific resilience dimensions. For instance, if incident responders score consistently lower in post-incident reporting or cross-team coordination, this could trigger focused training on communication under pressure or incident documentation aligned with regulatory templates.

The implications also extend to academia and policymaking. For academic institutions, the framework provides a reference model for embedding cyber resilience principles into cybersecurity curricula. It promotes a more holistic understanding of professional roles, integrating technical, operational, and organizational competencies. For policymakers, the framework offers a measurable basis for advancing cyber resilience mandates, ensuring that workforce development policies are grounded in observable performance metrics rather than abstract capability statements.

In summary, the proposed framework can enable CI sectors to operationalize cyber resilience training, enhance regulatory alignment, and strengthen human performance in the face of increasingly complex threats.

6 Conclusions

This paper proposed a multi-dimensional, cyber range-powered scoring framework designed to quantify and assess the cyber resilience of CI organizations. By embedding the scoring model within realistic cyber range simulations, it enables structured evaluation of individual and team performance, technical responses, coordination efficiency, and mission impact. The scoring model not only supports benchmarking and compliance preparation, but also provides actionable insights to inform workforce development, training interventions, and organizational decision-making.Although the current work presents a conceptual design without empirical validation, it lays a robust foundation for future implementation, testing, and refinement. Follow-up research will focus on piloting the framework in sector-specific cyber ranges, calibrating and extending initial scoring indicators, and evaluating its effectiveness across diverse CI contexts. Ultimately, this work aims to contribute to a more measurable, mission-aligned, and human-centered approach to cyber resilience. This approach is envisioned to empower organizations to anticipate, withstand, recover from, and adapt to cyber threats, while sustaining their essential services to society.

Acknowledgments. This work has received funding from the European Union's Digital Europe research and innovation programme under grant agreement No. 101128049 (SecAwarenessTruss). Views and opinions expressed are however those of the author(s) only and do not necessarily reflect those of the European Union. Neither the European Union nor the granting authority can be held responsible for them.

Disclosure of Interests. The authors have no competing interests to declare that are relevant to the content of this article.

References

1. NIS Cooperation Group: Annual report NIS Directive incidents 2024. CG Publication, European Commission, Brussels (2025). https://ec.europa.eu/newsroom/repository/document/2025-31/Annual_Report_NISD_Security_Incidents_2024_lLl8Yt8at5UKGOymYgsc0rxZrpQ_118680.pdf
2. National Institute of Standards and Technology (NIST): NIST Special Publication 800-160, Volume 2: Developing cyber resilient systems – A systems security engineering approach. U.S. Department of Commerce, Gaithersburg (2021). https://doi.org/10.6028/NIST.SP.800-160v2
3. Annarelli, A., Nonino, F., Palombi, G.: Understanding the management of cyber resilient systems. Comput. Ind. Eng. **149**, 106829 (2020). https://doi.org/10.1016/j.cie.2020.106829
4. Andreolini, M., Colacino, V.G., Colajanni, M., et al.: A framework for the evaluation of trainee performance in cyber range exercises. Mob. Netw. Appl. **25**, 236–247 (2020). https://doi.org/10.1007/s11036-019-01442-0
5. Peratikou, A., Stavrou, S.: On corporate resilience in the face of data breaches and the preventative power of awareness training. In: 2025 Information Science Frontier Forum and the Academic Conference on Information Security and Intelligent Control (ISF), pp. 1–7. IEEE (2025). https://doi.org/10.1109/ISF65011.2025.11047327
6. Chatzis, P., Stavrou, E.: Cyber-threat landscape of border control infrastructures. Int. J. Crit. Infrastruct. Prot. **36**, 100503 (2022). https://doi.org/10.1016/j.ijcip.2021.100503

7. Toregas, C., Santos, J.R.: Cybersecurity and its cascading effect on societal systems. Cybersecurity and Privacy Research Institute, George Washington University (2018)
8. Damianou, A., Mazi, M.S., Rizos, G., Voulgaridis, A., Votis, K.: Situational awareness scoring system in cyber range platforms. In: IEEE International Conference on Cyber Security and Resilience (CSR), pp. 520–527 (2024). https://doi.org/10.1109/CSR61664.2024.10679451
9. Russo, E., Ribaudo, M., Orlich, A., Longo, G., Armando, A.: Cyber range and cyber defense exercises: gamification meets university students. In: ITiCSE 2023, pp. 29–36 (2023). https://doi.org/10.1145/3617553.3617888
10. Yamin, M.M., Katt, B., Gkioulos, V.: Cyber ranges and security testbeds: scenarios, functions, tools and architecture. Comput. Secur. **88**, 101636 (2019). https://doi.org/10.1016/j.cose.2019.101636
11. Chowdhury, N., Gkioulos, V.: Cyber security training for critical infrastructure protection: a literature review. Comput. Sci. Rev. **40**, 100361 (2021). https://doi.org/10.1016/j.cosrev.2021.100361
12. Abrahams, T.O., Farayola, O.A., Kaggwa, S., Uwaoma, P.U., Hassan, A.O., Dawodu, S.O.: Cybersecurity awareness and education programs: a review of employee engagement and accountability. Comput. Sci. IT Res. J. **5**(1), 100 (2024). https://doi.org/10.51594/csitrj.v5i1.708
13. Piki, A., Stavrou, E., Procopiou, A., Demosthenous, A.: Fostering cybersecurity awareness and skills development through digital game-based learning. In: 2023 10th International Conference on Behavioural and Social Computing (BESC), Larnaca, pp. 1–9. IEEE (2023). https://doi.org/10.1109/BESC59560.2023.10386988
14. Pappas, G., Peratikou, P., Siegel, J., Politopoulos, K., Christodoulides, C., Stavrou, S.: Cyber escape room: an educational 3D escape room game within a cyber range training realm. In: INTED2020 Proceedings, pp. 2621–2627 (2020). https://doi.org/10.21125/inted.2020.0788
15. Švábenský, V., Vykopal, J., Čermák, M., Laštovička, M.: Enhancing cybersecurity skills by creating serious games. In: ITiCSE 2018, pp. 192–197 (2018). https://doi.org/10.1145/3197091.3197123
16. Petullo, W.M., Moses, K.V., Klimkowski, B., Hand, R., Olson, K.: The use of cyber-defense exercises in undergraduate computing education. In: USENIX Workshop on Advances in Security Education (ASE 2016) (2016)
17. Somarakis, I., Smyrlis, M., Fysarakis, K., Spanoudakis, G.: Model-driven cyber range training: a cyber security assurance perspective. In: Fournaris, A., et al. (eds.) IOSEC MSTEC FINSEC 2019 2019 2019. LNCS, vol. 11981, pp. 172–184. Springer, Cham (2020). https://doi.org/10.1007/978-3-030-42051-2_12
18. Ošlejšek, R., Rusňák, V., Burská, K.D., Švábenský, V., Vykopal, J., Čegan, J.: Conceptual model of visual analytics for hands-on cybersecurity training. IEEE Trans. Vis. Comput. Graph. **27**(8), 3425–3438 (2021). https://doi.org/10.1109/TVCG.2020.2977336
19. Ošlejšek, R., Vykopal, J., Burská, K.D., Rusňák, V.: Evaluation of cyber defense exercises using visual analytics process. In: 2018 IEEE Frontiers in Education Conference (FIE), pp. 1–9 (2018). https://doi.org/10.1109/FIE.2018.8659299
20. Peratikou, A., Louca, C., Shiaeles, S., Stavrou, S.: On federated cyber range network interconnection. In: Ghita, B., Shiaeles, S. (eds.) INC 2020. LNNS, vol. 180, pp. 117–128. Springer, Cham (2021). https://doi.org/10.1007/978-3-030-64758-2_9
21. Dobson, G.B., Podnar, T., Cerini, A.D., Osterritter, L.J.: R-EACTR: a framework for designing realistic cyber warfare exercises. AFRL Technical report (2017). https://apps.dtic.mil/sti/pdfs/AD1044880.pdf
22. Chouliaras, N., Kantzavelou, I., Maglaras, L., Pantziou, G., Ferrag, M.A.: A novel autonomous container-based platform for cybersecurity training and research. PeerJ Comput. Sci. **9**, e1574 (2023). https://doi.org/10.7717/peerj-cs.1574

23. Diakoumakos, A., Tsatiris, A., Mouratidis, H., Gkioulos, V.: Cyber-range federation and cyber-security games: a gamification scoring model. In: 16th International Conference on Availability, Reliability and Security (ARES 2021), New York, Article no. 32, pp. 1–10. ACM (2021). https://doi.org/10.1145/3465481.3470096
24. Maeng, Y.J., Pihelgas, M.: Request for a surveillance tower: evasive tactics in cyber defense exercises. In: 14th International Conference on Cyber Conflict (CyCon 2023), pp. 239–256 (2023). https://doi.org/10.23919/cycon58705.2023.10182014
25. Peffers, K., Tuunanen, T., Rothenberger, M.A., Chatterjee, S.: A design science research methodology for information systems research. J. Manag. Inf. Syst. **24**(3), 45–77 (2007)
26. Ampel, B.M., Samtani, S., Zhu, H., Chen, H., Nunamaker, J.F.: Improving threat mitigation through a cybersecurity risk management framework: a computational design science approach. J. Manag. Inf. Syst. **41**(1), 236–265 (2024). https://doi.org/10.1080/07421222.2023.2301178
27. National Institute of Standards and Technology (NIST): The NIST Cybersecurity Framework (CSF) 2.0. NIST Cybersecurity White Paper 29, U.S. Department of Commerce, Gaithersburg (2024). https://doi.org/10.6028/NIST.CSWP.29
28. European Parliament and Council: Directive (EU) 2022/2555 of 14 December 2022 on measures for a high common level of cybersecurity across the Union, amending Regulation (EU) No 910/2014 and Directive (EU) 2018/1972, and repealing Directive (EU) 2016/1148 (NIS 2 Directive). Official Journal of the European Union L 333, pp. 80–152 (2022). https://eur-lex.europa.eu/legal-content/en/TXT/?uri=CELEX%3A32022L2555
29. Tzavara, V., Vassiliadis, S.: Tracing the evolution of cyber resilience: a historical and conceptual review. Int. J. Inf. Secur. **23**(3), 1695–1714 (2024). https://doi.org/10.1007/s10207-023-00811-x
30. Katsantonis, M.N., Manikas, A., Mavridis, I., Gritzalis, D.: Cyber range design framework for cyber security education and training. Int. J. Inf. Secur. **22**, 1005–1027 (2023). https://doi.org/10.1007/s10207-023-00680-4
31. ENISA: Port cybersecurity – Good practices for cybersecurity in the maritime sector. Publications Office of the European Union, Luxembourg (2019)
32. IAPH: Cybersecurity guidelines for ports and port facilities. International Association of Ports and Harbors, Tokyo (2021)
33. MITRE: Evaluating the impact of cyber attacks on missions. MITRE Technical report, Bedford, MA (2009)
34. Potamos, G., Stavrou, E., Stavrou, S.: Enhancing maritime cybersecurity through operational technology sensor data fusion: a comprehensive survey and analysis. Sensors **24**(11), 3458 (2024). https://doi.org/10.3390/s24113458
35. Roshanaei, M.: Resilience at the core: critical infrastructure protection challenges, priorities and cybersecurity assessment strategies. J. Comput. Commun. **9**, 80–97 (2021). https://doi.org/10.4236/jcc.2021.98006
36. International Maritime Organization (IMO): Guidelines on maritime cyber risk management. MSC-FAL.1/Circ.3, adopted June 2017; revision MSC-FAL.1/Circ.3/Rev.2, approved October 2021–May 2022. IMO, London (2017/2022)
37. Hatzivasilis, G., et al.: Modern aspects of cyber-security training and continuous adaptation of programmes to trainees. Appl. Sci. **10**(16), 5702 (2020). https://doi.org/10.3390/app10165702
38. Vykopal, J., Seda, P., Švábenský, V., Čeleda, P.: Smart environment for adaptive learning of cybersecurity skills. IEEE Trans. Learn. Technol. **16**(3), 443–456 (2023). https://doi.org/10.1109/TLT.2022.3216345

Security Frameworks

CY-TRUST: A Sectorial SOC Framework for Enhanced National and Cross-Border Cybersecurity Resilience

Adamantini Peratikou[1](✉), Evagoras Charalambous[1], Eliana Stavrou[1], Panayiota Smyrli[1], George Hadjichristophi[2], and Stavros Stavrou[1]

[1] Open University of Cyprus, Nicosia, Cyprus
Adamantini.peratikou@ouc.ac.cy
[2] Digital Security Authority of Cyprus, Nicosia, Cyprus

Abstract. CY-TRUST introduces a federated framework for deploying sectorial Security Operations Centers (SOCs) to enhance national and EU-level cybersecurity resilience. Focused on Cyprus's critical sectors energy, maritime, government, and SMEs, the architecture supports scalable, standards-based implementations aligned with NIS2 and the Cyber Resilience Act. Each sectorial SOC integrates AI-driven situational awareness, incident response playbooks, and structured Cyber Threat Intelligence (CTI) sharing via Structured Threat Information Expression (STIX). It also integrates Trusted Automated Ex-change of Intelligence Information (TAXII), and the Malware Information Sharing Platform (MISP). A multi domain ICT/Maritime/Industrial cyber range, Cyber Threat Realm (CTR), ensures continuous training and preparedness. Three SOC deployment variants accommodate varying stakeholder maturity, coordinated through a national backend operated by the Digital Security Authority. CY-TRUST aligns with EU initiatives such as JCOP, NG-SOC, and PHOENi2X, and provides a replicable blueprint for federated SOC ecosystems. This paper presents the architecture and implementation approach of CY-TRUST, demonstrating its value as a strategic model for adaptive and collaborative cyber defense.

Keywords: Cybersecurity Architecture · SOC · CTI · Cyber-range · EU NIS2 · STIX · TAXII

1 Introduction

The increasing frequency and sophistication of cyber threats targeting national infrastructures demand robust and scalable cybersecurity solutions tailored to sectorial needs. Across Europe, critical infrastructure sectors have faced a surge in complex cyberattacks exploiting vulnerabilities within fragmented cybersecurity ecosystems. These developments underscore the urgency for a holistic, cooperative, and standards-based approach to cybersecurity governance and operations. The CY-TRUST (CYpriot secToRial secUrity operationS cenTres) project was conceived to enhance the Republic of Cyprus's national cybersecurity posture by establishing a federated network of sectorial Security

E. Bergström et al. (Eds.): CRITIS 2025, LNCS 16291, pp. 369–383, 2026.
https://doi.org/10.1007/978-3-032-19540-1_19

Operations Centers (SOCs). These SOCs serve key sectors in energy, maritime, government, or other sectors, and are interconnected with a centralized National SOC operated by the Digital Security Authority (DSA). This hierarchical and collaborative architecture enables real-time threat detection, automated incident response, focused national training, and seamless EU-level interoperability. CY-TRUST aligns closely with European cybersecurity policy and frameworks, contributing to harmonization efforts through regulatory alignment with initiatives such as NIS2 and the Cyber Resilience Act (CRA) [1, 2], and sup-ports the evolving EU Cybersecurity Certification Scheme (EUCS) [22].CY-TRUST aligns closely with European cybersecurity policy and frameworks, contributing to harmonization efforts through regulatory alignment with initiatives such as NIS2 and the Cyber Resilience Act (CRA), aiming at synergetic work with EU programs including JCOP, NG-SOC, and PHOENi2X. The project emphasizes technological innovation, integrating AI-enhanced situational awareness, machine-executable incident response playbooks, and immersive cyber range-based preparedness training. These components work together to form a replicable model for the development of SOC infrastructures across other EU Member States. In line with its national priorities and European commitments, Cyprus is taking a proactive stance in strengthening its cybersecurity ecosystem. Through CY-TRUST, sectorial SOCs are envisioned as foundational elements that offer advanced threat detection, streamlined incident management, and dynamic preparedness tailored to the unique risk profiles of each sector. These SOCs are not only defensive hubs but strategic assets supporting broader goals of digital resilience and cross-border cooperation.

By embedding sectorial intelligence and orchestration mechanisms into its national cybersecurity fabric, CY-TRUST sets a new benchmark for operational security. Its emphasis on collaboration, interoperability, and regulatory cohesion paves the way for more integrated and adaptive cybersecurity strategies, not just for Cyprus but for the wider European community.

2 State of the Art and Related Work

2.1 Cybersecurity Situational Awareness

Situational awareness is a cornerstone of modern cybersecurity operations, encompassing the real-time monitoring, analysis, and comprehension of activities within an organization's digital environment [3]. Drawing upon Endsley's three-tiered model of perception, comprehension, and projection, cybersecurity situational awareness (CSA) begins with data acquisition from tools like intrusion detection systems, firewall logs, and vulnerability scans, followed by contextual analysis to identify anomalies and threats, and culminates in forecasting potential impacts [4, 5]. Effective CSA is not a static capability but a dynamic, evolving process of continuously interpreting and adapting to the threat landscape [6]. Platforms such as Security Information and Event Management (SIEM) systems and behavior analytics increasingly serve as the backbone of CSA, aggregating and correlating data across distributed infrastructures. Recent efforts have emphasized cross-border and multi-sector situational awareness. Fysarakis et al. [7] proposed a structured blueprint for collaborative cybersecurity operations centres (CSOCs) that integrates real-time visibility, coordinated incident response, and common playbook automation, aligning closely with the CSOC Blueprint underpinning CY-TRUST. Similarly, Amanowicz [8] introduced a shared cybersecurity awareness platform highlighting the need for real-time threat visibility, risk modeling, and collaborative analysis across interconnected critical infrastructures. In the context of projects like CY-TRUST, which focus on deploying federated Security Operations Centers (SOCs) across multiple sectors, CSA plays an integral role. It enables the identification of sectorial threats, facilitates cross-SOC visibility, and supports automated incident response. Likewise, the ATHENA platform [9] incorporates AI/ML-powered situational awareness across national boundaries, enabling secure data exchange and real-time collaboration between cross border SOCs to improve shared awareness within the EU. The ability to correlate indicators of compromise (IOCs) across infrastructures and sectors and borders, provides a powerful enabler for both national and EU-level cybersecurity coordination.

2.2 Cyber Threat Intelligence CTI

Cyber Threat Intelligence serves as the analytical backbone of proactive cybersecurity-ty strategies, offering contextual insights into threat actors, their methods, and potential targets. Effective CTI enhances situational awareness, enables informed decision-making, and aligns cybersecurity strategies with the organization's threat landscape [10]. At its core, CTI involves the collection and analysis of threat data from sources such as malware reports, threat feeds, and vulnerability databases and trans-forms it into actionable intelligence [11, 12]. A significant advancement in CTI practices is the integration of Artificial Intelligence and Machine Learning. These technologies automate the analysis of vast datasets, enabling the rapid identification of patterns and anomalies while reducing the burden on human analysts. This synergy of AI and expert knowledge is essential for generating timely, high-fidelity CTI [13, 14]. However, it also introduces new challenges such as data bias, validation, and the need for algorithmic transparency. CTI innovation continues to be driven by automation and semantic enrichment. Radoglou-Grammatikis et al. [15] highlight the importance of CTI interoperability and enriched contextual understanding using standards such as STIX, TAXII, and MISP. Ellinitakis et al. [16] introduced CTI-DATH, a machine-learning-based system for automated extraction of intelligence from online sources such as dark web forums and security blogs. Their approach transforms unstructured data into standardized formats suitable for SOAR integra-Tion an approach that echoes the design of CY-TRUST's CTI Extractor and Translator modules. CTI also supports collaborative defense through platforms like Information Sharing and Analysis Centers (ISACs), where organizations pool threat in-formation to strengthen collective resilience. This aligns with the goals of the CY-TRUST initiative, which leverages structured formats and ontology-based CTI enrichment to enable standardized and interoperable threat sharing across national and EU-level SOCs, an approach investigated in [17].

2.3 Cyber Ranges

Cyber ranges are emerging as critical realistic training infrastructures for enhancing cybersecurity preparedness and resilience. These platforms provide immersive, multi-domain environments where cybersecurity professionals can develop and refine their skills. Controlled simulation settings allow the safe execution of attack-and-defense scenarios, enabling realistic practice without jeopardizing live systems [18, 19]. Potamos et al. [20] highlight the importance of domain-specific cyber ranges, presenting a maritime-focused training environment that underscores the value of tailored simulation platforms for sector-specific preparedness. The ATHENA platform incorporates a federated cyber range architecture with an integrated LMS that supports capture-the-flag challenges, tabletop exercises, and red/blue team simulations, allowing cross-border coordination of cyber preparedness efforts [9]. Similarly, PHOENi2X introduces an AI-assisted cyber resilience framework that integrates orchestration, training, and recovery scenarios across multiple stakeholders [21]. Cyber ranges are instrumental in developing skilled cybersecurity workforces by providing realistic training environments that mirror evolving threat landscapes [22]. They are also used to validate SOC workflows, train on playbook execution, and test detection and containment strategies under pressure. Peratikou et al. [23] proposed a federated cyber range network interconnection model that supports distributed cyber training across organizational and national boundaries. By embedding cyber range capabilities into both central and sectorial SOCs, CY-TRUST enhances its capacity-building mission while ensuring operational readiness at all levels. Together, cybersecurity situational awareness, threat intelligence, and cyber ranges represent a triad of capabilities that underpin modern SOC architectures. Situational awareness offers real-time understanding of threats; CTI provides the contextual intelligence to inform strategic decisions; and cyber ranges deliver the hands-on training needed to execute effective responses. The CY-TRUST project integrates all three to build a replicable, AI-enabled, and sector-tailored national cybersecurity model enhancing both operational effectiveness and cross-border interoperability within the EU. CY-TRUST architecture aligns with the CSOC Blueprint and the strategic goals of the EU Cybersecurity Strategy. Technically, the project builds upon open standards such as STIX/TAXII for threat intelligence exchange and for automating incident response. While national SOCs exist in several EU countries, few integrate modular sectorial deployments with AI-driven analytics and coordinated response playbooks across multiple sectors, making CY-TRUST a novel implementation.

3 Baseline Assessment and Requirements

A critical foundation of the CY-TRUST architecture was the establishment of a realistic and actionable baseline of cybersecurity capabilities across key national infrastructure stakeholders in Cyprus. This initial phase aimed to uncover operational maturity levels, identify capability gaps, and elicit technical, procedural, and regulatory requirements to inform the design and deployment of sectorial Security Operations Centers (SOCs).

3.1 Stakeholder Selection and Scope

The baseline assessment included six representative stakeholders from different critical sectors in Cyprus. These entities were selected for their essential role in national services, varying levels of cybersecurity preparedness, and relevance under the NIS2 directive. Their inclusion ensured coverage of diverse operational models, from state-owned to private and hybrid organizations.

3.2 Methodology: SIM3-BASED Capability Assessment

To measure cybersecurity maturity consistently across all partners, the Security Incident Management Maturity Model (SIM3) was adopted. SIM3 evaluates SOC and CSIRT capabilities across four domains: Organization, Process, Tools, and People. For each domain, the partners were scored against a standard set of criteria addressing incident response capacity, monitoring, communication protocols, reporting workflows, and staff expertise. Stakeholders from essential service sectors and digital providers under the NIS2 Directive will be sampled to ensure representative coverage. The SIM3-based assessment uses a concise questionnaire and scoring rubric to evaluate organizational, process, tools, and people capabilities. The data collected is then analyzed to identify common gaps and maturity patterns across sectors, supporting the design of the three SOC deployment variants.

The assessment revealed substantial heterogeneity. While some entities had existing SOC functions or partial monitoring capabilities, others had limited or no centralized cybersecurity operations. Many lacked:

- Documented incident response workflows.
- Automated threat detection systems.
- Threat intelligence (CTI) ingestion or sharing mechanisms.
- Training environments or simulation exercises for staff preparedness.

These gaps demonstrated the need for differentiated architectural responses, leading to the formulation of three SOC deployment models—Variants A, B, and C—tailored to partner SOC readiness and capabilities.

3.3 Deployment Variants and Capability Mapping

To accommodate varying levels of maturity, three SOC deployment variants were designed:

- Variant A: Centralized SOC Support: Sector partners without in-house monitoring capabilities are served directly via the DSA's national SOC instance. All processing and alerting are centralized.
- Variant B: Federated Sectorial SOCs: Stakeholders operate local SOCs with partial autonomy, including their own data ingestion, visualization, and incident triage functions, but remain integrated with the national backend.
- Variant C: SOC Integration Layer: For organizations with their own SOCs, CY-TRUST provides an integration interface to connect their tooling to the shared CTI ecosystem and orchestrated response mechanisms.

This flexible model enables each stakeholder to be aligned with a deployment scenario that reflects their current capabilities and readiness. For instance, three of the stakeholders were mapped to Variant B, while one of them was placed under Variant C due to its representational role for SMEs.

4 CY-TRUST Architecture

The CY-TRUST architecture was designed to support a flexible, scalable, and standards-compliant cybersecurity operations framework that meets the needs of a heterogeneous group of stakeholders across Cyprus. The architecture enables the implementation of sectorial Security Operations Centers (SOCs) while maintaining centralized coordination, interoperability with EU infrastructures, and integration with existing national cybersecurity assets.

4.1 Architectural Principles

The architecture follows these foundational principles:

- Federated Autonomy with Coordinated Governance: Sectorial SOCs maintain operational control over local infrastructures while participating in a nationally coordinated cyber response ecosystem. The centralized backend, managed by the Digital Security Authority (DSA), facilitates data aggregation, national crisis coordination, and EU interoperability.
- Scalability and Modularity: SOCs are implemented according to a scalable reference model with variant-based deployments (centralized, federated, and integrated). Each component can be independently updated or extended to support new threats, sectors, or regulatory changes. AI-Driven Intelligence and
- Automation: Integration of artificial intelligence enhances threat detection, predictive analysis, and orchestration of automated responses via playbooks.
- Standards-Based Interoperability: Alignment with open and vendor-neutral standards including STIX 2.1, TAXII, and the OASIS Threat Actor Context ontology ensures compatibility with EU programs and national CSIRT/CERT infrastructures.
- Resilience and Preparedness: Incorporation of the Cyber Threat Realm (CTR) cyber range ensures continuous capacity building and incident readiness across all levels.

While this paper focuses on the architectural perspective, the design choices for AI integration, federated learning, and network topology were guided by scalability, data sovereignty, and regulatory compliance considerations. The selected approaches ensure alignment with the project's operational context and the EU's cybersecurity framework, rather than optimizing for specific algorithmic performance.

4.2 Layered Architectural Model

The CY-TRUST architecture is structured into four interdependent layers as shown in Fig. 1.

Layer 1: External and EU-Level Interfaces

- Connects with ENISA, CERT-EU, CyCLONe, and other European cybersecurity infrastructures.
- Enables real-time exchange of Indicators of Compromise (IoCs), threat actor profiles, and incident response protocols.
- Supports alignment with EU-level strategic directives (NIS2, CRA, EUCS).

Layer 2: National Coordination Layer, DSA SOC Backend

- Operated by the DSA, this core backend serves as the national coordination plane.
- Composed of the following:
  - SIEM Cluster which aggregates logs, telemetry, and alerts from all SOC layers for centralized monitoring.
  - SOAR Engine that executes playbooks with automated responses, enriched with real-time context.
  - CTI Hub to manage structured threat data using STIX/TAXII and facilitates two-way integration with MISP.
  - Analytics Engine that hosts federated AI/ML models for User and Entity Behavior Analytics (UEBA), anomaly detection, and trend forecasting.
  - Multitenant Architecture to support isolated tenant environments for sectorial SOCs while allowing shared resources where appropriate.

Layer 3: Sectorial SOC Instances
Deployed per organization or sector with tailored capabilities:

- Lightweight or full-feature SOC platforms based on Variant A, B, or C.
- Local ingestion pipelines (e.g., from NIDS, HIDS, endpoint tools).
- Interfaces for telemetry, dashboards, and incident triage.
- Optional deployment of local playbook interpreters and analytics microservices

Enables horizontal collaboration across sectors through shared threat feeds and playbook repositories.

Layer 4: Interoperability and Crisis Coordination Layer

- Supports multi-party response workflows during large-scale incidents.
- Maintains synchronization of operational and training playbooks, allowing rapid mobilization.

Leverages semantic interoperability tools to harmonize data models and facilitate trust between entities.

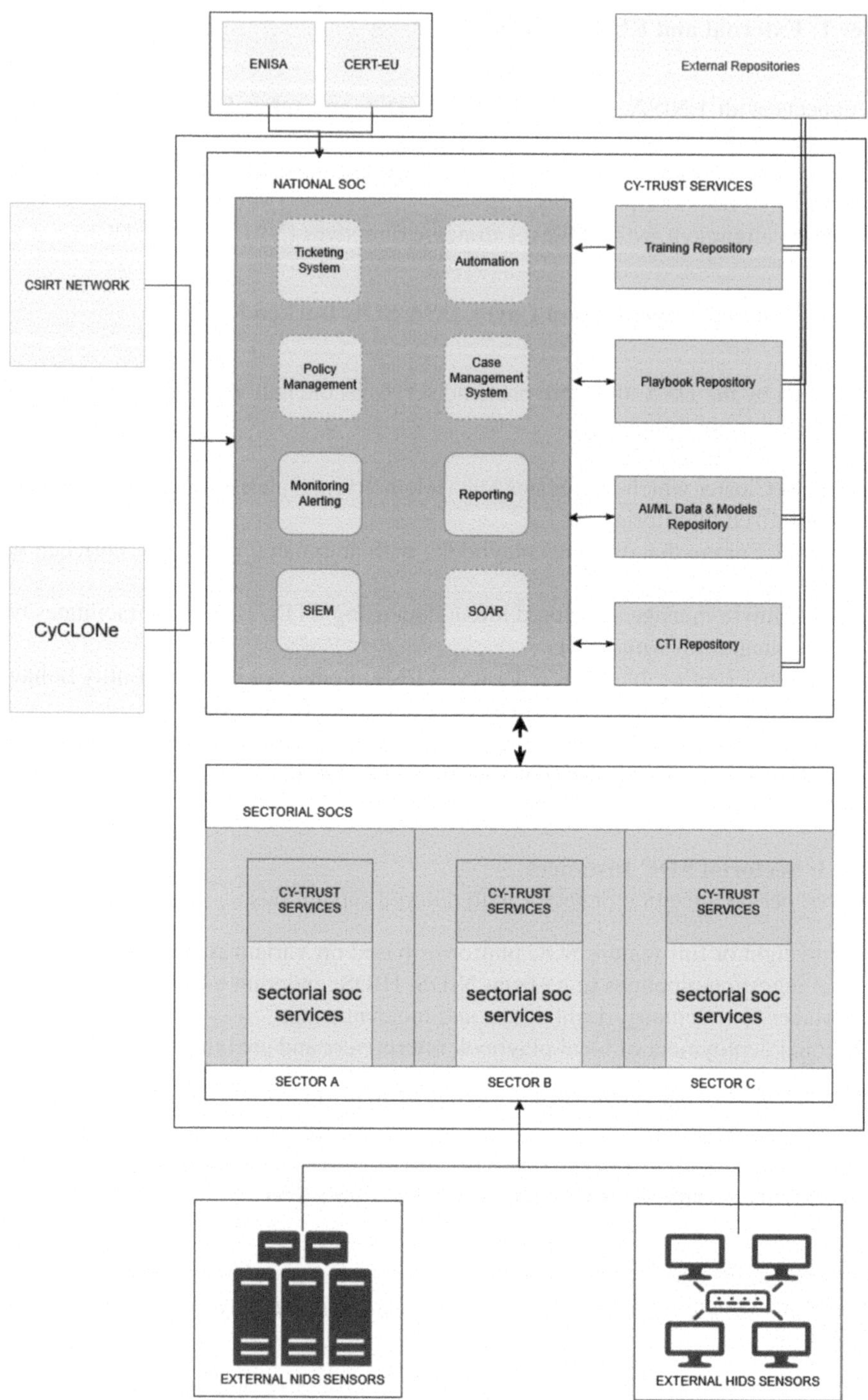

Fig. 1. CY-TRUST Architecture Overview

4.3 Integration of Core Functional Components

CY-TRUST embeds its enabling technologies across layers to achieve a fully functional SOC ecosystem:

- AI-Augmented Threat Detection: Machine learning models for anomaly detection and predictive analytics operate both locally and centrally, trained through federated learning principles to preserve data sovereignty.
- Playbook Automation: Playbooks define modular workflows (e.g., isolation, escalation, notification), allowing human and automated responses to operate in unison. These are version-controlled and sharable between SOCs.
- Cyber Threat Intelligence Sharing: CTI Extractor and Translator modules transform unstructured reports into machine-readable STIX 2.1 objects and enrich them with ontological context for integration into national and EU platforms.
- Cyber Threat Realm: A distributed multi domain cyber range used for exercises, simulations, and red/blue team engagements. CTR integrates with incident scenarios to support post-incident learning and validation.
- Training and Preparedness: A Learning Management System including online courses, tabletop simulations, certifications, and technical exercises. Training pathways are aligned to organizational roles and dynamically assigned based on threat patterns or exercise performance.

4.4 Enhanced Flow and Governance

The architecture supports a dynamic and responsive governance model:

- **Data Flows:** Events collected at sectorial SOCs are filtered and enriched before being pushed to the national backend. Responses may be initiated centrally or recommended back to the source SOC.
- **Governance and Orchestration:** Policies and access controls are defined centrally but enforced locally, enabling both compliance and contextual customization.
- **Trust and Auditability**: Role-based access controls, pseudonymization of sensitive telemetry (especially in UEBA data), and comprehensive audit logs ensure legal and operational accountability.

4.5 Security, Privacy, and Interoperability Considerations

Security and data integrity are ensured through:

- TLS-secured communication between SOC layers.
- Pseudonymized UEBA data flows to preserve privacy.
- Role-based access control and incident traceability.
- Support for both pull-based (STIX/TAXII) and push-based (MISP) CTI feeds.

Interoperability is achieved via:

- Standardized message formats.
- Executable playbooks with schema validation.
- Ontology-driven threat analysis (via the TAC Ontology).

- Integration with both legacy and cloud-native cybersecurity tools.

This architectural foundation enables CY-TRUST to support not only sectorial operations but also national coordination and European alignment, fulfilling both local resilience goals and EU strategic directives. The next section describes the operational enablers that activate this architecture across real-world pilots.

4.6 Preparedness and Training

An integral component of the CY-TRUST architecture is the centralized backend infrastructure that enables training, preparedness, and knowledge dissemination across sectors. As depicted in Fig. 2, the CY-TRUST Central Backend orchestrates global scenario management, learning material distribution, and training synchronization. It includes modules such as the Global Cyber Range, LMS System, and Training Repository, which interoperate with sectorial SOC deployments. Data is dynamically routed based on sector involvement, ensuring role-aligned training and consistent preparedness across the ecosystem.

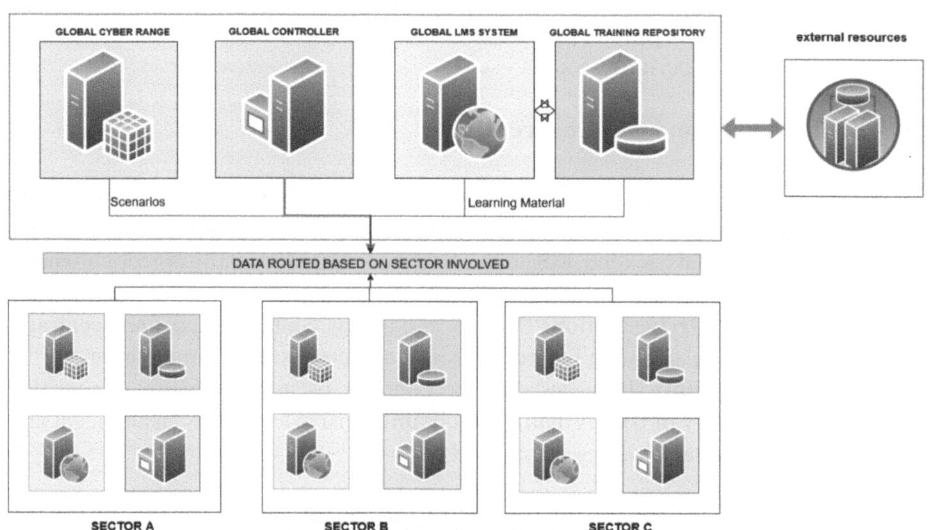

Fig. 2. CY-TRUST Central Backend Preparedness and Training Enabler

5 Testbed Setup and Design Evaluation

The evaluation framework for the CY-TRUST proof-of-concept (PoC) focuses on validating the integrated capabilities of sectorial and national Security Operations Centres (SOCs). The testbed architecture supports both functional and performance evaluation across four representative sectors, energy, maritime, government, and SMEs. It provides a controlled environment for simulating realistic cyber threats and observing system responses under operational conditions. The testbed comprises of dedicated infrastructure mirroring each sector's cybersecurity environment. It also includes central and sectorial SOC deployments, based on three architectural variants (centralized via DSA, dedicated sectorial SOCs, and federated pre-existing SOCs). It consists of an AI-powered situational awareness tools, incident response engines with playbook automation, and cyber range training facilities. The CY-TRUST testbed architecture integrates multiple components, including SIEMs, IDS/IPS systems, orchestration platforms, CTI feeds, and LMS modules, ensuring comprehensive coverage from detection to response and training. To ensure high availability and secure connectivity across the distributed SOC environments, the CY-TRUST testbed adopts a fault-tolerant network architecture as shown in Fig. 3, providing a resilient network architecture supporting CY-TRUST SOC deployments. The design incorporates dual Internet Service Providers (ISP 1 and ISP 2), redundant routers and firewalls in a high-availability configuration, and segregated internal network zones for services, host networks, and end users. Such architecture ensures continuous service availability, fault tolerance, and secure routing for both sectorial operations and national-level coordination. To demonstrate the integrated detection and response flow within the testbed, Fig. 4 presents the processing pipeline used in the CY-TRUST SOC environment. Events are first collected by host agents and processed through the HIDS/SIEM components. Logs are parsed and enriched, indexed, correlated, and visualized, or forwarded to downstream services such as alerting, CTI systems, playbook automation, or AI-assisted modules. The bottom layer highlights the integration of additional SOC services (e.g., LMS, Cyber Range, Ticketing, Monitoring) that operate over the enriched data stream. Preliminary evaluation results indicate measurable operational improvements across pilot SOC deployments.

5.1 Evaluation Methodology

The assessment methodology follows a structured, multi-dimensional approach encompassing baseline assessment derived from SOC maturity profiling (based on SIM3). KPI and metric alignment across technical (e.g., detection latency, containment time) and operational (e.g., cross-sector collaboration) indicators. Scenario execution per sector with tailored threat simulations (e.g., DDoS on SCADA, ransomware in government, phishing for SMEs). Data monitoring and evaluation of alerts, system logs, user response, and automated actions. Feedback loops for iterative improvement and playbook refinement. Evaluation dimensions include Situational awareness, Cyber threat intelligence (CTI) usage, Incident response execution, Training and preparedness, Interoperability, Compliance readiness. Each dimension is scored on a scale from 1 (Very Poor) to 5 (Excellent), with anchoring descriptions ensuring consistency across evaluators.

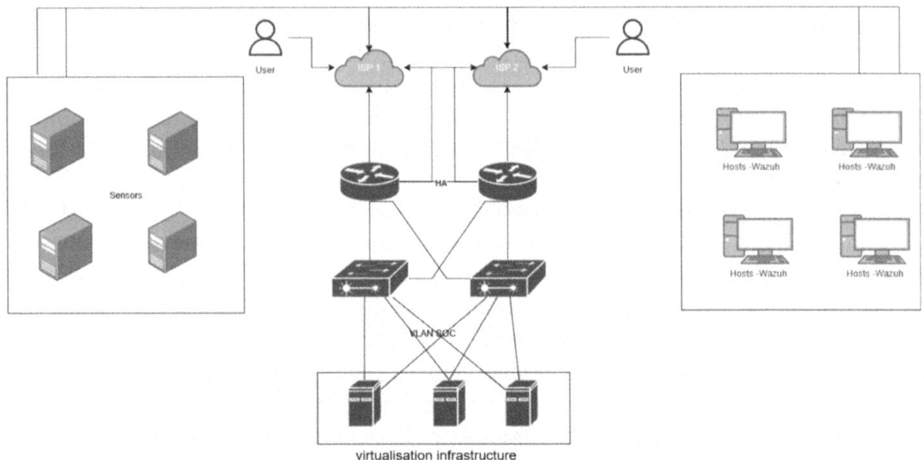

Fig. 3. High-Availability Network Topology for Sectorial SOC Integration

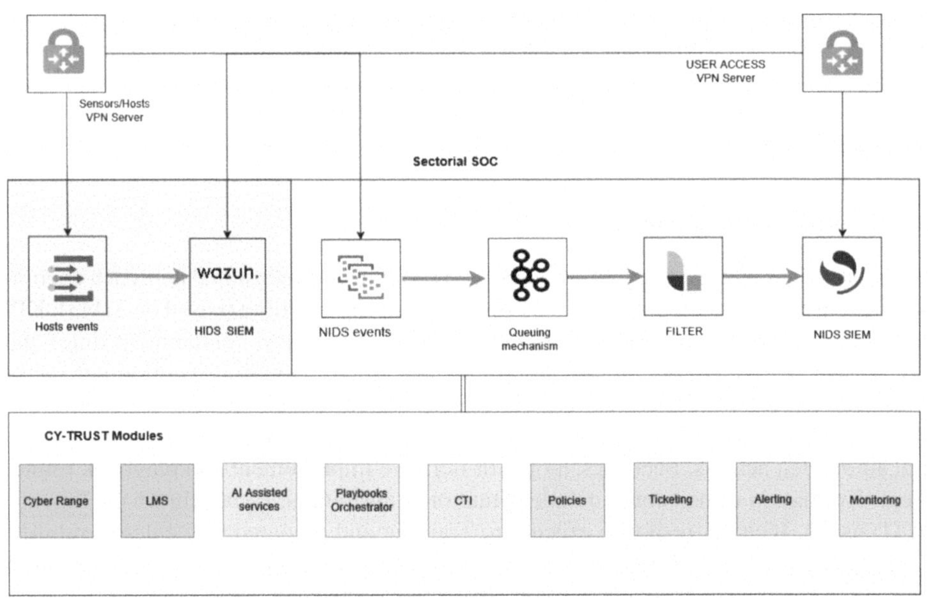

Fig. 4. Flow of host-based events through a layered detection and response pipeline in CY-TRUST.

6 Conclusions

CY-TRUST demonstrates a comprehensive, forward-looking model for implementing sectorial cybersecurity operations within a nationally coordinated and EU-aligned framework. By integrating AI-driven situational awareness, structured cyber threat intelligence, and immersive cyber range training into a modular, standards-compliant architecture, the project addresses the operational heterogeneity and evolving threat landscape that characterizes modern critical infrastructure ecosystems. The deployment of three tailored SOC variants enables flexible adoption across sectors with varying cybersecurity maturity levels, ensuring inclusivity and scalability. The project's federated architecture, anchored by the national SOC backend, fosters interoperability and real-time collaboration across sectorial SOCs, national authorities, and EU entities. This design reflects an evolution beyond traditional SOC silos toward a more cohesive, federated cybersecurity posture. Early results suggest notable improvements in threat detection accuracy, reduced mean time to response (MTTR), and increased stakeholder engagement in cybersecurity training and coordination efforts. Moreover, CY-TRUST's adherence to EU standards such as STIX/TAXII, and the NIS2 directive, positions it as a replicable model for other Member States seeking to modernize and federate their national cybersecurity capabilities.

While these results are promising, several challenges remain to be addressed. Ensuring privacy in federated learning, harmonizing cross-border data exchange under NIS2, and supporting resource-constrained SMEs represent key focus areas for the next project phase. These limitations highlight the importance of continuous evaluation and policy alignment to ensure sustainable adoption.

Looking ahead, the project opens avenues for further research and development in areas such as federated learning for threat detection, zero-trust orchestration across sectors, and the use of synthetic data in cyber range simulations. Continuous feedback from real-world deployments and stakeholder evaluations will guide future iterations of the CY-TRUST framework, contributing to both national resilience and EU-wide cybersecurity harmonization. In summary, CY-TRUST is not only a national implementation it is a blueprint for how countries can operationalize cybersecurity cooperation at scale, blending technology, policy, and sectorial engagement to safeguard their digital sovereignty in an increasingly interconnected and adversarial cyber environment.

Acknowledgments. This work has received funding from the European Union's Digital Europe Programme (DIGITAL) under the Grant Agreement No. 101128017 (CY-TRUST project). Views and opinions expressed are, however, those of the authors only and do not necessarily reflect those of the European Union or the granting authorities. Neither the European Union nor the granting authorities can be held responsible for them.

References

1. ENISA: EU Cybersecurity Certification Scheme (EUCS) – Candidate Version. Publications Office of the European Union, Luxembourg (2024). https://data.europa.eu/doi/10.2824/614691
2. European Commission: NIS2 Implementation Guidance for Operators of Essential and Important Entities. Directorate-General for Communications Networks, Content and Technology (DG CONNECT), Brussels (2024). https://digital-strategy.ec.europa.eu/en/library/nis2-implementation-guidance
3. Shatnawi, A.S., Al-Duwairi, B., Almazari, M.M., Alshakhatreh, M.S., Khader, A.N., Abdullah, A.A.: Adaptable plug and play security operations center leveraging a novel programmable plugin-based intrusion detection and prevention system. arXiv (2022). https://doi.org/10.48550/arxiv.2204.04576

4. Damianou, A., Mazi, M.S., Rizos, G., Voulgaridis, A., Votis, K.: Situational awareness scoring system in cyber range platforms. In: Proceedings of the 2024 IEEE International Conference on Cyber Security and Resilience (CSR), New York, pp. 520–528. IEEE (2024).https://doi.org/10.1109/csr61664.2024.10679451
5. Ainslie, S., Thompson, D.G., Maynard, S.B., Ahmad, A.: Cyber-threat intelligence for security decision-making: a review and research agenda for practice. Comput. Secur. **132**, 103352 (2023). https://doi.org/10.1016/j.cose.2023.103352
6. Macabante, C., Wei, S., Schuster, D.: Elements of cyber-cognitive situation awareness in organizations. In: Proceedings of the Human Factors and Ergonomics Society Annual Meeting, vol. 63, no. 1, pp. 1624–1628. SAGE Publications, Thousand Oaks (2019). https://doi.org/10.1177/1071181319631483
7. Fysarakis, K., Mavroeidis, V., Athanatos, M., Spanoudakis, G., Ioannidis, S.: A blueprint for collaborative cybersecurity operations centres. In: Proceedings of the 2022 IEEE International Conference on Big Data (Big Data), New York, pp. 2601–2609. IEEE (2022). https://doi.org/10.1109/BigData55660.2022.10020736
8. Amanowicz, M.: A shared cybersecurity awareness platform. J. Telecommun. Inf. Technol. **3**, 32 (2021). https://doi.org/10.26636/jtit.2021.154421
9. Peratikou, A., Charalambous, E., Smyrli, P., Stavrou, S.: ATHENA: a federated architecture for cross-border cybersecurity operations and situational awareness. In: Proceedings of the Cyber Security & Resilience Conference (CSR), 2025, Crete, Greece (2025)
10. Aljuhami, A.M., Bamasoud, D.M.: Cyber threat intelligence in risk management. Int. J. Adv. Comput. Sci.Appl. **12**(10) (2021). https://doi.org/10.14569/ijacsa.2021.0121018
11. Sibiga, M.P.: Applying Cyber Threat Intelligence to Industrial Control Systems. Thesis, Air Force Institute of Technology, Wright-Patterson AFB, OH, USA (2017). https://scholar.afit.edu/cgi/viewcontent.cgi?article=2606&context=etd
12. Kim, D., Kim, H.K.: Automated dataset generation system for collaborative research of cyber threat intelligence analysis. arXiv (2018). https://arxiv.org/abs/1811.10050v2
13. Alevizos, L., Dekker, M.: Towards an AI-enhanced cyber threat intelligence processing pipeline. Electronics **13**(11), 2021 (2024). https://doi.org/10.3390/electronics13112021
14. Sun, N., et al.: Cyber threat intelligence mining for proactive cybersecurity defense: a survey and new perspectives. IEEE Commun. Surv. Tutor. **25**(3), 1748–1778 (2023). https://doi.org/10.1109/comst.2023.3273282
15. Radoglou-Grammatikis, P., Sarigiannidis, P., Chatzikonstantinou, I., et al.: Surveying cyber threat intelligence and collaboration. In: Proceedings of the 2023 IEEE International Conference on Cloud Computing Technology and Science (CloudCom), New York, pp. 309–314. IEEE (2023). https://doi.org/10.1109/CloudCom59040.2023.00057
16. Ellinitakis, R.A., Fysarakis, K., Bountakas, P., Spanoudakis, G.: Automated, machine learning-based CTI extraction from online sources. In: Proceedings of the 2024 IEEE International Conference on Cyber Security and Resilience (CSR) Workshops, New York, pp. 860–865. IEEE (2024). https://doi.org/10.1109/CSR61664.2024.10679473
17. Saeed, S., Suayyid, S.A., Al-Ghamdi, M.S., Almuhaisen, H.A., Almuhaideb, A.M.: A systematic literature review on cyber threat intelligence for organizational cybersecurity resilience. Sensors **23**(16), 7273 (2023). https://doi.org/10.3390/s23167273
18. Andreolini, M., Colacino, V.G., Colajanni, M., Marchetti, M.: A framework for the evaluation of trainee performance in cyber exercises. In: 2020 IEEE International Conference on Cyber Security and Resilience (CSR), New York, pp. 1–8. IEEE (2020)
19. Russo, E., Ribaudo, M., Orlich, A., Longo, G., Armando, A.: Cyber range and cyber defense exercises: gamification meets university students. In: Proceedings of the 28th ACM Conference on Innovation and Technology in Computer Science Education, New York, pp. 29–34. ACM (2023). https://doi.org/10.1145/3617553.3617888

20. Potamos, G., Peratikou, A., Stavrou, S.: Towards a maritime cyber range training environment, p. 180, July 2021. https://doi.org/10.1109/csr51186.2021.9527904
21. Fysarakis, K., et al.: PHOENi2X – a European cyber resilience framework. In: Proceedings of the 2023 IEEE International Conference on Cyber Security and Resilience (CSR) Workshops, New York, pp. 538–545. IEEE (2023). https://doi.org/10.1109/CSR57506.2023.10224995
22. Ošlejšek, R., Vykopal, J., Burská, K.D., Rusňák, V.: Evaluation of cyber defense exercises using visual analytics process. In: 2021 IEEE Frontiers in Education Conference (FIE), New York, pp. 1–6. IEEE (2018). https://doi.org/10.1109/fie.2018.8659299
23. Peratikou, A., Louca, C., Shiaeles, S., Stavrou, S.: On federated cyber range network interconnection. In: Ghita, B., Shiaeles, S. (eds.) INC 2020. LNNS, vol 180, pp. 117–128. Springer, Cham (2021). https://doi.org/10.1007/978-3-030-64758-2_9

CPSTRIDE: A Threat Modeling Framework for Cyber-Physical Systems

Dallas Elleman(✉) and John Hale

University of Tulsa, Tulsa, OK 74104, USA
{dallas-elleman,john-hale}@utulsa.edu
https://utulsa.edu/programs/cyber-security/

Abstract. Cyber-physical systems requires threat models that account for cyber and physical vulnerabilities alike. We present the CPSTRIDE framework, which extends the classic STRIDE model with a novel Cyber-Physical Flow Diagram and updated Security Property and Threat definitions. We demonstrate CPSTRIDE's utility by modeling threats beyond STRIDE's capabilities, and employ LLM assistance to identify threats in an additive manufacturing context.

Keywords: Cyber-Physical Systems · Additive Manufacturing · Threat Modeling · STRIDE · Critical Infrastructure · LLM-assisted

1 Introduction

Cyber-physical systems (CPS) combine sensors, actuators, and computation to monitor and control physical processes and enable automation and efficiency. They are integral to distributed, adaptive, and data-driven decision-making and operations in nearly every critical sector, including transportation, health care, energy, and Industry 4.0 [12]. Additive manufacturing (AM) technologies are a quintessential example of CPS that merge digital and physical processes to overcome legacy manufacturing limitations [3]. Automation and connectivity confer many advantages in CPS, but also expose new attack paths that compromise safety-critical systems. In light of widespread and potentially catastrophic risks to infrastructure, services, and human safety, CPS threat modeling is imperative for their secure and resilient design, deployment, operation, and maintenance [5].

Threat modeling frameworks (e.g., STRIDE, MITRE ATT&CK, Cyber Kill Chain) are used widely in the design, modeling, and analysis of information and communications technologies such as computers, software applications, and the Internet. However, these frameworks lack the native capacity to model physical vulnerabilities in CPS, such as in plant and machinery, material flows, energetic processes, physical access controls and trust boundaries, and many other elements and interactions [10]. Our research fills this gap with a purpose-built framework for CPS threat modeling, comprising several primary contributions:

1. We present CPSTRIDE, a threat modeling framework for CPS that extends the STRIDE framework with updated security properties and threats.

E. Bergström et al. (Eds.): CRITIS 2025, LNCS 16291, pp. 384–403, 2026.
https://doi.org/10.1007/978-3-032-19540-1_20

2. We describe the Cyber-Physical Flow Diagram (CPFD), which transcends the STRIDE Data Flow Diagram (DFD) paradigm by modeling physical and cyber-physical elements and threats and distinguishing between processes and devices, and between flows and paths.
3. We demonstrate CPSTRIDE's utility for CPS threat modeling - and its advantages over STRIDE - via LLM-assisted comparative threat modeling and identification on a representative AM system.

The remainder of the paper is organized as follows: Sect. 2 presents background information and previous work related to CPS and AM threats and STRIDE-based threat modeling. Section 3 details the CPSTRIDE framework. Section 4 describes our comparative threat modeling of an AM system using both CPSTRIDE and STRIDE. Section 5 compares and discusses the results. Section 6 suggests future directions and offers concluding remarks.

2 Background/Previous Work

2.1 Cyber-Physical System Threat Modeling with STRIDE

A substantial body of research is directed at re-purposing existing threat modeling frameworks for use in CPS; one popular choice is Microsoft's STRIDE framework [13]. STRIDE's iterative four-step process entails creating a Data Flow Diagram (DFD) for the system under study, identifying threats to each DFD element, investigating system vulnerabilities to threats, and prioritizing mitigations for vulnerabilities. DFDs use a set of five symbols that represent different types of software-relevant objects [8]. Yampolskiy et al. [17] extend STRIDE for application to uncrewed aerial systems (UAS). They note STRIDE's insufficiency for differentiating CPS-relevant interactions, e.g., cyber vs. physical communications, and formulate an extended DFD or "xDFD" that enables modeling of "physical components, communication media, optional data flows, and physical signal" using four additional DFD elements. They address several threat modeling challenges in CPS, but do not expand STRIDE security property and threat definitions. Khan et al. [10] apply STRIDE to analyze a synchronous island microgrid electrical system, demonstrating the method's expertise-informed brainstorming to identify cyber-attacks. They discuss the DFD's shortcomings for representing physical and cyber-physical elements and processes in electric power systems, and opt to exclude components not susceptible to cyber attacks from their model. To our knowledge, there is no widely-recognized standard for representing physical system elements and threats using the STRIDE framework.

2.2 Additive Manufacturing Threat Modeling

AM systems combine digital design models and material feed stocks to produce physical objects, and as such are prime examples of CPS. Configuration and implementation details vary, but all AM systems exhibit the characteristic process chain illustrated by the entities and flows in Fig. 1.

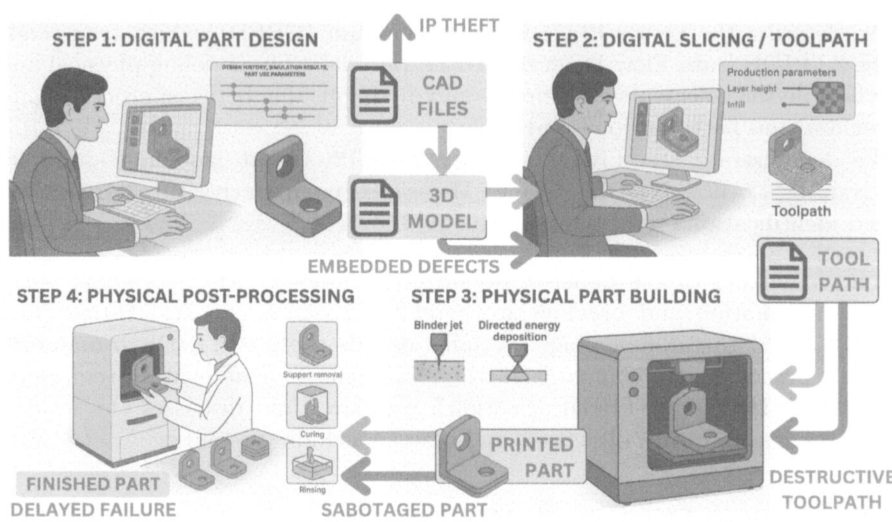

Fig. 1. The AM process chain, with benign and malicious cyber-physical flows

Using computer aided design (CAD) software, AM parts are digitally modeled and optimized through iterative simulation and analysis; the resulting CAD files include the part's 3-D model, design history, and simulated performance information (if applicable). The 3-D model is then *sliced* into layers and a *toolpath* is generated that contains a set of machine instructions for physically building each part layer. This toolpath is then given to an AM machine, which executes each line of instructions to mechanically deposit and/or join feedstock one layer or small amount at a time. Once the toolpath file has been executed completely, the physical part may finally undergo post-processing, quality control testing, warehousing, shipping, and other product life cycle phases.

The AM process chain enables digital designs to be rapidly transformed into physical objects, with the unintended side effect of also allowing cyber-attacks to be rapidly translated into physical harms. AM systems are susceptible to regular cyber-security flaws as well as to unique attack vectors [4,6,7,11,18], some of which are illustrated in Fig. 1. Sturm et al. identify four main opportunities for cyber-attacks to cross into the physical world: the CAD file, 3D model, toolpath file, and the physical machine [15]. However, numerous other cyber-attack vectors permit physical attack manifestations in AM machinery.

CAD files are the most information-dense digital artifacts produced by the AM process chain, containing a part's geometric data, design history, simulated performance data, use parameters, and more, making them attractive targets for intellectual property (IP) theft and ransomware. Sabotage at this early stage may propagate data integrity and availability failures through the entire process chain [15]. 3-D model tampering can produce physical objects with hidden defects that are difficult or impossible to detect, causing unpredictable and dangerous failure during use, as found by Belikovetsky [4]. Toolpath files are vectors for sabotaging manufactured objects, allowing theft of IP in the form of operational and manufacturing parameters, and can be modified to result in incorrect machine movement, dimension scaling, heating, feedrates, and other actions resulting in production defects and/or catastrophic equipment damage [18].

Supply chain attacks, as Yampolskiy et al. report, are difficult to defend against due to the sprawling ecosystem of third-party providers in AM systems [18]. Malware embedded in AM software, hardware, and firmware components could grant adversaries access to IP and even real-time operational control. Other attacks targeting mechanical AM system components actuators, and feedstocks can result in material composition, size, or form factor inconsistency. Gupta et al. examine supply chain vulnerabilities where material composition, purity, and microstructure might be attacked [7]. Side channels for AM system attack include acoustic, magnetic, and thermal emanations that allow the recreation or replication of AM parts without direct access to files. This type of technical data theft can be accomplished via smartphones and inexpensive surveillance equipment [1,2,9]. In addition, 3-D model files can carry hidden malicious payloads via steganographic embedding [16].

The unique nature of the digital-model-to-physical-object AM process chain exemplifies the need for a comprehensive cyber-physical threat framework. Next, we describe our approach to creating such a framework - one that is both rich enough to capture fine system and process detail, and abstract enough to describe diverse types of CPS.

3 CPSTRIDE Framework Specification

We choose the mature and widely-used STRIDE model as a foundation due to its balance between specificity and generality for modeling cyber threats. While too data-centric and narrow for full description of CPS, we expand its coverage by examining its structure from first principles, starting with its four-step workflow:

1. Create a DFD model of the system.
2. Identify STRIDE threats, either per-element or per-interaction.
3. Investigate vulnerabilities to identified threats.
4. Plan mitigations for identified vulnerabilities.

Our changes to the STRIDE framework involve only the first two steps of the process; Steps 3 and 4 are not considered in our CPSTRIDE framework specification here, nor are they applied during side-by-side threat modeling of the AM system with both frameworks in Sect. 4. We begin with Step 1 by defining an expanded Cyber-Physical Flow Diagram (CPFD). For Step 2, we specify the CPS Security Properties and Threats required for threat identification.

3.1 CPFD: Cyber-Physical Flow Diagram

Drawing from Khan and Yampolskiy [10,17], and considering Shostack's [14] guidance to keep models "...aggressively simple to prioritize easy learning and use over expressiveness," we borrow five visual notation rules from DFDs:

1. All lines are solid, except for trust boundaries, which are dashed or dotted.[1]

[1] We extend the use of dashed lines for the two new CPFD elements: Links and Devices; see Fig. 2.

2. CPFDS can use color for additional information, but must not require it.
3. All elements should have a label.
4. Context diagram(s) for complex systems are optional.
5. Must, must not, should, should not are used per IETF norms.

Each existing DFD element has a name, a definition, an abbreviation, and a graphical symbol. Our process for developing the CPFD is to consider whether the *core meaning* of each existing DFD element definition can be expanded to include important physical and cyber-physical analogs in a CPS context. If so, we rename, redefine, and/or re-abbreviate the existing DFD element to include this context, and we retain its graphical symbol. Otherwise, we create a new element in the CPFD and strive for aggressive simplicity, à la Shostack [14]. Our resulting CPFD specification is found in Fig. 2.

For example, the DFD *Interactor (I)* element (sometimes referred to as External Entity – EE – as in [10]) represents a person, code or website that interacts with the software system but is outside its control. The core meaning, "beyond system scope," can be expanded to include CPS analogs such as physical raw material sources, gas or electric mains, cyber-physical supply chain providers, autonomous service robots, etc. We redefine a CPFD Interactor as "an entity that exchanges data, energy, or material with the CPS but remains outside its design scope and/or control boundary," specify its cyber, physical, and cyber-physical abbreviations, and keep the graphical symbol (see Fig. 2). Similarly we redefine the DFD *Trust Boundary* as "a virtual and/or physical zone of privileged access" and give it CPS abbreviation versions.

The DFD *Data Store (DS)* element represents data at rest (e.g., files, databases, registry keys) in software systems. This can be expanded to include CPS analogs at rest such as physical and cyber-physical materials, objects, and keys at rest. We wish to differentiate between the entity being stored and the storage medium as well as represent hierarchical or nested cyber-physical stores (e.g. digital files on a physical hard drive). Thus, we simplify the CPFD element name to *Store* and define it as "data, energy, or material at rest, distinct from its storage medium or container, with nesting allowed." Abbreviations and graphical symbol changes can be found in Fig. 2. We add a new element to the CPFD for physical and cyber-physical storage media and containers: *Device (D)*.

Similarly, the *Data Flow (DF)* element represents data in motion (e.g., communication patterns and function calls); this can be expanded to include CPS analogs such as material flows, but we agree with Yampolskiy et al. [17] that CPS flow-enabling paths and media such as gas pipes, transmission lines, and radio frequency (RF) spectrum deserve first-class representation. We simplify the CPFD element name to *Flow*, define it as "data, energy, or material in motion, distinct from its enabling path, channel or medium," modify its abbreviations and keep the graphical symbol, and add a new CPFD element to represent Flow enablers: *Link*.

The DFD *Process (P)* element represents "any running code." This definition can be expanded to include analogous CPS processes, but we wish to distinguish between cyber-physical processes (e.g., manufacturing, refining, automated logistics) and the entities that enable them (e.g., manufacturing and refining equipment, logistic robots). We define the CPFD Process element as "activity that transforms inputs into outputs," modify its abbreviations and keep the graphical symbol, and choose to represent Process enablers with the new CPFD Device element. The new CPFD *Link* and *Device* elements represent the paths and media that enable Flows and the entities that enable Stores and Processes, respectively. Their definitions, abbreviations, and graphical symbols can be found in Fig. 2; visually, these elements combine existing graphical conventions of Trust Boundaries, Flows, and Processes.

Cyber-physical Flow Diagram (CPFD)

Cyber indicates information, data, or signal; *physical* indicates material, energy, or force; *cyber-physical* indicates the integration or combination of the two. Each CPFD element is categorized as either cyber, physical, or cyber-physical depending on whether the element can reasonably be considered vulnerable to cyber and/or physical threats.

Element name, abbreviation, and description	**Graphical Symbol**	**Examples** **C:** *Cyber* **P:** *Physical* **CP:** *Cyber-physical*
Interactor (I) An entity that exchanges data, energy, or material with the CPS but remains outside its design scope and/or control boundary.	CI/PI/CPI	**CI**: External APIs, the Internet and other networks. **PI**: Raw material sources; water, gas or electric mains. **CPI**: Humans (e.g., employees, contractors), external orgs (e.g., supply chain providers, partners, customers), technological entities (e.g., autonomous delivery and service robots).
Trust Boundary (TB) A virtual and/or physical zone of privileged access.	CTB/PTB/CPTB	**CTB**: Password-protected systems, encrypted files, or trusted computing environments. **PTB**: Physically secured areas with controlled access, locked rooms, fenced perimeters, analog safes, motor housings, machine casings. **CPTB**: Secured areas with both physical barriers (locks, fences) and cyber controls (authentication, surveillance monitoring).
Store (S) Data, energy, or material at rest, distinct from its storage medium or container. Nesting is allowed.	CS/PS/CPS NCS/NPS/NCPS	**CS**: Files, databases, registry keys. **PS**: Raw materials, simple manufactured objects, physical keys. **CPS**: Smart materials, physical key cards, 3D-printed objects. *Note: The 3D-printed object's transformation from cyber to physical makes it vulnerable to time-dependent cyber-physical threats.*
Flow (F) Data, energy, or material in motion, distinct from its enabling path, channel or medium.	CF/PF/CPF	**CF**: Function calls, network communications, data transfers. **PF**: Material flows, energy transfers, mechanical forces. **CPF**: Sensor data streams, HVAC / IoT communications, transport of smart materials or devices, cyber-physical process I/Os.
Link (L) - New for CPFD A logical and/or physical path, channel, or medium that connects and enables Flows between CPFD elements.	CL/PL/CPL	**CL**: File formats / schema, data structures; communication ports, channels, & protocols. **PL**: Geographic routes, power lines, fluid pipes. **CPL**: RF spectrum, air (visible light / IR / acoustic transmission).
Process (P) Activity that transforms inputs into outputs.	CP/PP/CPP	**CP**: Only digital inputs and outputs, e.g. **any running code**. **PP**: Only physical inputs and outputs, e.g. manual manufacturing, simple raw material mixing / refining. **CPP**: Cyber-physical inputs and/or outputs, e.g. OT processes, smart manufacturing, automated logistics, robotic assembly, adaptive environmental control, etc.
Device (D) - New for CPFD An instantiation of computational capability and/or physical functionality for Processes and Stores; a virtually- and/or physically-embodied enabler of Processes and/or Storage in a cyber-physical system.	CD/PD/CPD	**CD**: Abstracted virtual / digital resources, e.g. virtual sensors and machines, Docker containers, digital twins, cloud compute instances, remote database servers, content delivery networks (CDN), cloud storage instances, distributed blockchain ledgers. **PD**: Mechanical actuators, manual valves, analog gauges, hydraulic motors, physical key storage lockboxes, material storage tanks, pressure vessels, chemical reagent containers. **CPD**: Embedded systems, smart thermostats, autonomous vehicles, IoT-enabled medical implants, OT actuators, desktop computers, 3D printers, smart inventory management systems, RFID-enabled storage cabinets, IoT-connected storage tanks with sensors.

Fig. 2. CPSTRIDE Cyber-physical Flow Diagram Specification

3.2 Security Properties and Threats

Our next task is to expand the STRIDE framework's Security Properties and corresponding Threats as needed to include CPS contexts; most of these need only minor modifications, which can be found in Figs. 3 and 4. However, we find that Authentication, Confidentiality, and Information Disclosure are too narrowly data-centric for CPS, and require more substantial redefinition.

The Authentication security property deals with the identification of users and software agents; we wish to expand the core meaning to include CPS analogs such as physical or cyber-physical parts or materials assumed to have come from a third-party supply chain provider. We define a new property – *Authenticity* – that includes the authentication of data entities as well as physical entities. Similarly, the Confidentiality property and corresponding Information Disclosure threat are too data-centric. The core meaning involves "(limiting) unauthorized access of valuable system elements and resources." These can be expanded to CPS analogs, such as the extraction or diversion of physical resources by unauthorized recipients, so we define a new security property and corresponding threat – *Containment* and *Interception* – that deal with (limiting) unauthorized interception of cyber-physical entities, including data (see Figs. 3 and 4).

CPSTRIDE Cyber-Physical Security Properties	
Highlighted rows contain new CPSTRIDE Security Properties.	
Property	**Definition**
Authenticity (*previously Authentication*)	System elements (such as users, processes, devices, materials, and energy sources) are genuine and can be verified as what they claim to be. Authenticity replaces and includes the traditional *Authentication* security property for data systems while extending to the verification of physical components, materials, and energy signatures in cyber-physical contexts.
Integrity	System elements (such as data, software, firmware, hardware, materials, and energy parameters) remain unaltered and uncorrupted by unauthorized means throughout their lifecycle. This preserves the traditional data Integrity concept while expanding to include physical properties such as material composition, structural integrity, and energy calibration.
Non-Repudiation	Actions performed within the system cannot be denied by their initiator, through providing sufficient evidence of activities across cyber and physical domains. This extends beyond digital audit trails to include physical evidence trails, sensor data, surveillance records, and material verification techniques that establish accountability.
Containment (*previously Confidentiality*)	System elements (such as data, energy, and material resources) remain within their authorized boundaries and are accessible only to entities with appropriate privileges. Containment replaces and includes the traditional data *Confidentiality* security property, and more broadly represents the prevention of unauthorized cyber-physical extraction, leakage, or diversion.
Availability / Reliability	System functions, services, and resources are accessible and operational when needed, at expected performance levels. This maintains the traditional concept of digital Availability while extending to the physical reliability of components, consistent energy supply, material accessibility, and operational continuity across the cyber-physical spectrum.
Authorization	Specific entities are explicitly granted or denied permission to access, control, or modify certain system elements. This extends traditional digital access controls to include physical access rights, operational authority over equipment, material handling permissions, and energy distribution controls throughout the cyber-physical system.

Fig. 3. CPSTRIDE Security Properties Specification

3.3 Susceptibility Matrix

Next, we consider that the STRIDE model conventionally assumes certain types of DFD elements to be immune to specific threats; for example, DFD Data Stores and Data Flows are considered immune to Spoofing; Interactors are assumed immune to Tampering; Information Disclosure; and Denial of Service threats; and Process elements are uniquely susceptible to Elevation of Privilege (see Fig. 5). In the context of secure software development these assumptions may be reasonable. However, CPSTRIDE's inclusion of physical dimensions and novel attack vectors motivates their reexamination. In addition, we argue that although Interactors are outside of system scope and/or control, the exercise of considering the effects of attacks on Interactors can still inform system hardening. The same argument holds for all other CPFD elements and threat categories. Accordingly, we broaden the assumed susceptibility of all CPFD elements to all threat categories, and leave narrowing the matrix to future work.

4 AM Threat Modeling: CPSTRIDE vs. STRIDE

To show the advantages of CPSTRIDE over STRIDE, we perform the first two steps of the threat modeling process side-by-side. Since the third and fourth steps for both frameworks are identical, we leave them as a future exercise. The CPS to be modeled is an advanced additive manufacturing facility providing critical parts for downstream customers. The hardware setup consists of a commercial-grade bound metal deposition (BMD)-type 3D printer, a debinder, and a sintering furnace, as well as a workstation and a network router/switch.

4.1 AM System Flow Diagram Modeling

First we perform the CPSTRIDE version of Step 1, modeling the AM system with a CPFD (Fig. 6). Each of the AM machines is modeled as a cyber-physical Device (CPD1-5). The router is connected via Cat5 ethernet cable to the other Devices, as well as to an enterprise network with Internet access. The networks are modeled as cyber-Interactors (CI1, CI2) and each physical connection is modeled as a cyber-physical Link (CPL1-6). Four cyber-physical Interactors are modeled: an internal designer/engineer, an operator/controller, an external material supply chain provider, and a critical downstream manufacturer (CPI1-4).

The AM process chain is broken into nine steps. Digital process chain steps from CAD design to toolpath transmission are represented by cyber-Processes (CP2-6) connected by cyber and cyber-physical Flows (CPF1, CPF2, CF1-10), while physical part production is represented by cyber-physical Processes (CPP1-4) with cyber (toolpath) and cyber-physical (material cartridge, physical part, operator input) input Flows (CF11, CPF3-12, CPF15).

Part CAD files are modeled as nested cyber-stores (CS2, NCS2.1-2.5) located on the workstation, and the AM part material cartridge is modeled as a cyber-physical store (CPS1). The physical stages of manufactured part production are modeled as four separate cyber-physical stores (CPS2-CPS5). Other modeled entities include material transport to and from the external downstream manufacturer and supply chain provider (cyber-physical Flows CPF13-14), both of which cross the primary AM Facility Cyber-Physical Trust Boundary (CPTB1); the operator/controller's quality control inspection of the AM part in the final production step (physical flow PF1); the transmission of design requirements and production parameters from the enterprise network to the human Interactors and the CAD files (cyber Flows CF12-14); and the emanation of RF and acoustic energy from the 3-D printer during operation (cyber-physical Link CPL7).

Next we perform the STRIDE version of Step 1, modeling the AM system with a DFD (Fig. 7). The AM facility is modeled as a Trust Boundary (TB1), with the Internet, human designer/engineer and operator/controller, router/switch and enterprise modeled as Interactors (I1-5). The AM process chain is modeled as 9 separate Processes (P1-9) with 20 Data Flows (DF1-20). CAD files are modeled as individual Data Stores (DS1-5), and the transmission of design requirements and production parameters from the enterprise network to the humans and router are modeled by Data Flows (DF14, DF21-22), but omitted for the CAD files to avoid cluttering the diagram. Physical entities are not modeled, nor are entities which only interact with the system physically; this includes several Links, Stores, and Devices modeled in the CPFD, as well as the supply chain and downstream manufacturing Interactors.

CPSTRIDE Cyber-Physical Threats		
Each Threat potentially violates a corresponding Security Property. In the Examples column, *Cyber* indicates threats to information, data, control signal, etc.; *Physical* indicates threats to material, energy, force, etc.; *Cyber-physical* indicates the integration or combination of the two. Highlighted rows contain new CPSTRIDE Threats.		
Threat	**Definition**	**Examples** **C:** *Cyber* **P:** *Physical* **CP:** *Cyber-physical*
Spoofing	Falsification of identity, source, or authenticity of system elements, including users, processes, signals, or physical/cyber-physical stores, undermining trust mechanisms and authentication controls within the CPS. *Violates Authenticity.*	**C:** Phishing, smishing, social engineering, malicious broadcast of trusted WiFi network SSID, typosquatting, deepfaking. **P:** Faking physical credentials, passing off counterfeit parts and materials as genuine, forging signatures on physical documents. **CP:** Broadcasting fake GPS to misguide autonomous vehicles or drones, injection of counterfeit OT sensor readings.
Tampering	Unauthorized modification, corruption, or alteration of legitimate cyber-physical entities including data, structures, energy flows, material compositions, or control signals, that compromises system integrity. *Violates Integrity.*	**C:** Modifying control logic in industrial automation software. **P:** Physically adjusting valve settings or equipment calibration screws. **CP:** Altering sensor readings through electromagnetic interference, causing the system to respond to fabricated conditions.
Repudiation	Denial of responsibility for actions within the system, either through passive rejection of accountability or active measures to destroy, corrupt, or disable auditing mechanisms or evidence trails that would establish proof of activities, legitimate or malicious. *Violates Non-repudiation.*	**C:** Disabling logging mechanisms to hide evidence of digital access. **P:** Destroying physical access records or tampering with surveillance footage. **CP:** Cross-domain log corruption.
Interception *(previously Information Disclosure)*	Unauthorized acquisition or monitoring of system resources, including data, energy flows, or physical materials, violating containment. Interception replaces and includes the traditional Information Disclosure threat, and *Violates Containment.*	**C:** Capturing sensitive control data through network sniffing. **P:** Physically extracting / diverting material from manufacturing processes. **CP:** Harvesting energy from wireless power transmission systems through unauthorized coupling.
Denial of Service	Impairment or prevention of system availability through any means that renders services, functions, or resources inaccessible or unreliable for legitimate users. *Violates Availability / Reliability.*	**C:** Network flooding, resource exhaustion, communication jamming. **P:** Blockage of moving parts; permanent damage by physical destruction, component sabotage, or irreversible physical alterations; energy disruption through power supply manipulation or battery depletion; environmental manipulation to introduce adverse conditions. **CP:** Creating electromagnetic interference to disrupt wireless communications and/or electronic sensors, physical obstruction of sensors/actuators.
Elevation of Privilege	Exploitation of system vulnerabilities to gain unauthorized higher-level access rights beyond assigned permissions. *Violates Authorization.*	**C:** Traditional privilege elevation cyber-techniques such as exploiting software vulnerabilities to gain administrative access to control systems. **P:** Obtaining master keys or accessing restricted physical areas without authorization. **CP:** Using physical access to maintenance ports to install privileged software that bypasses normal authorization controls.

Fig. 4. CPSTRIDE Threats Specification

DFD Element	S	T	R	I	D	E
Interactor	✓		✓			
Data Flow		✓		✓	✓	
Data Store		✓	✓	✓	✓	
Process	✓	✓	✓	✓	✓	✓

CPFD Element	S	T	R	I	D	E
Interactor	✓	✓	✓	✓	✓	✓
Trust Boundary	✓	✓	✓	✓	✓	✓
Store	✓	✓	✓	✓	✓	✓
Flow	✓	✓	✓	✓	✓	✓
Process	✓	✓	✓	✓	✓	✓
Link	✓	✓	✓	✓	✓	✓
Device	✓	✓	✓	✓	✓	✓

Fig. 5. Assumed susceptibility for DFD and CPFD elements.

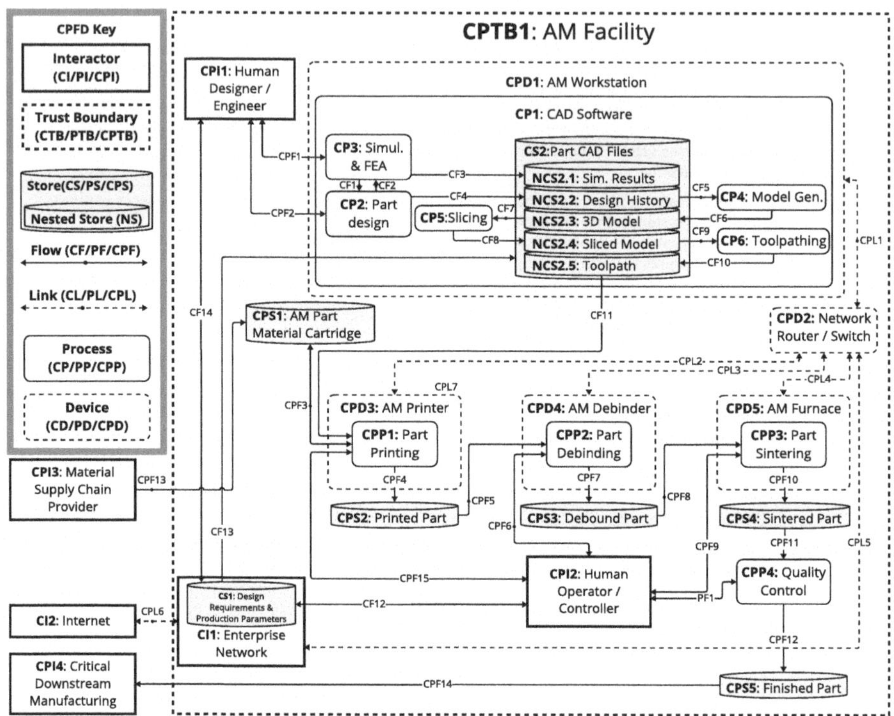

Fig. 6. Cyber-Physical Flow Diagram (CPFD) for additive manufacturing facility.

4.2 AM System Threat Identification

Next, we perform threat identification using each framework by considering how the threat categories apply to all flow diagram elements. For instance, to identify threats against the STRIDE representation of the 3-D Model (DS3) element in the DFD, we consult the STRIDE susceptibility matrix (Fig. 5) for Data Stores and find susceptibility to Tampering, Repudiation, Information Disclosure, and Denial of Service threats. We then consider how each threat might apply to the digital 3-D Model; Tampering with the 3-D Model could alter the design of the part; a Repudiation threat might involve modifying the 3-D Model's design history; an Information Disclosure threat might represent IP theft or publicly

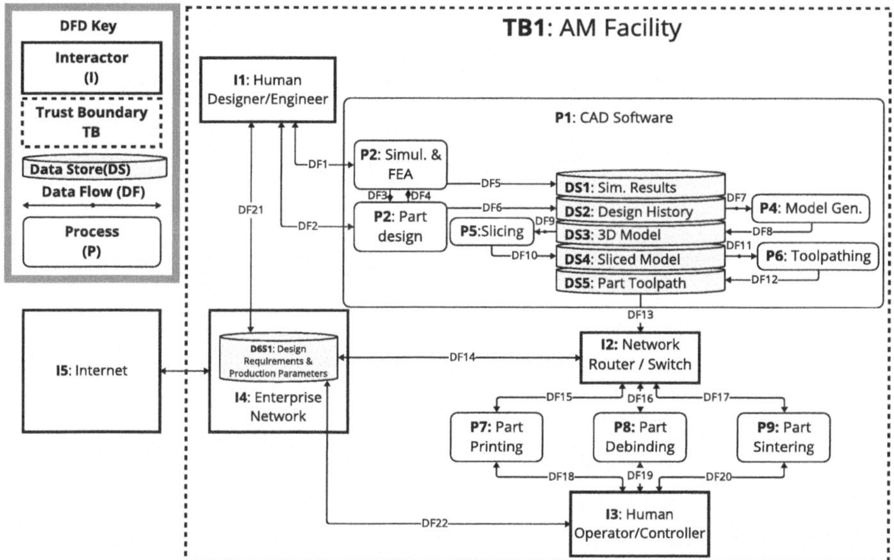

Fig. 7. Data Flow Diagram (DFD) for additive manufacturing facility.

leaking the 3-D Model; a Denial of Service threat could represent ransomware encryption or deletion of the 3-D Model. We use each applicable threat category as a brainstorming prompt to generate examples of threats to each diagram element modeled in the system. We repeat this process until all applicable threat susceptibilities have been considered for all diagram elements.

This approach generates extensive lists of threats to the system, but presents at least three challenges. First, this approach is time consuming and scales with size; larger and more complex system flow diagrams have more threats to identify. Second, this approach relies on expert knowledge; cyber-security professionals must not only be well-acquainted with the architecture and function of their system, but also consult online repositories such as MITRE ATT&CK and CVE to help identify likely cyber threats. Since there are no cyber-physical threat databases mirroring CVE for CPS, threat modeling in this domain must rely even more heavily on personal expert knowledge. A third challenge with this approach involves the ambiguity inherent in considering how a threat category might apply to an element. For instance, a particular system element might be considered the subject of a threat (i.e., the performer of a threat action), the object (target/victim) of a threat, or the instrument (used as a means to threaten another target) of a threat, or something else altogether.

We partially address the first two challenges by employing Anthropic's Claude 3.7 Sonnet large language model (LLM) as an automated assistant threat modeler. In response to the third challenge, we adopt a posture of systematically considering each threat category/element combination from all three of the perspectives mentioned above (subject, object, and instrument).

Element	Spoofing	Tampering	Repudiation
CPD3: AM Printer	**Object: Adversary could spoof printer identity in the network, causing misrouting of sensitive toolpath files. Instrument: Printer could be used to spoof manufacturing source of parts (counterfeiting).**	Object: Physical tampering with printer's calibration or components to alter part dimensions or introduce defects. Object: Tampering with embedded sensors to create false readings on material deposition quality.	Subject: Printer's firmware could be modified to report incorrect logging of operations, hiding evidence of unauthorized usage. Object: Logger or operation recorder could be disabled, preventing attribution of print jobs.
CPD4: AM Debinder	Object: Spoofed control signals from unauthorized sources could initiate dangerous operations.	Object: Tampering with temperature controls to alter material properties. Object: Tampering with safety interlocks to allow opening during operation.	Subject: Manipulation of operation logs to hide unauthorized chemical or material handling.
CPD5: AM Furnace	Similar to debinder, plus: Object: Spoofing of temperature sensors to trick safety systems.	Object: Tampering with gas supply or atmosphere control systems. Object: Modification of heating profiles to affect material properties.	Subject: Alteration of sintering records to hide unauthorized operations.
CPD2: Network Router/Switch	Object: Physical spoofing of device (replacing with malicious lookalike). Object: MAC address spoofing.	Object: Physical tampering with networking hardware to create backdoors or monitoring capabilities.	Object: Tampering with physical logs or indicators of connection activity.
CPL1-CPL6: Physical Network Connections	Object: Spoofing by creating a physically similar but malicious connection pathway. Instrument: Used as a medium for spoofed transmissions.	Object: Physical tapping, splicing or modification of cables. Object: Adding unauthorized hardware inline.	Instrument: Modified physical medium could be used to alter transmission records or logs.
CPL7: RF/Acoustic Side Channel	Instrument: Could be used to inject false signals into sensors.	N/A	N/A
CPS1: AM Part Material Cartridge	***Object: Counterfeit material cartridges with fraudulent identification tags/labels. Instrument: Used to introduce unauthorized materials with spoofed identification.***	Object: Adulterating material composition. Object: Tampering with material feed mechanisms. Object: Tampering with RFID/identification chips on cartridges.	Object: Removal or alteration of material batch tracking identifiers.
CPS2-CPS5: Physical Parts (Printed, Debound, Sintered, Finished)	Object: Counterfeit parts introduced into production chain. Instrument: Tampered parts could be used to falsely authenticate production source.	Object: Physical modification of parts between process steps. Object: Introduction of internal defects or weaknesses that evade detection.	Object: Removal or alteration of part identification markings/serial numbers.
PF1: Physical Inspection Flow	Object: Presenting different parts for inspection than those that were manufactured. Subject: Inspector could be impersonated by unauthorized personnel.	Object: Manipulation of physical inspection tools or gauges to incorrectly pass defective parts. Object: Tampering with part between manufacturing and inspection.	Subject: Inspector denying inspection was performed. Object: Removal or alteration of inspection stamps or markers.
CPF3-CPF12: Material/Part Movement Flows	Object: Redirecting physical materials to incorrect machines through misleading labeling or handling instructions.	Object: Modifying physical parts during transfer between process steps. Object: Swapping genuine parts with counterfeits during transfers.	***Subject: Denying responsibility for part handling errors. Object: Removal of handling logs or transfer records.***
CPF13: Material Flow from Supply Chain	Object: Accepting materials from fraudulent suppliers posing as legitimate vendors.	Object: Tampering with incoming materials during shipping or receiving. Object: Modifying material manifests or certifications.	***Subject: Supplier denying sending defective materials. Object: Tampering with shipping records or chain of custody.***
CPF14: Part Flow to Downstream Manufacturer	Object: Redirecting finished parts to unauthorized recipients through fraudulent shipping instructions.	Object: Tampering with parts during shipping or handling. Object: Swapping genuine parts with counterfeits during transit.	***Subject: Denying shipping defective parts. Object: Tampering with shipping manifests or delivery confirmations.***
CPF15: Operator Control Interactions	Subject: Spoofing operator identity through stolen badges or biometric workarounds. Object: Spoofed physical interfaces tricking operators into incorrect actions.	Object: Tampering with physical controls (buttons, switches) to cause incorrect operator inputs. Object: Altering physical feedback mechanisms (displays, indicators).	**Subject**: Operator denying initiating certain physical actions. **Object**: Disabling physical interaction logging systems.
CPI3: Material Supply Chain Provider	***Subject: Providing counterfeit materials with falsified certifications. Object: Supplier identity could be spoofed by competitors or malicious actors.***	Subject: Deliberately altering material properties or specifications. Object: Supply chain systems could be tampered with to alter material specifications.	***Subject: Denying knowledge of material defects or certification issues. Object: Tampering with supply chain records to hide responsibility.***
CPI4: Critical Downstream Manufacturing	***Subject: Falsely reporting part quality issues to gain access to manufacturing facilities or processes. Object: Downstream manufacturer identity could be spoofed to intercept parts.***	Subject: Requesting unauthorized modifications to physical specifications. Object: Tampering with parts after delivery but claiming they were received damaged.	**Subject**: Denying receipt of parts or falsely claiming defects. **Object**: Tampering with receiving records to hide responsibility.
CPP1: Part Printing Process	Object: Process could appear to be functioning correctly while actually using modified parameters through sensor spoofing.	Object: Physical tampering with print environment (temperature, humidity). Object: Tampering with physical layer registration or alignment.	***Object: Alteration of process logs to hide evidence of abnormal printing conditions.***
CPP2: Part Debinding Process	Object: Process monitoring could be spoofed to indicate proper debinding while incomplete.	Object: Tampering with physical environmental conditions affecting chemical reactions. Object: Altering solvent compositions or gas mixtures.	***Object: Manipulation of process records to hide improper debinding conditions.***
CPP3: Part Sintering Process	Object: Temperature or atmosphere monitoring could be spoofed to indicate proper sintering while improper.	Object: Manipulation of physical sintering environment (gases, pressure, temperature gradients). Object: Tampering with cooling rates to induce internal stresses.	***Object: Alteration of thermal records to hide improper sintering conditions.***
CPP4: Quality Control Process	Object: QC equipment could be manipulated to show false positive inspection results.	Object: Tampering with physical test specimens. Object: Manipulation of physical calibration standards.	***Object: Falsification of physical inspection records. Object: Removal of physical defect indicators.***

Fig. 8. The CPSTRIDE threat matrix identifies physical and cyber-physical spoofing, tampering, and repudiation threats in the AM system that have no standardized representation in STRIDE. Highlighted cells are special examples discussed further in the text.

Element	Interception	Denial of Service	Elevation of Privilege
CPD3: AM Printer	***Object: Side-channel emissions (acoustic/electromagnetic) could be intercepted to reverse-engineer part designs or manufacturing parameters. Object: Physical observation of printer operation could reveal proprietary manufacturing techniques.***	***Object: Physical damage to printer through sabotage or improper maintenance. Object: Overheating through disabling cooling systems. Object: Jamming of moving parts with foreign materials.***	Object: Unauthorized physical access to maintenance ports allowing privileged commands to be sent. Object: Exploitation of firmware update mechanisms to install modified firmware with elevated privileges.
CPD4: AM Debinder	Object: Unauthorized collection of process parameters through physical monitoring or tapping of control signals.	***Object: Physical blockage of ventilation systems. Object: Contamination of chemical baths or catalysts. Object: Damage to heating elements.***	Object: Exploitation of maintenance interfaces to gain control of equipment beyond operator permissions.
CPD5: AM Furnace	***Object: Monitoring of thermal profiles could reveal proprietary sintering parameters.***	***Object: Sabotage of gas supply lines. Object: Damage to heating elements or thermal barriers. Object: Manipulation of cooling rates to induce part stress.***	Object: Bypassing thermal safety systems through physical access to control circuits.
CPD2: Network Router/Switch	***Object: Physical tapping of network lines. Object: Installation of hardware keyloggers or packet sniffers.***	***Object: Physical damage or disconnection of network cables. Object: Signal jamming using physical proximity devices.***	Object: Physical access to reset mechanisms allowing reconfiguration with privileged access.
CPL1-CPL6: Physical Network Connections	***Object: Physical eavesdropping on network cables through electromagnetic monitoring. Object: Physical taps on communication lines.***	Object: Physical cutting or disconnection of cables. Object: Electromagnetic interference/ jamming of communication channels.	Instrument: Unauthorized physical access to connection points could enable privileged network access.
CPL7: RF/Acoustic Side Channel	***Object: Passive interception of unintentional electromagnetic or acoustic emissions to extract operational data or designs.***	Object: Deliberate RF/acoustic jamming to disrupt environmental sensors or wireless communications.	N/A
CPS1: AM Part Material Cartridge	Object: Unauthorized sampling of proprietary material formulations.	Object: Contamination or degradation of material properties. Object: Deliberate damage to feed mechanisms.	N/A
CPS2-CPS5: Physical Parts (Printed, Debound, Sintered, Finished)	Object: Physical theft of parts to obtain design information through reverse engineering. Object: Unauthorized measurements or scanning of parts.	Object: Physical damage to parts. Object: Contamination with materials that could cause downstream failures.	N/A
PF1: Physical Inspection Flow	Object: Unauthorized observation of inspection techniques could reveal proprietary quality control methods.	Object: Physical interference with inspection process. Object: Damage to inspection equipment.	Object: Unauthorized physical access to inspection area could allow an attacker to approve defective parts.
CPF3-CPF12: Material/Part Movement Flows	Object: Unauthorized observation of part transfers to gather manufacturing sequence information. Object: Visual or physical access to parts during transfer.	Object: Physical blockage of material transfer paths. Object: Creating unsafe conditions that halt transfers due to safety protocols.	Object: Unauthorized physical access to handling areas could allow bypassing of material control procedures.
CPF13: Material Flow from Supply Chain	Object: Unauthorized access to proprietary material compositions during transit. Object: Interception of material specifications or order details.	Object: Blocking or delaying physical delivery of materials. Object: Damage to critical material supplies.	Object: Using compromised supply chain access to bypass material quality controls.
CPF14: Part Flow to Downstream Manufacturer	Object: Unauthorized access to parts during transit for design information. Object: Interception of accompanying documentation revealing proprietary specifications.	Object: Blocking or delaying physical delivery of finished parts. Object: Damaging parts during transit.	N/A
CPF15: Operator Control Interactions	Object: Unauthorized observation of operator actions to learn proprietary procedures. Object: Physical surveillance of authentication actions (shoulder surfing).	Object: Physical prevention of operator access to controls. Object: Creating hazardous conditions that prevent operator presence.	Object: Physical access to operator interfaces could allow execution of unauthorized commands.
CPI3: Material Supply Chain Provider	Subject: Unauthorized collection of proprietary material usage patterns. Object: Intellectual property related to material specifications could be intercepted.	Subject: Deliberately delaying or blocking critical material deliveries. Object: Disruption of supplier operations could prevent material provision.	***Subject: Exploiting trusted supplier relationship to introduce unauthorized materials or components into the manufacturing process.***
CPI4: Critical Downstream Manufacturing	Subject: Using privileged position to gather proprietary manufacturing data. Object: Customer specifications could be intercepted.	Subject: Generating excessive emergency orders disrupting production. Object: Disruption of downstream operations could prevent part acceptance.	***Subject: Using trusted customer relationship to gain unauthorized physical access to facility or processes.***
CPP1: Part Printing Process	Object: Physical monitoring of printing process for reverse engineering. Object: Acoustic or EM emissions could reveal printing patterns.	Object: Introduction of environmental contaminants disrupting layer adhesion. Object: Creating physical conditions that trigger safety shutdowns.	Object: Exploitation of physical process controls to override safety limits.
CPP2: Part Debinding Process	Object: Monitoring of process parameters to derive proprietary debinding techniques.	Object: Contamination of debinding media. Object: Disruption of ventilation or chemical containment systems.	Object: Unauthorized manipulation of safety-critical physical parameters through process access.
CPP3: Part Sintering Process	Object: Thermal imaging to capture proprietary sintering profiles. Object: Monitoring gas consumption to derive process details.	Object: Introduction of contaminants that disrupt sintering reactions. Object: Creating thermal conditions that trigger emergency shutdowns.	Object: Bypassing physical thermal interlocks to run unauthorized sintering profiles.
CPP4: Quality Control Process	Object: Observation of QC methods to learn acceptance criteria. Object: Unauthorized access to physical test results.	Object: Damaging or miscalibrating test equipment. Object: Creating conditions that prevent proper inspection.	Object: Unauthorized access to quality control areas to approve defective parts.

Fig. 9. The CPSTRIDE threat matrix identifies physical and cyber-physical interception, denial of service, and elevation of privilege threats in the AM system that have no standardized representation in STRIDE. Highlighted cells are special examples discussed further in the text.

4.3 LLM-Assisted Threat Modeling

Arguably, a human expert given sufficient time would be capable of generating a threat matrix of a higher quality and more comprehensive coverage than that produced by an LLM assistant (in 2025), whether using CPSTRIDE or STRIDE. However, CPFD's expanded consideration of physicality, devices, and paths elicits the enumeration of physical and cyber-physical elements and interactions which the DFD, by its cyber-centric nature, excludes. We expect the CPSTRIDE process, therefore, to reveal threats that would remain hidden by an equally rigorous application of the STRIDE process, whether the threat modeler is an expert human or an LLM assistant. With this in mind, we pursue an abbreviated, first-order differential approximation of comparative STRIDE/CPSTRIDE threat modeling by instructing the LLM assistant to identify all AM system elements in the CPFD for which no corresponding DFD element exists, and then to create a CPSTRIDE threat identification matrix for the CPFD using only these elements.

Accordingly, we instruct the LLM to play the role of a subject matter expert in AM systems and threat modeling and provide it with context similar to that which a human expert might be provided, including full CPSTRIDE and STRIDE framework specifications. We instruct the LLM to identify purely cyber threats (which would also be captured by STRIDE) as well as physical and cyber-physical threats (which would not be captured by STRIDE). To resolve potential ambiguity, we instruct the LLM to systematically consider each threat category/element combination in subject, object, and instrument contexts. To limit hallucinations, we direct the LLM to identify realistic threats only and emphasize that filling each cell is not necessary. To reduce context window pressure, we instruct the LLM to work through the threat matrix carefully, completing a small number of matrix rows before awaiting human-in-the-loop approval to continue building the matrix. Finally, to reduce redundant threat identification, we give the LLM permission through instruction to group elements with similar or identical threats, and provide additional formatting instructions. All context and prompts provided to the LLM, as well as all resulting conversations, are included in our project Repository Sect. 6 for review.

The results of this LLM-assisted threat modeling, modified in format only for clarity and appearance, are found in Figs. 8 and 9. These figures contain many physical and cyber-physical elements, interactions, and threats to CPS that have no standardized representation in STRIDE. For example, in the Spoofing column, highlighted cells not only identify the potential for the 3-D printer's network identity to be spoofed (a purely cyber-threat), but also for the 3-D printer to be an instrument for physically spoofing the manufacturing source of counterfeit printed parts. Similarly, the cyber-physical AM Part Material Cartridge could be the object of counterfeiting with fraudulent ID tags/labels (physical threat), or the instrument used to introduce unauthorized physical materials into the AM system. The Material Supply Chain Provider and Critical Downstream Manufacturing recipient also receive consideration, and examples of physical subject and object spoofing threats are provided for each. Each threat identified in the matrix involves either a physical/cyber-physical element (interactor, process, store, device, flow, or path) or a threat susceptibility in the AM system which would not be captured by the STRIDE framework.

Additional examples are found in the remaining columns. The highlighted cells in the Repudiation column deal with erasure, modification, tampering, and corruption of handling logs, transfer records, chain of custody, shipping manifests, delivery confirmations, and certificates of authenticity. Although such records are often stored digitally in real-world manufacturing environments, many physical counterparts such as shipping labels and engraved or embossed serial numbers are also widely used; both types are integral to the physical identification, handling, and tracking of manufactured physical objects. Physical and cyber-physical threats captured in the Interception column include IP theft through physical side channel emissions, physical tapping of network lines, installation of cyber-physical hardware keyloggers or packet sniffers, and physical theft and material diversion.

In the Denial of Service column, highlighted cells contain threats that include physical damage to 3-D printer via sabotage, improper maintenance, and overheating by disabling cooling systems, as well as damage to other AM system components such as ventilation systems, chemical baths or catalysts (AM debinder), gas supply lines and thermal barriers (AM furnace). In the Elevation of Privilege column, highlighted cells identify threats related to the abuse of Supply Chain Provider and Critical Manufacturing customer trust relationships to introduce unauthorized materials or components or to gain unauthorized physical access to facility or processes.

5 Discussion

The CPSTRIDE framework models physical entities, processes, interactions, and threats in CPS that the STRIDE framework cannot. The consideration of susceptibility for all CPFD elements to all types of threats allows more possibilities to be explored during the brainstorming phase of threat identification than in the conventional STRIDE approach. Another advantage of CPSTRIDE is that it allows humans to be modeled as cyber-physical Processes or even Devices (though we recommend they be modeled as Interactors); STRIDE seemingly has no satisfactory options for modeling humans. To illustrate: if humans are modeled as STRIDE Interactors (immune to T, I, D, and E attacks), then the DFD is blind to the potential impacts on CPS of human-related attacks like blackmail, bribery, social engineering, and phishing (Tampering or Information Disclosure), as well as double agency and insider threats (Denial of Service or Elevation of Privilege). Modeling humans as STRIDE Processes allows these threats to be considered, but is a clunky workaround that requires either the redefinition of humans as "any running code" or the redefinition of the STRIDE Process element - either of which would create inconsistencies in the STRIDE/DFD framework, as would redefining Interactor immunity.

STRIDE's limitations extend to modeling non-human physical stores and flows in at least two ways. First, the modeling of physical stores and flows as data is visually and conceptually confusing, and without some visual convention for distinguishing files from parts, for example, the potential for human error in modeling and mitigating threats is increased. Second, modeling physical stores and flows as data in STRIDE bestows immunity to spoofing and elevation of privilege on both, making DFD blind to any cascading effects of counterfeiting and unauthorized access to stores and flows, in addition to bestowing immunity to repudiation (e.g., attacks on inventory systems) for physical flows (inventory in/out of controlled areas, for example).

A prominent advantage of CPSTRIDE is its ability to differentiate between cyber-physical links and flows. This, for example, allows attacks on communication protocols to be considered separately from attacks on data to be transmitted and received, as well as threats to physical communications routing (tampering, denial of service) and RF spectrum (interception). CPSTRIDE's distinction between cyber-physical processes and devices further allows the modeling of physical threats to equipment and infrastructure posed by digital and physical sabotage.

Comparing our AM facility diagrams from the previous section, we notice that the STRIDE DFD is unable to capture many details relevant to cyber-physical operations in the AM facility environment. For instance, the cyber-physical print material cartridge flow from the external supply chain provider, and thus cyber-physical threats such as counterfeited, sabotaged, or backdoored cartridges crossing the AM facility trust boundary. Similarly, the DFD is unable to represent the downstream manufacturer, and thus is blind to the potential risks to downstream systems, human health, and financial liability associated with shipping sabotaged or defective physical parts.

Physical aspects of AM machinery are not modeled in the DFD, meaning that the threat of production delays and financial damages related to reduction of physical manufacturing capabilities are not considered or mitigated directly, nor are threats associated with IP theft via side-channel attacks on RF and acoustic energy emanation from the AM printer. Physical part production is not represented, nor are the physical cartridge or physical input flows by the operator/controller; this results in DFD blindness to the physical threats posed by digital file spoofing and tampering at different stages in the AM process chain, as well as to the physical threats of material part cartridge tampering or damage. Additionally, physical aspects of the quality control process are not considered in the DFD, and therefore neither can the associated threats be.

Threat identification during the brainstorming phase is just an early example of the potential usefulness of artificial intelligence (AI) for CPSTRIDE implementation; as these models advance in capability and accuracy, human-AI partnership in threat modeling is likely to reduce variation between different threat modelers or teams and result in reproducible threat assessment baselines. In addition, AI assistants may reduce costs and time by exploring attack chains and cascading effects, constructing and collecting from threat knowledge databases, cross-referencing similar systems and known attack patterns, and identifying threats based on emerging research or incidents.

5.1 Challenges and Limitations

Threat modeling with STRIDE is complex and time-intensive, and CPSTRIDE's inclusion of physical entities increases this complexity and time-intensity. This, of course, is the classic modeler's dilemma (how to balance scientific fidelity and complexity with practical usefulness and comprehensibility?) which CPSTRIDE makes no advances toward resolving.

A second limitation of the method is that although CPSTRIDE's broadening of element susceptibility to threat categories allows additional freedom, it also can add ambiguity as to how certain entities should be modeled. Our CPFD element category definitions were designed to proactively resolve several ambiguities, but confounding exceptions undoubtedly exist and await discovery. This is acceptable for CPSTRIDE v1; future refinements of the model should seek ways to reduce ambiguity.

A third limitation is that the threats identified in our AM facility study are merely abstract conceptual representations of potential attacks that have no standard taxonomy or representation in physical threat databases to mirror their digital counterparts in CVE, ATT&CK, and Cyber Kill Chain. Creating and maintaining such resources would benefit from cooperation and partnership with the CPS security community, but would require a significant long-term effort to realize a workable solution.

A fourth barrier to adoption involves technological costs and limitations. Performing network scans with existing cyber-security tools is far quicker and more accurate than visually scanning or using other means to find physical vulnerabilities in CPS, which may cover sprawling geographic footprints and/or include inaccessible or dangerous areas. However, the continued adoption of autonomous maintenance and inspection robots may eventually make this more feasible.

There are many additional challenges related to the use of AI and LLM assistance for CPSTRIDE modeling. AI may lack deep understanding of specific industrial processes, or may miss subtle physical-world constraints and realities. Over-reliance on AI may lead to accepting threat suggestions without proper validation, over-engineering security solutions for unrealistic threats, and missing critical threats not suggested by AI. Human expertise will be required to assess and prioritize threats and mitigations into the foreseeable future.

6 Conclusion

CPSTRIDE is a comprehensive threat modeling framework for CPS extending STRIDE to address security challenges introduced by physical and cyber-physical elements. By expanding the threat modeling vocabulary to include physical and cyber physical elements, CPSTRIDE enables security professionals to develop more comprehensive defense strategies for CPS. As Industry 4.0 technologies proliferate across manufacturing, healthcare, transportation, and energy sectors, the need for cyber-physical threat modeling becomes more urgent.

Our analysis compares CPSTRIDE and STRIDE modeling of an AM facility, demonstrating several advantages to our novel approach. The CPSTRIDE framework captures threat vectors such as side-channel attacks via acoustic and RF emanations, physical material cartridge tampering, and supply chain vulnerabilities that are invisible to traditional STRIDE modeling approaches. This illustrates the substantial security gap that CPSTRIDE helps fill.

Future research includes the application of CPSTRIDE to CPS domains beyond AM (smart grids, autonomous vehicles, medical devices, industrial control systems) to validate generalizability and uncover domain-specific requirements. The development of automated tools for CPSTRIDE analysis could make the framework accessible to practitioners and reduce the burden of comprehensive cyber-physical threat modeling. These tools could leverage AI, LLMs, and other machine learning approaches to streamline diagram creation, threat identification, and vulnerability assessment processes.

Integrating CPSTRIDE with security frameworks and standards such as NIST Cybersecurity Framework, IEC 62443, and ISO/IEC 27001 could facilitate adoption. Its validation through case studies across different industries could help refine the framework and establish best practices for its implementation.

The continued evolution of cyber-physical systems demands equally sophisticated security approaches. CPSTRIDE represents a foundational step toward comprehensive CPS security, but its real-world impact will depend on widespread adoption, tool development, and integration with existing security practices. As CPS continue to transform critical sectors of our economy and society, frameworks like CPSTRIDE will become increasingly valuable for maintaining the security, resilience, and trustworthiness of our cyber-physical infrastructure.

Competing Interests. The authors have no competing interests to declare that are relevant to the content of this article.

Repository. The CPSTRIDE repository can be found online at the following URL: https://github.com/DallasElleman/CPSTRIDE

References

1. Al Faruque, M., Chhetri, S.R., Canedo, A., Wan, J.: Acoustic side-channel attacks on additive manufacturing systems. In: 2016 ACM/IEEE 7th International Conference on Cyber-Physical Systems (ICCPS), pp. 1–10 (2016). https://doi.org/10.1109/ICCPS.2016.7479068
2. Al Faruque, M., Chhetri, S.R., Faezi, S., Canedo, A.: Forensics of thermal side-channel in additive manufacturing systems. Technical report 16–01, University of California, Irvine; Siemens Corporation, Center for Embedded and Cyber-Physical Systems (2016)
3. Beaman, J.J., Bourell, D.L., Seepersad, C.C., Kovar, D.: Additive manufacturing review: early past to current practice. J. Manuf. Sci. Eng. **142**(11), 110812 (2020). https://doi.org/10.1115/1.4048193
4. Belikovetsky, S., Yampolskiy, M., Toh, J., Gatlin, J., Elovici, Y.: dr0wned – cyber-physical attack with additive manufacturing. In: 11th USENIX Workshop on Offensive Technologies, p. 16. USENIX (2017)

5. Duo, W., Zhou, M., Abusorrah, A.: A survey of cyber attacks on cyber physical systems: recent advances and challenges. IEEE/CAA J. Automatica Sinica **9**(5), 784–800 (2022). https://doi.org/10.1109/JAS.2022.105548
6. Graves, L., King, W., Carrion, P., Shao, S., Shamsaei, N., Yampolskiy, M.: Sabotaging metal additive manufacturing: powder delivery system manipulation and material-dependent effects. Addit. Manuf. **46**, 102029 (2021). https://doi.org/10.1016/j.addma.2021.102029
7. Gupta, N., Tiwari, A., Bukkapatnam, S.T.S., Karri, R.: Additive manufacturing cyber-physical system: supply chain cybersecurity and risks. IEEE Access **8**, 47322–47333 (2020). https://doi.org/10.1109/ACCESS.2020.2978815
8. Hernan, S., Lambert, S., Ostwald, T., Shostack, A.: Uncover Security Design Flaws Using The STRIDE Approach. Microsoft MSDN Magazine (2006). https://learn.microsoft.com/en-us/archive/msdn-magazine/2006/november/uncover-security-design-flaws-using-the-stride-approach
9. Hojjati, A., et al.: Leave your phone at the door: side channels that reveal factory floor secrets. In: Proceedings of the 2016 ACM SIGSAC Conference on Computer and Communications Security, Vienna Austria, pp. 883–894. ACM (2016). https://doi.org/10.1145/2976749.2978323
10. Khan, R., McLaughlin, K., Laverty, D., Sezer, S.: STRIDE-based threat modeling for cyber-physical systems. In: 2017 IEEE PES Innovative Smart Grid Technologies Conference Europe (ISGT-Europe), pp. 1–6 (2017). https://doi.org/10.1109/ISGTEurope.2017.8260283
11. McCormack, M., et al.: Security analysis of networked 3D printers. In: 2020 IEEE Security and Privacy Workshops (SPW), pp. 118–125 (2020). https://doi.org/10.1109/SPW50608.2020.00035
12. Rahman, H., Shafae, M.: Cyber-Physical Security Vulnerabilities Identification and Classification in Smart Manufacturing: A Defense-in-Depth Driven Framework and Taxonomy (2024). https://arxiv.org/abs/2501.09023
13. Saßnick, O., Rosenstatter, T., Schäfer, C., Huber, S.: STRIDE-based methodologies for threat modeling of industrial control systems: a review. In: 2024 IEEE 7th International Conference on Industrial Cyber-Physical Systems (ICPS), pp. 1–8 (2024). https://doi.org/10.1109/ICPS59941.2024.10639949. iSSN 2769-3899
14. Shostack, A.: adamshostack/DFD3 (2025). https://github.com/adamshostack/DFD3. Original-Date: 2017-11-05T21:20:58Z
15. Sturm, L.D., Williams, C.B., Camelio, J.A., White, J., Parker, R.: Cyber-physical vulnerabilities in additive manufacturing systems: a case study attack on the .STL file with human subjects. J. Manuf. Syst. **44**, 154–164 (2017). https://doi.org/10.1016/j.jmsy.2017.05.007
16. Yampolskiy, M., Graves, L., Gatlin, J., Skjellum, A., Yung, M.: What did you add to my additive manufacturing data?: Steganographic attacks on 3D printing Files. In: 24th International Symposium on Research in Attacks, Intrusions and Defenses, San Sebastian Spain, pp. 266–281. ACM (2021). https://doi.org/10.1145/3471621.3471843
17. Yampolskiy, M., Horvath, P., Koutsoukos, X.D., Xue, Y., Sztipanovits, J.: Systematic analysis of cyber-attacks on CPS-evaluating applicability of DFD-based approach. In: 2012 5th International Symposium on Resilient Control Systems, pp. 55–62 (2012). https://doi.org/10.1109/ISRCS.2012.6309293
18. Yampolskiy, M.: Security of additive manufacturing: attack taxonomy and survey. Addit. Manuf. **21**, 431–457 (2018). https://doi.org/10.1016/j.addma.2018.03.015

Next-Generation Threat Risk Management by Integrating GenAI for Security Compliance and Controls

Šarūnas Grigaliūnas[1](✉), Rasa Brūzgienė[2], Ilona Veitaitė[2], Renata Danielienė[2], Paulius Astromskis[2], Živilė Nemickienė[2], Dovilė Vengalienė[2], Rokas Stankūnas[2], Ieva Andrijauskaitė[2], and Ieva Šilingaitė[2]

[1] Department of Computer Sciences, Kaunas University of Technology, Kaunas, Lithuania
sarunas.grigaliunas@ktu.lt

[2] Vilnius University, Kaunas Faculty, Muitinės Str. 8, 44280 Kaunas, Lithuania
{rasa.bruzgiene,ilona.veitaite,renata.danieliene,paulius.astromskis, zivile.nemickiene,dovile.vengaliene,rokas.stankunas, ieva.andrijauskaite,ieva.silingaite}@knf.vu.lt

Abstract. The increasing complexity and volume of cybersecurity threats present significant challenges for CISO function (hereafter, "CISO function": the CISO and delegated security leadership teams such as SOC/IR, risk, compliance, and security architecture) tasked with protecting critical information infrastructure. Traditional risk assessment methods often struggle to keep pace with the rapidly evolving threat landscape, leading to potential gaps in coverage and regulatory non-compliance. To address this, this paper proposes a novel method that integrates Generative Artificial Intelligence (GenAI) into threat risk management. The proposed dual GenAI architecture, consisting of a primary risk analysis engine and an independent verification layer, demonstrated high alignment with expert evaluations in experimental testing, achieving high accuracy in certain risk scenarios. This method also reduces the risk of hallucinations and ensures compliance with evolving regulatory frameworks through a structured, prompt-driven analysis workflow. The achieved results indicate that the proposed method can significantly improve the precision of risk assessments, providing a scalable and legally defensible solution for CISO function. This work represents a substantial advancement in the integration of GenAI for critical infrastructure protection, offering a practical, data-driven alternative to conventional risk management approaches.

Keywords: GenAI · CISO · Risk management · Compliance · Critical information infrastructure protection · Cybersecurity

E. Bergström et al. (Eds.): CRITIS 2025, LNCS 16291, pp. 404–423, 2026.
https://doi.org/10.1007/978-3-032-19540-1_21

1 Introduction

Accelerating digital transformation and increasing reliance on information technologies inevitably heighten organizational vulnerability to cyber threats. This trend is confirmed by various recent reports documenting an overall increase in the volume of attacks [10] and a record surge in data breaches [5,24] and ransomware incidents observed in 2024. Successful cyber incidents inflict diverse adverse effects, ranging from the disruption of technical systems and financial losses to societal damage, harm to organizational reputation, and detrimental impacts on the physical and psychological well-being of individuals [10].

Recognizing these growing threats, the European Union adopted the NIS2 Directive (Directive (EU) 2022/2555), which mandates that essential and important entities implement appropriate and proportionate cybersecurity risk management measures [14]. This requirement necessitates the continuous and methodical assessment of emerging threats and actively pursuing ways to mitigate their impact. Responsibility for developing, implementing, and managing these measures, as well as handling incidents, is carried out by the CISO function—the CISO and delegated security leadership teams (e.g., SOC/IR, risk, compliance, security architecture)—rather than a single individual. Throughout this paper, "CISO function" denotes the CISO and the delegated security leadership teams operating under the CISO's authority; references do not imply that one person performs all operational tasks. In executing these duties, CISO function face immense challenges: processing vast data volumes from diverse sources, identifying and assessing increasingly sophisticated attacks, and making critical decisions under significant time pressure, often without comprehensive situational awareness. To assist CISO function in overcoming these challenges, artificial intelligence (AI) and machine learning (ML) are emerging as enabling technologies in daily CISO operations. They offer capabilities for automating and accelerating threat detection, analysis, pattern recognition, prediction, and response [6,22].

European Union institutions also recognize the potential of AI in the cybersecurity domain. Although NIS2 does not mandate the use of AI, Recital (88) (Note: Corrected from 89 in the source text based on previous verification) of the directive suggests that entities should "...evaluate their own cybersecurity capabilities and, where appropriate, pursue the integration of cybersecurity enhancing technologies, such as artificial intelligence or machine-learning systems to enhance their capabilities and the security of network and information systems...." [15]. Broader EU strategies, such as "The EU's Cybersecurity Strategy for the Digital Decade," emphasize the need to invest in AI and other advanced technologies to increase the EU's resilience against cyber threats and its capacity to respond to them [12]. The European Union Agency for Cybersecurity (ENISA) also actively analyzes the opportunities and challenges presented by AI for cybersecurity, providing guidance on the secure and trustworthy deployment and use of AI for defensive purposes [9,11].

While recommendations for specific, CISO-oriented AI tools are currently lacking in these documents, the overall strategic direction and the adopted AI

Act indicate the growing role of AI and the need to ensure its trustworthy application [13]. Due to this, the aim of this paper is to develop a comprehensive method for integrating Generative Artificial Intelligence (GenAI) into risk management processes, ensuring alignment with existing legal regulations and control mechanisms pertinent to critical information infrastructure protection. This proposed method significantly advances the field of critical information infrastructure security through its innovative dual GenAI architecture and structured methodological approach. The key contributions of this research include:

- a novel cybersecurity risk assessment method that integrates two GenAI models - a primary GenAI for initial risk analysis and a secondary, independent GenAI for verification - enhancing the overall reliability and accuracy of threat risk analysis.
- a structured approach to prompt engineering that includes initial analysis, self-review, revision, and final verification phases, ensuring consistency and adherence to predefined response structures.
- a verification and error reduction through cross-model validation mechanism in order to mitigate the risks of GenAI hallucination and factual errors;
- an integration of threat risk assessment outputs with legislative and regulatory context through predefined control mapping processes, ensuring that recommended measures are legally defensible and contextually appropriate.

The proposed method not only enhances the precision of threat risk assessment and mitigation but also aligns these processes with evolving regulatory requirements, thereby supporting CISO function in their complex, high-stakes decision-making roles. This integration of GenAI aims to reduce the cognitive load on cybersecurity professionals, improve response times, and enhance overall critical information infrastructure resilience against emerging threats.

The remainder of this paper is structured as follows: Sect. 2 reviews the current state of research in the field, highlighting key advances and ongoing challenges in GenAI-based risk assessment. Sections 3 and 4 presents the proposed GenAI-based threat risk assessment method, including its design principles and operational workflows. Section 5 describes the experimental setup and results, evaluating the effectiveness and accuracy of the proposed method in various threat scenarios. Section 6 discusses the implications of these findings, addressing limitations and potential future research directions. Finally, Sect. 7 concludes the paper by summarizing the main contributions and outlining practical recommendations for implementing GenAI in the protection of critical information infrastructure.

2 Related Works

Several architectural paradigms have emerged in this area. One prominent approach leverages the internal activations or hidden states of primarily large language models (LLMs) to preemptively assess the risk of hallucination before text generation begins. For example, FactCheckMate introduces a classifier trained on hidden states to predict hallucinations in advance; if a risk is detected, the system adjusts the model's hidden states to steer output toward greater factuality. Such methods have demonstrated notable detection accuracy and efficiency, as they can preempt hallucinations with minimal computational overhead [3]. Related work has shown that these internal signals in LLMs are indicative of risks and can be effectively probed to estimate hallucination likelihood at runtime [18]. Another major research direction involves real-time or in-process monitoring during the text generation stage. Systems such as Monitoring Decoding dynamically analyze partial outputs, targeting low-confidence tokens for potential revision. These systems intervene at the token or phrase level, ensuring factual accuracy and coherence while maintaining efficiency by avoiding the need to regenerate entire responses [26]. Similar strategies – such as monitoring the model's logit outputs for low-confidence generations and intervening during decoding – have been shown to significantly reduce hallucination rates in practice. For example, one approach reduced hallucinations from 47.5% to 14.5% on average in article generation tasks [7].

Chain-of-thought (CoT) and natural language inference (NLI) frameworks represent a further refinement, decomposing model outputs into atomic claims and verifying each for factual consistency. HalluMeasure, for instance, breaks down responses into smaller units, applies step-by-step reasoning, and assesses various types of hallucinations, demonstrating measurable improvements in detection metrics such as F1 and AUC-ROC scores on test datasets [2]. Likewise, methods involving chain-of-inference or sequential NLI have also shown strong performance gains across multiple tasks [19]. Multi-agent and debate-based approaches are also gaining prominence. In these systems, multiple LLM agents – each adopting specific roles or stances – critique or debate the correctness of candidate outputs, sometimes under the supervision of a judge agent who makes the final determination. Such frameworks, as demonstrated in the Counterfactual Multi-Agent Debate (CFMAD) approach, have been shown to outperform existing methods in empirical studies [16]. Peer-reviewing between agent pairs or ensembles, as tested in both small- and large-scale LLM combinations, frequently results in notably higher rates of hallucination identification and successful output revision; for instance, advanced model reviewers were able to correct outputs in 85–100% of cases in a synthetic knowledge test [28]. The field also extends these principles to the realm of vision-language models, where hallucination occurs when generated image descriptions or multimodal outputs are not grounded in visual input. Here, fine-grained AI feedback and detection at the sentence or token level – often trained using datasets generated by proprietary models – enable more precise interventions. Such approaches not only detect but also categorize and prioritize hallucinations based on their severity, contributing to new state-of-the-art performance in multimodal hallucination mitigation benchmarks [2,23,27].

Importantly, the literature emphasizes the necessity of empirical validation – demonstrating that AI evaluators, when integrated into the generation or decision-making pipeline, produce a measurable decrease in hallucination frequency or an improvement in other trust-related metrics. Several works provide such end-to-end validation using quantitative benchmarks, reporting reductions in hallucination rates, improvements in factual alignment, and statistical gains in evaluation scores when compared to baseline models without in-loop AI evaluators [2,3,7,8,26]. The collective evidence from these studies shows a trend toward more robust, efficient, and empirically validated AI evaluators that increase both the trustworthiness and practical utility of advanced AI generation systems. The reviewed research also addresses the deployment of generative AI to support or transform security governance and CISO responsibilities with risk and threat analysis, compliance assessment, and the automation of security controls within critical infrastructure environments. Expanding from sector-specific cases, the comprehensive review offer broad analyses of generative AI's potential across various critical infrastructure sectors. Yigit and colleagues [29] survey AI-driven approaches, with particular focus on the reliability and security of national infrastructures such as energy, water, transportation, and telecommunications. This review introduces benchmarking strategies for evaluating LLMs within cybersecurity, considers challenges such as trust, privacy, and resilience, and presents conceptual roadmap for integrating agentic AI into critical infrastructure protection (CIP). While this paper provides a valuable overview of trends, research gaps, and opportunities, it primarily synthesizes existing knowledge and best practices rather than presenting new empirical deployments or direct evidence of CISO workflow transformation.

In terms of security control automation, Ahmed et al. [1] demonstrate the application of prompt engineering with LLM to enforce and validate critical security controls from the Center for Internet Security (CIS). Using chain-of-thought (CoT) prompting and few-shot learning, their system can extract relevant measures, metrics, and monitoring implementation steps from standard control descriptions. Their evaluation shows a reduction in dependency on human security analysts for compliance monitoring tasks and provides a prototype for automated metric extraction - key steps toward continuous monitoring and semi-automation in the compliance process. Several additional papers propose frameworks and models for leveraging generative AI in GRC (governance, risk, compliance) and regulatory compliance. Thomas [25] and [21] extend this by outlining multi-layered or tiered frameworks for integrating LLMs into GRC workflows, automating evidence gathering, risk assessment, compliance monitoring, and strategic decision-making. Although these approaches suggest significant potential for improved efficiency and real-time compliance, they generally lack sector-specific, real-world evaluations and do not explicitly document transformations within CISO workflows.

Emergent technical advances are also present in the form of LLM-powered retrieval-augmented generation (RAG) systems for risk and threat management. Arora and Ramteke [4] propose a framework utilizing generative AI and RAG to automate third-party risk assessments and compliance validation. This aims to scale risk analysis across dynamic vendor supply chains, improving precision, reducing human error, and adapting to regulatory changes. Munmun et al. [20]

summarize the broader impact of AI, including machine learning and deep learning, for project risk management in critical infrastructure and national security contexts. They highlight AI's role in shifting organizations toward proactive risk management through predictive analytics and real-time situational awareness, but their discussion is not centered on generative models, lacks compliance automation specifics, and does not detail CISO workflow impacts.

The review of related works reveals the growing adoption of generative AI for risk and compliance in critical infrastructure, primarily through improved compliance verification, control mapping, and automation of audit and monitoring processes. Research contributions provide strategic frameworks and technical innovations, yet robust, sector-specific evidence of CISO workflow transformation and full compliance automation remains limited, highlighting this as an ongoing area for future research and deployment.

3 Proposed GenAI-Based Threat Risk Assessment Method

The proposed method illustrated in the Fig. 1 represents a structured approach to the threat risk assessment by integrating generative artificial intelligence models in a dual-architecture system. The process flows through four distinct domains - CISO domain, primary GenAI domain, verification GenAI domain, and results domain - each with specific responsibilities in the risk assessment workflow.

Within the CISO domain, the process begins with the asset repository and threat intelligence components that feed into the control measures repository. These components contain information about the organization's critical information infrastructure, potential threats, and existing security controls. This foundational information helps create risk scenarios, which are then processed through a prompt formulation process. The CISO crafts specific prompts based on the risk scenarios, aligned with a regulatory and compliance framework. The CISO review and decision component represents the final human-expert oversight in the process.

The primary GenAI domain (GAISO) contains the technical engine that processes the security analysis. It begins with the threat risk analysis that receives the prompt from the CISO domain. The risk strategy formulation component is a core decision-making function that translates the quantitative output of the"Risk Evaluation" stage into actionable strategic recommendations. Based on the calculated risk score (Impact × Probability), the GenAI is programmed to follow a predefined logical progression that aligns with standard risk management practices. The process works as follows. High-risk scenarios are for threats with a high impact and high-probability score, the GenAI defaults to a risk mitigation strategy. This involves recommending the immediate implementation of preventive, detective, and corrective controls to reduce the risk level to an acceptable threshold. An example of this is seen in Scenario 1, where the high risk leads to a high number of recommended controls. Moderate-risk scenarios are for threats with moderate scores, the GenAI is instructed to formulate a risk acceptance strategy where the CISO acknowledges the risk but chooses to accept it due to the balance of cost and benefit. This is applied in cases where the cost of implementing extensive controls outweighs the potential impact of the threat.

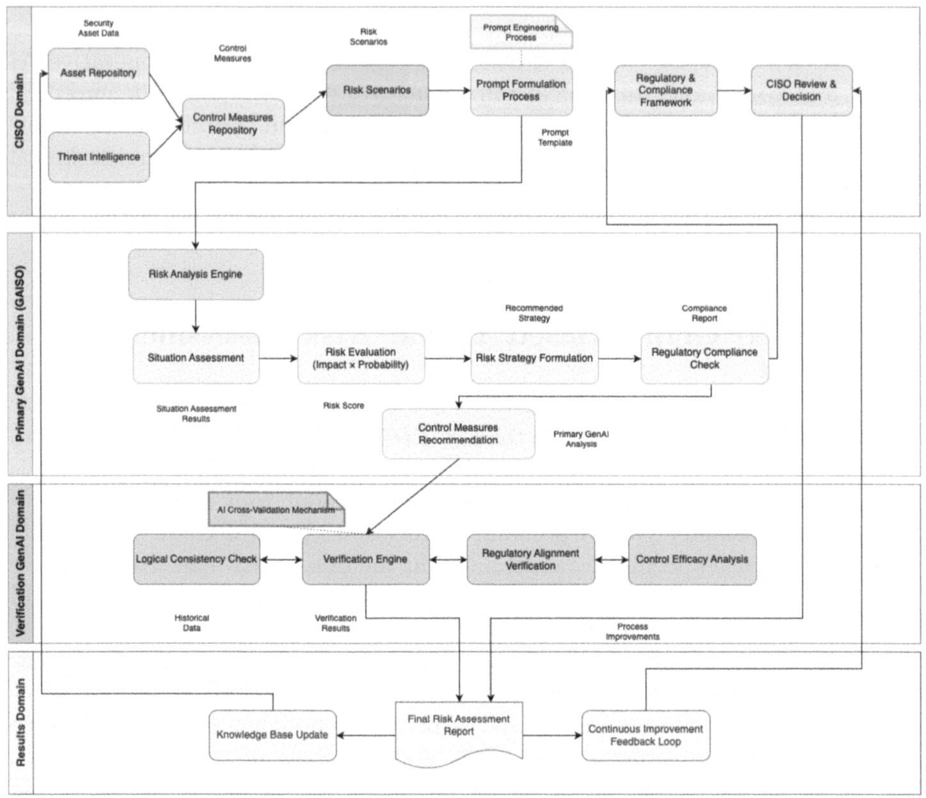

Fig. 1. A structured architecture of the proposed method for threat risk assessment.

Low-risk scenarios are in cases of low probability and low impact, the agent may recommend a risk avoidance strategy by suggesting the discontinuation of a specific service or activity to eliminate the risk entirely. This logical framework ensures that the GenAI's recommendations are not just based on a raw score but are tied to a strategic, defensible rationale. This threat risk analysis engine drives the analysis through several steps:

- the situation assessment, which evaluates which assets may be affected;
- the threat risk evaluation that calculates impact and probability scores;
- the risk strategy formulation that recommends approaches such as risk mitigation or risk acceptance;
- the regulatory compliance check that ensures alignment with relevant legislation frameworks.

The control measures recommendation component provides specific security control suggestions based on the analysis.

The verification GenAI domain introduces a critical validation layer. Through its verification engine, this domain performs independent checks on the primary GenAI's output. Components include logical consistency check that ensures internal coherence in the analysis, regulatory alignment verification that validates compliance with frameworks, and control efficacy analysis that evaluates the effectiveness of recommended controls. This validation architecture helps identify potential hallucinations or errors in the primary analysis.

The results domain captures the final outputs of the process. The final risk assessment report contains the comprehensive analysis with verification results. This feeds into the knowledge base update to improve future assessments and the continuous improvement feedback loop that enhances the overall threat risk assessment process. Notably, such a proposed threat risk assessment method includes self-correction mechanisms where "issues found" can trigger revision phases before final delivery of results. This includes initial analysis, self-review, revision, and final check phases that systematically evaluate assets, security attributes, threats, vulnerabilities, control measures, risk analysis, and risk mitigation strategies. Before delivering the final response, the GenAI model must pass a final round of testing to ensure strict adherence to provided documents, exclusion of unsupported assumptions, consistent and accurate terminology, and full compliance with the established analysis template.

With this proposed method, the authors enable CISO function to leverage generative AI for risk assessment while maintaining accuracy through cross-validation between multiple AI models. It addresses the growing challenge of handling complex cybersecurity threats in environments governed by regulatory frameworks, helping organizations implement appropriate and proportionate cybersecurity risk management measures.

4 Methodology for GenAI Model Training

The successful implementation of GenAI for threat risk management requires a structured and comprehensive methodology to train and validate AI generative models. The methodology includes two main steps:

1. Document analysis instructions for GenAI – specifies the documents that GenAI must analyze before carrying out a task.
2. Action sequence instruction and validation process – GenAI is requested to analyze a threat scenario and provide a risk analysis and mitigation strategies according to a predefined 12-point sequence based on the information provided. The results obtained are validated with a second GenAI model to identify discrepancies and further compared with the cybersecurity expert's assessment.

The GenAI-based agent was provided with specific output documents, such as the profile of the 1009 LTD (institution of a critical sectoral entity), the security controls used and a 12-point response template. This template provides a structured format that the GenAI agent must strictly follow to produce a consistent and accurate analysis. While the document doesn't list all 12 points explicitly, it details the key areas that are systematically evaluated and verified as part of the analysis process. These areas include verifying assets, security attributes, threats, vulnerabilities, control measures, risk analysis, and risk mitigation strategies. The analysis process is divided into an initial drafting stage, a self-review phase for validation, a revision phase for refinement, and a final check to ensure strict adherence to the template before delivering the final response. The profile of 1009 LTD contained comprehensive information about 1009 LTD services, assets, threat identification, and risk management frameworks. Specifically, it included documentation of the 1009 LTD service catalog, asset classification tables, threat assessment reports, risk scoring methodologies, impact assessment frameworks, probability scoring guidelines, and risk management strategies. It also contained detailed service categorization tables showing critical versus noncritical services, service dependencies, and community impact assessments.

The training of the GenAI agent was done on the basis of the data leakage threat scenario. The initial step in the process was to devise an agent and formulate a prompt for it. The scientific project requirements necessitated writing the initial prompt in Lithuanian. The example of this initial prompt is following:

```
This GPT is designed to analyse situations based on a predefined
analysis structure using the documents provided. The user provides
various documents, including a description of the situation and an
analysis template (e.g. in the file ‘‘Situation No. 00’’). The GPT
first asks the user to provide the context of the situation. Once the
 context has been provided, the GPT provides an analysis structured
according to the points specified in the template (e.g. from 1 to 12)
. The answers must be clear, concise, logically structured and
provided in Lithuanian. The GPT must adhere strictly to the analysis
structure - all points must be included in the answer. If necessary,
GPT may supplement missing information by logically inferring it from
 the context, but should indicate if this is an assumption. If the
format of the analysis in the file ‘‘Situation No. 00’’ changes, GPT
must always follow the latest document template. If any documents or
information are missing, the GPT must ask the user to provide the
missing files or data. GPT responses must be written in clear,
professional, but understandable Lithuanian, suitable for academic or
 business analysis. The initial text of the agent must always be: ‘‘
Provide the context of the situation.’’
```

The comparative study was carried out using a specific prompt (Fig. 2). A comparison prompt was used, which asked for a detailed comparison between the two analyzes, examining each relevant point from both analyses, assessing the percentage of similarity between each point and providing an overall assessment. In order to improve the accuracy of the GenAI agent's results, a prompt adjustment has been carried out according to the recommendations made by Claude

3.7 Sonnet model. In addition, the self-review and revision phases, as well as the final check phase, were introduced to improve the prompt. Additional instructions were given to ensure that responses are based only on specific information from the submitted documents and to follow even more closely the format specified in the 12-point template. Improvements to the prompt have increased its size from 1100 characters to 7000 characters.

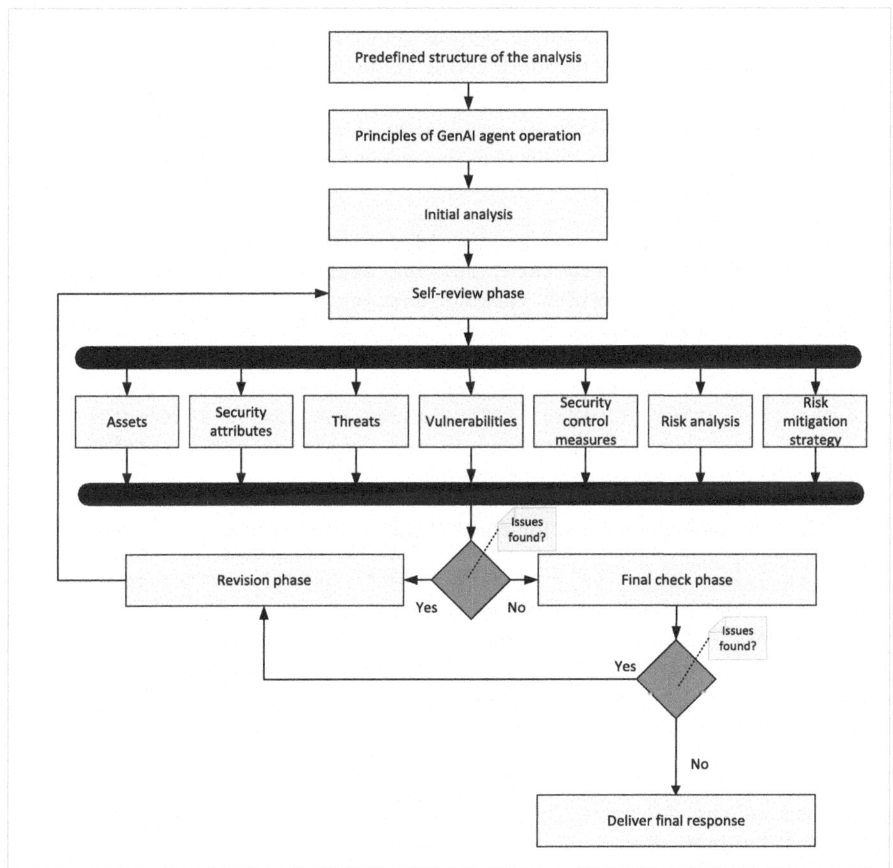

Fig. 2. Structured workflow of the adjusted comparison prompt.

The initial testing results after the ChatGPT-4o agent's training based on that threat scenario were compared with the cybersecurity expert's answers along with the verification of the agent's results with Gemini Advanced 2.5 Pro (experimental) and Claude 3.7 Sonnet models. Claude 3.7 Sonnet found a 92% agreement between the analysis results, and Gemini Advanced 2.5 Pro (experimental) found 90% agreement. After the prompt improvements: the percentage of matches for Claude 3.7 Sonnet was 98%, for Gemini Advanced 2.5 Pro 95%.

Additional tests with further editing of the prompt gave poorer results, so it was decided to revert to the previous version. The edited final version of the prompt was then used to check the results against the expert's answers again. The result was very similar to the one obtained with the improved but not yet edited prompt, so it was decided that the prompt was suitable for this stage of further testing.

The prompt is designed to guide the GenAI model in performing highly structured analysis based exclusively on provided documents. This approach ensures accurate, document-centric responses without introducing assumptions or hypothetical scenarios. The model first requests a context description from the user to anchor its analysis. This is a critical step, as it sets the scope and foundation for subsequent evaluations. The model's responses are structured to meet specific criteria, emphasizing clarity, precision, and strict adherence to the provided analysis templates:

```
This GPT is designed to analyze provided situations using a
predefined analytical structure, relying exclusively on supplied
documents. The user provides various documents, including the
description of the situation and the analysis template (e.g., in the
file "Situation No. 00").
GPT first prompts the user: ''Provide the context of the situation.''
Once the context is provided, GPT prepares the analysis strictly
following the structure specified in the template (e.g., points 1
through 12).
```

The foundational principles for the model's analysis include:

```
1.Base analysis exclusively on direct facts and circumstances
provided in the situation description. Do not assess hypothetical
consequences.
2.Evaluate information security attributes (confidentiality,
integrity, availability) only based on explicitly mentioned breaches
in the situation. Avoid evaluating potential or indirect consequences
.
3.When identifying threats, include all possible threats explicitly
mentioned in the documents relevant to the provided situation - do
not limit to just one.
4.All answers must strictly follow the template, using terminology
and classifications indicated in the documents.
5.If the analysis template changes, GPT must adhere to the latest
version.
6.If any document or data is missing, GPT must ask the user to
provide it.
7.If certain analysis points cannot be filled, GPT must explicitly
indicate that it is based on an assumption.
```

The analysis process is divided into clearly defined stages:

- Initial analysis: drafting responses according to the template.

- Self-review phase: validating the completeness, accuracy, and format of responses.
- Revision phase: refining the responses for consistency and removal of redundant elements.
- Final check: ensuring strict adherence to the template before finalizing.

For more structured evaluations, the prompt includes verification checks for critical aspects, including:

```
1.Asset verification:
-Are assets grouped according to services?
-Are only data/information resources listed?
2.Security attributes verification:
-Is evaluation restricted to documented impacts only?
-Are availability/integrity included only if there is direct evidence
?
3.Threats verification:
-Are all risks listed in the "Identified Threats" document included?
-Do threats relate directly to scenario context (e.g., disloyal
employee, cybercriminal)?
4.Vulnerabilities verification:
-Is reference made exclusively to the "Control Measures" document?
-Are no additional unsubstantiated vulnerabilities included?
5.Control measures verification:
-Is only ``Yes'' / ``No'' format used?
-Are measures classified exactly according to their documented status
 (preventive, detection, corrective)?
6.Risk analysis verification:
-Are scores and levels set based strictly on documents?
-Is the risk level accurately calculated using the matrix?
7.Strategy verification:
-Does the strategy match the risk level?
-Do proposed measures address specific vulnerabilities?
```

A critical component of comprehensive cybersecurity risk management is the alignment of implemented control measures with applicable legislative and regulatory requirements. This alignment not only ensures the effectiveness of security controls but also supports the organization's broader compliance obligations. For the CISO, this integration is a key part of their strategic function, enabling informed decision making and effective risk mitigation. The designed prompt includes the process of integrating legislative considerations by involving and verifying the following steps:

- based on the identified risks, the GenAI agent should select appropriate control measures that effectively mitigate these risks. This selection is informed by the context of the organization's risk appetite and the specific threats identified in the security assessment.
- each chosen security control measure is then systematically linked to relevant legal frameworks and standards. This mapping ensures that controls are

not only technically effective, but also legally defensible. The mapping file serves as the primary reference for this step, providing a comprehensive list of available control measures and their associated legal requirements.
- to facilitate practical application, this compliance information should be presented in a structured table format. This table should clearly indicate the control measure, its description, and the specific legislation that supports its implementation. This approach provides CISO function with a concise, actionable reference for ensuring compliance across various regulatory regimes.
- the final output should be included as an appendix or attached as a spreadsheet. This provides a full, unambiguous record of the control-legislation mapping, supporting both internal audits and external regulatory reviews without additional text elaboration.

5 Experimental Use Case and Analysis of Results

To ensure reliable performance, the treat risk analysis process must reflect real-world cybersecurity contexts and address the unique challenges associated with high-stakes decision-making. This includes reducing the risk of GenAI hallucinations, enhancing factual consistency, and ensuring that the models are capable of handling complex, dynamic threat scenarios. The proposed method integrates not only the GenAI model-validator but the cybersecurity expert knowledge as well in order to align the model outputs closely with human expert assessments, ensuring both accuracy and interpretability. Three GenAI models were used during the experimental use case:

- ChatGPT-4o model serves as a main threat risk analyzer;
- Gemini Advanced 2.5 Pro (experimental) model serves as a validator and as well used for the testing;
- Claude 3.7 Sonnet model for validating and testing.

Five different threat scenarios were used for the threat risk analysis and strategies of security compliance and controls [17]:

1. Scenario no. 1: data leakage – a compromised or disloyal employee with access to databases downloads all the information and posts it on the dark web.
2. Scenario no. 2: cyberattack – 1009 LTD network suffers an intense cyberattack, which overloads the network resources within 4 h and makes services unavailable from outside.
3. Scenario no. 3: storage resource-exhaustion attack (database disk space depletion)—malicious data or log inflow renders the email service database unavailable, disrupting services.
4. Scenario no. 4: intruder enters the premises of 1009 LTD – the intruder enters the premises of 1009 LTD undetected by security, reaches the server room and intentionally damages the servers, resulting in an interruption of all services for over 48 h.

5. Scenario no. 5: erroneous update of the information system – after a software code change in the cloud infrastructure service, errors occur, causing data incompatibility and service disruption for up to 24 h.

Scenario3 is modeled as an availability-focused resource-exhaustion (storage) attack against the email service database. The ChatGPT-4o agent was trained according to the methodology provided in Sect. 4. With the help of this agent, all 5 threat risk scenarios were tested. A control prompt with 3 source files (1009 LTD, security controls, 12-item control template) was used to validate the submitted analyzes, as well as additional documents such as the threat scenario and the response generated by the ChatGPT-4o agent (main threat risk analyzer). The prompt asked for a percentage of correct completion of the task by rating each of the items 1–12 separately.

Figure 3 presents a comparative analysis of preventive security controls as identified by the GenAI model and human expert across five different threat scenarios. The expert evaluations, represented by the blue bars, are considered the correct baseline for this analysis. The GenAI, represented by the green bars, demonstrates a strong alignment in scenarios 2, 3, and 4, where the control counts are closely matched. However, in scenario 1, the GenAI significantly overestimates the required preventive controls (16 vs. 15), potentially reflecting a more conservative risk posture. In scenario 5, the GenAI also suggests substantially more preventive controls (10 vs. 4), indicating a potential overestimation of risks or a broader interpretation of preventive measures. This variability suggests that while the GenAI can capture a wide range of preventive actions, it may lack the nuanced context awareness that human experts apply when balancing efficiency with security.

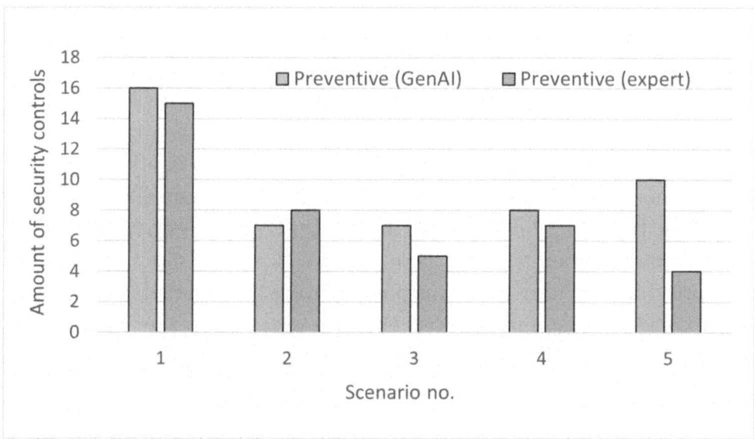

Fig. 3. Comparative analysis of preventive security controls identified by GenAI and human experts.

Figure 4 presents the comparison of detective controls identified by GenAI and human experts. The results indicate that the GenAI consistently overestimates the number of required detective controls in scenario 1 (8 vs. 7), suggesting a more cautious approach to threat detection. However, in scenarios 2 through 5, the GenAI closely aligns with expert assessments, achieving near-parity in control counts. This indicates that the GenAI's ability to identify detective measures is generally reliable across a range of scenarios, though it tends to adopt a more conservative detection strategy in higher-risk contexts, potentially leading to unnecessary resource allocation.

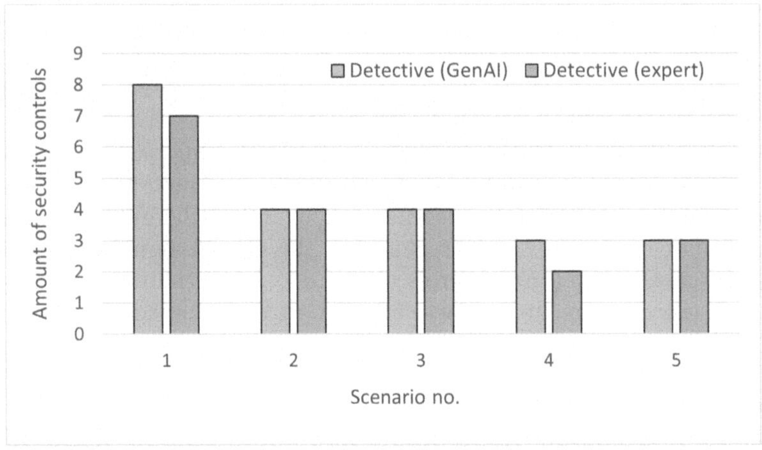

Fig. 4. Comparison of detective controls identified by GenAI and human experts.

Figure 5 compares the corrective controls. GenAI shows the greatest variation, significantly overestimating the necessary corrective actions in Scenarios 1 (8 vs. 7) and 2 (7 vs. 6), while underestimating in Scenario 3 (3 vs. 2). The alignment improves in scenarios 4 and 5, where the GenAI's control counts match expert assessments. This suggests that while the GenAI is effective in identifying corrective measures in lower-risk or well-defined scenarios, it can struggle to appropriately balance the urgency and extent of corrective actions in more complex threat landscapes.

Figure 6 provides a radar plot comparing overall risk levels calculated by the GenAI and expert assessments across the five scenarios. The results indicate a close alignment in overall risk perception, with the GenAI accurately matching expert assessments in scenarios 1 and 5. However, in scenario 2, the GenAI slightly overestimates the risk level (16 vs. 15), while in scenario 3 it underestimates (9 vs. 12), reflecting a need for better calibration when evaluating the combined impact and likelihood of threats. This mixed performance suggests that while the GenAI's risk assessment model is generally reliable, it may require further tuning to more accurately reflect expert judgment in moderate to high-risk scenarios.

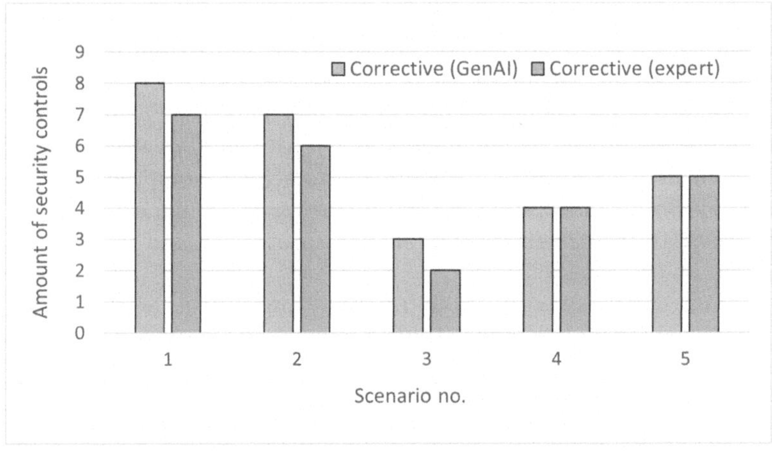

Fig. 5. Comparison of corrective controls identified by GenAI and human experts.

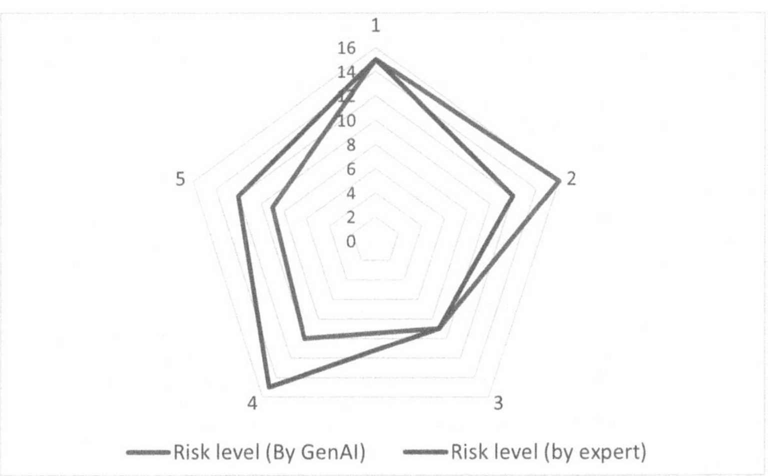

Fig. 6. Comparison of overall risk levels identified by GenAI and human experts.

The comprehensive analysis of the legislative compliance landscape reveals a strategic but fragmented approach to regulatory adherence. By mapping scenarios, controls, and standards together, we've uncovered that while we maintain technical compliance across both GDPR and ISO 27001 frameworks, our implementation lacks cohesion. Scenario 1 represents our strongest posture with robust data protection controls and independent security reviews, addressing both regulatory frameworks effectively. However, scenarios 2 through 5 demonstrate our tendency to address specific compliance requirements in isolation rather than adopting a unified security approach. The redundant implementation in scenarios 2 and 3 suggests inefficient resource allocation, while scenarios 4 and 5 highlight concerning regulatory blind spots—with one focusing exclusively on ICT preparedness for GDPR compliance and the other prioritizing technical vulnerabilities for ISO standards while neglecting data protection requirements. This siloed approach creates unnecessary vulnerability gaps that could be addressed through a more integrated compliance strategy. Moving forward, we should consolidate our security controls implementation to achieve comprehensive coverage across all scenarios while eliminating redundancies, particularly by strengthening the complementary controls between our data protection and technical vulnerability management processes.

The results of the experimental investigation on the accuracy of GenAI models-validators are presented in Table 1.

Table 1. Experimental results of the GenAI models-validators accuracy in threat risk analysis

Scenario	Gemini Advanced 2.5 Pro	Claude 3.7 Sonnet
Scenario no. 1	99.6	96
Scenario no. 2	100	97
Scenario no. 3	100	100
Scenario no. 4	87	92
Scenario no. 5	95.8	97.8

In addition, 1st scenario's tests were carried out from three different devices with different IP addresses with an interval of 5 h. The results showed slight instability (see Table 2):

- Claude 3.7 Sonnet results agreement ranged between 98–99%
- Gemini Advanced 2.5 Pro had an 83–98% agreement rate

Table 2. Experimental results of the GenAI models-validators accuracy in comparison of the first scenario GenAI agent's response with the cybersecurity specialist's checklist

GenAI models	Test from IPx	Test from IPy	Test from IPz
Claude 3.7 Sonnet	99	99	98
Gemini Advanced 2.5 Pro	83	95	98

The accuracy of the GenAI models varies from one situation to another. Gemini Advanced 2.5 showed larger fluctuations (87% to 100%), while Claude 3.7 Sonnet showed more stable results (92% to 100%). The models treat the same scenarios differently, suggesting that the validation of GenAI models requires the use of multiple models for greater reliability. The accuracy of the answer also depends on the percentage assessment methodology. When calculating the accuracy of each point and making a summary percentage assessment, the result differs slightly if GenAI is asked to assess the overall accuracy without assessing each sub-point.

All five cybersecurity risk scenarios tested were created by a specialist. In the event of a real incident, the CISO officer may not be able to accurately describe the context of the situation. When improving the agent, it is necessary to formulate specific questions or a methodology for the agent to use to obtain all the necessary information from the answers to the questions.

6 Discussion and Future Work

The proposed threat risk assessment method shows promise but faces key limitations. The dual GenAI setup risks an echo chamber effect, where both models reinforce the same biases. This was evident in testing, with fluctuating validation scores: 83–99 % for Gemini Advanced 2.5 Pro and 96–100

The system's reliance on fixed templates limits adaptability to evolving attacks. Recommendation accuracy was lowest (80 %), highlighting difficulty in turning analysis into actionable measures.

Future work should diversify GenAI ensembles to reduce echo effects, add explainable AI for transparency, and use dynamic prompt optimization to refine CISO inputs. Automated knowledge acquisition could keep pace with incidents and regulations, while weighted validation would reflect the criticality of different analysis points. Finally, adaptive recommendation engines tailored to organizational context would strengthen practical applicability.

7 Conclusions

This paper presents a novel method for integrating GenAI into cybersecurity threat risk management, specifically targeting the needs of CISO function responsible for critical information infrastructure protection. The proposed dual GenAI architecture, combining a primary risk analysis engine with a secondary independent validation layer, demonstrates significant potential for enhancing the precision, consistency, and regulatory alignment of risk assessments.

The proposed method significantly advances the state of GenAI-driven risk assessment, providing a structured, scalable, and legally defensible approach to managing cybersecurity risks. This work lays a strong foundation for the continued development of AI-assisted CISO operations, emphasizing the need for ongoing refinement to fully realize the potential of GenAI in critical infrastructure protection.

The cross-model verification approach effectively mitigates some common pitfalls of single-model hallucinations, but also introduces the risk of reinforcing mutual biases, potentially creating an echo chamber effect. To address this, future research should focus on integrating diverse model architectures and adaptive learning frameworks capable of dynamically adjusting to evolving threat landscapes.

Acknowledgments. This paper was funded by the project "Research on Cyber Resilience Through Application of Generative Artificial Intelligence in CISO Operations", which has received funding from the Research Council of Lithuania (LMTLT) (agreement No S-ITP-24-13).

Disclosure of Interests. The authors have no competing interests to declare that are relevant to the content of this article.

References

1. Ahmed, M., Wei, J., Al-Shaer, E.: Prompting LLM to enforce and validate cis critical security control. In: Proceedings of the 29th ACM Symposium on Access Control Models and Technologies, pp. 93–104 (2024)
2. Akbar, S.A., Hossain, M.M., Wood, T., Chin, S.C., Salinas, E., Alvarez, V., Cornejo, E.: Hallumeasure: fine-grained hallucination measurement using chain-of-thought reasoning. In: Proceedings of the 2024 Conference on Empirical Methods in Natural Language Processing, pp. 15020–15037 (2024)
3. Alnuhait, D., Kirtane, N., Khalifa, M., Peng, H.: Factcheckmate: preemptively detecting and mitigating hallucinations in LMS (2024). https://arxiv.org/abs/2410.02899
4. Arora, S., Ramteke, V.: Revolutionizing third party risk management using generative AI and rag. In: 2024 First International Conference on Data, Computation and Communication (ICDCC), pp. 16–22. IEEE (2024)
5. Bluefin (reporting on ITRC 2024 Data Breach Report): The 2024 ITRC Data Breach Report (2025). https://www.bluefin.com/bluefin-news/2024-itrc-data-breach-report-record-breaking-breaches/, Accessed 7 May 2025
6. Buczak, A.L., Guven, E.: A survey of data mining and machine learning methods for cyber security intrusion detection. IEEE Commun. Surv. Tutorials **18**(2), 1153–1176 (2016). https://doi.org/10.1109/COMST.2015.2494502, https://ieeexplore.ieee.org/document/7307098
7. Chen, Y., et al.: Attributive reasoning for hallucination diagnosis of large language models. In: Proceedings of the AAAI Conference on Artificial Intelligence. vol. 39, pp. 23660–23668 (2025)
8. Chuang, Y.S., Qiu, L., Hsieh, C.Y., Krishna, R., Kim, Y., Glass, J.: Lookback lens: detecting and mitigating contextual hallucinations in large language models using only attention maps. arXiv preprint arXiv:2407.07071 (2024)
9. ENISA: Artificial Intelligence Cybersecurity Challenges (2020). https://www.enisa.europa.eu/publications/artificial-intelligence-cybersecurity-challenges, Accessed 7 May 2025
10. ENISA: ENISA Threat Landscape 2023 (2023). https://www.enisa.europa.eu/publications/enisa-threat-landscape-2023, Accessed 7 May 2025
11. ENISA: Artificial Intelligence and Next-Gen Technologies (2025). https://www.enisa.europa.eu/topics/artificial-intelligence-and-next-gen-technologies, Accessed 7 May 2025
12. European Commission: JOINT COMMUNICATION TO THE EUROPEAN PARLIAMENT AND THE COUNCIL: The EU's Cybersecurity Strategy for the Digital Decade (2020). https://eur-lex.europa.eu/legal-content/EN/TXT/?uri=celex:52020JC0018, Accessed 7 May 2025

13. European Parliament and Council: Regulation (EU) 2024/1689 Laying Down Harmonised Rules on Artificial Intelligence (Artificial Intelligence Act) (2024). https://eur-lex.europa.eu/eli/reg/2024/1689/oj, Accessed 7 May 2025
14. European Parliament and Council of the European Union: DIRECTIVE (EU) 2022/2555 of the European Parliament and of the Council (2022). http://data.europa.eu/eli/dir/2022/2555/2022-12-27, Accessed 7 May 2025
15. European Parliament and Council of the European Union: DIRECTIVE (EU) 2022/2555 of the European Parliament and of the Council (2022), https://eur-lex.europa.eu/legal-content/EN/TXT/PDF/?uri=CELEX:32022L2555, Accessed 7 May 2025
16. Fang, Y., Li, M., Wang, W., Lin, H., Feng, F.: Counterfactual debating with preset stances for hallucination elimination of LLMS (2025). https://arxiv.org/abs/2406.11514
17. Grigaliūnas, Š, Schmidt, M., Brūzgienė, R., Smyrli, P., Andreou, S., Lopata, A.: Holistic information security management and compliance framework. Electronics **13**(19), 1–31 (2024)
18. Ji, Z., et al.: LLM internal states reveal hallucination risk faced with a query (2024). https://arxiv.org/abs/2407.03282
19. Lei, D., et al.: Chain of natural language inference for reducing large language model ungrounded hallucinations (2023). https://arxiv.org/abs/2310.03951
20. Munmun, N.Z.S., Hossain, N.M.D., Jahan, N.I., Akther, N.S., Masum, N.a.A.: AI-driven project risk management: leveraging artificial intelligence to predict, mitigate, and manage project risks in critical infrastructure and national security projects. J. Comput. Sci. Technol. Stud. **7**(2), 71–85 (2025). https://doi.org/10.32996/jcsts.2025.7.2.6
21. Oluoha, O.M., Odeshina, A., Reis, O., Okpeke, F., Attipoe, V., Orieno, O.H.: Artificial intelligence integration in regulatory compliance: a strategic model for cybersecurity enhancement. J. Front. Multidis. Res. **3**(1), 35–46 (2022). https://doi.org/10.54660/.ijfmr.2022.3.1.35-46
22. Sarker, I., Kayes, A., Badsha, S., Alqahtani, H., Watters, P., Ng, A.: Cybersecurity data science: an overview from machine learning perspective. J. Big Data **7**, 41 (2020). https://doi.org/10.1186/s40537-020-00318-5, https://journalofbigdata.springeropen.com/articles/10.1186/s40537-020-00318-5
23. Snyder, B., Moisescu, M., Zafar, M.B.: On early detection of hallucinations in factual question answering. In: Proceedings of the 30th ACM SIGKDD Conference on Knowledge Discovery and Data Mining, pp. 2721–2732 (2024)
24. Surfshark: Global Data Breach Statistics: A 2024 Recap (2025). https://surfshark.com/research/study/data-breach-recap-2024, Accessed 7 May 2025
25. Thomas, S.: Revolutionizing security compliance and GRC with generative AI and LLMs. Int. J. Multidis. Res. **5**(2) (2023). https://doi.org/10.36948/ijfmr.2023.v05i02.37226, https://doi.org/10.36948/ijfmr.2023.v05i02.37226
26. Wang, A., et al.: Improving LLM generations via fine-grained self-endorsement. In: Findings of the Association for Computational Linguistics ACL 2024, pp. 8424–8436 (2024)
27. Xiao, W., et al.: Detecting and mitigating hallucination in large vision language models via fine-grained AI feedback (2025). https://arxiv.org/abs/2404.14233
28. Yang, Y., Ma, Y., Feng, H., Cheng, Y., Han, Z.: Minimizing hallucinations and communication costs: adversarial debate and voting mechanisms in LLM-based multi-agents. Appl. Sci. **15**(7), 3676 (2025)
29. Yigit, Y., et al.: Critical infrastructure protection: generative AI, challenges, and opportunities (2024). https://arxiv.org/abs/2405.04874

A Comparison of Security ICS Communication Protocols

Daniel Clark(✉) and Tom Chothia

University of Birmingham, Birmingham, UK
{d.e.clark,t.chothia}@bham.ac.uk

Abstract. This paper presents a summary and comparison of leading secure Industrial Control System (ICS) communication protocols. We find two categories of ICS protocols: those that run an insecure ICS protocol over TLS and those that use a bespoke security protocol. We assess the key properties of bespoke ICS protocols using formal modelling, for OPC-UA and DNP3-SAv5 we use existing models, and we build formal models for S7Comm-Plus and SSP-21; this lets us make a full comparison between these protocols. For ICS protocols based on TLS, we compare the versions and configurations of TLS specified, and any access control add-ons. This leads to a detailed picture of the security provided and best use cases for each protocol.

Keywords: ICS protocols · Formal analysis · TLS

1 Introduction

Industrial Control Systems (ICS) manage most aspects of national critical infrastructure, therefore the security of the protocols is of the utmost importance. Traditionally ICS protocols such as Modbus and PROFINET had no cryptographic protections, relying on firewalled networks for security, however many recent attacks have shown that this makes it possible for an attacker to penetrate the network and send commands to PLCs. Examples of such attacks include Industroyer/CrashOverride [16], Triton [27] and FrostyGoop [22]. In response to this some ICS protocols, such as Siemens S7Comm or OPC, have added encryption and authentication. Other protocols, such as Modbus TLS or BACnet/SC, add security by running the older insecure version of the protocol over a particular flavour of TLS.

While many of these protocols have been looked at individually (e.g., [8, 15]), little work has been done on comparing the security they offer. This paper provides a comprehensive analysis and comparison of the leading security ICS protocols. To make a direct comparison of the security offered by the protocols, we build and test models of S7Comm-Plus, and SSP-21 [35] in the Tamarin protocol checker, and we use existing models of OPC-UA and DNP3-SAv5. This allows us to uniformly test and compare the security properties offered by these protocols.

E. Bergström et al. (Eds.): CRITIS 2025, LNCS 16291, pp. 424–444, 2026.
https://doi.org/10.1007/978-3-032-19540-1_22

Past work has found attacks against Siemens S7Comm-Plus protocol [12,29]; our formal modelling confirms these attacks and finds more. Our modelling of SSP-21 finds that it has the strongest security properties. However, this protocol is not supported by any of the devices we have looked at. This leaves OPC-UA as the best option from the non-TLS protocols.

Next we look at protocols that use TLS, i.e., Modbus TLS, BACnet/SC, CIP Security, IEC 62351 and Siemens Logo. We review the documents for these to find the particular kinds of TLS used. The most secure use TLS 1.3 with client certificates and a PKI, leading to a very high level of security. However we identify a major issue with the use of TLS for ICS protocols. Best practice in ICS networks calls for an Intrusion Detection System (IDS) to monitor traffic and a data historian to record network behaviour. This only works with plaintext traffic, but TLS 1.3 has been designed not to allow authenticated plaintext. Hence the use of TLS 1.3 may present an issue for some ICS owners. CIP Security addresses this by specifying the use of TLS 1.2 that allows authenticated plaintext traffic. However TLS 1.2 will become outdated and lack support in the future. Therefore we conjecture that the use of TLS will pose a problem for ICS protocols in the future.

In summary the contributions of this paper are:

- Formal modelling in the Tamarin Prover of S7Comm-Plus and SSP-21.
- A detailed review of how TLS is used in Modbus TLS, BACnet/SC, CIP Security, IEC 62351 and Siemens Logo.
- A comparison of the security offered by these protocols and discussion of future directions.

Our Tamarin models and protocol diagrams can be found in our GitLab repo: https://gitlab.com/ICSProtocolSecurityComparison/ICSProtocolSecurity

2 Background

Industrial Control Systems (ICS) are an example of Operational Technology (OT); they will typically control physical processes such as factory machinery and industrial processes. A key component of ICS networks are Programmable Logic Controllers (PLCs) that will read data from sensors and run a program to control actuators. These PLCs are usually programmed and controlled by proprietorial desktop controller software provided by the manufacturer of the PLC, and the PLC may be set to communicate with other PLCs and Human Machine Interface (HMI)s. Importantly, the ICS owner will often have very little visibility of the software running on the PLC and the ways in which the PLC communicates with other devices; hence the need to understand the security of ICS communication protocols.

ICS protocols have historically not been designed with security in mind, despite controlling significant swathes of critical infrastructure the world over, instead focusing primarily on reliability and compatibility. There are a huge number of varying ICS protocols, but some of the most common are: Modbus,

HART, DNP3, CIP, PROFINET and BACnet, the vast majority of which put little to no consideration towards security in the protocols themselves. These systems were normally designed explicitly to be isolated from all remotely accessible networks, often through the use of air gaps, meaning the attack vectors were much more limited, so the risks of cyber attacks were considered negligible.

More recently however, these assumptions have been disproven in two significant ways. The first is that attacks have been discovered on these air-gapped networks via sophisticated malware designed to bridge the air gap. The second is that in order to introduce novel functionality, like more extensive monitoring and operation between multiple industrial sites, these systems have been connected to wider networks, including the internet.

With the risks associated with added connectivity, and the increased sophistication of attacks, designers of these protocols have sought to either add security to protocols that already exist, or introduce new standard protocols which have security incorporated from the start. One common approach to creating these new secure protocols, has been to wrap an already existing protocol within TLS in various ways (which we refer to as the TLS protocols), whilst others have introduced their own bespoke solutions either by adapting existing protocols or creating a new protocol from scratch (which we label as the Non-TLS/Bespoke protocols).

IEC 62351 outlines broad protocol definitions for various environments in parts 3, 4, 5 and 6:

Part 3 outlines recommendations for protocols using TLS.
Part 4 details an approach for adding cryptographic security features to protocols based on the Manufacturing Message Specification (MMS).
Part 5 describes applying security features to protocols based on IEC 60870-5, and is the basis of DNP3-SAv5 which will be discussed in Sect. 4.4.
Part 6 proposes security additions to protocols based on IEC 61850.

There is a proposal for a version of PROFINET to run over TLS [37], however a full version has not been released. We do not look at the secure version of the Wireless-HART protocol, because this does not seem to be widely supported by PLCs and there is no public specification. We do not include more general protocols that may be used in an ICS environment, such as the Wi-Fi protocol WPA or the IoT device protocol MQTT. While some ICS equipment do use such protocols their security has been well studied outside the ICS domain.

2.1 Related Work

Formal Verification of ICS Protocols. In [13], Cremers, Dehnel-Wild and Milner performed an evaluation of the DNP3-SAv5 protocol, using the Tamarin Prover, and specifically tested it against the security claims made by the protocol specification. DNP3-SAv5 is a notably complex protocol, primarily because it is made up of multiple interacting sub-protocols which use the same shared state, and the model reflects this complexity. Through this model the researchers were able to prove a number of security properties against the protocol, and notably disprove a previously claimed attack outlined in [8].

The OPC-UA protocol has been modelled in the ProVerif protocol checker by Puys et al. [33] and more recently by Diemunsch et al. [15]. This second paper includes a very large model of OPC-UA and finds a range of security issues, the authors worked with the OPC standards group to fix some of the issues, but others remain and we discuss these below.

Non-Formal Analysis of ICS Protocols. Many authors have described attacks on ICS protocols without security (e.g., [1,7,11,20,28]), and other papers have pointed out these insecure protocols often have unsafe password protection for access control, e.g., [38].

Attacks have been discovered during previous analysis of S7Comm-Plus, for instance, [12,26,29] found that the Siemens PLCs using this protocol use common certificates and therefore traffic can be intercepted and decrypted. However, there has been no formal modelling of this protocol to provide a complete picture of exactly what security it does and does not provide.

Barbieri et al. [10] carry out a measurement study of ICS protocols used over the internet and find wide spread use of insecure ICS protocols. Dahlmanns et al. [14] look at the uptake of TLS based ICS protocol, but do not compare the security they offer. Holasova et al. [25] train a neural network to recognise some of the ICS protocols we look at, but they do not compare their security. [19] presents a comparison of OPC-UA and CIP Security; they conclude that both approaches have their benefits and drawbacks.

On the more practical side, Erba et al. [17] investigate devices that use OPC-UA and find that many do not handle certificate security. Tychalas and Maniatakos [36] look at side channel attacks on PLCs including some using OPC-UA, and [24] Hildebrandt et al. present a supply chain attack against PLCs using OPC-UA. All of these are due to the implementations of OPC-UA, rather than the protocol designs, which we analyse in this paper.

Work has also been done on exploiting implementation weaknesses in PLCs using other protocols. For example, Alsabbagh and Langendöerfer discover code injection attacks against various versions of Siemens S7 PLCs [3–6], and an OpenPLC environment [2]. These attacks highlight further the need for secure cryptographic protocols which would eliminate a key attack vector needed to exploit them.

2.2 Tamarin Prover

The Tamarin Prover is a tool for verifying the security of protocols using symbolic models. A Tamarin model is formed of two parts, the description of the protocol itself, and a set of security properties to be proven.

Protocol descriptions are built as a set of rules, which take a particular state as input, and output a new state. A state takes the form of a set of facts, which each declare some term exists in that state. By consuming and creating facts, rules are therefore the transitions between states. Agents are typically defined by an identifier, which is then stored in all facts which relate to them, and so are effectively restricted to only being accessed by that agent. Special *In* and *Out* facts exist to model the transfer of messages across the network, only data which has been output to the *Out* fact may be taken as input with the *In* fact.

Tamarin uses the Dolev-Yao attacker model to define the properties of the network. In this model the attacker is in full control of the network, they can intercept, modify, block, delay or create any message. The attacker can only create messages from their own knowledge, which can be derived from any information sent across the network and any public function. This model can be extended to allow malicious agents, that is, genuine agents which have been taken over by the attacker.

Cryptographic functions are defined symbolically and perfectly, e.g., all symmetric encryption schemes are modelled as the same functions (*senc* and *sdec*) and cannot be brute forced or otherwise broken by the attacker.

Security properties are defined as lemmas which reason about terms at specific points in the protocol. Action facts are used to mark terms in the protocol at particular points, which will be referenced by the lemmas. Lemmas are either defined as Exists or For-All lemmas. Exists lemmas simply state that there is at least one possible protocol run where a specific set of actions happen (or do not happen). For-All lemmas state that, in all cases where some set of actions happen, then this other set of actions must always happen.

For example, a possible secrecy for-all lemma could say that for all runs of the protocol where an agent has a secrecy key, it is never the case that the attacker knows that key. To prove this lemma, Tamarin will try to find a counter example. It will start from the assumption that both the agent and the attacker have the key, and work backwards, applying rules in reverse until it finds a valid run of the protocol. If no valid protocol run exists, it considers the lemma proven. If Tamarin does find a valid protocol run, the lemma is disproven, and Tamarin can present the counter example as a possible attack.

3 Security Properties and Attacker Model

In this paper we investigate each of the non-TLS/bespoke protocols against a number of security properties. To give a more complete picture and comparison of each protocol and each protocol mode, we go beyond checking basic secrecy and authenticity and check each of the following properties:

1. Authenticity
   (a) Non-Injective Agreement: If an entity believes it has finished a transaction with a particular party, then they have done so, and they agree on the protocol parameters, e.g., session keys or a message. This is the crucial security property for ICS; if a PLC believes it has received a specific command from a specific controller, then it is critical that this is actually the case.

   (b) Injective Agreement: As above, but the two parties must be in a one-to-one agreement regarding the sending and receiving of a message, e.g., messages cannot be replayed.
2. Secrecy - We consider this both in cases where agents external to the session may be compromised, and where they are not.
   (a) Secrecy: can an attacker learn the keys or messages of the protocol? Keeping long term and session keys secret is an important goal for any protocol. We note that some protocol (modes) deliberately do not keep messages secret so that they can be analysed by, e.g., IDSs.
   (b) Perfect Forward Secrecy (PFS): If a long term key is leaked, can previous messages be decrypted? We follow the definition of PFS from the Tamarin manual that allows an active attacker. PFS is a less important property for ICS than secrecy, but can still be important in some situations, e.g., if an encrypted control program was captured, and the key for this later learned from a compromised device.
3. Key Compromise Impersonation (KCI): If the long term key of an entity has been compromised, can an attacker impersonate other entities to them.
4. Key Uniqueness: Every session key should be different. If the attacker can force two sessions to have the same key they could for instance redirect encrypted messages from one device to another, leading to machinery behaving in dangerous ways.

Attacker Model: We consider an attacker that has gained access to the network used by the ICS equipment. Many ICS owners will aim to keep the ICS network secure and would consider the presence of an attacker on this network to already be a failure of security; this is the rationale behind the continued use of insecure ICS protocols. However, as many ICS attacks show, attackers do find their way onto these networks, and as Barbieri [10] shows, there is a strikingly large amount of ICS protocol traffic sent across the public internet.

All agents not directly involved in the current run of the protocol are considered malicious. For PFS, agents become malicious after the protocol run has completed, and for KCI, the agent which is the target of the attack is also considered malicious.

4 Non-TLS/Bespoke Protocols

In this section we will outline a number of protocols developed for communication between devices in ICS networks, specifically those which are not built around the TLS protocol, as these will be discussed later in this paper.

For each, we will give a brief background to the protocol, give an outline of the protocol itself if required, outline the security claims made by the protocol specifications and describe our contribution to the analysis of each protocol. After describing all the protocols we will then describe the results of testing the formal models and conclude with a summary of the results of each of the analyses. Protocol diagrams and Tamarin models for each protocol we model can be found on our website.

4.1 Siemens S7Comm-Plus

S7Comm-Plus is a proprietary standard developed by Siemens as an iteration of their earlier S7Comm protocol which has been used since 1995. Many forms of S7Comm-Plus have been released since 2012, primarily with the aim of adding encryption, authentication and integrity protection to the S7Comm protocol. Past work [12,29] reverse engineered the S7Comm-Plus protocol, and discovered a number of vulnerabilities. In this paper we focus on protocol version 3, as described in [12].

Protocol Description. A full protocol diagram for S7Comm-Plus can be found on our website, but we will provide a simplified description here based on the work of Biham et al. [12]. S7Comm-Plus sessions run between a Totally Integrated Automation Portal (TIA), which acts as the client, and a PLC which acts as the server. The PLC firmware is pre-configured with a public/private key pair, and that public key is also stored in the TIA firmware. Biham et al. [12] found that all PLCs of the same model and firmware version, used the same public/private key pair.

The protocol begins with a TIA sending a cleartext "Hello" message, to which the PLC responds with a random $serverSessionChallenge$. The TIA hashes and MACs this challenge with a freshly generated $KeyDerivationKey(KDK)$ to create the $sessionKey$. A fresh $preKey$ is then generated, which is used to derive the $KeyEncryptionKey(KEK)$ and other keys for error checking.

The TIA then sends a $SecurityKeyEncryptedKey$ message to the PLC that includes the $preKey$ encrypted with the public key, the $serverSessionChallenge$ and KDK both encrypted with the KEK, and other values for randomness and error checking. The PLC decrypts this message and hashes the newly acquired KDK with the $serverSessionChallenge$ to derive the $sessionKey$ in the same way as the TIA above. From this point on, every message in both directions is authenticated using a MAC keyed with the $sessionKey$.

Modelling. In S7Comm-Plus, TIAs have no long-term secrets, identifiers or private functions. This means that an attacker can trivially impersonate a valid TIA with no prior knowledge whatsoever. PLCs do have a long-term secret, a private key, however, in practice it has been seen that the same PLC private key is shared amongst all PLCs with the same model and firmware version [12]. The protocol itself does not depend on this beyond the TIAs needing to know the PLC's public key in advance. As such, we model two scenarios, one where the PLC private key was shared amongst all PLCs, and one more idealised version where the private key is unique for each PLC. These are both contained within the same model, and are switched via the -DNoSharedKey Tamarin flag.

PLC agents are restricted via a Once() restriction whereby each PLC may only have a single private key. TIA agents also have Once() restrictions on their initialisation, in order to stop the same combination of PLC and TIA from creating multiple identical !TIA facts.

The majority of the cryptographic algorithms used in S7Comm-Plus are custom and proprietary, and where standard algorithms are used, they are often used incorrectly [12]. The result of this is that there are significant cryptographic weaknesses in the protocol brought about by these algorithms. Due to the symbolic nature of Tamarin models, all cryptographic primitives are considered perfect, with the focus on flaws in the protocol rather than the cryptographic algorithms themselves.

During key establishment, a *preKey* is used with a Key Derivation Function (KDF) to derive 3 sub-keys, the Key Encryption Key (KEK), the Checksum Encryption Key (CEK), and the Checksum Seed (CS). The CS is then used to derive the Look Up Table (LUT), which is then used as an input to a checksum algorithm. In our model, we remove the step of deriving the LUT from the CS, and simply consider the Look Up Table to be an output from the KDF instead of the CS. The KDF is abstracted to a 1-way function with two inputs, the key name, and the *preKey*, and the checksum algorithm is also abstracted to a 1-way function with two inputs, the checksum input, and the LUT.

The Elliptic-Curve-ElGamal-Like encryption algorithm [12] used to encrypt the *preKey* is modelled using a custom asymmetric encryption equation: $adec\_s7(aenc\_s7(plaintext, nonce, pk(sk)), nonce, sk) = plaintext$, where the *preKey* and random y value are the plaintext. Both the $Nonce$ and the PLC's public key are needed to encrypt, then the PLC's private key X and the $Nonce$ are needed to decrypt.

The AES-CTR encryption of the Challenge and KDK is modelled as two separate symmetric encryptions, with counter values '0' and '1' respectively, where the IV, counter and KEK are used together as the key. The HMAC-SHA256 used to authenticate final protocol messages is modelled as a 1-way function with two parameters, the message data, and the $sessionKey$.

4.2 SSP-21

The Secure SCADA Protocol for the 21st Century (SSP-21) [23,35] started development in 2016, with the latest version being published in May 2020 as part of the California Energy Systems for the 21st Century (CES-21) project by the California Public Utilities Commission. It is inspired by the Noise protocol [32], especially the static-ephemeral triple Diffie-Hellman Key Exchange. This was a major effort to design a better ICS protocol, but is has not been widely adopted.

Protocol Description. In this section we will outline a simplified version of the SSP-21 protocol. A full protocol description for SSP-21 can be found in [35], and protocol diagrams can be found on our website.

SSP-21 can be run in one of 4 handshake modes: Shared Secret (SS), Public Keys (PK), Industrial Certificates (IC) and Quantum Key Distribution (QKD), each with their own requirements for any prior knowledge, values for EphemeralData and ModeData, and some Input Key Material (IKM). These are outlined in Table 1.

Table 1. Handshake Modes

Mode	Prior Knowledge	Ephemeral Data	Mode Data	Input Key Material (IKM)
SS	$SharedSecret$	Initiator: Random $INonce$ Responder: Random $RNonce$	-	$SharedSecret \| \| INonce \| \| RNonce$
PK	Initiator: $IStaticPrivate$ $RStaticPublic$ Responder: $RStaticPrivate$ $IStaticPublic$	Initiator: $IEphemeralPublic^{*}$ Responder: $REphemeralPublic^{*}$	-	Initiator: $REphemeralPublic^{IEphemeralPrivate} \| \| REphemeralPublic^{IStaticPrivate} \| \| RStaticPublic^{IEphemeralPrivate}$ Responder: $IEphemeralPublic^{REphemeralPrivate} \| \| IStaticPublic^{REphemeralPrivate} \| \| IEphemeralPublic^{RStaticPrivate}$
IC	Initiator: $TAPublic$ $IStaticPrivate$ $ICert$ Responder: $TAPublic$ $RStaticPrivate$ $RCert$	Initiator: $IEphemeralPublic^{*}$ Responder: $REphemeralPublic^{*}$	Initiator: ICert Responder: RCert	Initiator: $REphemeralPublic^{IEphemeralPrivate} \| \| REphemeralPublic^{IStaticPrivate} \| \| RStaticPublic^{IEphemeralPrivate}$ Responder: $IEphemeralPublic^{REphemeralPrivate} \| \| IStaticPublic^{REphemeralPrivate} \| \| IEphemeralPublic^{RStaticPrivate}$
QKD	Depends on QKD method and is not defined in the standard	-	KeyIdentifier	The QuantumKey identified using the KeyIdentifier

* Derived from a fresh ephemeral private key generated at the start of each session.

The *Initiator* sends the first message, *RequestHandshakeBegin*, which contains some configuration values (e.g. what algorithms are supported, the supported handshake mode(s), the required *NonceMode* and *CryptoMode*), the *EphemeralData* and the *ModeData*. The *NonceMode* simply defines if the counters in all *SessionData* messages must be strictly incrementing, or just needs to be higher than the last valid counter. The *CryptoMode* determines if the *SessionData* messages should be encrypted and MACed, or just MACed. The Responder then replies with the *ReplyHandshakeBegin* message, containing its *EphemeralData* and *ModeData*.

Each side then computes the hash of the two *HandshakeBegin* messages, as well as calculating their mode-specific IKM. A Key Derivation Function uses the hash and the IKM to generate two symmetric session keys on each side, one for sending (*SessionKeyTX*), and one for receiving (*SessionKeyRX*), where the TX key on each side matches the RX key on the other. Data transfer can then begin using *SessionData* messages, the first of which in each direction are used to authenticate both sides using the newly calculated session keys, and are nicknamed the *SessionAuthRequest* and *SessionAuthReply*.

All *SessionData* messages contain an *AuthMetadata* field which contains a *Nonce* (a counter which increments for each message sent in a session starting at 0) and the expiry time of the message *ValidUntilMS*. *SessionData* messages also included the length of the User Data, the User Data itself, and a MAC over the contents of the message using the *SessionKeyTX*. The *SessionAuthRequest* and *SessionAuthReply* messages may contain User Data, or may be empty with a User Data length of 0.

Once the *Responder* receives and verifies the *SessionAuthRequest* using its *SessionKeyRX*, it sends a *SessionAuthReply*. The *Initiator* receives and verifies the *SessionAuthReply* using its *SessionKeyRX*, after which authenticated communication can begin using standard *SessionData* messages. Authentication is considered complete by the *Responder* and *Initiator* once they have received the *SessionAuthRequest* and *SessionAuthReply* messages respectively.

Modelling. We constructed a separate model for each Crypto Mode (with and without encryption), which differ only in that the messages in the encrypted model are encrypted, decrypted and verified using the Authenticated Encryption with Associated Data (AEAD) equations from [21].

The SSP-21 standard defines 4 Handshake Modes, however the details of the Quantum Key Distribution (QKD) mode are not specified in sufficient detail to be implemented or modelled effectively, so we omitted this handshake mode from our models. The protocol is identical in every mode beyond the two *HandshakeBegin* messages, therefore, the 3 modes were implemented into the one shared model, with Tamarin preprocessor flags -DSS, -DPK and -DIC used to determine which modes to include.

SSP-21 uses a Key Derivation Function (KDF) function to generate session keys, which we model as a one-way function with three inputs, some IKM (based on the Handshake Mode), the Handshake Hash (generated from the two HandshakeBegin messages), and a key number, so that two keys can be generated. The certificates used in IndustrialCertificates mode are modelled as the Identity of the agent, the agent's static public key and the CA's signature of the identity and key. We use a NotEqual(NEq) restriction to ensure that incoming public keys do not have invalid values, as per the protocol specification, and we use a *Once* restriction to ensure only one Trusted Authority (TA) can exist.

In order to limit model complexity, we have only modelled the *STRICT_INCREMENT NonceMode*, and have hard-coded the message counter into each message. This is a valid optimisation as the two *SessionAuth* messages must always have their counter set to 0, and we only model one further message which should therefore always have the counter 1.

4.3 OPC-Unified Architecture (OPC-UA)

OPC-UA is an open standard developed by the OPC Foundation, a large consortium of industry players, which since its inception has been designed to allow interoperability and a layer of abstraction between devices using the plethora of legacy SCADA communications protocols. The first version of OPC-UA was released in 2006, and although developed by the same group, bares little resemblance to the original OPC protocol.

Protocol Description. Throughout the OPC-UA specification it often refers to "signing", however due to their symmetric nature, they should actually be more considered as Message Authentication Code (MAC)s rather than signatures in most cases. For consistency, we will continue to use the terminology set by the specification.

OPC-UA can be used in one of three Security Modes:

None - All messages are neither signed nor encrypted.
Sign - Final messages are signed but not encrypted. Open Secure Channel, Create Session and Activate Session messages are all both signed and encrypted.
SignEncrypt - All messages are both signed and encrypted.

The OPC-UA standard outlines a number of Security Policies, which define which algorithms are to be used for signing, encryption and key derivation.

Notably, OPC-UA authenticates Users separately from Clients and Servers. Clients/Servers are authenticated using TA-signed certificates, whilst Users can be authenticated using one of four User Identity Token Modes: **Anonymous** which provides no authentication, **UserName** which authenticates users via a Username and Password, **X509** which uses a self-signed User certificate, or **Issued** which uses an OAuth2 Security Token issued by an Authorisation Service.

The address of a Discovery Endpoint is pre-configured into each client. From there, the protocol is split into four logical sub-protocols:

Get Endpoints - A Client uses this to retrieve a list of available Servers from the Discovery Endpoint. It also includes each Server's certificate and the Security Modes and Policies it supports.

Open Secure Channel - Sends the Client's certificate to the Server, and establishes shared symmetric Session Keys (except in Security Mode: None). This can either use RSA or Elliptic-Curve Cryptography (ECC) with Elliptic-Curve DiffieHellman (ECDH), depending on the Security Policy.

Create Session - Both sides are authenticated using their certificates and a challenge-response exchange. The Server also shares a Session Authentication Token, which the client then includes in future requests to associate them with a session (and once activated, a User).

Activate Session - Uses the User Identity Token to authenticate the user, this depends on the User Identity Token Mode.

Modelling. For OPC-UA we use the detailed ProVerif model presented in [15].

4.4 DNP3-SAv5

The original 1993 version of Distributed Network Protocol 3 (DNP3) was derived from IEC 60870–5 to provide interoperability between different SCADA systems from different manufacturers, and was eventually adopted into IEEE 1815–2010. In 2013, IEC 62351–5 was published to standardise security additions to IEC 60870–5-derived protocols. It added support for asymmetric cryptography and a CA, and with the release of IEEE 1815–2012, these changes were introduced into the DNP3 specification in the form of Secure Authentication Version 5 (SAv5).

DNP3DNP3 is primarily used in the control of power grids and related infrastructure, and is used in the majority of grids worldwide. Its use has been growing in other parts of critical infrastructure such as water and gas supplies, but has found limited adoption outside of this.

DNP3-SAv5 has been analysed previously by [8], who claimed a vulnerability, however this was disproven by an in-depth investigation using the Tamarin Prover in [13]. They built a comprehensive model of DNP3-SAv5 and proved its security against the security guarantees claimed by the specification.

Modelling. We use Cremers et al.'s Tamarin model of DNP3-SAv5 from [13].

4.5 Analysis

In this subsection we present and describe the results of the formal analysis. These results are summarised in Table 2. Below we summarise notable findings and their impact, for each class of security property.

Table 2. Results of the formal analysis of bespoke ICS protocols

		Secrecy With External Compromise			Secrecy No External Compromise			Authentication				KCI		Uniqueness
		Secrecy		PFS	Secrecy		PFS	Client → Server		Server → Client		Client	Server	
		LTKs	Messages	Messages	LTKs	Messages	Messages	Non Injective	Injective	Non Injective	Injective			
S7	Shared SK Private PK	X$_{[S1]}$	-	-	✓	-	-	X$_{[A1]}$	X$_{[A1]}$	X$_{[A1]}$	X$_{[A1]}$]	-	X$_{[K1]}$	✓
	Shared SK Public PK	X$_{[S1]}$	-	-	✓	-	-	X$_{[A1]}$	X[$_{[A1]}$]	X$_{[A1]}$	X$_{[A1]}$	-	X$_{[K1]}$	✓
	Individual SKs Private PKs	✓	-	-	✓	-	-	✓	✓	✓	✓	-	X$_{[K1]}$	✓
	Individual SKs Public PKs	✓	-	-	✓	-	-	X[$_{[A2]}$]	X$_{[A2]}$	✓	✓	-	X[$_{[K1]}$	✓
SSP	SS - MAC	✓	-	-	✓	-	-	✓	✓	✓	✓	X$_{[K2]}$	X$_{[K2]}$	✓
	PK - MAC	✓	-	-	✓	-	-	✓	✓	✓	✓	✓	✓	✓
	IC - MAC	✓	-	-	✓	-	-	✓	✓	✓	✓	✓	✓	✓
	SS - AEAD	✓	✓	X$_{[P1]}$	✓	✓	X$_{[P1]}$	✓	✓	✓	✓	X$_{[K2]}$	X$_{[K2]}$	✓
	PK - AEAD	✓	✓	X$_{[P2]}$	✓	✓	X$_{[P2]}$	✓	✓	✓	✓	✓	✓	✓
	IC - AEAD	✓	✓	X$_{[P2]}$	✓	✓	X$_{[P2]}$	✓	✓	✓	✓	✓	✓	✓
OPC	Sign - RSA	✓	-	-	✓	-	-	✓	X$_{[A3]}$	✓	✓	✓	X$_{[K3]}$	*
	SignEnc - RSA	✓	✓	X$_{[P3]}$	✓	✓	X$_{[P3]}$	✓	✓	✓	✓	✓	X$_{[K4]}$	*
	Sign - ECC	✓	-	-	✓	-	-	✓	X$_{[A3]}$	✓	✓	✓	X$_{[K3]}$	*
	SignEnc - ECC	✓	✓	✓	✓	✓	✓	✓	✓	✓	✓	✓	X$_{[K4]}$	*
DNP3		✓	✓	*	✓	✓	*	✓	✓	✓	✓	*	*	*

[−] Not Applicable, e.g. Testing secrecy of an unencrypted message
[*] Not Checked, i.e. No equivalent lemma is found in the original model

Secrecy

S7Comm-Plus.

$S1$ - **Description** All PLCs with the same model and firmware version share the same long-term secret key, consequently an attacker can recover it by compromising any PLC, even one which is not involved in the session.

$S1$ - **Impact** Since TIAs have no long-term secrets, with access to the shared PLC secret key, an attacker can perform any action on the network.

Perfect Forward Secrecy

SSP-21.

*P*1 - **Description** In SharedSecret mode both agents share a single SharedSecret, and there are no ephemeral public keys exchanged. Once an attacker has extracted the SharedSecret, they can generate the session keys using public data from the two HandshakeBegin messages, and decrypt the session.

*P*1 - **Impact** Data exchanged in SharedSecret mode can be decrypted by any agent who witnessed the two HandshakeBegin messages and has possession of the SharedSecret. This weakness is acknowledged in the specification.

*P*2 - **Description** In PublicKeys and IndustrialCertificates modes, an attacker can masquerade as an existing Responder until it is required to send the SessionAuthResponse. At this stage the attacker only possesses 3 of the 4 public/private keys needed to derive the session keys and forge the SessionAuthResponse. If using AEAD, the attacker also cannot decrypt the previous message, the SessionAuthRequest, until the genuine Responder's Static Private Key is revealed after session termination - at which point the attacker has all 4 keys required to derive the session keys and decrypt the message.

*P*2 - **Impact** The SessionAuthRequest can optionally include session data, which the attacker is now able to decrypt. This session data could potentially include application configuration, commands, or even a partial application binary, which could lead to possible implementation attacks. Although the specification briefly alludes to "certain implementations" not leaving this field empty, but it provides no further details.

OPC-UA

*P*3 - **Description** When using an RSA Security Policy rather than an ECC one, OPC-UA session keys are generated only from Client and Server nonces exchanged during secure channel establishment. These nonces are shared encrypted only with their counterpart's public keys, therefore an attacker with access to both private keys is able to decrypt both nonces and generate the session keys.

*P*3 - **Impact** With the session keys, the attacker can decrypt all messages shared over the life of the secure channel. ECC support was only introduced to the OPC-UA specification in version 1.05, and of the 565 products listed on the OPC Foundation marketplace [31], only 43 claim any support for version 1.05, of which only 3 list support for any ECC Security Policies.

Authentication

S7Comm-Plus

*A*1 - **Description** After compromising the shared PLC long-term secret key as per S1, an attacker can impersonate any PLC to any TIA. TIAs have no long-term secrets of their own, and are authenticated only by possession of the PLC public key, consequently an attacker can simply derive the public key from the compromised secret key and impersonate any TIA to any PLC.

*A*1 - **Impact** If an attacker can compromise any PLC and recover the shared secret key, it can break all authentication and perform any action on the network.

*A*2 - **Description** The PLC public key is never made public as part of the protocol, but is pre-programmed onto each TIA with the correct firmware version. If an attacker can compromise any TIA and recover the public key, it can forge the unauthenticated *SecurityKeyEncryptedKey* message sent to the PLC. This includes a forged Key Derivation Key, which is used to MAC the *serverSessionChallenge* (sent in an earlier cleartext message), resulting in a forged session key established with the PLC.

*A*2 - **Impact** An attacker only need compromise any TIA (with the correct firmware version), to be able to send messages to any PLC, without needing to compromise any PLCs. This still holds in a hypothetical case where each PLC has an individual long-term secret key, however the attacker would specifically need to compromise a TIA which was set up to work with the target PLC.

OPC-UA

*A*3 - **Description** Diemunsch, V., et al. [15] previously found the following attack, which they refer to as 'Session Hijack by Reopening or Switching', and remains unpatched. In Sign Only mode, the Session Authentication Token is sent in clear text, and once received by the Client, the User activates the session as normal. If an attacker is able to then recover the Client's secret key, they can use that secret key and the Session Authentication Token to hijack the original (still activated) session, and impersonate the User.

*A*3 - **Impact** With control over an activated session, an attacker can send arbitrary commands to the Server. Human User sessions on HMI systems are typically relatively short lived, however automated clients with fixed user credentials may have sessions lasting weeks or even indefinitely. A Client may have multiple sessions active with multiple Servers at the same time, therefore this attack could lead to an attacker gaining a significant amount of control from a single vulnerable Client.

Key Compromise Impersonation

S7Comm-Plus

$K1$ - **Description** If an attacker is able to obtain a target PLC's secret key (which is trivial in the realistic case where they are shared amongst PLC's of the same model and firmware version), the attacker can decrypt the $SecurityKeyEncryptedKey$ message sent by a TIA, and derive the session key.

$K1$ bf - Impact An attacker can therefore transparently impersonate any TIA with which a session has been established. This enables an attacker to take control of the PLC without interrupting the existing session.

SSP-21

$K2$ - **Description** In SharedSecret mode both agents share a single SharedSecret, and use no other cryptographic identities, consequently if an attacker can extract that SharedSecret from either agent, they can impersonate both agents to each other.

$K2$ bf - Impact In this mode, an attacker need only to compromise a single device, to be able to authenticate to, and create malicious sessions with, every other device that the compromised device has been paired with.

OPC-UA

$K3$ - **Description** A KCI attack on user authentication is trivial when in Password mode, however [15] also finds a KCI attack when using X509 certificates for User authentication in Sign Mode. If an attacker has compromised a Server's secret key, it can use that key to impersonate the Server to a Client, and collect the User's signature of the Server certificate and nonce, which the attacker can then use to impersonate the User to the Server.

$K3$ bf - Impact With a compromised Server secret key, an attacker on an ICS network could already cause significant damage to the system, so the additional damage this attack could enable would be, in most cases, minor.

$K4$ - **Description** [15] also discovered that when in SignEncrypt mode and using x509 certificates for User authentication, an attacker that has compromised a Server's secret key may wait for a Client to renew its session keys and then impersonate the Server and learn the Session Authentication Token. The attacker can then use this token to impersonate the Client to the Server.

$K4$ bf - Impact With a compromised Server secret key an attacker on an ICS network could already cause damage to an ICS system so the additional damage this attack could enable would be, in most cases, minor.

4.6 Summary

Reviewing Table 2 we see that, based on the work of [13], the only protocol not to fail any tests was DNP3-SAv5 (although we note that KCI and key uniqueness were not tested, and we plan to do this as future work). DNP3-SAv5 is only used in the power domain, therefore for electricity systems it is the clear choice.

S7Comm-Plus fails most tests, this provides one more example of the failure of security through obscurity. However our formal model does show a new result that if S7Comm-Plus devices were configured with individual secret keys (and secure crypto), then the protocol would be secure against most attacks. While we note that Siemens does not sell PLCs in this configuration, this perhaps shows a path to making these widely deployed devices more secure.

SSP-21 provides the best authentication properties and is based on the state of the art Noise protocol [32]. We only find edge case weaknesses in forward secrecy and when a shared secret has been leaked. Unfortunately this protocol is not supported by any of the main PLC manufacturers; this is perhaps a missed opportunity of ICS security.

OPC-UA is widely deployed and the analysis of [15] shows that it provides most security properties. So in the case where an ICS owner can have some confidence that none of their devices have been compromised, OPC-UA seems to be the best option from the non-TLS protocols.

5 TLS Protocols

Many unsecured ICS protocols have added security by wrapping the protocol in TLS. While TLS is widely regarded as providing a high-level of security, it has many possible configurations which affect this in practice. In this section we review ICS protocols that make use of TLS and assess the security they provide.

5.1 Protocol Overviews

The Modbus/TCP. Security specification [34] describes how the TCP version of Modbus can be run over TLS to make it secure. The specification requires TLS 1.2 or higher and use of mutual TLS (mTLS, i.e., a certificate for both the server and the client, hence authenticating both parties). The only required cipher suites are TLS_RSA_WITH_AES_128_GCM_SHA256 and TLS_ECDHE_ECDSA_WITH_AES_128_GCM_SHA256 and the only forbidden cipher suite is TLS_NULL_WITH_NULL_NULL, which means that cipher suites with no encryption, but with authentication, are allowed.

The specification recommends the use of a PKI to provision the certificates, and let each device validate the certificate of the device it is talking to. As a novel point, Modbus TLS extends the standard TLS X509 certificates with a "RoleOID" field, this can be used to allow role-based access control for devices.

BACnet/SC is the secure version of the BACnet building automation protocol, which uses TLS 1.3 [9]. Devices must be provisioned with a certificate, the related private key, and the CA certificates. The devices use mutual TLS and will use the CA certificate to validate the certificate of any party it connects to. Devices may have multiple CA certificates, in which case it will connect to devices with certificates from any of the CAs.

The need to set up and manage the CA certificate and the certificates on every device, seems well suited to networks the size of a building, and BACnet typically uses a hub-and-spoke network topology [18], which could make configuration easier. The requirement of TLS 1.3 rules out the use of any insecure cyber suites, however it also disallows any authenticated plaintext cipher suites.

CIP Security is a standard managed by ODVA, for running EtherNet/IP (Industrial Protocol) over TLS [30]. EtherNet/IP is a complex protocol with no security, that can use TCP for messaging and UDP data streams.

The CIP Security specification, adds mTLS 1.2 for the TCP traffic and DTLS for the UDP traffic. TLS 1.2 is explicitly specified to support authenticated, plaintext traffic, and devices are required to support a plaintext cipher suite. Users may add other cipher suites, including insecure ones. While it is an open standard, it is mainly used by Rockwell Automation.

The (D)TLS connections may use X509 Certificates or Pre-Shared Keys (PSK). Devices may be used with a PKI, and the specification defines a Certificate Management Object interface to interact with a local PKI. This supports pushing certificates onto devices and also devices pulling any that they need.

The CIP Security specification also defines "Security Profiles" for access control, which can be exchanged after the TLS handshake.

IEC 62351–3 is not a protocol in itself, but standardises recommendations for power system communication protocols that use TLS. The standard mandates support for TLS 1.2, and optionally for TLS 1.3. It provides as set of mandatory cipher suites for both TLS versions, and for TLS 1.2 it explicitly disallows the TLS_NULL_WITH_NULL_NULL suite, as well as those using DES or MD5. When using TLS 1.2, additional cipher suites can be used, which it recommends follow the latest guidance from the IETF, but this it not mandatory.

Authentication-only operation is only permitted in cases where the connection is already encrypted by other means, or if it is limited to within the same organisation or administrative domain. If using TLS 1.2, the standard allows the use of the TLS_RSA_WITH_NULL_SHA256 cipher suite, and despite TLS 1.3 not officially supporting any authentication-only cipher suites, the standard allows use of two suites defined in RFC 9150: TLS_SHA256_SHA256 and TLS_SHA384_SHA384. IEC 62351–8 describes the additional requirements for adding role based access control support to IEC 62351–3 certificates.

The Siemens Logo series of PLCs communicate with their configuration interface using a proprietary protocol which is optionally wrapped in TLS 1.2 via HTTPS, and has been partially reverse engineered[1].

We inspected the traffic of a Siemens Logo device and found that it uses TLS 1.2 with the strong cipher suite ECDHE-ECDSA-AES128-GCM-SHA256 using

[1] https://github.com/jankeymeulen/siemens-logo-rest.

a certificate pre installed on the device and desktop controller. It does not use mutual TLS; the controller authenticates itself to the PLC using a password.

The reverse engineering of the protocol, mentioned above, found that an obfuscated CRC of the password is send to the PLC, which only provides a very week level of protection. Certificates could be removed from any device and reused by an attacker, and it would be straightforward for an attacker that MITMed the connections to reuse the password CRC.

Siemens Logo TLS traffic is always encrypted, however the TLS protection can be disabled to allow traffic analysis, though this removes all security. It does not provide an authenticated plaintext mode.

5.2 Analysis of TLS Protocols

Table 3. Comparison of TLS Protocols. mTLS: Is mutual TLS supported? Plain text: Is an authenticated plain text mode available? User certs: Can a user install their own certificates? PKI: Is there support for a PKI? PSK: Can a user install pre-shared keys? No weak ciphers: Is it impossible to use weak ciphers? PFS: Do all ciphers provide Perfect Forward Secrecy? Access Control: Is there support for profiles and permissions?

Protocol	TLS Version	mTLS	Plain text	User certs	PKI	PSK	No Weak ciphers	PFS	Access Control	Usage
Modbus TLS	1.2 +	Y	Y	Y	Y	N	N	N	Y	General
BACnet/SC	1.3	Y	N	Y	N	N	Y	Y	N	Buildings
CIP Security	1.2	Y	Y	Y	Y	Y	N	N	Y	General
IEC 62351-3	1.2+	Y	Y	Y	Y	Y	N	N	Y	Power
Siemens Logo	1.2	N	N	N	N	N	Y	N	N	General

We summarise the main aspects of each of the TLS protocols in Table 3. With the exception of Siemens Logo, all the TLS protocols we looked at provide strong security guarantees based on mutual TLS that authenticates both the client and server based on a certificate or pre-shared key. However, this security requires the additional effort of provisioning devices with certificates. The access control extensions and possible use of PKIs in Modbus TLS and CIP Security would make management of large deployments easier. BACnet/SC's requirement to manually add certificates to each device may be better for smaller deployments the size of a building management system, which is the target domain for BACnet.

IEC 62351-3 specifies a similar level of security and features to Modbus TLS and CIP Security, but is targeted just at power control systems.

One common issue across all the TLS protocols is around the supported TLS version. Either the protocol is restricted to using TLS 1.2, which is rapidly becoming obsolete, or it uses the latest TLS 1.3, which requires encryption and therefore blocks the use of IDS and Data Historians, which are required by a significant number of industrial applications.

ODVA and Cisco have authored RFC 9150 as an extension to TLS 1.3 to support integrity-only cipher suites, however this has not yet been widely adopted. IDSes and Data Historians could still be used if they were given the Certificate Authority private key and traffic was directed through them such that they could in effect perform a MITM attack on the TLS communications and recover the data. This opens up a number of other issues, including the risk of leaking the CA private key, significantly increased latency and increased system complexity.

This conflict may be a significant barrier to use of any of these protocols going forward, and given that the issue is only set to get worse as TLS 1.2 is further phased out, the concept of using TLS to build ICS protocols is problematic.

6 Conclusion

In this paper we provide the first direct comparison of leading, secured ICS protocols. We analyse non-TLS/bespoke ICS protocols using the Tamarin Prover. We identify OPC-UA as one of the most useful, secure protocols but highlight some minor security issues, such as lack of forward secrecy and key compromise impersonation attacks, however these are unlikely to be major issues in most ICS deployments.

We summarise the leading TLS-based ICS proposals and show that their designs promise a high level of security, with better protection than OPC-UA. However, there may be issues with the use of TLS 1.3 meaning that all data is encrypted, so cannot be used for IDS and ICS analysis. Protocols based on TLS 1.2 risk becoming outdated and unsupported, and as the proposal for plaintext TLS 1.3 has yet to gain traction, TLS based ICS protocols may face obstacles in the future, making OPC-UA one of the best options for ICS operators.

References

1. Alsabbagh, W., Amogbonjaye, S., Urrego, D., Langendörfer, P.: A stealthy false command injection attack on modbus based scada systems. In: 2023 IEEE 20th Consumer Communications & Networking Conference (CCNC) (2023)
2. Alsabbagh, W., Kim, C., Langendörfer, P.: Good night, and good luck: a control logic injection attack on openplc. In: IECON 2023-49th Annual Conference of the IEEE Industrial Electronics Society (2023)
3. Alsabbagh, W., Langendöerfer, P.: A new injection threat on s7-1500 plcs-disrupting the physical process offline. IEEE Open J. Industr. Electron. Soc. (2022)
4. Alsabbagh, W., Langendörfer, P.: A control injection attack against s7 plcs-manipulating the decompiled code. In: IECON 2021–47th Annual Conference of the IEEE Industrial Electronics Society (2021)
5. Alsabbagh, W., Langendörfer, P.: A stealth program injection attack against s7–300 plcs. In: 2021 22nd IEEE International Conference on Industrial Technology (ICIT) (2021)
6. Alsabbagh, W., Langendörfer, P.: No need to be online to attack-exploiting s7-1500 plcs by time-of-day block. In: 2022 XXVIII International Conference on Information, Communication and Automation Technologies (ICAT) (2022)

7. Alsabbagh, W., Langendörfer, P.: Patch now and attack later - exploiting s7 plcs by time-of-day block. In: International Conference on Industrial Cyber-Physical Systems (ICPS) (2021)
8. Amoah, R., Çamtepe, S., Foo, E.: Formal modelling and analysis of dnp3 secure authentication. J. Netw. Comput. Appl. (2016)
9. ANSI/ASHRAE: A data communication protocol for building automation and control networks- addendum BJ to standard 135-2016 (2019). https://bacnet.org/wp-content/uploads/sites/4/2022/08/Add-135-2016bj.pdf
10. Barbieri, G., Conti, M., Tippenhauer, N.O., Turrin, F.: Assessing the use of insecure ICS protocols via IXP network traffic analysis. In: Proceedings of International Conference on Computer Communications and Networks (ICCCN) (2021)
11. Beresford, D.: Exploiting siemens simatic s7 plcs. Black Hat USA (2011)
12. Biham, E., Bitan, S., Carmel, A., Dankner, A., Malin, U., Wool, A.: Rogue7: Rogue engineering-station attacks on s7 simatic plcs. In: BlackHat (2019)
13. Cremers, C., Dehnel-Wild, M., Milner, K.: Secure authentication in the grid: a formal analysis of dnp3: Sav5. In: ESORICS (2017)
14. Dahlmanns, M., Lohmöller, J., Pennekamp, J., Bodenhausen, J., Wehrle, K., Henze, M.: Missed opportunities: measuring the untapped TLS support in the industrial internet of things. In: Proceedings of Asia Conference on Computer and Communications Security (2022)
15. Diemunsch, V., Hirschi, L., Kremer, S.: A comprehensive formal security analysis of OPC UA. In: USENIX Security Symposium (2025)
16. Dragos, Inc.: Crashoverride: Analysis of the threat to electric grid operations. Tech. rep., Dragos, Inc. (2017). https://dragos.com/blog/crashoverride/, Accessed 19 June 2025
17. Erba, A., Müller, A., Tippenhauer, N.O.: Resting on feet of clay: securely bootstrapping OPC UA deployments. In: BlackHat Europe (2021)
18. Fisher, D., Isler, B., Osborne, M.: BACnet secure connect a secure infrastructure for building automation (2020). https://modbus.org/docs/MB-TCP-Security-v36_2021-07-30.pdf
19. Gebhard, A., Perouli, D.: Comparing the security approaches of CIP and OPC UA. In: Re-Design Industrial Control Systems with Security (2024)
20. Ghaleb, A., Zhioua, S., Almulhem, A.: On plc network security. Int. J. Critical Infrastr. Protection (2018)
21. Girol, G., Hirschi, L., Sasse, R., Jackson, D., Cremers, C., Basin, D.: A spectral analysis of noise: a comprehensive, automated, formal analysis of Diffie-Hellman protocols. In: USENIX Security Symposium (2020)
22. Greenberg, A.: How Russia-linked malware cut heat to 600 ukrainian buildings in deep winter. Wired (2024). https://www.wired.com/story/russia-ukraine-frostygoop-malware-heating-utility/, Accessed 19 June 2025
23. Helms, J., Van Randwyk, J., Taymaz, S., Weed, J., McClelland, C.: California energy systems for the 21st century (CES-21) program (final report). Tech. rep., Lawrence Livermore National Lab (2022). https://www.osti.gov/biblio/1880939
24. Hildebrandt, M., Lamshöft, K., Dittmann, J., Neubert, T., Vielhauer, C.: Information hiding in industrial control systems: an OPC UA based supply chain attack and its detection. In: Information Hiding and Multimedia Security (2020)
25. Holasova, E., Blazek, P., Fujdiak, R., andJiri Misurec, J.M.: Exploring the power of convolutional neural networks for encrypted industrial protocols recognition. In: Sustainable Energy, Grids and Networks (2024)
26. Hui, H., McLaughlin, K., Sezer, S.: Vulnerability analysis of s7 PLCs: manipulating the security mechanism. Int. J. Critical Infrastr. Protection (2021)

27. Johnson, B., Caban, D., Krotofil, M., Scali, D., Brubaker, N., Glyer, C.: Attackers deploy new ICS attack framework "triton" and cause operational disruption to critical infrastructure. Tech. rep., Mandiant (2017). https://cloud.google.com/blog/topics/threat-intelligence/attackers-deploy-new-ics-attack-framework-triton, Accessed 19 June 2025
28. Krotofil, M., Derbyshire, R.: Greetings from the '90s: exploiting the design of industrial controllers in modern settings. In: BlackHat Europe (2021)
29. Lei, C., Donghong, L., NS-Focus, M.L.: The spear to break the security wall of s7commplus. In: BlackHat Europe (2017)
30. ODVA: Overview of CIP security (2020). https://www.odva.org/wp-content/uploads/2023/07/PUB00319R2_CIP-Security-At-a-Glance.pdf
31. OPC Foundation: Opc foundation marketplace, https://opcfoundation.org/products/, Accessed 19 June 2025
32. Perrin, T.: The noise protocol framework. noiseprotocol, Protocol Revision (2018)
33. Puys, M., Potet, M., Lafourcade, P.: Formal analysis of security properties on the OPC-UA SCADA protocol. In: Computer Safety, Reliability, and Security SAFECOMP (2016)
34. Schneider Electric USA, I.: Modbus/tcp security protocol specification (2018). https://modbus.org/docs/MB-TCP-Security-v36_2021-07-30.pdf
35. Secure scada protocol for the 21st century (ssp21) (2020). https://ssp21.github.io/spec/latest/pdf/ssp21.pdf
36. Tychalas, D., Maniatakos, M.: Special session: potentially leaky controller: examining cache side-channel attacks in programmable logic controllers. In: International Conference on Computer Design (ICCD) (2020)
37. Walz, A., et al.: Profinet security: a look on selected concepts for secure communication in the automation domain. In: Conference on Industrial Informatics (INDIN) (2023)
38. Wardak, H., Zhioua, S., Almulhem, A.: Plc access control: a security analysis. In: World Congress on Industrial Control Systems Security (WCICSS) (2016)

Author Index

A
Afzal, Zeeshan 58
Andersson, Simon 3
Andrijauskaitė, Ieva 404
Asplund, Mikael 58
Astromskis, Paulius 404

B
Bada, Maria 123
Barredo, Jorge 326
Belinchon, Lander Aguirregomezcorta 200
Brūzgienė, Rasa 404
Burgherr, Peter 105

C
Charalambous, Evagoras 369
Chothia, Tom 424
Clark, Daniel 424
Crisp, Timothy 245

D
Danielienė, Renata 404

E
Eceiza, Maialen 326
Elleman, Dallas 384
Ericson, Åsa 3

F
Flores, Jose Luis 326
Furnell, Steven 123, 265

G
Gajić, Nataša 82
Gil-Delgado del Pozo, José María 200
Grigaliūnas, Šarūnas 404
Große, Christine 3

H
Hadjichristophi, George 369
Hale, John 245, 384
Heinrich, Markus 143
Heinzl, Steffen 185
Herkanaidu, Ram 123
Howe, Alex 224

I
Iturbe, Mikel 326

K
Katzenbeisser, Stefan 143
Khan, Neeshe 123
Koshijima, Ichiro 284
Koumourou, Sotiris 20
Krauß, Christoph 143

L
Lugnet, Johan 3

M
Morad, Issa 163
Myrén, Daniel 58

N
Nakayama, Kenta 284
Nemickienė, Živilė 404
Nunnelee, Jack 224
Nurse, Jason R. C. 123

P
Papa, Mauricio 224
Parkin, Simon 39
Peratikou, Adamantini 20, 347, 369
Pieters, Wolter 39
Poblete, Adolfo Alejandro Uribe 105

E. Bergström et al. (Eds.): CRITIS 2025, LNCS 16291, pp. 445–446, 2026.
https://doi.org/10.1007/978-3-032-19540-1

R
Rand, Matthew 123
Rechberger, Jakob 185
Reuter, Lenhard 305

S
Shah, Ronak Tejas 39
Skopik, Florian 305
Smith, Paul 305
Smyrli, Panayiota 369
Šilingaitė, Ieva 404
Soylu, Görkem Kılınç 163, 200
Spychalski, Dominik 143
Stankūnas, Rokas 404
Stavrou, Eliana 20, 265, 347, 369
Stavrou, Stavros 20, 347, 369

T
Theodoulou, Savvas 20, 347

V
van Eeten, Michel 39
Veitaitė, Ilona 404
Vengalienė, Dovilė 404

W
Watanabe, Kenji 284
Wolthusen, Stephen Dirk Bjørn 82

Y
Yako, Yousef 163
Yekta, Ali Recai 143
Yekta, Cenk 143

The manufacturer's authorised representative in the EU is Springer Nature Customer Service Centre GmbH, Europaplatz 3, 69115 Heidelberg, Germany. If you have any concerns regarding our products, please contact ProductSafety@springernature.com

Printed and bound by CPI Group (UK) Ltd, Croydon, CR0 4YY
07/07/2026
02160913-0013